Second Edition

CRIMINAL JUSTICE AND CRIMINOLOGY RESEARCH METHODS

Second Edition

CRIMINAL JUSTICE AND CRIMINOLOGY RESEARCH METHODS

Peter B. Kraska
Eastern Kentucky University

W. Lawrence Neuman
University of Wisconsin at Whitewater

Boston   Columbus   Indianapolis   New York   San Francisco   Upper Saddle River
Amsterdam   Cape Town   Dubai   London   Madrid   Milan   Munich   Paris   Montreal   Toronto
Delhi   Mexico City   Sao Paulo   Sydney   Hong Kong   Seoul   Singapore   Taipei   Tokyo

Editorial Director: Vernon Anthony
Acquisitions Editor: Eric Krassow
Editorial Assistant: Lynda Cramer
Director of Marketing: David Gesell
Marketing Manager: Cyndi Eller
Marketing Assistant: Crystal Hernandez
Senior Marketing Coordinator: Alicia Wozniak
Project Manager: Holly Shufeldt
Cover Art Director: Jayne Conte
Cover Designer: Karen Salzbach
Cover Art: Fotolia
Full-Service Project Management and Composition: Integra Software Services Pvt. Ltd.
Text Printer: Edwards Brothers
Cover Printer: Lehigh-Phoenix Color Corp.
Text Font: Minion

Credits and acknowledgments for materials borrowed from other sources and reproduced, with permission, in this textbook appear on the appropriate page within text.

Library of Congress Cataloging-in-Publication Data
Kraska, Peter B.
  Criminal justice and criminology research methods / Peter B. Kraska, W. Lawrence Neuman. — 2nd ed.
    p. cm.
  Includes bibliographical references and index.
  ISBN-13: 978-0-13-512008-8
  ISBN-10: 0-13-512008-X
  1. Criminology—Research—Methodology.   2. Criminal justice, Administration of—Research—Methodology.
  I. Neuman, William Lawrence   II. Title.
  HV6024.5.K73 2012
  364.072—dc23

                                                                                  2011027098

10 9 8 7 6 5 4 3 2 1

ISBN 10:   0-13-512008-X
ISBN 13: 978-0-13-512008-8

BRIEF CONTENTS

Preface xxi

PART 1 Disciplinary, Theoretical, and Philosophical Foundations 1

    Chapter 1 Criminal Justice and Criminology Research: Mapping the Terrain 2

    Chapter 2 The Nature of Science and Research 27

    Chapter 3 Philosophical and Theoretical Foundations 50

PART 2 Considerations in Research Preparation 79

    Chapter 4 The Ethics and Politics of Crime and Justice Research 80

    Chapter 5 Research Design and Measurement 101

    Chapter 6 Sampling in Crime and Justice Research 126

PART 3 Quantitative Data Collection and Analysis 147

    Chapter 7 Experimental and Quasi-Experimental Crime and Justice Research 149

    Chapter 8 Survey and Interview Methods 172

    Chapter 9 Nonreactive Research: Content Analysis and Existing Documents/Statistics 203

    Chapter 10 Analysis of Quantitative Data 227

PART 4 Qualitative Research, Mixed Methods, and Presenting Research 255

    Chapter 11 The Nature of Qualitative Research 257

    Chapter 12 Crime and Justice Ethnographic Field Research 276

    Chapter 13 Historical, Academic Legal, and Mixed Methods Research 311

    Chapter 14 Presenting Crime and Justice Research 338

    Appendix A Epistemology Elaborated 357

    Appendix B All About Researching and Reviewing Literature 367

    Appendix C Qualitative Data Analysis Techniques 381

Bibliography 392

Index 419

Credits 426

CONTENTS

Preface xxi

Part 1   Disciplinary, Theoretical, and Philosophical Foundations   1

Chapter 1   CRIMINAL JUSTICE AND CRIMINOLOGY RESEARCH: MAPPING THE TERRAIN   2

Knowledge, Research, and Power   2
Research Defined   4

The Relevance of Research   4

What Do We Research?   5

Who Are the Researchers?   7
Professors in Practice   7
Governmental Research   8
Practitioner-Based Research   8
Journalists as Researchers   8
■ HIGHLIGHT 1.1: Missing Children Hysteria   9
Student Research   9

How Do We Conduct Research?   10
Quantitative and Qualitative Research   10
COLLECTING QUANTITATIVE DATA   11
COLLECTING QUALITATIVE DATA   14

Why Do We Conduct Research?   18
Basic Research   18
Applied Research   19
Beyond the Basic–Applied Distinction   20
The Four Purposes of Research   20
EXPLORATION   20
■ HIGHLIGHT 1.2: A Sample of Potential Exploratory Research Topics   21
DESCRIPTION   22
EXPLANATION   22
EVALUATION   23
*Conclusion   25 •   Key Terms   25 •   Review Questions   25
Practicing Research   25 •   Notes for Additional Study   26*

Chapter 2   THE NATURE OF SCIENCE AND RESEARCH   27

CSI and Science   28

Alternatives to Research-Based Knowledge   28
Authority   29
Tradition   29
■ HIGHLIGHT 2.1: Experts Duel over Benefits of Stamping Out Graffiti   30
Common Sense   30

Media/Political Myths   31

Personal Experience   31

How Social Science Works   33

Science and Social Science   33

■ HIGHLIGHT 2.2: The Horse-Slasher: Origins of Science in Criminology   34

The Social Science Community   35

The Norms of the Social Science Community   36

Sharing Knowledge: The Role of Scholarly Publications   37

Steps in the Scientific Research Process   39

The Steps   39

Research Step Examples   41

QUANTITATIVE EXAMPLE: CHILD ABUSE   41

QUALITATIVE EXAMPLE: VIOLENT CRIMINALS   43

■ HIGHLIGHT 2.3: A Maverick Criminologist   44

Scientific Research and Time   45

Cross-sectional Research   45

Longitudinal Research   46

*Conclusion   48   •   Key Terms   48   •   Review Questions   49
Practicing Research   49   •   Notes for Further Study   49*

Chapter 3   PHILOSOPHICAL AND THEORETICAL FOUNDATIONS   50

Making Sense of Hurricane Katrina   50

Philosophical Foundations   51

The Three Approaches   52

POSITIVIST SOCIAL SCIENCE FEATURES   53

PSS CONCLUSION   54

INTERPRETIVE SOCIAL SCIENCE FEATURES   54

ISS CONCLUSION   56

CRITICAL SOCIAL SCIENCE FEATURES   57

■ HIGHLIGHT 3.1: A Splinter in Your Mind: CSS and *The Matrix*   59

CSS CONCLUSION   60

Philosophical Conclusion   60

■ HIGHLIGHT 3.2: Participatory Action Research   61

Theory in Crime and Justice Research   62

Why Theory?   62

The Parts of a Theory   63

ASSUMPTIONS   63

CONCEPTS   63

RELATIONSHIPS AMONG CONCEPTS   64

Approaches to Developing Theory: Deductive–Inductive   64

Causal Explanation and Testing Hypotheses   66

■ HIGHLIGHT 3.3: What Is Grounded Theory?   66

The Language of Variables and Hypotheses   67

TYPES OF VARIABLES   69

From the Research Question to Hypotheses   70

Causal Theory and Hypotheses   70

THE HYPOTHESIS AND CAUSALITY   70

TESTING AND REFINING A HYPOTHESIS   70

■ **HIGHLIGHT 3.4: Ten Ways to State Causal Relations between Religious Attendance and Criminality   71**

TYPES OF HYPOTHESES   71

Potential Errors in Causal Explanation   72

TAUTOLOGY   73

TELEOLOGY   73

ECOLOGICAL FALLACY   73

REDUCTIONISM   73

SPURIOUSNESS   74

■ **HIGHLIGHT 3.5: Night-Lights and Spuriousness   74**

Summary of Theory   75

Philosophy and Theory Conclusion   75

Key Terms   76   •   Review Questions   76   •   Practicing Research   77   •   Notes for Further Study   77

Part 2   Considerations in Research Preparation   79

Chapter 4   THE ETHICS AND POLITICS OF CRIME AND JUSTICE RESEARCH   80

Preparing to Research Felony Fights   80

Ethics in Crime and Justice Research   81

The Utilitarian Balance   82

Ethical Issues Involving Research Participants   84

■ **HIGHLIGHT 4.1: An Early Chronology of Research Subject Abuse in the United States   84**

PHYSICAL HARM, PSYCHOLOGICAL ABUSE, AND LEGAL JEOPARDY   86

DECEPTION   88

■ **HIGHLIGHT 4.2: Crime and Justice Researchers Breaking the Law   89**

INFORMED CONSENT   89

COVERT OBSERVATION   90

■ **HIGHLIGHT 4.3: Deep Cover Example   91**

Special Populations and New Inequalities   91

SPECIAL POPULATIONS AND COERCION   91

CREATING NEW INEQUALITIES   92

PRIVACY, ANONYMITY, AND CONFIDENTIALITY   92

Codes of Ethics in Crime and Justice Research   94

Policing Research: The Case of Institutional Review Boards   94

■ **HIGHLIGHT 4.4: Academy of Criminal Justice Sciences Code of Research Ethics   95**

Science and Politics   96

Research Ideals versus Political Realities   96

The Influence of Funding   97

Governmental and Corporate Secrecy   98

Conclusion   99   •   Key Terms   99   •   Review Questions   99   Practicing Research   100   •   Notes for Further Study   100

Chapter 5   RESEARCH DESIGN AND MEASUREMENT   101

     ■ HIGHLIGHT 5.1: Does Police Surveillance Using Closed Circuit Television Work? 102

Designing Research Questions   103

     The Best Ways to Select Topics   103

     ■ HIGHLIGHT 5.2: Techniques for Narrowing a Topic into a Research Question 105

     ■ HIGHLIGHT 5.3: Examples of Bad and Good Research Questions 106

Measurement: Fear of Crime and Executions   106

     ■ HIGHLIGHT 5.4: IQ Norms and the Death Penalty 108

Conceptualizing and Operationalizing: An Overview   109

     ■ HIGHLIGHT 5.5: Juvenile Probation Officer Morale 111

     Quantitative Conceptualization and Operationalization   112

     ■ HIGHLIGHT 5.6: Studying Turnover and Pay Among Texas JPOs 113

Reliability and Validity   113

     Reliability and Validity in Quantitative Research   114

         RELIABILITY   114

         FOUR TYPES OF VALIDITY   115

         CRITERION VALIDITY   115

     Relationship between Reliability and Validity   116

     Other Uses of the Words *Reliable* and *Valid*   117

A Guide to Quantitative Measurement   117

     Levels of Measurement   117

         FOUR LEVELS OF MEASUREMENT   118

         CONTINUOUS AND DISCRETE VARIABLES   119

     Specialized Measures: Scales and Indexes   119

     ■ HIGHLIGHT 5.7: Measuring Crime Rate Increases Using the UCR 120

         INDEXES AND SCALES   120

         UNIDIMENSIONALITY   120

Index Construction   121

     The Purpose   121

     Weighting   122

Scales   122

     The Logic and Purpose   122

     Likert Scales   122

         THURSTONE SCALING   123

         Conclusion 124 • Key Terms 124 • Review Questions 125   Practicing Research 125 • Notes for Further Study 125

Chapter 6   SAMPLING IN CRIME AND JUSTICE RESEARCH   126

Sexual Coercion and Sampling: A Cautionary Tale   126

     ■ HIGHLIGHT 6.1: Researching a Serious Problem: Rape on Campus 127

Probability Sampling   129

     Populations, Cases, and Sampling Frames   129

     Why Random?   129

Types of Probability Samples   130
SIMPLE RANDOM   130
SYSTEMATIC SAMPLING   133
STRATIFIED SAMPLING   133
CLUSTER SAMPLING   135
RANDOM-DIGIT DIALING   136
■ HIGHLIGHT 6.2: A Detailed Look at the NCVS Survey Sample Method   136
How Large Should a Sample Be?   137
■ HIGHLIGHT 6.3: National Violence against Women Study Sampling   138

Nonprobability Sampling   139
Haphazard or Convenience Sampling   140
Quota Sampling   140
Purposive or Judgmental Sampling   141
Snowball Sampling   141
Deviant Case Sampling   141
Sequential Sampling   142
Theoretical Sampling   142

Mixed Sampling Approaches for Hidden Populations   143
■ HIGHLIGHT 6.4: Two Classic Research Examples Using Snowball Sampling
                 and Hidden Populations   144
*Conclusion   145   •   Key Terms   145   •   Review Questions   145
Practicing Research   146   •   Notes for Further Study   146*

Part 3   Quantitative Data Collection and Analysis   147

**Chapter 7   EXPERIMENTAL AND QUASI-EXPERIMENTAL CRIME
AND JUSTICE RESEARCH   149**
The Experiment as the "Gold Standard"   150
A History of the Experiment in Social Science Research   150
Experimental Research in Crime and Justice Studies   151
Choosing an Experiment: Factors to Consider   152
The Importance of Random Assignment   153
How to Randomly Assign   154
Matching versus Random Assignment   154

Experimental Design Logic   155
The Language of Experiments   155
PARTS OF THE EXPERIMENT   155
STEPS IN CONDUCTING AN EXPERIMENT   156
STAYING IN CONTROL   157

Types of Design   157
Classical Experimental Design   157
Other Experimental Designs   157
TWO-GROUP POSTTEST-ONLY DESIGN   157
LATIN SQUARE DESIGN   158
SOLOMON FOUR-GROUP DESIGN   158
FACTORIAL DESIGNS   158

Preexperimental or Weak Experimental Designs   159

ONE-SHOT CASE-STUDY DESIGN   159

ONE-GROUP PRETEST-POSTTEST DESIGN   159

Quasi-Experimental Designs   160

INTERRUPTED TIME SERIES   161

EQUIVALENT TIME SERIES   161

■ HIGHLIGHT 7.1: Unraveling the Mystery of the Crime Drop   162

Internal and External Validity   162

The Logic of Internal Validity   162

Threats to Internal Validity   162

SELECTION BIAS   162

HISTORY   163

MATURATION   163

TESTING   163

INSTRUMENTATION   163

EXPERIMENTAL MORTALITY   163

STATISTICAL REGRESSION   163

DIFFUSION OF TREATMENT OR CONTAMINATION   164

COMPENSATORY BEHAVIOR   164

EXPERIMENTER EXPECTANCY   164

External Validity   165

Population Validity   166

Reactivity   166

Practical Considerations   167

Planning and Pilot Tests   167

Instructions to Subjects   167

Upholding Treatment Integrity   167

Postexperiment Interview   167

Meta-Analysis of Experiments   168

■ HIGHLIGHT 7.2: Straightening Out Offenders: A Meta-Analysis of Military-
Style Boot Camps   168

Beware of Naïvete   169

*Conclusion   169   •   Key Terms   170   •   Review Questions   170
Practicing Research   170   •   Notes for Further Study   171*

Chapter 8   SURVEY AND INTERVIEW METHODS   172

Getting It Straight from the Horse's Mouth   173

A History of Survey Research   173

Survey Research in Crime and Justice Studies   174

Choosing to Survey: Factors to Consider   174

■ HIGHLIGHT 8.1: Researching Homeland Security   175

The Logic of Survey Research   176

What is a Survey?   176

Steps in Conducting a Survey   176

Constructing the Questionnaire   178

Principles of Good Question Writing   178

Avoid Jargon, Slang, and Abbreviations   179
Avoid Ambiguity, Confusion, and Vagueness   179
Avoid Emotional Language and Prestige Bias   180
Avoid Double-Barreled Questions   180
Avoid Leading Questions   180
Avoid Asking Questions that Are Beyond Respondents' Capabilities   180
Avoid False Premises   180
Avoid Overlapping or Unbalanced Response Categories   181

Aiding Respondent Recall   181

Getting Honest Answers   182
Questions on Sensitive Topics   182

Open-Ended and Closed-Ended Questions   182

■ HIGHLIGHT 8.2: The Critical Role of Self-Report Surveys   183

Agree/Disagree or Ratings?   185

Questionnaire Design Issues   185
Length of Survey or Questionnaire   185
Question Order or Sequence   186

■ HIGHLIGHT 8.3: Sample Questions and Findings from Policing Schools Survey   186

Format and Layout   187
Cover Letter and Questionnaire Layout   187

How to Avoid Nonresponses   187

Types of Surveys: Advantages and Disadvantages   189

Mail and Self-Administered Questionnaires   189
Advantages   189
Disadvantages   189

Telephone Interviews   189
Advantages   189
Disadvantages   189

Face-to-Face Interviews   190
Advantages   190
Disadvantages   190

Web Surveys   191
Advantages   191

■ HIGHLIGHT 8.4: Web Surveys Sent to Correctional Agencies   191
Disadvantages   192

Interviewing   192

The Role of the Interviewer   192

■ HIGHLIGHT 8.5: Interviewing Street Youth and Anomie Theory   194

Stages of an Interview   195

Interviewer Bias   196

Pilot Testing   196

The "Meaning" Difficulty in Survey Research   197

Ethical Survey Research   198

■ HIGHLIGHT 8.6: Kraska's Five Minutes of Pain   199

*Conclusion   199 • Key Terms   200 • Review Questions   200
Practicing Research   200 • Notes for Further Study   201*

Chapter 9   NONREACTIVE RESEARCH: CONTENT ANALYSIS AND EXISTING DOCUMENTS/STATISTICS   203

Digging up Data   204
- ■ HIGHLIGHT 9.1: Death on the Roadside   205

Nonreactive Research in Crime and Justice Studies   205
- ■ HIGHLIGHT 9.2: To Map or Not to Map—Derek Paulsen's Crime-Mapping Experiment with the Police   206

Factors to Consider When Choosing Nonreactive methods   208

Nonreactive Research Methods   208

The Logic of Nonreactive Research   208
- ■ HIGHLIGHT 9.3: Caught on Camera: Nonreactive Shoplifting Study   209

Varieties of Nonreactive Observation   209

Recording and Documentation   210

Quantitative Content Analysis   210

What Is Content Analysis?   210

Topics Appropriate for Content Analysis   211

Measurement and Coding   212
- GENERAL ISSUES   212
- WHAT IS MEASURED?   212

Coding, Validity, and Reliability   213

Manifest Coding   213

Latent Coding   213

Intercoder Reliability   213

Content Analysis with Visual Material   214

How to Conduct Content Analysis Research   214
- QUESTION FORMULATION   214
- UNITS OF ANALYSIS   215
- SAMPLING   215
- VARIABLES AND CONSTRUCTING CODING CATEGORIES   216

Inferences   216

Existing Documents/Statistics   217

Topics Appropriate for Existing Documents/Statistics Research   218

Locating Data   218
- LOCATING DOCUMENTS   218
- ■ HIGHLIGHT 9.4: Counting Death: The Morgue versus Surveys   219
- LOCATING EXISTING STATISTICS   219

Reliability and Validity   220
- UNITS OF ANALYSIS AND VARIABLE ATTRIBUTES   221
- VALIDITY   222
- RELIABILITY   222
- ■ HIGHLIGHT 9.5: Racial Assault with a Baseball? Measuring Race-Motivated Aggression   223
- MISSING DATA   223

Example of Existing Documents/Statistics Research   223

*Conclusion   224   •   Key Terms   225   •   Review Questions   225
Practicing Research   225   •   Notes for Further Study   226*

Chapter 10   ANALYSIS OF QUANTITATIVE DATA   227

    Dying for Statistics   227

    Dealing with Data   229

        Coding Data   229

        Entering Data   229

        Cleaning Data   230

        ■ HIGHLIGHT 10.1: Neuman's Dealings with Data   231

    Results with One Variable   232

        Frequency Distributions   232

        Measures of Central Tendency   233

        Measures of Variation   234

        ■ HIGHLIGHT 10.2: Calculating z-Scores   237

    Results with Two Variables   237

        A Bivariate Relationship   237

        Seeing the Relationship: The Scattergram   239

            WHAT IS A SCATTERGRAM?   239

            HOW TO CONSTRUCT A SCATTERGRAM   239

            WHAT CAN WE LEARN FROM THE SCATTERGRAM?   239

        ■ HIGHLIGHT 10.3: Graphing Accurately   240

        Bivariate Tables   241

            WHAT IS A BIVARIATE TABLE?   241

            CONSTRUCTING PERCENTAGED TABLES   241

            READING A PERCENTAGED TABLE   244

            BIVARIATE TABLES WITHOUT PERCENTAGES   245

        Measures of Association   246

    Inferential Statistics   248

        The Purpose of Inferential Statistics   248

        Statistical Significance   248

        ■ HIGHLIGHT 10.4: Chi-Square   249

        Levels of Significance   250

        Type I and Type II Errors   250

    Being Critical: Ethics and Statistics   252

        ■ HIGHLIGHT 10.5: Statistical Programs on Computers   252

        Conclusion   253   •   Key Terms   253   •   Review Questions   254

        Practicing Research   254   •   Notes for Further Study   254

**Part 4   Qualitative Research, Mixed Methods,
and Presenting Research   255**

Chapter 11   THE NATURE OF QUALITATIVE RESEARCH   257

    Home-Grown Terrorism Data   257

    Qualitative Research Basics   260

    Qualitative "Versus" Quantitative Research   260

        Linear and Nonlinear Paths   261

Objectivity and Integrity 262

Reliability and Validity 263

RELIABILITY 263

VALIDITY 264

Features of Qualitative Research 264

Grounded Theory 264

The Context Is Critical 265

Bricolage 266

The Case and Process 266

Interpretation 267

Qualitative Document Analysis (QDA) 267

The General Idea of QDA 267

POSSIBLE APPLICATIONS OF QDA 268

■ HIGHLIGHT 11.1: Deciphering Meaning from a Photograph 269

How to Conduct QDA (Steps) 270

■ HIGHLIGHT 11.2: Semiotics and the Study of Crime and Justice 271

■ HIGHLIGHT 11.3: Visual Crime and Justice Studies 273

QDA Wrap-Up 274

Conclusion 274 • Key Terms 275 • Review Questions 275
Practicing Research 275 • Notes for Further Study 275

Chapter 12 CRIME AND JUSTICE ETHNOGRAPHIC FIELD RESEARCH 276

Home-Brewing Steroids: Generating Grounded Theory 277

The Roots of Ethnographic Field Research 278

Early Beginnings 278

Chicago School of Sociology 278

Conceptual/Theoretical Underpinnings 279

■ HIGHLIGHT 12.1: An Excerpt from Clifford Geertz's Famous Description of a Balinese Cockfight 280

Ethnographic Field Research in Crime and Justice Studies 281

Appropriate Questions for Ethnographic Field Research 282

The Logic of Field Research 282

What Is Ethnographic Field Research? 282

Steps in a Field Research Project 284

FLEXIBILITY 284

ORGANIZED FLEXIBILITY 284

Choosing a Site and Gaining Access 285

Selecting a Site 285

WHERE TO OBSERVE 285

LEVEL OF INVOLVEMENT 286

GATEKEEPERS 286

INFORMANTS 287

Strategy for Entering 287

Planning 287

Negotiation 288

Disclosure 288

Entering the Field 289

Presentation of Self 289

■ HIGHLIGHT 12.2: Entering the Field with Active
Burglars 289

Researcher as Instrument 290

An Attitude of Strangeness 290

■ HIGHLIGHT 12.3: Enjoying Militarism 290

Building Rapport 291

Charm and Trust 291

Understanding 292

Relations in the Field 292

Roles in the Field 292

Preexisting versus Created Roles 292

Negotiations and Danger 292

Learning the Ropes 293

Stress 293

Normalizing Crime and Justice Research 293

Acceptable Incompetent 294

Maintaining Relations 294

Small Favors 294

Conflicts in the Field 294

Appearing Interested 295

Observing and Collecting Data 295

Watching and Listening with Care 295

Keenly Observant 295

Argot or Specialized Language 296

Taking Notes 296

Types of Field Notes 297

Data Quality in Ethnographic Field Research 300

The Meaning of Quality 300

Reliability in Field Research 300

Validity in Field Research 301

Sampling 301

The Field Research Interview 302

Focus Group Research 302

The Field Interview 302

Life History 304

■ HIGHLIGHT 12.4: The Life History or Life Story Interview 304

Types of Questions in Field Interviews 305

Leaving the Field 306

Ethical Dilemmas of Field Research 307

Deception 307

Confidentiality 307

Involvement with Criminals/Deviants 307

Publishing Ethnographic Field Reports 307

Conclusion 308 • Key Terms 308 • Review Questions 308
Practicing Research 309 • Notes for Further Study 309

Chapter 13 HISTORICAL, ACADEMIC LEGAL, AND MIXED METHODS RESEARCH 311

Historical Research 312

The General Idea of Historical Research 312
THE SPECIFIC CASE OF HISTORICAL-COMPARATIVE RESEARCH 313

■ HIGHLIGHT 13.1: Seeing Past Events in a New Light, Racial Boundaries in the United States 314

Major Features of Historical Research 314

How to Conduct Historical and Historical-Comparative Research 315
PRIMARY SOURCES 315

■ HIGHLIGHT 13.2: Using Archival Data 315

■ HIGHLIGHT 13.3: World War II, Military Justice, and Racism 316
SECONDARY SOURCES 317
RUNNING RECORDS 317
RECOLLECTIONS 317

■ HIGHLIGHT 13.4: Women of the Klan 318

Limits of Secondary Sources 319

Limits of Primary Sources 319

Steps Taken in a Historical Research Project 321

Conclusion to Historical Research 322

Academic Legal Research (ALR) 322

Justifying ALR 322

The General Idea of ALR 323

■ HIGHLIGHT 13.5: A Quick Guide to Using Westlaw and Westlaw Campus 325
THE SPECIFIC CASE OF SOCIO-LEGAL RESEARCH 326

How to Conduct Legal Research 327

Conclusion to Legal Research 329

Mixed Methods Research 330

Beyond Conflict and Exclusion 330

The General Idea of Mixed Methods Research 330

■ HIGHLIGHT 13.6: Discovering the Benefits of Mixed Methods Research 331

Major Features of Mixed Methods Research 332

How to Conduct Mixed Methods Research 334

Conclusion to Mixed Methods Research 336

Conclusion 336 • Key Terms 336 • Review Questions 336
Practicing Research 337 • Notes for Further Study 337

Chapter 14   PRESENTING CRIME AND JUSTICE RESEARCH   338

      Communing with Our Audience   338

      Why Write a Report?   339

      Writing Considerations   339

           Your Audience   339

           Style and Tone   340

           Organizing Thoughts   341

           Back to the Library   342

      The Writing Process   342

           ■ **HIGHLIGHT 14.1: Suggestions for Ending Writer's Block   343**

           Rewriting   343

      The Quantitative Research Report   344

           Abstract or Executive Summary   344

           ■ **HIGHLIGHT 14.2: Suggestions for Rewriting   345**

           Introduction and Presenting the Problem   346

           Describing the Methods   346

           Results and Tables Section   346

           Discussion Section   346

           Drawing Conclusions   347

      The Qualitative Research Report   347

           ■ **HIGHLIGHT 14.3: Why Qualitative Research Reports Are Longer   347**

           Ethnographic Field Research Reports   348

           Historical Research   349

           ■ **HIGHLIGHT 14.4: Features to Consider in the Historical-Comparative Research Report   350**

      The Research Proposal   351

           Proposals to Fund Research   351

      What Happens to the Research?   353

           Conclusion   354   •   Conclusion to the Book   354 Key Terms   355   •   Review Questions   355   •   Practicing Research   355   •   Notes for Further Study   355

Appendix A *Epistemology Elaborated   357*

Appendix B *All About Researching and Reviewing Literature   367*

Appendix C *Qualitative Data Analysis Techniques   381*

Bibliography   392

Index   419

Credits   426

PREFACE

Learning research methods is fundamental to a quality education. Most criminal justice and criminology programs, at the graduate and undergraduate levels, require students to take at least one methods course. The reasons are simple but profound. First, producing knowledge lies at the heart of the academic enterprise. Researchers produce knowledge about crime and criminal justice through various methods, and then disseminate that knowledge to students, each other, and the public at large. This book examines the deep significance of what it means to produce knowledge, and how the knowledge we accept as legitimate helps to form our perceptions of reality. The creation of credible knowledge through rigorous scientific methods is a powerful pursuit.

Second, the practice of research, and the use of research-based knowledge, has become a mainstream part of criminal justice and social life. In the new millennium, we can no longer think of research as an academic pursuit just for other academics. Today's crime and justice students must learn to be critical consumers, if not competent producers, of research-based knowledge. We strive to illuminate the significance and relevance of research—presenting the research as not just something to study but as essential for sharpening critical thinking skills for academics and practitioners, and cultivating competent decision making.

Given our combined fifty-one years of experience teaching research methods, we realize that it is a challenging course for both students and instructors. As a result, we have carefully crafted a book designed to maximize the chances for a semester of successful learning. Our efforts have centered on truly *engaging* students to learn an essential yet difficult subject. Engagement occurs through the following:

- Frequent reference to grounded and interesting research examples
- An accessible style without sacrificing rigor
- Cutting-edge coverage of a wide array of research developments in our field
- A pedagogically friendly presentation of the material
- A consistent demonstration of how research methods are directly relevant to our discipline, the practicing criminal justice system, society as a whole, and to the student.
- A commitment to putting the knowledge gained into practice through thought-provoking highlights and a comprehensive collection of attention-grabbing research exercises.

We believe we have created a book that both professors and students will appreciate. Professors will like its comprehensive, balanced, and engaging coverage of the material; students will appreciate its straightforward style and its portrayal of research methods as interesting and relevant.

Listed below are the major features of this text that has been designed to keep students engaged in the semester-long process of learning about crime and criminal justice research methods.

- **Relevant and accessible without sacrificing academic rigor.** Students need to understand from the beginning why studying research methods is relevant to the practicing field, them as individuals, and crime and justice studies. Chapter 1 places a high level of emphasis on this theme, and it is reinforced throughout the book. Relevance must be demonstrated through easy-to-relate examples such as *The Matrix* movies, numerous real-life student research examples, major events and issues such as Hurricane Katrina, homeland security, the war on terrorism, domestic violence, and criminal justice practitioner morale and burnout. Every research example and exercise have been chosen to demonstrate to students how fascinating and worthwhile research can be in our field. *This mode of presentation communicates a tone of relevance, gritty reality, connectedness, and a strong sense that research actually matters.*
- **Beyond the nuts and bolts.** Students will more effectively commit to a class and a book if they have a clear sense of the big picture—where the subject matter ties in. This requires students to think about research methods beyond the typical how-to approach, and confront issues about

- the why of knowledge (an introduction to epistemological issues),
- the role of knowledge and research in our discipline and the practicing world,
- the thinking behind science (its spirit, ethos, assumptions, and methods), and
- the controversies and ethical issues facing the field of research methods

As we emphasize throughout the book, the goal here is to develop *critical thinking skills* of students as both users and consumers of research.

- **Highly pedagogically friendly.** Learning from textbooks can be difficult. This book employs numerous techniques to make learning the material easier.

  - Rather than scattering hundreds of disconnected studies throughout the book as illustrations, this book integrates some of the same main examples throughout the various chapters to maintain continuity of thought. Similarly, it presents some of the authors' research projects as illustrations and then revisits these throughout the book. We also reference our own students' research projects to give the reader a sense that research is not something beyond their reach.
  - The ideas, concepts, and issues presented in each chapter are integrated into subsequent chapters as the book moves forward. We refer to these repeatedly throughout the rest of the text. The objective is a well-integrated book.
  - We use numerous visual aids, which include figures and photographs. The figures are designed to represent complicated ideas in simple, concrete form. The photographs help ground the ideas and maintain reader interest.
  - The Highlights are substantive and well integrated into the subject matter. They are not merely interesting peripheral reading. Key terms are boldfaced and their definitions reviewed in the margins. We routinely use summary tables that distill in visual form the more lengthy and involved sections of the book.
  - Each of the four major sections of the book is explained in depth for the reader and provides clear direction; these parts help tie together the fourteen chapters.
  - A state-of-the-art visual media component accompanying this text includes virtual role-playing exercises and mini power-point guided lectures over key components of the text.

- **Learning beyond research methods.** We strongly believe that a research methods course harbors high potential not only to teach the students about research methods but also, in the process, to teach them about criminal justice and criminology and crime, crime control and justice. This book demonstrates to students the wide range of research interests and approaches that our field pursues. We include examples from international studies; what works in policing (and what doesn't); juvenile and adult correction research; and a wide array of evaluation research, forensics, feminist studies, juvenile justice, crime theory, and criminal justice theory. The examples we choose are designed to showcase our fascinating field of study as well as teach students about research methods.

- **A balanced approach to a diverse and highly dynamic field of study**. Our relatively young field of study is evolving rapidly. As the field of criminal justice and criminology has grown and matured, there has been rising interest in, and acceptance of, qualitative research, mixed methods research, and philosophy of science issues. Existing methods textbooks have not kept pace with these developments: Qualitative research is covered superficially, quantitative and qualitative methods are viewed as mutually exclusive, and philosophy of science issues is hardly addressed. *Criminal Justice and Criminology Research Methods* adopts a more inclusive and up-to-date approach, capturing and embracing our field's expanding methodological diversity. (However, this inclusive stance should not be interpreted as a lack of commitment to our traditional methods. The coverage of traditional methods is more rigorous and comprehensive than any other text in the field.)

COMPREHENSIVE YET FLEXIBLE

This book is comprehensive in its coverage. However, the structure and style of presentation applies well to many different types of methods courses. The survey research conducted for this book found that criminal justice and criminology instructors have a variety of goals and areas of emphasis for their particular courses. A few examples of how this book might accommodate this diversity include the following:

- Some instructors prefer to emphasize quantitative methods and spend less time on qualitative. The quantitative chapters are certainly thorough enough to accommodate this approach; if an instructor requires only the ethnographic field research chapter, students will still be exposed to a much more in-depth coverage of qualitative methods than other texts provide. The quantitative analysis chapter could easily be used along with an SPSS learning module as a way to further pursue a quantitative focus.
- There are also instructors who want their students to gain an in-depth education about both quantitative and qualitative methods. This book's balanced coverage is ideal.
- There are a few instructors who want their students to understand the basics of quantitative research, but they tend to focus more on qualitative methods. Before the publication of this text, their only option was to use a supplemental book on qualitative methods.
- Finally, this text—while written primarily for undergraduate students—is well suited for a master's level graduate course, particularly if the professor supplements the book with other materials such as journal articles. Another way to increase the rigor of a graduate course would be to require students to complete most, if not all, of the Practicing Research exercises. Over the last twenty-two years, Kraska has listened to many professors complain about the lack of an adequate methods textbook for graduate students in criminal justice/criminology. This text works quite well at the graduate level.

ACKNOWLEDGMENTS

The people at Pearson have been wonderful to work with—approaching what they do with professionalism, enthusiasm, and fun. Tim Peyton has been a great support and is really operating at the cutting edge of today's textbook market. Eric Krassow has done an adept job taking over this project midstream and competently moving it along to completion. Rex Davidson has provided exceptionally skilled assistance and has always remained patient despite some frustrating author missteps. And Moganambigai Sundaramurthy has done an exceptional job copy-editing this work.

The numerous anonymous reviewers significantly improved this textbook. I appreciate their insightful suggestions and obvious passion for quality research methods courses. I would also like to thank Eastern Kentucky University (EKU), and especially my friend and Chair Vic Kappeler for providing a supportive and intellectually rich research and writing environment. Numerous EKU graduate students contributed significantly to this book as well. Ashley Farmer provided invaluable assistance with creating a leaner and more user-friendly second edition. I learned a great deal from those students who used various versions of this text while I worked on it over the last few years. Their insights and criticisms helped tremendously. Special mention should go to my friend and former student John Brent, now a doctoral student at the University of Delaware. Besides contributing his fascinating study on human fighting for the text, John has also worked hard on making the book much more student friendly.

I thank the following reviewers of the second edition:

Peggy C. Bowen, Alvernia University; David Burlingame, Grand Valley State University; Steven F. Kappeler, Eastern Kentucky University; Lauren O'Neill Shermer, Widener University; Nicolette Parisi, Temple University; Debra Ross, Grand Valley State University; Gregory Thompson, San Diego State University; and Shun-Yung Kevin Wang, The College of New Jersey.

Finally, and most important, I am forever grateful for the beautiful life partnership I have with Shannon Leigh Weer. She contributed significantly to this project in editing my writing, exchanging ideas (many of which I borrowed from her), and filling in the holes I left in our family while putting in some long hours of work. My three daughters deserve thanks as well: Katie (nineteen years old) for helping me think through how best to present complex material, and Cora (eight years old) and Ella (two years old) for being a constant reminder of what's most important in life.

PART ONE

Disciplinary, Theoretical, and Philosophical Foundations

The first three chapters answer some basic questions about knowledge, its construction, and its use within crime and justice studies. The discussion revolves around central questions: What do we study and why? How do we know what we know? What are the best ways to generate valid, reliable, and legitimate knowledge?

These first three chapters are extremely important. The rest focus on how we research—techniques of the research process—and on how to conduct and assess research. Although this information is vital, we must first construct the big picture or road map—one that includes information and ideas about our discipline (what we study and who conducts research), theory (what theory is and why it is essential to research), and philosophy (the various philosophical and ethical issues associated with its production). The aim is to help you more competently, and with a greater level of critical awareness, navigate your way through either producing or consuming criminal justice research. In short, a solid theoretical and philosophical foundation is crucial for developing the necessary skills to critically assess research studies and claims to legitimate knowledge.

These first chapters, then, outline the larger context of crime and criminal justice research. Our goal is to help educate you *about* research methods in crime and justice (C&J) studies, as well as how to research and how to apply it properly. Chapter 1 discusses what we research and identifies who the researchers are. It also provides an overview in abbreviated form of how research is conducted. It points out the various reasons we conduct research as well as provides an outline of how the study of research methods is tangibly beneficial to you, the student. Chapter 2 examines the nature of crime and justice research. It details those sources of everyday knowledge that most of us rely on and some of their shortcomings, and then describes the history, standards, and process of social science research. It includes important sections on the dimension of "time". Finally, Chapter 3 first presents three philosophical approaches available to us for conducting crime and justice research:

1. positivist social science;
2. interpretive social science; and
3. critical social science.

The differences and similarities of each are presented. The second part of Chapter 3 provides a detailed examination of theory, its role in conducting quality research, and its various types.

We hope this foundational road map serves you well for the remainder of the book.

Criminal Justice and Criminology Research: Mapping the Terrain

Knowledge, Research, and Power
The Relevance of Research
  Research Defined
What Do We Research?
Who Are the Researchers?
  Professors in Practice
  Governmental Research
  Practitioner-Based Research
  Journalists as Researchers
      Highlight 1.1 Missing Children Hysteria
  Student Research
How Do We Conduct Research?
  Quantitative and Qualitative Research
      Collecting Quantitative Data
        ■ *Experimental Research*
        ■ *Survey and Interview Research*
        ■ *Nonreactive Research*
            □ *Existing Documents/Statistics Research*
            □ *Content Analysis*
      Collecting Qualitative Data
        ■ *Ethnographic Field Research*

        ■ *Qualitative Document Analysis*
        ■ *Historical Research*
        ■ *Academic Legal Research*
        ■ *Mixed Methods Research*
Why Do We Conduct Research?
  Basic Research
  Applied Research
  Beyond the Basic–Applied Distinction
  The Four Purposes of Research
      Exploration
      *Highlight 1.2 A Sample of Potential
          Exploratory Research Topics*
  Description
  Explanation
  Evaluation
Conclusion
Key Terms
Review Questions
Practicing Research
Notes for Additional Study

KNOWLEDGE, RESEARCH, AND POWER

Welcome to the fascinating world of crime and justice research. This chapter is designed to orient you to research in our particular field of study, crime and justice studies. Let's start by looking at how the activity of research fits into the big picture.

The quest for knowledge is a defining feature of human history. Seeking the truth, being liberated from ignorance, and trying to answer that ever-elusive question, "what is really the case?" underpins nearly every aspect of humankind's evolution. What we ultimately agree on as being accurate and useful knowledge forms the basis for what we define and view as reality. However, agreeing on the proper methods to search for and validate what is knowledge—such as traditional myths, religious texts, or scientific research methods—has been a source of struggle and conflict for centuries.

The struggle is not over. Today's headlines demonstrate that large differences still remain over how best to determine what we know. The media dub one dimension of this conflict the "science wars."[1] Several contemporary issues are illustrative. Are the scientific studies documenting global warming and its causes valid, or are they skewed because of climatologists' ideological leanings? Should the scientifically tested "theory of evolution" be placed on the same educational plane as the biblically based notion of "intelligent design"? Are recent dramatic drops in reported violent crime in the United States due mainly to social, economic, and demographic factors as explained in numerous academic studies, or are they caused simply by getting tough with law violators, regardless of what the "experts" say?

These questions point to an interesting paradox: As research-based knowledge in our society grows exponentially in both size and influence, so has the level of skepticism about its legitimacy.[2] As in the past, what we know and how we determine what we know are under serious dispute.

Besides long-standing differences in worldviews (religion vs. science), a central factor driving this dispute can be found in the close relationship between knowledge and power. Put simply, *knowledge generates power, and conversely, power generates knowledge* (see Figure 1.1). Let's look at what this **knowledge–power dynamic** entails.

The research methods detailed in this book are specifically designed to generate knowledge. Research-based knowledge, if perceived as legitimate and accurate, holds tremendous capacity to influence others. For example, medical doctors assume that the prescription drugs they dispense are safe only because of the research findings generated by pharmaceutical companies (an assumption currently under serious dispute). We assume that the knowledge associated with a drug we place in our mouth is legitimate and we won't be harmed as a result; that's power!

Conversely, with regard to power generating knowledge, the government helps to pay for the research and development of new drugs by these companies. The drug companies that develop these drugs are given the responsibility to determine their safety and effectiveness through conducting experimental research. The U.S. government's and the drug company's power, therefore, determine what illnesses are targeted, which drugs are developed and researched, and how these studies are going to be conducted. Hence, these two entities' interests—making the largest profit possible, keeping political interest groups happy, and safely treating illness—guide what is researched and how that research is conducted. In other words, their power influences the knowledge generation process (power generates knowledge).

In today's information-based society, scientific research methods produce one of our most authoritative sources of knowledge. It consequently wields considerable power, and often lies at the center of today's most pressing issues and conflicts (i.e., knowledge generates power). It is at

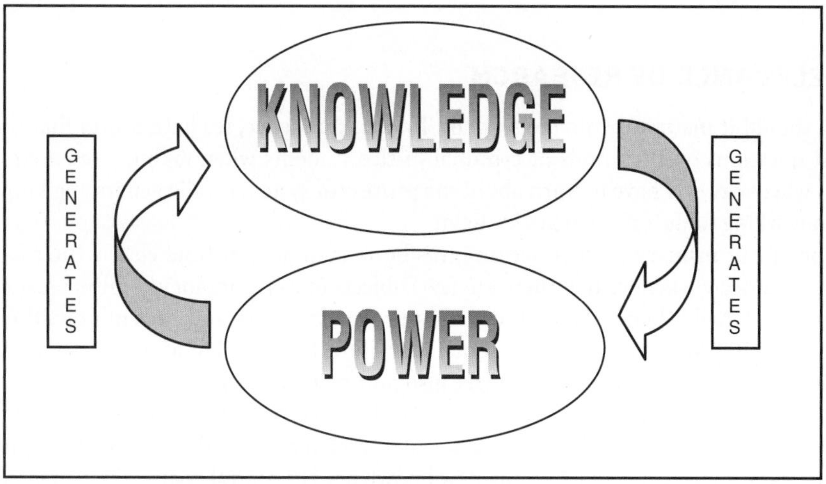

KNOWLEDGE–POWER DYNAMIC

The idea that knowledge generates power and, conversely, power generates knowledge.

FIGURE 1.1 The Knowledge–Power Dynamic.

the same time subject to manipulation by people or institutions that are attempting to wield power to further their own interests (i.e., power generates knowledge).

Nowhere is this knowledge–power dynamic more relevant than in the study of crime and criminal justice. The trends and issues we research are highly contested and loaded with vested interests: the causes and pains of violence against children, the state execution of convicted murderers, the recent history of terrorism and how to control it, the use and distribution of illegal drugs, and the rapid growth in the number of criminal laws. People's views on these types of topics vary dramatically. Where some see oppression, others see justice; where some see a violation of human rights, others see the upholding of public order; where some see myth and hysteria, others see fact and reality.

Our field of study possesses tremendous potential to shed much needed empirical light on these types of topics and issues. The knowledge–power dynamic, however, instructs us on the importance of generating credible knowledge only through the most rigorous social scientific methods, independent, to the extent possible, of dominant interests. Put in a different way, research holds tremendous power to influence, yet the researcher must be diligent to resist being unduly influenced by those in power.

Research Defined

CRIME AND JUSTICE RESEARCH

A collection of social science methods applied systematically to generate knowledge about crime and justice phenomena.

At its core, then, research is all about producing knowledge. The Old French word *recerchier* means "an intense search for knowledge." We'll define **crime and justice research** as *a collection of social science methods applied systematically to generate knowledge about crime and justice phenomena.* This book details numerous social science methods that systematically generate knowledge, including surveys, interviews, experiments, ethnographic field research, existing data, and historical analyses. Consider that at this exact moment tens of thousands of people in our field—practitioners, academics, students, and other interested parties—are using these methods to collect evidence and data about a range of topics and problems. They are, for example,

- developing and testing theories about the why of crime,
- questioning taken-for-granted assumptions about how to control crime,
- evaluating traditional and cutting-edge criminal justice practices,
- documenting the prevalence of criminal violence in U.S. society, and
- exploring the consequences of crime for its victims.

These research pursuits are clearly needed, engaging, and relevant to real-world problems. In the context of the big picture, crime and justice research really does matter.

THE RELEVANCE OF RESEARCH

But why should it matter to you, the student. In our experience, we have found that one of the foremost questions on the minds of criminal justice students when taking a research methods course is why: Why do I have to learn about the process of systematically generating knowledge if I plan on working in the criminal justice field?

One of our primary goals in writing this book is to demonstrate clearly the relevance of research. We sincerely believe that there are few subjects in a criminology/criminal justice degree program more tangibly beneficial to students, future practitioners, and current practitioners than research methods. This chapter, and the remainder of the book, will reinforce this point; for now, let's review a few of the more important (see also Summary Table 1.1).

We hope one benefit is obvious—crime and justice research is interesting. The various objects of study reviewed next and their associated research methods will hopefully pique your interest to learn. Generating and learning new knowledge is a central goal of the higher education system, and it can be an intellectually stimulating and rewarding experience.

SUMMARY TABLE 1.1	Tangible Benefits of Research Methods for Students

- Generating new knowledge is interesting and rewarding in and of itself.
- Sharpens critical thinking skills.
- Promotes being a critical consumer of research-based knowledge.
- Begins the process of becoming a proficient researcher.
- Highly beneficial in today's increasingly research-oriented workplace; promotes evidence-based practices.

This is not to minimize research method's practical benefits. Understanding the philosophies of knowledge generation (found in Chapter 3), as well as the ins and outs of conducting research, will sharpen your **critical thinking** skills. Rather than taking for granted what you know, and what others tell you is the "truth," research methods mandate that knowledge claims be assessed analytically, using the criteria of *reason* and *evidence*. Aside from religion and superstition, we human beings can only accurately assess "what is really the case" using evidence and reason. Research methods provide us a powerful framework for enacting effectively our ability to think critically.

CRITICAL THINKING

A type of thinking that scrutinizes knowledge claims using the criteria of reason and evidence.

For example, this book should provide you with the skills to assess the strength of a hypothetical statement a professor might make to her or his students: "Due to a long-running culture of violence and revenge, the United States incarcerates more of its citizens than any country in the world." Three knowledge claims would need to be assessed to determine the probable accuracy of this assertion:

1. Has violence and revenge been a historical feature of U.S. culture?
2. Does the United States incarcerate more of its citizens than any other country?
3. What evidence indicates that 1 and 2 above are causally related?

Dissecting this type of knowledge claim is essential for the closely related benefit of becoming a *critical consumer of research*. Research-based knowledge claims are a pervasive part of our lives in commercials, newspapers, political campaigns, the workplace, and the doctor's office. By being a more informed citizen, you will be able to critically analyze research in your everyday decision making.

We assume that a large percentage of students using this book either plan to work or are currently working in some crime and justice–related field. (A few might even be inspired to pursue a career as a crime and justice researcher.) Whatever the case, understanding research methods can be highly beneficial in the workplace. All crime and justice agencies are becoming more data, information, and research oriented. Today's police or correctional administrator would be lost without a basic understanding of how to manage, solve problems, and make effective decisions using research-based information. Evidence-based practice and thinking are rapidly becoming the norm rather than the exception.

The authors have witnessed this transformation firsthand in dozens of criminal justice agencies. We've also witnessed college graduates making themselves invaluable to an organization because of their research method education and skills. One of Kraska's former students who was a police practitioner is a good example. He worked his way quickly into the ranks of administration, ultimately becoming police chief, due in part to his abilities to answer complex agency and community questions using the research techniques he learned in a research methods course.

WHAT DO WE RESEARCH?

You should now have a better sense of criminal justice research's relevance and how it fits into today's ever-changing society. Let's examine next *what exactly we research*—referred to as our **objects of study.** The range of our objects of study in criminology/criminal justice is vast. In fact, because our field of study is a relatively new one and growing rapidly, the boundaries around what we study are still being drawn.

OBJECTS OF STUDY

The specific crime and justice phenomena that we decide to research.

Notice that we even had to use two labels for our field—criminology and criminal justice. *Criminology* is usually seen as the study of crime, including how it is defined, and its causes, control, and nature. *Criminal justice* examines crime control policies and the criminal justice system, and its components. Many perceive of criminology as theoretically oriented and criminal justice as practically oriented. We have two reasons for preferring to use the unifying label **crime and justice studies** (sometimes we'll use crime and criminal justice studies). First, it's far less cumbersome. Second, the split between criminology and criminal justice seems to be based more on old academic turf wars than actual substantive differences. When we consider the actual research, teaching, and intellectual interests of professors working in both fields, the commonalities and overlap far outweigh the differences. Criminology researchers increasingly study practical crime control matters, and there is an entire body of theoretical scholarship on crime control/criminal justice topics (Kraska 2006).

This difficulty in labeling our field is a testament to our diversity. As noted, our area of study is both theoretically and practically oriented. We research technical/practical questions (e.g., how to best supervise police officer patrol time) as well as sophisticated theoretical issues (e.g., explaining the massive increase in incarceration over the last thirty years). Crime and justice studies is also multidisciplinary, meaning it is influenced by numerous academic fields such as sociology, anthropology, biology, economics, geography, political science, history, psychology, psychiatry, philosophy, public administration, international and comparative studies, and legal jurisprudence, among others. Multiple academic lenses result in a wide diversity of perspectives, numerous areas of study, and a highly eclectic selection of research methods (revisited in Chapter 3). In short, our diversity allows for a good deal of freedom in what we study and options for how to research.

We refer to all that we study in our field as **crime and justice phenomena.** This includes all topics, activities, issues, questions, and trends that revolve around crime, crime control, and the criminal justice system. Assuming you are a criminology or criminal justice major, it is likely that research has been conducted on nearly every topic brought up in your other courses. Some of these topics are very controversial—crimes committed by the U.S. government—and some are extremely technical—whether less-than-lethal weaponry (pepper spray, for example) reduces injuries for police and corrections officers. International research has also become commonplace, and research on terrorism and our reaction to terrorism are increasingly popular subjects.

Table 1.1 shows the data we have collected specifically for this book (with the help of a very capable research assistant, Robert Seaver). We examined the content of every article in four of our

---

CRIME AND JUSTICE STUDIES

A phrase that combines the two highly interrelated fields of study, *criminal justice* and *criminology*.

CRIME AND JUSTICE PHENOMENA

The full range of possible objects of study in our field, which includes all topics, activities, issues, questions, and trends that revolve around crime, crime control, and the criminal justice system.

TABLE 1.1	Prevalence of Crime and Justice Objects of Study (1995–2004)

	N size	Percent
Crime	310	23
Corrections	192	14
Juvenile justice	176	13
Police	166	12
Our discipline, crime and justice studies	115	8.5
Race	93	7
Gender	85	6
International	73	5
Criminal law	53	4
Courts	48	3.5
Victims	36	2.5
Media	19	1.5
TOTAL	1,366	100

Source: The four journals included *Criminology, Justice Quarterly, Journal of Criminal Justice,* and *Crime and Delinquency.*

best-known and respected academic journals over a ten-year period (a total of 1,366 cases). We hoped to obtain a clearer picture, through quantitative documentation, of various dimensions of research in our field. One of the things we examined (what researchers refer to as variables) was the different objects of study found in these journals and their prevalence. Studies usually include more than one object of study—we coded only the primary focus of the research.

As you can see, crime was, not surprisingly, the most researched topic (310 articles, or 23 percent of the total), followed by studies on the correctional subsystem (192 articles, or 14 percent of the total), then the juvenile justice system, and finally the police (13 and 12 percent, respectively). Race and gender issues were featured in 178 articles (13 percent), and international/comparative topics in 73 articles.

WHO ARE THE RESEARCHERS?

It would be misleading to give the impression, however, that crime and criminal justice research is found only in journals monopolized by academic researchers. Research and statistics have become an integral part of professional and bureaucratic life as well. Nonacademic practitioners—in policing, courts, prisons, probation, juvenile justice, the legal community, journalists, government researchers, nongovernmental organizations (NGOs), and activist/interest group organizations—all conduct, with increasing regularity, a wide range of different kinds of research.

Professors in Practice

Many crime and justice academics also work as paid consultants and as pro bono researchers for the government, NGOs, and even special-interest groups. A common arrangement is paid-for consulting work, where an academic researcher is hired by an agency or organization to research a particular topic. A county jail, for example, needs to know the likely size of its inmate population in ten years, or a community group opposed to legalized gambling wants to know if there is a relationship between casinos and crime. These studies are occasionally published in academic journals, but they are generally used for bureaucratic or political reasons. The various research arrangements are too numerous to review, but Figure 1.2 provides a cursory look.

Academic Researchers at Colleges and Universities

- Academics researching for scholarly publications
- Academics researching for private or public C&J organizations
- Academics researching as part of expert witness testimony work
- Academics researching for activist organization (e.g., Amnesty International)
- Academics researching for educational institutions (e.g., research on teaching efficacy)
- Academics researching for foreign countries

Practitioner-based Research at Federal, State, and Local Level

- Practitioners embarking on their own research for agency purposes
- Practitioners conducting research in concert with academic researchers

Professional Researchers Working Outside Academe

- Researchers working in research division of large organization (e.g., NIJ, British Home Office, state-level research department, research department within police agency, Government Accounting Office)
- Researchers working in interest group (e.g., Cato Institute, American Bar Association; Human Rights Watch)

Print/Media Journalists

Students

- Students conducting research as part of class project
- Students conducting research in concert with academic researcher

FIGURE 1.2   Who Carries Out Crime and Justice Research?

One noteworthy variety is in the area of **expert witness research** and testimony. Numerous academics in our field contract out their research expertise to law firms or the government for civil and criminal legal cases. Dr. James W. Marquart, an expert in the area of corrections, has presented his academic research findings in numerous death penalty cases. His research examined whether inmates released from death row, a result of the landmark Supreme Court decision in *Furman v. Georgia*, were at risk of committing additional violent crimes. He did not find evidence to support the hypothesis of future danger. His data and analysis raised questions about the reliability of psychiatrists' expert-witness predictions that a typical murderer poses a future danger to society—in some states a legal requirement for imposing the death penalty.[3]

Governmental Research

Governments also conduct a great deal of crime and justice research at the federal, state, local, and even international levels. In fact, generating scientifically based knowledge has been a centerpiece of attempts at criminal justice reform worldwide. The U.S. Department of Justice oversees the National Institute of Justice (NIJ) and the Bureau of Justice Statistics (BJS), two large departments dedicated to crime and justice research. The BJS administers the **National Crime Victimization Survey (NCVS),** the primary source of information on criminal victimization in the United States. Every year, they collect data from a nationally representative sample of 42,000 households on the frequency and consequences of criminal victimization. The NIJ is a research agency responsible for awarding and overseeing research grants targeted at crime control and justice issues. The NIJ is the most commonly used source of research funding for crime and justice academics. The Federal Bureau of Investigation, also a branch of the Department of Justice, collects and analyzes data on reported crimes and arrests (found in the *Uniform Crime Reports*), as well as on hate crimes and numbers of police officers killed and assaulted while on duty.

Most individual states have their own criminal justice research office, and local criminal justice agencies, such as police departments or probation departments, engage in various degrees of research. These can range from large-scale projects involving millions of dollars to a single officer in a police or probation agency who is responsible for constructing an annual report (usually a college graduate who had paid close attention in her research methods course).

Practitioner-Based Research

The fact is that in the real world of today's criminal justice apparatus, research is ubiquitous and unavoidable. Criminal justice practitioners—aside from those working in research-oriented governmental agencies such as NIJ—generate on a daily basis, sometimes with the assistance of academics, massive amounts of data and analysis in areas such as family violence, violent youth crime, arrests, illegal drug use among arrestees, gangs, prison disciplinary infractions, and probation revocations. Katz (2003) describes one program, for instance, in which 56 percent of all U.S. police departments collect street-level data on gangs in their jurisdictions. These data are sent to the BJS, where academic researchers use them for their own studies. The BJS conducts a similar program for generating national-level data on hate crimes.

Crime and justice researchers often rely heavily on these types of practitioner-generated data (UCR data, for example). These data are also being used within the system for identifying crime patterns (see crime-mapping example used in Chapter 9), developing risk models to help in sentencing offenders, and constructing elaborate classification systems for incarcerated offenders.

Journalists as Researchers

Journalists also conduct crime and justice research. Your authors have worked extensively with investigative print journalists from credible publications and have found them without exception to be adept, conscientious, and resourceful researchers. They dig deep to understand what they are studying using multiple field research techniques. They also collect and analyze quantitative

HIGHLIGHT 1.1

Missing Children Hysteria

The missing children myth discussed in this chapter is illustrative of the vital yet difficult position in which crime and justice researchers can find themselves. John Walsh is the host of the long-running and popular *America's Most Wanted*. Walsh's son was a victim of stranger-abduction and was subsequently murdered. Imagine how difficult it is to disprove and critique, using the cold facts found in statistics, Walsh's assertion that 1.5 million children are abducted per year and that "this country is littered with mutilated, decapitated, raped and strangled children" (Glassner 1999: 63). Politicians since Ronald Reagan have capitalized on this fear and much of the media uncritically reports hearsay as facts. Researchers are placed in the unenviable position of trying to explain the "scientific facts" of the matter, juxtaposed against the reality that there are indeed real victims with deep emotional pain. Of course, in the end it does no one any good to grossly exaggerate the problem. As many criminologists note, public policy based on raw emotion, unjustified fear, and distorted facts will yield few benefits and many negative, albeit unintended, consequences.

data, oftentimes obtaining sensitive documents from government officials using the Freedom of Information Act. It was actually the careful research conducted by *Los Angeles Times* journalists that debunked the most often cited crime myth in our field—the missing children phenomenon (see Highlight 1.1).

President Ronald Reagan called it the nation's most dire domestic problem. If the statistics had been true, he would have been right: The mainstream media, and many politicians, were claiming that 1.5 million children were abducted each year and that 50,000 of those children were never found. Many Americans became highly fearful that strangers would abduct their children. Two skeptical *Los Angeles Times* journalists collected data directly from the federal government by filing a Freedom of Information Act request and discovered that a more realistic number of children abducted by strangers was closer to 100. Subsequent research has found no indication that the problem has worsened over the last forty years. Included in the 1.5 million were all teenage runaways (nearly three-quarters of which were found in less than twenty-four hours) and *children involved in* divorced or divorcing parental disputes.

The distortion of this phenomenon is still occurring. On a *Today Show* program, the anchor reported with alarm that there are 58,000 stranger-kidnappings per year—whereas the Justice Department's figures show just 115.[4] Later in this chapter, we highlight the rich sources of ideas for exploratory research projects found in journalistic accounts of recent events.

Student Research

Finally, let's not forget students. Advances in information technology enable nearly any student to engage in meaningful, quality crime and justice research. We have found students to be very capable and creative researchers (see Figure 1.3). More are using written surveys, in-depth interviews, field observations, and even the analysis of preexisting governmental data to supplement their semester papers. Our research methods students have conducted fascinating studies on snake handling in rural churches, the growth of the criminal justice system, prescription drug dealing, the why of steroid use and trafficking, police domestic violence policies, military

- College and university professors in academic journals
- College and university professors in practice
- Governmental research at federal, state, and local levels
- Practitioner-based research
- Journalists as researchers
- Students as researchers

FIGURE 1.3 Summary of Crime and Justice Researchers Discussed.

marijuana eradication exercises, Internet sexual predators, and the history of drug panics. We will use numerous student research projects as examples of quality research throughout this text.

HOW DO WE CONDUCT RESEARCH?

This next section briefly overviews the main data collection techniques covered in this book. In later chapters, you will read about these techniques in detail and learn how to use them; for now, we are providing you with a sense of where we're headed. The techniques are grouped into (1) quantitative techniques—collecting data in the form of numbers—and (2) qualitative techniques—collecting data in the form of words or pictures. It takes practice, creativity, and skill to match an object of study to an appropriate data collection technique. Table 1.2 ranks a few of these various methods in crime and justice studies from most commonly used to least commonly used.

Quantitative and Qualitative Research

QUANTITATIVE AND QUALITATIVE RESEARCH

Quantitative research uses numerically based data, and qualitative research uses text, language, and visually based data.

All the research methods discussed in this book are split into two categories, **quantitative and qualitative.** We will explore in depth the differences between these two; for now, think of *quantitative research as using numerically based data, and qualitative research as using text, language, and visually based data.* Traditionally, there has been some ill will between the followers of the two. Some have found it difficult to understand or appreciate the worth of the other approach. Thus, Levine (1993: 12) wrote, "quantitative social science," which he called "real social science," faced opposition but it "won the battle." Denzin and Lincoln (2003) argued that qualitative research has expanded greatly and is "rapidly displacing" outdated quantitative research.

As will be discussed in Chapter 3, the debate has deep philosophical roots and is far from frivolous. Fortunately, though, over the past decade, the combative stance between those advocating one approach over the other has begun to give way to a new methodological tolerance. Instead of thinking in terms of one versus the other (mutual exclusivity), most methodologists now view both qualitative and quantitative approaches as having unique strengths, weaknesses, and compatibilities (see Table 1.2). Chapter 13 will discuss how these two approaches can complement one another by mixing them together in a single study or series of studies (called mixed methods research). Summary Table 1.2 reviews some of the key differences between quantitative and qualitative approaches.

TABLE 1.2	Prevalence of Research Methods Used in Crime and Justice Research	
	N size	**Percent**
Secondary data set	522	35
Survey	292	20
Secondary data research	266	18
Interview	137	9
Legal	94	6.5
Content analysis	55	4
Experiment	50	3
Participant observer	46	3
Historical	21	1.5
TOTAL	1,483	100

Table 1.3 illustrates that 54 percent of women who reported that their husband had ever hit/beat them also reported instances of sexual violence.

SUMMARY TABLE 1.2 Quantitative vs. Qualitative Approaches

Quantitative Approach	Qualitative Approach
Measure objective facts	Construct social reality, culture
Focus on variables	Focus on interactive process, meaning
Reliability is key	Authenticity is key
Data are quantitative; precise measurement	Data are qualitative: words, images, categories
Analysis looks for statistical relationships	Analysis looks for patterns, themes, holistic features
Research is detached	Researcher is involved
Deductive process (top down)	Inductive process (bottom up)

Source: From W. Lawrence Neuman, *Social Research Methods, Qualitative and Quantitative Approaches,* 6/e. Published by Allyn and Bacon, 75 Arlington St., Boston, MA 02116. Copyright © 2006 by Pearson Education. Reprinted by permission of the publisher. Adapted from John W. Creswell. *Research Design: Qualitative and Quantitative Approaches.* Thousand Oaks, CA: Sage Publications, 1994; Normal K. Denzin and Yvonna S. Lincoln. "Introduction." (2003) and Egon G. Guba and Yvonna S. Lincoln. *Competing Paradigms in Qualitative Research.* (1994) In *Strategies of Qualitative Inquiry,* 2/e. Norman K. Denzin and Yvonna S. Lincoln. Thousand Oaks, Sage Publications, pp. 1–45 and 105–117 respectively; Amir B. Marvasti. *Qualitative Research in Sociology.* Thousand Oaks, CA: Sage Publications, 2004; Barbara Mostyn. "The Content Analysis of Qualitative Research Data: A Dynamic Approach." In *The Research Interview: Uses and Approaches,* ed. M. Brenner et al. New York: Academic Press, 1985, pp. 115–145; and Abbas Tashakkori and Charles Teddlie. *Mixed Methodology: Combining Qualitative and Quantitative Approaches.* Thousand Oaks, CA: Sage Publications, 1998.

COLLECTING QUANTITATIVE DATA.

Experimental Research. Whereas experiments were used in only 3.5 percent of articles, all academics agree that they are critical to the scientific process and are usually seen as the apex of quantitative scientific robustness. **Experimental research** uses the logic and principles you learned in any good high school science course—what we'll refer to in Chapters 2 and 3 as the "natural science" model (Chapter 7 details experimental research). Experiments can be conducted in laboratories or in real-life settings. They usually, but not always, involve a relatively small number of people and address a well-focused question. They are most effective for explaining phenomena or evaluating whether a program works.

In most experiments, the researcher divides the people being studied into two or more groups. He or she then treats both groups identically, except that one group but not the other is given a condition he or she is interested in: the "treatment." The researcher measures the reactions of both groups precisely. By controlling the setting for both groups and giving only one group the treatment, the researcher can conclude that any differences in the reactions of the groups over a set period of time are due to the treatment alone.

One of the earliest and most well-known experiments in crime and justice research was the Cambridge-Somerville Youth Study (Powers and Witmer 1951). The researchers selected boys younger than age ten and assigned them at random to a control group and a treatment group. The treatment group received numerous advantages, including school tutoring, medical and psychiatric attention, summer camp, and significant one-on-one contact with youth counselors. The control group received whatever assistance would normally be provided to any youth, for example, a public education. The program was deemed an initial success because from all indications the boys in the treatment group that had previous difficulties did well compared to the control group.

However, Joan McCord's well-known follow-up research, where she contacted and reexamined the participants over a longer time period, found that members of the treatment group "were more likely to have been convicted for crimes indexed by the FBI as serious street crimes;

EXPERIMENTAL RESEARCH

A method that divides people being studied into two or more groups, applying a treatment to one of the groups and determining if there are any differences in the reactions of the groups over a set period of time.

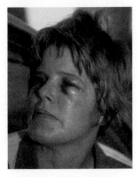

Despite concerted efforts by researchers and the criminal justice system, domestic violence remains a pervasive threat to women and children in all strata of our society.

SURVEY AND INTERVIEW RESEARCH

A method that uses a written questionnaire or formal interview to gather quantitative data on the backgrounds, behaviors, beliefs, or attitudes of a large number of people or agencies.

they had died an average of five years younger; and they were more likely to have received a medical diagnosis as alcoholic, schizophrenic, or manic-depressive" (McCord 2001: 188). She speculated that this counterintuitive finding might have been the result of juvenile delinquents attending summer camp together and reinforcing and encouraging one another's deviant values. (Can you think of any other reasons? Perhaps, for example, something that might have happened at that summer camp?)

Experimental research is the exception in crime and justice research rather than the rule. It is difficult to conduct and expensive to administer. In those instances where researchers have overcome these barriers, it has generally yielded important, unexpected findings, and has generated a good deal of controversy. The most comprehensive body of experimental research studied the deterrent effect of mandatory arrest for domestic violence offenders, commissioned by the National Institute of Justice. This series of experiments was unique: Sherman's initial study, which demonstrated that arrest did reduce future reporting of abuse by victims, was replicated numerous times to retest Sherman's impressive and controversial findings (Piquero et al. 2005). Replicating a research study is crucial to the scientific process because it determines if a study's results will hold true for different researchers in different locations or settings.

Survey and Interview Research.   In contrast to experiments, survey research is used often in our field (20 percent of journal articles rely centrally on survey research). **Survey and interview research** uses a written questionnaire or formal interview to gather quantitative data on the backgrounds, behaviors, beliefs, or attitudes of a large number of people or agencies (see Chapter 8 on survey research). Usually, they ask a large number of people or organizations dozens of questions in a short time frame. The researcher does not manipulate a situation or condition to see how people react, as in an experiment; he or she carefully records answers from many people who have been asked the same questions. Often researchers select the people or agencies for a survey using a random sampling technique so they can legitimately generalize information from a few people (e.g., one thousand) to many more (e.g., several million) (random sampling is discussed in Chapter 6).

In a provocative but important piece, "Ain't No Faggot Gonna Rob Me: Anti-Gay Attitudes of Criminal Justice Undergraduate Majors," Cannon (2004) used survey research to examine the attitudes of undergraduate criminal justice majors toward gays and lesbians. He surveyed a random sample of 1,055 criminal justice and non–criminal justice majors at four universities. He measured attitudes using a multiple-item scale—asking those surveyed their opinions about such statements as "male homosexuality is a perversion" and "lesbians just can't fit into our society."

In comparing the two groups' answers, he found that criminal justice majors held more negative opinions of gays and lesbians than did non–criminal justice majors. Interestingly, however, criminal justice majors were no more likely to have negative opinions than were political science, education, or business majors (psychology majors were the least biased). He also discovered that criminal justice majors who had taken a class that had discussed gay and lesbian issues held significantly more positive attitudes toward gays and lesbians than those who had not.

The NCVS is another good example. Instead of relying on crimes reported to the police (Uniform Crime Reports, or UCR), the NCVS measures the incidence of crime by actually asking real people about their direct experiences. Hagan and colleagues (2005) recently used this approach, conducting victimization survey research to document the genocide of Africans in the Darfur region of Sudan. Aside from determining the likely number of civilians killed, his research team was also able to demonstrate that the killings were "racially motivated, state supported, and militarily unjustified" (Hagan et al. 2005: 552).

NONREACTIVE RESEARCH

The unobtrusive collection of data that have usually been left behind by others.

Nonreactive Research.   Being asked personal questions by a researcher unknown to the respondent is clearly obtrusive. The next category of data collection involves the unobtrusive collection of data, or what is usually referred to as **nonreactive research** (the researcher studies crime and justice phenomena without affecting it). This type of research often collects and uses only what others have left behind (Webb 1981). Two nonreactive techniques are examined.

African Union soldiers patrol the village of Kerkera, located between El-Fasher, the capital of northern Darfur and Kuma. In August of 2007, the UN Security Council voted unanimously to deploy up to 26,000 peacekeepers to try to stop the violence in Darfur.

Existing Documents/Statistics Research.   The first nonreactive method, and the most common type of research in crime and justice studies, is **existing documents/statistics research.** It involves the collection and reanalysis of existing quantitative data. It is often derived from publicly available sources of information such as census bureau data, governmental crime data, economic data, and governmental survey research. The researcher reorganizes or combines the information in new ways to address a research question. As detailed in Chapter 9, some of these data can be easily accessed over the Internet. However, at times this method can require a good deal of ingenuity—especially when the researcher is gathering old data buried in the basements of government buildings or gaining access to bureaucratically sensitive data on death row inmates.

Koetting and Schiraldi (1997) conducted path-breaking international/comparative research using existing statistics. They were interested in identifying those countries with the highest incarceration rates. They compiled data from sources such as International Criminal Police Organization (Interpol), the Council of Europe, the United Nations, and the U.S. Department of Justice. The researchers found that the United States had the highest rate of incarceration compared to all other countries that were studied—with rates that exceeded even that of the occupied regions of Israel (i.e., the West Bank and Gaza Strip). The most recent data available on comparative incarceration rates are found in Chapter 10.

An interesting piece by Tark and Kleck (2004) in the journal *Criminology* examined nearly 27,595 crime incidents found in the NCVS governmental database to determine whether self-protection measures used by the victim reduced the likelihood of property loss and injury, compared to nonresistance. They found strong evidence that all forms of resistance reduced injury and property loss, with extreme forceful resistance—using a gun, for instance—having the strongest impact. The authors assert that their findings raise doubts about the commonly held belief that resistance during the commission of a crime only worsens the situation, and recommend victim self-protection measures as a "wise course of action."

Content Analysis.   **Content analysis** is another nonreactive technique used to examine the content, or information and symbols, contained in written documents or other

EXISTING DOCUMENTS/ STATISTICS RESEARCH

A method that involves the collection and reanalysis of existing quantitative data.

CONTENT ANALYSIS

A nonreactive method used to examine the content, or information and symbols, contained in written documents or other communication media.

communication media (e.g., photographs, movies, song lyrics, and advertisements). To conduct quantitative content analysis, a researcher identifies a body of material to analyze (e.g., television programs, newspaper articles, governmental records, and academic journal articles) and then creates a system for recording specific aspects of that body's content. The system might include counting how often certain words or themes appear. After the researcher systematically records what was found, she or he analyzes it, often using graphs or charts. Content analysis lets a researcher discover and document specific features in the content of a large amount of material that might otherwise go unnoticed.

Scholars have devoted a significant amount of attention and research to the role the media play in the construction of our views and opinions regarding crime and justice phenomena. In order to study this process, they often employ quantitative content analysis (see Summary Table 1.3). Chermak (1995) conducted one of the better-known studies in this area. Using an array of complex sampling techniques, Chermak coded the content of 2,158 newspaper stories and 506 television stories to describe the nature of crime reporting and crime victimization media coverage. This comprehensive work documented quantitatively what many criminologists believed but had little empirical validation for: The media present a highly distorted and sensationalized picture of crime, offenders, and victims.

Kubrin (2005), in an example of content analysis using both quantitative and qualitative approaches, studied rap music. He examined the lyrics of all rap albums that had gone platinum (sold over a million copies) between the years 1992 and 2000, comprising 1,922 songs. He drew a random sample of 632 songs and coded them for themes such as gun violence, retaliatory violence, objectification of women, and yearning for respect. He found that 68 percent referenced respect, 65 percent referenced violence, and 22 percent referenced the objectification of women.

COLLECTING QUALITATIVE DATA.

Ethnographic Field Research.   Some disciplines conduct most of their research out in the field—in the real-world settings of their subject matter. Anthropologists study humans by immersing themselves into the everyday lives of different groups' culture. Criminology has a rich history of this type of anthropological work, generally referred to as ethnographic field research.

ETHNOGRAPHIC FIELD RESEARCH

A method in which the researcher engages the natural environment of his or her subjects and strives for an up close, personal, and highly detailed understanding of the research subjects' culture.

Ethnographic field research strives for an up close, personal, and highly detailed understanding of its research subject's culture. It requires time, patience, resourcefulness, and caution. Imagine involving yourself as an observer (and in some cases participant) in the real world of an inner-city drug dealer, a White supremacist skinhead, a corrupt police or correctional officer, a criminal motorcycle gang member, armed robbers, a bouncer at a strip club, a BASE jumper, a graffiti artist, a wealthy cocaine trafficker, a juvenile prostitute, a victim of domestic violence, an incarcerated serial murderer, or a "dumpster diver." This type of research epitomizes the notion of a researcher fully immersing herself or himself into the subject matter.

SUMMARY TABLE 1.3	Quantitative Data-Gathering Techniques
Quantitative Techniques	**Examples**
Experiments	Cambridge-Somerville Youth Study and Domestic Violence Mandatory Arrest
Surveys	CJ Major Anti-Gay Attitude; Police SWAT Growth; Darfur Genocide
Existing Data/Statistics	International Incarceration Rates and Self-Protection against Crime
Content Analysis	Media Presentation of Crime; Rap Music Lyrics

Ethnographic field research begins with a loosely formulated idea or topic. Next, researchers select a social group or site for study. Once they gain access to the group or site, they adopt a social role in the setting and begin observing. The researchers observe and interact in the field setting for a period lasting from a few months to several years. They get to know personally the people being studied and may conduct hundreds of informal interviews. They take detailed notes about the settings they immerse themselves in, their interactions and observations of those being studied, participants' use of language, the conflicts and tensions, espoused values, and participant actions. During the observation, they consider what they observe and refine or focus ideas about its significance. Finally, they leave the field site, analyze their notes and experience, and prepare written reports.

A landmark study on armed robbery conducted by Wright and Decker (1997) provides a good example of crime and justice field research. Unlike most previous research on this topic, which tends to focus on armed robbers after they have been arrested and incarcerated, these two authors actually spent time in the natural environment of active armed robbers in St. Louis, Missouri. This street-level view of armed robbery offered fresh insights into the methods, motives, and meanings of committing armed robbery from the robbers' point of view. Much of their study contains verbatim quotes from conversations with armed robbers on such topics as how and why criminals select certain victims and not others. The authors drew on their rich field experience to suggest more effective avenues for robbery prevention and future research.

Jeff Ferrell (1993) also conducted an important ethnography. He spent three years as a participant-observer with a group of graffiti artists. He spent hundreds of hours in dark railroad yards, abandoned buildings, alleys, and other discarded spaces in inner-city Denver. He studied the inner workings and culture of these underground artists. He also researched the political reaction to their work and the processes involved in "criminalizing" this activity. The book is rich in graphic descriptions of the settings, emotions, and motivations of his research subjects. Ferrell (1993: 197) concluded that creating graffiti represents, for its artists, not criminality but a stylized form of cultural resistance to governmental and corporate control: "It stands as a sort of decentralized and decentered insubordination, a mysterious resistance to conformity and control, a stylish counterpunch to the belly of authority."

Qualitative Document Analysis (QDA). **Qualitative document analysis (QDA)** (or what is sometimes referred to as qualitative content analysis) attempts to make theoretical sense of *documents* by analyzing their cultural meaning. The content of documents is generally seen as its "text," but recently this genre of inquiry includes visual images as well (still pictures and video images). Kubrin's rap research (discussed previously), for instance, deciphered the predominant cultural themes within rap lyrics (toughness, revenge, respect, etc.) as a means to better understand the formation of some young men's identity and the connection between their identities and the larger cultural context within which they are formed. It is worth noting that Kubrin could have incorporated as well a content analysis of the visual images used on the album covers or associated videos—images of guns, expensive cars and jewelry, drugs, sexually objectified women, or scenes of physical violence.

Chapter 11 will examine the qualitative analysis of documents and images in more depth.

QUALITATIVE DOCUMENT ANALYSIS (QDA)

A nonreactive method that attempts to make theoretical sense of documents (text or visual) by analyzing their cultural meaning.

Historical Research. **Historical research** examines past events systematically in an effort to accurately describe and account for what has happened in the past (Berg 2007). It involves the collection and analysis of historical facts, dates, figures, and events in order to tell a story—one that is accurate; identifies the driving forces at play; details the individual personalities of key figures; and captures the social, political, and/or cultural circumstances surrounding the phenomenon studied. Of course, in the reconstructing and telling of this story, the researcher's perspectives and interpretations become part of the analysis. Historians, in fact, fully acknowledge the interpretive nature of their work and routinely concede to the reader the point of view(s) through which they are working.

Criminology/criminal justice has a rich but scattered literature on the history of crime and the various components of the criminal justice system. Fascinating historical work has been done

HISTORICAL RESEARCH

A method that examines past events systematically in an effort to accurately describe and account for what has happened in the past.

on parole, police, juvenile justice, homicide, and drug laws, to name just a few. David Garland (2005) published a noteworthy piece of historical scholarship in the journal *Law and Society Review*. Garland targets an ugly chapter in American history: the 4,000 officially reported lynchings of African Americans between 1882 and 1940.[5] He was specifically interested in the several hundred lynchings that constituted a "public event," meaning that large crowds (sometimes numbering in the thousands) attended the torture and killing of these individuals. Garland (2005: 94) describes the scene:

> Professional photographers set up shop at the scene of these lynchings and did a brisk business selling photo-souvenirs of the event. Images of mutilated black bodies, some of them horribly burned and disfigured, were purchased as picture postcards, and passed between friends and families like holiday mementoes, dutifully delivered by the U.S. mail.

HISTORICAL-COMPARATIVE RESEARCH

A method that examines aspects of social and political life across different cultures and eras.

An important branch of historical research is labeled historical-comparative research. Its emergence coincides with crime and justice studies' increasing interest in international/comparative research. **Historical-comparative research** examines aspects of social and political life across different cultures and eras. Sometimes researchers focus on one historical period or several, compare one or more cultures, or mix historical periods and cultures. It combines theory with data collection. As with field research, a researcher begins with a loosely formulated question and then refines that question during the research process. Researchers often use a mix of evidence, including existing statistics, documents (e.g., books, newspapers, diaries, photographs, and maps), observations, and interviews.

Anthony Marx (1998) conducted an interesting historical-comparative study of criminal justice and racial oppression in the United States, South Africa, and Brazil, which all had a large subordinate African populations. He asked why a racially oppressive criminal justice system, Jim Crow–type segregation, and an apartheid system did not develop in Brazil. Marx spent six years examining the histories of the three nations; traveling to numerous research centers, archives, and libraries in each country; and interviewing hundreds of people in English and Portuguese. He concluded that government-supported political oppression against Africans arose in countries that had violent conflict among Whites (the U.S. Civil War and South Africa's Boer War). Racially dominating Blacks was a way to unify all Whites around national goals and to override regional, political, and class differences among them. This dynamic was not present in Brazil.

Academic Legal Research.   Methods textbooks in crime and justice studies overlook an obvious fact when reviewing research—we study the law. Note in Table 1.2 that 6.5 percent of academic publications use legal research as their primary method; a much higher percentage incorporate legal research as a secondary method. In fact, research focusing on criminal justice phenomena often has a legal dimension. A few examples help demonstrate this fact. If a study on special weapons and tactics (SWAT) teams finds that the most common form of SWAT deployments are for drug raids, then it would be prudent to analyze Supreme Court rulings, legislative statutes, and the case law associated with drug searches using SWAT teams—often called no-knock or quick-knock drug raids. Studying "super-max" prisons as a disciplinary tool in the U.S. prison system would require research on the case law and legal challenges relevant to this practice. Inquiring into the differences in how the criminal justice system handles crack versus powder cocaine would involve an examination of federal drug laws and their judicial interpretation. Clearly, an examination of macroshifts in how the U.S. Supreme Court applies the Bill of Rights to criminal justice operations would require a detailed analysis of case law.

Many think of legal research as something that practicing attorneys and paralegals conduct to convince the court of an argument about the law. We can label this "technical legal research."

What we're concerned with in this book, however, is **academic legal research.** Although it uses some of the same techniques as technical legal research, academic legal research is simply the systematic collection and analysis of legal-related documents to generate knowledge about a given crime and justice subject. Academic legal research is published in law journals, social science journals, and scholarly books.

Collins and Vaughn (2004) provide a good example of academic legal research published in the *Journal of Criminal Justice.* Mike Vaughn, the second author, has published a large volume of work using legal research methods found in leading journals. The authors studied the civil liability of sexual harassment in criminal justice agencies. They collected all federal lower court judicial decisions that had applied the case law for sexual harassment established in three recent Supreme Court rulings. Through a detailed qualitative analysis of these cases, the authors identify trends in how the courts are dealing with lawsuits filed against criminal justice agencies for sexual harassment. Among other findings, the analysis of case law demonstrated that criminal justice agencies will be held liable for violating sexual harassment laws unless they: (1) immediately investigate all sexual harassment complaints, (2) transfer the harassing employee to a different unit, (3) administer appropriate disciplinary action where warranted, and (4) thoroughly train and educate all employees in the appropriate response and handling of sexual harassment. Notice that these research findings provide clear policy prescriptions for criminal justice organizations.

Mixed Methods Research. We mentioned earlier that quantitative and qualitative research methods each have their own unique strengths. Most researchers are moving beyond "one-versus-the-other" thinking and recognizing the cumulative strength of using both. **Mixed methods research,** then, is simply the mixture of quantitative and qualitative techniques in a single study or series of studies on the same topic. About 6 percent of articles examined used a combined approach. (See Summary Table 1.4.)

The SWAT research mentioned earlier provides a good example. One objective of this research was to inquire into whether the rapid growth in size and use of SWAT teams signaled a blurring of the traditional line delineating civilian police from the U.S. military. Survey research of police departments serving 50,000 people or more yielded an interesting finding: 46 percent of departments received training from "active-duty military experts in special operations." Because of the limitations of survey research, it could not shed light on the nature of this arrangement. Eighty-one follow-up in-depth interviews, from a sample of respondents, provided important qualitative insights into what was occurring. The following is a representative quote from a SWAT commander:

> We've had special forces folks come right out of the jungles of Central and South America. These guys get into the real shit. All branches of the military service are involved in providing training to law enforcement. U.S. Marshals act as liaisons between the police and military to set up the training—our go-between. I just received a piece of paper from a four-star general who tells us he's concerned about the type of training we're getting. We've had teams of Navy Seals and Army Rangers

ACADEMIC LEGAL RESEARCH

The systematic collection and analysis of legal-related documents to generate knowledge about a given crime and justice subject.

MIXED METHODS RESEARCH

A mixture of quantitative and qualitative techniques in a single study or series of studies on the same topic.

SUMMARY TABLE 1.4	Qualitative Data-Gathering Techniques
Qualitative Techniques	**Examples**
Field research	Armed robbery ethnography; Urban graffiti ethnography
Qual. document analysis	Rap lyric research
Historical research	American lynching research
	United States, South Africa, Brazil racial oppression
Legal research	Civil liability of sexual harassment
Mixed methods research	SWAT research

come here and teach us everything. We just have to use our judgment and exclude the information like: "at this point we bring in the mortars and blow the place up." (Kraska and Kappeler 1997: 13)

Notice how the qualitative information found in this passage complements the strength of survey research's ability to document quantitatively what is a nationwide phenomenon.

WHY DO WE CONDUCT RESEARCH?

The eight research methods just reviewed—experiments, surveys, nonreactive, ethnography, qualitative document analysis, historical, academic legal research, and mixed methods–are all conducted for a varying reasons. This section will examine the various reasons we conduct research. As you'll discover, some researchers examine crime and justice phenomena purely out of intellectual curiosity, with little or no concern about how the findings might be used to affect a problem or help others make better decisions. They pursue knowledge for knowledge's sake. Others focus on pragmatic research projects, attempting to solve problems, assist in more rational decision making, or reform policy. These two orientations are referred to as basic research and applied research, respectively. As we'll discover, the line that distinguishes these two types in crime and justice research can be blurry. Let's explore each in more detail.

Basic Research

BASIC RESEARCH

A genre of research that generates knowledge for the sake of knowledge.

DISINTERESTED KNOWLEDGE

Knowledge not pursued for any instrumental purpose, but merely for the sake of making ethical, intellectual, and theoretical sense of our world.

Basic research generates knowledge for the sake of knowledge. What does this mean? Put simply, generating knowledge is an end in and of itself. It has no utility beyond making us more knowledgeable. The traditional notion of a university was that it was a place where scholars pursued knowledge only for the purpose of better understanding humans, society, or the natural environment. A university professor was to generate **disinterested knowledge**—knowledge not pursued for any instrumental purpose, but merely for the sake of making ethical, intellectual, and theoretical sense of our world. This is why basic research is sometimes still referred to as "pure" research—an attempt no doubt to distance it from the negative trappings of the knowledge–power dynamic discussed earlier.

Whereas crime and justice studies is more of an applied discipline, basic research still plays a critical role. We produce foundational knowledge refuting or supporting theories that explain crime, theorize major historical and contemporary shifts in our reaction to crime, and examine how both fit into our social structure and culture. This type of basic research is the source of most new ideas, insights, and differing ways of thinking about our field of study. Its primary audience is the academic community.

The worth of basic research can be hard for some to appreciate. It seems to epitomize the academic "egghead" residing in the ivory tower uninterested in making an impact on the real world. This is especially true in a field dealing with people's suffering: We should only produce knowledge capable of ameliorating real-world problems. Two justifications for basic research are worth considering.

First, there is room for a small group of scholars to approach their research with the same mind-set as an astronomer or a paleontologist. Studying stars or dinosaurs has few practical benefits, yet uncovering their hidden secrets is a fascinating pursuit that interests millions of people. Some researchers approach crime and justice phenomena the same way. They find the same type of intellectual value in researching the why of serial murdering, the history of drug laws, the growth of the surveillance society, or the subculture of the police. Gaining clearer insight and better understanding about these topics should be seen as valuable in and of itself.

Still, doesn't basic research have any worth beyond enhancing our knowledge? Absolutely. The second reason is that basic research provides a foundation of understanding that can change the way we think and how we approach problems. The really big breakthroughs in understanding and significant advances in knowledge usually come from basic research and scholarship. It is, indeed, the source of most of the tools—methods, theories, and ideas—that applied researchers use.

How we deal with juvenile delinquency, for example, is directly related to our perceptions of its causes. Using scientific methods in developing and testing juvenile crime theory might seem at first irrelevant to police officers, juvenile probation officers, or social workers dealing with youthful offenders. Yet it is basic research that stimulates new ways of thinking about juvenile deviance and crime, which in turn harbors the potential to revolutionize and dramatically improve what practitioners do. Crime control policies and practices will be ineffective and misguided if they fail to filter their real-world practices through a scientifically generated body of basic knowledge.

Applied Research

Applied research can also build new knowledge, but for a different purpose. Those involved in applied research conduct a study to address a specific concern or to offer solutions to a problem. Applied researchers rely on studies usually conducted over a short time period designed to yield practical results that people can use. For example, the student government of University X wants to know whether the number of University X students who are arrested for driving while intoxicated will decline if it sponsors alcohol-free parties next year. Applied research, probably in the form of an experiment, would be most applicable for this situation.

A great deal of applied research is conducted in criminal justice agencies, social service agencies, interest groups, and educational institutions. The goal is to base real-world decision making on solid research—or what we can refer to as **evidence-based practice.** Applied research affects practitioner decisions such as starting a new program to reduce heroin addiction with an alternative prescription drug or assessing the effectiveness of adopting a new police response to reduce spousal abuse.

Applied research does not fit the idealized and romantic image of a social researcher having total freedom to pursue knowledge without any impediments. The idealized researcher is independent, has sufficient funds for a study, and maintains complete control over what to study and how to study it. A contrast to this image of the autonomous researcher is the reality of applied research.

Applied research often depends on others for research funds, and the researcher is expected to find answers to the sponsor's questions. Someone other than the researcher usually decides the topic and scope of the research question. Other conditions of funding may include restrictions to examine certain issues but not others, limits on the time to complete a study, specification of the techniques to be used or people to be contacted in a study, and directions about how and when to disseminate findings. This is not meant to imply that applied research is inherently biased; rather, it is just more sensitive to the power–knowledge dynamic.

Applied research is central to crime and justice studies. Most crime and justice academics would agree that our collective mission, as a part of the knowledge generation process, includes the reduction of crime and its associated harms, the promotion of justice, and the enhancement of government responsiveness.

All of these pursuits require quality research that assists in these efforts. The mandatory arrest experiments discussed earlier are a solid example. The research question pursued was precise and relevant to police and the victims of domestic violence: Does arresting the abuser reduce the likelihood of future violence? Similarly, hundreds of experimental and applied research studies have inquired into the effectiveness of efforts targeted at rehabilitating offenders. Francis Cullen (2005) emphasizes the critical role researchers have played in "saving rehabilitation."

> These scholars rejected the "nothing works" professional ideology and instead used
> rigorous science to show that . . . offenders were not beyond redemption, and that

APPLIED RESEARCH

A genre of research where a study is conducted to address a specific concern or to offer solutions to a problem.

EVIDENCE-BASED PRACTICE

The notion that justice practices should be based on research-generated knowledge.

treatment programs rooted in criminological research were capable of meaningfully reducing recidivism. Their story is a reminder that, under certain conditions, the science of criminology is capable of making an important difference in the correctional enterprise, if not far beyond.

Given its criticality to crime and justice studies and the practicing world, applied research will be incorporated throughout this book (although, as seen below, it will most often be referred to as *evaluation research*).

Beyond the Basic–Applied Distinction

Although instructive, the basic–applied distinction has its shortcoming in organizing our particular field of study. There are two general audiences for applied research in our field. The first is those agencies sponsoring an applied study. We discussed earlier how many academics contracted out by agencies, and practitioners themselves, conduct research to solve or shed light on an immediate organizational problem. These types of studies are only occasionally published in academic journals.

The second audience for applied research is other academics, and only indirectly for practitioners. Crime and justice research emphasizes the importance of publishing applied research in academic journals as a means to develop the field's body of *practical knowledge* (this is not to infer that *theoretical knowledge* is not practical). Crime and justice studies has developed a rich body of applied work found in most of its leading journals. The hope is that our field can accrue a useable body of practical knowledge for crime and justice practitioners and policy makers to draw from (i.e., evidence-based practice).

Clearly, much of the research and the researchers in our field, therefore, do not fit comfortably into the basic–applied dichotomy. Many do both simultaneously. Developing our basic knowledge about the causes of crime, for instance, is also a practical endeavor in guiding crime control policy. Determining whether criminal justice punishment deters crime is an intensely researched theoretical field, which simultaneously is trying to answer the evaluative question of whether deterrence works to control crime.

The Four Purposes of Research

The basic–applied dichotomy, although an important distinction for learning about the nature of research, has its limitations. Let's now look at a more specific categorization of research purposes. The purposes of crime and criminal justice research can be organized into four groups based on what the researcher is trying to accomplish:

- *explore* a new phenomenon or issue,
- *describe* a phenomenon,
- *explain* why something occurs, and
- *evaluate* practices and policy.

It is important to be aware from the outset that many crime and justice studies combine elements of these differing purposes. We have already noted how *evaluation* research targeted at determining what works to control crime can also be attempting to test the *explanatory* strength of deterrence theory. Likewise, we could *explore* the underground world of graffiti artists by providing a rich *description* of that setting.

EXPLORATORY RESEARCH

Research in which the primary purpose is to examine a little understood issue or phenomenon to develop new ideas and move toward refined research questions.

EXPLORATION.   **Exploratory research** investigates new crime and justice territory. New territory can include studying new subjects, trying out new research methods, or looking into the feasibility of undertaking a more in-depth study. Earlier we mentioned that our young discipline is still charting its boundaries. Combine this with an ever-mutating crime and crime control situation, and conditions are perfect for exploratory researchers. Whereas many disciplines are left with merely reanalyzing a new twist on previous research, opportunity abounds in crime and justice for discovering new frontiers of knowledge. Please take note of Highlight 1.2, which demonstrates the myriad exploratory research ideas available to our field.

The goals of the exploratory researcher are to uncover new and potentially important crime and justice phenomena and to formulate more precise questions that future research can answer. Exploratory research may be the first stage in a sequence of studies. A researcher sometimes needs to conduct an exploratory study to know enough to design and execute a second, more systematic and extensive study.

Exploratory researchers must be creative, open-minded, and flexible; adopt an investigative stance; and explore all sources of information. They ask out-of-the-box questions and take advantage of serendipity, those unexpected or chance factors that have larger implications. For example, Kraska and several graduate students have been working on an exploratory research project for the past several years that began with a simple story conveyed by a real estate agent. While looking for a new house, Kraska was told a heart-wrenching story. A twenty-eight-year-old father of three children was delivering supplies in a small truck. He crossed over double yellow lines to pass another vehicle (that was traveling at fifteen miles an hour below the posted speed limit). He did not see the oncoming car, which turned out to be occupied by his own uncle, resulting in a head-on collision (no substance abuse was involved). The uncle died and the nephew lived, and despite strong pleas from the entire family system (including his wife and three children), the nephew was sentenced to six years imprisonment in state prison as his actions were seen as sufficient grounds to convict him of involuntary manslaughter.

HIGHLIGHT 1.2
A Sample of Potential Exploratory Research Topics

This highlight presents a revealing illustration of the immense exploratory research possibilities in our field. We examined several newspaper Web sites during a two-week period while writing this chapter (e.g., CNN, *Washington Post*, January 24 to February 6, 2006). We scanned headline topics looking for potential objects of study that have not been researched or that little is known about. The following topics would all make for potentially worthwhile exploratory research projects:

- Stolen body parts are sold in a black market scheme to be used in legitimate medical procedures (subject: body-part trafficking) (CNN).
- High-potency methamphetamine from Mexico fills in supply gaps resulting from domestic law enforcement efforts (subject: mutating methamphetamine market due to law enforcement pressure) (*Los Angeles Times*).
- Soldier convicted of negligent homicide in torture-related death receives no jail time (subject: commission of crimes during the prosecution of Iraq War) (CNN).
- Corporate executives receive jail time while corporations themselves receive no official punishment (subject:

individual corporate offenders being used as scapegoats) (*Mother Jones*).
- Crime scene investigators claim criminals are using tactics learned on television to clean up and cover up their crimes (e.g., bleach eliminates all traces of blood) (subject: unintended consequences of *CSI* cultural fad) (CNN).
- Off-duty police officer is shot and killed by another officer (subject: friendly fire casualties in war on crime) (CNN).
- Saddam Hussein trial deteriorates into chaos (subject: international criminal courts and trials of major political figures) (BBC News).
- Retail giant Target, Inc., uses its own state-of-the-art forensics lab to assist local and federal police with difficult crimes (subject: public/private security blur) (*Washington Post*).

These examples collected from a cursory examination of current events should demonstrate that the crime and justice field is wide open for generating new knowledge about a host of undiscovered issues and phenomena. Think about which research methods discussed earlier might be used to generate knowledge about these various subjects.

Note that the nephew had no intention (*mens rea*) of killing his uncle; only 15 years ago, it would have been defined not as a crime but a tragic accident. This story piqued Kraska's research interests, leading to a long-term, state-funded exploratory research project. Notice the exploratory tone found in the text of the grant proposal:

The overall purpose of this proposed research is to identify, document, and theorize a potential macro-change in criminal law and its application. Redefining accidents and acts of negligence as serious criminality has profound implications for our society and the criminal justice system. We could view this phenomenon in several different ways:

- the erosion of "intent" (or *mens rea*) as a necessary element in an event being defined as serious crime;
- an extension of the criminal law into what were once considered accidents in the least, and civil law events at the most;
- an increasing tendency in society to criminalize harmful events that have been traditionally defined as mere accidents, acts of negligence, or the result of "risky" behavior.

DESCRIPTION.   We may have a more highly developed idea about a crime and justice phenomenon and want to describe it. **Descriptive research** presents a detailed picture of a situation, social setting, or relationship. Much of the crime and justice research found in scholarly journals, or used for making policy decisions, has a descriptive purpose.

DESCRIPTIVE RESEARCH

Research in which the primary purpose is to "paint" a picture using words or numbers and to present a profile, a classification or types, or an outline of steps to answer the questions such as who, when, where, or how.

In descriptive research, the researcher begins with a well-defined subject and conducts research to describe it accurately. The outcome of a descriptive study is a detailed picture of the subject. For example, results may indicate the percentage of people who hold a particular view or engage in specific behaviors—for example, that 10 percent of parents physically abuse their children. Recall Hagan's research on the Darfur genocide—one of the researcher's central goals was to describe the event both quantitatively and qualitatively.

A descriptive study presents a picture of what is, how something occurs, or who is involved. Exploring new issues or explaining why something happens is less of a concern for descriptive researchers than describing how things are. Descriptive research employs most data-gathering techniques—surveys, field research, legal research, content analysis, and historical research. Experimental research is not used for descriptive purposes.

Robin Haarr (2007) has completed some fascinating descriptive research (it is also exploratory). She works as both a university professor and a researcher for the Swiss government as part of a program designed to provide assistance to the country Tajikistan. Tajikistan experienced a civil war from 1992 to 1997, which caused the deaths of 60,000 people and resulted in economic ruin for the country. Haarr was brought in to deal with the problems of violence against women and child abuse in Tajik society.

Through survey research and group interviews (discussed in Chapter 12 as *focus groups*), Haarr was able to establish a baseline description, both quantitative and qualitative, of the attitudes about and prevalence of wife abuse (see Table 1.3). Aside from raising awareness about the problem, the baseline numbers will be used to determine the extent to which proposed measures to reduce violence against women in Tajikistan are having an impact (i.e., evaluation research).

EXPLANATORY RESEARCH

Research in which the primary purpose is to explain why events occur and to build, elaborate, or test theory.

EXPLANATION.   When you encounter an issue that is already known and have a description of it, you might begin to wonder why things are the way they are. The desire to know why, to explain something, is the purpose of **explanatory research.** It builds on exploratory and descriptive research and goes on to identify the reason something occurs. Explanatory research looks for causes and reasons. For example, a descriptive researcher may discover that 10 percent of parents

TABLE 1.3	Physical and Sexual Violence Perpetrated by One's Husband	
Question: Has Your Husband Ever Hit/Beat You?	**Experienced Sexual Violence**	
	n	**%**
Yes	77	54.2
No	91	36.0
sign = .00		

Source: Haarr, Robin N. (2005). *Violence against women in marriage: A general population study in Khatlon Oblast, Tajikistan,* p. 36. NGO Social Development Group. Reprinted by permission.

abuse their children, whereas the explanatory researcher is more interested in learning why parents abuse their children. As discussed further in Chapters 2 and 3, explanatory research is extremely important in crime and criminal justice studies.

Explanatory research can be either quantitative or qualitative (or it can be both) and it can employ nearly every major research method covered in this text. Recall that Garland's historical research on American public lynchings had an explanatory objective. Along with a rich description of these events, he explained lynchings as both a means to racial domination and as a type of cultural backlash to the enlightenment notion of civilized punishment.

EVALUATION.   Evaluation research attempts to determine the effectiveness of a program, policy, or method. It is the most widely used type of research conducted for, and used in, criminal justice bureaucracies (both public and private). Its overall objective is to discover what works and how to best accomplish goals—what we referred to earlier as evidence-based practice. It can be conducted using most methods discussed in this book; consequently, it will be discussed throughout.

EVALUATION RESEARCH

Research in which the primary purpose is to assess the effectiveness of a program, policy, or way of doing something.

Evaluation research brings with it an ethic of accountability and critical thinking—at least within the parameters of the question, what works? Oftentimes practices and policies are not questioned due to:

1. engrained tradition ("we've always done it that way"),
2. their comfortable fit with prevailing ideology ("getting tough on juvenile delinquents is what people and politicians want"), or
3. the fear of losing a source of funding ("we don't want to know if these Homeland Security grants are actually accomplishing anything; we need the money").

Evaluation research, in its ideal form, sets aside all these rationalizations; asks the hard question of whether a practice is working; and then unflinchingly provides an answer using rigorous experiments, survey research, existing data analysis, and qualitative techniques. Francis Cullen's comments discussed earlier, about applied research testing of the efficacy of correctional rehabilitation programs, embodied this evaluative spirit.

The Drug Abuse Resistance Education (D.A.R.E.) program is another excellent example. This is a nationwide program (which is also implemented in forty-two other countries), costing taxpayers millions of dollars to expose children to preventive information about illegal drugs. This program is extremely popular with politicians, schools, students, the police, and parents. In fact, many of you reading this text probably attended a D.A.R.E. program. The D.A.R.E. program's many proponents make it difficult for those who raise questions about its effectiveness to be listened to. The federal government nonetheless has sponsored numerous evaluative studies to determine if this program is accomplishing its central objective: reducing the likelihood of children using illegal drugs as they grow up.

The political and public support of D.A.R.E. makes it difficult for many to accept the legitimacy of rigorous academic studies that have raised serious questions about its efficacy.

Rosenbaum and Hanson (1998) conducted a difficult-to-ignore experimental study using random assignment and multiple control groups. They tracked longitudinally all participants in their control and treatment groups from the sixth grade to twelfth grade (over a five-year period during what are considered to be the drug-prone years). The authors found that D.A.R.E. had no preventive effect on its participants as compared to the control groups. If judged solely on its central objective, D.A.R.E. failed. D.A.R.E. probably had some positive outcomes—fostering more positive police–community relations, and helping politicians, school officials, and the police feel good about being involved in antidrug actions. However, a body of disinterested research has raised serious doubts about whether these actions reduce drug use among teenagers.

Not surprisingly, D.A.R.E. advocates have used these negative findings to argue that more D.A.R.E. efforts are needed, not fewer, especially during the high school years. Failure is often construed by those with vested interests in a program as a reason to do more of the same. Consistent with the power–knowledge dynamic discussed earlier, ethical and political conflicts often arise in crime and justice evaluation research because people have opposing interests in the results.

The real-world practices of those working in the criminal justice system, and of course all those other entities that can have an impact on the crime problem, are of serious consequence. Their policies and everyday practices have a profound impact on the health and welfare of victims of crime, arrestees, convicted offenders, and public safety. The death penalty is a poignant example. Much of the debate on the death penalty boils down to an evaluative question: Does the execution of convicted murderers deter future murders? The answer, determined by evaluative research, could literally mean the difference between life and death.

The death penalty example raises one final point about evaluation research and critical thinking. By inquiring only into what works, ethical concerns get pushed to the periphery. What if we found that closely monitored police surveillance cameras and microphones in all public and business spaces reduced crime? Or we discovered that giving psychotropic drugs to all children as they grow would make for a more effective and easier socialization process, thereby reducing crime? Just because something works does not mean it is ethically desirable or a just course of action. Evaluative findings should always be tempered with careful ethical deliberation and discussion.

Conclusion

One of our main objectives in this chapter has been to demonstrate the relevance and importance of research methods not only in academe, but also in the real world of criminal justice. Research and the knowledge it produces harbor significant potential to influence and make a difference. We warned as well, though, about the importance of maintaining a balance between making a difference and maintaining distance. The essence of the knowledge–power dynamic is recognizing the power of research-based knowledge to influence, while guarding against the influence of power.

We also hope that you have gained a big-picture appreciation for what research in criminology/criminal justice is all about. By presenting a broad overview of what we research, why we research, and how we conduct research, our aim has been to familiarize you up front with the basics so that the more detailed material in the rest of the book will be easier to assimilate.

Key Terms

knowledge–power dynamic *3*

crime and justice research *4*

critical thinking *5*

objects of study *5*

crime and justice studies *6*

crime and justice phenomena *6*

expert witness research *8*

National Crime Victimization Survey (NCVS) *8*

quantitative and qualitative research *10*

experimental research *11*

survey and interview research *12*

nonreactive research *12*

existing documents/ statistics research *13*

content analysis *13*

ethnographic field research *14*

qualitative document analysis (QDA) *15*

historical research *15*

historical-comparative research *16*

academic legal research *17*

mixed methods research *17*

basic research *18*

disinterested knowledge *18*

applied research *19*

evidence-based practice *19*

exploratory research *20*

descriptive research *22*

explanatory research *22*

evaluation research *23*

Review Questions

1. What is the knowledge–power dynamic and what does it have to do with crime and justice research?
2. How do we define research?
3. What are some of our major objects of research in crime and justice studies?
4. Who conducts crime and justice research and for what purposes?
5. What are the four major quantitative research methods reviewed in this text?
6. What are the four major qualitative research methods reviewed in this text?
7. What are the major differences between basic and applied research, and how do they sometimes overlap?
8. When is exploratory research used, and what can it accomplish?
9. What types of results are produced by a descriptive research study?
10. What is explanatory research? What is its primary purpose?
11. What is evaluation research and why is it so important for crime and justice studies?
12. What are the tangible benefits of learning research methods for students?

Practicing Research

1. Contact a professor in your academic program, or e-mail a professor in another academic program, and ask about his or her research activities. Find out if that person is conducting research through a grant, for journal publication, for a sponsor, or perhaps as an expert witness.
2. In the library, find a research article that uses one of the four quantitative methods reviewed in this chapter (experiments, surveys, unobtrusive measures, or content analysis). Do the same for qualitative methods. Discuss in small groups.
3. Using the same method found in Highlight 1.2, locate three more exploratory research topics. Being aware that you've been exposed only to limited information about different research methods, speculate about how you might go about researching these three topics.
4. Look through several issues of the journal *Criminology and Public Policy* and select an evaluation study that you find interesting/relevant. Read through the article and the essays in response to that article, and write an essay about what you discovered and learned.

Notes For Additional Study

1. The "science wars" can also be found in academia. The following Web site is dedicated to exploring its trends and debates: http://members.tripod.com/ScienceWars/.

2. For an excellent discussion of this phenomenon see Ulrich Beck's (1992), *Risk Society, toward a New Modernity.*

3. Marquart et al.'s (1989) research actually concentrated on specifically whether jurors could accurately predict dangerousness. As part of this analysis, though, it examined the role of expert witnesses that testified with 100 percent certainty that the convicted murderer would kill again even if incarcerated.

4. An excellent Web site that examines the statistical facts that underlie many social issues is George Mason University's "STATS" (www.stats.org). The statistics used in this section were derived from this reputable Web site, and from Kappeler and Potter (2006).

5. This research is found in two articles (Kraska and Cubellis 1997; Kraska and Kappeler 1997) and a book (Kraska 2001).

6. The following is a powerful Web site that provides a wealth of visual information on lynching: http://withoutsanctuary.org. It includes a slide show of James Allen's nonreactive research collecting and buying photographs of lynchings all over the United States. The images are quite graphic and disturbing, but document effectively a disturbing chapter in U.S. history.

7. Mark Lanier and Stuart Henry's (2004) two classroom textbooks provide excellent and updated discussions of the role biology and genetics might play in crime causation.

The Nature of Science and Research

CSI and Science

Alternatives to Research-Based Knowledge

Authority

Highlight 2.1 Experts Dual over Benefits of Stamping out Graffiti

Tradition

Common Sense

Media/Political Myths

Personal Experience

How Social Science Works

Science and Social Science

Highlight 2.2 The Horse-Slasher: Origins of Science in Criminology

The Social Science Community

The Norms of the Social Science Community

Sharing Knowledge: The Role of Scholarly Publications

Steps in the Scientific Research Process

The Steps

Quantitative Research Steps

Qualitative Research Steps

Research Step Examples

Quantitative Example: Child Abuse

■ Select a Topic

■ Focus the Question
■ Design the Study
■ Collect the Data
■ Analyze the Data
■ Interpret the Data
■ Inform Others

Qualitative Example: Violent Criminals

■ Select a Topic
■ Focus the Question
■ Design the Study
■ Collect the Data
■ Analyze the Data
■ Interpret the Data

Highlight 2.3 A Maverick Criminologist

■ Inform Others

Scientific Research and Time

Cross-sectional Research

Longitudinal Research

Conclusion

Key Terms

Review Questions

Practicing Research

Notes for Further Study

CSI AND SCIENCE

The recent popularity of police investigation shows that feature prominently the use of forensic science to solve crimes has perpetuated many myths and misperceptions.

Images of scientists working closely with the police and courts to solve crimes have captured the public's imagination. Highly scientific forensic procedures and language form the backdrop for the highly popular *CSI* television shows (set in Las Vegas, New York, and Miami). Americans probably know more about the ins and outs of a crime scene investigation than they do the Fourth, Fifth, Sixth, or Eighth Amendments to the U.S. Constitution (a testable assertion?). Criminal justice and criminology academic programs are inundated with requests from prospective students to major in forensic science, forensic criminology, or forensic psychology. Despite the myriad myths these shows perpetuate—one being that all police departments have a CSI division, which most do not—they do reflect an important reality in today's crime control apparatus. Hard science and the legal system are increasingly interrelated and interdependent. The best example is forensic DNA testing. This type of scientific testing and evidence is often central to police detective work, the appeal of death penalty cases, and in expert witness research and testimony. Understanding the nature and workings of science, therefore, is critical to understanding not only crime and justice research methods but also the daily operations of the criminal justice system.

This chapter concentrates on the nature and workings of science. Chapter 1 provided an overview of where we're headed. The next two chapters take a step back and examine the underlying thinking and ideas behind crime and justice research methods. As will be discussed in Chapter 3, *science* usually refers to quantitative methods of knowledge generation alone (the natural science model). The notion of *social science*, though, encompasses a much broader range of methods, including quantitative, qualitative, and mixed methods approaches. Not that long ago the typical research methods textbook covered only natural science techniques (what Chapter 3 will refer to as *positivist social science*). Even now, many texts devote only a single chapter to the discussion of qualitative methods. Much has changed, however, and most researchers now accept and employ numerous methods of knowledge production alongside and in cooperation with the natural science model. Before we explore further the nature of science in crime and justice studies, let's look at those nonscientific forms of knowledge we rely on in our everyday lives.

ALTERNATIVES TO RESEARCH-BASED KNOWLEDGE

The public's understanding of crime and criminal justice phenomena and issues is wrought with misguided assumptions, distorted interpretations, outright myths, and hardened ideological positions (Kappeler and Potter 2006). Most people have learned what they know about crime and justice phenomena and issues by an alternative to scientific research. Some of that knowledge is based on personal experience and common sense. Most of it is based on the information and images put forth by politicians, governmental agencies, and especially the media.

The social scientist, at least ideally, takes no knowledge claim for granted. In the attempt to generate new knowledge, this skeptical stance mandates the questioning of all conventional thinking. In this process, existing knowledge claims are refuted, substantiated, or modified. The elevated concern over missing children discussed in Chapter 1 is a good example.

Although knowledge produced through scientific methods does not by any means produce perfect knowledge, it is definitely a more structured, organized, evidence-based, and systematic process than the four alternatives discussed below.[1] However, researchers should guard against devolving into an elitist mind-set in which all "common" knowledge is dismissed and only research-based knowledge is deemed worthy. Most academic social science ideas and theories, no matter how abstract or complex, have their origins in everyday thinking, experiences, and common sense.

Authority

We gain knowledge from parents, teachers, and experts as well as from books, television, and other media. When we accept something as being true just because someone in a position of authority says it is true, we are using **authority knowledge** as a basis of knowing. Relying on the wisdom of authorities is a quick, simple, and cheap way to learn something. Authorities often spend time and effort to learn something, and you can benefit from their experience and work.

Relying on authorities also has limitations. It is easy to overestimate the expertise of other people. You may assume that they are right when they are not. Authorities may speak on fields they know little about; they can be plain wrong. An expert in one area may try to use her or his authority in an unrelated area. Have you ever seen television commercials in which an expert in football uses that expertise to try to convince you to buy a car? In addition, there are these questions: Who is or is not an authority? Whom do you believe when authorities disagree?

Politicians are sometimes taken as unquestionable authoritative sources of knowledge about the law, crime, and criminal justice issues. After all, they're lawyers who pass laws for a living. We only have to recall Ferrell's research on graffiti artists to be discussed in this chapter to appreciate the hazards of relying on politicians. Politicians were actively constructing these activities as a serious criminal threat being committed by violent gangs. From the moral panic that ensued, much of the public obviously accepted this interpretation uncritically. Ferrell's ground-level research produced an alternate view, one not based on rallying voters, but on a close inspection of the actual lived culture of graffiti artists. (Of course, the scientific spirit mandates that Ferrell would have been obligated to disclose any evidence that his research subjects were actually a gang of criminals committing acts of violence, if that were the case.) Highlight 2.1 provides an instructive example of how even "experts" can vehemently disagree about important issues.

History is full of past "authorities" that we now see as being misinformed. For example, some "experts" of the past measured criminality by counting bumps on the skull; other "experts" used bloodletting to cure diseases. Their errors seem obvious now, but can we be certain that today's experts will not become tomorrow's fools? Also, too much reliance on authorities can be dangerous to a democratic society. An overdependence on experts in homeland security efforts, for example, could keep most of us in the dark while the homeland security politicians and experts promote ideas that strengthen their power and position. When we have no idea of how the experts arrived at their knowledge, we lose some of our ability to make judgments for ourselves.

Tradition

People sometimes rely on tradition for knowledge. Tradition is a special case of authority—the authority of the past. **Traditional knowledge** means you accept something as being true because it's the way things have always been. For example, in eastern Kentucky coal oil is a cure-all for most injuries, whether horse or human. No one knows how or why it works, just that it has always been used. Tradition is the basis of the knowledge for the cure.

Here is an example from the criminal justice field. Police administrators assumed for decades that having patrol officers drive around randomly in the communities they served would prevent crime. Many road-patrol officers were skeptical, but the uncritical acceptance of traditional knowledge kept them quiet. It was not until some pioneering police executives in the Kansas City Police Department designed and implemented, with some help from academic researchers, an experiment to test whether preventative patrol had an impact on crime. The results made clear that this traditional practice accomplished little as far as reducing crime. Thirty years later police researchers are still exploring how best to deploy police services (discussed further in Chapter 8).

Not all research efforts debunk traditional knowledge. Some versions of traditional knowledge tell us that the most effective way to discipline the children who engage in serious wrongdoing is not only to make them accountable for their actions, but also to do it within the context of a caring community, so that the process is one of inclusion rather than exclusion. This is the essence of numerous restorative justice programs around the world—punishment processes that stress the

AUTHORITY KNOWLEDGE

A basis of knowledge in which we rely on what someone in a position of authority says.

TRADITIONAL KNOWLEDGE

A basis of knowledge in which we accept something as being true because of a long-running custom or belief.

HIGHLIGHT 2.1
Experts Duel over Benefits of Stamping Out Graffiti

As discussed in Chapter 1, Jeff Ferrell did ethnographic research on Denver's underground graffiti artists. Some criminologists believe that graffiti is one of the more visible indicators of disorder in a community, leading to increased crime. James Q. Wilson and George Kelling are well known for positing this "broken windows" theory of crime, and its associated solution: aggressive suppression tactics used by police to fix the "broken windows." Kelling has worked as a consultant to many cities, attempting to reduce crime based on what is sometimes called a "zero-tolerance approach."

He and his associates were hired by Denver, Colorado, city officials to help the Denver police department implement a "broken windows" crime-reduction program. The effort has generated controversy, primarily because Kelling's approach represents a move away from what is traditionally seen as a more liberal, community-oriented policing and toward a conservative, punitive-oriented policing. Consequently, the *Rocky Mountain News* published two essays debating the pros and cons of this program, one written by George Kelling and the other by Bernard Harcourt (another police social scientist). Harcourt bases his argument on research findings. He cites research that raises serious doubts about Kelling's repeated assertion that the crime drop that occurred in New York during the late 1990s was due primarily to broken windows policing. After citing an additional study, Harcourt writes,

> "broken windows" is a cute slogan that's good marketing. But it rests on a faulty theory. There is no reliable empirical evidence that disorder causes crime. The most rigorous empirical analysis, conducted by Robert Sampson at Harvard and Stephen Raudenbush at the University of Chicago, suggests that disorder and crime have common antecedents in structural disadvantage and lack of neighborhood trust.

Kelling actually ends up agreeing with Harcourt in his reply: "let us concede up front that from a 'scientific' perspective, the studies that are available provide mixed evidence...." He makes his central counterargument through a quote from the former chief of police in New York and current chief of the Los Angeles Police Department, William Bratton:

> What particularly galls police about these critiques is that ivory-tower academics—many of whom have never sat in a patrol car, walked or bicycled a beat, lived in or visited regularly troubled violent neighborhoods, or collected any relevant data of their own "on the ground"— cloak themselves in the mantle of empirical "scientist" and produce "findings" indicating that broken windows has been disproved. Worse, they allege that police have little to do with the declines in crime. Police don't have time for these virtual-reality theories; they do their work in the real world.

Notice the hostility, by both Bratton and Kelling, toward those who conduct research. We can only imagine that they would be readily embracing and touting the virtues of social scientific research if the research findings supported their theory and programs. It is also important to note that many researchers in our field have spent considerable time in the field either as former practitioners or as engaged researchers. This highlight illustrates both the hazards of relying on expert opinions and that research-based knowledge can be politically controversial.

Source: Prepared using Kelling et al. (2006), Harcourt (2006), and Kilzer (2006).

caring reintegration of offenders. These programs have held up fairly well under the scrutiny of evaluation (Morrison and Ahmed 2006).

Common Sense

*COMMON SENSE
KNOWLEDGE*

A basis of knowledge in which we rely on commonly accepted, ordinary reasoning.

We know a lot about the social world from ordinary reasoning or **common sense knowledge.** We rely on what everyone knows and what "just makes sense." For example, it "just makes sense" that murder rates are higher in nations that do not have a death penalty, because people are less likely to kill if they face execution for doing so. This and other widely held commonsense beliefs, such as that poor youth are more likely to commit deviant acts than those from the middle class, are questionable (at least based on the available evidence).

Common sense is valuable in daily living, but it can allow logical fallacies to slip into our thinking. For example, the gambler's fallacy says, "If I have a long string of losses playing a lottery, the next time I play, my chances of winning will be better." In terms of probability and the facts, this is false. Also, common sense contains contradictory ideas that go unnoticed because people use the ideas at different times—for example, "opposites attract" and "birds of a feather flock together." Common sense can originate in tradition. It is useful and oftentimes correct, but it also contains errors, misinformation, contradiction, and prejudice.

Media/Political Myths

Television shows, movies, and newspaper and magazine articles are important sources of information about social life. For example, most people who have no contact with criminals or the criminal justice system learn about crime and justice by watching television shows and movies, and by reading newspapers. A major area of study in crime and justice studies deals with how media portrayals of crime, crime victims, police, and corrections do not accurately reflect social reality. Instead, the writers who invent or adapt real life for television shows and movie scripts distort reality either out of ignorance or because they rely on authority, tradition, and common sense. Their primary goal is to entertain, not educate, but these media still have a potent educative effect.

A good example is the highly popular *CSI* television shows mentioned earlier. They present a feeling of gritty reality about the underworld of crime and the "scientists" who put people behind bars using cutting-edge forensics. Most crime and justice majors are surprised to find out that the premises behind the show are for the most part false. Very few police departments have a crime lab. Almost all crime labs are separate, centralized agencies operating at the state level. Homicide detectives, not lab technicians, run all murder investigations, including conducting all interviewing of suspects. And the typical lab technician, who has a chemistry-based degree in forensic science, rarely goes out into the field; instead, he or she spends a large portion of his or her time analyzing a several-month backlog of evidence samples and filling out reports (Pratt et al. 2006).

The media help to construct and maintain the myths of a culture. For example, the media routinely show that most people who receive welfare are African American (actually, the large majority are White), that most people who are mentally ill are violent and dangerous (only a minuscule percentage actually are), and that most people who are elderly are senile and in nursing homes (again, a tiny minority). In addition, mass media "hype" can create the idea that a major problem exists when it may not. People are misled by visual images more easily than other forms of "lying"; this means that stories or stereotypes that appear on film and television can have a powerful effect on people. For example, television repeatedly shows low-income, inner-city, African-American youth using illegal drugs. Eventually, most people "know" that urban Blacks use illegal drugs at a much higher rate than other groups in the United States, even though this notion is false.

Before the media get too much blame, however, it is critical to consider the sources of the media's information. Academics have documented the general pattern involved in the construction of crime and justice media myths.[2] In reality, the media are only one component in a three-way dynamic between media interests, governmental official interests, and politicians' interests. The **media knowledge** often feed off uncritically the information provided to them by government agencies and politicians, and vice versa. The back and forth interplay between these three stakeholders can ratchet up the level of drama to a point of hysteria (or what social construction theorists call a "moral panic"), particularly if the theme they are constructing resonates with its customers (us). Just a few examples of themes in which this trio mutually ratcheted up the level of sensationalism include crack babies, juvenile super-predators, missing children, car jackings, gang violence, and an ever-worsening crime problem.

Personal Experience

If something happens to us, that is, if we personally see it or experience it, most of us accept it as true. **Personal experience knowledge** has a strong and lasting impact. It is a forceful source of knowledge, so much so that an academic's professional research interests can sometimes be traced back to childhood experiences. Lived experiences are even the data used by some types of researchers (an approach known as *phenomenology*).

MEDIA KNOWLEDGE

A basis of knowledge in which we rely on the media's construction of the truth, which often relies on claims made by politicians and government officials.

PERSONAL EXPERIENCE KNOWLEDGE

A basis of knowledge in which we rely on our own lived experiences.

Experiences, then, are definitely an essential building block of our reality. The difficulty is that they can also be unreliable, distort reality, and deceive us into believing things that aren't true. Kraska's youthful experiences as a fly-out fishing guide in Alaska provide a good example. Making landings and takeoffs in small rivers and ponds, running river rapids in powerboats, fishing in grizzly bear–populated streams, and luging on flotation devices down steep glaciers never once led to an injury or accident. Over several years of experience, he learned to assume that accidents don't happen—the myth of invincibility. Unfortunately, this erroneous assumption has led to numerous errors in judgment and injuries as he's aged.

There are actually four errors of personal experience that reinforce each other and can occur in other areas as well.

<table>
<tr><td>

OVERGENERALIZATION

Statements that go far beyond what can be justified based on the data or empirical observations that one has.

</td><td>

1. **Overgeneralization** occurs when we have some evidence that we believe and then assume that it applies to many other situations. Limited generalization may be appropriate; under certain conditions, a small amount of evidence can explain a larger situation. The problem is that people often generalize well beyond the limited evidence derived from their own personal experience.

   When people know little or nothing about many individuals, areas, and situations, they tend to generalize from the little they do know. For example, over the years, Neuman has known five blind people. All of them were very friendly. Can he conclude that all blind people are friendly? Do the five people with whom he had personal experience fully represent all blind people?

   Research often casts serious doubts on personal experience and self-knowledge. People misjudge themselves; eyewitness accounts such as those used in criminal justice tend to be highly inaccurate; most people's estimates of the chance of being involved in an accident are far off from actual probabilities; and people are easily misled by appearances, such as purchasing an SUV for its perceived safety.[3]

</td></tr>
<tr><td>

SELECTIVE OBSERVATION

Making observations in a way that simply reinforces preexisting thinking, rather than attempting to observe in a balanced and critical manner.

</td><td>

2. **Selective observation** occurs when we take special notice of people or events and generalize from them. People often focus on or observe particular cases or situations, especially when they fit preconceived ideas. We often seek out evidence that confirms what we already know or believe and ignore the range of cases and contradictory information. We are sensitive to features that confirm our ideas—features that might otherwise go unnoticed.

   For example, someone might believe that the majority of African Americans are poor, live on welfare, and are prone to criminality. Because all of these beliefs are actually far off the statistical mark, they are obviously rooted in an ideology based in racial prejudice and stereotypes. However, this person will likely find plenty of evidence for his or her beliefs because he or she will notice only those pieces of evidence that reinforce his or her ideology. The entertainment/media industry unfortunately provides plenty of images and themes that reinforce these views.

</td></tr>
<tr><td>

PREMATURE CLOSURE

Making a judgment or reaching a decision and ending in an investigation before one has the amount or depth of evidence required by scientific standards.

</td><td>

3. **Premature closure** reinforces the first two errors. Premature closure occurs when we feel we have all the answers and do not need to listen, seek information, or raise questions any longer. Unfortunately, most of us take the easy route and examine only a few pieces of evidence or look at events for a short while and then think we have it figured out. We look for evidence to confirm or reject an idea and stop when a small amount of evidence is present. In a word, we jump to conclusions: I know three people who smoked six packs of cigarettes a day and lived to be eighty years old; therefore, people who smoke lots of cigarettes will live to age eighty.

</td></tr>
<tr><td>

HALO EFFECT

Allowing the prior reputation of persons, places, or things to color one's evaluations, rather than attempting to evaluate in a neutral, equal manner.

</td><td>

4. The last error is the **halo effect.** It comes in various forms, but it says we overgeneralize from what we believe to be highly positive or prestigious sources of knowledge. We give things or people we respect a halo. We let the prestige rub off on other things or people about which we know little. The White House might publish a report with an introduction from the president that warns that "reported violent crime" in schools has increased significantly. The halo effect might inhibit reporters from scrutinizing the veracity of this knowledge claim. What they might be overlooking, of course, is that school officials, in times of zero tolerance,

</td></tr>
</table>

SUMMARY TABLE 2.1	Alternative Sources of Knowledge
Source of Knowledge	**Examples**
Authority knowledge	Homeland Security and broken windows experts
Traditional knowledge	Kansas City patrol experiment Restorative justice
Common sense knowledge	Death penalty
Media knowledge	CSI and crack myths
Personal experience knowledge	Eyewitness accounts Racial prejudice

might be defining a much broader range of youth behaviors as police matters; hence, reporting rates increase, not actual school violence incidents. Summary Table 2.1 reviews each alternative source of knowledge along with the major examples provided.

HOW SOCIAL SCIENCE WORKS

Carefully following a set of processes to create new knowledge is the essence of science. Let's look at the meaning of science and social science; it is a subject that we will examine in more detail in Chapter 3.

Science and Social Science

When most people hear the word *science*, the first image that comes to their mind is one of test tubes, computers, rockets, and people in white lab coats. These outward trappings are a part of the natural sciences. The natural sciences—biology, chemistry, physics, and zoology—deal with the physical and material world (e.g., rocks, plants, chemicals, stars, blood, electricity, dinosaur bones, etc.). The natural sciences are the basis of new technology and receive a lot of publicity.

The social sciences, such as anthropology, psychology, political science, education, criminal justice criminology, and sociology, involve the study of people—their beliefs, personalities, behavior, interaction, cultures, institutions, and so forth. Fewer people associate these disciplines with science. They are sometimes called soft sciences. This is not because their work is sloppy or lacks rigor but because their subject matter, human social life, is fluid, formidable to observe, and hard to measure with traditional scientific instruments. (Try measuring sexism in a test tube.) David Silverman (2004: 224) summarizes current thinking on broadening the notion of science: "It is an increasingly accepted view that research becomes scientific by adopting methods of study *appropriate* to its subject matter. Social science is thus scientific to the extent that it uses appropriate methods and is rigorous, critical, and objective in its handling of data." Science in this view, therefore, includes all social scientific research methods—assuming they meet the criteria of being systematic, rigorous, and critical.

Science must be understood as a human-constructed social institution. It has not always been around; it is a human invention for producing knowledge. Before science became fully entrenched in our society, people used only prescientific or nonscientific methods. These included the alternatives discussed previously and other methods (e.g., oracles, mysticism, astrology, and sacred texts). Such prescientific systems were an unquestioned way to produce knowledge. They are still pervasive in modern society—any large bookstore has large sections devoted to premodern forms of knowing (e.g., the New Age, spiritual, paganism, or religious sections).

What people now call science grew from a major shift in thinking that began with the Age of Reason or the Enlightenment in Western European history, between the 1600s and the early 1800s. The Enlightenment ushered in a wave of new thinking. It included a faith in logical reasoning, an emphasis on experiences in the material world, a belief in human progress, and a questioning of traditional religious authority. Science originally concentrated only on the natural

---

HIGHLIGHT 2.2

The Horse-Slasher: Origins of Science in Criminology

Scholars have long debated the origins of scientific criminology. Nicole Rafter (2004) has contributed significantly to this discussion in "The Unrepentant Horse-Slasher: Moral Insanity and the Origins of Criminological Thought." Whereas most have settled on Lombroso's *Criminal Man,* published in 1876, as the defining work, Rafter researched how and when European and American Enlightenment thinking began affecting the understanding of crime in the late 1700s. She examined the work of three early psychiatrists who attempted to shift explanations of crime from the religious-based notion of sinner to the scientific condition labeled "moral insanity." Her research method was historical: "I followed debates about moral insanity in literature covering the period from 1785 through 1885, focusing in particular on material in the *American Journal of Insanity* [the professional journal of U.S. psychiatrists] and the *Journal of Mental Science* [the equivalent journal of British psychiatrists]."

One leading theorist she studied, James Prichard, defined *moral insanity* as "a form of mental derangement in which … the moral and active principles of the mind are strangely perverted and depraved; the power of self-government is lost or greatly impaired; and the individual is found to be incapable of conducting himself with decency and propriety in the business of life" (1835: 4). In 1885, another psychiatrist reported a "perfect example" of moral insanity—a normal man, by all accounts, except that

as a boy he whipped a younger brother, almost killing him, and then was apprehended for cutting the throat of a valuable horse belonging to a neighbour. He confessed to this act and to maiming and killing other animals as well. Jailed for twelve months, he returned and tried to strangle a younger brother. An attempt to smother an infant sibling and several thefts led to a 7-year penitentiary sentence. His next escapade was the result of an accident. B and his father were at a neighbour's one evening, and while paring apples, the old man accidently cut his hand … severely. B … became restless, nervous, pale, and went to a nearby farm where he cut the throat of a horse, killing it. While hiding in the woods, he raped a little girl … He … went on to castrate a horse, gash its neck and abdomen, and amputate part of its tongue. Sent to an insane asylum, he escaped, and attempted rape and committed a number of minor offenses. Back in the asylum he tried to castrate a fellow inmate and punctured the stomach of another with a fork.

---

world, but it soon spread to the study of social life as well. Highlight 2.2 provides a revealing and fascinating early application of natural science thinking to understanding crime.

The advancement of science or of fields within science, such as criminology, does not just happen. It is punctuated by the triumphs and struggles of individual researchers. It is also influenced by significant social events, such as war, depression, government funding, or shifts in public support.[4] Many have tried to make theoretical sense of how science progresses. One of the more well known is Thomas Kuhn (1963, 1970, 1979). He turned the scientific world on its head when he demonstrated that scientific knowledge does not progress in an orderly incremental fashion, from error to truth, based on the research evidence. Instead, as illustrated in Figure 2.1, knowledge is constructed within a community of people who carry with them a host of professional, personal, and cultural interests. New knowledge or new methods of knowledge generation often pose, therefore, a serious threat to the dominant way of thinking (or a *paradigm*). Significant progressions in thought require what Kuhn describes as a "revolution." In short, at least for Kuhn, constructing knowledge is as much a cultural-political process as it is a scientific one. Kuhn's analysis targeted the natural sciences. **Kuhn's progression of knowledge** is a cultural-political process, as much as it is a scientific one, and is even more applicable for the social science such as crime and justice studies.

Social science, then, refers to both a system for producing knowledge and the knowledge produced from that system. The system evolved over many years and is slowly but constantly changing. It combines assumptions about the nature of the world and knowledge; an orientation toward knowledge; and sets of procedures, techniques, and instruments for gaining knowledge. It is visible in a social institution called the social scientific community.

The knowledge of social science is organized in terms of theories. For now, **theory** can be defined as a system of interconnected ideas that condenses and organizes knowledge for purposes

KUHN'S PROGRESSION OF KNOWLEDGE

The idea that scientific knowledge does not progress in a simple linear and cumulative fashion; rather, knowledge progresses in the context of a community, meaning that professional, personal, and cultural interests play important roles.

THEORY

A system of interconnected ideas that condenses and organizes knowledge for purposes of understanding and/or explanation

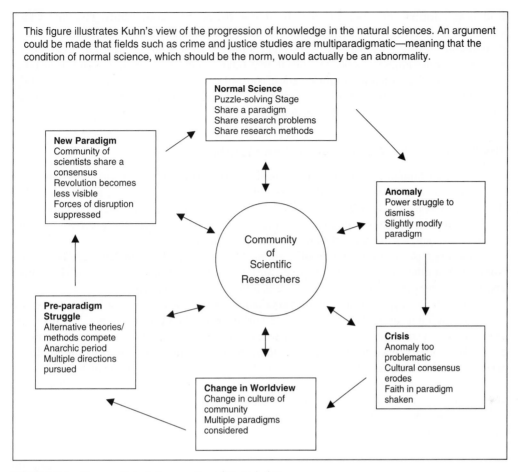

This figure illustrates Kuhn's view of the progression of knowledge in the natural sciences. An argument could be made that fields such as crime and justice studies are multiparadigmatic—meaning that the condition of normal science, which should be the norm, would actually be an abnormality.

Normal Science
Puzzle-solving Stage
Share a paradigm
Share research problems
Share research methods

New Paradigm
Community of
scientists share a
consensus
Revolution becomes
less visible
Forces of disruption
suppressed

Anomaly
Power struggle to
dismiss
Slightly modify
paradigm

Community
of
Scientific
Researchers

**Pre-paradigm
Struggle**
Alternative theories/
methods compete
Anarchic period
Multiple directions
pursued

Crisis
Anomaly too
problematic
Cultural consensus
erodes
Faith in paradigm
shaken

Change in Worldview
Change in culture of
community
Multiple paradigms
considered

FIGURE 2.1   Thomas Kuhn's Progression of Knowledge.

of understanding and/or explanation. Several types of crime and justice theory are discussed in Chapter 3. Theory is like a map; it helps people visualize and comprehend the complexity of their surroundings and explains why things happen.

Social scientists gather qualitative and quantitative data using specialized techniques, and then use these data to support or reject theories. **Data** are the empirical evidence or information that one gathers carefully according to rules or procedures. The data can be quantitative (i.e., expressed as numbers) or qualitative (i.e., expressed as words, pictures, or objects). **Empirical evidence** refers to observations that people experience through their senses—touch, sight, hearing, smell, and taste. This confuses people because researchers cannot use their senses to directly observe many aspects of the social world about which they seek answers (e.g., intelligence, attitudes, opinions, feelings, emotions, power, authority, etc.). Researchers have many specialized techniques to observe and indirectly measure such aspects of the social world.

The Social Science Community

As noted by Kuhn, science is given life through the operation of the scientific community, which sustains the assumptions, attitudes, and techniques of science. The scientific community is both a collection of people and a set of norms, behaviors, and attitudes. In crime and justice studies, the boundaries of this community and its membership are defined loosely. Chapter 1 described our area of study as one that includes many different groups both inside and outside academia. There is no membership card or master roster. Many people treat a doctoral degree in a social scientific

DATA

The empirical evidence or information that one gathers carefully according to rules or procedures. Data can be quantitative (i.e., expressed as numbers) or qualitative (i.e., expressed as words, pictures, or objects).

EMPIRICAL EVIDENCE

Observations that people experience through the senses—touch, sight, hearing, smell, and taste.

field as an informal entry ticket to membership in the research community. The PhD, which stands for doctorate of philosophy, is an advanced graduate degree beyond the master's that prepares one to conduct independent research. Some researchers do not have PhDs and not all those who receive PhDs enter occupations in which they conduct research; they may have other responsibilities (e.g., teaching, administration, consulting, clinical practice, advising, etc.). At the core of the social scientific community are researchers who conduct studies on a full-time or part-time basis, usually with the help of assistants who are students.

The Norms of the Social Science Community

Behavior in any human community is regulated by social norms. The social scientific community is governed by a set of professional norms and values that researchers learn and internalize during many years of schooling and practice.[5] Like other social norms, professional norms are ideals of proper conduct. Because researchers are real people, their prejudices, egos, ambitions, personal lives, and the like may affect their professional behavior.

The five basic norms of the social scientific community are listed in Table 2.1. They differ from those in other social institutions (e.g., business and government) and set social scientists apart. Researchers check on each other to see that the norms are followed.

Consistent with the norm of **universalism,** scientists will admire a brilliant, creative researcher even if he or she has strange personal habits or a disheveled appearance. Scientists may argue intensely with one another and tear apart a research report as part of the norm of organized skepticism. They usually listen to new ideas, no matter how strange. Following **disinterestedness,** scientists are detached and take results, including from their own research, as being tentative. They enjoy having other researchers read and react to their research, and some have led fights against censorship. This is consistent with the norm of **communalism.**

Scientists also expect strict **research honesty** in the conduct and reporting of research and become morally outraged when anyone cheats at research. These norms do not apply to all research communities. Communalism, for example, breaks down when it conflicts with the profit motive. As the publication of research findings of scientists working in the tobacco, pharmaceutical, and computer chip industries have been suppressed or delayed by corporate officials for whom the profit

---

UNIVERSALISM

The scientific norm that says research should be judged only on the basis of scientific merit.

DISINTERESTEDNESS

The scientific norm that mandates researchers should strive to be impartial and open to unexpected findings and new ideas.

COMMUNALISM

The scientific norm that says that producing knowledge is a public act and the findings should be available for all to use. In order for it to be accepted into the community, it must be rigorously reviewed.

RESEARCH HONESTY

The scientific norm that demands utmost honesty in all aspects of the research process; dishonesty, fraud, or cheating is a major taboo.

TABLE 2.1 Norms of the Social Scientific Community

Universalism. Regardless of who conducts research (e.g., old or young, male or female) and regardless of where it was conducted (e.g., United States or France, Harvard or Unknown University), the research is to be judged only on the basis of scientific merit.

Organized skepticism. Scientists should not accept new ideas or evidence in a carefree, uncritical manner. They should challenge and question all evidence and subject each study to intense scrutiny. The purpose of their criticism is not to attack the individual, but to ensure that the methods and ideas used in research can stand up to close, careful examination.

Disinterestedness. Scientists should aspire to be neutral, impartial, receptive, and open to unexpected observations or new ideas. They should not be rigidly wedded to a particular idea or point of view. They should accept, even look for, evidence that runs against their positions and should honestly accept all findings based on high-quality research.

Communalism. Scientific knowledge must be shared with others; it belongs to everyone. Creating scientific knowledge is a public act, and the findings are public property, available for all to use. The way in which the research is conducted must be described in detail. New knowledge is not formally accepted until other researchers have reviewed it and it has been made publicly available in a special form and style.

Honesty. This is a general cultural norm, but it is especially strong in scientific research. Scientists demand honesty in all research; dishonesty or cheating in scientific research is a major taboo.

motive overrode the scientific norm of communalism.[6] The section on ethics in Chapter 4 details similar situations in which the norms of science are violated because of the influence of politics.

Sharing Knowledge: The Role of Scholarly Publications

The glue that binds communities together is communication about knowledge. Formal communication between crime and justice researchers takes place in academic journals, scholarly books, and in paper presentations at conferences. They share information about the topic they're studying, new ideas and theories, methods used to collect data, and the findings of their work. Chapter 5 discusses in detail how to find and use these information resources.

Scholarly publications represent the building blocks of knowledge. There are dozens of journals that specifically address crime and justice phenomena (see Figure 2.2). You have already been exposed to several of these in Chapter 1—both in the research examples and in the research presented to you. Crime and justice research finds itself in an interesting place, though, due to its multidisciplinary nature. Studies on crime and justice could appear in any of the fields discussed in Chapter 1 (e.g., sociology, anthropology, biology, economics, geography, political science, history, psychology, psychiatry, philosophy, public administration, international and comparative studies, and legal jurisprudence). This means we have a massive network of information.

Let's consider what happens once a researcher completes a study. First, he or she writes a description of the study and the results as a research report or a paper in a special format. Often, he or she gives an oral presentation of the paper at a meeting of a professional association, such as the Academy of Criminal Justice Sciences or the American Society of Criminology, and sends a copy of it to a few research colleagues for their comments and suggestions. Next, the researcher must decide in what format to publish. Most often, publication in an academic journal is preferred. Sometimes, however, the work might warrant a full-length scholarly book, or the researcher might include it in an edited collection of articles within a scholarly book. Whatever its final form, creating original research manuscripts is akin to craftwork. A lot of thought, creativity, and careful, meticulous construction go into a quality research publication.

Before an article is published in an academic journal, though, it must undergo a review process. Once the researcher sends copies of the article to a scholarly journal, such as *Theoretical*

These are just a sample of the approximately 300 journals used in crime and justice studies:
American Criminal Law Review
Australian and New Zealand Journal of Criminology
Canadian Journal of Criminology and Criminal Justice
Crime and Delinquency
Criminal Justice: The International Journal of Policy and Practice
Crime, Media, Culture
Criminology
Criminology and Public Policy
Critical Criminology
Howard Journal of Criminal Justice
International Journal of Comparative and Applied Criminal Justice
Journal of Criminal Justice
Justice Quarterly
Policing and Society
Punishment and Society
Theoretical Criminology
Violence against Women

FIGURE 2.2   A Sample List of Crime and Justice Journals.

The following is an example of a blind review letter received for a recent submission to the journal, Justice Quarterly, for a paper eventually titled, "Criminal Justice Theory: Toward Legitimacy and an Infrastructure" (Kraska 2006). Notice that the reviewer, even though this is the second time she/he has had to read the article under review, still provides a high level of detail and constructive criticism. This would be considered a well-done review. This reviewer helped to substantially improve the final product.

Justice Quarterly

REVIEWER COMMENTS TO THE AUTHOR

Manuscript Number: 05-009RR
Manuscript Title: Why Not Criminal Justice Theory? A Call for Developing an Infrastructure
Reviewer Number: 2

Shout of thanks for all the hard work

This is a revise and resubmit, and therefore I will not repeat my general comments from the first review. I believe the author has addressed many of the issues raised by all three reviewers and that the paper has been improved thereby. I do have some remaining concerns.

Abstract: "studies" should be singular. Here and throughout the paper: use of "theorize" as a transitive verb is not correct. It is intransitive.

p.2 I would drop the opening paragraph. It is vague; the third sentence contradicts the first; and the reader knows no more about the subject at the end of it than before reading it. The second paragraph is a good place to start. It would be useful to cite an authority on social science theory, such as Blalock, regarding the importance of theory in general.

p.3 and throughout: the author uses abbreviations such as CJ and CJS without introducing them; I would spell out.

p.3 Second paragraph: Sherman calls criminal justice "applied criminology," which is an apt term for the "how to and what works" functions that the author is decrying here.

p.4. I am not sure what the author means by "target of analysis" in first paragraph.

p.4 second paragraph: there are a number of other works that, like Henderson and Boostrom, provide empirical support for the author's claims in this passage. I could send them if they are needed.

p.5. I agree with the author's examples of objects of criminal justice theory that are not crime related. There are others that he does not mention, especially at the individual agent level, such as employee satisfaction, disaffection, and turnover.

p.6 third line in p.#1 is confusing or incomplete. In making this argument, the author could mention that insisting that criminal justice study focus on its impact on crime is akin to insisting that organizational studies of firms focus on profit. If organizational study had done that, most of its literature would not exist.

good analysis! Not a footnote?

1

FIGURE 2.3 Sample Article Review Letter.

Criminology or *Justice Quarterly*, the editor of that journal (a respected academic who has been chosen by other researchers to oversee the journal) sends the paper to several referees for a **blind review.** In other words, neither the author nor the reviewers know the identities of one another. The referees are usually researchers who have conducted similar studies. This process reinforces the norm of universalism, because referees judge the paper on its merits alone. They evaluate the research on the basis of its clarity, originality, standards of good research, and contribution to the

BLIND REVIEW

A process of judging the merits of a research report in which the peer researchers do not know the identity of the person who conducted a study and the researcher does not know the identity of the evaluators in advance.

field. The referees return their evaluations to the editor, who decides to either reject the paper or ask the author for revisions or accept it for publication. Figure 2.3 presents an example of a journal article review received for a manuscript that was sent to the journal *Justice Quarterly*.

The quality of a journal is reflected in the extent to which its articles are methodologically and theoretically solid, and that they advance knowledge. Some well-established journals have a high rejection rate (85 percent), whereas some have a high acceptance rate (65 percent).

Almost all academic fields use peer referees for publication, but not all use the blind review process. Criminology, criminal justice, sociology, psychology, and political science use blind reviews for almost all scholarly journals. By contrast, fields such as legal studies, biology, history, and economics use a mix of review processes—including sometimes using only one reviewer who is known to the author. Blind reviews with many referees slow the process and lower acceptance rates.[7] It is a purposively cautious method of ensuring quality control that advances the norms of organized skepticism and universalism.

Publishing a scholarly book involves a somewhat different review process. Because the publisher of a book makes decisions based as much on financial concerns as academic ones, the review process includes an assessment of a book's scholarly and market strength.[8] Traditionally, the most prestigious books were published by an academic press (e.g., Oxford University Press or the University of Chicago Press), but most recently high-quality scholarly books are published by an array of outlets.

Unlike a magazine or newspaper author who is paid for writing, researchers are not paid for publishing in scholarly journals. In fact, they may have to pay a small fee to help defray costs just to have their papers considered. The reward is the chance to impact their field of study by making their research available to their academic peers, and interested practitioners and students. Likewise, the referees are not paid for reviewing papers. They consider it an honor to be asked to conduct the reviews and a responsibility of membership in the social scientific community.

A researcher gains prestige and honor within the social scientific community, respect from peers, and a reputation as an accomplished researcher through such publications. In addition, an impressive record of respected publications helps a researcher obtain grants, fellowships, job offers, a following of students, improved working conditions, and increases in salary.[9] Researchers also have an opportunity to impact the practicing world. Finally, a scholarly article or book that breaks new theoretical/research ground could impact the literature far beyond the author's career (or even life).

Perhaps you will have an opportunity to publish a scholarly journal article or book one day. And even if you do not publish personally, the knowledge disseminated in these journals and books will either directly or indirectly impact your life, work, and thinking.

STEPS IN THE SCIENTIFIC RESEARCH PROCESS

The Steps

Conducting research requires following a sequence of steps. Although all research starts with a research idea (objective), the order of these steps varies depending on whether a quantitative or qualitative approach is used. There are seven well-known steps that apply to both quantitative and qualitative studies (see Figure 2.4). Notice that even though these are presented as steps—indicating a linear process—in the real world of research, the steps are often reordered, particularly when it comes to qualitative research.

Quantitative Research Steps.   The process of conducting a quantitative study begins with a researcher selecting a topic. Quantitative researchers typically start with a general area of academic or professional interest, such as the effects of domestic violence, reasons for delinquency, impact of homelessness, or privatization of prisons. A general interest in a topic, though, is too broad for conducting an actual study. This is why the next step is crucial. The researcher must narrow it down to, or focus on, a specific research question that can be addressed

QUANTITATIVE RESEARCH STEPS

Those basic research steps used in concluding quantitative research.

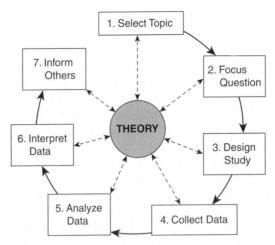

FIGURE 2.4 Generic Steps in the Research Process. *Source:* From W. Lawrence Neuman, *Social Research Methods, Qualitative and Quantitative Approaches,* 6/e. Published by Allyn and Bacon, 75 Arlington St., Boston, MA 02116. Copyright © 2006 by Pearson Education. Reprinted by permission of the publisher.

in the study. This requires a careful review of the research literature (see Appendix B), exploratory trips into the field, and the developing of testable research ideas (hypotheses, discussed in Chapter 3) that come from an awareness of crime and justice theory (discussed in Chapter 3).

For example, a broad topic of interest—let's say, the reasons for delinquency—could be transformed into a focused research question: Is childhood physical abuse and neglect a cause of delinquency among juveniles? A rather vague topic is focused into a specific causal question for a specific group of people. Designing the study, the next step, requires making decisions about the type of cases or sample to select, the time frame of the research (cross-sectional or longitudinal; see below), how to measure what's being studied (discussed later as *variables*), and what research technique (e.g., questionnaire, experiment) to employ. At this stage as well, theory informs decision making.

After designing the study, a researcher begins to collect data using the research method selected. A quantitative researcher will very carefully record and verify the data and then transfer these data into computer-readable format. Once the data are organized, the researcher begins the fifth step—statistical analysis (see Chapter 10). This involves manipulating the data or numbers using computer software to create charts, tables, graphs, and statistics. Often the research ends up with a large quantity of computer-generated output that provides the researcher with a condensed picture of the data.

The researcher next has to give meaning to or interpret the data. By looking at the analyzed data, using theoretical knowledge on the research topic and question, and drawing on previous published research, a researcher attempts to shed light on the original research question. A researcher also considers alternative interpretations of the data, compares the results of this study with previous studies, and draws out its wider implications. Informing others means writing a report about the study in a specific format (described in Chapter 14) and presenting a description of the study and results to professional audiences in an academic publication. In addition, it often entails recommendations for practice based on the researcher's findings.

QUALITATIVE RESEARCH STEPS

Those basic research steps used in concluding qualitative research.

Qualitative Research Steps.   Like the quantitative researcher, a qualitative researcher will select a topic, design a study (Chapter 11), collect data (Chapters 12 and 13), analyze data (see Appendix C), and interpret data. However, the qualitative researcher often collects, analyzes, and interprets data simultaneously, or goes back and forth between these steps. Using an example from Chapter 1, Wright and Decker selected the topic of armed robbery and then collected, analyzed, and interpreted their field-generated data simultaneously over a two-year period. Their theoretical insights developed over time, eventually leading them to view armed robbery in new and unique ways.

Qualitative research is generally geared toward exploratory, descriptive, and theoretical research objectives. From firsthand involvement or observation with the phenomenon being studied, it builds from the ground level up to developing new theoretical insights (in Chapter 3 called *grounded theory*). When interpreting data, most quantitative researchers test hypotheses they previously developed, whereas qualitative researchers tend to create new concepts and/or construct novel theoretical interpretations that help to make sense of their object of study. The last step, to inform others, is similar for both approaches, but here again, qualitative research differs in that it usually provides a rich narrative report filled with detailed descriptions and in-depth theoretical and conceptual discussion of the findings' significance (see Chapter 14). It less often includes policy recommendations, but this practice is becoming increasingly common.

Research Step Examples

To give you a better feel for how these seven steps work in practice, summaries of quantitative and qualitative published studies are outlined below. Both studies explore the role of child abuse and neglect in juvenile crime. The quest to understand the causes of juvenile delinquency, and in turn adult criminality, is intense and complex. Interestingly, some influential theorists do not view serious physical abuse and neglect as important causal factors in juvenile and adult crime—but there is serious debate about the issue. Remember that science by nature is skeptical and cautious, even if an association may seem obvious to the rest of us. There has to be carefully collected evidence, meticulous analysis, and intellectually honest interpretation, following the steps outlined below.

The quantitative research example found below uses an existing database to test the impact that child abuse has on delinquency and whether two popular crime theories, which tend to reject the abuse–delinquency connection, also play a role. The second example reviews the steps taken by Lonnie Athens when conducting a landmark qualitative study of dangerous, violent criminals.

QUANTITATIVE EXAMPLE: CHILD ABUSE.   This example is found in the article "Can Control Theory Explain Parental Abuse and Delinquency? A Longitudinal Analysis," published in the

As this section discusses, there is a debate in criminology as to the impact child abuse has on the future likelihood of violence and/or lawbreaking. The two studies reviewed here lend support to the child abuse/future violence relationship.

Journal of Research in Crime and Delinquency (Rebellon and Gundy 2005). The authors both work at the University of New Hampshire and have an interest in the relationship between a child's family life and juvenile delinquency. Cesar Rebellon has published numerous articles exploring the why of juvenile crime; this piece represents another piece of the puzzle.

Select a Topic.   The more specific topic the authors are interested in is the effect, if any, child abuse has on a juvenile's criminal behavior.

Focus the Question.   The previous scientific literature demonstrates a "growing consensus that physical parental abuse is associated with higher levels of delinquent behavior" (Rebellon and Gundy 2005: 47). Rebellon and Gundy realize as well from the literature that some prominent crime theorists minimize the causal importance of child abuse. They argue that abuse and neglect are simply one dimension of bad parenting, which leads to "low self-control" in children (Gottfredson and Hirschi 1990). Low self-control, therefore, is the key causal variable in juvenile criminality (what researchers call an *independent variable*). Rebellon and Gundy aimed to examine the abuse–delinquency connection and to test the veracity of two varieties of "control theory" in relation to the child abuse–crime connection. The two theories tested are known as "self-control theory" and "social bonding theory." (These theories may be familiar to those of you who have taken a course in crime theory.)

Design the Study.   In order to examine the abuse–delinquency relationship, and the two control theories, the authors designed a study in which they could track a number of juveniles over a long enough time period to determine what factors were influencing their behaviors. As discussed below, this is known as a longitudinal design. They also needed valid measures of the major variables involved: (1) child abuse, (2) juvenile crime, (3) self-control (low), and (4) "social bonding." They argue that survey research is the best method for collecting data on these variables.

Collect the Data.   Designing a robust study often involves an attempt to overcome the limitations of previous research. Rebellon and Gundy noted serious flaws in previous data sets and decided to use existing data from a famous study, the National Youth Survey. This research began in 1976 with a nationally representative sample of 1,725 adolescents between the ages of eleven and seventeen. One of each participant's parents was also interviewed. The participants were then resurveyed over a multiyear period to record changes. The study included numerous measures of control theory. It measured juvenile crime through self-report measures of property and violent crimes. It measured child abuse as an affirmative response to the question of whether the child had ever been "beaten up by a parent." (Although this is a questionable and limited measure of child abuse, the authors had to work with the data collected in the 1970s.)

Analyze the Data.   The authors' analysis was divided into three parts. They first examined the statistical relationship between physical parental abuse and property crime and violent crime (see Rebellon and Gundy 2005, Figure 2.1, p. 262). The second part examined the relationships among abuse and social bonding measures. The third part explored the extent to which abuse predicts future delinquency when controlling for numerous variables—including social bonding and self-control variables. They employed what researchers call "multivariate analysis," which is a statistical procedure that determines the strength and direction of the effect of numerous variables (called *independent variables*) on the variable the researchers are trying to explain (called *dependent variables*).

Interpret the Data.   The authors discovered a robust relationship between parental abuse and juvenile crime. In their own words, they "found that physical child abuse contributes to violent offending as well as property offending and that neither self-control theory nor social bonding theory appears capable of explaining the relationship." This study provides additional evidence for the child abuse–juvenile crime relationship using a robust methodology. It also raises questions about Gottfredson and Hirschi's claims that child abuse is not an important explanatory variable for making sense of juvenile delinquency.

Inform Others.   In publishing this article in a leading journal, the authors will be assured that this study will become a part of a growing understanding of the role that domestic violence plays in juvenile crime. It also provides some "falsification" evidence for control theories of crime. In line with the ethic of critical thinking, "falsifying" theories is as important as substantiating them in the quest to advance scientific knowledge. The authors state only one, yet important, practical implication: "the present results suggest that efforts aimed at controlling parental abuse ... might serve to control delinquency."

QUALITATIVE EXAMPLE: VIOLENT CRIMINALS.   In what is considered a classic qualitative study, in 1989 Lonnie Athens published a scholarly book summarizing his twenty years of research on the link between childhood abuse and violent crime in *The Creation of Dangerous Violent Criminals*. Norman K. Denzin, a leading figure in qualitative research, characterized Athens's work as "the most far-reaching, provocative, and profound analysis of violent conduct available in the criminological literature."

Select a Topic.   Athens's study was an attempt to understand why certain people become dangerous, violent criminals. From this broad interest, Athens became interested in discovering how children are transformed into seriously violent people.

Focus the Question.   Athens was a student of the sociologist Herbert Blumer. His early thinking about his topic was largely shaped by Blumer's theory of symbolic interaction. This school of thought suggests that criminals must be studied from their own experiences and perspective to learn what shaped them and how they define their situation. Athens stated, "In reading this book one should find that one is undergoing similar thoughts and feelings as the subjects" (what Chapter 3 will refer to as *verstehen*). Athens was concerned with only a particular impulsive type of violent criminal—those who had exhibited extremely violent behavior toward another with little or no provocation.

Design the Study.   Rather than going into the study with clearly defined hypotheses to test, Athens designed an exploratory study that would be open to the perspectives and experiences of his subjects. He also decided that, for his purposes, it was better to study fifty people in great depth than to study, say, 500 people superficially. Athens used in-depth personal interviews with his subjects as his primary data collection technique. His strategy was to get the dangerous and violent criminals to talk about the formative experiences they, not the researcher, felt were significant for their lives.

Collect the Data.   In applying his research strategy, Athens spent many hundreds of hours interviewing a group of eight male adult offenders imprisoned for committing serious violent crimes and who had been previously convicted of at least two serious violent crimes. He also conducted in-depth interviews with a group of thirty young adult violent offenders, both male and female. Their ages ranged from early to late teens, and all were serving time in a correctional institution for those who had committed serious violent crimes. All the subjects candidly admitted to Athens to having committed previous violent criminal acts for which they were never arrested or convicted.

Analyze the Data.   Athens's main strategy for analyzing the enormous volume of data he collected was to look for patterns in the developmental experiences of his violent subjects. He wondered if these subjects had certain common and unique social experiences that might in turn provide the basis for their impulsive violence.

Interpret the Data.   Athens uncovered four significant experiences that were commonly endured by his research subjects. All four experiences were suffered at an early stage in each subject's life, usually in early adolescence. The first experience was brutalization. Brutalization comprises three important experiences: (1) violent subjugation, in which the subject is beaten into fear and submission; (2) personal horrification, in which the subject helplessly witnesses the abuse of a primary loved one, such as a mother or sibling; and (3) violent coaching, in which the subject

HIGHLIGHT 2.3

A Maverick Criminologist

It's not every day that a Pulitzer Prize–winning author targets an academic researcher's work for a major new book. What is more remarkable is that Lonnie Athens is not a typical high-profile professor from a well-known university. He instead appears to be a fairly typical professor at a small university, teaching a regular load of classes, in a small criminal justice department. It speaks to the power of his qualitative research and theory, therefore, that his life's work would be honored in Richard Rhodes's *Why They Kill: The Discoveries of a Maverick Criminologist*. The book combines an autobiography of Professor Athens as well as a detailed and thorough examination of how Athens's theory is applicable to a wide range of historical events and famous acts of violence.

Chapters 1 through 9 provide an entertaining and insightful examination of Athens's childhood, his beginning work as a graduate student, and finally his work as an academic researcher. The story reveals an extremely violent childhood and a difficult path taken by Athens to produce his research and work in academe (hence the descriptor *maverick*). His qualitative research was conducted during a time when crime and justice research was fairly intolerant of any methodology other than traditional quantitative science.

Athens's qualitative work was often not well received and he suffered numerous setbacks; still, he persevered. Much of his frustration came from trying to find funding (see the last section in this chapter on funding and research). He wrote his mentor, Herbert Blumer, in 1987:

> I was denied research grants by every granting agency in America at least a half a dozen times. The research director at one government agency candidly told me that my work resembled art more than science, to which I promptly replied, "good science and good art may have more in common than you realize." … After years of hitting my head against the wall, I finally realized that I must either do my study with my own resources or not do it at all."

Athens's first book, *The Creation of Dangerous Violent Criminals*, was published in 1989 by Routledge Press. Athens now teaches as a full professor at Seton Hall University. He serves as a consultant and expert witness on capital murder and murder cases, is cited extensively in the research literature, and has been featured in dozens of major newspapers.

is coached, often by the primary abuser, on the value of violence as a means to resolve conflicts and gain respect. Of the three, Athens emphasized personal horrification as the most important.

The second experience Athens discovered was belligerency, which involved the subject's introspection and resolution, because of the brutalization, to someday respond in kind to the violence they themselves have experienced and to the violence experienced by their loved ones. In other words, the subjects internalize an "eye for an eye" revenge ethic. The third experience was violence performance, in which the subjects participated in a fight that they "won," and in the process had hurt someone seriously. The fourth experience was virulency, in which a violent label was put on the subjects by their peers, and the subjects experienced satisfaction at the fear (and respect) that others now feel toward them. In short, the subjects gained status, prestige, and even a measure of perceived safety, by being considered "crazy" and a "bad ass."

As summarized in Table 2.2, Athens asserts that it is this fourfold process that transforms a nonviolent child into a dangerous and violent criminal. As opposed to locating the causes of criminal

TABLE 2.2 Athens's Theory of Violentization	
Stage One:	**Brutalization** (coarse and cruel treatment at the hands of others)
	• *Violent subjugation* (authority figures use violence to force submission)
	• *Personal horrification* (witness to loved one's violent subjugation)
	• *Violent coaching* (significant other provides violent instruction)
Stage Two:	**Belligerency** (solve problem of being brutalized by taking violent action against others who provoke)
Stage Three:	**Violence performances** (carrying out acts of violence against others; "successful" attempts are key)
Stage Four:	**Virulency** (gains respect and status through others' fear)

behavior in personality disorders or self-control problems, as conventional wisdom often does, Athens argues that a "violent situation comes into being when defined by an individual as a situation that calls for violence—that an actor responds to the circumstance as he or she defines it" (Athens 1997: 23).

Inform Others.   Athens's study was published as a scholarly book. Over seventy other researchers have cited his work. His research was also the subject of a highly acclaimed book, *Why They Kill: The Discoveries of a Maverick Criminologist*, written by a Pulitzer Prize–winning author, Richard Rhodes (Vintage 2000) (see Highlight 2.3). Although Athens includes an entire chapter on policy implications (e.g., curbing child abuse will curb crime), his most recent work critiques the lack of political will in the United States to prevent the creation of dangerous and violent criminals by taking child abuse more seriously (Athens 1997).

SCIENTIFIC RESEARCH AND TIME

Another important dimension of science and research we'll examine in this chapter is time. The element of time can be perplexing. Rebellon and Gundy were studying what causes delinquency today, yet they were using data collected from youth in the mid-1970s. Does this mean their findings apply only to youth in the decade of the 1970s, making it in a sense historical? Notice also that Athens conducted his qualitative research over a long period of time and at the same time he was looking back in time to the subjects' most formative experiences. However, his research focus was a mere snapshot in time of the perceptions and memories of the subjects themselves. Finally, a famous work by Michel Foucault (1977) examined the history of discipline and punishment beginning in the eighteenth century, yet his research goal was to shed light on the nature of contemporary social control. He characterized his work, thus, as a "history of the present."[10]

The social sciences have struggled since their inception with the notions of past, present, and future. What constitutes studying the past: a hundred years ago, last year, or yesterday? How do we study the present when the moment we conceive it, it transforms into the past? And if the central goal of quantitative science is prediction (and through accurate predictions we can control our environment), aren't these predictions made possible only through a study of the past (trend analysis)?

An awareness of the time dimension in research will assist in generating quality knowledge. Some studies give us a snapshot of a single, fixed point in time and then analyze it in detail. Others provide a moving picture that allows the reader to follow events, people, or social relations over a long period of time. The time dimension in research is divided into two groups: studying a single point in time, termed cross-sectional research, versus examining multiple time points, longitudinal research. We will also examine briefly the time implications in qualitative research.

Cross-sectional Research

Most crime and justice research takes a snapshot approach. It studies a phenomenon at one point in time. This **cross-sectional research** approach is generally the simplest and least costly alternative. Cross-sectional research can be exploratory, descriptive, explanatory, or evaluative, but it is most consistent with a descriptive approach to research. Its disadvantage is that it cannot capture social processes or change. This makes it an inferior approach for explanatory research because of the difficulty in establishing whether the proposed cause actually preceded the effect.

CROSS-SECTIONAL RESEARCH

Any study that examines information on many cases at one point in time.

We have already reviewed numerous studies focusing on a cross section of time. A few include Cannon's (2004) survey of undergraduate criminal justice majors on their views of gays and lesbians; Hagan's (2005) victimization research documenting the Darfur genocide; Tark and Kleck's (2004) use of National Crime Victimization Survey (NCVS) data to determine whether self-protection measures reduce injury and property loss; Haarr's (2007) survey research on wife battering in Tajikistan; and Kubrin's (2005) content analysis of rap lyrics. It might be confusing to think of Kubrin's research as cross-sectional, since he studied nine years' worth of albums that had sold enough copies to "go platinum." The key is that he did not study changes in the albums over time; he instead analyzed the entire nine years as a single cross section in time.

Longitudinal Research

Researchers using **longitudinal research,** then, examine features of people or other units at more than one point in time. It is usually more complex and costly than cross-sectional research, but it is also more powerful, especially when researchers seek answers to questions about trends and/or cause and effect. Exploratory, descriptive, explanatory, and evaluation research all employ longitudinal approaches. Rebellon and Gundy's study on the abuse–delinquency link discussed earlier used longitudinal methods. Chapter 1 reviewed several examples of longitudinal research including Rosenbaum's D.A.R.E. evaluation, Sherman's mandatory arrest for domestic violence experiment, and research by McCord using the Cambridge-Somerville Youth Study. We will now consider three types of longitudinal research: time series, panel, and cohort.

1. **Time-series research** is a longitudinal study in which the same type of information is collected on a group of people or other units across multiple time periods. Researchers can observe stability or change in the features of the units or can track conditions over time. Time-series research often relies on preexisting data, such as the Uniform Crime Reports (UCR), NCVS, or U.S. Census data.

   As seen in Figure 2.5, information from time-series data can be very revealing. A time-series study by Pettit and Western (2004) on imprisonment rates among Black and White men in the United States in the period 1964–1997 found that during a major rise in incarceration rates in the 1980s (up by 300 percent), African-American men were eight times more likely than White men to go to jail. Young Black men who did not attend college were more likely to be incarcerated, with nearly one in three spending some time behind bars. These rates doubled for Black men who failed to complete high school.

2. The **panel study** is a powerful type of longitudinal research. It is more difficult to conduct than time-series research. In a panel study, the researcher observes exactly the same people, group, or organization across time periods. Panel research is formidable to conduct and very costly. Tracking people over time is often difficult because some people die or cannot be located. Nevertheless, the results of a well-designed panel study are valuable. Even short-term panel studies can clearly show the impact of a particular life event. The most important

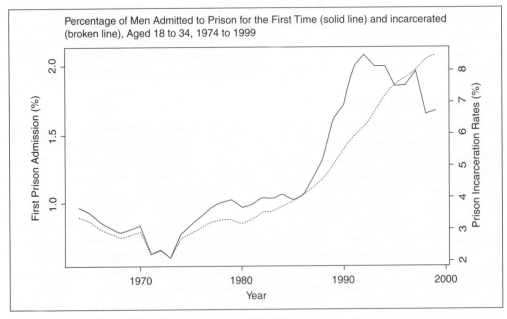

FIGURE 2.5 Time-Series Graph Depicting African-American Incarceration Rates. *Source:* Pettit, Becky and Bruce Western (2004). "Mass imprisonment and the life course: Race and class inequality in U.S. incarceration." *American Sociological Review.* 69:151–169. Reprinted by permission of American Sociological Association and the authors.

CROSS-SECTIONAL: Observe a collection of people at one time.

February 2006

TIME SERIES: Observe different people at multiple times.

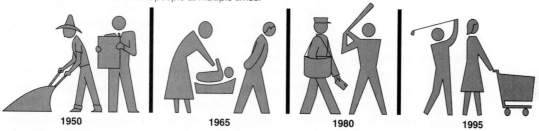

1950   1965   1980   1995

PANEL: Observe the exact same people at two or more times.

1985   1995   2005

COHORT: Observe people who shared an experience at two or more times.

Married in 1962   1982   2002

CASE STUDY: Observe a small set intensely across time.

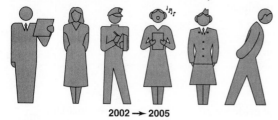

2002 → 2005

FIGURE 2.6 The Time Dimension in Social Research. *Source:* From W. Lawrence Neuman, *Social Research Methods, Qualitative and Quantitative Approaches,* 6/e. Published by Allyn and Bacon, 75 Arlington St., Boston, MA 02116. Copyright © 2006 by Pearson Ecducation. Reprinted by permission of the publisher.

criminological panel study in the United States is the NCVS. Recall that it collects vicitmization data on 42,000 households over a three-year period, and then resamples another panel for the next three years. The Cambridge-Somerville Youth Study used by McCord, the National Youth Survey used by Rebellon and Gundy, and Rosenbaum's experimental research on the effectiveness of D.A.R.E. are all solid examples of panel studies.

3. A **cohort study** is similar to a panel study, but rather than observing the same people, a category of people who share a similar life experience in a specified time period is studied. Cohort analysis is "explicitly macroanalytic," which means researchers examine the category as a whole for important features (Ryder 1992: 230). The focus is on the cohort, or category, not on specific individuals. Commonly used cohorts include all people born in the same year (called birth cohorts), all people hired at the same time, all people who retire in a one- or two-year time frame, and all people who graduate in a given year. Unlike panel studies, researchers do not have to locate the same people for cohort studies. They need only identify those who experienced a common life event.

4. Marvin Wolfgang conducted an important and massive birth-cohort study of over 5,000 Chinese individuals born in 1973. Less than 2 percent of the birth cohort had a record of delinquency by age seventeen. In contrast to cohort levels of delinquency found in other studies—including those in Philadelphia, Racine (Wisconsin), Stockholm (Sweden), and London (England), which typically show delinquency rates about 30 percent—the Chinese birth cohort had extremely low rates (Friday et al. 2005) (see Figure 2.6).

COHORT STUDY

Longitudinal research in which information about a category of cases or people that shared a common experience at one time period is traced across subsequent time periods.

Conclusion

Most of us were taught in high school science courses that science involves the objective search for factual truths through mathematical means. This innocent view of crime and justice research suggests that generating scientifically based knowledge is a pure process that operates in a sociopolitical vacuum, totally insulated from the pressures or concerns of the larger society. This is of course the way it ought to be. We attempt to paint a more realistic picture that researchers and consumers of research must be aware of. Researchers face economic, professional, political, and governmental pressures that can limit what they can study, how they conduct research, or how they disseminate the findings of research. Remember, as discussed at the outset of this book, knowledge generates power and power can generate, or at least impede, the advancement of knowledge.

In this chapter, we learned about the differences between ordinary sources of knowledge and research-based knowledge. We also examined the workings of the social science community—its practices, norms, and values. We toured the typical steps in the research process and we explored how the dimension of time impacts research. The next chapter will delve even deeper into the nature of the scientific production of knowledge, examining three major philosophical approaches to research in our field. Our aim is to provide a foundational backdrop for understanding research as a critical consumer and/or producer.

Key Terms

authority knowledge *4*
traditional knowledge *4*
common sense knowledge *5*
media knowledge *6*
personal experience knowledge *6*
overgeneralization *7*

selective observation *7*
premature closure *7*
halo effect *7*
Kuhn's progression of knowledge *9*
theory *9*
data *10*

empirical evidence *10*
universalism *11*
disinterestedness *11*
communalism *11*
research honesty *11*
blind review *12*
quantitative research steps *14*

qualitative research steps *15*
cross-sectional research *20*
longitudinal research *21*
time-series research *21*
panel study *21*
cohort study *23*

Review Questions

1. What sources of knowledge are alternatives to crime and justice research?
2. What role does the media play in our knowledge about crime and criminal justice? Why is crime and justice research usually better than the alternatives to research-based knowledge?
3. What is the scientific community? What is its role?
4. What are the norms of the scientific community? What are their effects?
5. How does a study get published in a scholarly crime and justice journal?
6. What steps are involved in conducting a quantitative research project?
7. What steps are involved in conducting a qualitative research project?
8. What are some of the differences between the steps involved in quantitative versus qualitative research?
9. What is cross-sectional versus longitudinal data and research?
10. How do time-series, panel, and cohort studies differ?

Practicing Research

1. Over the next week, carefully observe and record how your personal experiences affect what you know (your personal knowledge). Using the four errors to personal experience (e.g., overgeneralization), consider the extent to which your experiences (1) substantiate what you already know, (2) have forced you to modify what you already know, (3) or provided strong evidence that refuted your personal knowledge. The key to this exercise is to observe and document through writing a process that is normally taken for granted (the construction of our personal knowledge-base through personal experiences). Finally, think about how this experientially based knowledge might be tested using three of the research methods discussed in Chapter 1.

2. Using the scientific norms found in Table 2.1 (universalism, organized skepticism, disinterestedness, communalism, honesty), think of several problematic hypothetical situations that illustrate the importance of each to maintaining the integrity of the knowledge production process. For example, the norm of universalism is an attempt to ward against a situation where only certain researchers and research institutions are seen as producing legitimate studies (i.e., elitism).

3. Select one quantitative and one qualitative research method from the following list of methods discussed in Chapter 1:

1. Experimental research
2. Survey and interview research
3. Existing documents statistics research
4. Content analysis
5. Ethnographic field research
6. Qualitative document analysis
7. Historical research
8. Academic legal research
9. Mixed methods research

Using the research steps outlined in this chapter, construct a hypothetical study on any topic of your choice. Each step should be constructed around the topic and research method you have selected.

4. Using the Internet search engine "Google Scholar" (discussed in Chapter 4), conduct a search using the following key words: time-series criminal justice. Select and find one of these articles either online or in your library. Read through the article and determine the purpose of the study and what types of longitudinal data are used. Select one of the time-series graphs displayed in the article and write a short narrative explaining what it is depicting. We realize that at this point in the book, the details of the article may be confusing. The purpose of this exercise is simply to begin the process of reading and making sense of research using longitudinal data.

Notes for Further Study

1. For more on fallacies, see Babbie (1998: 20–21), Kaplan (1964), and Wallace (1971).
2. See Kappler and Potter (2007) and Bohm and Walker (2006).
3. On the limits to self-knowledge, Wilson and Dunn (2004); on inaccurate eyewitness accounts, Wells and Olson (2003); on inaccurate risk evaluation, Gowda and Fox (2002), Paulos (2001); on SUVs, Bradsher (2002).
4. The rise of science is discussed in Camic (1980), Lemert (1979), Merton (1970), Wuthnow (1979), and Ziman (1976). For more on the historical development of the social sciences, see Eastrope (1974), Laslett (1992), Ross (1991), and Turner and Turner (1991).
5. For more on the social role of the scientist, see Ben-David (1971), Camic (1980), and Tuma and Grimes (1981).
6. See Altman (1997), Markoff (1997), and Meier (1998).
7. See Clemens and Powell (1995: 446).
8. Ibid., 444.
9. For more on the system of reward and stratification in science, see Cole and Cole (1973), Cole (1978), Fuchs and Turner (1986), Gaston (1978), Gustin (1973), Long (1978), Meadows (1974), and Reskin (1977).
10. Foucault's (1977) work was also the inspiration for the notion of the "knowledge-power dynamic" used throughout this book.

Philosophical and Theoretical Foundations

Making Sense of Hurricane Katrina

Philosophical Foundations

  The Three Approaches

    Positivist Social Science Features

    PSS Conclusion

    Interpretive Social Science Features

    ISS Conclusion

    Critical Social Science Features

    Highlight 3.1 A Splinter in Your Mind: CSS and The Matrix

    Highlight 3.2 Participatory Action Research

    CSS Conclusion

  Philosophical Conclusion

Theory in Crime and Justice Research

  Why Theory?

  The Parts of a Theory

    Assumptions

    Concepts

    Relationships among Concepts

      ■ *Kinds of Relationships*

      ■ *Propositions and Hypotheses*

  Approaches to Developing Theory: Deductive–Inductive

    ■ *Deductive Direction*

    ■ *Inductive Direction*

  Highlight 3.3 What Is Grounded Theory?

Causal Explanation and Testing Hypotheses

The Language of Variables and Hypotheses

  ■ Types of Variables

From the Research Question to Hypotheses

Causal Theory and Hypotheses

  ■ The Hypothesis and Causality

  ■ Testing and Refining a Hypothesis

Highlight 3.4 Ten Ways to State Causal Relations between Religious Attendance and Criminality

  ■ Types of Hypotheses

Potential Errors in Causal Explanation

  ■ Tautology

  ■ Teleology

  ■ Ecological Fallacy

  ■ Reductionism

  ■ Spuriousness

Highlight 3.5 Night-Lights and Spuriousness

Summary of Theory

Philosophy and Theory Conclusion

Key Terms

Review Questions

Practicing Research

Notes for Further Study

MAKING SENSE OF HURRICANE KATRINA

Catastrophic natural disasters, despite all the suffering and pain they inflict, often play out ultimately as stories of human triumph, heroism, and community solidarity. We construct them as testaments to the true decency of humankind. The urgent task at hand to take care of each others' most basic needs trumps, at least temporarily, some of our uglier societal faults, such as class/race/gender divisions and prejudices, self-centeredness, entrenched political conflict, and a lack of social caring.

Hurricane Katrina, which hit the coasts of Alabama, Louisiana, and Mississippi on August 29, 2005, was different. While human triumph and decency were evident, the lasting legacy of Katrina will be a storm that washed away the surface veil of denial and neglect and lay bare those same ugly societal faults usually glossed over. It similarly seemed to stir up and inflame some of our deepest contemporary fears: poor racial minorities free to loot and victimize others, a sign of things to come as the result of global warming, and a government so inept in homeland security matters that it failed on almost all accounts.

U.S. soldiers are guarding Hurricane Katrina victims waiting to leave the Superdome in New Orleans, Louisiana. Research can help us to make sense of these complex crime and justice events.

Just as with the terrorist attacks of September 11, 2001, we have a strong and collective desire to make sense of these types of catastrophic events, both for therapeutic reasons and to prevent or minimize the harm they cause. What exactly does "making sense" mean though? Making sense for some people means resorting to the spiritual (e.g., it must be God's will), for others it means filtering the event through a rigid ideology to reaffirm the truth of that ideology (e.g., it's the fault of our welfare system—only the welfare-dependent individuals weren't able to get out of New Orleans). For the social scientist, it means using theory and research to examine with rigor and intellectual honesty the many questions in need of answering.

As Chapters 1 and 2 have demonstrated, crime and justice researchers have numerous research and theoretical avenues available to them for answering a multitude of different questions. In fact, the nature of the research question directs the research employed and the theoretical focus. Answering the question of how effectively the criminal justice system reacted to the Katrina disaster, for example, would likely require quantitative evaluation research, and perhaps a system's theoretical outlook. Or, asking why the media and governmental officials exaggerated and distorted the crime threat in the aftermath of the disaster might involve what this chapter will call an interpretive approach to generating knowledge and the use of social constructionist theory. Another possible question might explore why crime rates tend to plummet during times of disaster. This would likely involve quantitative explanatory research relying perhaps on survey research.

This chapter will build on our discussion of the nature and workings of the social sciences by discussing the place of philosophy and theory in research methods.

PHILOSOPHICAL FOUNDATIONS

Many people question whether the social sciences, such as crime and justice studies, are real science. As noted in the previous chapter, they think only of physics, chemistry, and biology—the natural sciences. In this section, we examine in even more depth the meaning of science, particularly in relation to the social sciences. We are concerned here more with broad approaches to producing knowledge than with specific techniques for gathering and examining data—an area of study formally referred to as **epistemology.** Epistemology looks at the question, how do we know what we say we know? It deals with such issues as, what constitutes legitimate knowledge?

Epistemological questions are important, with a long and rich history of debate. They have been asked repeatedly since the social sciences originated. Classical theorists such as Auguste Comte, Sigmund Frued, Émile Durkheim, Karl Marx, and Max Weber, along with contemporary thinkers such as Karl Popper, Michel Foucault, Richard Bernstein, Anthony Giddens, and Jurgen Habermas, have pondered these questions. A good deal of epistemological discussion and debate has taken place in crime and justice studies as well. Much of it has centered on whether the field should value alternative approaches to research that fall outside the natural science model (e.g., quantitative versus qualitative).[1]

EPISTEMOLOGY

A philosophical concept that asks how we know what we say we know, and what constitutes legitimate knowledge.

Crime and justice researchers choose from three epistemological alternatives: positivist approach, interpretive approach, and critical approach. Each has its own set of philosophical assumptions and principles and its own stance on how to do research. They are rarely declared explicitly in research studies, and some researchers have only a vague awareness of them. Yet, they play an important role, helping to:

- set standards for what constitutes good research and legitimate knowledge,
- spell out the role of values in research,
- guide ethical research behavior, and
- clarify the ultimate purpose of research.

Much of the confusion and conflict between these three approaches comes from the traditional and overly rigid definition of science. This book relies on more updated thinking, viewing crime and justice studies as a large tent that values a diversity of thinking and approaches to knowledge production. Certainly the positivist approach as noted below is the most often used and is essential to our field, but this in no way should diminish the importance of the other two approaches.

Besides, understanding the philosophical foundations of research has four important benefits (See Summary Table 3.1). First, specific research techniques (e.g., experiments and ethnographies) will make more sense if we are aware of the logic and assumptions on which they are based. Second, the approaches presented here help us to understand the diverse, and sometimes conflicting, perspectives we may encounter as we read crime and justice research studies. Third, understanding each approach allows for an informed choice among alternatives for the type of research we may want to pursue. And fourth, an awareness of each approach's deep assumptions, shortcomings, and strengths is essential for developing our skills as critical consumers and producers of research.

The Three Approaches

We need to begin with the meaning of science. It was not written in stone or handed down in a sacred text; it has been an evolving human creation. Until the early 1800s, only philosophers and religious scholars who engaged in armchair speculation studied or wrote about human behavior. The classical theorists made a major contribution to modern civilization when they argued that the social world could be studied using science. They contended that rigorous, systematic observation of the social world, combined with careful, logical thinking, could provide a new and valuable type of knowledge about human relations. In modern times, science has become the accepted way to gain knowledge.

Once the idea of a science of the social world gained acceptance, the issue became, what might the social sciences look like? Some people looked to the already accepted natural science model (e.g., physics, biology, and chemistry) and copied their methods. Their argument was simple: The legitimacy of the natural sciences rests on the scientific method, so social scientists should adopt the same approach.

Many researchers accepted this answer, but it posed a difficulty. Some scholars saw human beings as qualitatively different from the objects of study in the natural sciences (stars, rocks, plants, chemical compounds, etc.). Humans think and learn, have an awareness of

---

SUMMARY TABLE 3.1   Benefits of Understanding Philosophical Foundations

1. Better understanding of data-gathering techniques.
2. Better comprehension of research studies.
3. More informed choice of research method.
4. Develops skills as critical consumers and producers of research.

SUMMARY TABLE 3.2   Philosophical Features of Each Approach
1. The ultimate purpose of research
2. Assumptions about the nature of reality
3. Views on free will versus determinism
4. Assumption about what constitutes good evidence

themselves and their past, establish highly complex meaning systems (language and culture), possess motives and reasons, write poetry, and exercise free will. These unique human characteristics meant that a special science is needed to appropriately capture the complexity of human social life.

The three approaches to research detailed below—positivist social science, interpretive social science, and critical social science—capture the thinking behind the development of social science research.[2] Summary Table 3.2 reviews features of each approach to be examined. Appendix A reviews four additional features of each of the three approaches.

POSITIVIST SOCIAL SCIENCE FEATURES.   Positivist social science (PSS) is used widely, and positivism, broadly defined, is the approach of the natural sciences. In fact, most people assume that the positivist approach is science. Positivism arose from a nineteenth-century school of thought by the Frenchman who founded sociology—Auguste Comte (1798–1857).

PSS researchers prefer precise quantitative data and often use experiments, surveys, and statistics. They emulate the hard sciences emphasizing rigorous, exact measures and the statistical testing of hypotheses. **Positivist social science,** thus, *is a method for combining deductive logic with precise empirical observations in order to discover and confirm a set of probabilistic causal laws that can be used to predict general patterns of human activity*.

POSITIVIST SOCIAL SCIENCE

One of three major approaches to crime and justice research that emphasizes discovering causal laws, careful empirical observations, and value-free research.

1. *Purpose of PSS.* Perhaps the most important distinction between PSS, ISS, and CSS is what they assume is their purpose—in other words, the ultimate objective of research. The ultimate **purpose of research for PSS** is scientific explanation—to discover and document universal causal laws of human behavior. Developing causal laws provides us a tool, in turn, that allows us to predict, based on probability statements of what will likely occur in the future. In this way, we can exercise control over our external environment. Put simply, if we know the cause of something, we can better control its effect. This is the premise behind using PSS as a tool to control crime and administer justice rationally.

PURPOSE OF RESEARCH FOR PSS

The purpose of research for PSS is scientific explanation—to discover and document universal causal laws of human behavior.

This instrumental form of knowledge sees research results as a tool or instrument that people use to master or control events in the world around them. Consequently, PSS has a more technical perspective toward applying knowledge. It is perceived as a valuable tool for solving problems and enhancing the quality of decisions in organizations.

2. *Nature of Reality.* Modern positivists adopt an essentialist orientation to reality: Reality is real; it exists "out there" and is waiting to be discovered. Human perception and intellect may be flawed, and reality may be difficult to pin down, but it does exist. Moreover, social reality is not random; it is patterned and has order. Without this assumption (i.e., the world is not chaotic and without regularity), logic and prediction would be impossible.

According to **essentialism** what people see and touch (i.e., empirical reality) is not overly complex. Thus, quantitative measurements of crime, race, and gender may be difficult but still accomplishable. An essentialist assumption about time is that it is linear or flows in a straight line. This means that what happened in the past will not be directly repeated, because time moves in only one direction—forward to the future.

ESSENTIALISM

A philosophical position that views reality and causal processes as fairly straightforward and determinable through scientific observation.

DETERMINISM

An approach to human agency and causality that assumes human actions are largely caused by forces external to individuals that can be identified.

3. *Free Will versus Determinism.* PSS looks at how external forces and pressures (e.g., child abuse) that operate on individuals, groups, organizations, or societies produce outcomes (resulting in adult criminality). Although few positivists believe in absolute **determinism,** PSS downplays an individual's subjective or internal reasons and any sense of free choice or volition. Mental processes are less central than the structural forces or conditions beyond individual control that exert influence over choices and behavior. Although individual people may feel that they can act freely and can make any decision, positivists emphasize the powerful pressures and situations that operate on people to shape most, if not all, of their actions. Even positivists who use rational choice explanations focus less on how individuals reason and make choices than on identifying sets of conditions that allow them to predict what people will choose. They assume that once they know external factors, individual reasoning will largely follow a machinelike rational logic of decision making.

Consequently, researchers can estimate the odds of a predicted behavior. In other words, scientific causal laws enable us to make accurate predictions of how often a social behavior will occur within a large group. The causal laws cannot predict the specific behavior of a specific person in each situation. However, they can say that under conditions X, Y, and Z, there is a 95 percent probability that half of the people will engage in a specified behavior.

4. *Good Evidence.* PSS is dualist; it assumes that the cold, observable facts are fundamentally distinct from ideas, values, or theories. Empirical facts exist apart from personal ideas or thoughts. We can observe them by using our senses (sight, smell, hearing, and touch) or special instruments that extend the use of our sense organs (e.g., telescopes, microscopes, and Geiger counters). Knowledge of observable reality obtained using our senses allows us to separate true from false ideas about social life.

INTERPRETIVE SOCIAL SCIENCE (ISS)

An approach to research that emphasizes the systematic analysis and detailed study of people and text to arrive at understandings and interpretations of how people construct and maintain meaning within their social worlds.

PSS CONCLUSION.   Many PSS assumptions will reappear when you read about quantitative research techniques and measurement in later chapters. A positivist approach implies that a researcher begins with a cause–effect relationship that he or she logically derives from a possible causal law in general theory. He or she logically links the abstract ideas to precise measurements of the social world. The researcher remains detached, neutral, and objective as he or she measures aspects of social life, examines evidence, and replicates the research of others. These processes lead to an empirical test of and confirmation for the laws of social life as outlined in a theory. Summary Table 3.3 provides a summary of PSS.

VERSTEHEN

Max Weber's concept defined as empathetic understanding used by ISS researchers as their primary goal.

INTERPRETIVE SOCIAL SCIENCE FEATURES.   Interpretive social science (ISS) can be traced to German sociologist Max Weber (1864–1920). Weber emphasized a social science that strove empathetic understanding, or **verstehen**, of the everyday lived experience of people in specific cultural settings. Weber embraced *verstehen* and felt that we must learn the personal reasons, motives, and cultural context that shape a person's internal feelings and guide decisions to act in particular ways. Here's how one criminologist describes this concept:

SUMMARY TABLE 3.3   Positivist Social Science Features
1. Ultimate purpose is to discover causal laws; control.
2. Reality is empirically evident; out there to be discovered.
3. Free will minimized; determinism stressed.
4. Good evidence stems from neutral observation/measurement.

I can't seem to find an ethnographic moment away from Max Weber. His notion of *verstehen* all but overwhelms me. . . . He showed up regularly in one of my research projects: the documentation of the roadside shrines that families and friends build for loved ones lost to automotive violence. Sometimes the rush of sympathetic understanding overtakes me at the edge of a roadway as a big automobile blasts by, offering me the visceral proximity of violent death. . . . Such moments sparkle with human possibility, with intellectual excitement, because they ground analysis in experience—and because they situate our analysis and experience inside the everyday lives of others. (Ferrell 2004a: 299)

Jeff Ferrell (2002) conducted a unique ethnography where he photographed and inquired into the interpretive meaning of roadside memorials. His research aimed to raise people's awareness about the high level of vehicular violence we seem to tolerate in our society.

The interpretive approach is the systematic analysis and detailed study of people and text to arrive at understandings and interpretations of how people construct and maintain meaning within their social worlds.

1. *Ultimate Purpose of ISS.* The goal of interpretive research is to develop an understanding of social life and discover how people construct meaning in natural settings—in a word, *verstehen.* An interpretive researcher wants to learn what is meaningful or relevant to the people being studied, or how individuals experience daily life. The researcher does this by getting to know a particular social setting and seeing it from the point of view of those in it. Recall Wright and Decker's research of armed robbers in Chapter 1 and Athens's research on violent criminals in Chapter 2.

    The researcher must take into account the social actor's reasons and the social context of action. For example, a physical reflex such as eye blinking is human behavior that is rarely an intentional social action (i.e., done for a reason or with human motivation), but in some situations, it can be such a social action (i.e., a wink). Human action, therefore, has little inherent meaning. People construct meaning by interacting with others. Interpretative social scientists' **ultimate purpose** thus is to learn about how the world works so they can acquire an in-depth understanding of other people, appreciate the wide diversity of lived human experience, and better acknowledge shared humanity. Instead of viewing knowledge as a kind of tool or instrument, ISS researchers try to capture the inner lives and subjective experience of ordinary people.

2. *Nature of Reality.* The interpretive approach sees human social life intentionally created out of the purposeful actions of interacting social beings. In contrast to the positivist view that social life is out there waiting to be discovered, ISS states the social world is largely what people perceive it and construct it to be. Social life exists as people experience it and give it meaning. It is fluid and fragile. People construct it by interacting with others in ongoing processes of communication, conflict, and negotiation. What we call crime, for example, is a human construction that varies across time and place. Consider that when your authors were growing up, a fistfight among children at school was seen at worst as a situation requiring parental involvement. Today, many states require by law that any incidence of so-called violence on school grounds to be reported to the police—even at the elementary school level. What was previously handled as a minor childhood transgression is increasingly being redefined as serious criminality (Kappeler and Potter 2006).

    ISS assumes that this ongoing construction of meaning creates our reality (referred to as the **social construction of reality**). There is no inner essence that causes the reality people see; it is a product of social and political processes. For example, when you see a chair, there is no "chairness" in it; rather, what you see as a chair arises from what a people

ULTIMATE PURPOSE (ISS)

ISS's purpose is to acquire an in-depth understanding of other people, appreciate the wide diversity of lived human experience, and better acknowledge shared humanity.

SOCIAL CONSTRUCTION OF REALITY

An orientation toward reality that assumes the beliefs and meanings people construct and use in a social context fundamentally shape social reality.

of a particular society define, accept, and understand to be a chair. Imagine coming from a culture that had no chairs. A chair would have no meaning—it would be merely a peculiar inanimate object (until someone sat on it).

3. *Free Will versus Determinism.* Whereas PSS assumes determinism, ISS emphasizes voluntary individual free choice, sometimes called **human agency.** ISS sees people as having volition and being able to make conscious choices. Social settings and subjective points of view help to shape the choices a person makes, but people create and change those settings and have the ability to develop or form an alternative point of view. ISS researchers emphasize the importance of taking into account individual decision-making processes, subjective feelings, and ways to understanding events.

4. *Good Evidence.* Good evidence in positivism is observable, quantitatively measurable, precise, and independent of theory and values. By contrast, ISS sees PSS, by reducing human experience to numbers, as distorting the true nature of human social life. Evidence about social action cannot be isolated from the context in which it occurs or the meanings assigned to it by the social actors involved. As Weber (1978: 5) said, "Empathic or appreciative accuracy is attained when, through sympathetic participation, we can adequately grasp the emotional context in which the action took place."

For ISS, facts are fluid and embedded within a culture or subculture; they are not impartial, objective, and neutral. The so-called "facts" can have several meanings and can be interpreted in multiple ways.

For example, we might all agree when standing in a forest looking at a tree that it is a tree (assuming we all use the same symbolic sound "tree" to represent this massive brown, gray, and green object in front of us). PSS views this scene as clear evidence of an objective fact. ISS, however, would argue that there is a tremendous amount of ambiguity in what this object means (what is its reality), depending on whether a corporate logging executive or passionate conservationist is interpreting its meaning. To one it's a commodity to be cut down and used for human consumption and profit; to the other it's a living organism essential for the health and well-being of our natural environment (example modified from Blumer): one object—two very different realities based on differing interpretive values.

ISS CONCLUSION.   The interpretive approach existed for many years as the loyal opposition to positivism. Although some positivist social researchers resist viewing the interpretive approach as scientific research (see Chapter 2), most now concede its credibility as a means to produce knowledge. You will read again about the interpretive outlook in the latter part of this book concentrating on qualitative research—especially historical, ethnographic field research, and qualitative document analysis. The interpretive approach is the foundation of social research

These two photographs illustrate the point in this section about how one object (in this case, the wilderness) can possess two very different realities based on differing interpretive values.

SUMMARY TABLE 3.4 Interpretive Social Science Features

1. Ultimate purpose is Max Weber's verstehen; understand social meaning in context.
2. Reality/meaning is a social/human construction.
3. Assumes human agency; people have volition.
4. Good evidence is verified through research subjects.

techniques that are sensitive to context, that get inside the ways others see the world, and that are more concerned with achieving an empathic understanding than with testing lawlike theories of human behavior. Summary Table 3.4 provides an overview of the interpretive approach.

CRITICAL SOCIAL SCIENCE FEATURES. **Critical social science (CSS)** agrees with many of the criticisms the interpretive approach directs at PSS, but it adds some of its own and disagrees with ISS on some points. This approach's roots are traced to Karl Marx (1818–1883) and Sigmund Freud (1856–1939), and was elaborated on by Theodor Adorno (1903–1969), Erich Fromm (1900–1980), and Herbert Marcuse (1898–1979). In crime and justice studies, the areas of scholarship most associated with CSS include a broad-based area of interest usually referred to as critical criminology, as well as feminist criminology and race-based criminology. The common thread running through each is a concern for researching oppression and injustice, the role of the criminal justice system in that oppression and injustice, and the measures needed to eliminate or improve these conditions.

CRITICAL SOCIAL SCIENCE (CSS)

A critical process of inquiry that generates liberating knowledge so as to reveal structural and cultural inhibiting forces in an attempt to help people change their living conditions and build a better world for themselves.

As outlined below, CSS researchers critique ISS for being too subjective and relativist. CSS sees the interpretive approach as treating people's ideas and subjective experiences as more important than actual economic and political conditions. By focusing on localized, microlevel, short-term settings, ISS tends to ignore the broader and long-term context. CSS believes researchers should link both microprocesses and concerns to macrostructures and concerns (the larger economic system, for example). To CSS researchers, ISS and PSS are passive, as they fail to take a value position or actively help people to see false illusions around them so that they can improve their lives. *In general, then, CSS defines social science as a critical process of inquiry that generates liberating knowledge so as to reveal structural and cultural inhibiting forces in an attempt to help people change their living conditions and build a better world for themselves.*

1. *Ultimate Purpose of CSS.* The **purpose of critical research** is not simply to study the social world but to change it. CSS researchers conduct research to critique and transform inhibiting social conditions by revealing the underlying sources of these conditions and empowering people, especially less powerful people. More specifically, they uncover deep-seated ideologies, reveal hidden truths, and help people to change the world for themselves. In CSS, the purpose is "to explain a social order in such a way that it becomes itself the catalyst which leads to the transformation of this social order" (Fay 1987: 27).

PURPOSE OF CRITICAL RESEARCH

The purpose of CSS is to study the social world in order to transform it.

The CSS researcher asks normally unmentionable questions, exposes hypocrisy, and investigates oppressive conditions. "The point of all science, indeed all learning, is to change and develop out of our understandings and reduce illusion. . . . Learning is the reducing of illusion and ignorance; it can help free us from domination by hitherto unacknowledged constraints, dogmas and falsehoods" (Sayer 1992: 252).

For CSS, then, knowledge is not an instrument for people to manipulate, nor is it a capturing and rendering of people's inner, subjective experiences; instead, knowledge means active change in the world. Knowledge can free people from the shackles of past thinking and help them take control of events around them. It is not a thing to be possessed, but a process that combines greater awareness with taking action. The relevance of knowledge is its ability to connect consciousness with people engaging in concrete actions, reflecting on the consequences of those actions, and then advancing consciousness to a new level in an ongoing cycle.

2. *Nature of Reality*. CSS bridges a divide between PSS and ISS. It shares PSS's premise that there is an empirical reality independent of our perceptions, and agrees with ISS's position that we simultaneously construct what we take to be reality from our subjective experiences, cultural beliefs, and social interactions. Although seemingly irreconcilable, CSS views this, and many other societal contradictions, as operating in a **dialectical** fashion. Put simply, *PSS reality and ISS reality mutually transform one another; it's not one or the other in operation but both transforming and influencing each other simultaneously.*

Similarly, causal mechanisms in society often have internal contradictions and operate in a paradoxical manner, creating structural conflicts. They may contain forces or processes that appear to be opposites, or to be in conflict, but are actually parts of a single larger process. A biological analogy helps illustrate this idea. We see birth and life as the opposites of death. Yet, death begins the day we are born and each day of living moves us toward death as our body ages and decays. There is a contradiction between life and death; to live we move toward its opposite, death. Living and dying appear to be opposites, but actually they are two parts of a single process. Discovering and understanding such paradoxical processes, what CSS researchers call the dialectic, is a central task in CSS.

Laying bare and making sense of society's paradoxes and contradictions reveal what critical social scientists refer to as "deep structure." An example would be how the deep structure of patriarchy—a cultural and structural system of male privilege—shapes and structures the everyday actions of men and women. With theoretical insight and careful investigation, researchers can uncover these deep structures, expose the unfair assumptions and the power they wield, and then help to reconstruct them in a way that no longer disadvantages or harms women. (Patriarchy is also seen by feminists as quite harmful to boys and men as well.) Feminist CSS researchers would certainly argue that the educative power of knowledge has made advances in the United States—but would quickly point out how far we still have to go. They would note the virulent backlash in contemporary U.S. society against the deconstruction of patriarchy and the complete lack of progress made with regard to women's oppression in much of the rest of the world.

For CSS, therefore, social change and conflict are not always apparent or easily observable. As illustrated in Highlight 3.1, using the *Matrix* movies, the social world is full of illusion, myth, and distortion. These illusions, what some CSS theorists call **dominant ideology,** benefit and work to the advantage of those with cultural, political, and economic power. Responsible research, from this perspective, should expose the flaws in dominant ideology and work to empower those who are oppressed by it.

3. *Free Will versus Determinism*. CSS blends determinism and voluntarism into a single idea labeled **bounded autonomy.** Bounded autonomy suggests that free will, choices, and decision making are not unlimited or open ended; rather, they stay within restricted boundaries of options—both culturally and materially derived. In other words, a CSS researcher identifies a range of options, or at least what people see as being realistic alternatives, and allows for some volition among those options. People make choices, but the choices are confined to what they feel is possible. Material factors (e.g., natural resources, physical abilities) and cultural-subjective schemes (e.g., beliefs, core values, deeply felt norms) set what people feel to be possible or impossible, and people act based on what they believe is possible.

4. *Good Evidence*. CSS researchers believe that our observations and experiences with empirical reality are not pure, neutral, and unmediated; rather, preexisting ideas, beliefs, and interpretations color what we see and how we interpret it. Our knowledge of empirical reality can capture the way things really are, yet in an incomplete manner, because our experiences of it depend on ideas and beliefs. What the PSS researcher calls facts are actually only interpretation of the "real" within a framework of preconstructed values, theory, and meaning.

In CSS, theory is a type of map telling researchers where to look for facts and how to interpret them once they are uncovered. It claims this is true in the natural sciences as well. For example, a biologist looks into a microscope and sees red blood cells—a fact based on

---

DIALECTICAL

The idea that two seemingly contradictory elements or processes actually interact in a mutually transformative manner, with each transforming one another.

DOMINANT IDEOLOGY

That ideology (type of thinking, beliefs) that benefits and works to the advantage of those with cultural, political, and economic power.

BOUNDED AUTONOMY

This idea suggests that free will, choices, and decision making are not unlimited or open ended; rather, they stay within restricted boundaries of options— both culturally and materially derived.

HIGHLIGHT 3.1

A Splinter in Your Mind: CSS and *The Matrix*

A journalist friend of Kraska went to New Orleans immediately after Katrina hit. He told a revealing story that might help you better understand the philosophical underpinnings of critical social science. The journalist was slogging through four feet of water helping an elderly woman into a boat. He saw a boy about ten years old enthusiastically carrying some supplies over his head. Curious about where the boy was going, he asked if he needed help. The boy politely refused, and then the journalist asked, "Hey, what do you think of all this?" The boy said, in a deep New Orleans accent, "Man, New Orlean's took the red pill." The journalist didn't figure out until later what the comment meant and then he was amazed. The young boy was referring to a key moment in the movie, *The Matrix.*

Many aren't aware that *The Matrix's* central objective, according to its creators, was to make an action movie infused with deep philosophical meaning. Numerous scholarly books and articles have teased out its philosophical significance.[3] For those not familiar with *The Matrix* movies (there are three of them), the premise is pure science fiction: The world is dominated by highly advanced machines that enslave humans for the production of energy. They keep millions of humans pacified by plugging their minds into an elaborate computer-programmed virtual world, which allows them to lead normal albeit wholly illusionary lives (the Matrix). There are a few rogue humans, though, who have managed to unplug themselves from the Matrix, forming a resistance movement. A central philosophical moment occurs when the resistors contact a plugged-in human named Neo (the ONE as an anagram) and give him the choice to unplug from the Matrix and see the truth. Morpheus, the leader of the resistance movement, attempts to explain to Neo about the nature of reality in providing him the choice to unplug from the Matrix.

MORPHEUS: As children, we do not separate the possible from the impossible, which is why the younger a mind is the easier it is to free, while a mind like yours can be very difficult.

NEO: Free from what?

MORPHEUS: From the Matrix. Do you want to know what it is, NEO?

NEO: (Nods his head.)

MORPHEUS: It's that feeling you have had all your life. That feeling that something was wrong with the world. You don't know what it is but it's there, like a splinter in your mind, driving you mad, driving you to me. But what is it? The Matrix is everywhere, it's all around us, here even in this room. You can see it out your window, or on your television. You feel it when you go to work, or go to church or pay your taxes. It is the world that has been pulled over your eyes to blind you from the truth.

NEO: What truth?

MORPHEUS: 'That you are a slave, Neo. That you, like everyone else, was born into bondage . . . kept inside a prison that you cannot smell, taste, or touch. A prison for your mind. Hold out your hands. (*Morpheus places a red pill and a blue pill in each hand.*) This is your last chance. After this, there is no going back.

You take the blue pill and the story ends. You wake in your bed and you believe whatever you want to believe. You take the red pill and you stay in Wonderland and I show you how deep the rabbit-hole goes. Remember that all I am offering is the truth. Nothing more.*

Of course, Neo takes the red pill and the truth—an ugly yet at the same time very liberating and rewarding truth—is revealed.

The young boy from New Orleans was espousing a central philosophical tenet of CSS. The hurricane washed away the Matrix of denial and ignorance, exposing the raw reality of poverty, inequality, structural racism, ecological degradation, and system dependency. ISS taught us that reality can be seen as relative—a mere human construction. Critical social science agrees, yet still believes that there is an underlying reality (truth) behind our ideologies and myths. It sees research as a way to awaken us to what really is the case, or the truth, so that we work toward informed change (praxis). It asks us to break free from the Matrix, embrace the real, and work toward creating a more humane, just, free, and peaceful existence. Although this may sound more spiritual than scientific, it is important to note that many serious scientific researchers share this view of scientific knowledge's ultimate goal.

_____

* _The Matrix_ used courtesy of Warner Bros. Entertainment Inc. TM & © Warner Bros. Entertainment Inc.

a theory about blood and cells and a biologist's education about microscopic phenomena. Without this theory and education, a biologist sees only meaningless spots. Clearly, then, facts and theories are interrelated. And if all theory has values embedded within them, then values play a critical role in all research.

CSS CONCLUSION.   As seen in Summary Table 3.5, the CSS approach captures many of the more important criticisms of both the positivist and interpretive approaches. It constitutes an important presence and influence in crime and justice studies. It is also unique in that it allows for researchers to fully collaborate with those most directly effected by what they are researching – an approach know as "participatory action research" (see Highlight 3.2). Despite CSS's critique of positivism, it is important to realize that there is actually a large range of activism associated with CSS (from passive rhetoric to serious activist work), as there is with positivist social science. Remember that these categories are ideal types, and most researchers incorporate elements of all three orientations at some time in their work. We have already discussed several researchers—such as Francis Cullen, Todd Clear, Robin Haarr, and John Hagan—who rely primarily on the PSS approach, and yet are committed to bringing about social changes consistent with the value position of social justice. (For those readers that would like to learn more about CSS, Appendix A provides a more thorough discussion).

Philosophical Conclusion

You have learned two important things in this section. First, there are competing approaches to crime and justice research based on philosophical assumptions about the purpose of science and the nature of social reality. Second, the ideal-type approaches answer basic questions about research differently. The three different approaches to knowledge production outlined in this chapter should not be viewed as opposing camps. In the real world of actual people conducting research, the lines between them are blurry and overlapping. As mentioned in Chapter 1, it is increasingly common to combine various elements of each approach in a single study. Perhaps it is best to think of them as one large bag of golf clubs—some irons, some putters, and some drivers—all designed for different tasks and purposes but used in the same game. Despite their differences, all the approaches share the view that the social sciences strive to create systematically gathered, empirically based theoretical knowledge through public processes that are self-reflective and open ended. We'll learn the specifics of each set of clubs in subsequent chapters (Chapters 8–11 cover PSS, and Chapters 12–15 cover ISS and CSS).

SUMMARY TABLE 3.5   Critical Social Science Features
1. Ultimate purpose is consciousness-raising leading to change.
2. Reality is multilayered and complex, yet it exists.
3. Both volition and determinism—bounded autonomy.
4. Evidence is theory dependent and should reveal deeper kinds of evidence.

HIGHLIGHT 3.2
Participatory Action Research

Participatory action research (PAR) is applied research that treats knowledge as a form of power and abolishes the line between research and social action. There are several types of PAR, but most share common characteristics:

- those who are being studied participate in the research process;
- research focuses on power inequities with the goal of empowerment;
- research seeks to raise consciousness and theoretical awareness;
- research is tied directly to practical/political action; and
- research views theory and practice as mutually transformative (see Figure 3.1).

Action researchers try to equalize power relations between themselves and research subjects, and they avoid having more control, status, and authority than those they study. These researchers try to advance a cause or improve conditions by constructing knowledge that enlightens and empowers. They are explicitly political, not value neutral. PAR assumes that ordinary people can become aware of oppressive conditions and learn to take actions that can bring about improvement.

The goals of participatory action research are to democratize the knowledge-creation process, reveal injustices, highlight the centrality of social conflict, and emphasize the importance of engaging in collection action to alter oppressive cultural and structural conditions (Carr and Kemmis 1986). This requires the research participants to assume an active role in formulating, designing, and carrying out the research. Applied to practitioners working in an organization, PAR is "simply a form of self-reflective enquiry undertaken by participants in organizational situations in order to improve the rationality and justice of their own practices, their understanding of these practices, and the situations in which the practices are carried out" (Carr and Kemmis 1986: 162). Can you think of an example of how this approach might be applied in criminal justice agencies or non-criminal justice crime control initiatives?

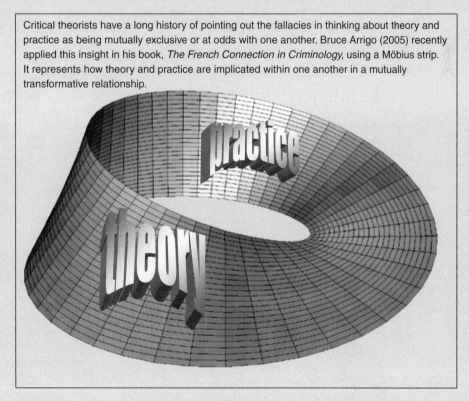

Critical theorists have a long history of pointing out the fallacies in thinking about theory and practice as being mutually exclusive or at odds with one another. Bruce Arrigo (2005) recently applied this insight in his book, *The French Connection in Criminology,* using a Möbius strip. It represents how theory and practice are implicated within one another in a mutually transformative relationship.

FIGURE 3.1 Möbius Strip Depicting the Relationship between Theory and Practice.

THEORY IN CRIME AND JUSTICE RESEARCH

Why Theory?

THEORY

A system of interconnected ideas that condenses and organizes knowledge for purposes of understanding and/or explanation.

PERSONAL THEORETICAL FRAMEWORK

The idea that each of us carries with us an enormous stock of theoretical knowledge essential for making sense of our surroundings.

Just as the three different epistemological approaches provide the broad framework for how a study proceeds, so can theories. A **theory** is in its simplest terms a speculation as to why? We defined it formally in Chapter 2 as a system of interconnected ideas that condenses and organizes knowledge for purposes of understanding and/or explanation.

Theory should not be viewed as something exclusively owned by "high-minded" academics. It is an essential force in all of our lives. We carry around an enormous stock of theoretical knowledge—what we might call our **personal theoretical framework** (PTF)—that allows us to understand our immediate surroundings and larger environment, and to navigate through that environment (see Figure 3.2). Filtering our observations and actions through our numerous theoretical lenses allows us to notice patterns and trends that indicate what might happen in the future (i.e., prediction). Our competence in problem solving is directly tied to our theoretical skills and abilities. Why isn't my car turning over? The clicking sound indicates a dead battery. Why is my significant other treating me poorly? I hurt her or his feelings yesterday with a callous comment. Why did Hurricane Katrina destroy New Orleans? Fifty years of environmental destruction eliminated the vast stretches of cypress forests and marshlands that had acted as a natural flood barrier.

Whereas most of us take little notice of our speculations as to why, social scientists ask and attempt to answer these types of *why* questions in a careful, methodical manner. In fact, most would rank the development, substantiation, and/or refutation of theory as the highest goal of academic research. However, as we learned in Chapter 1, even when explanation is not the stated objective, such as in evaluation research, theory is still present in the formulation

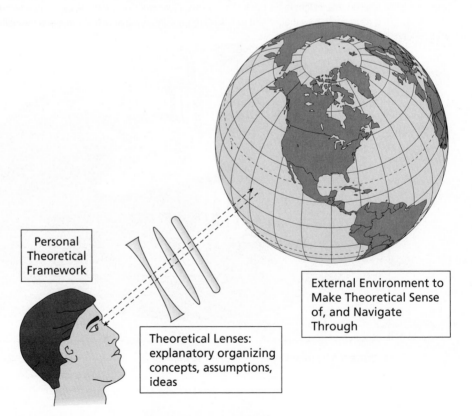

FIGURE 3.2 Personal Theoretical Framework (PTF).

of the research questions, in the interpretation of the data, and in the implications of our findings. Almost all research involves some theory, so the question is less whether you should use theory than how you should use it.

Theory and research, then, are interrelated. Researchers interweave a story about crime and justice phenomena (the theory) with what they observe when they examine it systematically (the data). Only the naive researcher mistakenly believes that theory is irrelevant to research or that a researcher just collects the data. Researchers who attempt to proceed without theory will likely collect data of little use. They easily fall into the trap of hazy and vague thinking, faulty logic, and imprecise concepts. They find it difficult to converge onto a crisp research issue or to generate a lucid account of their study's purpose. They find themselves adrift as they attempt to design or conduct empirical research.

The reason is simple. Theory frames how we look at and think about a topic. It gives us organizing concepts and ideas, provides basic assumptions, directs us to the important questions, and suggests ways for us to make sense of data. Theory enables us to connect a single study to the immense base of knowledge to which other researchers contribute. Peering through differing theoretical lenses allows us to understand crime and justice phenomena in different ways.

The Parts of a Theory

ASSUMPTIONS.   Theories contain built-in assumptions and statements about the nature of things. We accept **theoretical assumptions** as a necessary starting point, such as assumptions about the nature of human beings, social reality, or a particular phenomenon. Assumptions often remain hidden or unstated. One way for a researcher to deepen his or her understanding is to identify the assumptions on which a theory is based. Crime and criminal justice theories operating from what is known as a social constructionist orientation, for example, harbor the deep assumption that reality is relative. It's the same assumption found in interpretive social science (ISS). Crime, thus, is whatever we construct it to be, and how we construct it will all depend on the time in history, political climate, or cultural leanings of the time. Only twenty years ago, if a driver missed a stop sign and hit another vehicle, resulting in the death of a motorist, that was defined as an accident. In today's safety-conscious society, more jurisdictions are redefining these situations as a serious act of criminality deserving prison time (Kraska 2006).

THEORETICAL ASSUMPTIONS

Hidden or unstated ideas about the nature of human beings, social reality, or social processes that underlie a theory or theoretical framework.

CONCEPTS.   **Concepts** are the building blocks of theory.[4] A theoretical concept is an idea expressed as a symbol or in words. Natural science concepts are often expressed in symbolic forms, such as Greek letters (e.g., p). Most social science concepts are expressed as words.[5]

Concepts are everywhere, and we use them all the time. Height is a simple concept from everyday experience. What does it mean? It is easy to use the concept of height, but describing the concept itself is difficult. It represents an abstract idea about physical relations. How would you describe it to a very young child or a creature from a distant planet that was totally unfamiliar with it? A new concept from a crime and justice theory may seem just as alien when you encounter it for the first time.

Recall Hagan's research on genocide in the Darfur region of Africa. He examined the appropriateness of using the organizing concept of "criminal genocide" to help make theoretical sense of this tragic and ongoing event. *Genocide* is defined as the intentional annihilation of a large group of people, especially those of a particular ethnic, racial, or religious group through mass execution or the imposition of conditions calculated to bring about their destruction (starvation, rape, transference of children, etc.). Notice how this one concept could help organize an entire research project—both its methods and its interpretations.

CONCEPTS

An abstract idea expressed as a word.

The definition of a concept helps to link theory with research. An important goal of all research is to clarify and refine concepts. Weak, contradictory, or unclear definitions of concepts restrict the advance of knowledge. For instance, after noting that there are many definitions of a gang, but little consensus, Ball and Curry (1995: 239) argued that lack of a clear, consistent definition seriously hampered our understanding of the phenomenon of gangs. An unclear definition could result in researchers overdefining what constitutes a gang, and consequently focusing on various harmless forms of youths hanging out in groups.

Some concepts take on a range of values, quantities, or amounts. Examples of this kind of concept are amount of income, temperature, density of population, years of schooling, and degree of violence. When used in a quantitative research study, social scientists call these **variables** (simply defined as concepts that vary). Variables are classified depending on their location in a causal relationship. The cause variable, or the one that identifies forces or conditions that act on something else, is the **independent variable.** The variable that is the effect or is the result or outcome of another variable is the **dependent variable.** We will learn more about independent and dependent variables later in this chapter.

RELATIONSHIPS AMONG CONCEPTS.   In addition to making assumptions and providing concepts, theories specify relationships among concepts. Theories posit relationships between differing concepts and attempt to determine the nature of that relationship (e.g., the relationship between fear of crime and criminal justice growth). By outlining an entire complex of assumptions, concepts, and interconnections, a theory often states why a specific relationship does or does not exist.

Kinds of Relationships.   If two concepts are interrelated, a theory specifies what kind of relationship exists: Whether they are related strongly or weakly, directly or indirectly; whether they accelerate or accentuate one another, or depress or reduce each other. One concept might relate to another alone, or only when it is in combination with other conditions and concepts (these are called an interaction effect and a contingent relationship and are discussed later in the book). A theory may identify a concept as a necessary (i.e., essential and required) precondition for another concept, or state that it is sufficient (i.e., it may be involved but does not have to be present).

Propositions and Hypotheses.   Many theories contain propositions, or statements, about the connection among concepts. For example, high levels of fear of crime will result in criminal justice system growth. This **proposition** is a theoretical statement that specifies the relationship between two or more concepts (variables) and says something about the kind of relationship it is. A researcher will try to learn the truthfulness of a proposition by evaluating whether it conforms to empirical evidence or data. To do this he or she converts the proposition into a **hypothesis**, delineating the relationship between the two variables (e.g., as fear of crime increases, so will the size of the criminal justice system).

A hypothesis, then, is an empirically testable version of a proposition. It is a tentative statement about a relationship between variables. Researchers are uncertain as to its truthfulness, or whether it actually operates in the empirical world.

In sum, propositions in a theory are converted into hypotheses for empirical testing, and after the hypothesis has been evaluated, the empirical results inform us whether the proposition is likely to be truthful, or if it needs to be modified or rejected. Sometimes researchers develop propositions after they examine empirical evidence, and in some types of research they proceed without using hypotheses. We'll examine the specifics of hypothesis testing in the next section.

Approaches to Developing Theory: Deductive–Inductive

Researchers approach the building and testing of theory from two directions—deductive and inductive. **Deductive theorizing** begins with abstract thinking. It logically connects the

---

*VARIABLES
(INDEPENDENT AND
DEPENDENT)*

Concepts that vary. An independent variable is the effect, result, or outcome of the dependent variable.

*INDEPENDENT
VARIABLE*

The cause variable, or the one that identifies forces or conditions that act on something else.

DEPENDENT VARIABLE

The variable that is the effect or is the result or outcome of another variable.

PROPOSITION

A theoretical statement that specifies the relationship between two or more concepts (variables).

HYPOTHESIS

An empirically testable version of a theoretical proposition that has not yet been tested or verified with empirical evidence. It is most often used in deductive theorizing.

*DEDUCTIVE
THEORIZING*

An approach to developing or confirming a theory that begins with abstact concepts and theoretical relationships and works toward more concrete empirical evidence.

ideas of a preexisting theory to concrete evidence, then tests these ideas against the evidence. **Inductive theorizing** begins with specific observations of empirical evidence. On the basis of its observations and evidence, it constructs a more abstract set of ideas and concepts that explain the object of research. In practice, many researchers are flexible and approach the activity of theorizing deductively and inductively (see Figure 3.3). Let's explore these in more depth.

Deductive Direction. To theorize in a *deductive direction*, we begin with abstract concepts or a theoretical proposition that outlines the logical connection among concepts and then move toward concrete, empirical evidence. Thus, we start with ideas and then test our thinking against observable empirical evidence. The biologically based theories of crime you read about in Chapter 1 use deductive theorizing. They might begin with the theoretical proposition that the biologically based personality trait of extroversion will predispose a person to commit crime. Researchers would turn this abstract proposition into a tangible empirical hypothesis; that is, a population of prison inmates will more likely be extroverted as compared to a group of free citizens. The theorizing proceeded deductively from the abstract level logically to a more concrete, empirical level. Deductive theorizing is generally aligned more with positivist social science.

Inductive Direction. While deductive theorizing begins with a theory, inductive theorizing begins with engaging the empirical world. Observing the empirical world invariably leads to speculating about why, thinking in increasingly abstract ways, and developing organizing concepts that help us categorize our thinking. Whereas deductive theorizing requires us to begin with a clearly thought-out theoretical picture, inductive theorizing enables us to begin with a general topic and some vague ideas that we then refine and elaborate into more exact theoretical concepts. Inductive theorizing is most commonly associated with interpretive social science and critical social science.

> **INDUCTIVE THEORIZING**
>
> An approach to developing or confirming a theory that begins with concrete empirical evidence and works toward more abstract concepts and theoretical relationships.

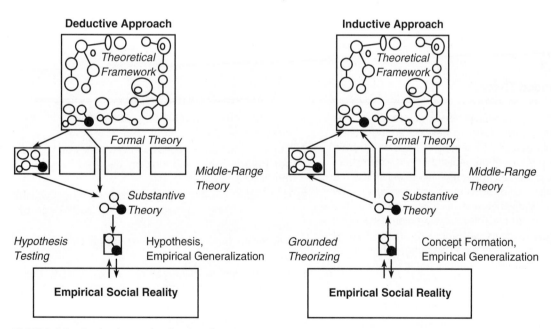

FIGURE 3.3 Deductive and Inductive Theorizing. *Source:* From W. Lawrence Neuman, *Social Research Methods, Qualitative and Quantitative Approaches,* 6/e. Published by Allyn and Bacon, 75 Arlington St., Boston, MA 02116. Copyright © by Pearson Education. Reprinted by permission of the publisher.

Ryan Bussard, a graduate student who worked with Kraska, recently completed a research project on illicit steroid manufacturing and trafficking. He began his research with no preconceived theories—just a willing research informant that sold illicit steroids to bodybuilders, competitive athletes, and recreational weight lifters. Bussard let the experience unfold naturally and allowed the data to cumulate into a theoretical narrative. He slowly found out how and why his informant became a steroid dealer. He ran a type of postmodern operation in which he ordered the precursor chemicals and supplies to manufacture his own cutting-edge steroids from numerous international drug companies found on the internet (ostensibly a legal transaction). He then located the recipes from bodybuilding Web sites for how to "cook" these materials into potent drugs. He was able to routinely convert a $500.00 purchase of supplies from foreign Internet sites into enough steroids to support his own use, as well as make $15,000.00 profit. Bussard constructed a theory based on the theoretical concepts "opportunity" and "rational-choice" to make sense of his data.

Ryan Bussard's research is an example of what Glaser and Straus called **grounded theory** (see Highlight 3.3). You will learn more about grounded theory in Chapters 6 and 12. It involves formulating new theoretical ideas from the ground up instead of testing existing theoretical ideas. A researcher builds theoretical generalizations out of the process of trying to explain, interpret, and render meaning from observed data.

Causal Explanation and Testing Hypotheses

In order to understand how exactly theory relates to research we need now to examine what social scientists mean by a "causal explanation," and how a researcher goes about designing and executing empirical tests of these explanations. **Causal explanation** refers to a cause and effect relationship. We use it all the time in everyday language. What do we mean when we say cause? For example, you may say that poverty causes crime or that looseness in morals causes an increase in child abuse. This does not tell how or why the causal process works. Researchers try to be more precise and exact when discussing causal relations.

GROUNDED THEORY

A type of inductive crime and justice theory often used in qualitative research that builds toward abstract theory by making comparisons of ground-level empirical observations.

CAUSAL EXPLANATION

A type of theoretical explanation about why events occur and how things work expressed in terms of causes and effects, or as one factor producing certain results.

HIGHLIGHT 3.3
What Is Grounded Theory?

Grounded theory is "a qualitative research method that uses a systematic set of procedures to develop an inductively derived theory about a phenomenon" (Strauss and Corbin 1990b: 24). The purpose of grounded theory is to construct theories that are grounded in the research evidence itself. It is an inductive method for discovering and developing new theory. In it, the researcher sees microlevel events as the foundation for a more macrolevel explanation. Grounded theory shares several goals with more positivist-oriented theory, yet retains qualitative data-gathering techniques. It seeks explanations that are comparable to the evidence, and it is precise, rigorous, and capable of replication.

Glaser and Strauss are the originators of grounded theory (Glaser and Strauss 1967). In fact, much of the credit can be given to their work for the renewed and sustained interest in qualitative research. Although this approach has evolved considerably, their original defining features still hold true (Charmaz 2006: 5):

1. Simultaneous involvement in data collection and analysis
2. Constructing analytic codes and categories from data, not from preconceived logically deduced hypothesis (positivism)
3. Using the constant comparative method, which involves making comparisons during each stage of analysis
4. Advancing theory development during each step of data collection and analysis
5. Memowriting to elaborate categories, specify their properties, define relationships between categories, and identify gaps
6. Sampling aimed toward theory construction, not for population representativeness
7. Conducting the literature review *after* developing independent analysis

We need three things to establish causality:

1. temporal order
2. association
3. the elimination of plausible alternatives

Let us examine briefly what we mean by each.

The **temporal order** condition means that a cause must come before an effect. This commonsense assumption establishes the direction of causality: from the cause toward the effect. You may ask, how can the cause come after what it is to affect? It cannot, but temporal order is only one of the conditions needed for causality. Temporal order is necessary but not sufficient to infer causality. Sometimes people make the mistake of talking about cause on the basis of temporal order alone. For example, when Kraska worked as a fishing guide, one of his clients noticed that whenever he threw a rock in the water his friend next to him hooked into a king salmon. He inferred cause to an undisputable pattern: Throw rock, catch fish. Does that mean the rock throwing "caused" the king salmon to hit the lure? It is very unlikely (although these fisherpersons will likely go to their graves thinking it did). As another more serious example, race riots occurred in four separate cities in 1968, one day after an intense wave of sunspots. The temporal ordering does not establish a causal link between sunspots and race riots. After all, all prior human history occurred before some specific event. The temporal order condition simply eliminates from consideration potential causes that occurred later in time.

Relationships between two variables can be positive or negative. Researchers imply a positive relationship if they say nothing. A positive relationship means that a higher value on the causal variable (independent variable) goes with a higher value on the effect variable (dependent variable). For example, an increased demand for marijuana is related to an increase in marijuana manufacturing. A negative relationship means that a higher value on a causal variable goes with a lower value on the effect variable. For example, an increased demand for heroin might mean a decrease in the demand for other illicit drugs. Figure 3.4 presents a typical model representing the relationship between variables.

A researcher, then, needs an **association** for causality. Two phenomena are associated if they occur together in a patterned way or appear to act together. Remember, the fisherpersons experienced a perfect one-to-one association between rock throwing and fish catching. It is easy to mistake association for causality. The media report studies all the time that infer causality when in actuality they are referring to a simple association. For example, "people taking vitamin C are eleven times less likely to be sick on an annual basis than those that don't." Of course, this strong association seems like solid evidence that vitamin C reduces the risk of getting sick, when in fact a better explanation is that those conscientious enough to take a daily vitamin are probably living an all-around healthier lifestyle than those who don't. This is a good example of the importance of eliminating alternative explanations when a researcher is interested in demonstrating that an effect is due to the causal variable and not to something else.

The Language of Variables and Hypotheses

A **variable**, simply defined, is a concept that varies. Variables take on two or more values. Once you begin to look for them, you will see variables everywhere. For example, sex is a variable: It can take on one of two values: male or female. (Some studies may include other categories such as transgender.) Marital status is a variable: It can take on the value of never married single, married, divorced, or widowed. Type of crime committed is a variable: It can take on values of robbery, burglary, theft, murder, and so forth. Family income is a variable: It can take on values from zero to billions of dollars. A person's attitude toward abortion is a variable: It can range from strongly favoring legal abortion to strongly believing that abortion should be a crime. The values or the categories of a variable are its **attributes** (e.g., "murder" "assault").

TEMPORAL ORDER

The commonsense notion that the cause must come before an effect.

ASSOCIATION

The co-occurrence of two events, characteristics, or factors such that when one happens/is present, the other one is likely to happen/be present as well.

VARIABLE

A concept that varies, or an empirical measure that can take on multiple values.

ATTRIBUTES

The categories or levels of a variable.

"It has long been known that officially recorded rates of most forms of crime are higher in economically disadvantaged areas. The conventional view has been that disadvantage increases the motivation to offend but there are a number of findings which are difficult to reconcile with this view. A growing body of research evidence drawn from studies of individual families suggests that economic and social stress exert their effects on crime by disrupting the parenting process. The research reported here confirms this hypothesis for Australian families and points to the importance of increasing family supports and parenting skills as a means of reducing juvenile involvement in crime."

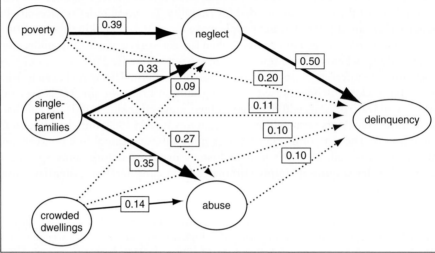

FIGURE 3.4 Causal Diagram of the Relationship between Economic/Social Stress and Juvenile Delinquency. *Source:* Weatherburn, Don, and Bronwyn Lind. (1998). "Poverty, Parenting, Peers and Crime-Prone Neighborhoods," *Trends and Issues in Crime and Criminal Justice,* Australian Institute of Criminology, no. 85.

Looking at Figure 3.5, note that "male" is not a variable, as it describes a category of sex and is an attribute of the variable "sex." Yet, a related idea, "degree of masculinity," is a variable. It describes the intensity or strength of attachment to attitudes, beliefs, and behaviors associated with the concept of "masculine" within a culture. "Married" is not a variable: It is an attribute of the variable "marital status." Related ideas such as "number of years married" or "depth of commitment to a marriage" are variables. Likewise, "robbery" is not a variable: It is an attribute of the variable "type of crime." "Number of robberies," "robbery rate," "amount taken during a robbery," and "type of robbery" are all variables because they vary or take on a range of values.

Quantitative research redefines concepts into the language of variables. As the examples of variables and attributes illustrate, slight changes in definition change a nonvariable into a

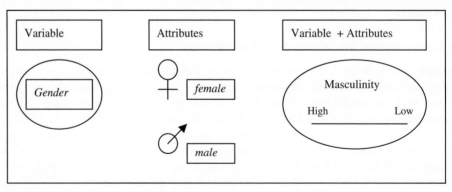

FIGURE 3.5 Variables and Attributes.

variable concept. As discussed above, concepts are the building blocks of theory; they organize thinking about the social world. Clear concepts with careful definitions are essential in developing quality variables.

TYPES OF VARIABLES. Quantitative research focusing on causal relations usually begins with an effect, then searches for its causes. Variables are classified depending on their location in a causal relationship. The cause variable, or the one that identifies forces or conditions that act on something else, is the independent variable. The variable that is the effect or is the result or outcome of another variable is the dependent variable. The independent variable is *independent of* prior causes that act on it, whereas the dependent variable *depends on* the cause.

It is not always easy to determine whether a variable is independent or dependent. Answering two questions helps you identify the independent variable. First, does it come before other variables in time? Independent variables come before any other type. Second, if the variables occur at the same time, does the author suggest that one variable has an impact on another variable? Independent variables affect or have an impact on other variables. Research topics are often phrased in terms of the dependent variables because dependent variables are the phenomenon or object of study to be explained. For example, suppose a researcher examines the reasons for an increase in the crime rate in Dallas, Texas, the dependent variable is the crime rate.

A basic causal relationship requires only an independent and a dependent variable. A third type of variable, the **intervening variable,** appears in more complex causal relations. It comes between the independent and dependent variables and shows the link or mechanism between them. Advances in knowledge depend not only on documenting cause-and-effect relationships, but also on specifying the mechanisms that account for the causal relation. In a sense, the intervening variable acts as a dependent variable with respect to the independent variable and acts as an independent variable toward the dependent variable.

> *INTERVENING VARIABLE*
>
> A variable that comes between the independent and dependent variables and shows the link or causal mechanism between them.

In a classic example, French sociologist Émile Durkheim developed a theory of suicide that specified a causal relationship between marital status and suicide rates. (Refer to Figure 3.6.) Durkheim found evidence that married people are less likely to commit suicide than single people. He believed that married people have greater "social integration" (i.e., feelings of belonging to a group or family). He thought that a major cause of one type of suicide was that people lacked a sense of belonging to a group. Thus, his theory can be restated as a three-variable relationship: Marital status (independent variable) causes the degree of social integration (intervening variable), which affects suicide (dependent variable). Specifying the chain of causality makes the linkages in a theory clearer and helps a researcher test complex explanations.[6]

Simple theories have one dependent and one independent variable, whereas complex theories can contain dozens of variables with multiple independent, intervening, and dependent variables. For example, a theory of criminal behavior (dependent variable) identifies four independent variables: an individual's economic hardship, opportunities to commit crime easily,

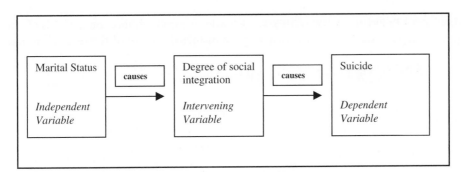

FIGURE 3.6 Intervening Variable According to Durkheim.

membership in a deviant subgroup of society that does not disapprove of crime, and lack of punishment for criminal acts. A multicausal explanation usually specifies the independent variable that has the greatest causal effect (revisit Figure 3.4).

From the Research Question to Hypotheses

A **causal hypothesis** is a proposition to be tested or a tentative statement of a relationship between two variables. All quantitative research must move from a broad topic to specific and testable hypotheses. The leap from a well-formulated research question to hypotheses is a short one. Hints about hypotheses are embedded within a good research question. For example, are **attention deficit hyperactivity disorder** (ADHD)-diagnosed children more prone to engage in delinquency than non-ADHD children? We would have to ask which is the independent variable. The independent variable would be ADHD, because it must logically precede delinquency. The researcher also asks what the direction of the relationship is. The hypothesis could be, ADHD children will have the greatest chances of being involved in delinquency as compared to non-ADHD children. This hypothesis answers the research question and makes a prediction. Several hypotheses are usually developed for one research question. (We want you to recognize that this particular study would be fraught with conceptual and ethical difficulties.)

You may be wondering where theory fits into the process of moving from a topic to a hypothesis I can test. Recall that theory takes many forms. Researchers use general theoretical issues as a source of topics. Theories provide concepts that researchers turn into variables as well as the reasoning or mechanism that helps researchers connect variables into a research question. A hypothesis can both answer a research question and be an untested proposition from a theory. Researchers can express a hypothesis at an abstract, conceptual level or restate it in a more concrete, measurable form.

Causal Theory and Hypotheses

THE HYPOTHESIS AND CAUSALITY.   We can think of *hypotheses* as guesses about how a causal relationship works; they are stated in a value-neutral form. A causal hypothesis is a tentative statement of a relationship between two variables; they have five characteristics (see Table 3.1). For example, the hypothesis that attending religious services reduces the probability of criminality can be restated as a prediction: Persons who attend religious services frequently have a lower propensity to commit crimes than do people who rarely attend religious services. The prediction can be tested against empirical evidence. The hypothesis should be logically tied to a research question and to a theory (the relationship between religiosity and crime). Researchers test hypotheses to answer the research question or to find empirical support for a theory.

Causal hypotheses can be stated in several ways. Sometimes the word *cause* is used, but this is not necessary. For example, as seen in Highlight 3.4, a causal hypothesis between religious attendance and criminality can be stated in ten different ways. Note how these variations of casual assertion are found not only in scientific research but in our everyday language as well.

TESTING AND REFINING A HYPOTHESIS.   Knowledge rarely advances on the basis of one test of a single hypothesis. In fact, it is easy to get a distorted picture of the research process by

TABLE 3.1   Five Characteristics of a Causal Hypothesis
1. It has at least two variables.
2. It expresses a causal or cause–effect relationship between the variables.
3. It can be expressed as a prediction or an expected future outcome.
4. It is logically linked to a research question and a theory.
5. It is falsifiable; that is, it is capable of being tested against empirical evidence and shown to be true or false.

HIGHLIGHT 3.4

Ten Ways to State Causal Relations between Religious Attendance and Criminality

1. Religious attendance causes reduced crime.
2. Religious attendance leads to reduced crime.
3. Religious attendance is related to reduced crime.
4. Religious attendance influences the reduction of crime.
5. Religious attendance is associated with reduced crime.
6. Religious attendance produces reduced crime.
7. Religious attendance results in reduced crime.
8. If people attend religious services, then the likelihood of crime will be reduced.
9. The higher the number of religious services attended, the lower the likelihood of crime will be.
10. Religious attendance reduces the likelihood of crime.

---

focusing on a single research project that tests one or two hypotheses. Knowledge develops over time as researchers throughout the scientific community test many hypotheses. It grows from shifting and culling through many hypotheses. Each hypothesis represents an explanation of a dependent variable. If the evidence fails to support some hypotheses, they are gradually eliminated from consideration. Those that receive support remain in contention.

Remember that scientists are a skeptical group. Support for a hypothesis in one research project is not sufficient for them to accept it. The principle of replication says that a hypothesis needs several tests with consistent and repeated support to gain broad acceptance, or, in Kuhn's words a "consensus position."

TYPES OF HYPOTHESES.   Hypotheses are links in a theoretical causal chain and are used to test the direction and strength of a relationship between variables. When a hypothesis defeats its competitors, it supports the researcher's explanation. A curious aspect of hypothesis testing is that researchers treat evidence that supports a hypothesis differently from evidence that opposes it. They give negative evidence more importance. The idea that negative evidence is critical when evaluating a hypothesis comes from the logic of disconfirming hypotheses.[7]

A hypothesis is never proved, but it can be disproved. A researcher with supporting evidence can say only that the hypothesis remains a possibility or that it is still in the running. Negative evidence is more significant because the hypothesis becomes tarnished or soiled if the evidence fails to support it. This is because hypotheses make predictions. Negative and disconfirming evidence shows that the predictions are wrong. Positive or confirming evidence for a hypothesis is less critical because alternative hypotheses may make the same prediction.

Quantitative researchers test hypotheses using what is called a **null hypothesis.** Most researchers, especially experimenters, frame hypotheses in terms of a null hypothesis based on the logic of the disconfirming hypotheses. They look for evidence that will allow them to accept or reject the null hypothesis. Most people talk about a hypothesis as a way to predict a relationship. The null hypothesis does the opposite. It predicts no relationship. For example, Sarah believes that students who live on campus in dormitories get higher grades than students who live off campus and commute to college. Her null hypothesis is that there is no relationship between residence and grades. Researchers use the null hypothesis with a corresponding alternative hypothesis or **experimental hypothesis.** The experimental hypothesis says that a relationship exists: Students' on-campus residence has a positive effect on grades.

For most people, the null hypothesis approach seems like a backward way of hypothesis testing. Null hypothesis thinking rests on the assumption that researchers try to discover a relationship, so hypothesis testing should be designed to make finding a relationship more demanding. A researcher who uses the null hypothesis approach only directly tests the null hypothesis. If evidence supports or leads the researcher to accept the null hypothesis, he or she concludes that the tested relationship does not exist. This implies that the experimental hypothesis is false. On the other hand, if the researcher can find evidence to reject the null hypothesis, then the alternative hypotheses remain a possibility. The researcher cannot prove the alternative; rather, by testing the null hypotheses, he or she keeps the alternative hypotheses in contention.

NULL HYPOTHESIS

A hypothesis that states there is no significant effect of an independent variable on a dependent variable.

EXPERIMENTAL HYPOTHESIS

A hypothesis paired with the null hypothesis with two independent variables in which it is unclear whether one or the other variable, or both in combination, produces an effect.

Potential Errors in Causal Explanation

Developing a good theory, and testing that explanation properly, requires avoiding common logical errors. These errors can enter at the beginning of the research, or while interpreting and analyzing quantitative data. It is easiest to think of them as fallacies or false explanations that may appear to be legitimate on the surface. The five we'll review include (1) tautology, (2) teleology, (3) ecological fallacy, (4) reductionism, and (5) spuriousness. Figure 3.7 shows each in visual form.

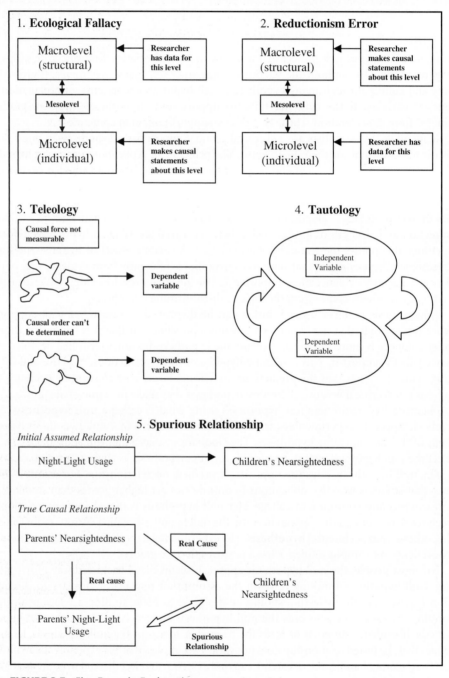

FIGURE 3.7   Five Errors in Explanation.

TAUTOLOGY. A **tautology** is a form of circular reasoning in which someone appears to say something new but is really talking in circles and making a statement that is true by definition. Tautologies cannot be tested with empirical data. For example, Neuman heard a news report about a representative in the U.S. Congress who argued for a new crime law that would send many more fourteen- and fifteen-year-olds to adult courts. When asked why he was interested only in harsh punishment and not prevention, the representative said that offenders would learn that crime does not pay and that would prevent crime. He believed that the only prevention that worked was harsh punishment. This sounded a bit odd when he heard it. So, he reexamined the argument and realized it was perfectly tautological (i.e., it contained a logic error in causal reasoning). The representative essentially claimed that punishment resulted in prevention, because he had redefined prevention as being the same as punishment. Logically, he said punishment caused prevention because harsh punishment was prevention.

TELEOLOGY. A **teleology** is something directed by an ultimate purpose or goal, and it takes two forms. It may be associated with events that occur because it is in "God's plan." In other words, an event occurs because God, or a deity, predetermined that it must occur. It appears when saying something occurs because it is part of the natural unfolding of an all-powerful inner spirit or *Geist* (German for "spirit"). Thus, society develops in a certain direction because of the "spirit of the nation" or a "manifest destiny." This is similar to arguments that use human nature as a cause, as in, "crime occurs because it is just human nature," or, "Timothy McVeigh blew up the Murrah Building in Oklahoma City because he's evil" (discussed further in Chapter 12).

ECOLOGICAL FALLACY. The **ecological fallacy** arises from a mismatch of units of analysis. It refers generalizing beyond what the evidence warrants. Ecological fallacy occurs when a researcher gathers data at a higher or an aggregated unit of analysis but wants to make a statement about a lower or disaggregated unit. It is a fallacy because what happens in one unit of analysis does not always hold for a different unit of analysis.[8] Thus, if a researcher gathers data for large aggregates (organizations, entire countries, etc.) and then draws conclusions about the behavior of individuals from those data, he or she is committing the ecological fallacy. We can avoid this error by ensuring that the unit of analysis we use in an explanation is the same as or very close to the unit on which we collect data.

Consider crime rates in Asia as an example. Japan has considerably lower rates of homicide and other forms of violent crime than does the United States. One possible reason for this is the community-based, mutual-help organizations (called *Jichikai*) to which over 90 percent of Japanese households belong (Rifkin 1995). These organizations are basically neighbors looking after neighbors. Underlying these organizations is the Confucian tradition of community cooperation and harmonious relations. The problem of ecological fallacy enters in, to the extent that criminologists attribute individual-based characteristics as accounting for the lower criminality of the Japanese. This, in effect, places the explanation not at the proper unit of analysis (i.e., the community), but at a lower or disaggregated unit (i.e., the individual). The ecological fallacy in this case is attributing to the individual what should properly be associated with the community.

REDUCTIONISM. Another problem is **reductionism.** This error occurs when a researcher explains macrolevel events using evidence derived from specific individuals. It is a mirror image of the mismatch error in the ecological fallacy. A researcher who has data on how individuals behave but makes statements about the nature of social dynamics is committing the error of reductionism.

As with the ecological fallacy, we can avoid this error by ensuring that the unit of analysis in our explanations is very close to the one for which we have evidence. Researchers who fail to think precisely about the units of analysis and those who do not couple data with the theory are likely to commit the ecological fallacy or reductionism. They make a mistake about the data appropriate for a research question, or they may seriously overgeneralize from the data.

TAUTOLOGY

A form of circular reasoning in which someone appears to say something new but is really talking in circles and making a statement that is true by definition.

TELEOLOGY

An error in explanation in which the causal relationship is empirically untestable because the causal factor does not come earlier in time than the result, or because the causal factor is a vague, general force that cannot be empirically measured.

ECOLOGICAL FALLACY

An error in which empirical data about associations found among large-scale units of analysis are greatly overgeneralized and treated as evidence for statements about relationships among much smaller units.

REDUCTIONISM

An error in explanation in which empirical data about associations found among small-scale units of analysis are greatly overgeneralized and treated as evidence for statements about relationships among much larger units.

Consider the example of white-collar crime in the case of the Enron debacle. Most people are willing to explain and therefore react to this event in individual terms: "Ken Lay, the CEO, was corrupt and a criminal"; "the accountants were dishonest." These are reductionist explanations. They ignore the cultural reality of the organization into which large corporations and accountant firms were socialized. Crime and justice research at the organizational level might reveal that, indeed, cultural norms and values, as well as the structural arrangements in the organization, were such that individuals were being tacitly encouraged to break the law. To broaden our focus even more, numerous large corporations were involved in similar practices during this time period. Does not this indicate something about the larger structural forces at play in the free market system? Corporate structure and culture cannot simply be reduced to the criminal tendencies of individuals.

SPURIOUS RELATIONSHIP

An apparent causal relationship that is actually false because of an alternative but unrecognized cause.

SPURIOUSNESS.   Just because two variables are associated does not mean they are casually related. A **spurious relationship** is a noncausal relationship. Because any association between two variables might be spurious, researchers are cautious when they discover that two variables are associated; upon further investigation, it may not be the basis for a causal relationship. It may be an illusion.

Spuriousness occurs when two variables are associated but are not causally related because there is actually an unseen third factor that is the real cause. The third variable causes both the apparent independent variable and the dependent variable. It accounts for the observed association. In terms of conditions for causality, the unseen third factor represents a more powerful alternative explanation.

In crime and justice research, opposing theories help people figure out which third factors are relevant for many topics (e.g., the causes of crime or the reasons for war or child abuse). Confusion abounds, for example, about the relationship between drugs and crime. Some people believe that taking illegal drugs causes suicide, violent acts, and a host of other social problems. This "drugs are the problem" position points to the positive correlations between taking drugs and problems such as suicide and violence. If their assumption were accurate, ending drug use would eliminate these problems. Others argue, based on years of research evidence, that many people turn to drugs for numerous reasons, including emotional problems and living in impoverished communities (e.g., high unemployment rates, limited economic opportunity, poor health care, unstable families, high crime levels, few community services, high levels of fear of crime) (Gaines and Kraska 2005). The people with emotional problems who reside in impoverished communities are also more likely to commit suicide and engage in violence. Of course, reducing drug abuse alone will have only a limited effect because it ignores the root cause; illegal drug use is a symptom of larger social problems. The "drugs are the problem" argument is spurious because the assumed relationship between taking illegal drugs and crime is misleading. The emotional problems and impoverishment are the more likely causal variables.

Another very interesting everyday example of spuriousness is provided in Highlight 3.5 on the relationship between child vision and night-light use. Summary Table 3.7 reviews all five errors with additional examples.

HIGHLIGHT 3.5
Night-Lights and Spuriousness

For many years, researchers observed a strong positive association between the use of a night-light and children who were nearsighted. Many thought that the night-light was somehow causing the children to develop vision problems (as illustrated in Figure 3.7). Other researchers could think of no reason for a causal link between night-light use and developing nearsightedness. A 1999 study provided the answer. It found that nearsighted parents are more likely to use night-lights; they also genetically pass on their vision deficiency to their children. The study found no link between night-light use and nearsightedness once parental vision was added to the explanation. Thus, the initial causal link was misleading or spurious.

Source: *New York Times*, May 22, 2001.

SUMMARY TABLE 3.7	Summary of Five Errors in Explanation	
Type of Error	*Short Definition*	*Example*
1. Tautology	The relationship is true by definition and involves circular reasoning.	Crime is caused by people who choose to break the law.
2. Teleology	The cause is an intention that is inappropriate, or it has misplaced temporal order.	Crime is caused by the forces of evil overcoming the forces of good.
3. Ecological fallacy	The empirical observations are at too high a level for the causal relationship that is stated.	Crime is caused by inequality in society. Jason is poor. Jason is probably a criminal.
4. Reductionism	The empirical observations are at too low a level for the causal relationship that is stated.	Jason, who is a preacher's son, commits rape. Organized religion creates hypocrites prone to criminality.
5. Spuriousness	An unseen third variable is the actual cause of both the independent and dependent variable.	Drug users commit more crimes than non-drug users; the mind-altering effect of drugs causes crime. (Actual cause is having to obtain drugs in an illegal context due to drug laws.)

SUMMARY TABLE 3.8	The Parts and Aspects of Crime and Justice Theory

Four Parts of Social Theory
1. Assumptions
2. Concepts—vary by level of abstraction (concrete versus abstract), single versus concept clusters, simple versus complex (e.g., classifications, typologies), and scope (narrow versus broad)
3. Relationships—forms of relationships, propositions, and hypotheses
4. Units of analysis

Five Aspects of Social Theory
1. Direction of theorizing—deductive (abstract to concrete) or inductive (concrete to abstract)
2. Level of analysis—microlevel, mesolevel, macrolevel
3. Focus of theory—substantive theory or formal theory
4. Forms of explanation—causal, structural, or interpretative
5. Range of theorizing—empirical generalization, middle-range theory, or theoretical framework

Summary of Theory

Summary Table 3.8 summarizes the various aspects of crime and justice theory. In this chapter you learned about crime and justice theory—its parts, purposes, and types. The dichotomy between theory and research is an artificial one. The value of theory and its necessity for conducting good research should be clear. Researchers who proceed without theory rarely conduct top-quality research and frequently find themselves in a quandary. Likewise, theorists who proceed without linking theory to research or anchoring it to empirical reality are in jeopardy of floating off into pure speculation and conjecture.

PHILOSOPHY AND THEORY CONCLUSION

We began this chapter discussing the Hurricane Katrina disaster. This event is receiving quite a bit of research attention. As discovered in this chapter, researchers have many possible philosophical and theoretical avenues from which to choose. Some will focus on more technical questions, whereas others will attempt to raise consciousness about the class, gender, and racial implications. Even though these approaches differ on many philosophical and theoretical points, they all share the goal of generating credible and legitimate knowledge about this phenomenon.

We need to remember to keep our thinking about philosophical and theoretical dimensions of research straightforward. It is easy to lose sight, in the fog of numerous concepts and distinctions, of the big picture. Theory is simply figuring out the why of things. It contains concepts that help organize our thinking. Researchers are interested in developing and testing theory—which unavoidably means they also develop, measure, and test the organizing concepts associated with a theory. Epistemology, as used in this chapter, gets at the basic questions: (1) how we know what we know, and (2) how we go about knowing. Three social science traditions were reviewed, all of which are evident in crime and justice studies, and all of which approach knowledge and its construction somewhat differently. Besides better understanding the foundation of the various research techniques detailed in the rest of the book, appreciating epistemological differences will greatly enhance our critical thinking skills. No matter which tradition we might relate to best—PSS, ISS, or CSS—knowing each of their worldviews, and their critiques of the others' worldviews, will render us a far more informed, understanding, and incisive thinker.

One last point: Remember that all of the philosophical and theoretical distinctions reviewed in this chapter should not be viewed in mutually exclusive terms (qualitative versus quantitative, critical versus positivist). We have demonstrated that in the real-world reality of crime and justice research, these distinctions often intersect, overlap, and even sometimes break down completely (e.g., chapter 13 discusses the notion of mixed methods). Accomplishing the objective of figuring out what is really the case often overrides an allegiance that a researcher might feel toward a particular tradition.

Key Terms

epistemology *51*
positivist social science *53*
purpose of research for PSS *53*
essentialism *53*
determinism *53*
interpretive social science (ISS) *54*
verstehen *54*
ultimate purpose *55*
social construction of reality *55*
human agency *56*

critical social science (CSS) *57*
purpose of critical research *57*
dialectical *58*
dominant ideology *58*
bounded autonomy *58*
theory *62*
personal theoretical framework *62*
theoretical assumptions *63*
concepts *63*

variables (independent and dependent) *64*
independent variable *64*
dependent variable *64*
proposition *64*
hypothesis *64*
deductive theorizing *64*
inductive theorizing *65*
grounded theory *66*
causal explanation *66*
temporal order *67*
association *67*
variable *67*

attributes *67*
intervening variable *69*
causal hypothesis *70*
null hypothesis *71*
experimental hypothesis *71*
tautology *73*
teleology *73*
ecological fallacy *73*
reductionism *73*
spurious relationship *74*

Review Questions

1. What function does learning about the three philosophical approaches serve?
2. What is the purpose of crime and justice research according to each philosophical approach to knowledge production?
3. How does each of the three approaches view the nature of reality?
4. How does each of the three approaches view the free will versus determinism debate?

5. What is each of the three approaches' stances on "determining the truth?"
6. What is each of the three approaches' views on what constitutes good evidence?
7. How are the criticisms of positivism by the interpretive and critical science approaches similar?
8. Why is theory so vital to quality research?
9. How do concepts contain built-in assumptions? Give examples.
10. What is the difference between inductive and deductive approaches to theorizing?
11. Describe the differences between independent, dependent, and intervening variables.
12. Describe the process of developing and testing hypotheses from our central research questions.
13. Restate the following in terms of a hypothesis with independent and dependent variables: "The number of miles a person drives in a year affects the number of visits a person makes to filling stations, and there is a positive, unidirectional relationship between the variables."
14. What are the five potential errors in causal explanations? Give an example of each.

Practicing Research

1. Watch the first Matrix movie titled *The Matrix*. (Watching all three movies would be even better.) Find indications and evidence for each of the three major epistemological approaches outlined in this chapter: positivist social science, interpretive social science, and critical social science (recall Highlight 3.1). For example, the matrix itself is clearly founded on the fundamental principles of science and mathematics (PSS), yet the character's existence is characterized by multiple realities. In addition, *The Matrix* explores in-depth philosophical issues revolving around the tension between free will versus determinism (#4). Compare and discuss your findings with your classmates in small groups and in a large group discussion.
2. Find an article or book that relies predominantly on one of the three approaches to research (PSS, ISS, and CSS). Using the eight features of each approach detailed in the chapter, note how this study conforms (or does not) to each of the features.
3. Highlight 3.2 discusses action research. In order to get a better sense of how action research works, work in groups of four to five students. Designate one of the members as the "action researcher" and have that member try to determine from the other group members specific issues and problems that concern them. Once a common concern is established, the group as a whole should discuss the types of knowledge needed to effectively address the issue/problem. Each group in the class should then share and compare with the entire class their experiences and findings.
4. This chapter emphasizes the importance of hard work when selecting a worthwhile research topic. Using the techniques noted, develop three different potential research topics, and speculate about the research design you might use to produce knowledge about these topics. Make sure and document the process and sources you use in developing the topics.
5. Locate three academic research articles that involve the testing of causal hypotheses. Identify in each article the central hypotheses tested; the independent, dependent, or intervening variables examined; and the results of this testing.
6. Devise a list of three to five survey questions that ask people about their explanations for various phenomena that you find interesting (preferably crime and justice related). For example: What do you think explains the motivations of someone who wants to commit an act of terrorism against the United States? Ask follow-up questions if necessary to inquire thoroughly into their causal thinking. Carefully record their explanations, and then analyze these explanations, paying close attention particularly to the five errors in explanations discussed in Summary Table 3.7 and Figure 3.7. Discuss your findings in small groups.

Notes for Further Study

1. For an excellent review of these issues in criminology see DiCristina (1995).
2. Divisions of the philosophies of social science similar to the approaches discussed in this chapter can be found in Benton (1977), Blaikie (1993), Bredo and Feinberg (1982), Fay (1975), Fletcher (1974), Guba and Lincoln (1994), Keat and Urry (1975), Lloyd (1986), Miller (1987), Mulkay (1979), Sabia and Wallulis (1983), Smart (1976), and Wilson (1970).
3. Out of the dozens of possibilities, one of the best books on *The Matrix* is Lawrence (2004).
4. For more detailed discussions of concepts, see Chafetz (1978: 45–61), Hage (1972: 9–85), Kaplan (1964: 34–80), Mullins (1971: 7–18), Reynolds (1971), and Stinchcombe (1973).
5. Turner (1980) has provided an interesting discussion of how explanation and theorizing can be conceptualized as translation.
6. See Lieberson (1985: 185–187) for a discussion of basic and superficial variables in a set of causal linkages. Davis (1985) and Stinchcombe (1968) provide good general introductions to making linkages among variables in social theory.
7. The logic of disconfirming hypothesis is discussed in Singleton and associates (1988: 56–60).
8. The general problem of aggregating observation and making causal inferences is discussed in somewhat technical terms in Blalock (1982: 237–264) and in Hannan (1985).

PART TWO

Considerations in Research Preparation

You've heard the expression, "can't see the forest for the trees." The purpose of the first three chapters was to gain a macroperspective of the multitreed forest of crime and justice research methods. We now begin the process of examining the trees themselves. These next four chapters are preparatory. Each comprises numerous issues and details to consider during the planning and initial implementation of a research project. In the course of doing research we have to:

- come up with a worthwhile topic,
- discover what the preexisting literature says about that topic (see Appendix B),
- focus our topic into a workable research project,
- think through the ethical pitfalls and implications,
- construct an overall design for the research,
- plan how the variables and concepts used will be measured, and finally,
- determine what sampling techniques will be used.

Obviously, there is a lot to think through. For seasoned researchers, many of these tasks are almost second nature and oftentimes occur simultaneously. For the less experienced, though, they have to be approached systematically and sequentially. The effectiveness of our planning can mean the difference between successfully producing quality knowledge and failing on a number of fronts including an unclear research purpose, ethical violations, errors in logic, and flawed data.

While much of the material in this section refers to preparing for quantitative research, the ethics chapter and parts of the sampling chapter are quite relevant to qualitative research. Later in the book (Chapter 11) we will examine how to prepare for, and the nature of, qualitative research.

Understanding the material in these chapters is essential to becoming a critical consumer of research-based knowledge. When we review articles for journals, or even read about studies in the media, often the most glaring shortcomings revolve around issues of sampling, the reliability and validity of the measures used, response rates, ethics, research design, and the extent to which the researchers really understood the subject matter. The next four chapters discuss these research issues in depth.

The Ethics and Politics of Crime and Justice Research

Preparing to Research Felony Fights

Ethics in Crime and Justice Research

The Utilitarian Balance

Ethical Issues Involving Research Participants

Highlight 4.1 An Early Chronology of Research Subject Abuse in the United States

Physical Harm, Psychological Abuse, and Legal Jeopardy

- *Physical Harm*
- *Psychological Abuse*
- *Legal Harm*

Highlight 4.2 Crime and Justice Researchers Breaking the Law

Deception

Informed Consent

Covert Observation

Highlight 4.3 Deep Cover Example

Special Populations and New Inequalities

Special Populations and Coercion

Creating New Inequalities

Privacy, Anonymity, and Confidentiality

- *Privacy*
- *Anonymity*
- *Confidentiality*

Codes of Ethics in Crime and Justice Research

Policing Research: The Case of Institutional Review Boards

Highlight 4.4 Academy of Criminal Justice Sciences Code of Research Ethics

Science and Politics

Research Ideals versus Political Realities

The Influence of Funding

Governmental and Corporate Secrecy

Conclusion

Key Terms

Review Questions

Practicing Research

Notes for Further Study

PREPARING TO RESEARCH FELONY FIGHTS

Every semester your authors receive numerous requests from students to help think through a prospective research study. Questions center on formulating the topic idea, what type of research might be appropriate, and whether a research idea can be implemented. We had a particularly capable student–John Brent–ask about a website Kraska had mentioned in his research methods class. While working on another project, Kraska came across a disturbing website titled "Felony Fights." The creators of this business pay recently released prison inmates to fight each other, film the affair, and then package it on digital versatile discs (DVDs) that they sell on their website (and more recently in mainstream stores). The violence is graphic and brutal. Brent was wondering if he could convert this observation into an executable research project for his master's thesis.

Kraska first encouraged John to refine the idea by reading the preexisting literature and looking through other websites. What Kraska did not know at the time was that John had a background in "mixed martial arts" and understood immediately how Felony Fights fell within the larger phenomenon of competitive "cage-fighting." He and Kraska eventually discussed how to go about researching both the underground and state-approved dimensions to this rapidly growing activity—focusing primarily on ethnographic field research of competitive fighters and content analysis of websites such as Felony Fights. Eventually, John developed an exploratory research proposal that had to be approved by Eastern Kentucky University's "Internal Review Board" (discussed below) to ensure that this sensitive and potentially dangerous project would be conducted in an ethical fashion. He then spent a year and a half studying contemporary human fighting among the fighters themselves. Ultimately, John's hard work led to a fascinating paper, "Late Modern Bloodlust: From the Unthinkable to Primetime," that will be published in an academic journal.

In this chapter, we begin to discuss more concrete research ethical concerns as illustrated by John's experience.

ETHICS IN CRIME AND JUSTICE RESEARCH

Recall the D.A.R.E. evaluation experiments discussed in Chapter 1. There we had a research study that provided a treatment (D.A.R.E. education) to one group of children and no treatment to the control group. No differences were found, but what if the researchers had found that D.A.R.E. had a significant preventative effect, and that a large majority of the children in the control group ended up as hard-core drug abusers? Certainly we could have asked if it were ethical to deny such education to some of the research subjects for the sake of determining D.A.R.E.'s effectiveness.

Thinking through the ethics of a research project is an essential part of effective planning and preparation. We've actually already discussed the importance of ethical conduct in numerous sections found in the first three chapters of this book. The knowledge–power dynamic, for example, taught us that the knowledge generated from research could have tremendous power to influence. Wielding this power responsibly requires ethical conduct on the part of the researcher. Likewise, the researcher has to deal ethically with the potential influence of power interests in conducting research and disseminating findings. We discussed the ethical difficulties caused by research-funding sources that place direct and indirect pressure on applied researchers to study certain topics and to report certain findings.

We also noted how all evaluation research, even though its analysis is narrowly focused on what works, still has an ethical dimension that will have to be considered by someone.

We discussed as well the values of "disinterestedness," "honesty," "academic freedom," "critical thinking," "communalism," and "precision." These values must be a part of all researchers' decision-making filters. Each requires careful ethical deliberation and conduct. For example, survey research usually involves inputting quantitative data from each completed survey. There can often be some ambiguity about a response on a returned survey. The ethic of honesty requires that this response be labeled "missing data." However, a researcher could rationalize what the respondent probably meant, code the response in a way to bolster hoped-for outcomes, and reduce the amount of missing data in the study.

This type of unethical behavior is termed **scientific misconduct,** which includes research fraud and plagiarism. Scientific misconduct occurs when a researcher falsifies or distorts the data or the methods of data collection, or plagiarizes the work of others. **Research fraud** occurs when a researcher fakes or invents data that were not really collected, or falsely reports how research was conducted. **Plagiarism** is fraud that occurs when a researcher steals the ideas or writings of another or uses them without citing the source. Research institutes and universities have policies and procedures to detect misconduct, report it to the scientific community and funding agencies, and penalize researchers who engage in it (e.g., through a pay cut or loss of job).[1]

SCIENTIFIC MISCONDUCT

Occurs when a researcher falsifies or distorts the data or methods of data collection, or plagiarizes the work of others.

RESEARCH FRAUD

Occurs when a researcher fakes or invents data that were not really collected, or falsely reports how research was conducted.

PLAGIARISM

Fraud that occurs when a researcher steals the ideas or writings of another or uses them without citing the source.

The Utilitarian Balance

Table 4.1 reviews fifteen basic principles of ethical crime and justice research. Numbers 8–14 all address ethical concerns discussed in Chapters 1, 2, and 3. Numbers 1–7 are ethical principles revolving around the treatment of research participants (such as in the D.A.R.E. example). The concern over the treatment of research participants is particularly important in crime and justice research, where we're often researching highly sensitive, risky, private, and illegal phenomena (e.g., juvenile crime, rape, police brutality, and child abuse). Recall that Wright and Decker's research of active armed robbers mentioned in Chapter 1 presented significant dangers. Previous to that work, though, Scott Decker conducted even riskier research on inner-city gangs (Decker and Van Winkle 1996). Consider his thoughts on the potential dangers involved (remember that the dangers of this research are a preexisting condition and not caused by the research itself):

TABLE 4.1   Fifteen General Ethical Research Principles
1. Ethical responsibility rests with the individual researcher.
2. Do not exploit subjects or students for personal gain.
3. Some form of informed consent is highly recommended or required.
4. Honor all guarantees of privacy, confidentiality, and anonymity.
5. Do not coerce or humiliate subjects.
6. Use deception only if essential, and always accompany it with debriefing.
7. Use a research method that is appropriate to the topic.
8. Detect and remove undesirable consequences to research subjects.
9. Anticipate repercussions of the research or publication of results.
10. Identify the sponsor who funded the research.
11. Cooperate with host nations when doing comparative research.
12. Release the details of the study design with the results.
13. Make interpretations of results consistent with the data.
14. Use high methodological standards and strive for accuracy.
15. Do not conduct secret research.

One of the reasons we are interested in understanding gangs is because of the high level of violence associated with gang membership. However, as a researcher, I was not prepared for just how great the violence would be nor for the effect the personal nature of such violence would have on me. . . . As our study progressed, a number of members of our sample were killed. When the following article was submitted for publication, nine of the ninety-nine gang members in our sample had been killed. In the six-month time period during which the manuscript was reviewed, two more were killed. Since the publication of the article in 1996, five more members of our sample have been killed, two have been sent to prison for life, and one is in a wheelchair.

Conducting research on violent gangs can be dangerous and ethically sticky. Imagine how difficult it would be for a researcher to conduct an ethnography on these young men who obviously have no problem "playing around" with guns.

Clearly Decker had to be extremely careful in not engaging in any research practices that would unduly place him, research associates, or the gang members in harm's way. Some argue that this type of research is too risky and not appropriate. The principles regarding how researchers treat those people under study often conflict with the goal of generating worthwhile knowledge. Figure 4.1 illustrates the sort of balancing act researchers are expected to perform. The ethical approach here is known as **utilitarianism:** Do the potential benefits of the research—such as advancing the understanding of crime, improving criminal justice decision making, or helping research participants—outweigh the potential costs to research participants, such as potential physical harm, loss of dignity, self-esteem, privacy, or personal freedoms.

UTILITARIANISM

Asks the question, do the potential benefits of the research outweigh the potential costs to research participants?

This level of concern for research participants might seem confusing. Why would it be a problem to put research subjects through a high level of stress, for example, when television shows such as *Survivor* starve people, purposefully put them in harm's way, and cause them extreme emotional distress? After all, are not these reality shows a type of social experiment? The answer is yes; they are in a crude way an experiment and can be highly entertaining. However, the standards for real research are much stricter and higher than those in other areas. Professional crime and justice research requires both knowledge of proper research techniques (e.g., sampling) and a high degree of sensitivity for the ethical treatment of people involved in their research.

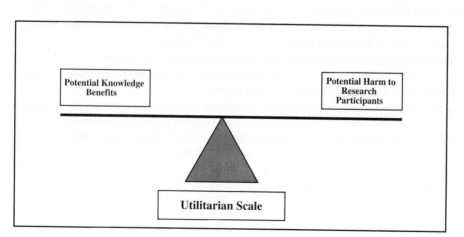

FIGURE 4.1   Balancing between the Benefits of Research and the Potential Harm to Participants.

Unfortunately, the Bad Blood scandal is not unique. During the Cold War era, the U.S. government periodically compromised ethical research principles for military and political goals. In 1995, reports revealed that the government authorized injecting unknowing people with radioactive material in the late 1940s. In the 1950s, the government warned Eastman Kodak and other film manufacturers about nuclear fallout from atomic tests to prevent fogged film, but it decided to not warn nearby citizens of the known health hazards. In the 1960s, the U.S. Army gave unsuspecting soldiers LSD (a hallucinogenic drug), causing serious trauma. Today, these are widely recognized to be violations of two fundamental ethical principles: Avoid physical harm and get informed consent.[4] These types of experiences have led to a high level of professional awareness about ethics in research.

PHYSICAL HARM, PSYCHOLOGICAL ABUSE, AND LEGAL JEOPARDY. Crime and justice research has the potential to harm a research participant in several ways: physical harms, psychological abuse, legal harm, and harm to a person's career or income. Researchers need to be aware of all potentials for harm or abuse and minimize them at all times.[5]

Physical Harm. A straightforward ethical principle is that researchers should not cause physical harm either for the research participants or research assistants working on a project. An ethical researcher anticipates risks before beginning research, including basic safety concerns. This can be especially true in crime and justice research, in which ethnographers often find themselves working in risky and dangerous settings.

Researchers must accept moral and legal responsibility for injury and terminate a project immediately if she or he can no longer guarantee the physical safety of the people involved. The **Zimbardo prison experiment** (Zimbardo 1972, 1973; Zimbardo et al. 1973, 1974) is a classic example. Male college students were divided into two role-playing groups: guards and prisoners. Before the experiment, volunteer students were given personality tests, and only those in the "normal" psychological range were chosen. Volunteers signed up for two weeks, and prisoners were told that they would be under surveillance and would have some civil rights suspended, but that no physical abuse was allowed. In a simulated prison in the basement of a Stanford University building, prisoners were deindividualized (dressed in standard uniforms and called only by their numbers) and guards were militarized (with uniforms, nightsticks, and reflective sunglasses). Guards were told to maintain a reasonable degree of order and served eight-hour shifts, while prisoners were locked up twenty-four hours a day.

ZIMBARDO PRISON EXPERIMENT

A famous research study in which student volunteers worked in a simulated prison environment as prisoners and guards.

The volunteers became very caught up in their roles—so much so, that the prisoners turned passive and disorganized, whereas the guards became aggressive, arbitrary, and dehumanizing. The experiment lasted only until its sixth day, when the head researcher, Zimbardo, called it off for ethical reasons. He felt that the risk of permanent psychological harm, and even physical harm, was too great.

Controversy about ethical violations has occurred within real prisons as well. From the 1940s up until the early 1970s, over 90 percent of all new pharmaceutical products were tested on prison inmates. Despite the international recognition of the Nuremburg Code of 1947, which developed clear standards for voluntary consent in all research involving human subjects, the United States became the only nation in the world to officially approve of the use of prisoners in experimental medical trials. U.S. doctors routinely injected and infected inmates with malaria, typhoid fever, herpes, cancer cells, tuberculosis, ringworm, hepatitis, syphilis, and cholera in attempts to research and treat such diseases.

Revelations about the Tuskegee Syphilis Study and the publication of a disturbing exposé by Jessica Mitford, *Kind and Unusual Punishment,* gradually exposed and reduced the support for prison medical experimentation. A governmental investigation and subsequent document known as the Belmont Report, published in 1979, resulted in such strict guidelines that medical research using inmates was no longer advantageous to the pharmaceutical industry.

One of the more tragic cases of medical research abuse on prisoners has only recently come to the attention of the public. It occurred at the Holmesburg penitentiary in Pennsylvania (see Highlight 4.1). Allen Hornblum's 1998 book, *Acres of Skin,* details how University of Pennsylvania researchers deliberately exposed prisoners to dangerous (sometimes lethal) substances without informing the inmates of the risks involved. Many of the inmates eventually died of health-related problems associated with these studies' treatments; 300 of the survivors who still suffer from the aftermath of these treatments filed a lawsuit in 2000 against the University of Pennsylvania, Dow Chemical, Inc., and Johnson and Johnson, Inc.

Interestingly, medical research on prisoners is witnessing a resurgence. Although national-level data are not being collected (a potentially valuable research project), several investigative journalists have documented various programs involving the testing of AIDS and hepatitus drugs.

Psychological Abuse.   One can imagine the stressful, embarrassing, anxiety-producing, and unpleasant situation Zimbardo's research subjects found themselves in. Researchers learn about how people respond in real-life, highly anxiety-producing situations by placing subjects in realistic situations of psychological discomfort or stress. Is it unethical to cause discomfort? The ethics of the famous Milgram obedience study are still debated.

Stanley **Milgram's obedience study** (Milgram 1963, 1965, 1974) attempted to discover how the horrors of the Holocaust under the Nazis could have occurred by examining the strength of social pressure to obey authority. After signing informed consent forms, subjects were assigned, in rigged random selection, to be a teacher and a confederate was the pupil. The director of the research project maintained an air of scientific authority and was dressed in a white lab coat. The teacher was to test the pupil's memory of word lists and increase the fictitious electric shock level if the pupil made mistakes. The pupil was located in a nearby room, so the teacher could hear but not see the pupil. The shock apparatus was clearly labeled with increasing voltage. As the pupil made mistakes and the teacher turned switches, the pupil also made noises, pretending to be in severe pain. The researcher was present and made comments, such as, "You must go on," to the teacher.

Milgram reported, "Subjects were observed to sweat, tremble, stutter, bite their lips, groan and dig their fingernails into their flesh. These were characteristic rather than exceptional responses to the experiment" (Milgram 1963: 375). The percentage of teachers who would shock to dangerous levels was dramatically higher than expected. Ethical concerns arose over the use of deception and the extreme emotional stress experienced by subjects. Some say that the precautions taken and the knowledge gained outweighed the stress and potential psychological harm that subjects experienced. Others believe that the extreme stress and the risk of permanent harm were too great. By today's standards, this research would likely not be allowed despite its valuable contribution to our knowledge about authority relations.

Only experienced researchers who take precautions before inducing anxiety or discomfort should consider conducting experiments that induce significant stress or anxiety. They should consult with others who have conducted similar studies and mental health professionals when planning the study, screen out high-risk populations (e.g., those with emotional problems or a weak heart), and arrange for emergency interventions or termination of the research if dangerous situations arise. Researchers should always get informed consent (to be discussed) before the research and debrief subjects immediately afterward.

Researchers should never create unnecessary stress, beyond the minimal amount needed to create the desired effect, or stress that has no direct, legitimate research purpose. Knowing the minimal amount comes with experience. It is better to begin with too little stress, risking no effects, than to create too much. If the level of stress could have long-term effects, the researcher should follow up and offer free psychological counseling.

Legal Harm.   A researcher is responsible for protecting research participants from increased risk of legal repercussions. If participation in research increases the risk of legal action, individuals will distrust researchers and be unwilling to participate in future research. Researchers may be able to secure clearance from law enforcement authorities before conducting certain types of research. For example, the U.S. Department of Justice provides written waivers for researchers studying criminal behavior.

Potential legal harm is one criticism of the well-known 1975 "**tearoom trade**" study by Laud Humphreys. Laud Humphreys (Humphreys 1975) was interested in male homosexual

MILGRAM'S OBEDIENCE STUDY

A famous research study in which researchers attempted to discover how people respond to the social pressure to obey authority.

HUMPHREYS'S "TEAROOM TRADE"

A famous research study in which the researcher observed men engaging in sexual acts in a public bathroom, and then tracked them down a year later to conduct covert interviews.

As James Marquart discovered, conducting research within a maximum-security facility can exact a toll on the researcher.

encounters in public restrooms (considered a serious crime at the time). About 100 men were observed engaging in sexual acts as Humphreys pretended to be a "watchqueen" (a voyeur and lookout). Subjects were followed to their cars, and their license numbers were secretly recorded. Names and addresses were obtained from police registers when Humphreys posed as a market researcher. One year later, in disguise, Humphreys used a deceptive story about a health survey to interview the subjects in their homes. Humphreys was careful to keep the names in safety deposit boxes, and identifiers with subject names were burned. He significantly advanced knowledge of homosexuals who frequent "tearooms" and overturned previous false beliefs about them. There has been controversy over the study: The subjects never consented; deception was used; and the names could have been used to blackmail subjects, to end marriages, or to initiate criminal prosecution.

A related ethical issue arises when a researcher learns of illegal activity when collecting data. A researcher must weigh the value of protecting the researcher–subject relationship and the benefits to future researchers against potential harm to innocent people. A researcher bears the cost of his or her judgment. For example, in his field research on police, Van Maanen (1982: 114–115) reported seeing police beat people and witnessing illegal acts and irregular procedures, but said, "On and following these troublesome incidents . . . I followed police custom: I kept my mouth shut." Field researchers often face difficult ethical/legal decisions.

Marquart (1986) conducted an ethnography of prison life by becoming a guard at a maximum security facility in the Texas Department of Corrections for nineteen months. He explains a key moment in legitimizing himself with both the guards and inmates when he defended himself successfully against a 300 -pound inmate who punched him in the forehead. Marquart's (2001: 43) experiences with prison violence continued:

> Full participation brought me face-to-face with actual fear and terror, emotions most field observers never encounter. It is difficult for me to describe how I felt when I saw officers punch, kick, and knock inmates senseless with riot clubs as they screamed and begged for mercy. On several occasions I assisted guards in restraining inmates while medics sutured their wounds without any anesthetic. . . . Violence in prison is banal and everyone must learn to cope. . . . I maintained a cold detachment. However, inwardly I was hurt because human suffering appalled me.

As Marquart's research demonstrates, observing illegal behavior may be central to a research project. A researcher who covertly observes and records illegal behavior and then supplies information to law enforcement authorities violates ethical standards regarding research participants and undermines future research. Yet, a researcher who fails to report illegal behavior indirectly permits criminal behavior and could be charged as an accessory to a crime (see Highlight 4.2). Is the researcher a professional seeking knowledge or a police undercover informant?

DECEPTION.   Has anyone ever told you a half-truth or lie to get you to do something? How did you feel about it? Crime and justice researchers follow the ethical principle of **voluntary consent:** Never force anyone to participate in research, and do not lie unless it is required for legitimate research reasons. The people who participate in crime and justice research should explicitly agree to participate. The right of a person not to participate becomes a critical issue whenever the researcher uses deception, disguises the research, or uses covert research methods.[6]

VOLUNTARY CONSENT

An ethical principle that people should never participate in research unless they explicitly and freely agree to participate.

HIGHLIGHT 4.2
Crime and Justice Researchers Breaking the Law

It is one thing to witness a crime take place as part of a research project, but what about participating in law-breaking? Conducting ground-level research on criminal behavior has in certain research projects translated into engaging in a criminal act to fit in, put the research subjects at ease, or avoid being physically harmed. It would be difficult to estimate how often this occurs—especially since few researchers would probably divulge such information. As discussed in more detail later in this chapter, Robert Seaver, a graduate student who worked with Kraska, conducted an online ethnography on Internet predators. He could have violated the law unknowingly when a respondent sent him some attached materials that included what was probably illegal pornography. If Seaver had downloaded those images (fortunately his research protocol prohibited opening any attached materials), he would have committed a crime (possession of illegal pornographic materials).

Some researchers have been open enough to admit breaking the law in the course of their research (Becker 1967; Ferrell 1993, 2006; Polsky 1969). Chapter 12 will feature additional research from Jeff Ferrell, who technically broke the law daily for eight months while engaging in an ethnographic study centered on "scrounging" (or what some call "dumpster diving"). Patricia and Peter Adler admitted using cocaine during their research on cocaine dealing: " . . . we broke the law through our 'guilty actions' by taking part in illegal behavior ourselves. Although we never dealt drugs (we were too scared to be seriously tempted), we consumed drugs and possessed them in small quantities. Quite frankly, it would have been impossible for a nonuser to have gained access to this group to gather the data presented here" (Adler and Adler 1994: 9).

Crime and justice researchers sometimes deceive or lie to participants in field and experimental research. A researcher might misrepresent his or her actions or true intentions for legitimate methodological reasons: If participants knew the true purpose, they would modify their behavior, making it impossible to learn of their real behavior, or access to a research site might be impossible if he or she told the truth. Experimental researchers often deceive participants to prevent them from learning the true hypothesis and to reduce reactive effects.

Deception is never preferable, though, if the researcher could accomplish the same thing without deception. Deception is acceptable only if there is a specific methodological purpose for it, and even then, it should be used only to the minimal degree necessary. A researcher who uses deception should obtain informed consent, never misrepresent risks, and always debrief the participants afterward if possible. He or she can describe the basic procedures involved and conceal only specific information about hypotheses being tested.

INFORMED CONSENT.   A fundamental principle of ethical research is this: Never coerce anyone into participating; participation must be voluntary. It is not enough to get permission from people; they need to know what they are being asked to participate in so that they can make an informed decision. Participants can become aware of their rights and what they are getting involved in when they read and sign a statement giving **informed consent,** a written agreement to participate given by people after they learn something about the research procedure.

The U.S. federal government does not require informed consent in all research involving human subjects. Nevertheless, researchers should get written consent unless there are good reasons for not obtaining it as judged by an institutional review board (IRB) (covert field research, use of secondary data, etc.) (see the discussion of IRBs on p. 94).

Informed consent statements provide specific information.[7] A general statement about the kinds of procedures or questions involved and the uses of the data are sufficient for informed consent. In a study by Singer (1978), one random group of survey respondents received a detailed informed consent statement and another did not. No significant differences were discovered. Indeed, people who refused to sign such a statement were more likely to guess or answer "no response" to questions. In their analysis of the literature, Singer and colleagues (1995) found that

INFORMED CONSENT

A statement, usually written, that explains aspects of a study to participants and asks for their voluntary agreement to participate before the study begins.

TABLE 4.2 Essential Elements Found in Informed Consent Statements

Informed consent statements contain the following:
1. A brief description of the purpose and procedure of the research, including the expected duration of the study
2. A statement of any risks or discomfort associated with participation
3. A guarantee of anonymity and the confidentiality of records
4. The identification of the researcher and of where to receive information about subjects' rights or questions about the study
5. A statement that participation is completely voluntary and can be terminated at any time without penalty
6. A statement of alternative procedures that may be used
7. A statement of any benefits or compensation provided to subjects and the number of subjects involved
8. An offer to provide a summary of findings

---

assuring confidentiality modestly improved responses when researchers asked about highly sensitive topics. In other situations, extensive assurances of confidentiality failed to affect how or whether subjects responded (see Table 4.2).

Signed informed consent statements are optional for most survey, field, and secondary data research, but are often mandated for experimental research. They are impossible to obtain in documentary research and in most telephone interview studies. The general rule is that the greater the risk of potential harm to participants, the greater the need for a written consent statement. In sum, there are many reasons to obtain informed consent and few reasons not to.

COVERT OBSERVATION. Obtaining informed consent is usually (but not always) easy in survey and experimental research, but some field researchers feel it is inappropriate when observing real-life field settings, and say they could not gain entry or conduct a study unless it were covert. Field researchers operate along a continuum from fully informed consent and disclosure to being completely covert. Borrowing from the language of espionage, Fine (1980) presented this range beginning with **deep cover** (the researcher tells nothing of the research role or objectives but acts as a full participant), to **shallow cover** (the researcher reveals that research is taking place but is vague about details), and **explicit cover** (the researcher fully reveals his or her purpose and asks permission). Figure 4.2 presents this as a continuum using field research into a correctional facility as the example. Marquart's research was a good example of shallow cover field research. Highlight 4.3 provides a fascinating example of a criminologist working on the far left end of the continuum.

Two arguments are made in favor of covert observation and exempting field research from informed consent (Miller and Tewksbury 2001). The first is that informed consent is impractical and disruptive in field research, and may even create some harm by disturbing the participants or

COVERT OBSERVATION

The role a field researcher adopts where he or she does not disclose to the research subjects the purpose or objective of the study.

DEEP COVER

The role a field researcher adopts where he or she completely disguises his or her true identity and research purposes.

SHALLOW COVER

The role a field researcher adopts where he or she reveals research is being conducted but is vague about its details.

EXPLICIT COVER

The researcher fully reveals his or her purpose and asks permission.

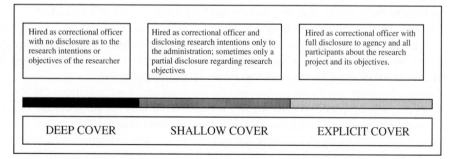

FIGURE 4.2 Covert Continuum in Field Research (Correctional Research Example).

HIGHLIGHT 4.3
Deep Cover Example

There are differing levels of deep cover. In an example on the far left end of the continuum, Martin-Sanchez Jankowski joined thirty-seven different urban street gangs from 1978 to 1988 in various parts of the country. He successfully joined and fully participated in gang life in African American gangs, Latino gangs, and an Irish gang. He conducted interviews with over 1,000 gang members and observed more than 5,000 acts of serious violence committed by them. He gained access to each of these gangs by posing as someone who wanted to join. In each instance, he was required to "fight" his way into the gang as part of his initiation—receiving a significant beating in many of these altercations, although never becoming seriously hurt. His fascinating deep cover research is found in the book *Islands in the Street: Gangs and American Urban Society* (1991). Dr. Jankowski earned his PhD at MIT, is now a full professor at the University of California, Berkeley, and directs the Center for Urban Ethnography at Berkeley.

the setting by upsetting the ongoing flow of activities. The problem with this reasoning is the moral principle that ensuring participant dignity may outweigh practical expediency for researchers. This reasoning obviously puts a higher value on doing research than on upholding honesty or privacy, and it assumes that researchers are better at judging the risk of being in a study than are the participants. The ideal moral-ethical standard is that researchers need to respect the freedom/autonomy of all the people they study and let them make their own decisions. Still, studying crime, criminogenic subcultures, secretive violence, or criminal justice practitioner wrongdoing may necessitate researcher secrecy. Miller (2001: 19), in making the case for covert research methods, argues that

> the study of crime invites and sometimes requires the covert methods as does examination of the clandestine nature of many facets of the formal social control apparatus. How other than through covert participant observation can topics such as undercover policing and inmate-correctional officer interaction be fully understood and evaluated? Those in the criminal justice system, as well as criminals, have vested interests in maintaining high levels of autonomy, which require degrees of secrecy. . . . Covert designs tender opportunities to reach important yet relatively unstudied topics.

Covert research remains controversial, and some researchers feel that all covert research is unethical.[8] Even those who accept covert research as ethical in some situations argue that it should be used only when overt observation is impossible.

Special Populations and New Inequalities

SPECIAL POPULATIONS AND COERCION.   Some populations or groups of research participants are not capable of giving true voluntary informed consent. It is unethical, for example, to involve "incompetent" people (children, mentally disabled, etc.) in research unless two conditions are met: a legal guardian grants written permission and the researcher follows all ethical principles against harm to participants.

It is also unethical to coerce people to participate, including offering them special benefits that they cannot otherwise attain. For example, it is unethical for a commanding officer to order a soldier to participate in a study, for a professor to require a student to be a research subject to pass a course, or for a prisoner to participate in medical research to receive some sort of preferential treatment.

Whether coercion to participate is involved can be a complex issue, and a researcher must evaluate each case. For example, a convicted criminal is given the alternative of imprisonment or participation in an experimental rehabilitation program. The convicted criminal may not believe

SUMMARY TABLE 4.1	Ethical Issues Involving Research Participants

- Physical harm, psychological abuse, and legal jeopardy—Bad Blood or Tuskegee Syphilis Study Example
  - Physical harm—Zimbardo Prison Study
  - Psychological abuse—Milgram's Experiments
  - Legal harm—Humphrey's Tearoom Trade/Marquart's Correctional Officer Study
- Deception
- Informed consent
- Covert observation—Deep and Shallow Cover; Jankowski Gang Example

in the benefits of the program, but the researcher may believe that it will help the criminal. This is a case of coercion, but the researcher must judge whether the benefits to the subject and to society outweigh the ethical prohibition on coercion.

CREATING NEW INEQUALITIES.   As noted in our D.A.R.E. hypothetical, another type of harm occurs when one group of people is denied a service or benefit as a result of participation in a research project. A researcher can reduce **new inequality** among research participants in three ways. First, subjects who do not receive the "new, improved" treatment continue to receive the best previously acceptable treatment. In other words, the control group is not denied all assistance, but they receive the best treatment available prior to the new one being tested. This ensures that people in the control group will not suffer in absolute terms, even if they temporarily fall behind in relative terms. Second, researchers can use crossover designs, whereby the control group for the first phase of the experiment becomes the experimental group in the second phase, and vice versa. Finally, the researcher carefully and continuously monitors results. If it appears early in the experiment that the new treatment is highly effective, the new treatment should be offered to those in the control group. Summary Table 4.1 reviews the major ethical issues involving research participants.

PRIVACY, ANONYMITY, AND CONFIDENTIALITY.   How would you feel if private details about your personal life were shared with the public without your knowledge? Crime and justice researchers must take precautions to protect participants' privacy.

Privacy.   Survey researchers invade a person's **privacy** when they probe into beliefs, backgrounds, and behaviors in a way that reveals intimate private details. Experimental researchers sometimes use two-way mirrors or hidden microphones to spy on subjects. Even if people are told they are being studied, they are unaware of what the experimenter is looking for. Field researchers may observe very private aspects of another's behavior or eavesdrop on conversations. In field experimentation and ethnographic field research, privacy may be violated without advance warning. When Humphreys (1975) served as a "watchqueen" in a public restroom where homosexual contacts took place, he observed very private behavior without informing the subjects. The ethical researcher violates privacy only to the minimum degree necessary and only for legitimate research purposes. In addition, she or he protects the information on research participants from public disclosure.

In a few situations, privacy is protected by law. One case of the invasion of privacy led to the passage of a federal law. In the Wichita Jury Study of 1954, University of Chicago Law School researchers recorded jury discussions to examine group processes in jury deliberations. Although the findings were significant and great precautions were taken, a congressional investigation followed and a law was passed in 1956 to prohibit the bugging of any grand or petit jury for any purpose, even with the jurors' consent.[9]

Anonymity.   Researchers protect privacy by not disclosing a participant's identity after information is gathered. This takes two forms: anonymity and confidentiality. **Anonymity**

NEW INEQUALITY

A type of research harm that occurs when one group of people is denied a service or benefit as a result of participation in a research project.

PRIVACY

Researchers invade a person's privacy when they probe into beliefs, backgrounds, and behaviors in a way that reveals intimate private details.

ANONYMITY

The ethical protection that participants remain nameless; their identity is protected from disclosure and remains unknown.

means that people remain anonymous, or nameless. For example, a field researcher provides a social picture of a particular individual, but gives a fictitious name and location, and alters some characteristics. The subject's identity is protected, and the individual is unknown or anonymous. Survey and experimental researchers discard the names or addresses of subjects as soon as possible and refer to participants by a code number only, to protect anonymity. If a researcher using a mail survey includes a code on the questionnaire to determine which respondents failed to respond, the respondent's anonymity is not being fully protected. Historical researchers use specific names in historical or documentary research. They may do so if the original information was from public sources; if the sources were not publicly available, a researcher must obtain written permission from the owner of the documents to use specific names.

Confidentiality.   Even if anonymity is not possible, researchers should protect confidentiality. Anonymity protects the identity of specific individuals from being known. **Confidentiality** means that information may have names attached to it, but the researcher holds it in confidence or keeps it secret from the public. The information is not released in a way that permits linking specific individuals to responses and is publicly presented only in an aggregate form (percentages, means, etc.).

A researcher may provide anonymity without confidentiality, or vice versa, although they usually go together. Anonymity without confidentiality means that all the details about a specific individual are made public, but the individual's name is withheld. Confidentiality without anonymity means that information is not made public, but a researcher privately links individual names to specific responses.

Attempts to protect the identity of subjects from public disclosure have resulted in elaborate procedures: eliciting anonymous responses, using a third-party list custodian who holds the key to coded lists, or using the random-response technique.

Confidentiality may protect participants from physical harm. For example, Neuman met a researcher who studied the inner workings of the secret police in a nondemocratic society. Had he released the names of informants, they would have faced certain death or imprisonment. To protect the subjects, he wrote all notes in code and kept all records secretly locked away. Although he resided in the United States, he was physically threatened by the foreign government and discovered attempts to burglarize his office.

Crime and justice researchers can pay high personal costs for being ethical. Rik Scarce, a doctoral sociology student at Washington State University, spent sixteen weeks in a Spokane jail for contempt of court. He was jailed because he refused to testify before a grand jury and break the confidentiality of research subjects involved in radical animal liberation groups. He had interviewed a research participant who was suspected of leading a group that broke into animal facilities and caused $150,000 damage. Two judges refused to acknowledge the confidentiality of his research data (Scarce 1995). Summary Table 4.2 reviews the major topics discussed regarding consent and confidentiality.

CONFIDENTIALITY

The ethical protection for those who are studied by holding research data in confidence or keeping them secret from the public, not releasing information in a way that permits linking specific individuals to specific responses.

SUMMARY TABLE 4.2   Consent and Confidentiality

- Special populations and new inequalities
  - Special populations and coercion—Prison Medical Research
  - Creating new inequalities—D.A.R.E. Hypothetical
- Privacy, anonymity, and confidentiality
  - Privacy—Grand Jury Bugging Research
  - Anonymity—Kraska Police Misconduct Research
  - Confidentiality—National Crime Victimization Survey Protocol and Scarce Jailed for Not Disclosing Sources

Codes of Ethics in Crime and Justice Research

CODES OF ETHICS

Principles and guidelines developed by professional organizations to guide research practice and clarify the line between ethical and unethical behavior.

Professional social science associations around the world have **codes of ethics.** The codes state proper and improper behavior and represent a consensus of professionals on ethics. All researchers may not agree on all ethical issues, and ethical rules are subject to interpretation, but researchers are expected to uphold ethical standards as part of their membership in a professional community.

Codes of research ethics can be traced to the Nuremberg Code, which was adopted during the Nuremberg Military Tribunals on Nazi war crimes held by the Allied powers immediately after World War II. The code, developed as a response to the cruelty of concentration camp experiments, outlines ethical principles and rights of human subjects. The principles in the Nuremberg Code dealt with the treatment of human subjects and focused on medical experimentation, but they became the basis for the ethical codes in social research. Similar codes of human rights, such as the 1948 Universal Declaration of Human Rights by the United Nations and the 1964 Declaration of Helsinki, also have implications for researchers.[10]

The Academy of Criminal Justice Sciences (ACJS) and the American Society of Criminology have professional codes of research ethics. Highlight 4.4 illustrates the ACJS's professional code. Codes of ethics do more than codify thinking and provide guidance; they also help universities and other institutions defend ethical research against abuses. For example, after interviewing twenty-four staff members and conducting observations, a researcher in 1994 documented that the staff at the Milwaukee office of the Wisconsin State Public Defender were seriously overworked and could not effectively provide legal defense for poor people. Learning of the findings, top officials at the office contacted the university and demanded to know who on their staff had talked to the researcher, with implications that there might be reprisals. The university administration defended the researcher and refused to release the information, citing widely accepted codes that protect human research subjects.[11]

Policing Research: The Case of Institutional Review Boards

Until recently, social science researchers were expected to exercise their own good professional judgment in designing and implementing ethical studies. As with other professionals (doctors, lawyers, psychologists), they were expected to follow a code of ethics, and any alleged violation of those ethics would be investigated and punished if appropriate. Biomedical research, on the other hand (due to egregious violations such as those in the Bad Blood experiment), has been much more closely regulated since the late 1970s. The primary enforcement mechanism came from a decentralized system of review bodies called **institutional review boards (IRBs).** These were established at universities, hospitals, and other research sites operating under federal oversight. An IRB is a preventative body; it is designed as a gatekeeper mechanism to ensure up front, before the research is conducted, that nothing potentially unethical will take place with regard to human participants. IRBs are staffed by researchers and community members.

INSTITUTIONAL REVIEW BOARDS (IRBS)

A committee at U.S. colleges and research institutes required by federal law to ensure that research involving humans is conducted in a responsible, ethical manner.

Until the mid-1990s, social science researchers, unlike medical researchers, did not need to seek the review of IRBs. However, the death of a young research participant at a University of Pennsylvania medical research study in 1999 created a far-reaching panic. The federal government terminated funding for several large medical research projects due to a lack of compliance with IRB rules and university rules. Most university officials responded with a sweeping requirement that all research activity should be routed through an IRB, including, in some cases, student research conducted as part of a course project. IRB approval of research has become the norm; at many universities a professor is not even allowed to write about his or her teaching experiences in an academic publication without prior approval by the IRB.

Your authors have been through the IRB process numerous times both in trying to get their own research and their students' research approved. The protocol is similar for most universities. The university establishes an IRB committee usually comprised of faculty members, knowledgeable staff, and sometimes a university attorney. If the study does not involve a protected class of people (such as juveniles), the researchers can ask for an expedited process where the committee

HIGHLIGHT 4.4
Academy of Criminal Justice Sciences Code of Research Ethics

Objectivity and Integrity in the Conduct of Criminal Justice Research.

1. Members of the Academy should adhere to the highest possible technical standards in their research.
2. Since individual members of the Academy vary in their research modes, skills, and experience, they should acknowledge the limitations that may affect the validity of their findings.
3. In presenting their work, members of the Academy are obliged to fully report their findings. They should not misrepresent the findings of their research or omit significant data. . . .
4. Members of the Academy should fully report all sources of financial support and other sponsorship of the research.
5. Members of the Academy should not make any commitments to respondents, individuals, groups, or organizations unless there is full intention and ability to honor them.
6. Consistent with the spirit of full disclosure of method and analysis, members of the Academy, after they have completed their own analyses, should cooperate in efforts to make raw data and pertinent documentation available to other social scientists, at reasonable costs, except in cases where confidentiality, the client's rights to proprietary information and privacy, or the claims of a field worker to the privacy of personal notes necessarily would be violated.
7. Members of the Academy should provide adequate information, documentation, and citations concerning scales and other measures used in their research.
8. Members of the Academy should not accept grants, contracts, or research assignments that appear likely to violate the principles enunciated in this Code, and should disassociate themselves from research when they discover a violation and are unable to correct it. . . .
10. When a member of the Academy is involved in a project with others, including students, there should be mutually accepted explicit agreements at the outset with respect to division of work, compensation, access to data, rights of authorship, and other rights and responsibilities. . . .
13. Human subjects have the right to full disclosure of the purposes of the research as early as it is appropriate to the research process, and they have the right to an opportunity to have their questions answered about

the purpose and usage of the research. Members should inform research participants about aspects of the research that might affect their willingness to participate, such as physical risks, discomfort, and/or unpleasant emotional experiences.
14. Subjects of research are entitled to rights of personal confidentiality unless they are waived.
15. Information about subjects obtained from records that are open to public scrutiny cannot be protected by guarantees of privacy or confidentiality.
16. The process of conducting criminal justice research must not expose respondents to more than minimal risk of personal harm, and members of the Academy should make every effort to ensure the safety and security of respondents and project staff. Informed consent should be obtained when the risks of research are greater than the risks of everyday life.
17. Members of the Academy should take culturally appropriate steps to secure informed consent and to avoid invasions of privacy. In addition, special actions will be necessary where the individuals studied are illiterate, under correctional supervision, minors, have low social status, are under judicial supervision, have diminished capacity, are unfamiliar with social research, or otherwise occupy a position of unequal power with the researcher.
18. Members of the Academy should seek to anticipate potential threats to confidentiality. Techniques such as the removal of direct identifiers, the use of randomized responses, and other statistical solutions to problems of privacy should be used where appropriate. Care should be taken to ensure secure storage, maintenance, and/or destruction of sensitive records.
19. Confidential information provided by research participants should be treated as such by members of the Academy, even when this information enjoys no legal protection or privilege and legal force is applied. . . .
21. All research should meet the human subjects' requirements imposed by educational institutions and funding sources. Study design and information-gathering techniques should conform to regulations protecting the rights of human subjects, regardless of funding.

Source: Academy of Criminal Justice Studies, Code of Ethics (March 21, 2000), Section III.B Nos. 1–8, 13–19, 21. Reprinted with permission of the Academy of Criminal Justice Sciences.

generally reviews and approves of the proposal with no questions asked. However, if the research involves protected classes, or if informed consent forms are not feasible, the IRB will require the researchers to go through a full review process where they will have to meet and answer direct questions posed by the board. Kraska went with John Brent to the Internal Review Board to help him make the case that asking underground fighters to sign an informed consent form would scare participants off, and could even be potentially dangerous for the John. After an hour-long session of tough questions and answers, the IRB ended up approving an oral consent protocol and allowed John to conduct his ethnography.

While IRBs are now the norm, their practices have clashed at times with the notion of "academic freedom" (discussed at length below). In 2004 a prominent panel of academics convened a professional conference to address what they view as a crisis in this research oversight system. They targeted specifically the inappropriate "mission creep" of institutional review boards into regulating an increasingly broad range of research activities. At many universities, all research, whether it uses human subjects or not, has to come under some form of review. According to the conference participants, the IRB system was designed specifically for biomedical research; applying it to social science disciplines such as criminology and criminal justice is beginning to seriously hamper researchers' ability to conduct meaningful studies. This steering committee's views might be particularly relevant in crime and justice research where a rigid rule of gaining informed consent, for example, would not be feasible when conducting field research on illegal or deviant subcultures (Ferrell and Hamm 1998). As noted earlier, these types of research often require, at least partially, the researcher to assume a covert role.

Although oversight is clearly needed for some research, many researchers feel that a university administration's desire to "cover all the bases" is eroding academic freedom. The University of Illinois's steering committee report (2005: 16) stated thus:

> Academic departments have the power to censure or discipline faculty who are not following ethical guidelines. When IRBs then try to apply regulations developed for traditional biomedica l research, they overlook the principles and guidelines that are already in place and have proven effective. Some would argue that self-regulation, as within a department, is not reliable, but the restraints IRBs impose are so much worse that it makes the "cure" (IRB oversight) much worse then the disease (difficulties in self-regulation).

Regardless of how this struggle resolves itself, ultimately, ethical research depends on the ethical and professional integrity of the individual researcher.

SCIENCE AND POLITICS

Research Ideals versus Political Realities

Our final topic for this chapter on ethics deals with an uncomfortable reality. Most of what we've examined in this book thus far has dealt with the ideals of social science research—how science generates and shapes knowledge in the best of circumstances. This chapter, and especially this section on science and politics , confronts some of the political realities of crime and justice research.

ACADEMIC FREEDOM

A guarantee that researchers and/or teachers are free to examine all topics and discuss all ideas without any restrictions, threats, or interference from people or authorities outside the community of teachers, scholars, and scientists.

Before we examine these realities, let's detail one more important academic ethic—**academic freedom.** Most people have heard about academic freedom, but few understand it. Academic freedom is the existence of an open and largely unrestricted atmosphere for the free exchange of ideas and information. In open democratic societies, many people value intellectual freedom and believe in providing scholars with freedom from interference. This idea is based on the belief that a free flow of ideas and information requires the advance of unbiased knowledge and freedom of expression.

Academic freedom is related to the autonomy of research. New ideas for research topics, the interpretation of findings, the development of theories or hypotheses, and the open public discussion and debate of ideas, even those that are unconventional, require academic freedom. Restrictions on academic freedom limit the growth of knowledge about society and undermine the integrity of the research process.

Galileo faced this issue about 400 years ago, before natural science was accepted. His astronomical findings, based on free-thinking science, contradicted official Church doctrine. Galileo was forced to recant his findings publicly, under the threat of torture. Silencing him slowed the advance of knowledge for a generation. The debate about Darwin's theory of evolution illustrates how even today scientific knowledge and popular beliefs conflict with one another.

Academic freedom, then, represents a fundamental ideal essential for quality, uncompromised research. The realities, however, can be different. As Chapter 1 established, the knowledge–power dynamic (knowledge generates power and power generates knowledge) teaches us that crime and justice research occurs within a context filled with political, cultural, and financial interests and pressure. The purpose of this section is to sensitize you about those forces that can corrupt or circumvent the integrity of the knowledge production process. This is not meant to diminish the importance of these ideals; however, *we cannot allow an adherence to the higher ideals of social science inquiry to disengage our critical thinking abilities.*

Consider the following example of what this means. A good friend of Kraska, Bankole Thompson, has his PhD in law from Cambridge University, and serves as a Supreme Court justice on a United Nations tribunal in Sierra Leone. Dr. Thompson has a strong belief in the highest ideals of the law. Whenever he and Kraska would talk about some of the real-world injustices associated with our U.S. legal system, he would get very agitated (at least in a Cambridge sort of way) and chastise Kraska for "not understanding the law." Dr. Thompson perceived Kraska as not respecting the law's highest ideals. His position is understandable: He has seen and dealt with unspeakable crimes committed by both individuals and governments. His reformist agenda of establishing U.S.-like autonomous legal order in Sierra Leone allows no room for questioning the highest ideals of law.

The problem with this position, as much as it should be respected and understood, is that it renders him unwilling to identify and assess the legal system's faults and weaknesses. His capacity for critical thinking has been disengaged. There is an alternative position. We (the authors of this book) obviously have a passion for social science research and its highest ideals. However, this belief should not cause us to be defensive apologists. The only route to becoming an adept critical thinker is to be educated about the ideals of research as well as the ways in which these ideals can fall short and are corrupted.

Similar situations have been documented about stem cell research, and in the anecdote that begins Chapter 3—Hurricane Katrina. Scientific research, funded by the U.S. government itself, predicted perfectly what would happen if a Category 4 storm hit New Orleans, right down to the 150,000 poor and disabled population that would not have the means to leave. Politicians, land developers, and especially government officials from the Federal Emergency Management Agency (FEMA) and the Department of Homeland Security ignored, reinterpreted, or altogether discounted these studies (Kraska and Gray 2006). The consequences of doing so should be obvious.

The Influence of Funding

Are you familiar with the saying "the one who pays the piper calls the tune"? This section will examine the role that **sponsored funding** has on the knowledge-generation process. Keep in mind the ethic of academic freedom while reading this section.

SPONSORED FUNDING

Research that is conducted under the sponsorship of an employer, contractor, government agency, or private agency.

The most common way that politics shapes crime and justice research, however, is through control over funds for doing research. Large-scale research projects can be expensive, costing as much as several million dollars. In the United States, most crime and justice research funding comes from the federal government (usually the U.S. Department of Justice's NIJ and BJS departments), with university and private foundation funding limited in amount, scope, and number. Thus, for large projects, most researchers are forced to seek funding from the federal and state government. Political priorities, therefore, can dictate what gets researched and even how that research is conducted. Governmental research funding also helps to fund doctoral programs, which means that the choice of what doctoral students research is sometimes structured around government-driven ideas.

Remember, when funds are allocated by the government, it has in mind certain research questions and priorities. The demise of community policing funding is a good example. Beginning in 1989 the U.S. government began a fifteen-year funding initiative to promote and study community policing reform and efforts. Crime and justice studies expended large amounts of intellectual and research energy on this topic. Abruptly, and for no credible scientific reason, this massive project came to a grinding halt. Funding priorities shifted dramatically after the September 11 terrorist attacks. The National Institute of Justice refocused the bulk of its attention from community policing initiatives to homeland security; consequently, so have the priorities of many researchers.

Of course, this homeland security example is only an anecdote. Is there long-term evidence that governmental funding is an important determinant in the knowledge-generation process in our field of study? Joachim Savelsberg and colleagues (2002, 2004) in two publications found in leading journals (*Criminology* and *Social Problems*) examined this research question in-depth. In their content analysis of 1,390 crime and justice journal publications, they examined the role of what they call "political funding" on what topics and ideas get researched. They found substantial evidence that political funding in criminology/criminal justice has a significant impact on its research agenda. They conclude with a caution to our field about relying so heavily on policy-based concerns driven by political funding.

> Potential benefits [of political funding] ought to be weighed against the risk of losing critical distance and abandoning issues that escape the eye of current policy debates. Perspectives from the tower may, under some circumstances, be more decisive to our understanding of crime and to the future of crime control than those that present themselves from the trenches. (Savelsberg and Flood 2004: 1036)

To put it in simpler terms, politically based funding can skew research priorities and compromise the notion of academic freedom. It is important to note, however, that Savelsberg's research also found that political forces did not affect whether the data the researchers collected supported the theories and programs studied. In other words, the manner in which the research was conducted appeared to be unaffected by the funding source.

Of course, if we were studying dinosaurs, not much would be at stake. However, when tackling crime and justice issues, it matters. The U.S. government has for the past twenty-five years favored a punitive approach to solving crime and drug problems. The majority of criminologists question—based on research evidence, logic, and sometimes their espoused values—whether this is the most effective and/or desirable approach. Todd Clear (1994), a leading figure in our field, expresses his views of how federal research funding only serves to perpetuate the political solution favored by the current governmental leadership:

> Even a major increase in support for research and development on crime problems will benefit us little without a simultaneous depoliticization of the federal crime research bureaucracy. The federal government has molded the crime research agenda into a finely-honed tool of politics, and in doing so goes far beyond any practice justified by electoral mandate. Over the last 12 years, topics for research were increasingly selected based on how well they fit the "get tough" philosophy of the Justice Department. Recommendations of external scholars and internal professional staff as to which research deserves support—though routinely solicited by the government—have been for the most part ignored.

Governmental and Corporate Secrecy

The final way in which politics can negatively influence the research process is through secrecy. Recall in Chapter 1 the use of a Freedom of Information Act request to obtain governmentally collected information. Governmental agencies and politicians often deal with sensitive information that they believe should not be made public. In the course of conducting research on the military and police, Kraska has been confronted numerous times with government agencies highly secretive about their activities and records. In theory, most of this information should fall within the public domain (taxpayers paid for it); however, when national security or privacy issues are at stake there can be legally justifiable reasons to keep certain types of information secret. As U.S. Homeland Security efforts grow, the difficulty of governmental secrecy will likely intensify, making it difficult for researchers to access important data. Indeed, part of the controversy of the U.S. Patriot Act is that it provides new and much broader exemptions for governmental agencies involved in the war on terror to keep what they deem to be sensitive information secret.

Secrecy barriers are even more problematic when researching the private sector. They have few legal obligations to share information with researchers. This makes it quite difficult to conduct in-depth research on privatized crime and justice agencies and operations, or the problem of white-collar/corporate crime.

Conclusion

John Brent's research project on cage fighting, as well as numerous other examples throughout this chapter, demonstrated the ethical dimensions and issues involved in generating knowledge. Clearly, researchers must always be aware of the power they hold in designing, conducting, and sharing their research. As noted in the history of prison medical research, they must also be diligent in guarding against the pressures that powerful interests can place on their work. This is especially true in a field where a single piece of evaluation research can determine the fate of a large-scale crime control program such as D.A.R.E. or prison educational efforts.

Ultimately, we as individuals must decide to conduct research in an ethical manner, to uphold and defend the principles of the social science approach we adopt, and to demand ethical conduct by others. The truthfulness of knowledge produced by crime and justice research and its use or misuse depends on individual researchers, reflecting on their actions and on how their work fits into society.

Key Terms

scientific misconduct 82
research fraud 82
plagiarism 82
utilitarianism 83
research atrocities 85
Zimbardo prison
    experiment 86

Milgram's obedience
    study 87
Humphreys's "tearoom
    trade" 87
voluntary consent 88
informed consent 89
covert observation 90

deep cover 90
shallow cover 90
explicit cover 90
new inequality 92
privacy 92
anonymity 92
confidentiality 93

codes of ethics 94
institutional review boards
    (IRBs) 94
academic freedom 96
sponsored funding 97

Review Questions

1. What is the primary defense against unethical conduct in research?
2. How do deception and coercion to participate in research conflict with the principle of voluntary consent?
3. Explain the ethical issues in the Milgram, Humphreys, and Zimbardo examples.
4. What is informed consent, and how does it protect research subjects?

5. What is the deep to shallow cover continuum?
6. What is the difference between anonymity and confidentiality?
7. Describe what an IRB is and describe the debate about their role in crime and justice research.
8. What is academic freedom and what does it have to do with politics in crime and justice research?
9. What influence can funding have on crime and justice research?

Practicing Research

1. Highlight 4.1 overviews some of the worst examples of violating research ethics. Select one of these events and learn more about it. Specifically, take note of the nature of the violations, the researcher's motivations, historical context, attempts to cover up the violations, the way in which the violations were uncovered, and the long-term consequences of the event (if any).

2. As an in-class exercise, set up a mock IRB board comprised of five to seven people. Other students in class should construct some hypothetical proposed research projects that involve the use of human subjects, dangerous situations, protected classes, and so on. Present these proposals to the mock IRB board. The IRB board should use the various ethical guidelines and principles found throughout the chapter to critique the proposals.

3. Select a published research article from a crime and justice journal. Use the article to construct an informed consent form that might be used in conjunction with this study.

4. Visit the National Institute of Justice website (www.ojp.usdoj.gov/nij/), click on the tab "funding," and examine the section titled, "Expired Solicitations." Read through the various topics for which NIJ has sought funding proposals and assess each (and in total) for their potential political agenda.

Notes for Further Study

1. Research fraud is discussed by Broad and Wade (1982), Diener and Crandall (1978: 154–158), and Weinstein (1979). Also see Hearnshaw (1979) and Wade (1976) on Cyril Burt. Kusserow (1989).

2. Lifton (1986) provided an account of Nazi medical experimentation.

3. See Jones (1981) and Mitchell (1997) on the Bad Blood case.

4. Diener and Crandall (1978: 128) discuss these examples.

5. See Warwick (1982) on types of harm to research participants. See Reynolds (1979: 62–68) on rates of harm in biomedical research. Kelman (1982) discusses different types of harms from different types of research.

6. For more on the general issue of the right not to be researched, see Barnes (1979), Boruch (1982), Moore (1973), and Sagarin (1973).

7. Informed consent requirements and regulations are discussed in detail in Maloney (1984). Also see Capron (1982) and Diener and Crandall (1978: 64–66).

8. The debate over covert research is discussed in Denzin and Erikson (1982), Homan (1980), and Sieber (1982). Also see Miller and Tewksbury (2000), especially sections 1 and 4.3.

9. For more on the Wichita Jury Study, see Dooley (1984: 338–339), Gray (1982), Robertson (1982), Tropp (1982:391), and Vaughan (1967).

10. See Beecher (1970: 227–228) and Reynolds (1979: 28–31, 428–441).

11. See "UW Protects Dissertation Sources," *Capital Times* (December 19, 1994), p. 4.

Research Design and Measurement

Highlight 5.1 Does Police Surveillance Using Closed Circuit Television Work?

Designing Research Questions
The Best Ways to Select Topics
Highlight 5.2 Techniques for Narrowing a Topic into a Research Question
Highlight 5.3 Examples of Bad and Good Research Questions

Measurement: Fear of Crime and Executions
Highlight 5.4 IQ Norms and the Death Penalty

Conceptualizing and Operationalizing: An Overview
Highlight 5.5 Juvenile Probation Officer Morale
Quantitative Conceptualization and Operationalization
Highlight 5.6 Studying Turnover and Pay among Texas JPOS

Reliability and Validity
Reliability and Validity in Quantitative Research
Reliability
■ *Stability Reliability*
■ *Representative Reliability*
■ *Equivalence Reliability*
Four Types of Validity
■ *Face Validity*
■ *Content Validity*

■ *Criterion Validity*
■ *Construct Validity*
Relationship between Reliability and Validity
Other Uses of the Words *Reliable* and *Valid*

A Guide to Quantitative Measurement
Levels of Measurement
Four Levels of Measurement
Continuous and Discrete Variables
Specialized Measures: Scales and Indexes
Highlight 5.7 Measuring Crime Rate Increases Using the UCR
Indexes and Scales
Unidimensionality

Index Construction
The Purpose
Weighting

Scales
The Logic and Purpose
Likert Scales
Thurstone Scaling

Conclusion

Key Terms

Review Questions

Practicing Research

Notes for Further Study

Let's begin this chapter with another student-conducted research project. Michele Grant—a fourth year undergraduate student—asked about conducting some research on "surveillance." A film (based on George Orwell's *1984*) shown in a media, entertainment, and criminal justice class had piqued her interest. She was first instructed to refine the idea by developing a focused research question through reading the preexisting literature.

HIGHLIGHT 5.1
Does Police Surveillance Using Closed Circuit Television Work?

In London, a police officer watches banks of television monitors. This scene shows only one component of a new high-tech operations room, believed to be the largest of its kind in the world.

Since the late 1990s, the British government has invested heavily in police-operated closed circuit television (CCTV) systems as a means to control crime. The government also put in place fairly rigorous data collection procedures in the hope of assessing whether this large outlay of money, and potential infringement on citizens' privacy, yielded sufficient benefits (reduction in crime and increase in public safety) to warrant its continued use and expansion. While the research is ongoing, two important studies, or meta-analyses, have been completed. These meta-analyses involved combining a large number of smaller evaluation studies on the effectiveness of CCTV into one large database in an attempt to determine the overall effectiveness of the program. Both of the following studies included research conducted in North America (Canada and the United States) as well as in Britain.

The first study was conducted by Brandon Welsh and David Farrington in 2002 ("Crime Prevention Effects of CCTV: A Systematic Review"). Using eighteen evaluation studies, the authors found that CCTV reduced crime by only 4 percent across all the programs evaluated. All nine of the programs showing a desirable effect on crime were administered in the United Kingdom; conversely, none of the programs administered in the United States and Canada yielded reductions. The researchers Welsh and Farrington also found that CCTV had no impact on violent crime—the bulk of the recorded reductions were for by vehicle crimes.

The second study was conducted in 2005 by Martin Gil and Angela Spriggs. They examined thirteen evaluations and found that only two resulted in a statistically significant decrease in crime attributable to the surveillance programs. They found, similar to Welsh and Farrington, that impulsive and violent crimes were not affected by police surveillance systems. Findings in both these studies were widely publicized in the British press. One headline captured the media's conclusion of the researchers' findings: "CCTV 'Not a Crime Deterrent.'" A photographic caption elaborates: "CCTV is not as useful in the fight against crime as was previously thought, according to government research" (see Internet link http://news.bbc.co.uk/2/hi/uk_news/2192911.stm).

After three weeks of learning, Michelle came back with the following question: "To what extent has the government established surveillance systems in public areas?" Perfect. Much to her surprise and delight, this basic descriptive question had not yet been systemically researched in the United States (Highlight 5.1 reviews a fascinating study).

In the first chapter we described the quest for knowledge as trying to answer, what really is the case? Pursuing this question through research requires a well-thought-out and carefully executed design. Designing a successful research study is as much art as it is science. It takes creativity and a good imagination as well as rational/logical thinking. Designing quantitative research such as surveys or experiments requires a different mind-set and set of skills than qualitative approaches such as historical, qualitative document analysis or ethnographic field research. It is increasingly common, though, for some types of projects to combine these approaches and mind-sets into a single project (discussed in Chapters 1 and 13 as mixed methods). For example, a classic quantitative experiment testing whether mandatory arrest reduces the incidence of domestic violence would probably include in today's research environment a qualitative component. This would likely involve in-depth interviews with domestic violence victims, police officers, courtroom players, and social service workers.

These qualitative data, as noted in Chapter 1, would be used to contextualize, clarify, and bring life to the quantitative findings. Drawing out a detailed plan of how a research project will look and proceed is an essential undertaking.

DESIGNING RESEARCH QUESTIONS

Our first step when designing a research project is to select a topic.[1] Coming up with the initial research idea can be a task in and of itself. The usual and still solid advice is to conduct research on something of interest. However, there are many different ways to select a topic.

The Best Ways to Select Topics

1. **Personal experience.** You can choose a topic based on something that happened to you or those whom you know. For example, you hear from your female friend that she was pulled over by a police officer for no apparent reason other than wanting her phone number. You realize that the topic of *police sexual harassment* might be a good research idea.

2. **Curiosity based on something in the media.** Sometimes you read a newspaper or magazine article or see a television program, and questions arise. Chapter 1 examined numerous headline media stories that could be converted into worthwhile exploratory research topics (see Highlight 1.2). Two included crime scene investigators claim criminals are using tactics learned on television to clean up and cover up their crimes (e.g., bleach eliminates all traces of blood) (subject: unintended consequences of *CSI* cultural fad); and "retail giant, Target, Inc., uses its own state-of-the-art forensics lab to assist local and federal police with difficult crimes (subject: public/private security blur)."

3. **The state of knowledge in a field.** Basic research is driven by new research findings and theories that push at the frontiers of knowledge. As theoretical explanations are elaborated and expanded, certain issues or questions need to be answered for the field to move forward. As such issues are identified and studied, knowledge advances. For example, you read about attitudes toward capital punishment and realize that most research points to an underlying belief in the innate wickedness of criminals among capital punishment supporters. You notice that no one has yet examined whether people who belong to certain religious groups that teach such a belief in wickedness support capital punishment, nor has anyone mapped the geographic location of these religious groups. Your knowledge of the field suggests a topic for a research project, beliefs about capital punishment, and religion in different regions.

4. **Solving a problem.** Applied research topics often begin with a problem that needs a solution. For example, as part of your job as a dorm counselor, you want to help college freshmen establish friendships with one another. Your problem suggests friendship formation among new college students as a topic.

5. **Personal values.** Some people are highly committed to a set of religious, political, or social values. For example, you are strongly committed to racial equality and become morally outraged whenever you hear about racial discrimination; your strong personal beliefs might point to "hate crimes" as a general topic.

6. **Everyday life.** Potential topics can be found throughout everyday life in old sayings, novels, songs, statistics, and what others say (especially those who disagree with you). Kubrin's research on violence and sexism in rap music, discussed at length in Chapter 2, was likely triggered by his everyday encounter with rap music.

Our overall suggestion is not *to wait for a good idea to arise just through thinking.* This doesn't usually happen. Quality topics come to us through reading the literature, developing our theoretical filters, paying attention to current events, and taking notice of problems in need of solving. Kraska recounted a story in Chapter 2 where he came upon a research topic from a story told to him by a realtor. If you recall, it had to do with a young father being sent to prison for accidentally killing his uncle in a car collision. The idea of researching the socio-legal trend of "criminalizing accidents and acts of stupidity" would not have surfaced if it weren't for Kraska's preexisting theoretical filters. Recognizing this event as a sign of a society becoming increasingly obsessed with safety and intolerant of "risky" behaviors came about from studying and reading. In other words, hard work generates solid research ideas, not just contemplating what interests us.

Note how Michelle Grant's broad research interest of surveillance was refined into the executable idea of surveying police departments about fixed surveillance systems in public spaces. All research begins with a topic, but a topic is only a starting point that researchers must narrow into a focused research question. Qualitative researchers often begin with vague or unclear research questions. The topic emerges slowly during the course of the study. The researchers often combine focusing on a specific question with the process of deciding the details of study design that occurs while they are gathering data. By contrast, quantitative researchers narrow a topic into a focused question as a discrete planning step before they finalize the study design. They use it as a step in the process of developing a testable hypothesis (to be discussed later) and to guide the study design before they collect any data.[2]

It might help at this point to contrast briefly how qualitative researchers develop an executable topic versus quantitative researchers. Qualitative researchers proceed inductively: They use early data collection to adjust and sharpen the research question(s) because they rarely know the most important issues or questions until after they become immersed in the data. Developing a focused research question is a part of the data collection process, during which the researcher actively reflects on and develops preliminary interpretations. The qualitative researcher is open to unanticipated data and constantly reevaluates the focus early in a study. He or she is prepared to change the direction of research and follow new lines of evidence. One of Kraska's graduate students began an ethnography on the general topic of how a small rural community's criminal justice system deals with domestic violence crimes. It wasn't until she was two-thirds of the way through it that she shifted her research attention on the dual arrest phenomenon. She found that the police and the courts had completely given up trying to determine who the real abuser was in a domestic violence situation and processed both partners as criminals.

Quantitative researchers, by contrast, focus on a specific research problem or question within a broad topic. They carefully read and think through what exactly their object(s) of study will be before proceeding. Emphasis is placed on whether what they want to study can feasibly be converted into quantitative data and tested statistically. For example, Chapter 1 discussed biologically based theories of crime. The first broad question might be, does biological makeup cause crime? After reading some of the literature, a researcher might run across Jans Jurgen Eysenck's (2006) proposition that extraverted people are more prone to criminality because of an autonomic nervous system that does not lend itself to easy socialization. Eysenck argued, therefore, that the personality trait of extroversion is biologically based. A measurable and testable research question might be, are attention deficit hyperactivity disorder (ADHD) children (a potential indicator of extroversion) more prone to engage in delinquency than non-ADHD children? Highlight 5.2 lists some other ways to focus a topic into a research question. These include: (1) examining the relevant academic literature; (2) talking the idea over with others; (3) applying the idea to a specific context; and, (4) defining the aim or desired outcome of the study.

The above example illustrates the practical limitations of designing a rigorous quantitative research project. We can only imagine all the possible explanations that we would have to control for to claim that our study substantiates Eysenck's theory. The last part of this chapter discusses

HIGHLIGHT 5.2

Techniques for Narrowing a Topic into a Research Question

1. **Examine the literature.** Published articles are an excellent source of ideas for research questions. They are usually at an appropriate level of specificity and suggest research questions that focus on the following:
   a. Replicate a previous research project exactly or with slight variations.
   b. Explore unexpected findings discovered in previous research.
   c. Follow suggestions for future research found at the end of an article.
   d. Extend an existing explanation or theory to a new topic or setting.
   e. Challenge findings or attempt to refute a relationship.
   f. Specify the intervening process and consider linking relations.

2. **Talk over ideas with others.**
   a. Ask people who are knowledgeable about the topic for ideas.
   b. Seek out those who hold opinions that differ from yours on the topic.

3. **Apply to a specific context.**
   a. Focus the topic onto a specific historical or time period.
   b. Narrow the topic to a specific society or geographic unit.
   c. Consider which subgroups or categories of people/ units are involved and whether there are differences among them.

4. **Define the aim or desired outcome of the study.**
   a. Will the research question be for an exploratory, explanatory, descriptive, or evaluation study?
   b. Will the study involve applied or basic research?

the difficulty in controlling for these factors. Other limitations include time, costs, access to resources, approval by authorities, ethical concerns, and expertise. If you have ten hours a week for five weeks to conduct a research project, but the answer to a research question will take five years, reformulate the research question more narrowly. Estimating the amount of time required to answer a research question is difficult. The research question specified, the research technique used, and the type of data collected all play significant roles. Experienced researchers are the best source of good estimates.

Access to resources is a common limitation. Resources can include the expertise of others, special equipment, or information. For example, a research question about burglary rates and family income in many different nations is almost impossible to answer because information on burglary and income is not collected or available for most countries. Some questions require the approval of authorities (e.g., to see medical records) or involve violating basic ethical principles (e.g., causing serious physical harm to a person to see the person's reaction). The expertise or background of the researcher is also a limitation. Answering some research questions involves the use of data collection techniques, statistical methods, knowledge of a foreign language, or skills that the researcher may not have. Unless the researcher can acquire the necessary training or can pay for another person's services, the research question may not be practical.

Highlight 5.3 provides examples of bad and good research questions. The most common problems found with bad research questions are as follows:

- The questions are not empirically testable (should child sexual offenders be chemically castrated?).
- The research topics are too general and not questions (war on drugs, juvenile crime).
- The research topics are not questions but variables (gun ownership, racial prejudice).
- The research questions are too vague (do the police control crime?).

Good research questions, on the other hand, are testable, specific, focused, and clear. Highlight 5.3 provides some examples of good solid research questions.

HIGHLIGHT 5.3
Examples of Bad and Good Research Questions

Bad Research Questions
Not empirically testable, nonscientific questions

- Should abortion be criminalized?
- Is it right to have capital punishment?
- Should parents be allowed by law to physically punish their children?

General topics, not research questions

- War on terrorism
- Aging in prison
- Child abuse in foster homes

Set of variables, not questions

- Capital punishment and racial discrimination
- Urban decay and gangs
- Victim of child abuse and child abuser

Too vague, ambiguous

- Do police affect delinquency?
- What can be done to prevent child abuse?

Need to be still more specific

Has the incidence of child abuse risen?
    How does abuse affect children?

Good Research Questions
Exploratory questions

- Has the incidence of new forms of child abuse appeared in Wisconsin in the past ten years?

- Are social work and criminal justice agencies working more closely to reduce the child abuse problem than they did in the past?

Descriptive questions

- Is child abuse, violent or sexual, more common in families that have experienced a divorce than in intact, never-divorced families?
- In what ways are criminal justice agencies collaborating with social service agencies to ameliorate the child abuse problem?

Explanatory questions

- Does the emotional instability created by experiencing a divorce increase the chances that divorced parents will physically abuse their children?
- Is a lack of sufficent funds or a lack of awareness the most important factor in explaining the lack of cooperation and collaboration between social service and criminal justice agencies when responding to child abuse?

Evaluation questions

- Has the joint task force program linking the police and child protective services acted to reduce the incidence of child abuse in community A?
- Has the divorced parents' education program helped to reduce the incidence of child abuse for those children in recently divorced families?

MEASUREMENT: FEAR OF CRIME AND EXECUTIONS

Once we have developed a focused and executable research question, or set of questions, we then begin to think about a host of decisions and activities that we have already discussed in Chapters 3 and 4. These aspects of designing our study include the following:

- figuring out the theoretical foundation we'll be working from (Chapter 3),
- researching and studying the relevant existing literature (see Appendix B),
- choosing a research method that best suits our research questions such as a survey or experimental design (Chapters 1, 7, 8),
- thinking through and planning for the potential ethical difficulties involved in our study (Chapter 4)
- determining what specific independent and dependent variables we'll be working with (Chapter 3), and
- determining how to measure these variables (this chapter!).

In this section of this chapter, we'll examine how we measure quantitatively the concepts/variables we are going to use in our study. Let's begin with a couple of examples that should demonstrate the importance of getting this right.

Do you fear crime? Are you worried of the possibility that you may fall victim to a criminal? Are you able to leave a night time class and walk to the back of a vacant parking lot without feeling afraid that something bad might happen? Have you or someone very close to you been the victim of a serious crime and how has this impacted your life? What kinds of crime victimization most worry you—burglary, murder, domestic violence, sexual assault, corporate crime, political crime, or a drug-induced assault? How often do you watch crime-oriented television shows or movies? What sorts of security precautions do you take in your everyday life to avoid being victimized (lock your car doors when you go into the store, avoid certain activities, set a security alarm when you go to bed, research a mutual fund company before you invest, etc.)? What situation has happened in the past month that produced a high level of anxiety about you being victimized?

All of these questions are attempting to elicit information about your fear of crime with regard to its quantity, degree, dimensions, or nature. This act of assessing the extent or nature of a concept, such as fear of crime, forms the basis of all research. Without accurate and reliable measures of our organizing concepts, credible research is impossible. Remember from the theory section in Chapter 3 that all research revolves around the concepts we construct and employ. They are representations of our objects of study, our independent and dependent variables, and our theoretical ideas and assumptions. The collection of data, whether quantitative or qualitative, involves accurately constructing, measuring, and assessing these concepts; and if our measurements are lacking, so will our research.

Thus, the way in which researchers measure variables is critical to the operation of our society. Today, governments and businesses have a tendency to measure most things quantitatively, and then use these numbers to make important decisions. The phenomenon of fear of crime, for instance, is a variable often measured in government-sponsored evaluation research. Criminologists agree that high levels of fear of crime in any community are destructive forces and, conversely, low levels of fear of crime are a key indicator of healthy communities. Accurately measuring the fear of crime, then, especially as a part of a crime-reduction or community-enhancement project is essential for determining its worth.

Another interesting example is intelligence tests and the death penalty. The U.S. Supreme Court recently ruled in *Atkins v. Virginia* (2002) that the measurement of a person's intelligence should be a factor for determining whether a convicted murderer is eligible for the death penalty. Most states have adopted an IQ cutoff point of either 70 or 75 (half the population have IQs of between 90 and 110, whereas 25 percent have higher IQs and 25 percent have lower IQs). Highlight 5.4 provides Delaware's statute revised as a result of the *Atkins* ruling, along with some interesting IQ tables.

Most assume IQ tests are an objective measure of someone's intelligence. Psychologists debate heatedly, though, on the meaning and measurement of the concept *intelligence*. And most intelligence tests only measure analytic reasoning—the capacity to think abstractly and to infer logically. Yet, undoubtedly, there are other types of intelligence, such as practical, emotional, spatial, social, and creative intelligence. If there are many forms of intelligence, but people narrowly limit measurement to one type, it seriously restricts how schools identify and nurture learning; how larger society evaluates, promotes, and recognizes the contributions of people; and how a society values diverse human abilities. It can even determine whether someone is executed. Measurement matters.

The manner in which researchers measure the numerous aspects of crime and criminal justice—such as criminal justice practitioner job satisfaction, the murder rate, incarceration rates, police surveillance systems, court-processing times, recidivism, terrorism, racism, sanity, victimization, militarization, fear of crime, or criminal justice practitioner morale—is the focus of this section.

HIGHLIGHT 5.4
IQ Norms and the Death Penalty

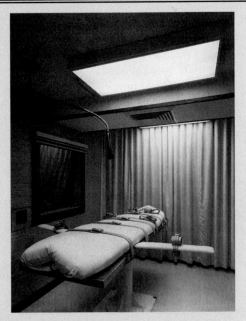

The U.S. Supreme Court ruling in *Atkins v. Virginia*, 536 U.S. 304 (2002) basically ruled it unconstitutional to execute a low-functioning, low-IQ individual. Numerous states have scrambled to pass new laws reflecting this change. The following is the wording used in Delaware's law.

Delaware Statute 11-4209
Burden of proof is on the defense. Before the Trial by a Judge.

Definition of Mental Retardation

"Seriously mentally retarded" or "serious mental retardation" means that an individual has significantly subaverage intellectual functioning that exists concurrently with substantial deficits in adaptive behavior and both the significantly subaverage intellectual functioning and the deficits in adaptive behavior were manifested before the individual became 18 years of age; "Significantly subaverage intellectual functioning" means an intelligent quotient of 70 or below obtained by assessment with 1 or more of the standardized, individually administered general intelligence tests developed for the purpose of assessing intellectual functioning; and "Adaptive behavior" means the effectiveness or degree to which the individual meets the standards of personal independence expected of the individual's age group, sociocultural background and community setting, as evidenced by significant limitations in not less than 2 of the following adaptive skill areas: communication, self-care, home living, social skills, use of community resources, self-direction, functional academic skills, work, leisure, health or safety.

To give a better sense of what an IQ of 70 means, examine the tables below.

One often-used classification is as follows.

Classification	IQ Limits	Percent Included
Very Superior	128 and over	2.2
Superior	120–127	6.7
Bright Normal	111–119	16.1
Average	91–110	50
Dull Normal	80–90	16.1
Borderline	66–79	6.7
Defective	65 and below	2.2

For years, mental deficiency was classified using the following labels that were later replaced due to their misuse.

IQ Range	Classification
70–80	Borderline deficiency
50–69	Moron
20–49	Imbecile
below 20	Idiot

The following classifications are now used to label the level of mental retardation in the United States.

IQ Range	Classification
50–69	Mild
35–49	Moderate
20–34	Severe
below 20	Profound

An interesting resource for death penalty information can be found at www.deathpenaltyinfo.org.

CONCEPTUALIZING AND OPERATIONALIZING: AN OVERVIEW

All researchers, whether quantitative or qualitative, use two processes: **conceptualization** and **operationalization** in measurement. Let's start with conceptualization. As we discussed in Chapter 3, *conceptualization* is the process of taking a rough or vague idea and refining it by giving it a conceptual or theoretical definition. A conceptual definition frames an idea in clear theoretical terms. There is no magical way to turn a vague idea into a precise conceptual definition. It involves thinking carefully, observing directly, consulting with others, reading what others have said, and trying possible definitions. It took Kraska several years of thinking, learning, and refining to develop a clear, measurable, and useful conceptual definition of the notion of police militarization. He eventually settled on a continuum-based definition (low to high militarization) that relied on four groups of empirical indicators. Conceptualizing his organizing concept in this way allows for both a qualitative measure and a potential quantitative measure (see Figure 5.1).

CONCEPTUALIZATION

The process of developing clear, rigorous, and systematic conceptual definitions for abstract ideas/concepts.

OPERATIONALIZATION

The process of moving from a construct's conceptual definition to specific activities or measures that allow a researcher to observe it empirically.

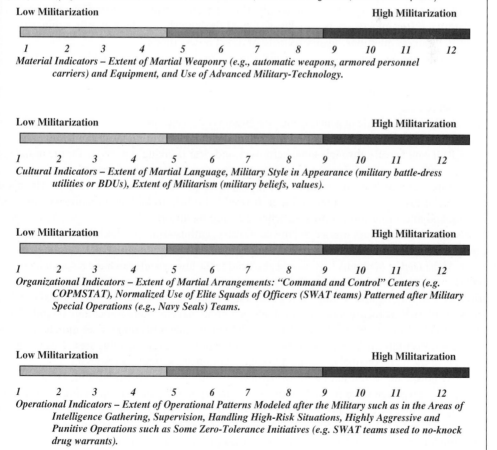

To militarize means adopting and applying the central elements of the military model to an organization or particular situation. Police militarization, therefore, is simply the process whereby civilian police increasingly draw from, and pattern themselves around, the military model. The figure below illustrates the four central dimensions of the military model which constitute tangible indicators of militarization.

Because the police have always been "militaristic" to some degree throughout their history, any analysis of militarization among civilian police has to focus on where the civilian police fall on the continuum and in what direction they are headed.

As you look at the continuum below ask yourself where you think today's police fall on these continuums, and where are they headed. You could also think about where different organizational subgroups fall (e.g. SWAT teams, Domestic Violence Units, Juvenile Gang Units, Homicide Squads).

Low Militarization   **High Militarization**

1 2 3 4 5 6 7 8 9 10 11 12
Material Indicators – Extent of Martial Weaponry (e.g., automatic weapons, armored personnel carriers) and Equipment, and Use of Advanced Military-Technology.

Low Militarization   **High Militarization**

1 2 3 4 5 6 7 8 9 10 11 12
Cultural Indicators – Extent of Martial Language, Military Style in Appearance (military battle-dress utilities or BDUs), Extent of Militarism (military beliefs, values).

Low Militarization   **High Militarization**

1 2 3 4 5 6 7 8 9 10 11 12
Organizational Indicators – Extent of Martial Arrangements: "Command and Control" Centers (e.g. COPMSTAT), Normalized Use of Elite Squads of Officers (SWAT teams) Patterned after Military Special Operations (e.g., Navy Seals) Teams.

Low Militarization   **High Militarization**

1 2 3 4 5 6 7 8 9 10 11 12
Operational Indicators – Extent of Operational Patterns Modeled after the Military such as in the Areas of Intelligence Gathering, Supervision, Handling High-Risk Situations, Highly Aggressive and Punitive Operations such as Some Zero-Tolerance Initiatives (e.g. SWAT teams used to no-knock drug warrants).

FIGURE 5.1 Measuring Police Militarization Using Continuums.

A solid conceptual definition has one clear, explicit, and specific meaning. There should be little ambiguity or vagueness. This is often difficult, especially in crime and justice research. Even the seemingly most basic concepts in our field, such as the proper definition and identification of "fear of crime," is heavily debated. Entire scholarly articles are devoted to conceptualizing key organizing concepts in our field. Gibbs (1989) tried to pin down a workable definition of *terrorism*, Ball and Curry (1995) discussed the complications in conceptualizing what constitutes a "street gang," Marenin (1996) has worked to clarify our notion of policing, and Kappeler has written extensively on the idea of crime and justice myths (Kappeler and Potter 2006). Although conceptualizing key organizing concepts can be frustrating for nonresearchers, as they don't understand this process, it is a necessity for researchers to have clear, unambiguous definitions of concepts to develop sound explanations and produce credible findings. Clear conceptualization is the bedrock of quality scholarship.

Some ideas such as worker morale are highly abstract and complex. They contain lower-level concepts within them such as job stress, which can be made even more specific—such as a feeling of strain or tension resulting from adverse circumstances. Other concepts are concrete and simple (e.g., age). A researcher needs to be aware of how complex and abstract a construct is.[3] For example, a concrete construct such as age is easier to define (e.g., number of years that have passed since birth) than a complex, abstract concept such as criminal justice practitioner morale or police militarization.

The researcher needs three things to measure: a clear concept, a method to measure that concept, and an ability to recognize what one is looking for.[4] For example, if we wanted to measure "criminal justice practitioner morale," we would first need to clearly define it. What does the construct of morale mean? As a construct that varies, it takes on different values—high-versus-low or good-versus-bad morale. Next, we create a measure of our construct. This could take the form of survey questions, an examination of agency records, and/or direct observations of criminal justice practitioners. Finally, we would distinguish morale from other things in the answers to survey questions, agency records, or direct observations.

Let's examine a hypothetical example where a juvenile probation officer is trying to come up with a research idea for his thesis. Paul Lemon decides to inquire into the workings of a juvenile probation department, focusing on the phenomenon of "workplace morale." He has a vague sense that the morale within the organization he works in is low and it seems to have an effect on his work, his life in general, and effectiveness of his agency's services to the probationers and the community.

Paul could create, through some hard work and clear thinking, a measure for the morale of juvenile probation officers. He would have to start with our everyday understanding of morale—something vague such as the extent to which people feel good or bad about their jobs. He might ask some of his friends how they define it. It would also help to look in a dictionary (an often overlooked and quite important step when developing an organizing concept). The *Oxford English Dictionary* defines morale as "the confidence, enthusiasm, and discipline of a person or group at a particular time: *their morale was high.*"

As detailed in Appendix B, he would also head to the library and search the research literature on organizational morale or criminal justice practitioner morale to see how others have defined and used it. Often this requires sorting through several definitions, and as the learning process unfolds, elements of each are incorporated into a single definition that embodies some finite boundaries of the core idea. Notice in Highlight 5.5 that even though juvenile probation officer morale is potentially a serious problem, crime and justice studies has not yet researched this area. This is a good example of the high potential in our field to conduct original, exploratory research.

By now, Paul would have a lot of definitions and needs to sort them out. Most say that morale is a spirit, feeling, or mental condition toward something, or a group feeling. We separate the two extremes of our concept. This helps us turn it into a variable. High morale involves confidence, enthusiasm, cheerfulness, feelings of togetherness, and willingness to endure hardship for the common good. Low morale is the opposite; it is a lack of confidence and enthusiasm, gloominess, selfishness, and an unwillingness to put forth effort for the common good.

HIGHLIGHT 5.5
Juvenile Probation Officer Morale

The juvenile probation officer (JPO) has been referred to as the workhorse of the juvenile justice system. Their functions include screening cases referred to juvenile and family courts, conducting presentence investigation of juveniles, and administering court-ordered supervision of juvenile offenders. Estimates are that nearly 2 million cases are handled per year by the juvenile justice court system, and that nearly every one of these cases was handled in some way by a juvenile probation department (juvenile probation departments screen all cases, make detention decisions, prepare investigation and presentence reports, and deliver aftercare services to released juvenile detainees). Given that more than half of all cases adjudicated result in an order of probation for the juvenile, and that juvenile probation officer caseloads can run as high as 80 to 120 probationers, the label *workhorse* seems apt (the norm is about fifty). Probation officer salaries are generally low—in Kentucky for example, some smaller juvenile probation departments in the poorer counties often start their officers at less than $16,000 per year. More than half of JPOs nationwide earn less than $30,000 per year.

High work volumes combined with low pay, along with tremendous public pressure on juvenile probation agencies to control crime while at the same time helping at-risk youth, points to the clear possibility of low morale, low job satisfaction, and poor-quality services to juveniles in need (of both help and supervision). Kraska has worked with several different juvenile probation agencies in Kentucky, Texas, and Alaska. His qualitative impression is that despite the amazing commitment most JPOs have toward their clients, low morale seems to plague both individual JPOs and juvenile probation organizations. Unfortunately, research in this area is seriously lacking. Although some limited research has been conducted on adult probation job morale issues, we had difficulty uncovering any research targeting issues of JPO morale, stress, or job satisfaction. Considering juvenile probation officers perform perhaps one of the most important jobs in criminal justice, this is a knowledge gap that needs filling.

(See Highlight 5.6, which provides state government-generated research on JPO turnover.)

Source: D. Thomas (1993), *The State of Juvenile Probation 1992: Results of a Nationwide Survey,* NCJ 159536.

Clearly we can see why low morale would be detrimental to the child recipients of a probation department's services (see Highlight 5.5).

Paul would need to construct examples of high or low juvenile probation worker morale. He might also want to refer to it in shorthand form, such as JPM. High JPM might include saying positive things about the workplace, not complaining about the extra work or hours involved, gaining some satisfaction in helping juvenile probationers, and being committed to accomplishing the organization's objectives. Low JPM might be indicated by chronic complaining, absenteeism, a rigid and mechanistic treatment of probationers, or officers looking for other jobs.

Morale involves a feeling toward something else; a person has morale with regard to something. Paul would list the various "somethings" toward which probation officers have feelings—for example, juvenile probationers, the probationer's guardians, the officer's pay, workload, supervisors, and the bureaucracy itself. This raises an issue that frequently occurs when developing a definition. Are there several kinds of JPM or are all these "somethings" aspects of one construct? There is no perfect answer. He will have to decide whether morale means a single, general feeling with different parts or dimensions, or several distinct feelings.

Conceptualization is a process of thinking through the meanings of a construct. By now, Paul knows that JPM is a mental state or feeling that ranges from high to low; it has several dimensions (morale regarding probationers, morale regarding the agency); it is a characteristic of a group; and it persists for a period of time. He now has a much more specific mental picture of what exactly he wants to measure. If he had not conceptualized, he would have tried to measure what he started with—how people feel about things.

To complete the conceptualization process, Paul needs to think about exactly what he intends to include within it. Conceptualization means we need to be very clear and precise in our thinking before we develop measures. It is only through this type of precision that we can proceed with operationalization. Operationalization links a conceptual definition like JPM to a specific set of quantitative measurement techniques or procedures. It constitutes our construct's

TABLE 5.1 Five Suggestions for Constructing a Measure

- Remember the conceptual definition. The underlying principle for any measure is to match it to the specific conceptual definition of the construct that will be used in the study.
- Keep an open mind. Do not get locked into a single measure or type of measure. Be creative and constantly look for better measures. Avoid what Kaplan (1964: 28) called the "law of the instrument," which means being locked into using one measurement instrument for all problems.
- Borrow from others. Do not be afraid to borrow from other researchers, as long as credit is given. Good ideas for measures can be found in other studies or modified from other measures.
- Anticipate difficulties. Logical and practical problems often arise when trying to measure variables of interest. Sometimes a problem can be anticipated and avoided with careful forethought and planning.
- Do not forget your units of analysis. Your measure should fit with the units of analysis of the study and permit you to generalize to the universe of interesting

OPERATIONAL
DEFINITION

The definition of a variable in terms of the specific actions to measure or indicate it in the empirical world.

operational definition (i.e., a definition in terms of the specific measurement operations or actions a researcher carries out). An operational definition is stated in a way that would make Paul's conceptual definition tangibly measurable. The key is for him to fit his measure to his conceptual definition. He must also consider the practical constraints within which he will conduct his research (time, money, available subjects, etc.). He could develop a new measure of JPM from scratch, or he could rely on measures developed by previous researchers. Table 5.1 presents five hints for coming up with a worthwhile measure.

Operationalization, then, links the language of theory with the language of empirical measures. Theory is full of abstract concepts, assumptions, relationships, definitions, and causality. Empirical measures describe how people concretely measure specific variables. They refer to specific operations or things people use to indicate the presence of a construct that exists in observable reality.

Quantitative Conceptualization and Operationalization

As Paul's JPM example illustrated, the measurement process for quantitative research is sequential: first conceptualization, followed by operationalization, followed by applying the operational definition or measuring to collect the data.

How would we give our JPM construct an operational definition? First, we should read the research reports of others and see whether a good indicator already exists. If there are no existing indicators, we must invent one from scratch. Morale is a mental state or feeling, so we measure it indirectly through people's words and actions. We might develop a questionnaire for the probation officers and ask them about their feelings toward the dimensions of morale in our definition. We might go to their workplace and observe them interacting with peers, guardians of juveniles, and other social service practitioners in different agencies. We might use agency personnel records for behavioral indicators of high or low morale (absences, letters of accommodation, performance reports, etc.). We might survey juvenile probationers, supervisors, the juvenile probation officers themselves, or guardians of juveniles to find out what they think about morale. Whichever indicator we choose, we further refine our conceptual definition as we develop it (e.g., write specific questionnaire questions). Ultimately, as we'll discuss later, we might develop a quantitative index of JPM, based on a series of survey questions that develop a comprehensive measure of our primary variable.

Please keep in mind that JPM could be a dependent variable caused by something else, or it could be an independent variable causing something else. It would depend on our theoretical focus. Are we studying JPM as the central object of study to be better understood (dependent variable) or

HIGHLIGHT 5.6
Studying Turnover and Pay Among Texas JPOs

This juvenile offender awaits sentencing after his conviction of second-degree murder for shooting his English teacher.

As a measure to stem the high rate of JPO turnover, the Texas state legislature in 1998 included an extra $10.2 million in their annual budget to increase the salaries of corrections and juvenile probation officers (see www.tjpc.state.tx.us/publications/Reports/RPTOTH200301.pdf). Previous research had documented a high turnover rate and that JPOs cited inadequate salaries as the primary factor. The trend needs to be reversed, according to the Texas Juvenile Probation Commission.

The importance of maintaining qualified officers is clear to department administrators. High turnover rates carry an expensive price tag in terms of financial resources for both county and state governments. More importantly, high turnover of probation, detention and corrections personnel has a negative impact on the effective rehabilitation of juveniles in the system.

The scope of this study included all state-run juvenile probation departments in Texas (Texas has numerous private-sector agencies as well). The data were collected using a state-mandated "Resignation/Termination Form," which was sent directly to a central database collection site. The second source involved a survey instrument sent to all juvenile probation departments on August 30, 2002, via e-mail. The survey included questions that supplied data "relating to the total number of officers (per position type) per department as of August 31, 2002, and provided the average salary per position type."

The student found that the turnover rate for probation officers decreased 28.8 percent from fiscal year 1999 to fiscal year 2002. The report stated that the salary supplements provided during fiscal year 2002 may have been a contributing factor to the decreased turnover rates during that period. Note how the researchers who conducted this study made certain that they only presented these findings as an association and not as a definitive causal factor.

Source: From Texas State Legislature (1998). www.tjpc.state.tx.us/publications/reports/RPTOTH200301.pdf

are we examining JPM as a critical variable used to explain the productivity of criminal justice workers (independent variable)? Highlight 5.6 describes an example of state government research conducted on JPO turnover in Texas. The Texas Department of Corrections realized that they had a serious problem with high JPO turnover rates and decided to research the problem.

RELIABILITY AND VALIDITY

The extent to which our measures are reliable and valid lies at the heart of whether the knowledge produced by a researcher is seen as credible, truthful, and worthwhile. Perfect reliability and validity are impossible to achieve (remember that all research traditions, PSS, ISS, and CSS, assume that research produces only tentative knowledge). Rather, they are ideals researchers strive for.

Reliability means dependability or consistency. It suggests that if the same measure is repeated or recurs under similar conditions, the same result will occur. The opposite of reliability is a measurement process that yields erratic, unstable, or inconsistent results. **Validity** suggests accuracy. It refers to how accurately a measure fits with reality. The absence of validity occurs if there is a poor fit between the concepts and measures that a researcher uses to describe, theorize, or analyze something and the actual reality of that something. Validity addresses the question of how well the social reality being measured through research matches with the constructs that researchers use to understand it.

RELIABILITY

The dependability or consistency of the measure of a variable.

VALIDITY

How well an empirical indicator and the conceptual definition of the construct that the indicator is supposed to measure fit together.

Reliability and Validity in Quantitative Research

RELIABILITY.   In quantitative research, measurement reliability means that the numerical results produced by an indicator do not vary because of characteristics of the measurement process or the measurement instrument itself. For example, you get on a bathroom scale and read your weight. You get off and get on again 100 times. You have a reliable scale if it gives you the same weight each time—assuming, of course, that you are not eating, drinking, changing clothing, stepping on a different part of the scale, and so forth. An unreliable scale will register varying weights, even though your true weight does not change. Another example is a car speedometer. If you drive at a constant slow speed on a level surface, but the speedometer needle jumps ten miles per hour, your speedometer is not a reliable indicator of how fast you are traveling. Actually, there are three types of reliability—stability, representative, and equivalence.

STABILITY RELIABILITY

Measurement reliability across time; a measure that yields consistent results at different time points, assuming what is being measured does not itself change.

Stability Reliability.   **Stability reliability** refers to how reliable a measure is across time. It addresses the question, does the measure deliver the same answer when applied in different time periods? The bathroom scale example just given is a simple example.

We can verify an indicator's degree of stability reliability by using the test-retest method. This has us retest or readminister the indicator to the same group of people. If what we measure is stable and the indicator has stability reliability, then we will get the same results each time. For example, let's say we have a hypothesis about the relationship between arrest and domestic violence. We measure our dependent variable (incidence of domestic violence) by using the official police version of events. Let's say I get somewhat confused in collecting this data, though, and I begin starting in the later years of the reports to record any claim of domestic violence by either party involved in the dispute, whether the police believed them or not. Changing my method of measuring for only certain years would seriously jeopardize stability reliability.

REPRESENTATIVE RELIABILITY

Measurement reliability across groups; a measure that yields consistent results for various social groups.

Representative Reliability.   **Representative reliability** is reliability across various groups or different populations of people. It addresses the question, does the measurement deliver the same answer when applied to different groups? An indicator has high representative reliability if it yields the same result for a construct when applied to different subpopulations (different classes, races, sexes, age groups, etc.). For example, we ask a question on a self-report questionnaire about a person's experiences with illegal drug use. If older people have a tendency to be more private and less candid in their answers than younger respondents, then the measure would have a low degree of representative reliability. To have representative reliability, the measurement would need to elicit accurate information from every age group.

EQUIVALENCE RELIABILITY

Measurement reliability across indicators; a measure that yields consistent results using different specific indicators, assuming that all measure the same construct.

Equivalence Reliability.   **Equivalence reliability** applies when researchers use multiple measurement indicators (e.g., several items in a questionnaire all measure the same construct). It addresses the question, does the measure yield consistent results across different measurement indicators? If several different indicators measure the same construct, then a reliable measure gives the same result with all indicators.

A special type of equivalence reliability, intercoder reliability, arises when there are several observers, raters, or coders of information (explained in Chapter 11). In a sense, each observer is an indicator. A measure is reliable if the observers, raters, or coders agree with each other. It is a common type of reliability reported in content analysis studies. For example, Kraska hires six students to scour through newspaper articles that include information about the prosecution of an accident or act of negligence as a serious crime. If all six of his assistants are equally skilled and trained at observing and recording the variables from the articles, he will be able to combine the information from all six into a single reliable set of measures. But if one or two students are inattentive or sloppy, then his measure will have lower equivalence reliability. Intercoder reliability is tested by cross-checking at random the manner in which the data were coded. In addition, special statistical techniques measure the degree of intercoder reliability. Summary Table 5.1 reviews all three types of reliability.

SUMMARY TABLE 5.1	The Three Types of Reliability
• Stability reliability	Example: coding domestic violence reports
• Representative reliability	Example: illegal drug use questionnaires
• Equivalence reliability	Example: conservatism and criminal justice students

FOUR TYPES OF VALIDITY.   There are also several types of measurement validity.

When a researcher says that a measurement indicator is valid, it is valid for a particular purpose and definition. The same indicator may be less valid or invalid for other purposes. For example, a measure of morale might be valid for measuring probation officers but invalid for measuring the morale of police officers.[5]

At its core, measurement validity refers to how well the conceptual and operational definitions mesh with each other: The better the fit, the greater the measurement validity. Validity is more difficult to achieve than reliability. We cannot have absolute confidence about validity, but some measures are more valid than others. The reason is that constructs are abstract ideas, whereas indicators refer to concrete observation. This is the gap between our mental pictures about the world and the specific things we do at particular times and places. Validity is part of a dynamic process that grows by accumulating evidence over time, and without it, all measurement becomes meaningless.

Face Validity.   The easiest to achieve and the most basic kind of validity is **face validity**. It is a judgment by the scientific community that the indicator really measures the construct. It addresses the question, on the face of it, do people believe that the definition and method of measurement fit? For example, few people would accept a measure of global warming using humidity levels. This would not be a valid measure of temperature (even though they might be correlated).

Content Validity.   **Content validity** addresses the question, is the full content of a definition represented in a measure? A conceptual definition holds ideas; it is a "space" containing ideas. Measures should sample or represent all ideas or areas in that conceptual space. Content validity involves three steps. First, specify the content in a construct's definition. Next, sample from all areas of the definition. Finally, develop one or more indicators that tap all of the parts of the definition.

An instructive example of content validity is the complexities of defining feminism. We could define it as a person's commitment to a set of beliefs creating full equality between men and women in areas of the arts, intellectual pursuits, family, work, politics, and authority relations. From this we could create a measure of feminism in which we ask two survey questions: Should men and women get equal pay for equal work? Should men and women share household tasks? Our measure would have low content validity because the two questions ask only about pay and household tasks. They ignore key areas of conceptual space (intellectual pursuits, politics, authority relations, and other aspects of work and family). For a content-valid measure, the researcher must either expand the measure or narrow the definition.[6]

CRITERION VALIDITY.   **Criterion validity** uses some standard or criterion to indicate a construct accurately. The validity of an indicator is verified by comparing it with another measure of the same construct in which a researcher has confidence.[7] There are two subtypes of criterion validity. The first is concurrent validity. To have **concurrent validity,** an indicator must be associated with a preexisting indicator that is already judged to be valid (i.e., it has face validity). For example, you create a new test to measure intelligence. For it to be concurrently valid, it should be highly associated with existing IQ tests (assuming the same definition of intelligence is used). This means that most people who score high on the old measure should also score high on the new one, and vice versa. The second subtype is **predictive validity**. It relies on the occurrence of a future event or behavior that is logically consistent to verify the

---

FACE VALIDITY

A type of measurement validity in which an indicator makes sense as a measure of a construct in the judgment of others, especially in the scientific community.

CONTENT VALIDITY

Measurement validity that requires that a measure represent all the aspects of the conceptual definition of a construct.

CRITERION VALIDITY

Measurement validity that relies on some independent, outside verification.

CONCURRENT VALIDITY

Measurement validity that relies on a preexisting and already accepted measure to verify the indicator of a construct.

PREDICTIVE VALIDITY

Measurement validity that relies on the occurrence of a future event or behavior that is logically consistent to verify the indicator of a construct.

SUMMARY TABLE 5.2	Summary of Measurement Reliability and Validity Types

Reliability (Dependable Measure)
- Stability—over time (verify using test-retest method)
- Representative—across subgroups (verify using split-half method)
- Equivalence—across indicators (verify using subpopulation analysis)

Validity (True Measure)
- Face—in the judgment of others
- Content—captures the entire meaning
- Criterion—agrees with an external source
  - Concurrent—agrees with a preexisting measure
  - Predicative—agrees with future behavior
- Construct—multiple indicators are consistent
  - Convergent—measures operate in similar ways
  - Discriminant—different ones differ

indicator of a construct. For example, the Scholastic Assessment Test (SAT) used to measure scholastic aptitude has high predictive validity if those students who get high SAT scores subsequently do well in college.

Construct Validity.   **Construct validity** addresses the question, does the measure actually measure accurately the object of study? This is the most basic form of measurement validity because it requires conceptual definitions that have clearly specified boundaries. There are two subtypes of construct validity.

The first kind applies when multiple indicators converge or are associated with one another. **Convergent validity** means that multiple measures of the same construct hang together or operate in similar ways. For example, I measure the construct "education" by asking people how much education they have completed, looking up school records, and asking the people to complete a test of school knowledge. If the measures do not converge (i.e., people who claim to have a college degree have no records of attending college, or those with college degrees perform no better than high school dropouts on my tests), then my measure has weak convergent validity. The second subtype, **discriminant validity,** is the opposite of convergent validity and means that the indicators of one construct hang together or converge, but also are negatively associated with opposing constructs. It says that if two constructs A and B are very different, then measures of A and B should not be associated (see Summary Table 5.1).

CONSTRUCT VALIDITY

A type of measurement validity that uses multiple indicators and has two subtypes: how well indicators of one construct converge and how well indicators of different constructs converge.

CONVERGENT VALIDITY

A type of measurement validity for multiple indicators based on the idea that indicators of one construct will act alike or converge.

DISCRIMINANT VALIDITY

Measurement validity for multiple indicators based on the idea that indicators of different constructs diverge.

Relationship between Reliability and Validity

Measurement reliability is necessary for validity and is easier to achieve. Although reliability is necessary to have a valid measure of a concept, it does not guarantee that a measure will be valid. It is not a sufficient condition for validity. A measure can produce the same result over and over (i.e., it has reliability), but what it measures may not match the definition of the construct (i.e., validity). In other words, a measure can be reliable but invalid. For example, you get on your bathroom scale. The weight registered by the scale is the same each time you get on and off. But then you go to a relative's house with a different scale—one that is certified as "official" and that measures "true weight"—and it says that you weigh twenty pounds less. The first scale's results are quite reliable (i.e., dependable and consistent), but it did not give a valid measure of your weight.

A diagram might help you see the relationship between reliability and validity. Figure 5.2 illustrates the relationship between the concepts by using the analogy of a target. The bull's-eye represents a fit between a measure and the definition of the construct.

A Bull's-Eye = A Perfect Measure

Low Reliability
and Low Validity

High Reliability
but Low Validity

High Reliability
and High Validity

FIGURE 5.2 Illustration of Relationship between Reliability
and Validity.

Other Uses of the Words *Reliable* and *Valid*

Reliability and validity are central terminology to all research methods. However, their meaning is easily confused. In addition to measurement reliability, researchers sometimes say a study or its results are reliable or valid when referring to the entire study's robustness—not just how well it measured its constructs. Reliability, for example, means that other researchers can reproduce the method of conducting a study or the results from it. If the mandatory arrest for domestic violence experiments yielded consistent results, they would be deemed overall as *reliable*, not referring necessarily just to measurement reliability. Similarly, validity is often referred to as general accuracy of the study, or its truthfulness. *Internal validity* means that within an experimental study there are no errors creating erroneous explanations internal to the design of the research project.[8] (See Chapter 8 for a discussion.) There is also *external validity*, which is used primarily in experimental research. It refers to the ability to generalize findings from a specific setting and small group to a range of settings and people (certainly similar to the meaning of *reliability*). It addresses the question, if something happens in a laboratory or among a particular group of subjects (e.g., college students), can the findings be generalized to the "real" (nonlaboratory) world or to the general public (nonstudents)?

A GUIDE TO QUANTITATIVE MEASUREMENT

Thus far, you have learned only about the principles of measurement. Quantitative research has a host of specialized measures and ideas to help in creating reliable and valid measures that yield numerical data for their variable constructs. This next section of the chapter is a brief guide to these ideas and a few of the techniques of measurement.

Levels of Measurement

Level of measurement is an important and widely used research methods idea. It states that we can measure a concept at different levels of precision and specificity. The level of measurement will depend on how a construct is conceptualized. When measuring crime victimization on a survey, for example, we could ask someone whether he or she has been victimized by a crime. The only possible answers are yes or no. We are limiting the level at which we measure our victimization variable to a simple two-choice category (a low level of measurement). We could have asked, though, how many times had they been the victim of a violent crime. This question would measure our variable at a more precise level—a specific numerical ranking with equal distances between the numbers (a much higher level of measurement). The way in which researchers conceptualize their variables determines the levels of measurement that they can use. It also has implications for how the data analysis will proceed. A wide range of powerful statistical procedures is available for the higher levels of measurement, but the types of statistics that can be used with the lowest levels are more limited.

*LEVEL OF
MEASUREMENT*

A system for organizing information in the measurement of variables into four levels, from nominal level to ratio level.

SUMMARY TABLE 5.3	Characteristics of the Four Levels of Measurement			
Level	Different Categories	Ranked	Distance Between Categories Measured	True Zero
Nominal	Yes			
Ordinal	Yes	Yes		
Interval	Yes	Yes	Yes	
Ratio	Yes	Yes	Yes	Yes

Source: From W. Lawrence Neuman, *Social Research Methods, Qualitative and Quantitative Approaches,* 6/e. Published by Allyn and Bacon, 75 Arlington St., Boston, MA 02116. Copyright © 2006 by Pearson Education. Reprinted by permission of the publisher.

FOUR LEVELS OF MEASUREMENT.   The four levels of measurement—nominal, ordinal, interval, and ratio—are categorized from lowest level of precision to highest.[9] The appropriate level of measurement for a variable depends first on how a construct is conceptualized, and second on the type of indicator or measurement that a researcher uses. Each level provides a different type of information (see Summary Table 5.2). **Nominal-level measurement** indicates only that there is a difference among categories, with no ranking of those categories implied. Typical nominal level variables include *gender* (male category or female category), *religion* (Protestant, Catholic, Jew, or Muslim), *racial heritage* (African, Asian, Caucasian, or Hispanic) or *occupation* (police officer, prosecutor, correctional officer, or probation officer). We could conceptualize and measure juvenile probation officer morale at the nominal level by asking a question that would only give us nonranked categories:

> Would you say morale is good in this agency? ____ yes, ____ no.

We might measure the fear of crime by asking what extra precautions a person takes in a given day to prevent being victimized: (1) lock doors to the house, (2) set a burglar alarm, (3) look in the backseat for someone hiding there, or (4) lock car doors while driving.

Ordinal-level measurement also provides us categories but these are assigned a ranking. Your grade earned in this course—A, B, or C (we won't consider the other two options)—is measured at the ordinal level. Survey research often asks people's opinions regarding some topic such as the death penalty, and the choices given are placed on ranked scale (Strongly Agree, Agree, Disagree, or Strongly Disagree). Our JPM variable would be measured at the ordinal level if we asked,

> How would you characterize morale in this agency? ___ Extremely High, ___ High, ____ Normal, ___ Low, ___ Extremely Low

Fear of crime might be measured at the ordinal level by asking how fearful a person feels while walking out to their car parked in a dark parking lot: (1) high fear, (2) moderate fear, (3) low fear, or (4) no fear. Notice that even though this measure gives a sense of degree, we still haven't measured a true numerical distance between these categories.

Interval-level measurement does everything the first two do plus it can specify the amount of distance between categories. Typical measurements at the interval level include temperature (5°, 45°, or 90°), IQ scores (95, 110, or 125), and annual crime rate. There is an equal numerical distance between the values within our variable. This is the level at which we are transforming social phenomena, such as worker morale, into what we normally think of as numerical data. If we constructed one indicator of JPM as *job turnover*, for example, we might record over a twenty-year period the annual amount of job turnover (e.g., 4 left in 1986, 12 in 1996, and 23 in 2006; of course, for these numbers to be comparable, we would have to control for annual number of JPOs in the agency). Measuring fear of crime at the interval level might be accomplished by asking how much money is spent in a given year on security measures specifically designed to prevent becoming a victim of a crime.

Ratio-level measurement does everything all the other levels do plus there is a true zero-point, which makes it possible to state relations in terms of proportion or ratios for example

NOMINAL-LEVEL MEASUREMENT

The lowest, least precise level of measurement for which there is a difference in type only among the categories of a variable.

ORDINAL-LEVEL MEASUREMENT

A level of measurement that identifies a difference among categories of a variable and allows the categories to be rank ordered as well.

INTERVAL-LEVEL MEASUREMENT

A level of measurement that identifies differences among variable attributes, ranks categories, and measures distance between categories, but there is no true zero.

RATIO-LEVEL MEASUREMENT

The highest, most precise level of measurement; variable attributes can be rank ordered, the distance between them precisely measured, and there is an absolute zero.

| TABLE 5.2 | Example of Levels of Measurement |

Variable (Level of Measurement)	How Variable is Measured
Religion (nominal)	Different religious denominations (Jewish, Catholic, Lutheran, Baptist) are not ranked, just different (unless one belief is conceptualized as closer to heaven).
Attendance (ordinal)	"How often do you attend religious services? (0) Never, (1) less than once a year, (3) several times a year, (4) about once a month, (5) two or three times a week, or (8) several times a week?" This might have been measured at a ratio level if the exact number of times a person attended was asked instead.
IQ score (interval)	Most intelligence tests are organized with 100 as average, middle, or normal. So higher or lower indicate distance from the average. Someone with a score of 115 has somewhat above average measured intelligence for people who took the test, whereas 90 is slightly below. Scores of below 65 or above 140 are rare.
Age (ratio)	Age is measured by years of age. There is a true zero (birth). Note that a forty-year-old has lived twice as long as a twenty-year-old.

Source: From W. Lawrence Neuman, *Social Research Methods, Qualitative and Quantitative Approaches,* 6/e. Published by Allyn and Bacon, 75 Arlington St., Boston, MA 02116. Copyright © 2006 by Pearson Education. Reprinted by permission of the publisher.

annual income ($12,500, $47,389, or $92,000) or years of formal schooling (1 year, 10 years, 13 years). In most practical research situations, the distinction between interval and ratio levels makes little difference. Table 5.2 provides some additional examples of the different levels of measurement.

CONTINUOUS AND DISCRETE VARIABLES. The idea of measuring variables at different levels of precision is also captured by an often-used distinction of **continuous variables** as opposed to **discrete variables.** Continuous variables have an infinite number of values or attributes that flow along a continuum. The values can be divided into many smaller increments; in mathematical theory, there is an infinite number of increments. Continuous variables are measured at the interval or ratio level. Examples include temperature, age, income, and crime rate. Discrete variables have a relatively fixed set of separate values or variable attributes. Instead of a smooth continuum of values, discrete variables contain distinct categories. They are measured at the ordinal and interval levels. Examples of discrete variables include gender (male or female), religion (Protestant, Catholic, Jew, Muslim, or atheist), or opinion (agree or disagree). Whether a variable is continuous or discrete affects its level of measurement.

Specialized Measures: Scales and Indexes

In this section we will look at several specialized quantitative measures usually referred to as scales and indexes. These are nothing more than techniques to bolster the fit between our constructs and our measurement of those constructs. They give us both a more refined and a precise measurement of our variables. **Scales** attempt to capture the intensity, direction, or potency of a variable construct (e.g., measuring feelings toward something using "very likely," "likely," "not sure," "unlikely," and "very unlikely"). **Indexes** are a measuring technique in which a researcher adds or combines numerous indicators of a construct into a single score (if you remember, a type of triangulation). An example is the FBI's Uniform Crime Reports, in which that agency combines numerous crime measures into a single crime index. The construct "property crime," for example, might be composed of a composite of individual types of crime including burglary, larceny-theft, motor vehicle theft, and arson (the FBI reasons that arson is a

CONTINUOUS VARIABLES

Variables measured on a continuum in which an infinite number of finder gradations between variable attributes are possible.

DISCRETE VARIABLES

Variables in which the attributes can be measured with only a limited number of distinct, separate categories.

SCALE

A class of quantitative data measure often used in survey research that captures the intensity, direction, level, or potency of a variable construct along a continuum. Most are at the ordinal level of measurement.

INDEXES

A measuring technique in which a researcher adds or combines numerous indicators of a construct into a single score.

HIGHLIGHT 5.7
Measuring Crime Rate Increases Using the UCR

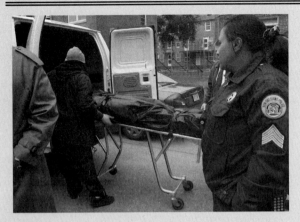

Making sense of trends in homicide is a difficult task for researchers. As this discussion illustrates, even research experts often disagree.

In June 2006, newspapers across the country reported a "significant increase" in violent crime. They relied on the Uniform Crime Report (UCR) put out by the FBI for their information. What few media outlets clarified, however, is that the UCR is not a measure of the crime rate; rather, it measures the rate at which the police report crime. This means that these statistics are dependent on the rate at which citizens report crime, the rate at which the police define an incident as a crime, and the year-to-year reliability of police reporting behavior to the FBI. Criminologists have raised serious questions about using the UCR as an accurate measure of the crime rate. One category of crime, however, is an exception: murder. Even so, murder statistics can be hard to decipher.

In 2005, the government and media were excited about reporting a 3.6 percent drop in the murder rate in 2004. Murders dropped 7.1 percent in cities with populations over 1 million, and 12.2 percent in towns with 10,000 or fewer people (Locy 2005). "This suggests that something fresh and positive is happening," said David Kennedy, director of the Center for Crime Prevention and Control at John Jay College of Criminal Justice in New York. "That's really striking." The difficulty is that murder rates are notoriously fickle. Consider that in the following year (2005) the press was reporting a "significant" rise in violent crime including murder (Eggen 2006). A *Washington Post* article asked another prominent criminologist about what this might mean: "James Alan Fox . . . said the increase should serve as a wake-up call in Washington. . . . We have to worry about not just homeland security but also hometown security" (Eggen 2006: 1). And then in 2008 and 2009, the UCR data demonstrated a significant drop in the murder rate (e.g., a 10 percent drop in the first half of 2009), and a smaller yet still significant drop in violent crime.

Probably the lesson to be learned for the student of research methods is the perils of trying to make sense of yearly fluctuations in the murder rate. Note how the graphic shows wide variations within short time periods, even though it is possible to discern high and low patterns over a longer period of time. (Please keep in mind as well that "reporting behavior" was likely quite different in the early 1900s than it is today.)

Source: From Bureau of Justice Statistics Web page, www.ojp.usdoj.gov/bjs/glance/hmrt.htm.

property crime because it destroys property). Highlight 5.7 examines in more depth the FBI's indexes and its finding that violent crime and murder is on the increase.

INDEXES AND SCALES.   You might find the words *index* and *scale* confusing at first because they are often used interchangeably. One researcher's scale is another's index. Both produce ordinal- or interval-level measures of a variable. To add to the confusion, scale and index techniques can be combined in one measure. Scales and indexes give a researcher more information about variables and make it possible to assess the quality of measurement. Scales and indexes increase reliability and validity, and they aid in data reduction; that is, they condense and simplify the information that is collected.

UNIDIMENSIONALITY

The principle that when using multiple indicators to measure a construct, all the indicators should consistently fit together and indicate a single construct.

UNIDIMENSIONALITY.   Scales and indexes should be unidimensional (one dimensional). **Unidimensionality** means that all the items in a scale or index fit together, or measure a single construct. Unidimensionality was hinted at in the previous discussions of construct and content validity. Unidimensionality means combining several specific pieces of information into a single score or measure, and having all the pieces measure the same thing.

INDEX CONSTRUCTION

The Purpose

We hear about indexes all the time. As mentioned above, U.S. newspapers report routinely from the FBI's crime index. The FBI's Part I Offenses index is the sum of police reports on seven so-called index crimes (criminal homicide, aggravated assault, forcible rape, robbery, burglary, larceny of $50 or more, and auto theft). The UCR and its various indexes are familiar to most U.S. citizens (see Chapter 1). Indexes are actually all around us. In this course, for example, if you take an exam of twenty-five questions, the total number of questions correct is a kind of -index. It is a composite measure in which each question measures a small piece of knowledge, and all the questions scored correct or incorrect are totaled to produce a single measure.

An example of an index is a crime and justice academic program quality index (see Table 5.3). Our theoretical definition says that a high-quality crime and justice program has six distinguishing characteristics: (1) a small number of students per faculty member, (2) a highly educated faculty, (3) more crime and justice books in the library, (4) admission requirements to the program, (5) more students who go on to advanced degrees, and (6) faculty members who publish books or scholarly articles. We score 100 programs on each item, and then add the scores for each to create an index score of program quality (PQI) that can be used to compare colleges.

TABLE 5.3	Criminal Justice Program Quality Index

In symbolic form, where:

Q = CJ program quality index

A quality-of-program index is based on the following six items:

R = number of students per faculty member

F = percentage of faculty with PhDs

B = number of books in library per student

D = admission requirements

A = percentage of graduates who go on to an advanced degree

P = number of publications per faculty member

Unweighted formula: $(-1)R + (1)F + (1)B + (-1)D + (1)A + (1)P = Q$

Weighted formula: $(-2)R + (2)F + (1)B + (-3)D + (1)A + (3)P = Q$

Old Ivy College

Unweighted: $(-1)13 + (1)80 + (1)334 + (-1)14 + (1)28 + (1)4 = 419$

Weighted: $(-2)13 + (2)80 + (1)334 + (-3)14 + (1)28 + (3)4 = 466$

Local College

Unweighted: $(-1)20 + (1)82 + (1)365 + (-1)25 + (1)15 + (1)2 = 419$

Weighted: $(-2)20 + (2)82 + (1)365 + (-3)25 + (1)15 + (3)2 = 435$

Big University

Unweighted: $(-1)38 + (1)95 + (1)380 + (-1)48 + (1)24 + (1)6 = 419$

Weighted: $(-2)38 + (2)95 + (1)380 + (-3)48 + (1)24 + (3)6 = 392$

Weighting

An important issue in index construction is whether to weight items. Unless it is otherwise stated, assume that an index is unweighted. Likewise, unless you have a good theoretical reason for assigning different weights, use equal weights. An unweighted index gives each item equal weight. It involves adding up the items without modification, as if each were multiplied by 1 (or −1 for items that are negative).

WEIGHTED INDEX

An index in which a researcher values or weighs some items more than others.

In a **weighted index,** a researcher values or weights some items more than others. The size of weights can come from theoretical assumptions, the theoretical definition, or a statistical technique such as factor analysis. Weighting changes the theoretical definition of the construct.

For example, we elaborate the theoretical definition of the PQI. We decide that the student–faculty ratio and number of faculty with PhDs are twice as important as the number of books in the library per student or the percentage of students pursuing advanced degrees. Also, the use of admission requirements and the number of publications per faculty member are three times more important than books in the library or percentage pursuing an advanced degree. This is easier to see when it is expressed as a formula.

The number of students per faculty member and the percentage who drop out have negative signs because, as they get larger, the quality of the college gets lower. The weighted and unweighted indexes can produce different results. Consider Old Ivy College, Local College, and Big University. All have identical unweighted index scores, but the colleges have different quality scores after weighting. Please note that oftentimes when collecting these types of comprehensive data, difficulties with missing cases arise.

SCALES

The Logic and Purpose

Scales are common in situations in which a researcher wants to measure how an individual feels or thinks about something. Some call this the potency of feelings. Scales also help in the conceptualization and operationalization processes. For example, a researcher believes that there is a single ideological dimension that underlies people's judgments about specific crime control policies (e.g., retribution and treatment). Scaling can help determine whether a single construct—for instance, conservative/liberal ideology—underlies the positions people take on specific criminal justice policies. Scaling produces quantitative measures used to test hypotheses.

Scaling measures the intensity, direction, level, or potency of a variable. Graphic rating scales are an elementary form of scaling. People indicate a rating by checking a point on a line that runs from one extreme to another. This type of scale is easy to construct and use. It conveys the idea of a continuum, and assigning numbers helps people think about quantities. Scales assume that people with the same subjective feeling mark the graphic scale at the same place (sometimes a questionable assumption). Figure 5.3 illustrates two examples of possible juvenile probation morale scales.

Likert Scales

LIKERT SCALES

A scale often used in survey research in which people express attitudes or other responses in terms of ordinal-level categories (e.g., agree, disagree) that are ranked along a continuum.

You have encountered **Likert scales** throughout your life; they are widely used in survey research. Likert scales are called additive scales because a person's score on the scale is computed by summing the number of responses the person gives. Likert scales usually ask people to indicate whether they agree or disagree with a statement. Other modifications are possible; people might be asked whether they approve or disapprove, or whether they believe something is "almost always true."

Likert scales need a minimum of two categories, such as agree and disagree. Using only two choices creates a crude measure and forces distinctions into only two categories. It is usually better to use four to eight categories. A researcher can combine or collapse categories after the data are collected, but data collected with crude categories cannot be made more precise later. The choices should be evenly balanced (e.g., "strongly agree," "agree" with "strongly disagree," "disagree").

How would you rate the overall morale of JPOs in this agency?

| 1 | 2 | 3 | 4 | 5 | 7 | 8 | 9 | 10 |

Low Morale   High Morale

How would you rate your personal level of morale within this department?

| 1 | 2 | 3 | 4 | 5 | 7 | 8 | 9 | 10 |

Low Morale   High Morale

FIGURE 5.3   Juvenile Probation Morale Graphic Rating Scale.

Researchers often combine many Likert-scaled attitude indicators into an index. The scale and indexes have properties that are associated with improving reliability and validity. An index uses multiple indicators, which improves reliability. The use of multiple indicators that measure several aspects of a construct or opinion improves content validity. Finally, the index scores give a more precise quantitative measure of a person's opinion. For example, each person's opinion can be measured with a number from ten to forty, instead of in four categories: "strongly agree," "agree," "disagree," and "strongly disagree."

THURSTONE SCALING.   During the late 1920s, Louis Thurstone developed scaling methods for assigning numerical values to a construct. These are now called **Thurstone scaling** or the method of equal-appearing intervals.[10] At its core, this type of scaling uses people with expertise in a particular area (judges) to sort items into a ranking that will result in a single numerical continuum.

For example, a nongovernmental human rights organization decides it needs a public fund drive to carry its message about the tragedy in Darfur in Africa to wider and more powerful circles (recall Hagan's research in Chapter 1). This is how the scale could help: The researcher conceptualizes the problem as a matter of the public's willingness to donate time and money to the Darfur genocide issue, and identifies three dimensions. The first is the public's awareness of the problem, the second is the public's knowledge of international events, and the third is the public's own financial and time constraints. However, unless the researcher knows how the three dimensions relate to the heart of the matter—that is, the public's willingness to make a donation of time or money—he or she cannot say which factor is the most important.

Thurstone scaling helps figure this out by developing many statements (e.g., more than 100) regarding the object of interest, and then uses judges to reduce the number to a smaller set (e.g., 20) by eliminating ambiguous statements. Each judge rates the statements on an underlying continuum (let's say favorable to unfavorable). The researcher examines the ratings and keeps statements based on two factors: (1) agreement among the judges and (2) the statement's location on a range of possible values. The final set of statements is a measurement scale that spans a range of values.

Thurstone scaling begins with a large number of statements that should cover all shades of opinion. Each should be clear and precise. Good statements refer to the present and are not capable of being interpreted as facts. They are unlikely to be endorsed by everyone, are stated as simple sentences, and avoid words such as *always* and *never*. Researchers get ideas for writing the statements from reviewing the literature, from the mass media, from personal experience, and from conducting interviews with knowledgeable people. The following are the sort of statements about human rights that the researcher would develop:

- I believe that human rights attracts far too little attention from governments.
- I think that the news media makes too much out of human rights issues in Africa.

THURSTONE SCALING

A scale in which the researcher gives a group of judges many items and asks them to sort the items into categories along a continuum, and then looks at sorting results to select items on which the judges are in agreement.

- I am not really sure where Darfur is.
- I am well aware of the criticisms human rights groups have of the United States.
- I think that one's time is just as important as one's money in solving problems like the Darfur genocide.
- I do not like to donate my money to human rights causes.

A researcher next locates 50–300 judges. The judges should be familiar with the object or concept in the statements. Each judge receives a set of statement cards and instructions. Each card has one statement on it, and the judges place each card in one of several piles. The number of piles is usually seven, nine, eleven, or thirteen. The piles represent a range of values (e.g., favorable to neutral to unfavorable) with regard to the object or concept being evaluated. Each judge places cards in rating piles independently of the other judges.

After the judges place all cards in piles, the researcher creates a chart cross-classifying the piles and the statements. For example, 100 statements and 11 piles results in a chart with $11 \times 100 = 1,100$ boxes. The number of judges who assigned a rating to a given statement is written into each box. Statistical measures (beyond the present discussion) are used to compute the average rating of each statement and the degree to which the judges agree or disagree. The researcher keeps the statements with the greatest between-judge agreement, or interrater reliability, as well as statements that represent the entire range of values. Thurstone scaling allows our human rights organization to construct an attitude scale or select statements from a larger collection of attitude statements that would help in determining funding opportunities and obstacles.

Conclusion

In this chapter you learned about designing research topics and the principles and processes of measurement. All researchers conceptualize—or refine and clarify their ideas into conceptual definitions. All researchers operationalize—or develop a set of techniques or processes that will link their conceptual definitions to empirical reality. The goal remains the same: to establish unambiguous links between a researcher's abstract ideas and the empirical world. If you recall from Chapter 3, this fundamental principle holds true whether the researcher operates from the positivist social science, interpretive social science, or critical social science traditions (or some combination of these three).

You also learned about the principles of reliability and validity. Reliability refers to the dependability of a measure; validity refers to its accurateness, or how well a construct and data fit together. In addition, you saw how the principles of measurement apply in the creation of indexes and scales.

Beyond the core ideas of reliability and validity, you now know the basic principles of good measurement: Create clear definitions for concepts, use multiple measurement indicators, and, as appropriate, weight and standardize the data. Proper conceptualization and measurement are a fundamental element in producing credible and worthwhile research.

Key Terms

conceptualization *109*
operationalization *109*
operational definition *112*
reliability *113*
validity *113*
stability reliability *114*
representative reliability *114*
equivalence reliability *114*

face validity *115*
content validity *115*
criterion validity *115*
concurrent validity *115*
predictive validity *115*
construct validity *116*
convergent validity *116*
discriminant validity *116*

level of measurement *117*
nominal-level
   measurement *118*
ordinal-level
   measurement *118*
interval-level
   measurement *118*
ratio-level measurement *118*

continuous variables *119*
discrete variables *119*
scales *119*
indexes *119*
unidimensionality *120*
weighted index *122*
Likert scales *122*
Thurstone scaling *123*

Review Questions

1. How does a researcher go about selecting and designing his or her research questions?
2. Explain the conceptualization and operationalization processes researchers use when measuring the phenomena under study.
3. What is the difference between reliability and validity, and how do they complement each other?
4. What are the differences between convergent, content, and concurrent validity? Can you have all three at once? Explain your answer.
5. What is the difference between the logic of a scale and that of an index?
6. Why is unidimensionality an important characteristic of a scale?
7. What are the advantages and disadvantages of weighting indexes?

Practicing Research

1. This chapter emphasizes the importance of hard work when selecting a worthwhile research topic. Using the techniques noted, develop three different potential research topics, and speculate about the research design you might use to produce knowledge about these topics. Make sure and document the process and sources you use in developing the topics.
2. This chapter explores the concept of morale as it applies to juvenile probation officers. This exercise will examine a related concept—police officer "burnout"—using a recent article published in the *Journal of Criminal Justice* [the formal citation is: Martinussen, M., Richardson, A. M., and R. J. Burke, (2007), "Job demands, job resources, and burnout among police officers." *Journal of Criminal Justice* 35, 3: 239–249]. This is a well-known journal that your library should carry. This exercise can be carried out as either an in-class exercise completed in small groups or an out-of-class written assignment.

    Using this article, complete the following:
    a. Identify the major variables used in this study. Describe exactly how the researchers measure these variables.
    Do they use scales or indexes (describe how these scales or indexes are used)? At what level of measurement did they measure the study's major variables?
    b. Using the three types of measurement reliability discussed in this chapter (stability, representative, and equivalence), assess the extent to which this study is reliable. What might be some ways that reliability could be improved?
    c. Using the various types of measurement validity that apply, assess and discuss the extent to which you think that the authors constructed valid measures.
    d. Provide your overall impression of this article's use of measurement and the relevance of this piece to criminal justice practice.

3. Find two research articles that rely on either an index or a scale for measuring its major independent and/or dependent variables. Using the keywords associated with either the scale or the index, try to find at least another two articles that have used the same scale or index for measuring variables. Compare and contrast how each article uses the scale or index as it relates to what you've learned in this chapter.

Notes for Further Study

1. Problem choice and topic selection are discussed in Campbell and associates (1982) and in Zuckerman (1978).
2. Exceptions are secondary data analysis and existing statistics research. In these situations, a quantitative researcher often focuses on the research question and develops a specific hypothesis to test after he or she examines the available data.
3. The words *concept*, *construct*, and *idea* are used more or less interchangeably, but their meanings differ. An idea is any mental image, belief plan, or impression. It refers to any vague impression, opinion, or thought. A concept is a thought, a general notion, or a generalized idea about a class of objects. A construct is a thought that is systematically put together, an orderly arrangement of ideas, facts, and impressions. The word *construct* is used here because its emphasis is on taking vague concepts and turning them into systematically organized ideas.
4. See Grinnell (1987: 5–18) for further discussion.
5. See Carmines and Zeller (1979: 17). For a discussion of the many types of validity, see Brinberg and McGrath (1982)
6. This was adapted from Carmines and Zeller (1979: 20–21).
7. For a discussion of types of criterion validity, see Carmines and Zeller (1979: 17–19) and Fiske (1982) for construct validity.
8. See Cook and Campbell (1979) for elaboration.
9. See Borgatta and Bohrnstedt (1980) and Duncan (1984: 119–155) for a discussion and critique of the topic of levels of measurement.
10. McIver and Carmines (1981: 16–21) have an excellent discussion of Thurstone scaling. Also see discussions in Anderson and colleagues (1983: 248–252), Converse (1987: 66–77), and Edwards (1957). The example used here is partially borrowed from Churchill (1983: 249–254), who described the formula for scoring Thurstone scaling.

Sampling in Crime
and Justice Research

Sexual Coercion and Sampling: A Cautionary Tale
    Highlight 6.1 Researching a Serious Problem:
        Rape on Campus
Probability Sampling
    Populations, Cases, and Sampling Frames
    Why Random?
    Types of Probability Samples
        Simple Random
        Systematic Sampling
        Stratified Sampling
        Cluster Sampling
        Highlight 6.2 A Detailed Look at the NCVS
            Survey Sample Method
        ■ *Probability Proportionate to Size (PPS)*
    Random-Digit Dialing
    How Large Should a Sample Be?
    Highlight 6.3 National Violence against Women
        Study Sampling

Nonprobability Sampling
    Haphazard or Convenience Sampling
    Quota Sampling
    Purposive or Judgmental Sampling
    Snowball Sampling
    Deviant Case Sampling
    Sequential Sampling
    Theoretical Sampling
Mixed Sampling Approaches for Hidden Populations
    Highlight 6.4 Two Classic Research Examples
        Using Snowball Sampling and Hidden
        Populations
Conclusion
Key Terms
Review Questions
Practicing Research
Notes for Further Study

SEXUAL COERCION AND SAMPLING: A CAUTIONARY TALE

A graduate student in one of Kraska's research methods classes decided to conduct a master's thesis project on women's experiences of sexual coercion while attending college. Other than a descriptive inquiry into the nature of the problem, this student, we'll call him Steve Randall, hoped to determine whether those female students who lived in sororities were more or less likely to be victims of some sort of coercive sexual experience compared to those who lived in normal on-campus residence halls. He did an excellent job reviewing the literature and developing his organizing concepts. He interviewed two leading researchers in this area of study via e-mail, he identified quality preexisting measures and indexes of sexual assault experiences to include in his survey, and he ultimately constructed a solid survey instrument (see Highlight 6.1 for a closer examination on this area of interest). He had difficulty deciding whom to survey. He eventually decided not to draw a sample from the larger population of university students, but instead to survey the entire population of female students at Eastern Kentucky University (EKU).

HIGHLIGHT 6.1
Researching a Serious Problem: Rape on Campus

Research-based knowledge has been instrumental in raising awareness about violence against women on college campuses.

Several major research studies have documented quantitatively, using sophisticated sampling procedures, the extent to which women in U.S. society are victims of sexual violence. The 1998 National Violence against Women Survey (cosponsored by the National Institute of Justice Centers for Disease Control and Prevention), for example, found that one in six women has experienced rape or attempted rape at some point in her life. Most have assumed that this high rate of sexual victimization would not be found on college and university campuses due to low rates of reported crimes. However, a series of national-level surveys is beginning to expose an unpleasant reality.

Following the lead of path-breaking work on college campus sexual victimization conducted by Walter DeKeseredy and Marty Schwartz (1998), a major U.S. study conducted by Bonnie Fisher and colleagues on the sexual victimization of college women reports that 2.8 percent of college women are the victims of rape or attempted rape per academic year. Bonnie Fisher's research estimates that in a college with 10,000 female students 350 rapes could occur in a year. However, only less than 5 percent will be reported to the police. These revealing findings were derived through a careful sampling protocol,

based on a telephone survey of a randomly selected, national sample of 4,446 women who were attending a 2- or 4-year college or university during fall 1996. The sample was limited to schools with at least 1,000 students and was stratified by the size of the total student enrollment (1,000–2,499; 2,500–4,999; 5,000–19,999; 20,000 or more) and the school's location (urban, suburban, and rural). Schools were randomly chosen using a probability proportional with the size of the total female enrollment. The sample was limited to schools with at least 1,000 students and they were then randomly selected using a sampling frame provided by the American Student List Company. This company provided the school address and telephone number for each student in the sample. Each sample member was sent a letter describing the study and research protocol approximately 2 weeks prior to when a trained female interviewer called using a computer-aided telephone interviewing system. The response rate was 85.6 percent.

(By the end of this chapter, the terminology used in this description of sampling methods used by the researcheSrs should be fully intelligible.)

Although on-campus sexual violence has not turned into a scandal for most colleges, it has rocked U.S. military academies. In particular, the Air Force Academy found itself embroiled in controversy. Because of documented instances of rape victims being castigated instead of their rapists, and a set of legal procedures in place that failed on all accounts, the top four officials at the academy were removed, and numerous research studies were mandated to further investigate the problem. In March and April 2004, the Department of Defense conducted its own research. It surveyed the entire population of research subjects (1,906 women from all 3 military academies). They also drew at random a representative sample of 3,107 men. The survey attempted to assess honestly the prevalence and nuances of the sexual violence problem. It was directed by Department of Defense Inspector General Joseph E. Schmitz (Vise 2005).

The research found that one in seven female students attending the nation's military academies had been sexually assaulted after becoming a cadet or midshipman. More than half the women studying there reported experiencing some form of serious sexual harassment on campus, according to survey responses. But few of those incidents, and only a third of the assaults, were reported to authorities.

Besides appointing new leadership, a host of new policies and procedures for assault victims has been implemented at all three academies in an attempt to improve reporting of sex crimes on military campuses. It is interesting to note that the research also found that men reported fifty-five sexual assaults, usually occurring in dormitory rooms and perpetuated by upper-class men.

Source: The seminal study in this area is Walter S. DeKeseredy and Martin D. Schwartz's (1998) *Woman Abuse on Campus: Results from the Canadian National Survey* (Thousand Oaks, CA: Sage Publications).

Steve decided on an Internet survey technique (even though he was cautioned on the potential pitfalls), in which he sent every female EKU student an e-mail cover letter with a link to a separate website containing the survey. After three weeks of waiting, he was quite excited to report that he had received over 1,700 surveys. On the surface, this seemed like great news. With the help of a friend, he coded and input all 60 variables found in the survey and 1,700 cases (returned surveys) into a statistical package called SPSS. (As discussed in Chapter 11, inputting data into this type of statistical package is similar to a computer spreadsheet.)

Steve assumed he had generated a wealth of reliable knowledge about his research topic. He even began to talk about disseminating his research findings to the wider university community through the campus newspaper, activist groups on campus, and possibly an academic journal publication. He had found a slightly higher-than-normal rate of victimization among his 1,700 respondents, and he found that women in a residential sorority were slightly more likely to report instances of sexual coercion as compared to regular university housing (see some examples of victimization rates in Highlight 6.3). The findings in this study could have had a major impact on university policy and procedures.

There was only one major snafu: EKU has over 9,000 female students, and the survey technique he used had garnered data from only 1,700 of them. Although this seemed like it should have been adequate, it also means that 7,300 female students self-selected out of the study. Could it be that those students who hadn't experienced victimization were more apathetic about the problem and did not bother linking to a separate website and filling out a survey? Likewise, perhaps the victims of sexual coercion were more motivated to fill it out. Of course, the converse could be true also: Victims would be more hesitant to fill it out.

The problem was that Steve had no idea why some women filled it out and others didn't. And because these 1,700 respondents were not chosen at random, he could not assume that they were representative of the total population of female students. What he had, then, was a data set based on about 19 percent of female EKU students who made the decision to respond, referred to as the "response rate." Anything lower than a 50–60 percent response rate in the social sciences is usually suspect. With only 19 percent responding, the findings could not be credibly generalized to all EKU female students—even with data from 1,700 respondents. When again asked for his advice, Kraska praised Steve for his efforts, but also had to caution him that it would be ethically irresponsible to disseminate his findings to the media and the campus community, given that neither the media nor the public would understand why his seemingly significant findings were based on a faulty foundation. Kraska did talk to Steve about how his data might still be publishable in an academic journal with some additional work and the proper clarification about its methodological limitations.

Researchers only occasionally attempt to examine an entire population, like what Steve had done. When they do—as in the case of the U.S. Census, for example—it is referred to as a census study. Most of the time, crime and justice researchers collect data from a select few cases among a larger population. Studying a smaller subset of cases from a larger set is known as **sampling.** In crime and justice studies, sampling isn't limited to just people; we could have a subset of reported crimes, legal case decisions, criminal justice processing decisions, newspaper article excerpts, or historical or international trends in crime control practices.

SAMPLING

A smaller set of cases that a researcher selects from a larger pool and generalizes to the population.

Most discussions of sampling come from quantitative research. Its goal is to get a representative sample, or a small collection of units from a much larger collection or population, so that the researcher can study the smaller group and produce accurate generalizations about the larger group. Researchers focus on the specific techniques that will yield highly representative samples (i.e., samples that are very much like the population). The sampling is based on theories of probability from mathematics (called probability sampling).

Crime and justice researchers have two motivations for using probability or random sampling. The first motivation is time and cost. For example, instead of trying to survey all 9,000 female college students, Steve would have been much better off targeting only 750 students, as long as they were chosen at random. The second motivation is accuracy. The results of a well-designed, carefully executed probability sample will produce results that are equally as accurate as trying to reach every single person in an entire population.

Qualitative research also uses sampling. It focuses less, however, on representativeness and more on how the sample or small collection of cases, units, or activities accurately illuminates an object of study (e.g., drug dealing, armed robbery, gang life, life at a domestic violence shelter, music albums, police magazine advertisements). The primary purpose of sampling in qualitative research is to collect specific cases, events, or actions that can clarify and deepen our understanding of crime and justice phenomena in a specific context. For example, a qualitative investigation into "home-grown terrorism" might focus on the specific case of the Oklahoma City bombing carried out by Timothy McVeigh (referred to in Chapter 12).

PROBABILITY SAMPLING

A specialized vocabulary is used in *probability sampling*. Before examining the techniques of probability sampling, it is important to understand its language. The sexual coercion research example has already introduced you to some basic and fairly easy-to-grasp concepts such as sampling, random selection, population, and representativeness.

Populations, Cases, and Sampling Frames

A researcher draws a sample from a larger pool of cases. A **sampling case** is the unit of analysis or case in a population. It can be a person, a group, an organization, a written document or symbolic message, or an event. The larger pool of cases is the **population.** To define and set the parameters of the population, a researcher specifies the target of analysis, the geographical location, and the temporal boundaries of populations.

A researcher begins with an idea of the population (e.g., all juvenile probation officers in a given city), and then defines it more precisely. A **target population** is the specific pool of cases that he or she wants to study. Steve defined his target population as all female students attending Eastern Kentucky University. The population needs an operational definition, similar to that used in the measurement process (see Chapter 5). A researcher operationalizes a population by developing a specific list that closely approximates all the cases in the population. This list, or set of boundaries, is called the **sampling frame.** We can choose from many types of sampling frames: telephone directories, county prosecutors in a given state, tax records, driver's license records, all the children in a particular school district, and so on. Although defining the parameters of a population sounds simple, it is often difficult because of flawed case lists. Steve's sampling frame, for example, seemed straightforward: an exhaustive list of e-mail addresses of all female students provided by the registrar's office. However, he ran into quite a few difficulties with students who use their personal e-mail accounts and not the university e-mail system. This could have been part of the reason for the low return rate.

A quality-sampling frame, then, is crucial to good sampling. Just as a mismatch between the theoretical and operational definitions of a variable creates invalid measurement, so does a mismatch between the sampling frame and the population causes invalid sampling. Although sampling frames almost always have some inaccuracies, researchers try to minimize mismatches. A **population parameter** is the true characteristics of the population. The parameter is never known with absolute accuracy for most populations, so researchers must estimate it on the basis of samples. They use information from the sample, in the form of statistics, to estimate population parameters (see Figure 6.1).

Why Random?

The notion of a probability sample comes from applied mathematics' reliance on random processes. The word *random* refers to a process that generates a mathematically random result. If the sample selection process operates in a truly random method (i.e., no discernable pattern), a

SAMPLING CASE

The name for a single unit to be sampled.

POPULATION

The abstract idea of a large group of many cases from which a researcher draws a sample and to which results from a sample are generalized.

TARGET POPULATION

The concretely specified large group of many cases from which a researcher draws a sample and to which results from a sample are generalized.

SAMPLING FRAME

A specific list or set of boundaries within a population from which a researcher chooses her or his sample (e.g., telephone directory, driver's license records).

POPULATION PARAMETER

A characteristic of the entire population that is estimated from a sample.

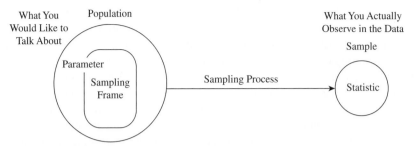

FIGURE 6.1   A Model of the Logic of Sampling.   *Source:* From W. Lawrence Neuman, *Social Research Methods, Qualitative and Quantitative Approaches,* 6/e. Published by Allyn and Bacon, 75 Arlington St., Boston, MA 02116. Copyright © 2006 by Pearson Education. Reprinted by permission of the publisher.

RANDOM SAMPLES

A sample in which the researcher uses a random number table or similar mathematical random process so that each sampling element in the population will have an equal probability of being selected.

SAMPLING ERROR

How much a sample deviates from being representative of the population.

researcher can calculate the probability of outcomes. In a true random process, each case has an equal probability of being selected (just think of the ping-pong ball system state lotteries use to select numbers at random). Today most researchers rely on computer programs to select cases in a purely random manner.

Random samples are most likely to yield a sample that represents the true characteristics of the population. As discussed in detail below, the randomness of the sample allows the researcher to make mathematical probability statements about the relationship between the sample and the population. Because the sample selected, even if done randomly, could still deviate somewhat from the entire population, statistical techniques determine the probable level of sampling error within a particular sample. (The notion of sampling error makes more sense if you think of flipping coins. Theoretically, ten flips of a coin should yield five heads and five tails. However, eight heads and two tails could happen, but it is not the most probable outcome.) This is why political pollsters, for example, say their findings have a probable accuracy within plus or minus three to five percentage points. This range represents the probable amount of **sampling error** within a sample. We'll discuss this further in the next section.

Types of Probability Samples

SIMPLE RANDOM SAMPLE

A random sample in which a researcher creates a sampling frame and uses a pure random process to select cases so that each sampling element in the population will have an equal probability of being selected.

SIMPLE RANDOM.   The **simple random sample** is the one on which other types are modeled. In simple random sampling, a researcher develops an accurate sampling frame, selects cases from the sampling frame according to a mathematically random procedure, and then locates the exact case that was selected for inclusion in the sample.

To generate a simple random sample, a researcher numbers all cases in a sampling frame, then uses a list of random numbers, or computer program, to decide which cases to select. He or she needs as many random numbers as there are cases to be sampled; for example, for a sample of 100, exactly 100 random numbers are needed. The researcher can get random numbers from a random-number table or statistical software. Random-number tables are available in most statistics and research methods books, including this one. The numbers are generated by a purely random process so that any number has an equal probability of appearing in any position.

If the researcher selects a case from the sampling frame, does he or she then return it to the sampling frame or keep it separate? Unrestricted random sampling is random sampling with replacement—that is, replacing a case after sampling it so it can be selected again. In simple random sampling without replacement, the most common approach, the researcher ignores cases already selected into the sample.

Let's illustrate the logic of simple random sampling using marbles from a jar. We have a large jar full of 5,000 marbles, some red and some white. The 5,000 marbles are our population, and the parameter we want to estimate is the percentage of red marbles in it. We randomly select 100 marbles (we close our eyes, shake the jar, pick one marble, and repeat the procedure 100 times). We now have a random sample of marbles. We count the number of red marbles in the sample to estimate the percentage of red versus white marbles in the population. This is a lot easier than counting all 5,000 marbles. Our sample has fifty-two white and forty-eight red marbles.

Does this mean that the population parameter is 48 percent red marbles? Maybe not. Because of random chance, our specific sample might not be quite accurate. We can check our results by dumping the 100 marbles back in the jar, mixing the marbles, and drawing a second random sample of 100 marbles. On the second try, our sample has forty-six white marbles and fifty-four red ones. Now we have a problem. Which is correct? How good is this random sampling business if different samples from the same population can yield different results? We repeat the procedure over and over until we have drawn 130 different samples of 100 marbles each (see Figure 6.2 for results). Most people might empty the jar and count all 5,000, but I want to figure out the worth of random sampling. We find that the results of my 130 different samples reveal a clear pattern. The most common mix of red and white marbles is 50:50. Samples that are close to that split are more frequent than those with more uneven splits. The population parameter appears to be 50 percent white and 50 percent red marbles.

Mathematical proofs and empirical tests demonstrate that the pattern found in Figure 6.2 appears for almost all phenomena—both natural and social phenomena. The collection of numerous different samples constitutes a **sampling distribution.** It is a distribution of different samples that shows the frequency of different sample outcomes from many separate random samples. The pattern will appear if the sample size is 1,000 instead of 100; if there are 10 colors of marbles instead of 2; if the population has 100 marbles or 10 million marbles instead of 5,000; and if the population is college students, automobiles, police departments, or criminal justice academic programs. In fact, the pattern will become clearer as more and more independent random samples are drawn from the population.

The bell-shaped pattern in the sampling distribution suggests that over many separate samples, the true population parameter will emerge (i.e., the 50:50 split in the preceding example). Of course, some samples, due to random chance, deviate from the population parameter, but they are exceptions. The distribution of many different random samples, as seen in the graph in Figure 6.2, is referred to as a normal or bell-shaped curve. Such a curve is theoretically important and is used throughout statistics.

The **central limit theorem** from mathematics tells us that as the number of different random samples in a sampling distribution increases toward infinity, the pattern of samples and the population parameter become more predictable. With a huge number of random samples, the sampling distribution forms a normal curve, and the midpoint of the curve approaches the population parameter as the number of samples increases. Of course, we want to conduct only one sample because we do not have the time or energy to draw 130 different samples. The central limit theorem allows us, though, to generalize from this one sample to the larger population. The theorem lets the researcher calculate the likeliness (probability) that our sample differs from our population parameter.

Random sampling does not guarantee that every random sample perfectly represents the population. Instead, it means that most random samples will be close to the true population most of the time. This allows us to calculate statistically the probability of a particular sample being inaccurate. A researcher estimates the chance that a particular sample is off or unrepresentative

SAMPLING DISTRIBUTION

A distribution created by drawing many random samples from the same population.

CENTRAL LIMIT THEOREM

A mathematical relationship that states that whenever many random samples are drawn from a population, a normal distribution is formed, and the center of the distribution for a variable equals the population parameter.

RED	WHITE	NUMBER OF SAMPLES
42	58	1
43	57	1
45	55	2
46	54	4
47	53	8
48	52	12
49	51	21
50	50	31
51	49	20
52	48	13
53	47	9
54	46	5
55	45	2
57	43	1
	Total	130

Number of red and white marbles that were randomly drawn from a jar of 5,000 marbles with 100 drawn each time, repeated 130 times for 130 independent random samples.

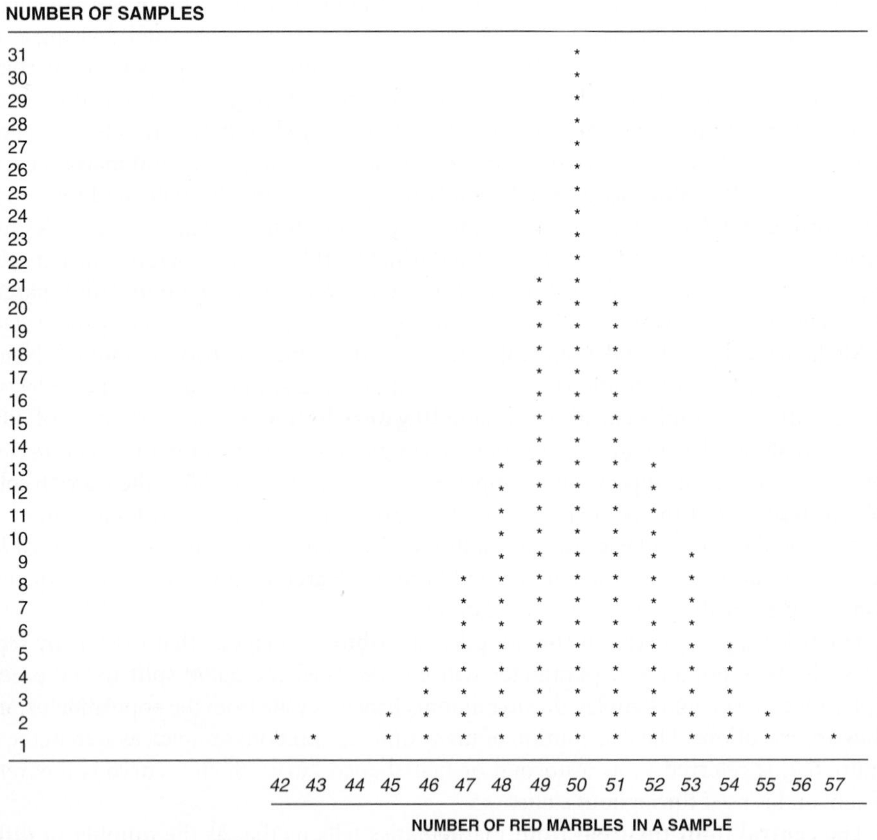

FIGURE 6.2 Example of Sampling Distribution. *Source:* From W. Lawrence Neuman, *Social Research Methods, Qualitative and Quantitative Approaches,* 6/e. Published by Allyn and Bacon, 75 Arlington St., Boston, MA 02116. Copyright © 2006 by Pearson Education. Reprinted by permission of the publisher.

CONFIDENCE INTERVALS

A range of values, usually a little higher and lower than a specific value found in a sample, within which a researcher has a specified and high degree of confidence that the population parameter lies.

(i.e., the size of the sampling error) by using information from the sample to estimate the sampling distribution. He or she combines this information with knowledge of the central limit theorem to construct what are called **confidence intervals.**

The confidence interval is a relatively simple but powerful idea. When researchers report findings, they sometimes mention something like "the margin of error being plus or minus two percentage points." A confidence interval is a range around a specific point used to estimate a population parameter. A range is used because the statistics of random processes do not allow a researcher to predict an exact point, but they allow the researcher to say with a high level of confidence (e.g., 95 percent certainty and 5 percent uncertainty) that the sample is representative of the true population. Using our marble example, we cannot say, "There are precisely 2,500 red marbles in the jar based on a random sample." We can say, "We are 95 percent certain that the population parameter lies between 2,450 and 2,550."

Crime and justice researchers rely heavily on the simple random sample as it helps generate reliable findings and it forms the basis of numerous other sampling techniques. In one of Kraska's studies on police SWAT teams, for example, he relied on a simple random sample of all police departments in the United States (a population supplied by an organization known as the Police Executive Research Forum) that served communities of 50,000 or more. This resulted in a survey being sent to

A SWAT team serves a drug-related search warrant. Determining the extent to which this type of activity constitutes a national trend requires careful sampling techniques.

almost 700 police departments, with 78 percent of police departments returning a useable instrument (known as the "response rate"). From this sample, Kraska was able to make reliable generalizations from his sample findings to the larger police institution (at least those agencies serving communities of 50,000 people or more).

SYSTEMATIC SAMPLING.   **Systematic sampling** is simple random sampling with a shortcut for random selection. Again, the first step is to number each case in the sampling frame. Instead of using a list of random numbers, a researcher calculates a sampling interval, and the interval becomes his or her quasi-random selection method. The **sampling interval** tells the researcher how to select cases from a sampling frame by skipping cases in the frame before selecting one for the sample.

For instance, we want to sample 300 police departments from a population of 3,000 departments. After a random starting point, we select every tenth department of the 3,000 to get a sample of 300. Our sampling interval is ten. In most cases, a simple random sample and a systematic sample yield equivalent results.

Systematic sampling cannot be substituted for simple random sampling that occurs when the cases in a sample are organized in some kind of cycle or pattern. For example, the 3,000 police departments were listed in order of number of police officers employed. Such a pattern would give us an unrepresentative sample if we chose every tenth case. Figure 6.3 illustrates simple random sampling and systematic sampling.

STRATIFIED SAMPLING.   In **stratified sampling,** a researcher first divides the population into subpopulations (strata) on the basis of supplementary information.[1] After dividing the population into strata, the researcher draws a random sample from each subpopulation. This way, the researcher controls the relative size of each stratum, rather than letting random processes control it. This guarantees true representation, or fixes the proportion of different strata within a sample.

In general, stratified sampling produces samples that are more representative of the population than simple random sampling if the stratum information is accurate. A simple example illustrates why this is so. Imagine conducting research in Alaska's two largest cities, Fairbanks and Anchorage, on crime problems associated with indigenous groups of people. The difficulty is that we want to study numerous different indigenous groups—Athabaskans, Aleuts, Tlinget, and Inuits—each of which forms only a small percentage of all Native American Alaskans living in these cities. The only way to ensure that a large enough number of an ethnic group is included in our study would be to stratify our sample. Researchers use stratified sampling when a stratum of interest (e.g., native indigenous groups) is a small percentage of a

SYSTEMATIC SAMPLING

A random sample in which a researcher selects every kth (e.g., 12th) case in the sampling frame using a sampling interval.

SAMPLING INTERVAL

The inverse of the sampling ratio that is used when selecting cases in systematic sampling.

STRATIFIED SAMPLING

A random sample in which the researcher first identifies a set of mutually exclusive and exhaustive categories, divides the sampling frame by the categories, and then uses random selection to select cases from each category.

1. Number each case in the sampling frame in sequence. The list of 40 names is in alphabetical order, numbered from 1 to 40.
2. Decide on a sample size. We will draw two 25 percent (10-name) samples.
3. For a *simple random sample,* locate a random number table (see excerpt; a fuller table appears in count the largest number of digits needed for the sample (e.g., with 40 names, two digits are needed; for 100 to 999, three digits; for 1,000 to 9,999, four digits). Begin anywhere on the random-number table (we will begin in the upper left) and take a set of digits (we will take the last two). Mark the number on the sampling frame that corresponds to the chosen random number to indicate that the case is in the sample. If the number is too large (over 40), ignore it. If the number appears more than

once (10 and 21 occurred twice in the example), ignore the second occurrence. Continue until the number of cases in the sample (10 in our example) is reached.
4. For a *systematic sample,* begin with a random start. The easiest way to do this is to point blindly at the random-number table, then take the closest number that appears on the sampling frame. In the example, 18 was chosen. Start with the random number, then count the sampling interval, or 4 in our example, to come to the first number. Mark it, and then count the sampling interval for the next number. Continue the end of the list. Continue counting the sampling interval as if the beginning of the list were attached to the end of the list (like a circle). Keep counting untill ending close to the start, or on the start if the sampling interval divides evenly into the total of the sampling frame.

No.	Name (Gender)	Simple Random	Systematic	No.	Name (Gender)	Simple Random	Systematic
01	Abrams, J. (M)			21	Hjelmhaug, N. (M)	Yes*	
02	Adams, H. (F)	Yes	Yes (6)	22	Huang, J. (F)	Yes	Yes (1)
03	Anderson, H. (M)			23	Ivono, V. (F)		
04	Arminond, L. (M)			24	Jaquees, J. (M)		
05	Boorstein, A. (M)			25	Johnson, A. (F)		
06	Breitsprecher, P. (M)	Yes	Yes (7)	26	Kennedy, M. (F)		Yes (2)
07	Brown, D. (F)			27	Koschoreck, L. (F)		
08	Catteline, J. (F)			28	Koykkar, J. (M)		
09	Cidoni, S. (M)			29	Kozlowski, C. (F)	Yes	
10	Davis, L. (F)	Yes*	Yes (8)	30	Laurent, J. (M)		Yes (3)
11	Droullard, C. (M)	Yes		31	Lee, R. (F)		
12	Durette, R. (F)			32	Ling, C. (M)		
13	Elsnau, K. (F)	Yes		33	McKinnon, K. (F)		
14	Falconer, T. (M)	Yes (9)		34	Min, H. (F)	Yes	Yes (4)
15	Fuerstenberg, J. (M)			35	Moini, A. (F)		
16	Fulton, P. (F)			36	Navarre, H. (M)		
17	Gneuwuch, S. (F)			37	O'Sullivan, C. (M)		
18	Green, C. (M)		START, Yes (10)	38	Oh, J. (M)		Yes (5)
19	Goodwanda, T. (F)	Yes		39	Olson, J. (M)		
20	Harris, B. (M)			40	Oritzy Garcia, L. (F)		

Excerpt from a Random-Number Table (for Simple Random Sample)

15010	18590	00102	42210	94174	22099
90122	38221	21529	00013	04734	60457
67256	13887	94119	11077	01061	27779
13761	23390	12947	21280	44506	36457
81994	66611	16597	44457	07621	51949
79180	25992	46178	23992	62108	43232
07984	47169	88094	82752	15318	11921

*Numbers that appeared twice in random numbers selected.

FIGURE 6.3 How to Draw Simple Random and Systematic Samples. *Source:* From W. Lawrence Neuman, *Social Research Methods, Qualitative and Quantitative Approaches,* 6/e. Published by Allyn and Bacon, 75 Arlington St., Boston, MA 02116. Copyright © 2006 by Pearson Education. Reprinted by permission of the publisher.

| TABLE 6.1 | Illustration of Stratified Sampling: Sample of 100 Personnel in County Sheriff's Department, Stratified by Position |

Position	Population N	Percent	Simple Random Sample N	Stratified Sample N	Errors Compared to the Population
Administrators	15	2.88	1	3	−2
Homicide detectives	25	4.81	2	5	−3
SWAT unit	25	4.81	6	5	+1
Gang unit	100	19.23	22	19	+3
Drug unit	100	19.23	21	19	+2
Dispatchers	75	14.42	9	14	+5
Secretarial staff	50	9.62	8	10	−2
Detention officers	75	14.42	5	14	+1
Road patrol officers	30	5.77	3	6	−3
Custodians	25	4.81	3	5	−2
Total	520	100.00	100	100	

Randomly select 3 of 15 administrators, 5 of 25 homicide detectives, and so on.

Note: Traditionally, N symbolizes the number in the population and *n* represents the number in the sample.

The simple random sample overrepresents gang and drug units but underrepresents administrators and road patrol officers. The stratified sample gives an accurate representation of each position.

Source: From W. Lawrence Neuman, *Social Research Methods, Qualitative and Quantitative Approaches,* 6/e. Published by Allyn and Bacon, 75 Arlington St., Boston, MA 02116. Copyright © 2006 by Pearson Education. Reprinted by permission of the publisher.

population and random processes could miss the stratum by chance. This guarantees that the sample represents the population with regard to the important strata (Table 6.1).

CLUSTER SAMPLING. **Cluster sampling** is much like simple random sample except that it randomly samples clusters first and then concentrates on individual cases. A cluster is a collective type of unit that includes multiple elements such as a criminal justice agency, universities, hospitals, or schools. The researcher will generally select a group of these clusters using a random process and then will randomly select individual cases to study within each cluster. Cluster sampling addresses two problems: (1) researchers lack a good sampling frame for a dispersed population and (2) the cost to reach a sampled case is very high.[2]

For example, there is no single list of all private policing personnel in the United States. Even if we got an accurate sampling frame, it would cost too much to reach the sampled companies who are dispersed all over the country. Instead of using a single sampling frame, researchers use a sampling design that would first draw a random sample of private security companies, and then draw a second sample of actual private police officers from within the clusters selected in the first stage of sampling. We randomly sample clusters, then randomly sample cases from within the selected clusters. This has a big practical advantage when we can create a good sampling frame of clusters. Once we get a sample of clusters, creating a sampling frame for cases within each cluster becomes manageable. A second advantage for geographically dispersed populations is that cases within each cluster are physically closer to one another. This may produce a savings in locating or reaching each case.

We draw several samples in stages in cluster sampling. In a three-stage sample, Stage 1 is random sampling of big clusters; Stage 2 is random sampling of small clusters within each selected big cluster; and the Stage 3 is sampling of cases from within the sampled small clusters.

CLUSTER SAMPLING

A type of random sample that uses multiple stages and is often used to cover wide geographic areas in which aggregated units are randomly selected and then samples are drawn from the sampled aggregated units, or clusters.

For example, we want a sample of individuals from Mapleville about their fear of crime. First, we randomly sample city blocks, then households within blocks, and then individuals within households. Although there is no accurate list of all residents of Mapleville, there is an accurate list of blocks in the city. After selecting a random sample of blocks, we count all households on the selected blocks to create a sample frame for each block. We then use the list of households to draw a random sample at the stage of sampling households. Finally, we choose a specific individual within each sampled household.

Cluster sampling is usually less expensive than simple random sampling, but it is less accurate. Remember that each stage in cluster sampling introduces sampling errors, so a multi-stage cluster sample has more sampling errors than a one-stage random sample.[3] Highlight 6.2 presents an example of how many sampling terms and ideas can be used together in one of our more important measures of crime—the National Crime Victimization Survey (NCVS).

Probability Proportionate to Size (PPS). Oftentimes, the clusters we are studying are not close in size. This means that we have to weigh some clusters more or less heavily to equalize the chances of cases within the cluster to be equalized. It is an equal probability selection method. Most studies employing a cluster sample in crime and justice research resort to this technique. It would certainly be necessary for our private policing example: One major private policing company, Wackenhut Corporation, has over 60,000 personnel, whereas a more specialized corporation, Blackwater, Inc., has only 5,000. This situation would necessitate using **probability proportionate to size (PPS)** sampling. (The rise of private security corporations handling global security issues, especially with regard to terrorism, is a needed and potentially very interesting exploratory study. So far, most of our knowledge about this aspect of the war on terrorism has been generated by investigative journalists.)

RANDOM-DIGIT DIALING. **Random-digit dialing (RDD)** is a sampling technique used in research projects in which the general public is interviewed by telephone.[4] It does not use the published telephone directory as the sampling frame.

Three kinds of people are missed when the sampling frame is a telephone directory: people without telephones, people who have recently moved, and people with unlisted numbers. Those without phones (e.g., the poor, transients, and those folks who have switched to cell or Internet phone services exclusively) are missed in any telephone interview study. Several kinds of people

PROBABILITY PROPORTIONATE TO SIZE (PPS)

An adjustment made in cluster sampling when each cluster does not have the same number of sampling elements.

RANDOM-DIGIT DIALING (RDD)

A method of randomly selecting cases for telephone interviews that uses all possible telephone numbers as a sampling frame.

HIGHLIGHT 6.2
A Detailed Look at the NCVS Survey Sample Method

Criminologists are increasingly relying on self-reported survey data to study criminal behavior, victimization, delinquency and drug consumption, fear of crime, and routine activities, among other topics. These surveys typically cover national and international populations and span large geographical areas. Because of the cost of random sampling in such studies and the difficulty in obtaining a comprehensive sampling frame, criminologists and other social scientists favor cluster sampling.

As already mentioned, the National Crime Victimization Survey is a very important survey in the United States for obtaining national estimates of crime victimization. The NCVS's cluster sampling is complex, involving three stages of sampling: counties or groups of counties, enumeration district, and housing unit. The methodology involves collecting data from a nationally representative sample of individuals aged twelve or older living in U.S. households. Basic demographic information, such as age, race, sex, and income, is collected to enable analysis of victimizations of various subpopulations. Interviews are translated for non-English-speaking respondents. The survey respondents are selected through the use of the U.S. Bureau of the Census. They select respondents for the NCVS using a rotating panel design. Households are randomly selected, and all age-eligible individuals in a selected household become part of the panel. Once in the sample, respondents are interviewed every six months for a total of seven interviews over a three-year period. The first and fifth interviews are face-to-face; the rest are by telephone when possible. After the seventh interview, the household is dropped from the panel and a new household is rotated into the sample. Interviews take about half an hour. The NCVS has consistently obtained a response rate of about 95 percent.

have unlisted numbers: people who want to avoid collection agencies; the very wealthy; and those who want privacy and want to avoid obscene calls, salespeople, and prank calls. In some urban areas in the United States, the percentage of unlisted numbers is as high as 50 percent. In addition, people change their residences, so directories that are published annually or less often have numbers for people who have left and do not list those who have recently moved into an area. A researcher using RDD randomly selects telephone numbers, thereby avoiding the problems of telephone directories. The population is telephone numbers, not people with telephones. RDD is not difficult, but it takes time and can frustrate the person doing the calling.

In RDD, a researcher identifies active area codes and exchanges, then randomly selects four-digit numbers. One problem is that the researcher can select any number in an exchange. This means that some selected numbers are out of service, disconnected, that of a pay phone, or that of a business; only some numbers are what the researcher wants—working residential phone numbers. Until the researcher calls, it is not possible to know whether the number is a working residential number. This means spending a lot of time getting numbers that are disconnected, numbers of businesses, and so forth. Research organizations often use computers to select random digits and dial the phone automatically. This speeds the process, but a human must still listen and find out whether the number is a working residential one. Highlight 6.3 provides another important study relying on random-digit dialing.

You are now familiar with several major types of probability samples (see Summary Table 6.1) and supplementary techniques used with them (e.g., PPS, within household, and RDD) that may be appropriate. Next, we turn to determining a sample size for probability samples.

How Large Should a Sample Be?

How large does a sample have to be? The best answer is, it depends. It depends on the kind of data analysis the researcher plans, on how accurate the sample has to be for the researcher's purposes, and on population characteristics. As we have seen with Steve Randall's sexual coercion study, a large sample size alone does not guarantee a representative sample. A large sample without random sampling or with a poor sampling frame is less representative than a smaller one with random sampling and an excellent sampling frame.

The question of sample size can be addressed in two ways. One is to make assumptions about the population and use statistical equations about random sampling processes. The calculation of sample size by this method requires a statistical discussion that goes beyond the level of this text.[5] The researcher must make assumptions about the degree of confidence (or number of errors) that is acceptable and the degree of variation in the population.

A second method is a rule of thumb. Researchers use it because they rarely have the information required by the statistical method and because it gives sample sizes close to those of the statistical method. Rules of thumb are based on past experience with samples that have met the requirements of

SUMMARY TABLE 6.1	Types of Probability Samples
Type of Sample	**Technique**
Simple random	Create a sampling frame for all cases, and then select cases using a purely random process (e.g., random-number table or computer program).
Systematic	Create a sampling frame, calculate the sampling interval 1/k, choose a random starting place, and then take every 1/k case.
Stratified	Create a sampling frame for each of several categories of cases, draw a random sample from each category, and then combine the several samples.
Cluster	Create a sampling frame for larger cluster units, draw a random sample of the cluster units, create a sampling frame for cases within each selected cluster unit, then draw a random sample of cases, and so forth.

HIGHLIGHT 6.3

National Violence against Women Study Sampling

Documenting quantitatively the extent to which women in U.S. society are victims of sexual and physical violence would be an important yet daunting task (as found in Chapter 1, a good example of descriptive research). In 1995, the National Institute of Justice (NIJ) paired up with the Centers for Disease Control and Prevention (CDC) to provide funds to two researchers at the University of Denver—Patricia Tjaden and Nancy Thoennes (1998)—to conduct a national telephone survey. The research was conducted from November 1995 to May 1996. Although Tjaden and Thoennes designed the survey instrument, the actual data collection process was administered by the survey company they hired, Schulman, Ronca, and Bucuvalas, Inc. (SRBI).

Hiring a separate company is not that unusual, especially if the research necessitates large sample sizes. This study, referred to as the National Violence against Women (NVAW) survey, sampled both women and men, allowing for comparisons between women's and men's experiences with violent victimization. The authors described the sampling technique as follows:

> The sample was drawn using a random-digit dialing system targeting households with a telephone in the United States. The sample was administered by U.S. Census region. Within each region, a simple random sample of working residential "hundreds banks" of phone numbers was drawn. (A hundreds bank is the first eight digits of any 10-digit telephone number; e.g., 301–608–38xx.) A randomly generated two-digit number was appended to each randomly sampled hundreds bank to produce the full 10-digit, random-digit number. Separate banks of numbers were generated for male and female respondents. These random-digit numbers were called by SRBI interviewers from their central telephone facility, where nonworking and nonresidential numbers were screened out. Once a residential household was reached, eligible adults (i.e., women and men 18 years of age and older) in each household were identified. A total of 8,000 women and 8,005 men 18 years and older were interviewed using a computer-assisted telephone interviewing system. To determine the representativeness of the sample, select demographic characteristics of the NVAW Survey sample were compared with demographic characteristics of the general

population as measured by the U.S. Census Bureau's 1995 Current Population Survey of adult men and women. Sample weighting was considered to correct for possible biases introduced by the fact that some households had multiple phone lines and multiple eligibles, and for over- and under-representation of selected subgroups. Although there were some instances of over- and under-representation, the overall unweighted prevalence rates for rape, physical assault, and stalking were not significantly different from their respective weighted rates. As a result, sample weighting was not used in the analysis of the NVAW Survey data.

The researchers needed to survey such a large number of people to identify an adequate number of crime victims. Note also that the researchers were able to verify the reliability of their sample by comparing it to U.S. Census data. A few of the more significant findings uncovered in this landmark research include the following:

- 52 percent of surveyed women said they were physically assaulted as a child by an adult caretaker and/or as an adult by any type of perpetrator.
- 1.9 percent of surveyed women said they had been physically assaulted in the previous twelve months. Based on these estimates, approximately 1.9 million women are physically assaulted annually in the United States.
- 18 percent of women surveyed said they experienced a completed or attempted rape at some time in their life, and 0.3 percent said they experienced a completed or attempted rape in the previous twelve months. Of the women who reported being raped at some time in their lives, 22 percent were under twelve years old and 32 percent were twelve to seventeen years old when they were first raped.
- Women experience significantly more partner violence than men do: 25 percent of surveyed women, compared with 8 percent of surveyed men, said they were raped and/or physically assaulted by a current or former spouse, cohabiting partner, or date in their lifetime.
- 8 percent of surveyed women and 2 percent of surveyed men said they were stalked at some time in their life; 1 percent of surveyed women and 0.4 percent of surveyed men said they were stalked in the previous twelve months.

TABLE 6.2	Sample Size of a Random Sample for Different Populations with a 99 Percent Confidence Level	
Population Size	**Sample Size**	**Population in Sample (Percent)**
200	171	85.5
500	352	70.4
1,000	543	54.3
2,000	745	37.2
5,000	960	19.2
10,000	1,061	10.6
20,000	1,121	5.6
50,000	1,160	2.3
100,000	1,173	1.2

the statistical method. One principle of sample sizes is, the smaller the population, the bigger the **sampling ratio** has to be for an accurate sample (i.e., one with a high probability of yielding the same results as the entire population). Larger populations permit smaller sampling ratios for equally good samples. This is because as the population size grows, the returns in accuracy for sample size shrink.

For small populations (under 1,000), a researcher needs a large sampling ratio (about 30 percent). For example, a sample size of about 300 is required for a high degree of accuracy. For moderately large populations (10,000), a smaller sampling ratio (about 10 percent) is needed to be equally accurate, or a sample size of around 1,000. For large populations (over 150,000), smaller sampling ratios (1 percent) are possible, and samples of about 1,500 can be very accurate. To sample from very large populations (over 10 million), one can achieve accuracy using tiny sampling ratios (0.025 percent) or samples of about 2,500. The size of the population ceases to be relevant once the sampling ratio is very small, and samples of about 2,500 are as accurate for populations of 200 million as they are for 10 million. The exception to this is when studying rare phenomena in a population. The National Crime Victimization Study, for example, samples 10,000–40,000 households a year to obtain data about numerous types of crime. This is referred to as the analysis of data on subgroups. If we want to analyze subgroups in the population, we need a larger sample. The National Violence against Women Survey discussed in Highlight 6.3 is similar in nature.

A related principle is that for small samples, small increases in sample size produce big gains in accuracy. Equal increases in sample size produce more of an increase in accuracy for small samples as opposed to large samples. For example, an increase in sample size from 50 to 100 reduces errors from 7.1 percent to 2.1 percent, but an increase from 1,000 to 2,000 only decreases errors from 1.6 percent to 1.1 percent.[6] Table 6.2 illustrates the various sample sizes needed as compared to the population size.

A researcher's decision about the best sample size to study depends on three things: (1) the degree of accuracy required, (2) the degree of variability or diversity in the population, and (3) the number of different variables examined simultaneously in data analysis. Everything else being equal, larger samples are needed if one wants a high level of accuracy, if the population has a great deal of variability or heterogeneity, or if one wants to examine many variables in the data analysis simultaneously. Smaller samples are sufficient when less accuracy is acceptable, when the population is homogeneous, or when only a few variables are examined at a time.

SAMPLING RATIO

The number of cases in the sample divided by the number of cases in the population or the sampling frame, or the proportion of the population in a sample.

NONPROBABILITY SAMPLING

Qualitative research generally does not involve drawing representative samples from a huge number of cases. For qualitative researchers, "it is their relevance to the research topic rather than their representativeness which determines the way in which the people to be studied are selected"

NONRANDOM SAMPLES

A sample in which the sampling elements are selected using something other than a mathematically random process.

HAPHAZARD SAMPLING

A nonrandom sample in which the researcher selects anyone he or she happens to come across.

QUOTA SAMPLING

A nonrandom sample in which the researcher first identifies general categories into which cases or people will be selected, and then he or she selects cases to reach a predetermined number of cases in each category.

(Flick 1998: 41). Qualitative researchers tend to use nonprobability or **nonrandom samples.** Unlike quantitative research, which preplans a selection approach based on mathematical theory, the qualitative researcher selects cases gradually, oftentimes during the course of the research itself, with the relevance of a case determining whether it is chosen.

Haphazard or Convenience Sampling

Haphazard sampling can produce unproductive samples and is not recommended. It selects cases based purely on convenience. The person-on-the-street interview conducted by television programs is an example of a haphazard sample. Another is a student research project where they ask whoever they run into to fill out a survey instrument or answer a few questions. Such haphazard samples are easy and may have entertainment value, but they can give a distorted view and seriously misrepresent the population.

Quota Sampling

Quota sampling is a vast improvement over haphazard sampling.[7] In quota sampling, a researcher first identifies relevant categories of people (male and female; or under age thirty, ages thirty to sixty, over age sixty, etc.), then decides how many to place in each category. Thus, the number of people in various categories of the sample is fixed. For example, a researcher decides to select five males and five females under age thirty, ten males and ten females aged thirty to sixty, and five males and five females over age sixty for a forty-person sample. It is difficult to represent all population characteristics accurately (see Figure 6.4). Quota sampling ensures that some differences are included in the sample. Targeted street interviews with different indigenous Alaskan Natives would be a good example.

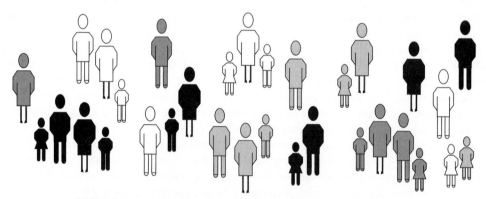

Of 32 adults and children in the street scene, select 10 for the sample:

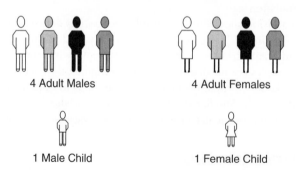

4 Adult Males   4 Adult Females

1 Male Child   1 Female Child

FIGURE 6.4 Quota Sampling. *Source:* From W. Lawrence Neuman, *Social Research Methods, Qualitative and Quantitative Approaches,* 6/e. Published by Allyn and Bacon, 75 Arlington St., Boston, MA 02116. Copyright © 2006 by Pearson Education. Reprinted by permission of the publisher.

A case from the history of sampling illustrates the limitations of quota sampling. George Gallup's American Institute of Public Opinion, using quota sampling, successfully predicted the outcomes of the 1936, 1940, and 1944 U.S. presidential elections. But in 1948, Gallup predicted the wrong candidate. The incorrect prediction had several causes (e.g., many voters were undecided, interviewing stopped early), but a major reason was that the quota categories did not accurately represent all geographical areas and all people who actually cast a vote.

Purposive or Judgmental Sampling

Purposive sampling is a valuable kind of sampling for special situations. It is used in exploratory research or in field research.[8] It uses the judgment of an expert in selecting cases or it selects cases with a specific purpose in mind. With purposive sampling, the researcher never knows whether the cases selected represent the population.

PURPOSIVE SAMPLING

A nonrandom sample in which the researcher uses a wide range of methods to locate all possible cases of a highly specific and difficult-to-reach population.

Purposive sampling is appropriate in selecting unique cases that are especially informative. For example, Richard Wright and Scott Decker targeted active armed robbers, Jeff Ferrell sampled graffiti artists, and Lonnie Athens selected his research subjects based on a history of committing serious violent crimes.

A researcher often uses purposive sampling, then, to select members of a difficult-to-reach, specialized population, such as prostitutes. It would be impossible to list all prostitutes and sample randomly from the list. Instead, subjective information (locations where prostitutes solicit, social groups with whom prostitutes associate, etc.) and experts (police who work on vice units, other prostitutes, etc.) identify a sample of prostitutes for inclusion in the research project. The researcher uses many different methods to identify the cases, because his or her goal is to locate as many relevant cases as possible.

Snowball Sampling

Crime and justice researchers are often interested in an interconnected network of people or organizations.[9] The network could be scientists around the world investigating global climate change, members of an organized crime family, or people on a college campus who have had sexual relations with each other. The crucial feature is that each person or unit is connected with another through a direct or indirect linkage. This does not mean that each person directly knows, interacts with, or is influenced by every other person in the network. Rather, taken as a whole, with direct and indirect links, most are within an interconnected web of linkages.

SNOWBALL SAMPLING

A nonrandom sample in which the researcher begins with one case, and then, based on information about interrelationships from that case, identifies other cases, and repeats the process again and again.

Snowball sampling, shown in Figure 6.5, is also called network, chain referral, or reputational sampling. It is a method for sampling (or selecting) the cases in a network. It is based on a snowball analogy: The sample begins small but becomes larger as it progresses down the "hill" of the research project. Snowball sampling, thus, is a multistage technique. It begins with one or a few people or cases and spreads out on the basis of links to the initial cases.

Ryan Bussard's research on illegal steroid trafficking is a good example (see Chapter 3). He started out his project with only one main informant and his sample snowballed the deeper he became involved in the project. He ended up with a sample of 20 different informants and 115 different steroid websites.

Deviant Case Sampling

DEVIANT CASE SAMPLING

A nonrandom sample, especially used by qualitative researchers, in which a researcher selects unusual or nonconforming cases purposely as a way to provide greater insight into social processes or a setting.

A researcher uses **deviant case sampling** (also called extreme case sampling) when he or she seeks cases that differ from the dominant pattern or that differ from the predominant characteristics of other cases. Similar to using purposive sampling, a researcher uses a variety of techniques to locate cases with specific characteristics. The goal is to locate a collection of unusual, different, or peculiar cases that are not representative of the whole. The cases are selected because they are unusual, and a researcher hopes to learn more about a phenomenon by considering cases that fall outside the general pattern or including what is beyond the main flow of events.

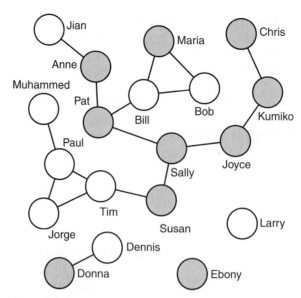

FIGURE 6.5   Snowball Sample—Steroid Informant Network.   *Source:* From W. Lawrence Neuman, *Social Research Methods, Qualitative and Quantitative Approaches,* 6/e. Published by Allyn and Bacon, 75 Arlington St., Boston, MA 02116. Copyright © 2006 by Pearson Education. Reprinted by permission of the publisher.

For example, a researcher is interested in studying juvenile crime. Of course, most juveniles who come to the attention of the juvenile justice system do poorly in school, come from low-income families, have unstable family backgrounds, and have a previous record of discipline problems. A researcher using deviant case sampling might seek juveniles who have committed a serious crime or crimes but who fall into the opposite profile: do well in school, come from a high-income family, have a stable family background, and have no record of previous discipline problems.

Sequential Sampling

SEQUENTIAL SAMPLING

A nonrandom sample in which a researcher tries to find as many relevant cases as possible, until time, financial resources, or his or her energy is exhausted, or until there is no new information or diversity from the cases.

Sequential sampling is similar to purposive sampling with one difference. In purposive sampling, the researcher tries to find as many relevant cases as possible. The principle is to get every possible case. In sequential sampling, a researcher continues to gather cases until the amount of new information or diversity of cases is filled. The principle is to gather cases until a saturation point is reached. In economic terms, information is gathered until the marginal utility, or incremental benefit for additional cases, levels off or drops significantly. It requires that a researcher continuously evaluate all the collected cases. For example, a researcher locates and plans in-depth interviews with sixty prisoners over seventy years old who have been institutionalized for thirty years or more. Depending on the researcher's purposes, getting an additional twenty prisoners, based on what they've learned from the sixty, would be unnecessary.

Theoretical Sampling

THEORETICAL SAMPLING

A nonrandom sample in which the researcher selects specific times, locations, or events to observe in order to develop a social theory or evaluate theoretical ideas.

In **theoretical sampling,** what is sampled (people, situations, events, time periods, etc.) comes from grounded theory. A growing theoretical interest guides the selection of sample cases. The researcher selects cases based on new insights they may provide. For example, a field researcher may be observing a site and group of people during weekdays. Theoretically, the researcher may question whether the people act the same at other times or other aspects of the site change. He or she could then sample other time periods (e.g., nights and weekends) to get a fuller picture and learn whether important conditions are the same.

Summary Table 6.2 reviews the various types of nonprobability sampling discussed.

SUMMARY TABLE 6.2	Types of Nonprobability Samples Discussed
Type of Sample	**Principle**
Haphazard	Get any cases in any manner that is convenient.
Quota	Get a preset number of cases in each of several predetermined categories that will reflect the diversity of the population, using haphazard methods.
Purposive	Get all possible cases that fit particular criteria, using various methods.
Snowball	Get cases using referrals from one or a few cases, and then referrals from those cases, and so forth.
Deviant case	Get cases that substantially differ from the dominant pattern (a special type of purposive sample).
Sequential	Get cases until there is no additional information or new characteristics (often used with other sampling methods).
Theoretical	Get cases that will help reveal features that are theoretically important about a particular setting/topic.

MIXED SAMPLING APPROACHES FOR HIDDEN POPULATIONS

In contrast to sampling the general population or visible and accessible people, sampling underground populations involves researching people who engage in clandestine or concealed activities, referred to as **hidden populations.** This is essential in crime and justice research where we study a host of criminal, deviant, underground, or highly sensitive situations.

Mixed sampling approaches illustrate the creative application of sampling principles, mixing qualitative and quantitative styles of research and combining probability with nonprobability techniques. Crime and justice studies has only limited experience using this approach but its potential usefulness to studying hidden crime, criminals, and crime victims should be obvious.

This approach was first developed in the area of AIDS research on the hidden populations of AIDS victims and illegal drug injectors. John Martin and Laura Dean (1993) sampled gay men from New York City. (Information regarding this is present in Martin and Dean's article "Bereavement Following Death from AIDS: Unique Problems, Reactions, and Special Needs," in their groundbreaking book, *Handbook of Bereavement,* which includes articles on the family survivors of crime victims, including those of the Holocaust.)

Martin and Dean started with a sampling frame that included men who lived in the city, were over age eighteen, were not diagnosed as having AIDS, and engaged in sex with other men. The authors began with a purposive sample using five diverse sources to recruit 291 respondents. They first contacted 150 New York City organizations with predominately homosexual or bisexual members. They next screened these down to ninety organizations that had eligible men for the study. From the ninety, they drew a stratified random sample of fifty-two organizations by membership size. They randomly selected five members from each of the organizations. Reports of Martin and Dean's study appeared in local news sources. This brought calls from which they got forty-one unsolicited volunteers. Another source of thirty-two men were referrals from respondents who had participated in a small pilot study. In addition, seventy-two men were identified at an annual New York City Gay Pride Parade. And fifteen eligible men were contacted at a New York City clinic and asked to participate.

They next used snowball sampling by asking each of the 291 respondents to give a recruitment packet to three gay male friends. Each friend who agreed to participate was also asked to give packets to three friends. This continued until it had gone five levels out from the initial 291 men. Eventually, 746 men were recruited into the study. Martin and Dean carefully compared their sample against two random samples of gay men in San Francisco, a random-digit dialing sample of 500, and a cluster sample of 823 using San Francisco census tracts. Their sample closely paralleled

HIDDEN POPULATIONS

A population of people who engage in clandestine, socially disapproved, or concealed activities and who are difficult to locate and study.

MIXED SAMPLING APPROACHES

An approach to sampling that involves mixing qualitative and quantitative styles of research and combining probability with nonprobability techniques.

those from San Francisco on race, age, and the percentage who were living an openly gay life. (Of course, it would have been much more robust to compare their sample to samples taken from New York City, but these data were not available to the researchers.)

Douglas Heckathorn (1997, 2002) used similar techniques in studying active illegal drug injectors in two small Connecticut cities and their surrounding areas. As of July 1996, 390 AIDS cases had been diagnosed in the towns; about half the cases involved illegal drug injection. The sampling was purposive in that each sampled case had to meet certain criteria. Heckathorn also used a modified snowball sampling with a dual reward system. He gave each person who completed an interview a monetary reward and a second monetary reward for recruiting a new respondent. The first person was asked not to introduce the new person to the researcher, at times referred to as masking (i.e., protecting friends). This gets around the "snitching" issue and "war on drugs" stigma, especially strong in the U.S. context. This modified snowball sampling is like sequential sampling in that, after a period of time, fewer and fewer new recruits are found, until the researcher comes to saturation or an equilibrium.

Heckathorn took significant steps to determine if the sample he collected using nonprobability sampling techniques was representative of the larger population under study. He found definitively in two separate analyses that these types of respondent-driven sampling techniques are capable of yielding a highly reliable sample.

A more recent study published in the *Journal of Drug Issues* used mixed sampling techniques to obtain data on 657 crack, powder cocaine, and heroin users and sellers that were hidden in the general population because they, for the most part, lived normal, working lives. The researchers found that using mixed nonprobability sampling techniques yielded a representative set of cases (Rees et al. 2004). Highlight 6.4 examines two additional examples of snowball sampling of hidden populations.

HIGHLIGHT 6.4

Two Classic Research Examples Using Snowball Sampling and Hidden Populations

Wright and colleagues (1996) provided a good example of a snowball sampling strategy. If you recall, their study attempted to contact active residential burglars in St. Louis, Missouri, to learn about the factors that go into targeting a house to burglarize. As they pointed out, "The most difficult aspect of using a snowball sampling technique is locating an initial contact or two" (p. 2). They solved the problem in this way:

> Fortunately, we were able to short-cut that process [i.e., frequenting known criminal hangouts] by hiring an ex-offender (who, despite committing hundreds of serious crimes, had few arrests and no felony convictions) with high status among several groups of black street criminals in St. Louis. This person retired from crime after being shot and paralyzed in a gangland-style execution attempt. He then attended a university and earned a bachelor's degree, but continued to live in his old neighborhood, remaining friendly, albeit superficially, with local criminals. We initially met him when he attended a colloquium in our department and disputed the speaker's characterization of street criminals. (pp. 2–3)

Sometimes a combination of snowball sampling and quota sampling can be used to shed light on complex criminological relationships. Consider the approach taken by Inciardi and colleagues (1996) in their research on the relationship of crime and crack cocaine:

> Selection of street and [drug] treatment respondents was guided by subsample quotas for gender, age, and ethnicity to ensure a demographically diverse sample. In the treatment programs, this generally meant returning repeatedly to interview every new client in the hard-to-fill subsamples (younger and white or Hispanic). On the street, subsample targets meant conducting the interview process in several selected neighborhoods to get the required race-ethnic diversity. Street respondents were located through standard multiple-starting-point "snowball sampling" techniques in the neighborhoods with high rates of cocaine use by street interviewers familiar with and well known in the target area. (pp. 61–62)

Conclusion

In this chapter, we learned about sampling. We learned about the types of sampling most often used in qualitative research. These techniques are not based on random processes and are therefore less concerned about scientific representativeness. Emphasis is placed instead on accurately capturing in close detail the phenomenon under study (recall Weber's notion of verstehen). Nonprobability sampling is essential because our objects of study often involve hidden and underground populations and phenomena. Understanding the subculture associated with police on-duty illegal drug use, for example, would require a careful selection of cases available to the researcher during the actual research process.

Quantitative research relies on probability sampling, which, if done correctly, produces a sample that represents the larger population under study. A researcher can in fact make probability statements about the chances that his or her findings represent true differences in the population under study or are due to sampling error. In addition to simple random sampling, we learned about systematic, stratified, and cluster sampling. The discussion of sampling error, the central limit theorem, and sample size demonstrated that random sampling can produce accurate and reliable findings.

This chapter also provided an initial and important example of moving beyond the quantitative versus qualitative mind-set and approaching the two as complementary. Mixing probability sampling and nonprobability sampling and then testing statistically whether the sample is representative of the larger population under study is a valuable technique for studying difficult or hidden populations in a reliable manner.

Before moving on to the next chapter, it may be useful to restate a fundamental principle of crime and justice research: In the real world of research, the steps are not as compartmentalized as we've presented them here. It is important to recognize the interconnections between the steps. Research design, ethical deliberation, learning from the literature, measurement, sampling, and specific research techniques are interdependent. Unfortunately, the constraints of presenting information in a textbook necessitate presenting the parts separately, in sequence. In practice, researchers think about data collection when they design research, peruse the literature, and develop measures for variables. Likewise, sampling issues influence research design, measurement of variables, and data collection strategies. As you will see in future chapters, quality research depends on simultaneously controlling quality at several different steps—research design, conceptualization, measurement, sampling, and data collection and handling. As we have unfortunately experienced firsthand, and as this chapter highlighted at the outset with the example of on-campus sexual violence, making an error in measurement or sampling can render an entire research project far less valuable, if not downright insignificant.

Key Terms

sampling *129*	simple random sample *132*	probability proportionate to size (PPS) *137*	purposive sampling *142*
sampling case *130*	sampling distribution *132*		snowball sampling *142*
population *130*	central limit theorem *132*	random-digit dialing (RDD) *137*	deviant case sampling *142*
target population *130*	confidence intervals *133*		sequential sampling *143*
sampling frame *130*	systematic sampling *134*	sampling ratio *140*	theoretical sampling *143*
population parameter *130*	sampling interval *134*	nonrandom samples *141*	hidden populations *144*
random samples *131*	stratified sampling *134*	haphazard sampling *141*	mixed sampling approaches *144*
sampling error *131*	cluster sampling *136*	quota sampling *141*	

Review Questions

1. What is probability sampling and why is it essential to quantitative research?
2. What is a sampling frame and population parameter and why are they important?
3. How do we conduct a simple random sample?
4. What is the logic behind stratified and probability proportionate to size sampling?
5. What is the population in random-digit dialing? Are sampling frame problems avoided? Explain.
6. How do researchers decide how large a sample to use?
7. How are the logic of sampling and the logic of measurement related?
8. List the seven types of nonprobability sampling techniques and give an example of each.
9. Why is snowball sampling an important technique for the qualitative researcher?
10. Explain how mixed sampling approaches can help in researching hidden populations.

Practicing Research

1. Assign each person in your class a number. Using the random numbers table in the back of this text, draw a random sample of ten classmates (assuming the class size is thirty or greater).
   a. What is the average height of the ten people in your sample?
   b. What is the average age of the people in your sample?
   c. Compare the two averages obtained from these samples with the actual population's average height and age (this will require you to calculate these two averages for the entire class).
   d. What was the sampling error for your simple random sample?
2. Locate and select two quantitative and two qualitative research articles found in crime and justice journals (you could select the sample police burnout article found in the last chapter's exercise). Describe the sampling techniques. Do the researchers use the same labels for the type of sample used in this text? Do they concede any limitations to their sampling technique?

What could they have done differently to strengthen their samples (remembering that qualitative and quantitative research are operating from different standards)?

3. The beginning of the chapter discusses the research topic, fear of crime. Using the purposive sampling technique, locate a sample of people who will answer a few simple questions you construct about their perceptions of fear of crime (relatives, fellow students, and people at a store). The purpose here is to gather qualitative data from a purposive sample—so the questions do not have to be formally presented, and the format might work better if conducted as an informal interview. Report your findings.
4. Think about whether you personally would have access to a "hidden population" engaged in some sort of deviant and/or criminal activity. Imagine how you might research these people and their activity, speculating specifically about various non-probability sampling techniques. (Think also about how you might present this idea as a research proposal to an IRB.)

Notes for Further Study

1. Stratified sampling techniques are discussed in more detail in Frankel (1983: 37–46), Kalton (1983: 19–28), Mendenhall and associates (1971: 53–88), Sudman (1976a: 107–130), and Williams (1978: 162–175).
2. Cluster sampling is discussed in Frankel (1983: 47–57), Kalton (1983: 28–38), Kish (1965), Mendenhall and associates (1971: 121–141, 171–183), Sudman (1976a: 69–84), and Williams (1978: 144–161).
3. For a discussion, see Frankel (1983: 57–62), Kalton (1983: 38–47), Sudman (1976a: 131–170), and Williams (1978: 239–241).
4. For more on random-digit dialing issues, see Dillman (1978: 238–242), Frey (1983: 69–77), Glasser and Metzger (1972), Groves and Kahn (1979: 20–21, 45–63), Kalton (1983: 86–90), and Waksberg (1978). Kviz (1984) reported that telephone directories can produce relatively accurate sampling frames in rural areas, at least for mail questionnaire surveys. Also see Keeter (1995).
5. See Kraemer and Thiemann (1987) for a technical discussion of selecting a sample size.
6. See Sudman (1976a: 99).
7. Quota sampling is discussed in Babbie (1998: 196), Kalton (1983: 91–93), and Sudman (1976a: 191–200).
8. For further discussion on purposive sampling, see Babbie (1998: 195), Grosof and Sardy (1985: 172–173), and Singleton and associates (1988: 153–154, 306). Bailey (1987: 94–95) describes "dimensional" sampling, which is a variation of purposive sampling.
9. For additional discussion of snowball sampling, see Babbie (1998: 194–196), Bailey (1987: 97), and Sudman (1976a: 210–211). Also see Bailey (1987: 366–367), Dooley (1984: 86–87), Kidder and Judd (1986: 240–241), Lindzey and Byrne (1968: 452–525), and Singleton and associates (1988: 372–373) for discussions of sociometry and sociograms. Network sampling issues are discussed in Galaskiewicz (1985), Granovetter (1976), and Hoffmann-Lange (1987).

PART THREE

Quantitative Data Collection and Analysis

The first part of this book provided a big picture roadmap examining some basic and fundamental precursors to understanding crime and justice research methods. We examined what we study, who conducts research, the relationship between theory and research, the effect of politics on research, and the philosophical ideas and concepts that underpin the varying approaches to knowledge production. The second part built on the first by examining the elements involved in planning and preparing to conduct research. We examined the ethics of research and how to focus our topic into a workable research project, think through ethical implications, operationalize and measure our variables, and use various sampling techniques.

We're now prepared to examine several specific quantitative data-gathering techniques. These include experiments, surveys/interviews, and nonreactive methods. Each method for collecting data is reviewed in detail, along with real-life examples of research relevant to both theory and criminal justice practice. We begin with experimental research. It is the easiest to grasp, it is used across many fields of science, and it is the most pure in terms of positivist social science standards. Chapter 8 examines survey and interview research in depth. Highlights in the chapter include the dos and don'ts of writing survey questions, how to design a quality questionnaire, methods used to enhance response rates, and the difficulties and possibilities in conducting interview research. Chapter 9 examines what we call nonreactive methods; these were overviewed in Chapter 1 as content analysis and existing documents/statistics research. If you remember, each of these methods was discussed in Chapter 1 with specific examples. These included:

- **Experiments:** Cambridge-Somerville Youth Study and Domestic Violence Mandatory Arrest
- **Surveys/Interviews:** Criminal Justice Major Anti-Gay Attitude; Police Militarization; Darfur Genocide
- **Existing Documents/Statistics:** International Incarceration Rates and Self-Protection against Crime
- **Content Analysis:** Media Presentation of Crime; Rap Music Lyrics

Chapter 10 looks at what we do with the data collected using these techniques. We review both how to manage our data and produce credible statistics.

Although these chapters focus only on quantitative methods, we point out when appropriate where qualitative approaches are relevant and complementary. These chapters should further demonstrate the richness of ideas and substantive research being conducted, as well as the importance of cultivating our critical thinking skills. Just a sampling of topics includes the following:

- the effectiveness of correctional boot camps
- explaining the 1990s crime drop
- 1,000 years of global warming data
- Head Start programs as crime control
- proactive police approaches to lowering crime
- homeland security
- homeless street youth
- death toll in war time
- dual arrest in domestic violence cases
- gangs and police gang units
- shoplifters caught on camera
- poverty, unemployment, and crime
- racial assault with a baseball

7

Experimental and Quasi-Experimental Crime and Justice Research

The Experiment as the "Gold Standard"

A History of the Experiment in Social Science Research

Experimental Research in Crime and Justice Studies

Choosing an Experiment: Factors to Consider

The Importance of Random Assignment
  How to Randomly Assign
  Matching versus Random Assignment

Experimental Design Logic
  The Language of Experiments
    Parts of the Experiment
    Steps in Conducting an Experiment
    Staying in Control

Types of Design
  Classical Experimental Design
  Other Experimental Designs
    Two-Group Posttest-Only Design
    Latin Square Design
    Solomon Four-Group Design
    Factorial Designs
  Preexperimental or Weak Experimental Designs
    One-Shot Case-Study Design
    One-Group Pretest-Posttest Design
  Quasi-Experimental Designs
    Interrupted Time Series
    Equivalent Time Series
  Highlight 7.1 Unraveling the Mystery of the Crime Drop

Internal and External Validity
  The Logic of Internal Validity

Threats to Internal Validity
  Selection Bias
  History
  Maturation
  Testing
  Instrumentation
  Experimental Mortality
  Statistical Regression
  Diffusion of Treatment or Contamination
  Compensatory Behavior
  Experimenter Expectancy
External Validity
  Population Validity
  Reactivity

Practical Considerations
  Planning and Pilot Tests
  Instructions to Subjects
  Upholding Treatment Integrity
  Postexperiment Interview

Meta-Analysis of Experiments
  Highlight 7.2 Straightening Out Offenders: A Meta-Analysis of Military-Style Boot Camps

Beware of Naïvete

Conclusion

Key Terms

Review Questions

Practicing Research

Notes for Further Study

Crime and criminal justice researchers have conducted large-scale experiments in an effort to determine what types of patrol work will impact the crime problem.

THE EXPERIMENT AS THE "GOLD STANDARD"

In October 1972 the Kansas City Police Department administered what has become one of the most well-known experiments in crime and justice research. It sought to determine whether the backbone of modern policing—preventative patrol—actually had a preventative effect on crime. As we discussed in Chapter 1, the study showed no significant differences between routine patrol work and intensified preventative patrol. The study had an enormous impact on the thinking of police academics and reformers—although the extent to which it actually modified police practices remains unclear. Many concluded simplistically from this single study that the police couldn't lower crime rates.

More than thirty years later, a few determined academics are attempting to test more carefully the same overall research question. David Weisburd and Lawerence Sherman in particular have led the field, conducting large-scale experiments on the impact police activities can have on crime. Two areas of study have managed to seriously question conventional thinking about police and crime: (1) hot spot policing, and (2) police control of illegal guns.[1] Weisburd, Sherman, and others have conducted numerous randomized field experiments in these two areas—almost all of which have shown the police capable, at least to some extent, of positively affecting the crime problem. Once again, experimental research is having a significant impact on crime control thinking and policies. (One should not assume that this means the police are necessarily capable of significantly reducing crime rates; this question is still being hotly debated.)

The experiment represents what David Farrington (2003) calls the "gold standard" of scientific quantitative research. Its goal is to determine cause and effect relationships. In general, it involves randomly dividing research subjects into a treatment group, which receives a treatment, and a **control group,** which receives no treatment. After the treatment has been applied, the researcher measures the extent to which the treatment had an effect on the treatment group (referred to as the **experimental group**) as compared to the control group. Statistically significant differences indicate that the treatment caused changes in the experimental group. Previous chapters have discussed numerous examples of the experimental method of data collection, including the Cambridge-Somerville youth experiment, correctional rehabilitation experiments, mandatory arrest for domestic violence experiments, D.A.R.E. evaluation experiments, Kansas City patrol experiment, Milgram experiment, and British police surveillance system experiments.

Experimental research embodies the principles of a PSS approach more directly than any other research technique.[2] It attempts to test the causal relationships between variables as stated in hypotheses. If you recall from Chapters 3 and 5, determining causality, the apex goal of PSS, is difficult and easily confusing. To make a **causal inference** from an experiment, we must meet the same requirements that are needed for any causal relationship: (1) cause must precede effect; (2) there must be an association between cause and effect; and (3) plausible alternatives must be eliminated. Establishing these requirements is fraught with difficulties. Most PSS-oriented researchers believe experimental research is best suited for the task because it allows for the direct testing and control for all three.

A HISTORY OF THE EXPERIMENT IN SOCIAL SCIENCE RESEARCH

We've discussed in Chapters 2 and 3 the rise of the scientific method for studying the natural world. In the social sciences, the experimental method began in psychology. It was not widely accepted in psychology, though, until after 1900. Wilhelm M. Wundt (1832–1920), a German

CONTROL GROUP

The group that does not get the treatment in experimental research.

EXPERIMENTAL GROUP

The group that receives the treatment in experimental research.

CAUSAL INFERENCE

To make a causal inference from an experiment, we must meet the same requirements that are needed for any causal relationship: (1) cause must precede effect, (2) there must be an association between cause and effect, and (3) the researcher must eliminate plausible alternatives.

psychologist and physiologist, introduced it during the late 1800s, establishing a laboratory for experimentation in psychology that became a model for many other social researchers. By 1900, researchers at many universities in the United States and elsewhere established psychology laboratories to conduct experimental social science research. Conducting scientific experiments displaced a more philosophical and introspective approach that was closer to interpretive social science (ISS). For example, William James (1842–1910), the foremost U.S. philosopher and psychologist of the 1890s, did not use or embrace the experimental method.

From the turn of the century to the time of World War II, the experimental method was refined and secured its place in the social sciences. The method's appeal was that it promised an objective, unbiased, scientific way to study human mental and social life at a time when the scientific study of social life was just gaining acceptance. Three trends helped speed the expansion of the experimental method in this period: the rise of behaviorism, the spread of quantification, and practical applications.

- Behaviorism is a school of psychology founded in the 1920s by the American John B. Watson (1878–1958) and extended by B. F. Skinner (1904–1990). It emphasized measuring observable behavior or outcomes of mental life and advocated the experimental method for conducting rigorous empirical tests of hypotheses.
- Quantification, or measuring social phenomena with numbers, also became popular between 1900 and 1940. Researchers reconceptualized social and psychological constructs so that they could be quantified, and other constructs (e.g., spirit, consciousness, will) were jettisoned from empirical research. An example is measuring mental ability by the IQ test. Originally developed by Alfred Binet (1857–1911), a Frenchman, the intelligence test was translated into English and revised by 1916. It was widely used, and the ability to express something as subjective as mental ability in a single score had public appeal as an objective way to rank and sort people.[3]
- People increasingly used experimental methods for solving real-world problems (applied research). Intelligence tests were adopted by the U.S. Army, for example, during World War I to sort thousands of men into different positions. The leader of the scientific management movement, Frederick W. Taylor (1856–1915), advocated the use of the experimental method in factories and worked with management to modify factory conditions to increase worker productivity.

Through the 1950s and 1960s, researchers continued to use the experimental method. They became concerned with sources of alternative explanations that could slip into experimental design. They created ways to reduce these possible sources of systematic error in experiments with new research designs and statistical procedures. Experiments became more logically rigorous, and, by the 1970s, methodological criteria were increasingly used to evaluate research. Experiments are highly repeated in the social sciences because of its logical rigor and simplicity and consistency with PSS assumptions.

EXPERIMENTAL RESEARCH IN CRIME AND JUSTICE STUDIES

In most social science disciplines, then, experiments are seen as the most credible method for developing and quantitatively testing theory. Recall that the PSS approach's ultimate purpose is scientific explanation—to discover and document universal causal laws of human and social behavior. Crime and justice research, though, attempts simultaneously to pursue this more traditional purpose as well as to develop a body of work that instructs us as how to best solve problems—referred to in Chapter 1 as applied and evaluation research. Experiments, in fact, are generally geared more toward evaluating the effectiveness of criminal justice and crime control practices than toward developing causal laws, although, as we discussed in Chapter 2, these goals sometimes overlap. (Of course, it is important to keep in mind that whenever we attempt to study cause and effect relationships, even if our objective is purely evaluative, our inquiry is still unavoidably explanatory.)

You might also recall that experimental research is fairly uncommon in our field. As Weisburd states, "Randomized experiments are noted more for their rarity than for the substantive importance in research and practice in criminology" (Weisburd 2000: 181). Some academics have bemoaned this fact and have been quite insistent that for our field to become more scientifically credible, we need to conduct more experiments (Farrington 2003; Sherman 2003; Weisburd 2000). They also see experimental research as essential in the development of evidence-based practical knowledge, such as might be found in medicine. Their influence, along with a more general trend toward developing more rigorous methods, has helped convince the National Institute of Justice and other state funding organizations to finance a small number of large-scale true experimental studies over the last twenty years.

Topics addressed by this new wave of large-scale experimental studies include the following:

- mandatory arrest for domestic violence
- the effectiveness of early childhood intervention in preventing future criminality
- the effectiveness of drug education programs such as D.A.R.E.
- the effectiveness of "hot spot" and problem-oriented policing
- the effectiveness of various types of community policing initiatives
- the effectiveness of intervention programs for juvenile offenders
- the effectiveness of rehabilitation programs for adult offenders
- the effectiveness of correctional boot camps
- the effectiveness of the Head Start program as a crime prevention technique

Notice again that these studies focus on evaluative research questions, or what some refer to as "what works scholarship." Due to the necessity of directly intervening in the operations of the criminal justice system, these studies usually require a high level of cooperation and collaboration from the practitioner community—after all, it is generally the practitioners who are responsible for implementing the treatment.

CHOOSING AN EXPERIMENT: FACTORS TO CONSIDER

The experiment is a powerful way to focus sharply on causal relations; it closely fits the canons of positivist science; and it has potential practical benefits in developing the best evidence-based practices. It also has its limitations. Let's consider the factors in deciding for or against using the experiment as a data-collection technique.

Ethical factors are perhaps the most often cited limitation of experiments in crime and justice research (Weisburd 2000). It is often unethical to manipulate many areas of criminal justice, crime, and juvenile delinquency for research purposes. The logic of an experiment has an experimenter induce a change in some focused part of social life, and then examine the consequences that result from the change or intervention. This means that the experiment is limited to research questions in which a researcher is able to practically manipulate conditions. It also means that applying a treatment or withholding one could be unethical. Remember the D.A.R.E. experiment, in which some students received D.A.R.E. education and others didn't? Imagine if D.A.R.E. had a large impact on subsequent drug use and the control group ended up with a much higher percentage of teens addicted to illegal drugs. Table 7.1 presents a list of things to consider when trying to determine the feasibility of conducting experiments in criminal justice settings. These nuggets of wisdom were developed by David Weisburd, drawing from decades of experience conducting experiments in real-world situations.

Experiments encourage researchers to isolate and target the impact that arises, usually from one causal variable. This strength in demonstrating causal effects is also a limitation in situations in which numerous causal variables are in operation simultaneously. The experiment is rarely appropriate for research questions or issues that require a researcher to examine the impact of dozens of diverse variables all together. Rarely do experiments permit assessing conditions across a wide range of complex settings or numerous settings all at the same time. Accumulated

TABLE 7.1	Eight Principles for Assessing Feasibility of Crime and Justice Experiments

1. When interventions involve the addition of resources, there are generally fewer ethical barriers.
2. There are fewer objections to experiments that test sanctions that are more lenient than existing criminal law penalties.
3. Experiments with lower public visibility will be easier to implement.
4. In cases in which treatment cannot be given to all eligible subjects, there is likely to be less resistance if random allocation is used. Applying treatments to groups of subjects through randomized cluster sampling based on a geographical location, as opposed to some individuals receiving treatment and others not, seems to lessen ethical concerns.
5. Randomized experiments are easier to develop if the subjects of intervention represent less serious threats to community safety (e.g., burglars vs. prostitutes).
6. Experimentation will be more difficult to implement when researchers try to limit the discretion of criminal justice agents who traditionally act with significant autonomy and authority.
7. It will be easier to develop randomized experiments in settings in which there is a high degree of hierarchical control.
8. When treatments are complex, involving multiple actions on the part of criminal justice agents, experiments can become prohibitively cumbersome and expensive and accordingly less feasible to develop.

Source: Adapted from David Weisburd (2000), Randomized experiments in criminal justice policy: Prospects and problems. *Crime and Delinquency*, 46(2): 191.

knowledge from many individual experiments, each focused on one or two variables, may advance understanding, yet the experiment is not appropriate for examining how numerous variables operate simultaneously.

THE IMPORTANCE OF RANDOM ASSIGNMENT

The act of randomly assigning research subjects to different groups is the defining feature of a true experiment. **Random assignment,** shown in Figure 7.1, is a method for assigning cases (e.g., individuals, organizations) to study groups for the purpose of making comparisons. It is a way to divide a collection of cases into two or more groups to increase one's confidence that:

1. the groups do not differ in a systematic way,
2. unknown, extraneous variables are controlled for, and
3. statistical techniques and reasoning that relies on randomization are used.

RANDOM ASSIGNMENT

Dividing subjects into groups at the beginning of experimental research using a random process, so the experimenter can treat the groups as equivalent.

It is a mechanical method determined through mathematics; the assignment is automatic, and the researcher cannot make assignments on the basis of personal preference or the features of specific cases.

Random assignment is random in the same sense we used it in the previous chapter on sampling: *Random* describes a process in which each case has an equal chance of being selected. Random selection lets a researcher calculate the odds that a specific case will be sorted into one group over another. A random process is one in which all cases have an exactly equal chance of ending up in one or the other group. The wonderful thing about a random process is that over many separate random occurrences, predictable things happen.

Random assignment controls for bias so that a desire to confirm a hypothesis or a research subject's personal interests do not enter into the selection process. Because the probability of selecting a case can be mathematically determined, the groups should be, within a probability range anyway, identical.

Random Assignment

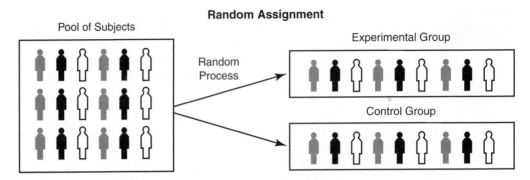

Random Sampling

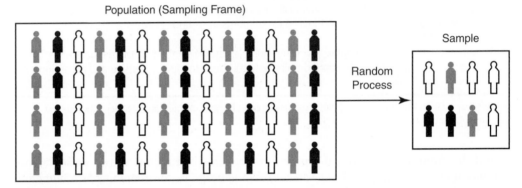

FIGURE 7.1 Random Assignment and Random Sampling. *Source:* From W. Lawrence Neuman, *Social Research Methods, Qualitative and Quantitative Approaches,* 6/e. Published by Allyn and Bacon, 75 Arlington St., Boston, MA 02116. Copyright © 2006 by Pearson Education. Reprinted by permission of the publisher.

How to Randomly Assign

Random assignment is quite simple to carry out. A researcher begins with a collection of cases (criminal justice agencies, juveniles, women, or whatever the unit of analysis is), and then divides them into two or more groups by a random process, such as asking people to count off, tossing a coin, or throwing dice. For example, a researcher wants to divide thirty-two people into two groups of sixteen. A simple random method is writing each person's name on a slip of paper, putting the slips in a hat, mixing the slips with eyes closed, and then drawing the first sixteen names for Group 1 and the second sixteen for Group 2. For larger experiments, group assignment is done with the assistance of a computer.

A specific situation can be unusual and the groups can differ. For example, it is possible, though extremely unlikely, that all cases with one characteristic will end up in one group (see the example in Figure 7.2).

Matching versus Random Assignment

If the purpose of random assignment is to get two (or more) equivalent groups, would it not be simpler to match the characteristics of cases in each group? Sometimes random assignment is not possible, and researchers opt instead to match cases in groups on certain characteristics, such as age and sex. **Matching** is an alternative to random assignment. It is a technique to control for certain variables. If a researcher wanted to study the effect of nutrition on educational testing performance among a group of prison inmates, he or she might want to control for the variable of IQ.

MATCHING

Used as an alternative to random assignment as a technique to control for certain variables.

Step 1: Begin with a collection of subjects.

Step 2: Devise a method to randomize that is purely mechanical (e.g., flip a coin).

Step 3: Assign subjects with "Heads" to one group   and "Tails" to the other group.

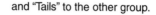

Control Group   **Experimental Group**

FIGURE 7.2   How to Randomly Assign.   *Source:* From W. Lawrence Neuman, *Social Research Methods, Qualitative and Quantitative Approaches,* 6/e. Published by Allyn and Bacon, 75 Arlington St., Boston, MA 02116. Copyright © 2006 by Pearson Education. Reprinted by permission of the publisher.

Matching the control and experimental group based on IQ levels would control for the variable influence of intelligence and better isolate the effect of nutrition.

Matching, however, presents a problem: What are the relevant characteristics to match on, and can one locate exact matches? Obviously, attempting to match groups based on all the potential variables in need of controlling would not be feasible. Generally, matching should only be attempted when random assignment is not possible.

EXPERIMENTAL DESIGN LOGIC

The Language of Experiments

We have already introduced you to numerous concepts used in experimental research design— control group, experimental group, treatment, research subjects, and randomization. Let's now examine these in more depth and see how they are used.

PARTS OF THE EXPERIMENT.   The experiment generally has seven parts. Not all experiments have all these parts, and some have all seven parts plus others.

- Treatment or independent variable
- Dependent variable
- **Pretest**
- **Posttest**
- Experimental group
- Control group
- Random assignment

PRETEST

Measurement of the dependent variable of an experiment prior to the treatment.

POSTTEST

Measurement of the dependent variable of an experiment after the treatment.

In most experiments, a researcher manipulates a situation to measure its effects. The *treatment* (or the stimulus or manipulation) is what the researcher modifies. The term is derived from medicine, in which a physician administers a treatment to patients; the physician intervenes in a physical or psychological condition to change it (the treatment of an aspirin given to affect a headache). It is the independent variable or a combination of independent variables. If a researcher wanted to study the impact fear of crime has on punitive attitudes, a researcher would first measure fear of crime (independent variable) and punitive attitudes (dependent variable). Instead of asking subjects whether they are fearful, such as we discussed in Chapter 6 on measurement, experimenters would put their subjects into either a high-fear or a low-fear situation (showing them a crime victimization video, for example) and then measure its impact on people's level of punitiveness (dependent variable).

TREATMENTS

What the independent variable in experimental research is often called.

Researchers go to great lengths to create **treatments** and uphold what they call the integrity of their treatments. Some treatments are as minor as giving different groups of subjects different instructions. Others can be as complex as staging contrived social situations or the implementation of a major new policy (mandatory arrest of domestic partner abusers). Researchers want the treatment to have an impact and produce specific reactions, feelings, or behaviors. Upholding treatment integrity means that the researcher constantly monitors the implementation of the treatment to ensure a consistent and robust treatment effect.

For example, several studies have been conducted on the effect of spouse-batterer intervention programs (independent variable) on convicted men's battering behavior (dependent variable) (Jackson et al. 2003). These studies have randomly assigned a group of batterers to either an experimental group that receives some sort of intervention program treatment or to a control group that does not. The findings have not been consistent: Some programs show a positive independent variable effect, whereas others show no effect. The researchers cite the extent to which the treatment was effectively administered—**treatment integrity**—as one likely reason for the differences in findings.

TREATMENT INTEGRITY

Upholding treatment integrity means that the researcher constantly monitors the implementation of the treatment to ensure a consistent and robust treatment effect.

Dependent variables or outcomes in experimental research are the physical conditions, social behaviors, attitudes, feelings, actions, or beliefs of subjects that change in response to a treatment. Most researchers try to triangulate their measure of the dependent variable (Chapter 5). For example, in one of the batterer experiments, over a twelve-month period the researchers measured the efficacy of the program by collecting information from offender's self-reports, victim's reports and interviews, and official measures of rearrest. They attempted to maximize measurement validity through multiple measures of their dependent variable. In addition, they measured the dependent variable multiple times over a twelve-month period.

STEPS IN CONDUCTING AN EXPERIMENT.   Unlike numerous other methods discussed in this book, the steps in conducting an experiment require a rigid sequential protocol that allows for little flexibility. These steps are as follows:

1. Begin with a straightforward hypothesis that is appropriate for experimental research.
2. Decide on an experimental design that will test the hypothesis within practical limitations.
3. Decide how to introduce the treatment or create a situation that induces the independent variable.
4. Develop a valid and reliable measure of the dependent variable.
5. Set up an experimental setting and conduct a pilot test of the treatment and dependent variable measures.
6. Locate appropriate subjects or cases.
7. Randomly assign subjects to groups (if random assignment is used in the chosen research design) and give careful instructions.
8. Gather data for the **pretest** measure of the dependent variable for all groups (if a pretest is used in the chosen design).
9. Introduce the **treatment** to the experimental group only (or to relevant groups if there are multiple experimental groups) and monitor all groups.
10. Gather data for posttest measure of the dependent variable.
11. Debrief the subjects by informing them of the true purpose and reasons for the experiment. Ask subjects what they thought was occurring. Debriefing is crucial when subjects have been deceived about some aspect of the experiment.
12. Examine data collected and make comparisons between different groups. Where appropriate, use statistics and graphs to determine whether the hypothesis is supported.

STAYING IN CONTROL. Control is crucial in experimental research.[4] A researcher wants to control all aspects of the experimental situation to isolate the effects of the treatment and eliminate alternative explanations. Aspects of an experimental situation that are not controlled by the researcher are alternatives to the treatment for change in the dependent variable and potentially undermine attempts to establish causality.

Experimental researchers sometimes use deception to control the experimental setting. **Deception** is when the researcher intentionally misleads subjects through written or verbal instructions, the actions of others, or aspects of the setting. It may involve the use of confederates or stooges—people who pretend to be other subjects or bystanders but who actually work for the researcher and deliberately mislead subjects. Through deception, the researcher tries to control what the subjects see and hear and what they believe is occurring. For example, in the Milgram experiments discussed in Chapter 4, the researchers misled the research subjects into thinking that they were actually punishing people through electrical shocks for not answering questions correctly. Most psychological experiments require some sort of deception because researchers don't want subjects to anticipate their hypotheses, thereby altering responses and behaviors.

DECEPTION

An experimenter lies to subjects about the true nature of an experiment or creates a false impression through his or her actions or the setting.

TYPES OF DESIGN

When designing an experiment, the researcher combines some selection of its various parts into a coherent study (e.g., pretests, control groups). Some designs lack pretests, some do not have control groups, and others have many experimental groups. As we'll review, certain widely accepted designs have specific names. The standard designs reviewed below are listed by name in research reports.

Classical Experimental Design

All experimental designs are variations of the **classical experimental design**—the type of design discussed so far—which has random assignment, a pretest and a posttest, an experimental group, and a control group.

CLASSICAL EXPERIMENTAL DESIGN

An experimental design that has random assignment, a control group, an experimental group, and a pretest and posttest for each group.

Lane et al. (2005), in the journal *Crime and Delinquency*, present an experiment on the effect that an intensive supervision juvenile probation program would have on juvenile probationers. The intensive probation program provides a much higher level of supervision, attention, and services than does regular probation. The study took place in fourteen counties in California and involved 539 high-risk youth—264 randomly assigned to the treatment group and 275 randomly assigned to the control group. Their pretest involved measuring the probationer's attitudes and difficulties with the law; the posttest reexamined their attitudes and remeasured their difficulties with the law (probation violations, arrests, etc.). The researchers found no significant differences between the two groups on all posttest measures. For example, 51 percent of the experimental group was arrested during the intervention period and 52 percent of the control group was arrested.

Zhang and Zhang (2005) also examined an intensive supervision program targeted at juveniles known as the Los Angeles County Repeat Offender Prevention Program (ROPP). This was a three-year program that compared 204 juvenile repeat offenders, with 106 randomly assigned to the ROPP program, and 98 receiving the same level of supervision and services as normal. The researchers found that the ROPP program significantly improved the experimental group's school performance (a noteworthy accomplishment); however, it had little overall impact on difficulties with the juvenile justice system. The authors note that the bulk of research on intensive supervision finds that it fails to produce measurable effects on subsequent criminal behavior. They question whether the integrity of the treatment used in this study was maintained consistently throughout the program.

TWO-GROUP POSTTEST-ONLY DESIGN

An experimental design that has all the parts of the classical design except a pretest. The groups are randomly assigned, reducing the chance that they differed before the treatment; but without a pretest, a researcher cannot be as certain that the groups began the same on the dependent variable.

Other Experimental Designs

TWO-GROUP POSTTEST-ONLY DESIGN. **Two-group posttest-only design** has all the parts of the classical design except a pretest. The random assignment reduces the chance that the groups differed before the treatment, but, without a pretest, a researcher cannot be as certain that the groups began the same on the dependent variable. Applied to our scared straight example on page 159, the researcher would measure differences between the groups after the application of the treatment (assuming the groups were similar), but would not use a pretest to establish baseline data from which to compare the groups.

LATIN SQUARE DESIGN

An experimental design used to examine whether the order or sequence in which subjects receive multiple versions of the treatment has an effect.

LATIN SQUARE DESIGN.   Researchers interested in how several treatments given in different sequences or time orders affect a dependent variable can use a **Latin square design.** For example, a criminology instructor has three learning modules to help teach students about crime mapping: one on map reading, another on using a compass, and a third on the longitude/latitude (LL) system. The modules can be taught in any order, but the teacher wants to know which order best helps students learn. In one class, students first learn to read maps, then how to use a compass, then the LL system. In another class, using a compass comes first, then map reading, then the LL system. In a third class, the instructor first teaches the LL system, then teaches compass usage, and ends with map reading. The teacher gives tests after each unit, and students take a comprehensive exam at the end of the term. The students were randomly assigned to classes, so the instructor can see whether presenting units in one sequence or another resulted in improved learning.

SOLOMON FOUR-GROUP DESIGN

An experimental design in which subjects are randomly assigned to two control groups and two experimental groups. Only one experimental group and one control group receive a pretest. All four groups receive a posttest.

SOLOMON FOUR-GROUP DESIGN.   A researcher may believe that the pretest measure has an influence on the treatment or dependent variable. A pretest can sometimes sensitize subjects to the treatment or improve their performance on the posttest (see the discussion of testing effect to come). Richard L. Solomon developed the **Solomon four-group design** to address the issue of pretest effects. It combines the classical experimental design with the two-group posttest-only design and randomly assigns subjects to one of four groups. For example, a juvenile probation officer wants to determine whether a new training method can improve her probationers' coping skills. She measures coping skills with a twenty-minute test of reactions to stressful events. Because the juvenile probationers might learn coping skills from taking the test itself, a Solomon four-group design is used. She randomly divides the juveniles into four groups. Two groups receive the pretest; one of them gets the new training method and the other gets the old method. Another two groups receive no pretest; one of them gets the new method and the other the old method. All four groups are given the same posttest, and the posttest results are then compared. If the two treatment (new method) groups have similar results, and the two control (old method) groups have similar results, then she knows pretest learning is not a problem. If the two groups with a pretest (one treatment, one control) differ from the two groups without a pretest, then she can conclude that the pretest itself may have an effect on the dependent variable.

FACTORIAL DESIGN

A type of experimental design that considers the impact of several independent variables simultaneously.

MAIN EFFECT/INTERACTION EFFECT

An effect of two independent variables operating simultaneously and in combination on a dependent variable. It is a larger effect that occurs from the sum of each independent variable working separately.

FACTORIAL DESIGNS.   Sometimes a research question suggests looking at the simultaneous effects of more than one treatment or independent variable. A **factorial design** uses two or more independent variables in combination. Every combination of the categories in variables (sometimes called factors) is examined. When each variable contains several categories, the number of combinations grows very quickly. The treatment or manipulation is not each independent variable; rather, it is each combination of the categories.

The treatments in a factorial design can have two kinds of effects on the dependent variable: main effects and interaction effects. Only **main effects** are present in one-factor or single-treatment designs. In a factorial design, specific combinations of independent variable categories can also have an effect. They are called interaction effects because the categories in a combination interact to produce an effect beyond that of each variable alone.

Interaction effects are illustrated in Figure 7.3, which uses data from a study by Ong and Ward (1999). As part of a study of 128 female undergraduates at the National University of Singapore, Ong and Ward measured which of two major ways subjects understood the crime of rape. Some of

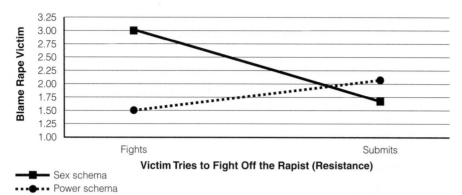

FIGURE 7.3 Blame, Resistance, and Schema. *Source:* From W. Lawrence Neuman, *Social Research Methods, Qualitative and Quantitative Approaches,* 6/e. Published by Allyn and Bacon, 75 Arlington St., Boston, MA 02116. Copyright © 2006 by Pearson Education. Reprinted by permission of the publisher.

the women primarily understood it as sex and caused by the male sex drive (sex schema); others understood it as primarily an act of male power and domination of a woman (power schema). The researchers asked the subjects to read a realistic scenario about the rape of a college student at their university. One randomly selected group of subjects read a scenario in which the victim tried to fight off the rapist. In the other set, she passively submitted. The researchers next asked the subjects to evaluate the degree to which the rape victim was to blame or was responsible for the rape.

Results showed that the women who held the sex schema (and who also tended to embrace traditional gender-role beliefs) more strongly blamed the victim when she resisted. Blame decreased if she submitted. The women who held a power schema (and who also tended to be non-traditionalists) were less likely to blame the victim if she had fought. They blamed her more if she had passively submitted. Thus, the subjects' responses to the victim's act of resisting the attack varied by, or interacted with, their understanding of the crime of rape (i.e., the rape schema held by each subject). The researchers found that the two rape schemas led subjects to interpret victim resistance in opposite ways for the purpose of assigning responsibility for the crime.

Preexperimental or Weak Experimental Designs

Some experimental designs lack the fundamental elements of a true experiment and are therefore of questionable value. These **preexperimental designs** are sometimes necessary, however, because of the difficulty of using the classical design. They all have weaknesses that make inferring a causal relationship more problematic.

ONE-SHOT CASE-STUDY DESIGN. Also called the one-group posttest-only design, the **one-shot case-study design** has only one group, a treatment, and a posttest. Because there is only one group, there is no random assignment.

> *Example.* The experimenter takes a group of forty juvenile probationers and provides all of them counseling during their time on probation. The researcher then measures, after the treatment has run its course, the recidivism rate of the probationers.

ONE-GROUP PRETEST-POSTTEST DESIGN. **One-group pretest-posttest design** has one group, a pretest, a treatment, and a posttest. It lacks a control group and random assignment.

> *Example.* The same researcher takes a group of forty juvenile probationers and sends them to a scared straight program in which seasoned adult inmates spend the day with them describing what they can look forward to if they continue to commit crimes. The

PREEXPERIMENTAL DESIGNS

Experimental designs that lack random assignment or use shortcuts and are much weaker than the classical experimental design. They can be substituted in situations in which an experimenter cannot use all the features of a classical experimental design, but have weaker internal validity.

ONE-SHOT CASE-STUDY DESIGN

An experimental design with only an experimental group and a posttest, no pretest.

ONE-GROUP PRETEST-POSTTEST DESIGN

A preexperimental design that has one group, a pretest, treatment, and a posttest. It lacks a control group and random assignment.

researcher measures the attitude of the youth using a rebelliousness scale as a pretest, applies the scared straight treatment, and then remeasures the youth to see if the program caused a change in attitude.

This is an improvement over the one-shot case study because the researcher measures the dependent variable both before and after the treatment. But it lacks a control group. The researcher cannot know whether something other than the treatment occurred between the pretest and the posttest to cause the outcome. (Notice also that the juveniles may be able to anticipate what the researchers are looking for in this simple pretest, posttest format.)

Quasi-Experimental Designs

QUASI-EXPERIMENTAL DESIGNS

Experimental designs that are stronger than preexperimental designs. They are variations on the classical experimental design, they do not include randomization, and they also sometimes lack a pretest or control group.

These next designs, like the classic design, make identifying a causal relationship more certain than do preexperimental designs, but they still lack a key element of a classic experiment. They are called *quasi* because they are variations of the classical experimental design. They do not include randomization and they also sometimes lack a pretest or control group. **Quasi-experimental designs** help researchers test for causal relationships in a variety of situations in which the classical design is not feasible or is inappropriate. In general, the researcher has much less control over the influence of extraneous variables.

Quasi-experimental techniques have proved invaluable in crime and justice studies for assessing cause and effect relationships in program evaluations and in what are called natural experiments. In a natural experiment, a researcher examines a naturally occurring event (i.e., no researcher manipulation of treatment or experimental groups) such as a change in law or criminal justice agency practice as if an experiment took place. The collection of data about this event usually occurs after the fact using preexisting data, although at times a researcher has foreknowledge of some upcoming change and collects data before, during, and after the change.

In Chapter 1, we mentioned James Marquart's death penalty research. His research examined whether inmates released from death row, due to the landmark Supreme Court decision *Furman v. Georgia* (treatment/independent variable), were at risk for committing additional violent crimes (dependent variable). This is an excellent example of examining post hoc a naturally occurring experiment.

Quasi-experiments, therefore, although not as robust as classical experiments, allow researchers to sidestep their inherent difficulty and expense. Table 7.2 displays a few of the major features associated with differing experimental designs.

TABLE 7.2 A Comparison of the Classical Experimental Design with Other Major Designs

Design	Random Assignment	Pretest	Posttest	Control Group	Experimental Group
Classical	Yes	Yes	Yes	Yes	Yes
One-shot case study	No	No	Yes	No	Yes
One-group pretest posttest	No	Yes	Yes	No	Yes
Static group comparison	No	No	Yes	Yes	Yes
Two-group posttest only	Yes	No	Yes	Yes	Yes
Time-series designs	No	Yes	Yes	No	Yes

Source: From W. Lawrence Neuman, *Social Research Methods, Qualitative and Quantitative Approaches,* 6/e. Published by Allyn and Bacon, 75 Arlington St., Boston, MA 02116. Copyright © 2006 by Pearson Education. Reprinted by permission of the publisher.

INTERRUPTED TIME SERIES. In an **interrupted time-series design**, a researcher uses one group and determines multiple pretest measures before a treatment occurs and then compares this to multiple posttest measures. This is a very popular approach because it allows researchers to access preexisting data associated with a trend, a new law, or a new program (the treatment), and then to examine the data from a single group to discern what changes occurred or did not occur as a result of the treatment. Many studies using time-series data have been conducted, for example, on the effect of incarceration rates (the treatment) on the crime rate (dependent variable)—using both UCR and NCVS data (Blumstein and Wallman 2005). The same technique can be applied to any situation in which data previous to and following some sort of significant change have been collected.

In essence, the researcher has data available that establishes baseline information about the object of study (a type of pretesting data). The researcher also has longitudinal data throughout the time period that a treatment (e.g., legislative change, new program implementation) has been enacted (posttesting data). *The treatment's impact is determined by the discontinuity in the pretest versus the posttest measurements.* There are numerous sophisticated statistical techniques using this sort of time-series data that help to control for the influence of extraneous variables.

Our continued examination of the global warming issue provides for an illustrative example. Visualize having longitudinal data that plot the annual temperature of Earth's surface for the last 1,000 years.

Now imagine asking whether the advent of widespread industrialization (along with the human production of carbon dioxide) has caused a rise in temperatures. These time-series data would allow a researcher to test statistically whether human activity (the independent variable) is the probable cause of a change in the dependent variable (Earth's surface temperature). Although this research may seem to be fairly straightforward, climatologists disagree heatedly over issues of measurement validity. Relying on ice-core samples or tree rings, or combining both, yields different findings. All three techniques, though, still substantiate the overall global warming hypothesis (correspondence with Andy Jacobsen at NOAA).

Let's now examine a typical crime and justice studies example. Gover, MacDonald, and Alpert (2003: 109), in the journal *Criminology and Public Policy*, used interrupted time-series analysis to examine the impact of a specialized domestic violence court in South Carolina on recidivism rates for abusers. They describe their research as follows:

> The recidivism rates of 189 defendants arrested for domestic violence before implementation of the court are compared with the rates of 197 defendants arrested after the court's establishment. There is a significant increase in domestic violence arrests after creation of the court. Moreover, those processed through the court have significantly lower rates of rearrest. A coordinated community response can increase the attention paid by law enforcement to domestic violence and reduce future incidence of violence.

Highlight 7.1 examines several other examples of crime and justice researchers using interrupted time series on important questions.

EQUIVALENT TIME SERIES. An **equivalent time-series design** is another one-group design that extends over a time period. Instead of one treatment, it has a pretest, then a treatment and posttest, then treatment and posttest, then treatment and posttest, and so on. For example, people who drive motorcycles were not required to wear helmets before 1975, when a law was passed requiring helmets. In 1981, the law was repealed because of pressure from motorcycle clubs. The helmet law was reinstated in 1998. The researcher's hypothesis is that wearing protective helmets results in a lower number of head injury deaths in accidents. The researcher plots head injury death rates in motorcycle accidents over time. He or she finds the rate was very high prior to 1975, dropped sharply between 1975 and 1981, then rose to pre-1975 levels between 1981 and 1998, and then dropped again from 1998 to the present. This pattern establishes a likely causal link between helmet use and motorcycle accident fatalities.

INTERRUPTED TIME-SERIES DESIGN

An experimental design in which the dependent variable is measured periodically across many time points, and the treatment occurs in the midst of such measures, often only once.

EQUIVALENT TIME-SERIES DESIGN

An experimental design in which there are several repeated pretests, posttests, and treatments for one group, often over a period of time.

HIGHLIGHT 7.1

Unraveling the Mystery of The Crime Drop

Chapter 5 discussed the fickle nature of crime rate statistics, examining an increase in reported violent crime from the UCR, and then a sudden decrease in 2008–2009. An important question that has preoccupied crime and justice research for several years has been the dramatic decrease in crime rates measured by both the UCR and NCVS in the 1990s. As one can imagine, plenty of people have attempted to exploit the difficult-to-explain decrease—conservatives claim a victory for the efficacy of the tougher law and order measures, whereas liberals point to an improved economy.

Time-series data and analyses are the central avenue for attempting to understand why this drop occurred. Unfortunately, due to the complex nature of making theoretical sense of macrophenomena such as national crime rates, the answers are now somewhat clearer but far from definitive. Perhaps the best and most comprehensive examination of this research question is found in the book, *The Crime Drop in America* (Blumstein and Wallman 2005). In a series of articles by prominent criminologists, the authors manage to shed light on the crime drop mystery, often relying on time-series analytical techniques. They find that the crime drop was likely driven by a confluence of factors, the most important being (and not in any causal order):

- a reduction in gun violence associated with the stabilization of the illegal drug market
- punitive criminal justice–based crime control measures such as the massive increase in incarceration (the authors note no effect from punitive legislation such as the "three strikes and you're out" law)

- a dramatically improved labor market and overall economy
- police efforts to increase gun control
- a slight effect due to changing demographics

Each article adds a new piece to the causal puzzle, culminating in a complex theoretical scenario that will likely satisfy few except for those methods professors and students who appreciate theoretical convolution.

We have to be careful, though, in assuming that the PSS approach found in analyzing time-series data is the only avenue for understanding this drop. Marc Ouimet (2004: 13) provides an international perspective by comparing what happened in the United States and Canada. Interestingly, similar drops in crime occurred in both countries during the same time period, yet Canada did not appreciably increase incarceration nor did that country institute get-tough policing measures. After a thorough review of the quantitative data, Ouimet concludes with a difficult-to-quantify answer (and one more closely aligned with the ISS approach). What explains the drop in both countries is a change in our collective values, or culture:

> The late 1980s and 1990s can be characterized by the progressive integration of a new ethos of moderation in drinking, drug use, sexual activity, and even tobacco use. Many behaviours that were seen as acceptable or were not the object of public outrage only twenty years ago are now gradually integrated into our moral conditioning.

INTERNAL AND EXTERNAL VALIDITY

The Logic of Internal Validity

In **internal validity,** the hypothesized independent variable alone affects the dependent variable. Extraneous variables (variables other than the treatment), which affect the dependent variable, are threats to internal validity. They threaten the researcher's ability to say that the treatment was the true causal factor producing change in the dependent variable. Thus, researchers try to rule out variables other than the treatment by controlling experimental conditions and through experimental designs. Three pioneers of social science experiments and quasi-experiments—Donald Campbell, Julian Stanley, and Thomas Cook—identified numerous factors within an experiment that could threaten internal validity. These well-established norms are not only helpful in conducting credible research but they also assist us in becoming more adept critical consumers of research-based knowledge.

Threats to Internal Validity

The following are ten common threats o internal validity.[5]

SELECTION BIAS. **Selection bias** is the threat that research participants will not form equivalent groups. It plagues designs without random assignment. It occurs when more subjects in one group have a characteristic that affects the dependent variable. Consider an experiment on the ability of people to dodge heavy traffic with all subjects assigned to one group coming from rural areas, and having all subjects who grew up in large cities in the other. An examination of pretest scores helps a researcher detect this threat, because no group differences are expected.

HISTORY.   This is the threat that an event unrelated to the treatment will occur during the experiment and influence the dependent variable. **History effects** are more likely in experiments that continue over a long time period. For example, halfway through a two-year experiment evaluating juvenile probation officer morale, a well-regarded officer is killed while doing a home visit, affecting morale among the other officers.

MATURATION.   This is the threat that some biological, psychological, or emotional process within the subjects and separate from the treatment will change over time. A **maturation effect** is more common in experiments conducted over long time periods. For example, consider an experiment on the effect counseling has on victims of severe domestic violence who have managed to leave their abusive relationship. Due to maturation, one might expect over a two-year period a natural amount of emotional healing to take place, aside from the effect of counseling.

TESTING.   Sometimes, the pretest measure itself affects an experiment. This **testing effect** threatens internal validity because something more than the treatment alone affects the dependent variable. The Solomon four-group design helps a researcher detect testing effects. For example, a researcher gives students an examination on the first day of class. The semester-long course is the treatment. He or she tests learning by giving the same exam on the last day of class. If subjects remember the pretest questions and this affects what they learned (i.e., paid attention to) or how they answered questions on the posttest, a testing effect is present. If testing effects occur, a researcher cannot say that the treatment alone has affected the dependent variable.

INSTRUMENTATION.   **Instrumentation** is related to stability reliability. It occurs when the instrument or dependent variable measure changes during the experiment. For example, in a weight-loss experiment, the springs on the scale weaken during the experiment, giving lower readings in the posttest. Another example might have occurred in an experiment by Bond and Anderson (1987) on the reluctance to transmit bad news. The experimenters asked subjects to tell another person the results of an intelligence test and varied the test results to be either well above or well below average. The dependent variable was the length of time it took to tell the test taker the results. Some subjects were told that the session was being videotaped. During the experiment, the video equipment failed to work for one subject. If it had failed to work for more than one subject or had worked for only part of the session, the experiment would have had instrumentation problems. (By the way, subjects took longer to deliver bad news only if they thought they were doing so publicly—that is, being videotaped.)

EXPERIMENTAL MORTALITY.   **Experimental mortality,** or attrition, arises when some subjects do not continue throughout the experiment. Although the word *mortality* means death, it does not necessarily mean that the subjects have died. If many subjects leave partway through an experiment, a researcher cannot know whether the results would have been different had the subjects stayed. In the Zhang and Zhang (2005) intensive supervision study discussed above, the researchers began with 327 juvenile probationers who were assigned to the two experimental groups. However, only 204 successfully completed the entire program. The researchers' analysis only considered the 204 cases, leaving the question open as to whether mortality could have impacted the findings.

STATISTICAL REGRESSION.   **Statistical regression** is not easy to grasp intuitively. It is a problem of extreme values or a tendency for random errors to move group results toward the average. It can occur in two ways.

HISTORY EFFECTS

A threat to internal validity due to something that occurs and affects the dependent variable during an experiment, but that is unplanned and outside the control of the experimenter.

MATURATION EFFECT

A threat to internal validity in experiments due to natural processes of growth, boredom, and so on that occurs during the experiment and affect the dependent variable.

TESTING EFFECT

A threat to internal validity that occurs when the very process of measuring in the pretest can have an impact on the dependent variable.

INSTRUMENTATION

A threat to internal validity that occurs when the instrument or dependent variable measures change during the experiment.

EXPERIMENTAL MORTALITY

Threats to internal validity due to subjects failing to participate through the entire experiment, especially if it is many participants or more from one group than another.

STATISTICAL REGRESSION

A threat to internal validity that is a problem of extreme values or a tendency of random errors to move group results toward the average.

One situation is when subjects are unusual with regard to the dependent variable. Because they begin as unusual, subjects are unlikely to respond further in one direction. For example, a researcher wants to see whether violent films make people act violently. He or she chooses a group of chronically violent criminals from a high-security prison, gives them a pretest, shows violent films, and then administers a posttest. To the researcher's shock, the criminals are slightly less violent after the film, whereas a control group of nonprisoners who did not see the film are more violent than before. Because the violent criminals were unusual and began at an extreme, a treatment could make them more violent; by random chance alone, they appear less extreme when measured a second time.[6]

A second situation involves a problem with the measurement instrument. If many research participants score very high (at the ceiling) or very low (at the floor) on a variable, random chance alone will produce a change between the pretest and the posttest. For example, a researcher gives eighty subjects a test, and seventy-five get perfect scores. He or she then gives a treatment to raise scores. Because so many subjects already had perfect scores, random errors will reduce the group average because those who got perfect scores can randomly move in only one direction—to get some answers wrong. An examination of scores on pretests will help researchers detect this threat to internal validity.

DIFFUSION OF TREATMENT

A threat to internal validity that occurs when the treatment "spills over" from the experimental group, and the control group subjects modify their behavior because they learn of the treatment.

DIFFUSION OF TREATMENT OR CONTAMINATION.   **Diffusion of treatment** is the threat that research participants in different groups will communicate with each other and learn about the other's treatment. Researchers avoid it by isolating groups or having subjects promise not to reveal anything to others who will become subjects. For example, subjects participate in a daylong experiment on a new way to memorize crime scene photos. During a break, treatment group subjects tell those in the control group about the new way to memorize, which control group subjects then use. A researcher needs outside information, such as postexperiment interviews with subjects, to detect this threat.

COMPENSATORY BEHAVIOR

A threat to internal validity that occurs when subjects in the control group modify their behavior to make up for not getting the treatment.

COMPENSATORY BEHAVIOR.   Some experiments provide something of value to one group of subjects but not to another, and the difference becomes known. The inequality may produce pressure to reduce differences, competitive rivalry between groups, or resentful demoralization. These types of **compensatory behavior** can affect the dependent variable in addition to the treatment. For example, one police unit within a department under study receives a treatment (an increase in pay) to produce gains in productivity. Once the inequality is known, participants in the control group become demoralized and intentionally attempt to undermine treatment integrity. It is difficult to detect this threat unless outside information is available (see the discussion of diffusion of treatment).

EXPERIMENTER EXPECTANCY

A type of reactivity and threat to internal validity due to the experimenter indirectly making subjects aware of the hypothesis or desired results.

EXPERIMENTER EXPECTANCY.   Although it is not always considered a traditional internal validity problem, the experimenter's behavior can threaten causal logic.[7] A researcher may threaten internal validity by indirectly communicating experimenter expectancy to subjects. Researchers may be highly committed to an experimental hypothesis, for example, and indirectly communicate their expectations about desired outcomes to the research subjects. For example, imagine a researcher who is highly committed to the notion that targeting high crime areas with intense police pressure will reduce crime rates. The researcher, who will invariably take some role in maintaining the integrity of the treatment, might inadvertently come across as a champion of this approach. The researcher's expectations could result in an informal change throughout a police department in how crimes are reported. For instance, knowing that the crime rate should be dropping due to their more intensive efforts, line-level police officers might be more lenient in how they officially define certain acts as serious crime or minor nuisances.

DOUBLE-BLIND EXPERIMENT

A type of experimental research in which neither the subjects nor the person who directly deals with the subjects for the experimenter knows the specifics of the experiment.

The **double-blind experiment** is designed to control researcher expectancy. In it, people who have direct contact with subjects do not know the details of the hypothesis or the treatment.

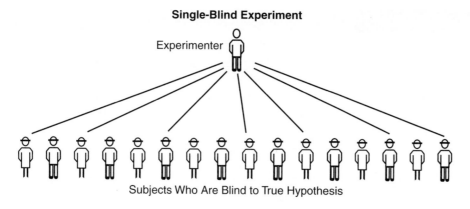

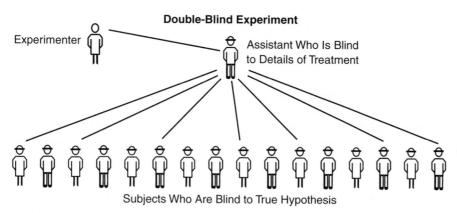

FIGURE 7.4 Double-Blind Experiments: An Illustration of Single-Blind, or Ordinary, and Double-Blind Experiments. *Source:* From W. Lawrence Neuman, *Social Research Methods, Qualitative and Quantitative Approaches,* 6/e. Published by Allyn and Bacon, 75 Arlington St., Boston, MA 02116. Copyright © 2006 by Pearson Education. Reprinted by permission of the publisher.

It is double blind because both the subjects and those in contact with them are blind to details of the experiment (see Figure 7.4). For example, a researcher wants to see if a new drug is effective. Using pills of three different colors—green, yellow, and pink—the researcher puts the new drug in the yellow pill, puts an old drug in the pink one, and makes the green pill a placebo—a false treatment that appears to be real (e.g., a sugar pill without any physical effects). Assistants who give the pills and record the effects do not know which color contains the new drug. Only another person who does not deal with subjects directly knows which colored pill contains the drug and examines the results. The double-blind design is nearly mandatory in medical research because experimenter expectancy effects are well recognized. These threats to internal validity are shown in Summary Table 7.1.

External Validity

Recall from Chapter 3 that a central objective of positivist research is the development of causal laws—regular and predictable patterns of human and social behavior that occur throughout society. Shadish and colleagues (2002: 39) defined external validity as the "validity of inferences about whether the identified causal relationship is maintained over variations in person, settings, time, or treatment variables." **External validity,** then, is the ability to generalize experimental findings to

EXTERNAL VALIDITY

The ability to generalize findings beyond a specific study.

SUMMARY TABLE 7.1	Major Threats to Internal Validity
1. Selection bias	Nonequivalent groups
2. History	Unrelated event occurs during the experiment that impacts dependent variable
3. Maturation	Natural processes of change that affect dependent variable
4. Testing	Testing itself impacts the dependent variable
5. Instrumentation	Unstable measuring instrument changes
6. Experimental mortality	Research subjects do not complete study
7. Statistical regression	Random errors move group results toward the average
8. Diffusion of treatment	Treatment effect spills over to control group
9. Compensatory behavior	Control group modify behavior to make up for not receiving the treatment
10. Experimenter expectancy	Experimenter's expectations impact research subjects' responses

events and settings outside the experiment itself. External validity problems are common in most crime and justice experiments because they usually occur within a local setting, raising questions about their generalizability. Campbell and Stanley (1963) described several important threats to external validity within experimental and quasi-experimental designs; we'll review two of the more important ones.

POPULATION VALIDITY.   In Chapter 6 we discussed the importance of being able to generalize from our sample to the larger population under study. An experiment that demonstrates a strong causal relationship for a particular group of juveniles or crime victims in a particular location may not be generalizable to all juveniles or crime victims. Many experiments, therefore, suffer from low levels of external validity. The only real tactics to combat this problem are to (1) conduct multiple-site studies, (2) select experimental subjects through random sample procedures, and/or (3) to replicate experiments for different groups and locations to determine if the treatment effects are similar. Scholars have examined carefully the numerous replications of the original Minneapolis mandatory arrest for domestic violence experiments. Overall, they have demonstrated that the original study lacked external validity due to the incongruent findings at the different research locations (Fagan 2005).

REACTIVITY

A general threat to external validity that arises because subjects are aware that they are in an experiment and being studied.

HAWTHORNE EFFECT

A reactivity effect named after a famous case in which subjects responded to the fact that they were in an experiment more than to the treatment.

DEMAND CHARACTERISTICS

A type of reactivity in which the subjects in experimental research pick up clues about the hypothesis and alter their behavior accordingly.

REACTIVITY.   Research participants might react differently in an experiment from the way they would in real life because they know they are in a study; this is called **reactivity.** The **Hawthorne effect** is a specific kind of reactivity.[8] The name comes from a series of experiments conducted by Elton Mayo at the Hawthorne, Illinois, plant of Westinghouse Electric during the 1920s and 1930s. Researchers modified many aspects of working conditions (e.g., lighting, time for breaks) and measured productivity. They discovered that productivity rose after each modification, no matter what it was. This curious result occurred because the workers did not respond to the treatment but to the additional attention they received from being part of the experiment and knowing that they were being monitored. Later research questioned whether this had occurred, but the name is used for an effect caused by the attention of researchers. A related effect is the effect of something new, which may wear off over time.

     Demand characteristics are another type of reactivity. Subjects may pick up clues about the hypothesis or goal of an experiment, and they may change their behavior to what they think is demanded of them (i.e., support the hypothesis) to please the researcher (note the intensive police patrol example above).

A last type of reactivity is the **placebo effect,** observed when subjects are given the placebo but respond as if they have received the real treatment. For example, in an experiment on stopping marijuana smoking, subjects are given either a drug to reduce their dependence or a placebo. If subjects who received the placebo also stop using marijuana, then participating in an experiment and taking something that subjects believed would help them quit had an effect. The subjects' belief in the placebo alone affected the dependent variable.

Each of these types of reactivity threatens the ability of the researcher to generalize the results of a study across various settings. Finding that a Head Start program reduces future criminality among one group of youth in Boston may not necessarily have the same impact in Miami.

PLACEBO EFFECT

When subjects do not receive the real treatment and instead receive a placebo or imitation treatment but respond as though they have received the real treatment.

PRACTICAL CONSIDERATIONS

Every research technique has "tricks of the trade" that are pragmatic strategies learned from experience. They often account for the difference between success and failure. Three are discussed here.

Planning and Pilot Tests

Experiments require an extra level of diligence in planning. During the planning phase, a researcher needs to anticipate all alternative explanations or threats to internal validity and how to avoid them (oftentimes found when reviewing the literature), constructs carefully thought-through variables and their measurements, develops a well-organized system for recording data, and pilot-tests any apparatus used (e.g., computers, video cameras, tape recorders). After the pilot tests, the researcher should interview the pilot subjects to uncover aspects of the experiment that need refinement.

Instructions to Subjects

Most experiments involve giving instructions to subjects to set the stage. A researcher should word instructions carefully and follow a prepared script so that all subjects hear the same thing. This ensures reliability. The instructions are also important in creating a realistic cover story when deception is used. Aronson and Carlsmith (1968: 46) noted, "One of the most common mistakes the novice experimenter makes is to present his instructions too briefly."

Upholding Treatment Integrity

Maintaining treatment integrity is critical to all experiments. It is also one of the more difficult tasks. Imagine running an experiment in which you are attempting to get 300 different probation officers to implement an intensive supervision program in the same manner, or where 20 different Head Start programs are treating the children in a similar and effective manner. The difficulties in upholding treatment integrity increase in proportion to the size and scope of the project, as well as the complexity of the treatment itself.

Postexperiment Interview

At the end of an experiment, the researcher should interview subjects for four reasons. First, if deception was used, the researcher needs to debrief the research participants, telling them the true purpose of the experiment and answering questions. Second, he or she can learn what the subjects thought and how their definitions of the situation affected their behavior. Third, he or she can explain the importance of not revealing the true nature of the experiment to other potential participants. And finally, an informal interview provides an excellent opportunity for collecting qualitative information from participants that might be helpful in thinking through and writing up the findings (i.e., mixed methods thinking).

META-ANALYSIS OF EXPERIMENTS

Comparison is the key to all research. By carefully examining the results of different experimental research studies, a researcher, policy maker, and student of crime and justice studies can learn a great deal about what works and what doesn't, the causal factors involved in explaining some phenomena, and the general threats to internal and external validity.

META-ANALYSIS

A study where all previous studies in a particular area are combined in an attempt to determine whether the causal factor studied has had an overall impact on the dependent variable.

There are several areas of research in which enough individual experiments have been completed using the same independent and dependent variables that all these studies are combined into a **meta-analysis.** A meta-analysis combines and compares the data and findings from all the studies and attempts to determine whether the causal factor studied (the treatment) has had an overall impact on the dependent variable. The objectives are to uncover robust empirical relationships, identify weaknesses in the research, provide summary statistics about overall effectiveness, and to overcome the inherent external validity problems found in most experimental studies. Meta-analysis fits with the canons of PSS and, in our example above on global warming, proves that a legitimate knowledge claim can be made only when an accumulated body of research points to a consistent pattern of findings. Meta-analyses of experimental studies that evaluate correctional rehabilitation programs are probably the most well known (see Cullen's work in Chapter 1), but other areas include the effectiveness of punishment as a crime deterrent and police arrest for domestic violence (Garner and Visker 2003; Weisburd 2000). Highlight 7.2 describes a good example of a meta-analysis completed on the research associated with programs attempting to rehabilitate juvenile offenders through boot camps.

HIGHLIGHT 7.2
Straightening Out Offenders: A Meta-Analysis of Military-Style Boot Camps

The boot camp model of incarceration has become highly popular in many southern states. A meta-analysis study of 29 programs found that overall it had no positive impact on recidivism rates.

We have already examined in this text the militarization of policing. Let's look at the militarization of rehabilitation. Since the late 1980s, many policy makers have been enamored with the idea of employing a militarized rehabilitation program,

known as "correctional boot camps" (Lutze 2006). The idea emanates from a popular sentiment in the United States: Serving in the U.S. armed forces creates discipline, a work ethic, and a sense of personal responsibility, all of which begins with the boot camp experience. Its punitive nature also has an appeal. The political popularity of this program has been similar, albeit not as widespread, as the already discussed D.A.R.E. program.

Doris MacKenzie and colleagues (2001) conducted a meta-analysis on twenty-nine experimental and quasi-experimental studies, evaluating the effectiveness of correctional boot camps. Nine of the twenty-nine studies showed a small reduction in recidivism among the experimental groups as compared to the control, eight showed the comparison group as having lower recidivism rates, and the remaining showed no differences between the groups. When combining all the data from these twenty-nine studies, the meta-analysis revealed no significant differences in recidivism between boot camp participants and comparison samples. The authors also found that the ineffectiveness of boot camps cannot be attributed to the methodology used or to the types of offenders studied.

BEWARE OF NAÏVETE

In light of what we learned from Karl Popper (falsification), Thomas Kuhn (paradigms), and the ISS and CSS approaches discussed earlier in this book, we must retain some skepticism about even the gold standard. Fittingly, the best critique of the experimental method comes from three methods experts who most consider to be the gurus of this approach—William Shadish, Thomas Cook, and Donald Campbell (2002). They strongly caution researchers not to naïvely assume that even well-executed experiments yield the true nature of things—a tendency called *naïve realism* or the naïve assumption model: "The experiment is not a clear window that reveals nature directly to us . . . . To the extent they do, it is through a very clouded windowpane." They explain that human biases and perspectives unavoidably cloud all aspects of the experimental process, leaving claims to objective truth problematic. "These [critical] analyses have taken some of the luster from the experiment as a centerpiece of science. The experiment may have a life of its own, but is no longer life on a pedestal" (Shadish, Cook, and Campbell 2002: 30). (The naïve assumption model will be discussed further in Chapter 9, in relation to interviews.)

Conclusion

In this chapter, we learned about the experimental method of data collection and the essential, yet still limited, role it plays in crime and justice studies. Experimental research, if the threats to internal validity are carefully controlled for, provides one of the best avenues available to the researcher for shedding light on causal relationships. Random assignment is key to effectively comparing two (or more) experimental groups. This chapter also examined how the parts of an experiment can be combined to produce different experimental designs. In addition to the classical experimental design, we learned about preexperimental and quasi-experimental designs and design notation. Finally, we demonstrated through numerous examples of experimental research the powerful role it plays in developing evidence-based and effective crime control practices.

We also discussed experimental research's limitations. Some questions cannot be addressed using experimental methods because control and experimental manipulation are impossible. Another limitation is that experiments usually test one or a few hypotheses at a time. This fragments knowledge and makes it necessary to synthesize results across many research reports. External validity is also a problem because most experiments rely on small groups and locales.[9] We did learn how the meta-analysis technique allows us to compare different experiments from different locales and/or programs in trying to determine which causes, programs, and interventions are most plausible (or not) overall.

Perhaps the greatest value of learning the experimental method is how beneficial it can be for developing our critical thinking skills. Learning the rigorous logic and protocol of the experiment allows us to more easily discern flaws in logic and protocol in any individual piece of research, as well as the limitations of the other types of research discussed in this text. Developing these critical filters is beneficial both as producers and consumers of research-based knowledge.

As a final note, we should not assume that the experiment's close alliance with the positivist approach renders it hostile to qualitative techniques. To the contrary, they can benefit experiments in numerous ways. For example, ethnographic techniques can be used to monitor the integrity of the treatment implementation. This might involve a researcher conducting informal interviews, observing participants, and videotaping members of an implementation team and possibly the research subjects themselves. These same techniques can be used during and after the research to gain greater insight into the research findings. Weisburd et al. (2006: 588) for example, in a study testing whether police crackdowns simply displace crime to new areas, provided a qualitative quote from their field research interviews to illuminate why they found little empirical evidence for crime displacement. Field notes from an informal interview revealed that prostitutes are very uncomfortable changing locations, even when police pressure on them to do so is high.

> I walked over (to the cemetery) and I didn't think I'd make money. It was unfamiliar to me . . . I didn't know the guys (clients). On Cornelison [her old territory] you recognize the guys. I know from being out there every day (on Cornelison) the cars, the faces. It's different. In my area, I know the people. Up on the hill—I don't really know the people at that end of town.

Key Terms

control group *150*
experimental group *150*
causal inference *150*
random assignment *153*
matching *154*
pretest *155*
posttest*155*
treatments *156*
treatment integrity *156*
deception *157*
classical experimental
   design *157*
two-group posttest-only
   design *157*

Latin square design *158*
Solomon four-group
   design *158*
factorial design *158*
main effect/interaction
   effect *158*
preexperimental designs
   159
one-shot case-study
   design *159*
one-group pretest-posttest
   design *159*
quasi-experimental
   designs *160*

interrupted time-series
   design *161*
equivalent time-series
   design *161*
internal validity *162*
selection bias *162*
history effects *163*
maturation effect *163*
testing effect *163*
instrumentation *163*
experimental
   mortality *163*
statistical
   regression *163*

diffusion of
   treatment *164*
compensatory
   behavior *164*
experimenter
   expectancy *164*
double-blind
   experiment *164*
external validity *165*
reactivity *166*
Hawthorne effect *166*
demand characteristics *166*
placebo effect *167*
meta-analysis *168*

Review Questions

1. What are the seven elements or parts of an experiment?
2. What is random assignment and why is it so crucial to the experiment?
3. Which design permits the testing of different sequences of several treatments?
4. How do the interrupted and the equivalent time-series designs differ?
5. What is the logic of internal validity and how does the use of a control group fit into that logic?
6. How does the Solomon four-group design show the testing effect?
7. What is the double-blind experiment and why is it used?
8. Do field or laboratory experiments have greater internal validity? External validity? Explain.
9. What is the difference between experimental and mundane realism?
10. What does it mean to uphold the integrity of the treatment, and what effect might not doing so have on internal validity?
11. What is external validity and how is it similar to reliability?

Practicing Research

1. Conduct a mock experiment. Any conceivable topic could work but it would have to be conducive to including a pretest, random assignment to a control group and treatment group, a treatment, and a posttest. Attempt to follow the basic steps in conducting an experiment. The topic idea and design should be kept simple. The idea here is to simply familiarize you with this technique, not to conduct a serious study. A brief final report should include the protocol used, how the data were collected, the findings, and a discussion of the major threats to internal and external validity.
2. As noted in this chapter, time-series studies are particularly important to our field. This exercise is designed to further your study of this method. Find and review the following well-written and straightforward article that uses this method.
   Gover, A. R., MacDonald, J. M., and G. P. Alpert (2003) "Combating domestic violence: Findings from an evaluation of a local domestic violence court." *Criminology and Public Policy* 3(1): 109–132.
   a. Why exactly did the authors characterize this study as using "interrupted time-series"?

   b. How did they go about testing the impact of the treatment?
   c. What does a significant reduction in re-arrests indicate? (Hint: There could be more than one interpretation of this finding.)
3. Find an experimental and a quasi-experimental article in the literature (the journals *Criminology and Public Policy, Justice Quarterly, Crime and Delinquency* and the *Journal of Experimental Criminology* are good places to look). Answer the following questions for the two articles found.
   a. What experimental research design did they use?
   b. What makes this study an experimental versus a quasi-experimental study?
   c. What are the major research questions; what are the major hypotheses tested?
   d. What are the independent, dependent, or intervening variables?
   e. How did the experiment control for other variables or factors influencing the dependent variable outside the treatment? Did they discuss issues of internal validity?
   f. What was their major finding and how it is relevant to our field?

4. The following article is a solid example of crime and justice research testing the efficacy of a program designed to help juvenile offenders. Using the same techniques discussed in Chapter 4, write a review of this piece that could be incorporated into a literature review.

   McGarrell, E. F., and N. K. Hippie (2007) "Family group conferencing and re-offending among first-time juvenile offenders: The Indianapolis experiment." *Justice Quarterly* 24(2):221–246.

5. Mainstream media routinely report the findings of experimental/time-series research, usually in reference to the medical field. Locate a recent story on the testing of a medical drug or technique using an experimental model. Attempt to find a more thorough discussion of the methods used—perhaps even the original article referenced. Critique the research on grounds of internal and external validity. This exercise often demonstrates the shaky ground on which much of our medical knowledge is produced.

Notes for Further Study

1. David Weisburd and Lawrence Sherman are prolific scholars. See their associated Web sites for a full list of their articles and books. David Weisburd: www.ccjs.umdedu/Faculty/faculty.asp?p=38. Lawrence Sherman: www.sas.upenn.edu/jerrylee/people/lsherman.htm.

2. Cook and Campbell (1979: 9–36, 91–94) argued for a modification of a more rigid positivist approach to causality for experimental research. They suggested a "critical-realist" approach, which shares some features of the critical approach outlined in Chapter 3.

3. See Hornstein (1988: 11).

4. For a discussion of control in experiments, see Cook and Campbell (1979: 7–9) and Spector (1981: 15–16).

5. For additional discussions of threats to internal validity, see Cook and Campbell (1979: 51–68), Kercher (1992), Spector (1981: 24–27), Smith and Glass (1987), and Suls and Rosnow (1988).

6. This example is borrowed from Mitchell and Jolley (1988: 97).

7. Experimenter expectancy is discussed in Aronson and Carlsmith (1968: 66–70), Dooley (1984: 151–153), and Mitchell and Jolley (1988: 327–329).

8. The Hawthorne effect is described in Roethlisberger and Dickenson (1939), Franke and Kaul (1978), and Lang (1992). Also see the discussion in Cook and Campbell (1979: 123–125) and Dooley (1984: 155–156). Gillespie (1988, 1991) discussed the political context of the experiments and how it shaped them.

9. See Graham (1992).

8

Survey and Interview Methods

Getting It Straight from the Horse's Mouth

A History of Survey Research

Survey Research in Crime and Justice Studies

Choosing to Survey: Factors to Consider
> Highlight 8.1 Researching Homeland Security

The Logic of Survey Research
What Is a Survey?
Steps in Conducting a Survey

Constructing the Questionnaire
Principles of Good Question Writing
Avoid Jargon, Slang, and Abbreviations
Avoid Ambiguity, Confusion, and Vagueness
Avoid Emotional Language and Prestige Bias
Avoid Double-Barreled Questions
Avoid Leading Questions
Avoid Asking Questions that Are Beyond Respondents' Capabilities
Avoid False Premises
Avoid Overlapping or Unbalanced Response Categories
Aiding Respondent Recall
Getting Honest Answers
Questions on Sensitive Topics
> Highlight 8.2 The Critical Role of Self-Report Surveys in Crime and Justice Survey Research
Open-Ended and Closed-Ended Questions
Agree/Disagree or Ratings?
Questionnaire Design Issues
Length of Survey or Questionnaire
Question Order or Sequence
■ *Organization of Questionnaire*
■ *Order Effects*
> Highlight 8.3 Sample Questions and Findings from Policing Schools Survey

Format and Layout
Cover Letter and Questionnaire Layout
How to Avoid Nonresponses

Types of Surveys: Advantages and Disadvantages
Mail and Self-Administered Questionnaires
Advantages
Disadvantages
Telephone Interviews
Advantages
Disadvantages
Face-to-Face Interviews
Advantages
Disadvantages
Web Surveys
Advantages
> Highlight 8.4 Web Surveys Sent to Correctional Agencies
Disadvantages
Interviewing
The Role of the Interviewer
> Highlight 8.5 Interviewing Street Youth and Anomie Theory
Stages of an Interview
Interviewer Bias
Pilot Testing

The "Meaning" Difficulty in Survey Research

Ethical Survey Research
> Highlight 8.6 Kraska's Five Minutes of Pain

Conclusion

Key Terms

Review Questions

Practicing Research

Notes for Further Study

GETTING IT STRAIGHT FROM THE HORSE'S MOUTH

Recall the fundamental question all researchers try to answer: What is really the case? Experiments produce evidence for this question by testing the impact of a treatment on a dependent variable. Surveys take a simpler route: They ask people. At the heart of survey research is the old expression, "get it straight from the horse's mouth."

If we want to know whether more people are being prosecuted for acts of negligence and stupidity (what we referred to earlier as *criminalizing negligence*), ask prosecutors about whether and how often they prosecute these types of cases. If we want to study illegal steroid use or sexual coercion behavior on college campuses, then we ask students about performance-enhancing drug use and sexual coercion. If we want to know what people's opinions are about executing juveniles or the mentally retarded, then we simply ask. If we want to know how the *CSI* series on television is affecting the average person's perceptions about policing and criminal investigations, then we ask the public. If we want to know the extent of governmental surveillance, then we ask the police about fixed surveillance systems they monitor (remember Michelle Grant's research). And finally, if we want to assess the extent of crime in a society, then one of the most productive approaches is to ask people about their experiences with crime (NCVS).

Surveys and interview research are merely formalized extensions of how we have gone about generating knowledge our whole lives. We ask people direct and indirect questions in the pursuit of knowing more about what is really the case. Thought about this way, the knowledge we've been accumulating has been founded in large part through simple surveys (asking people questions) from a very narrow sample (family, friends, educators) using a host of rough measuring instruments (e.g., "do you think that the *CSI* series is realistic?"; "do you think the police are actually monitoring that camera over there on the building?"). Survey research pursues the same goal but formalizes the process by carefully constructing questions in a way that the answers can be quantified (operationalization), asking a large representative sample of people, and following a carefully scripted research protocol.

The survey is the most widely used research technique in the social sciences, and in crime and justice studies, it is second only to secondary data analysis. It is also likely the method of research most often used by criminal justice practitioners. Despite its popularity, though, it is easy to conduct a misleading or meaningless survey. Good surveys require an awareness of some key principles and tactics, as well as concerted effort. In this chapter, we will examine the main ingredients of good survey research, as well as its limitations.

A HISTORY OF SURVEY RESEARCH

The modern survey can be traced back to ancient forms of the census. A census includes information on characteristics of the entire population in a territory. It is based on what people tell officials or what officials observe. For example, the *Domesday Book* was a famous census of early England conducted in 1085–1086 by William the Conqueror. It assessed the property available for taxation and the young men available for military service.

The survey has a long and varied history. Its use for social research in the United States and Great Britain began with social reform movements and social service professions documenting the conditions of urban poverty. From the 1890s to the 1930s, it was the major method of social research practiced by the Social Survey Movement in Canada, Great Britain, and the United States. By the mid-1940s, the modern quantitative survey had largely displaced it.

Three forces reshaped the social survey into modern quantitative survey research. First, researchers applied statistically based sampling techniques and precise measurement to the survey. They also created scales and indexes to gather systematic quantitative data on attitudes and opinions. Second, many others adapted the survey to applied areas. Market research emerged as a distinct field and adapted surveys to study consumer behavior. Journalists used surveys to measure public opinion and the impact of the radio. Government agencies used surveys to improve services for agricultural and social programs. And third, empirical social research was reoriented away from nonacademics using a mixture of methods to focus on local social problems, and toward "respectable" scientific methods modeled after the natural sciences. Social research became more professional, objective, and nonpolitical.[1]

Today, quantitative survey research is an essential part of most social science fields (crime and justice studies, communication, education, economics, political science, social psychology, and sociology). Many U.S. universities have centers for survey research, including the Survey Research Center at the University of California at Berkeley, the National Opinion Research Center (NORC) at the University of Chicago, and the Institute for Social Research (ISR) at the University of Michigan.

SURVEY RESEARCH IN CRIME AND JUSTICE STUDIES

If experiments are the gold standard in quantitative crime and justice methods, survey research is the backbone. Both of our major measures of crime rely on the survey method. The National Crime Victimization Survey (NCVS) is a massive ongoing crime survey program in which, as we've discussed before, a representative sample of people are asked a multitude of questions about their family's direct experiences with crime. The Uniform Crime Report (UCR) relies on police departments filling out surveys provided by the FBI, asking about arrests, reported crimes, and officers injured or killed in the line of duty. Although each survey is conducted in a very different manner, they both yield important data about the nature of crime in our society. Moreover, much of our knowledge about crime justice phenomena has come from surveys—shedding empirical light on the law, police, judiciary, corrections, and juvenile justice system.

Survey research has produced valuable knowledge about a host of critical criminal justice phenomena and trends. Because of surveys, we now know much more about child abuse, white-collar crime, police deviance, community policing, juvenile crime, correctional rehabilitation, the death penalty, violence against women, international criminal justice, homeland security programs, criminal justice administrative and management practices, and too many others to list. Chapters 1–8 of this book have relied heavily on survey-based research for its examples.

CHOOSING TO SURVEY: FACTORS TO CONSIDER

Researchers use surveys to collect data for all four purposes of research discussed in Chapter 1: exploratory, descriptive, explanatory, and evaluative. Surveys are an exceptional technique for exploring the numerous unexplored areas of research. Kraska's police militarization survey research, for example, was exploratory. The data collected were also descriptive, in that they quantitatively documented the rise and normalization of SWAT teams. Surveys, if done properly, can document accurately many types of crime and criminal justice behavior. Asking prosecutors how often in a year they have filed charges against someone for criminal negligence could provide strong quantitative evidence of an important trend.

Explanatory research is also possible—although establishing causal connections using survey research is difficult. Finally, a great deal of evaluation research is based on surveys. This research can be as simple as program recipients being asked about their level of satisfaction, or as complex as incorporating survey research techniques within a classic experimental design.

Surveys are also appropriate for research questions about self-reported beliefs, behaviors, practices, and policies. They are strongest when the answers people give to questions measure variables. Researchers usually ask about many things at one time in surveys, measure many variables (often with multiple indicators), and test several hypotheses in a single survey.

The following are examples of research questions appropriate for survey research:

1. *Behavior.* Have you used cocaine one or more times in the last thirty days? Have you carried a weapon (e.g., gun, knife, or club) on one or more of the thirty days preceding the survey? While on duty as a police officer, have you ever used an illegal drug?

2. *Attitudes/beliefs/opinions.* How safe would you feel being alone and outside in your area of town at night? In your opinion, how much of the illegal drug problem in your country is caused by the demand for drugs in the United States? In which areas does your state-level homeland security agency most need additional federal funding?

3. *Characteristics.* What country were you born in? What is the highest level of education that you completed? How many probation officers are currently employed in your department?

4. *Expectations.* Do you plan to purchase any home security devices in the next twelve months? Do you plan to alter any of your routine activities because of your fear of crime?

5. *Self-classification.* Into which social class would you put yourself and your family? Do you consider yourself a target of hate crime?

6. *Knowledge.* What would you estimate the overall addiction rate is for crack cocaine use? Is there a "crack house" in your neighborhood?

7. *Policies.* Does your prosecutor's office involve itself in the practice of "civil asset forfeiture"? Do you have a specific set of policies that regulates how forfeited dollars are spent in your office?

What are the strategic goals of the Department of Homeland Security (DHS)? Highlight 8.1 examines the notion of homeland security and the role survey research might play in producing knowledge about this new area of study.

HIGHLIGHT 8.1
Researching Homeland Security

Crime and justice scholars are in unfamiliar territory when it comes to researching the topic of homeland security. The first difficulty is that the concept is vague and expansive. It is a political construct that originated in the aftermath of September 11. In general, it is an attempt to join together many different activities into a single, all-encompassing view of security. It blurs the traditional lines between war and law enforcement, internal/domestic and external/national security, military and police, private security and public security, and local security and federal security. Under the broadly defined notion of *domestic threats,* the newly formed Department of Homeland Security works closely with the Department of Defense, and vice versa, while targeting a range of traditionally nonmilitary concerns such as gang violence, drug abuse, school violence, and immigration.

The vague nature of the concept can be found in the Department of Homeland Security's vision, mission, and goals:

Vision Preserving our freedoms, protecting America . . . we secure our homeland.

Mission We will lead the unified national effort to secure America. We will prevent and deter terrorist attacks and protect against and respond to threats and hazards to the nation. We will ensure safe and secure borders, welcome lawful immigrants and visitors, and promote the free-flow of commerce.

Strategic Goals

Prevention—Detect, deter, and mitigate threats to our homeland.

Protection—Safeguard our people and their freedoms, critical infrastructure, property, and the economy of our Nation from acts of terrorism, natural disasters, or other emergencies.

Response—Lead, manage, and coordinate the national response to acts of terrorism, natural disasters, or other emergencies.

Recovery—Lead national, state, local, and private sector efforts to restore services and rebuild communities after acts of terrorism, natural disasters, or other emergencies. See the DHS Web site www.dhs.gov/index.shtm.

These changes have occurred rapidly, and few crime and justice academics have attempted to research these shifts. An important exception has been the descriptive research conducted by the Rand Corporation on behalf of the U.S. Department of Justice (Davis et al. 2004). Its study examined the extent to which state and local police agencies were prepared for a terrorist event. Rand surveyed a nationally representative sample of all police and state law enforcement agencies and asked a series of questions that tried to determine:

1. steps taken to be prepared for a terrorist event, such as whether they established a terrorism unit within their agency;
2. local law enforcements' training activities, including that training provided by the U.S. military;
3. resource needs; and
4. the relationship between terrorism preparedness and federal funding.

As expected, this survey research documented a range of new activities and programs. More survey research is definitely needed, though, to keep track and make sense of this rapidly evolving phenomenon.

Army National Guard soldiers keep an eye out for signs of illegal activity along the U.S. border with Mexico. These types of arrangements that significantly blur the traditional roles of police and military pose a challenge to researchers interested in homeland security issues.

THE LOGIC OF SURVEY RESEARCH

What is a survey?

In experiments, researchers place people in groups, test one or two hypotheses with a few variables, control the timing of the treatment, note associations between the treatment and the dependent variable, and control for alternative explanations. By contrast, survey researchers sample many respondents who answer the same questions, measure many variables, test multiple hypotheses, and infer temporal order from questions about past behavior, experiences, or characteristics. For example, years of schooling or a respondent's race are prior to current attitudes. An association among variables is measured with statistical techniques (e.g., being abused as child covaries with committing crimes as an adult). They think of alternative explanations when planning a survey, measure variables that represent alternative explanations (i.e., control variables), then statistically examine their effects to rule out alternative explanations. This is why survey research is sometimes referred to as **correlational** (examining which independent variables best correlate with a dependent variable). Survey researchers use control variables to approximate the rigorous test for causality that experimenters achieve with their physical control over temporal order and alternative explanations.

CORRELATIONAL

Survey research is sometimes referred to as correlational research because it often examines which independent variables best correlate with a dependent variable, and rely on control variables to approximate the rigorous test for causality that experimenters achieve with their physical control over temporal order and alternative explanations.

Steps in Conducting a Survey

The survey researcher begins with a question and ends with empirical analysis and interpretation of the data collected about that question. The basic steps in a survey research project can be divided into the steps outlined in Figure 8.1.

The researcher must first decide on a topic. If you recall from Chapter 4, topic selection and refinement should involve reading the literature, and oftentimes talking to people in

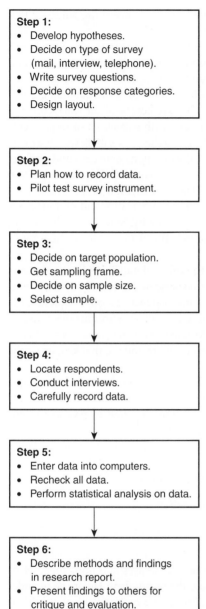

FIGURE 8.1 Steps in the Process of Survey Research
Source: From W. Lawrence Neuman, *Social Research Methods, Qualitative and Quantitative Approaches,* 6/e. Published by Allyn and Bacon, 75 Arlington St., Boston, MA 02116. Copyright © 2006 by Pearson Education. Reprinted by permission of the publisher.

the field. Once a topic is chosen, a survey researcher conceptualizes and operationalizes variables as questions. The questions are carefully constructed so that they accurately and reliably measure what they are supposed to measure. Sometimes these questions will make up a scale or index as discussed in Chapter 6. The researcher writes and rewrites questions for clarity and completeness, and organizes questions on the questionnaire based on the research question, the respondents, and the type of survey. (The types of surveys are discussed later.)

Oftentimes, a seasoned researcher will talk and interact directly with those types of people they will be surveying to ensure the relevance of the questions they're asking. In the police surveillance research example found in Chapter 4, Michelle Grant might have developed a much better instrument if she had visited police agencies that have fixed surveillance systems. Some researchers spend considerable time in the field before constructing their survey instrument. This firsthand experience allows her or him to construct a survey instrument that will fully capture a range of issues and phenomena unknown to the uninitiated. It also helps to use language that puts respondents at ease, and does not threaten or confuse.

The researcher must then develop a survey instrument—either a survey questionnaire or interview schedule. Respondents in a survey questionnaire read the questions themselves and mark answers. An interview schedule is a set of questions read to the respondent by an interviewer, who also records responses. To simplify the discussion, we will use only the word *questionnaire*.

When preparing a questionnaire, the researcher thinks ahead to how he or she will record and organize data for analysis. He or she pilot-tests the questionnaire with a small set of respondents similar to those in the final survey. If interviewers are used, the researcher trains them with the questionnaire. He or she asks respondents in the pilot test whether the questions were clear and explores their interpretations to see whether his or her intended meaning was clear.[2] The researcher also draws the sample during this phase (see Chapter 7). Robin Haarr, for example, in her research on wife battering in Tajikistan spent countless hours testing out her survey instrument on numerous Tajik people who were able to point out areas of confusion or insensitivity. Note, too, in this type of international survey research the obvious difficulties in accurately translating an instrument into a foreign language.

After the planning phase, the researcher is ready to collect data. This phase is usually shorter than the planning phase. He or she locates sampled respondents in person, by telephone, by mail, or by e-mail. Respondents are given information and instructions on completing the questionnaire or interview. The questions follow, and there is a simple stimulus–response or question–answer pattern. The researcher accurately records answers or responses immediately after they are given. After all respondents complete the questionnaire and are thanked, he or she organizes the data and prepares them for statistical analysis.

Survey research can be complex and expensive and it can involve coordinating many people and steps. The administration of survey research requires careful organization and accurate record keeping.[3] The researcher keeps track of each respondent, questionnaire, and interviewer, oftentimes using an identification number found on each questionnaire. Next, the researcher reviews responses on individual questionnaires, stores original questionnaires, and transfers information from the questionnaire items (variables) into spreadsheet software or a statistical software program, such as SPSS. Meticulous bookkeeping and labeling are essential.

CONSTRUCTING THE QUESTIONNAIRE

Principles of Good Question Writing

A good questionnaire forms an integrated whole. The researcher weaves questions together so they flow smoothly and in no way annoy, distract, or confuse the respondent. He or she includes introductory remarks and instructions for clarification and measures each variable with one or more survey questions.

There are two key principles for good survey questions:

1. Avoid respondent confusion.
2. Have empathy (always keep the respondent's perspective in mind).

Good survey questions yield valid and reliable measures of their constructs, and help respondents feel that they understand the question and that their answers are meaningful.

A survey researcher exercises extra care if the respondents are heterogeneous or have different life situations than his or her own. Researchers want each respondent to hear exactly the same question, but it is difficult to know whether the questions will be equally clear, relevant, and meaningful to all respondents. If respondents have diverse backgrounds and frames of reference, the same wording may not have the same meaning. Yet, tailoring the wording to each respondent makes comparisons almost impossible. Question writing, therefore, is more of an art than a science. It takes skill, practice, patience, and creativity. It requires, ironically, the same type of interpretive and empathetic thinking that the interpretive social science (ISS) approach values.

The basic principles of question writing are illustrated in the following eight things to avoid when writing survey questions.

AVOID JARGON, SLANG, AND ABBREVIATIONS.   Jargon and technical terms come in many forms. Plumbers talk about snakes, police talk about spraying people down (pepper spray), and lawyers talk about an Alford plea. Slang is a kind of jargon within a subculture and unless absolutely necessary should not be used. Also avoid abbreviations. NATO usually means North Atlantic Treaty Organization, but for a respondent, it might mean something else (National Association of Tactical Officers). Slang and jargon can be used if a specialized population is being surveyed, such as asking probation officers about *presentence investigation reports*. For the general public, use the language found in the newspaper or on television. A crime victimization survey conducted in the United States should be written with about an eighth-grade reading vocabulary. That level of literacy, however, would probably be too high if the same victimization survey were also being conducted in an area with high illiteracy rates.

AVOID AMBIGUITY, CONFUSION, AND VAGUENESS.   Ambiguity and vagueness plague most question writers. A researcher might make implicit assumptions without thinking of the respondents (empathy). For example, the question, "What is your income?" could mean weekly, monthly, or annual; family or personal; before taxes or after taxes; for this year or last year; and from salary or from all sources. The confusion causes inconsistencies in how different respondents assign meaning to and answer the question. Table 8.1 illustrates how professional researchers caught mistakes they made in wording and how they corrected them.

TABLE 8.1   Improving Unclear Questions

Here are three survey questions written by experienced professional researchers. They revised the original wording after a pilot test revealed that 15 percent of respondents asked for clarification or gave inadequate answers (e.g., don't know). As you can see, question wording is an art that may improve with practice, patience, and pilot-testing.

Original Question	Problem	Revised Question
Do you exercise or play sports regularly?	What counts as exercise?	Do you do any sports or hobbies, physical activities, or exercise, including walking, on a regular basis?
What is the average number of days each week you have butter?	Does margarine count as butter?	The next question is just about butter—not including margarine. How many days a week do you have butter?
[Following question on eggs] What is the number of servings in a typical day?	How many eggs is a serving? What is a typical day?	On days when you eat eggs, how many eggs do you usually have?

	Responses to Question		Percentage Asking for Clarification	
	Original	*Revision*	*Original*	*Revision*
Exercise question (% saying "yes")	48%	60%	5%	0%
Butter question (% saying "none")	33%	55%	18%	13%
Egg question (% saying "one")	80%	33%	33%	0%

Source: From W. Lawrence Neuman, *Social Research Methods, Qualitative and Quantitative Approaches*, 6/e. Published by Allyn and Bacon, 75 Arlington St., Boston, MA 02116. Copyright © 2006 by Pearson Education. Reprinted by permission of the publisher. Adapted from Floyd J. Fowler Jr. "How Unclear Terms Can Affect Survey Data." *Public Opinion Quarterly*, (1992): 56: 218–231.

AVOID EMOTIONAL LANGUAGE AND PRESTIGE BIAS.   Words have implicit meanings as well as explicit meanings. Likewise, titles or positions in society (e.g., president, expert) carry prestige or status. Words with strong emotional connotations, and stands on issues linked to people with high social status, can color how respondents hear and answer survey questions.

Use neutral language. Avoid words with emotional "baggage" because respondents may react to the emotionally laden words rather than to the issue. For example, the question, "What do you think about a policy to fight murderous terrorists who threaten to steal the freedoms of peace-loving people?" is full of emotional words—such as *murderous, freedoms, steal, fight,* and *peace.*

<dl>
<dt>*PRESTIGE BIAS*</dt>
<dd>A problem in survey research question writing that occurs when a highly respected group or individual is associated with an answer choice.</dd>
</dl>

Also avoid **prestige bias**—associating a statement with a prestigious person or group. Respondents may answer on the basis of their feelings toward the person or group rather than addressing the issue. For example, saying, "Most doctors say that marijuana smoke causes lung disease. Do you agree?" affects people who want to agree with doctors. Likewise, a question such as, "Do you support the president's policy regarding fighting terrorism in Uzbekistan?" will be answered by respondents who have never heard of Uzbekistan on the basis of their view of the president.

AVOID DOUBLE-BARRELED QUESTIONS.   Make each question about one and only one topic. A **double-barreled question** is a common error. It consists of two or more questions joined together. It makes a respondent's answer ambiguous. Asking a person to respond to two questions at once makes no sense. Thus, it would not be a good idea to ask a survey question such as, "Do you agree or disagree with U.S. drug policy and antiterror policies in Afghanistan?" The respondent may not be able to give just one answer. On the other hand, it may be perfectly appropriate to ask this question, which is not double barreled: "Do you agree or disagree with the United States linking its war on terror in Afghanistan with its drug policy?"

<dl>
<dt>*DOUBLE-BARRELED QUESTION*</dt>
<dd>A survey question that contains more than one issue and can create respondent confusion or ambiguous answers.</dd>
</dl>

AVOID LEADING QUESTIONS.   Make respondents feel that all answer choices are equally good. Do not let them become aware of an answer that the researcher wants. A **leading (or loaded) question** is one that leads the respondent to choose one response over another by its wording. There are many kinds of leading questions. For example, a leading question might be, "You don't really smoke marijuana, do you?"

Loaded questions can be stated to get either positive or negative answers. For example, "Should the mayor spend even more tax money on police salaries?" leads respondents to disagree, whereas "Should the governor fix the police-pay problem in our city?" is loaded for agreement.

<dl>
<dt>*LEADING (OR LOADED) QUESTION*</dt>
<dd>A question that leads the respondent to choose one response over another by its wording.</dd>
</dl>

AVOID ASKING QUESTIONS THAT ARE BEYOND RESPONDENTS' CAPABILITIES.   Asking something that few respondents know frustrates respondents and produces poor-quality responses. Respondents cannot always recall past details and may not know specific factual information. Asking respondents to make a choice about something they know nothing about (e.g., a technical issue in foreign affairs or an internal policy of an organization) may result in an answer, but one that is unreliable and meaningless. When many respondents are unlikely to know about an issue, use a full-filter question form (to be discussed).

Asking adult respondents how many times they were hit by their parents per month while growing up would likely result in no response or possibly an unreturned survey. A better lead-in question might be "Did your parents or legal guardians ever physically strike you in anger?" If the respondent answered yes, a follow-up open-ended question might be "From your recollection, how often did this occur?"

AVOID FALSE PREMISES.   Do not begin a question with a premise with which respondents may not agree, then ask about choices regarding it. Respondents who disagree with the premise will be frustrated and not know how to answer. A better question explicitly asks the respondent to assume a premise is true, then asks for a preference. For example, a question might ask, "The Department of Homeland Security works tirelessly to make us more secure. Would you be in favor of granting them more discretion in wire-tapping U.S. citizens suspected of terrorism?" The original statement may not be a fact, as stated in this survey question. A better approach would exclude this part of the question altogether.

AVOID OVERLAPPING OR UNBALANCED RESPONSE CATEGORIES. Response choices should be mutually exclusive, exhaustive, and balanced (mutually exclusive and exhaustive attributes were discussed in Chapter 6). *Mutually exclusive* means that response categories do not overlap. Overlapping categories that are numerical ranges (e.g., 5–10, 10–20, 20–30) can be easily corrected (e.g., 5–9, 10–19, 20–29).

The ambiguous verbal choice is another type of overlapping response category—for example, "Are you satisfied with your juvenile probation position or are there things you don't like about it?" Exhaustive means that every respondent has a choice—a place to go. For example, asking respondents, "Are you using your criminology or criminal justice major at your job?" leaves out respondents who are unemployed.

Keep response categories balanced. A case of unbalanced choices is the question, "What kind of job is the police chief doing: outstanding, excellent, very good, or satisfactory?" (see Summary Table 8.1).

Aiding Respondent Recall

Survey researchers have studied the ability of respondents to recall past behavior and events accurately when answering survey questions.[4] Recalling events accurately takes more time and effort than the seconds that respondents have to answer survey questions. Also, one's ability to recall accurately declines over time. Studies in crime victimization show that although most respondents can recall significant events that occurred in the past several weeks, half are inaccurate a year later. Survey researchers recognize that memory is less trustworthy than once assumed. It is affected by many factors—the topic (threatening or socially desirable), events occurring simultaneously and subsequently, the significance of an event for a person, and situational conditions (question wording and interview style).

The complexity of respondent recall does not mean that survey researchers cannot ask about past events; rather, they need to customize questions and interpret results cautiously. Researchers should provide respondents with special instructions and extra thinking time. They should also provide aids to respondent recall, such as a fixed time frame or location references. Rather than ask, "How often do you smoke marijuana?" they should ask, "How often did you smoke marijuana last month. Let's break it down per day." "On Monday the 1st, how many times did you smoke? Okay, now on Tuesday the 2nd, how many times did you smoke," and so forth.

Many respondents will **telescope**—compress time when asked about frequency, tending to overreport recent events. Two techniques reduce telescoping: situational framing (e.g., ask the respondent to recall a specific situation and then ask in more detail about it) and decomposition (e.g., ask several specifics and add them up). The following passage reveals how telescoping is specifically dealt with in the NCVS:

TELESCOPE

When survey research respondents compress time when answering about past events, overreporting recent events and underreporting distant past ones.

SUMMARY TABLE 8.1	Eight Things to Avoid in Writing Survey Questions

1. Avoid jargon, slang, and abbreviations.
2. Avoid ambiguity, confusion, and vagueness.
3. Avoid emotional language and prestige bias.
4. Avoid double-barreled questions.
5. Avoid leading questions.
6. Avoid asking questions that are beyond respondents' capabilities.
7. Avoid false premises.
8. Avoid overlapping or unbalanced response categories.

Telescoping is another problem in which incidents that occurred before the reference period are placed within the period. The effect of telescoping is minimized by using the bounding procedure previously described [i.e., bounding establishes a time frame to avoid duplication of crimes on subsequent interviews]. The interviewer is provided with a summary of the incidents reported in the preceding interview and, if a similar incident is reported, it can be determined whether or not it is a new one by discussing it with the victim. Events that occurred after the reference period are set aside for inclusion with the data from the following interview. (Maguire and Pastore 1997: 624–625)

To be sure, survey researchers who ask about past events or behavior, even within a bounded period (e.g., six months), need to do so with great care.

Getting Honest Answers

QUESTIONS ON SENSITIVE TOPICS.   As we've mentioned before, crime and justice research topics often involve sensitive issues and hidden behaviors that survey respondents may feel threatened about. Respondents may be reluctant to answer the questions or to answer completely and truthfully. Survey researchers who wish to ask such questions must do so with great care and great empathy, and must be extra cautious about protecting the results.[5]

We all try to present a positive image of ourselves to others. Consequently, respondents may be ashamed, embarrassed, or afraid to give truthful answers, or find it emotionally painful to confront their own actions honestly, let alone admit them to other people (e.g., "Do you sometimes hit your children in anger?"). They underreport behavior or attitudes they wish to hide or believe to be in violation of social norms. Alternatively, some may overreport positive behaviors or generally accepted beliefs (social desirability bias is discussed later). As discussed in Highlight 8.2, criminologists have generated a wealth of important knowledge about crime and lawbreaking through the use of **self-report surveys**.

SELF-REPORT SURVEYS

A survey technique that asks respondents to disclose information about their own behaviors—usually of a sensitive nature.

Survey researchers use many techniques to increase honest answering to questions about sensitive topics. One technique is to establish a comfortable setting before asking the questions. Guarantees of anonymity and confidentiality and an emphasis on the necessity of honest answers both help. It also helps to ask sensitive questions following a warm-up period of other nonthreatening questions and after creating an atmosphere of trust and comfort. A second technique is to use an enhanced phasing of questions. For example, consider the question, "Have you shoplifted?" This has an accusatory tone and uses the word *shoplift*, which implies committing an illegal act. Instead, get at the same behavior by asking, "Have you even taken anything from a store without paying for it?"

Researchers also try to reduce threat and make it easier for respondents to answer honestly about sensitive topics by providing contextual background information. They might provide a factual statement to respondents to put them at ease, such as "Incest, while a hidden phenomenon, is more common than most people think." Another technique to improve honest answers is to ask the respondent about other people's involvement in an activity, rather than one's own: "What would you estimate is the percentage of your police coworkers who have used some sort of illegal drug while on duty?"

The questioning format can also affect how respondents answer questions. Studies show that survey formats that permit greater respondent anonymity, such as a self-administered questionnaire or Internet-based survey, increase the likelihood of honest responses over formats that involve interacting with another person, such as in a face-to-face or telephone interview.[6]

OPEN-ENDED QUESTION

A type of survey research question in which respondents are free to offer any answer they wish to the question.

Open-Ended and Closed-Ended Questions

There has been a long debate about open-ended versus closed-ended questions in survey research.[7] An **open-ended question** (unstructured, free response) simply asks a question to which

HIGHLIGHT 8.2

THE CRITICAL ROLE OF SELF-REPORT SURVEYS

As surprising as it may seem, crime and justice researchers have had a great deal of success using self-report surveys in studying crime. The self-report method simply asks people about their delinquent behavior—its types and frequency. It solicits information directly from those who are breaking the law, and therefore avoids the problems associated with using police-generated data (UCR). Early researchers were skeptical that people would be willing to admit to lawbreaking on a survey instrument or in an interview. However, a large body of research has proven that this method, if done correctly, can yield reasonably valid and reliable data (Thornberry and Krohn 2000).

Delbert Elliot is probably the person most responsible for refining the self-report survey into a useful method. The success of the approach hinges on the researcher developing effective self-report scales (Chapter 6). These scales need four characteristics to yield worthwhile data:

- The scales must measure a wide range of criminal behaviors, including drug use, violence, property crime, sexual crimes, and so forth.
- The scales must include even the most serious crimes. Early studies did not include them and thus missed the opportunity to identify and study the more serious repeat offenders (who many assert commit the bulk of crime in society).
- The scales must measure adequately the incidence of self-reported criminal behavior by allowing respondents a wide range of options. It should capture effectively the offender who has committed three burglaries over his or her lifetime as well as those who have committed 300.

- Follow-up and open-ended questions should be used to ensure the accuracy of the self-reporting behavior. This also wards against including events that are trivial (not criminal) (modified from Thornberry and Krohn 2000).

Survey researchers have actually tested whether the survey instrument used—telephone, face-to-face interview, written questionnaire, and computer-assisted questionnaire—affects the outcome of self-report research. Overall, these studies have found few differences. A key factor, however, is the extent to which the respondents feel that their responses are completely confidential, especially in studies on alcohol and illegal drug use. This is why the computer-assisted self-administered interview (CASI) has proven to be quite a successful technique. It ensures in the respondent a high level of confidence that his or her answers are not traceable back to that individual and that the study has a high level of legitimacy and scientific value. It also appeals to juveniles who seem generally more comfortable with the idea of responding to an anonymous computer as opposed to an adult interviewer. Tourangeau and Smith (1996) examined a newer modification to CASI that incorporates an audio component, so the respondent is given verbal instructions by the computer (known as ACASI). They found this method is even more effective than CASI when it comes to self-reporting illegal drug use.

Source: This highlight draws extensively from an excellent article, "The Self-Report Method for Measuring Delinquency and Crime," written by two leading experts in crime theory and research, Terence P. Thornberry and Marvin D. Krohn (2000). In U.S. National Institute of Justice (Ed.), *Measurement and Analysis of Crime and Justice: Criminal Justice series*, vol. 4, pp. 33–83. Washington, D.C.: National Institute of Justice.

---

respondents can give any answer (e.g., "What is the most serious factor affecting morale in this agency?"). A **closed-ended question** (structured, fixed response) both asks a question and gives the respondent fixed responses from which to choose.

As detailed in Table 8.2 each form has advantages and disadvantages. The crucial issue is not which form is best. Rather, it is under what conditions a form is most appropriate. A researcher's choice to use an open- or closed-ended question depends on the purpose and the practical limitations of a research project. The demands of using open-ended questions, with interviewers writing verbatim answers followed by time-consuming coding, may make them impractical for a specific project.

Large-scale surveys have closed-ended questions because they are quicker and easier for both respondents and researchers. Yet something important may be lost when an individual's beliefs and feelings are forced into a few fixed categories that a researcher created. To learn how a respondent thinks, to discover what is really important to him or her, or to get an answer to a question with many possible answers, open-ended questions may be best. In addition, sensitive topics may be more accurately measured with closed-ended questions.

The disadvantages of a question form can be reduced by mixing open-ended and closed-ended questions in a questionnaire. Mixing them also offers a change of pace and helps interviewers establish rapport. Periodic probes (i.e., follow-up questions by interviewers) with closed-ended questions can reveal a respondent's reasoning.

CLOSED-ENDED QUESTION

A type of survey research question in which respondents must choose from a fixed set of answers.

TABLE 8.2	Closed-Ended and Open-Ended Questions

Advantages of Closed

- It is easier and quicker for respondents to answer.
- The answers of different respondents are easier to compare.
- Answers are easier to code and statistically analyze.
- The response choices can clarify question meaning for respondents.
- Respondents are more likely to answer about sensitive topics.
- There are fewer irrelevant or confused answers to questions.
- Less articulate or less literate respondents are not at a disadvantage.
- Replication is easier.

Advantages of Open

- They permit an unlimited number of possible answers.
- Respondents can answer in detail and can qualify and clarify responses.
- Unanticipated findings can be discovered.
- They permit adequate answers to complex issues.
- They permit creativity, self-expression, and richness of detail.
- They reveal a respondent's logic, thinking process, and frame of reference.

Disadvantages of Closed

- They can suggest ideas that the respondent would not otherwise have.
- Respondents with no opinion or no knowledge can answer anyway.
- Respondents can be frustrated because their desired answer is not a choice.
- It is confusing if many (e.g., 20) response choices are offered.
- Misinterpretation of a question can go unnoticed.
- Distinctions between respondent answers may be blurred.
- Clerical mistakes or marking the wrong response is possible.
- They force respondents to give simplistic responses to complex issues.
- They force people to make choices they would not make in the real world.

Disadvantages of Open

- Different respondents give different degrees of detail in answers.
- Responses may be irrelevant or buried in useless detail.
- Comparisons and statistical analysis become very difficult.
- Coding responses is difficult.
- Articulate and highly literate respondents have an advantage.
- Questions may be too general for respondents who lose direction.
- Responses are written verbatim, which is difficult for interviewers.
- A greater amount of respondent time, thought, and effort is necessary.
- Respondents can be intimidated by questions.
- Answers take up a lot of space in the questionnaire.

Source: From W. Lawrence Neuman and Bruce Weigand, *Criminal Justice Research Methods, Qualitative and Quantitative Approaches,* 1/e. Published by Allyn and Bacon, 75 Arlington St., Boston, MA 02116. Copyright © 2006 by Pearson Education. Reprinted by permission of the publisher.

Open-ended questions are especially valuable in early or exploratory stages of research. For large-scale surveys, researchers use open-ended questions in pilot tests, and then develop closed-ended question responses from the answers given to the open-ended questions. As discussed in Chapter 13, if open-ended questions are retained as qualitative data, they can be a valuable tool in conducting a minimalist type of mixed methods research that combines quantitative findings with qualitative insights.

TABLE 8.3	Rating Example: Public's Confidence in Major Institutions

"I am going to read you a list of institutions in U.S. society. Would you tell me how much respect and confidence you, yourself, have in each one: a great deal, quite a lot, some, or very little?"

Institution	Percent Choosing "A Great Deal" or "Quite a Lot"
Military	64
Police	*58**
Presidency	45
Supreme Court	44
Banks	43
Public schools	40
Television news	33
Organized labor	26
Congress	21
Big business	21
Criminal justice system	*20**

*Why do you think the police are ranked so high and the criminal justice system is ranked last behind Congress and big business?

Source: From W. Lawrence Neuman and Bruce Weigand, *Criminal Justice Research Methods, Qualitative and Quantitative Approaches,* 1/e. Published by Allyn and Bacon, 75 Arlington St., Boston, MA 02116. Copyright © 2000 by Pearson Education. Reprinted by permission of the publisher. Adapted from Jean Johnson. "Americans' Views on Crime and Law Enforcement." *National Institute of Justice Journal,* (Sept. 1997): 9–12.

Agree/Disagree or Ratings?

Survey researchers who measure values and attitudes have debated two issues about the responses offered.[8] Should a questionnaire item make a statement and ask respondents whether they agree or disagree with it, or should it offer respondents specific alternatives? Should the questionnaire include a set of items and ask respondents to rate them (e.g., approve, disapprove) or should it give them a list of items and force them to rank-order items (e.g., from most favored to least favored)?

It is best to offer respondents explicit alternatives. For example, instead of asking, "Do you agree or disagree with the statement, 'Men are better suited to police work'?" just ask, "Do you think men are better suited, women are better suited, or both are equally suited for police work?" Table 8.3 illustrates an example of asking respondents to simply rate their views along a continuum, as opposed to forcing them to rank-order.

Questionnaire Design Issues

LENGTH OF SURVEY OR QUESTIONNAIRE. How long should a questionnaire be or an interview last?[9] Researchers prefer longer questionnaires or interviews because they are able to obtain more information for less cost. The cost for extra questions—once a respondent has been sampled, has been contacted, and has completed other questions—is small. There is a point of no return, however. Many respondents will simply not bother to fill out a survey that seems too demanding. This is especially true when sending surveys to time-strapped criminal justice practitioners, or inattentive juveniles. A lengthy survey may result in low response rates or poor-quality responses.

There is no absolute proper length. The length depends on the survey format (to be discussed) and on the respondent's characteristics. A ten-minute telephone interview is rarely a problem. Mail questionnaires are more variable. A short (three or four pages) questionnaire is appropriate for the general population. Some researchers have had success with questionnaires as long as ten pages (about 100 items) with the general public, but responses drop significantly for longer questionnaires. Criminal justice practitioners will generally only devote eight to fifteen minutes to a written questionnaire, although it can be longer, depending on its importance to them. Face-to-face interviews lasting an hour are not uncommon, but are generally kept around thirty minutes. In special situations, face-to-face interviews as long as three to five hours have been conducted.

QUESTION ORDER OR SEQUENCE. A survey researcher faces three question sequence issues: organization of the overall questionnaire, question order effects, and context effects.

Organization of Questionnaire. In general, you should sequence questions to minimize the discomfort and confusion of respondents. A questionnaire has an opening, middle, and ending question. After an introduction explaining the survey, it is best to make opening questions pleasant, interesting, and easy to answer so that they help a respondent feel comfortable about the questionnaire. Avoid asking boring background, threatening, or complex questions first. Organize questions in the middle into common topics. Mixing questions on different topics causes confusion. Orient respondents by placing questions on the same topic together and introduce the section with a short introductory statement (e.g., "Now I would like to ask you questions about police in schools"). Make question topics flow smoothly and logically, and organize them to assist respondents' memory or comfort levels. Do not end with highly threatening questions, and always end with a thank you.

Order Effects. Researchers are concerned that the order in which they present questions may influence respondent answers.[10] This is known as **order effects**. Matthew DeMichele, a former graduate student who worked with Kraska and who is finishing his PhD in sociology, surveyed police departments in Kentucky about several "cutting-edge" police practices, including placing police officers in schools (Kraska and DeMichele 2001). In his pilot test he first included a question that asked respondents their opinion about police working in elementary schools, followed by a question concerning their own department's level of involvement. This order had the effect of making police in schools seem controversial, and therefore reduced respondents' willingness to admit their involvement. DeMichele simply removed the opinion-based question on the final form of the survey. Highlight 8.3 provides a more detailed look at the type of questions DeMichele used for this study.

ORDER EFFECTS

An effect in survey research in which a topic or some questions asked before others influence respondents' answers to later questions.

HIGHLIGHT 8.3
Sample Questions and Findings from Policing Schools Survey

For the survey "Cutting-Edge Police Tactics," researchers were attempting to document trends and issues associated with several controversial police developments, including civil asset forfeiture, public housing enforcement, fixed public surveillance systems, and police in public schools. The questions were kept quite basic in an attempt to reduce its length and reduce ambiguity. For example,

3. Does your department currently assign at least one officer to work within a school or several schools in your jurisdiction?
☐ Yes
☐ No

3a. Are these positions:
☐ Full-time
☐ Part-time
☐ Both

3b. How many officers are assigned to this duty? The researchers found that 46 percent of police departments in the state of Kentucky as of 2000 assigned at least one police officer to work in schools, and 63 percent of the 54 percent of departments that did not assign an officer had plans to do so within the next year (Kraska and DeMichele 2001). The researchers followed up with in-depth interviews to inquire more deeply into the respondent's opinions about this trend. The following opinion was typical:

We have tapped into the federal money but I still have my doubts. It seems that we now need the police for the typical stuff that has gone on for a long time in schools—vandalism, being disruptive, fighting, mouthing off to a teacher. I'm not sure about turning us [the police] into hall monitors and assistant principles. (respondent #24)

Format and Layout

There are two format or layout issues: the overall physical layout of the questionnaire and the format of questions and responses.

COVER LETTER AND QUESTIONNAIRE LAYOUT.   Layout is important, whether a questionnaire is designed for an interviewer or for the respondent.[11] Questionnaires should be clear, neat, and easy to follow. Give each question a number and put identifying information (e.g., name of organization) on questionnaires. Never cramp questions together or create a confusing appearance. A few cents saved in postage or printing will ultimately cost more in terms of lower reliability because of a lower response rate. Make a cover sheet or face sheet for each interview, for administrative use. Put the time and date of interview, the interviewer, the respondent identification number, and the interviewer's comments and observations on it. A professional appearance with high-quality graphics, space between questions, and good layout improves accuracy and completeness and helps the questionnaire flow.

Give interviewers or respondents instructions on the questionnaire. Print instructions in a different style from the questions (e.g., in a different color or font or in all capitals) to distinguish them. This is so that an interviewer can distinguish between questions for respondents and instructions intended for the interviewer alone.

The success of a mail survey can hinge on the effectiveness of the **cover letter**. It should be printed on high-quality paper, identifying the researcher, the purpose of the survey, guarantees of anonymity and/or confidentiality, and offering a telephone number for questions. It also helps to include an approximate time frame to complete the survey.

COVER LETTER

The letter that accompanies a mail-out survey and that provides the respondent all necessary information about the survey itself.

Details matter. Respondents will be turned off if they receive a bulky brown envelope with bulk postage addressed to Occupant or if the questionnaire does not fit into the return envelope. Always end with the statement: "Thank you for your participation." Interviewers and questionnaires should leave respondents with a positive feeling about the survey and a sense that their participation is appreciated.

How to Avoid Nonresponses

The failure to get a valid response from every sampled respondent weakens a survey. In addition to research surveys, people are asked to respond to many requests from charities, marketing firms, candidate polls, and so forth. Charities and marketing firms get low response rates, whereas government organizations get much higher cooperation rates. Nonresponse can be a major problem for survey research because if a high proportion of the sampled respondents do not respond, researchers may not be able to generalize results, especially if those who do not respond differ from those who respond (recall Steve's experience in Chapter 6).

Researchers have identified five types of nonresponse.[12]

1. Nonlocation (could not find a sampled respondent),
2. Noncontact (respondent was not at home or not reached after many attempts),
3. Ineligible (respondent was reached but was not the proper age, race, sex, citizenship, etc. for the survey purposes),
4. Refusal to participate (respondent was not willing to be interviewed), and
5. Incomplete participation (respondent stopped answering before the end or began answering every question with "do not know" or "no opinion").

Improving the overall survey response rate requires reducing each type of nonresponse.

Survey researchers can improve eligibility rates by careful respondent screening, better sample-frame definition, and multilingual interviewers. They can decrease refusals by sending letters in advance of an interview, offering to reschedule interviews, using small incentives (i.e., small gifts), adjusting interviewer behavior and statements (i.e., making eye contact, expressing sincerity, explaining the sampling or survey, emphasizing importance of the interview,

TABLE 8.4	Tips to Increase Mail Survey Response Rates

- Address the questionnaire to a specific person or organization, not "Occupant," and send it first class.
- Include a carefully written, dated cover letter on letterhead stationery. In it, request respondent cooperation, guarantee confidentiality, explicitly and convincingly explain the purpose and worth of the survey, and give the researcher's name and phone number.
- If appropriate, secure sponsorship of the survey from an organization that respondents will respect. For example, a survey to probation departments would probably be returned more readily if it were approved of by the American Probation and Parole Association (APPA).
- Always include a postage-paid, addressed return envelope.
- The questionnaire should have a neat, professional layout and reasonable page length. Criminal justice professionals will not likely fill out lengthy and time-consuming surveys.
- The questionnaire should be professionally printed and easy to read, with clear instructions.
- Send two follow-up reminder letters to those not responding. The first should arrive about one week after sending the questionnaire, the second a week later. It helps to send an additional copy of the survey if funds are available. Gently ask for cooperation and try to make clear why their participation is vital to the purpose of the research.
- Do not send questionnaires during major holiday periods.
- Do not put questions on the back page. Instead, leave a blank space and ask the respondent for general comments.
- Sponsors that are local and are seen as legitimate (e.g., government agencies, universities, large firms) get a better response.
- Include a small monetary inducement ($5–$10) if possible and appropriate. (This step would not be appropriate for a survey sent to an organization.)

clarifying promises of confidentiality, etc.). Survey researchers can also use alternative interviewers (i.e., different demographic characteristics, age, race, gender, or ethnicity), use alternative interview methods (i.e., phone versus face to face), or accept alternative respondents in a household.

There is a large body of literature on ways to increase response rates for mail questionnaires. Table 8.4 lists some of the more time-tested techniques for increasing response rates.[13] A meta-analysis of 115 articles on mail survey responses taken from 25 journals published between 1940 and 1988 revealed that cover letters, questionnaires of four pages or less, a return envelope with postage, and a small monetary reward all increase return rates (Yammarino et al. 1991).

Summary Table 8.2 provides a helpful overview of questionnaire design issues.

SUMMARY TABLE 8.2	Questionnaire Design Issues

- **Length of Survey or Questionnaire** (depends on time constraints/attention span of respondents)
- **Question Order or Sequence**
  - **Organization of Questionnaire** (organize to minimize the discomfort and confusion of respondents)
  - **Order Effects** (minimize any respondent bias by carefully ordering questionnaire items)
- **Format and Layout**
  - **Cover Letter and Questionnaire Layout** (cover letter has to establish legitimacy of research; questionnaire must appear highly professional and easy to use)
  - **Question Format** (make responses unambiguous)

TYPES OF SURVEYS: ADVANTAGES AND DISADVANTAGES

Mail and Self-Administered Questionnaires

ADVANTAGES. Researchers can give questionnaires directly to respondents or mail them to respondents who in turn will read instructions and questions, and then record their answers. This type of survey is by far the cheapest, and it can be conducted by a single researcher. A researcher can send questionnaires to a wide geographical area. The respondent can complete the questionnaire when it is convenient and can check personal/organizational records if necessary. Mail questionnaires offer anonymity and avoid interviewer bias. They are very effective, and response rates may be high for a target population that is well educated or has a strong interest in the topic or the survey organization. Mail surveys are particularly appropriate when a researcher wants to study criminal justice agencies. Most bureaucracies are used to paperwork and, assuming the target population feels the survey is worthwhile, it is possible to obtain fairly high response rates.

DISADVANTAGES. Because people do not always complete and return questionnaires, the biggest problem with mail questionnaires is a low response rate. Most questionnaires are returned within two weeks, but others trickle in up to two months later. Researchers can raise response rates by sending nonrespondents reminder letters, but this adds to the time and cost of data collection.

The mail questionnaire format limits the kinds of questions that a researcher can use. Questions requiring visual aids (e.g., "Look at this picture and tell me what you see"), open-ended questions, many contingency questions, and complex questions do poorly in mail questionnaires (see Table 8.5).

Telephone Interviews

ADVANTAGES. The telephone interview is a popular survey method because about 95 percent of the population can be reached by telephone. An interviewer calls a respondent (usually at home), asks questions, and records answers. Researchers sample respondents from lists or telephone directories, or use RDD, and can quickly reach many people across long distances. A staff of interviewers can interview 1,500 respondents across the nation within a few days and, with several callbacks, response rates can reach 90 percent. Although this method is more expensive than a mail questionnaire, special, reduced long-distance phone rates help. In general, the telephone interview is a flexible method with most of the strengths of face-to-face interviews but for about half the cost. Interviewers control the sequence of questions and can use some probes. A specific respondent is chosen and is likely to answer all the questions alone. The researcher knows when the questions were answered and can use contingency questions effectively.

Several kinds of computer-assisted technologies have been developed for use in telephone interviews such as **computer-assisted telephone interviewing (CATI)** and interactive voice response interviews. Advances and lower costs for computer technology in the late 1970s–1980s enabled professional survey research organizations to install systems.[14] With CATI, the interviewer sits in front of a computer and makes calls. Wearing a headset and microphone, the interviewer reads the questions from a computer screen for the specific respondent who is called, then enters the answer via the keyboard. Once he or she enters an answer, the computer shows the next question on the screen.

CATI speeds interviewing and reduces interviewer errors. It also eliminates the separate step of entering information into a computer and speeds data collection.

DISADVANTAGES. Relatively high cost and limited interview length are disadvantages of telephone interviews. In addition, respondents without telephones are impossible to reach, and

COMPUTER-ASSISTED TELEPHONE INTERVIEWING (CATI)

Survey research telephone interviewing in which the interviewer sits before a computer screen and keyboard, reads from the screen questions, and enters answers directly into the computer.

| TABLE 8.5 | Types of Surveys and Their Features | | | |

Features	Type of Survey			
	Mail Questionnaire	Telephone Interview	Face-to-Face Interview	Web Survey
Administrative Issues				
Cost	Cheap	Moderate	Expensive	Cheapest
Speed	Slowest	Fast	Slow to moderate	Fastest
Length (number of questions)	Moderate	Short	Longest	Moderate
Response rate	Lowest	Moderate	Highest	Moderate
Research Control				
Probes possible	No	Yes	Yes	No
Specific respondent	No	Yes	Yes	No
Question sequence	No	Yes	Yes	Yes
Only one respondent	No	Yes	Yes	No
Visual observation	No	No	Yes	Yes
Success with Different Questions				
Visual aids	Limited	None	Yes	Yes
Open-ended questions	Limited	Limited	Yes	Yes
Contingency questions	Limited	Yes	Yes	Yes
Complex questions	Limited	Limited	Yes	Yes
Sensitive questions	Some	Limited	Limited	Yes
Sources of Bias				
Social desirability	No	Some	Worse	No
Interviewer bias	No	Some	Worse	No
Respondent's reading skill	Yes	No	No	Some

Source: From W. Lawrence Neuman and Bruce Weigand, *Criminal Justice Research Methods, Qualitative and Quantitative Approaches,* 1/e. Published by Allyn and Bacon, 75 Arlington St., Boston, MA 02116. Copyright © 2006 by Pearson Education. Reprinted by permission of the publisher.

the call may come at an inconvenient time. Also, cell phones and Internet-based phones are rapidly changing the availability of respondents by phone. The use of an interviewer reduces anonymity and introduces potential interviewer bias. Open-ended questions are difficult to use, and questions requiring visual aids are impossible. Interviewers can note only serious disruptions (e.g., background noise) and respondent tone of voice (e.g., anger or flippancy) or hesitancy (see Table 8.5).

Face-to-Face Interviews

ADVANTAGES. Face-to-face interviews have the highest response rates and permit the longest questionnaires. They have the advantages of the telephone interview, and interviewers also can observe the surroundings and can use nonverbal communication and visual aids. Well-trained interviewers can ask all types of questions, ask complex questions, and use extensive probes.

DISADVANTAGES. High cost is the biggest disadvantage of face-to-face interviews. The training, travel, supervision, and personnel costs for interviews can be high. Interviewer bias is also greatest in face-to-face interviews. The appearance, tone of voice, question wording, and so forth of the interviewer may affect the respondent.

Web Surveys

Access to the Internet and e-mail did not become widespread across the advanced world until the late 1990s. For example, in 1994 only 3 percent of the U.S. population had e-mail, but by 2006 an estimated 75 percent of homes were connected to the Internet.[15] Highlight 8.4 provides an interesting example of using Web-based surveys to examine correctional programs that assist released inmates to secure work.

ADVANTAGES.   Web-based surveys over the Internet or by e-mail are very fast and inexpensive, allow flexible design, and can use visual images, or even audio or video. Commenting on the efficiency of e-mail or Web-based survey technologies compared to past methods, Dillman (2000: 352) observed, "These efficiencies include the nearly complete elimination of paper, postage, mail-out, and data entry costs . . . [they] also provide a potential for overcoming international boundaries as significant barriers . . . [and] the time required for survey implementation can be reduced from weeks to days, or even hours."

HIGHLIGHT 8.4
Web Surveys Sent to Correctional Agencies

Surveys of employers reveal a great reluctance to hire felony offenders. Most examinations have found that less than 50 percent of employers would hire an ex-offender. This number is further reduced by type of crime and multiple incarceration status. New security fears after September 11 have heightened worries about hiring ex-convicts, creating even tougher barriers for ex-offenders searching for employment.

Jessie Krienert (2005), is interested in a significant problem: The United States releases from incarceration over 1,600 convicted felons per day and nearly two-thirds of them will be rearrested for a felony or serious misdemeanor within three years. Most agree that a decent job would help to ameliorate this problem. However, no baseline data exist that documents the extent to which state correctional systems attempt to help inmates secure work after their release (prison-to-community employment programs).

Dr. Krienert sought to remedy this gap by conducting a simple pilot study. She collected data by using a Web-based survey technique that involved sending an e-letter to public information officers for all fifty state departments of corrections. The letter "served as both a pre-notification letter and an opportunity to participate in the survey via the Internet. The pre-notification letter also contained information on how to access a Web-based survey online. States (13) that did not have public e-mail correspondence were sent a hardcopy of the e-letter with a link to the online survey, and an invitation to participate." Only fifteen states responded to the initial e-mail, so she contacted the remaining thirty-five states a second time, eliciting a few more responses, and then a third time.

Ultimately, data collection resulted in response from 35 states (70 percent response rate). Twenty-six states (74.3 percent) filled out the survey online. Seven states (20 percent) returned the completed survey through the US Postal Service, and two states (5.7 percent) faxed in a hardcopy form. Five non-reporting states called or emailed, stating they would have to collect this information from their individual institutions and that they did not currently have the resources to perform such an undertaking, therefore could not participate. It is possible that other non-responding states faced similar barriers to completion.

This research revealed that none of the responding state correctional systems had a true prison-to-community work program, and only a few made nominal attempts to assist the inmate transition from prisoner to a gainfully employed member of society.

Dr. Krienert's research shows some promise for Web-based surveys—but it is illustrative that she still needed to supplement this technique with the traditional mail-out survey. Bureaucracies are creatures of habit, and crime and justice researchers should not assume that organizations have transitioned from paperwork-based operations to electronic. It should also demonstrate how even the most baseline descriptive questions have often not been researched in crime and justice studies.

Source: Jessie L. Krienert (2005), "Bridging the Gap between Prison and Community Employment: An Initial Assessment of Current Information," *Criminal Justice Studies,* vol. 18, no. 4 (293–303).

DISADVANTAGES.   Web surveys have three disadvantages or areas of concern: coverage, privacy and verification, and design issues. The first concern involves sampling, and unequal access and use of the Internet. Older, less educated, lower-income, and rural people are less likely to have access, and a majority without access now say they do not plan to acquire it in the future. In addition, many people have multiple e-mail addresses. As Tourangeau (2004a: 792) remarked, "The sampling problems with Web surveys are formidable."

A second concern involves protecting respondent privacy. This may be addressed technologically with secure Web sites and high confidentiality protection. Respondent verification to ensure that the sampled respondents alone participate and do so only once may also be resolved with a technical fix, such as giving each respondent a unique personal identification number (PIN) number, limiting who can complete the questionnaire.

A third concern involves the complexity of design. Researchers need to check and verify the compatibility of various Web software and hardware combinations for respondents using different types of computers. Researchers are just beginning to learn what is effective on this relatively new way to administer questionnaires. For example, it appears best to provide screen-by-screen questions and make each entire question visible on the screen at one time in a consistent format with drop-down boxes for answer choices. It is best to include a progress indicator (as motivation) such as a clock or waving hand. Visual appearance, such as the range of colors and fonts, should be limited for easy readability and consistency. Be sure to provide very clear instructions for any computer actions (e.g., use of drop-down screens) where they are needed and include "click here" instruction. Also, it is best to make it easy for respondents to move back and forth across questions (see Dillman 2000: 376–400 for a summary).

Table 8.5 overviews the various features of each kind of questionnaire used in survey research.

Interviewing

Interviews occur in many crime and justice settings. Criminal justice employers interview prospective employees, probation officers interview their clients, investigative journalists interview politicians and criminal justice administrators, police officers interview witnesses and crime victims, and social workers interview child abuse victims. **Survey research interviewing** is a specialized kind of interviewing. Its goal is to obtain accurate, quantitative-based information from another person. This approach to interviewing differs significantly from the type of interviews conducted by qualitative researchers discussed in Chapters 12–14, although many of the same tactics to extract and record worthwhile information are similar (see Chapter 13).[16]

SURVEY RESEARCH INTERVIEWING

A special type of interviewing designed to obtain specific and accurate quantitative-based information.

Quantitative and qualitative researchers often use interviews in a structured way to elicit information about a person's experiences, knowledge, feelings, values, and sometimes their secrets. It is important to recognize that the interview is a type of conversation between two people—and carries with it therefore all the emotional and cultural baggage of any human interaction. As the ISS approach would emphasize, the problem of accurately interpreting meaning is sticky. Communicating what a set of interviewers mean when they ask a question to numerous individuals, perhaps in many different contexts, is fraught with potential for misinterpretation. Careful controls and protocols have to be followed in order to approximate accurate and reliable quantitative data.

The interview, then, is a short-term, social interaction between two strangers with the explicit purpose of one person obtaining specific information from the other. The social roles are those of the interviewer and the interviewee or respondent. Information is obtained in a structured conversation in which the interviewer asks prearranged questions and records answers, and the respondent answers. As Table 8.6 illustrates, it differs in several ways from ordinary conversation.

The Role of the Interviewer

An important concern for interviewers is that many respondents are unfamiliar with the survey respondents' role and "respondents often do not have a clear conception of what is expected of them" (Turner and Martin 1984: 282). As a result, they substitute another role that may affect

TABLE 8.6	Differences between Ordinary Conversation and a Structured Survey Interview

Ordinary Conversation	The Survey Interview
1. Questions and answers from each participant are relatively equally balanced.	1. Interviewer asks and respondent answers most of the time.
2. There is an open exchange of feelings and opinions.	2. Only the respondent reveals feelings and opinions.
3. Judgments are stated and attempts made to persuade the other of particular points of view.	3. Interviewer is nonjudgmental and does not try to change respondent's opinion or beliefs.
4. A person can reveal deep inner feelings to gain sympathy or as a therapeutic release.	4. Interviewer tries to obtain direct answers to specific questions.
5. Ritual responses are common (e.g., "Uh huh," shaking head, "How are you?" "Fine").	5. Interviewer avoids making ritual responses that influence a respondent and also seeks genuine answers, not responses.
6. The participants exchange information and correct the factual errors that they are aware of.	6. Respondent provides almost all information. Interviewer does not correct a respondent's factual errors.
7. Topics rise and fall and either person can introduce new topics. The focus can shift directions or digress to less relevant issues.	7. Interviewer controls the topic, direction, and pace. He or she keeps the respondent "on task," and irrelevant diversions are contained.
8. The emotional tone can shift from humor, to joy, to affection, to sadness, to anger, and so on.	8. Interviewer attempts to maintain a consistently warm but serious and objective tone throughout.
9. People can evade or ignore questions and give flippant or noncommittal answers.	9. Respondent should not evade questions and should give truthful, thoughtful answers.

Source: Adapted from Raymond Gorden (1980), *Interviewing: Strategy, techniques and tactics,* 3rd ed. Homewood, IL: Dorsey Press, pp. 19–25; Seymour Sudman and Norman M. Bradburn (1983), *Asking questions: A practical guide to questionnaire design.* San Francisco, CA: Jossey-Bass, pp. 5–10.

their responses. Some people believe the interview is an intimate conversation or therapy session, some see it as a bureaucratic exercise in completing forms, some view it as a citizen referendum on policy choices, some view it as a testing situation, and some see it as a form of deceit in which interviewers are trying to trick or entrap respondents. Even in a well-designed, professional survey, follow-up research found that only about half the respondents understand questions exactly as intended by researchers. Respondents reinterpreted questions to make them applicable to their idiosyncratic, personal situations or to make them easy to answer.[17]

The role of interviewers is difficult. They obtain cooperation and build rapport, yet remain neutral and objective. They encroach on the respondents' time and privacy for information that may not directly benefit the respondents. They try to reduce embarrassment, fear, and suspicion so that respondents feel comfortable revealing information. They may explain the nature of survey research or give hints about social roles in an interview. Good interviewers monitor the pace and direction of the social interaction as well as the content of answers and the behavior of respondents.

Survey interviewers are nonjudgmental and do not reveal their opinions, verbally or nonverbally (e.g., by a look of shock). If a respondent asks for an interviewer's opinion, he or she politely redirects the respondent and indicates that such questions are inappropriate.

Interviewers do more than interview respondents. In fact, face-to-face interviewers spend only about 35 percent of their time interviewing. About 40 percent is spent in locating the correct respondent, 15 percent in traveling, and 10 percent in studying survey materials and dealing with administrative and recording details.[18] As seen in Highlight 8.5, crime and justice researchers

HIGHLIGHT 8.5
Interviewing Street Youth and Anomie Theory

The traditional academic presentation of research usually omits a great deal of interesting contextual and logistical information about how the research was actually carried out. Imagine a study that involved interviewing hundreds of homeless, hard-living youth in the inner city about their criminal activities. Certainly, numerous obstacles had to be overcome and an enormous amount of time and effort must have been devoted to interviewing, coding the data, inputting it into a statistical software program, analyzing the data, and then writing up the research report.

Stephen Baron, from Queen's University in Ontario, Canada, recently published an interesting piece of research testing the theory of anomie (discussed in Chapter 3) using survey interviewing as his primary data collection method. Baron interviewed 400 (265 male and 135 female) at-risk street youth who were both unemployed and homeless in a large Canadian city. Each youth was screened for inclusion in the study and then given a consent form that outlined their rights as a participant. Interviews were conducted on the street, parks, bus shelters, social services buildings, and fast-food restaurants. Interviews lasted an average of seventy minutes and each respondent was given a $20 food coupon.

Respondents were asked to self-report their involvement in crime and had to answer a range of questions relevant to the theory of anomie. For example, respondents were asked about breaking into cars, stealing food, selling drugs, using physical force to get money or things from another person, and "attacking someone with a weapon or fists injuring them so badly they probably needed a doctor" (Baron 2006: 215). Anomie questions inquired into the "youth's monetary goals, expectations for future financial success, and relative deprivation." Baron explored the numerous ways his study both supports and refutes the theory of anomie.

We asked Dr. Baron to relate some of his experiences. He made the following interesting observations. His description

should be helpful in giving a more accurate sense of what's involved in this kind of research:

I essentially spent a lot of time hanging around in places where these kids hung around, or did business. This meant the street, some parks, and in front of services for the street population. I began by approaching a group of five kids and went from there. These people were helpful in introducing me to other kids. And the kids were helpful in communicating to others that there was a study going on. This is important in that it helped establish my credibility on the street. This meant I had people who would just approach me and ask for an interview.

To make sure that I was getting people from different networks, I did the first part, introducing myself to a group or an individual on numerous occasions. Through observation I also learned that some people were social isolates, but by seeing them around all the time I was able to determine that they might be good candidates for the project. Further, since this is a transient population, you are always looking for the kids who had just come into town. Some of the challenges in getting participation flow from having people on the street who make their living there and do not have time to talk to you.

You have to catch the ebb and the flow of business and conduct your interviews when things are slow. This could be during bad weather, or it could be after a situation where the police have just arrested or confronted someone in the location where I was spending my time. This provided an opportunity to access people who were waiting for the situation to return to such that they felt comfortable conducting business again or that customers were coming again. It also depended on how efficient things were working in the system. If for example drug runners were delayed or people had not saved enough to pick up to start the day then there was down time. Similarly, since participants were given $20 in food coupons, there was some relationship between the availability of access to soup kitchens on certain days that could determine interest.

You also have to spend enough time to make sure you are getting people who are not high, or coming down, or getting sick. Further,

it was important to be around at all points in the day since different people seemed to be around at different times. You have to do all this in an environment where the police are asking your identity, and what you are doing hanging around since, as one police officer said to me, "There are only two reasons to be around here, buying or selling." You also have the interesting experience of people treating you as if you are homeless. The cigarettes tossed at me from people passing by and the sandwiches I got from street workers I passed on to those who needed them.

Source: Stephen W. Baron (2006), "Street Youth, Strain Theory, and Crime," *Journal of Criminal Justice*, vol. 34, (209–223).

sometimes conduct hundreds of interviews devoting large amounts of time in an effort to generate firsthand knowledge (in this case, about crime and homeless youth).

Stages of an Interview

The interview proceeds through stages, beginning with an introduction and entry. The interviewer greets the respondent, introduces herself, shows authorization if appropriate, and reassures and secures cooperation from the respondent. She is prepared for reactions such as, "How did you pick me?" "What good will this do?" "I don't know about this." "What's this about, anyway?" The interviewer can explain why the specific respondent is being interviewed.

The main part of the interview consists of asking questions and recording answers. Because the answers will eventually be coded as numerical data, the interviewer uses the exact wording on the questionnaire—no added or omitted words and no rephrasing. Consistency is of paramount importance. He or she asks all applicable questions in order, without returning to or skipping questions unless the directions specify this. He or she proceeds at a comfortable pace and gives nondirective feedback to maintain interest.

In addition to asking questions, the interviewer accurately records answers. This is easy for closed-ended questions, for which interviewers just mark the correct box. For open-ended questions, the interviewer's job is more difficult. He or she listens carefully, must have legible writing, and must record what is said verbatim without correcting grammar or slang. More important, the interviewer never summarizes or paraphrases. This causes a loss of information or distorts answers. For example, the respondent says, "I'm really concerned about my daughter's performance at school since the shootings. She's only thirteen years old and she doesn't seem to be dealing well with the trauma of witnessing such violence. We don't have health insurance or the money to get her into counseling and the school is only providing minimal help. I guess she'll just have to learn to live with it." If the interviewer simply writes, "concerned about her daughter's emotional health," much is lost.

The interviewer knows how and when to use probes. A **probe** is a neutral request to clarify an ambiguous answer, to complete an incomplete answer, or to obtain a relevant response. Interviewers recognize an irrelevant or inaccurate answer and use probes as needed.[19] There are many types of probes. A three- to five-second pause is often effective. Nonverbal communication (e.g., tilt of head, raised eyebrows, or eye contact) also works well. The interviewer can repeat the question or repeat the reply and then pause. He or she can ask a neutral question, such as, "Any other reasons?" "Can you tell me more about that?" "How do you mean?" "Could you explain more for me?"

Given this complexity and possible distortion, what should the diligent survey researcher do? Survey research should at least supplement closed-ended questionnaires with open-ended questions and probes. This takes more time, requires better-trained interviewers, and produces responses that may be less standardized and more difficult to quantify. But remember, qualitative quotes can illuminate effectively quantitative findings. Fixed-answer questionnaires based on the naïve assumption model imply a more simple and mechanical way of responding than occurs in many situations.

PROBE

A follow-up question in survey research interviewing that asks a respondent to clarify or elaborate on an incomplete or inappropriate answer.

The last stage is the exit, when the interviewer thanks the respondent and leaves. He or she then goes to a quiet, private place to edit the questionnaire and record other details such as the date, time, and place of the interview; a thumbnail sketch of the respondent and interview situation; the respondent's attitude (e.g., serious, angry, or happy); and any unusual circumstances. He or she notes anything disruptive that happened during the interview (e.g., "Officer received three calls for service that he had to route to other officers on duty"). The interviewer also records personal feelings and anything that was suspected (e.g., "Respondent became nervous and fidgeted when questioned about his marriage").

Interviewer Bias

Ideally, the actions of a particular interviewer will not affect how a respondent answers, and responses will not vary from what they would be if asked by any other interviewer. This goes beyond reading each question exactly as worded.

Survey researchers are still learning about the factors that influence survey interviews. They know that interviewer expectations can create significant bias. Interviewers who expect difficult interviews have them, and those who expect certain answers are more likely to get them. Proper interviewer behavior and exact question reading may be difficult, but the issue is larger. Interviewer bias can arise from expectations based on a respondent's age and race. In a major national U.S. survey, researchers learned that interviewers regularly coded Black respondents as being less intelligent and coded younger respondents as both less intelligent and less informed. Better interviewer training is needed to reduce such bias in survey results.[20] Listed below are six categories of interview bias that can adversely impact this type of research.

1. *Errors by the respondent.* Forgetting, embarrassment, misunderstanding, or lying because of the presence of others.
2. *Unintentional errors or interviewer sloppiness.* Contacting the wrong respondent, misreading a question, omitting questions, reading questions in the wrong order, recording the wrong answer to a question, or misunderstanding the respondent.
3. *Intentional subversion by the interviewer.* Purposeful alteration of answers, omission or rewording of questions, or fabricating answers.
4. *Interviewer's expectations.* Nonverbal and verbal cues that skew a respondent's answers based on his or her perception of the interviewer's expectations.
5. *Failure to probe properly.*
6. *Interviewer influence.* Adversely affect respondents due to the interviewer's appearance, tone, attitude, reactions to answers, or comments made outside of the interview schedule.

Pilot Testing

It is best to pilot-test survey interviews and questionnaires prior to implementation. In recent years, researchers have begun the systematic study of pilot tests in the survey process. Researchers examine how respondents answer questions during pilot tests. They use this information to refine the questionnaire or interviewing process. Listed below are several worthwhile pilot-test evaluation techniques (as seen in Dillman and Redine 2004; Fowler 2004; Martin 2004; Tourangeau 2004a, 2004b; Willis 2004; van der Zouwen and Smit 2004).

1. *Think-aloud interviews.* A respondent explains his or her thinking out loud during the process of answering each question.
2. *Retrospective interviews and targeted probes.* After completing a questionnaire, the respondent explains to researchers the process used to select each response or answer.
3. *Expert evaluation.* An independent panel of experienced survey researchers reviews and critiques the questionnaire.
4. *Behavior coding.* Researchers closely monitor interviews, often using audio- or videotapes, for misstatements, hesitations, missed instructions, nonresponse, refusals, puzzled looks, answers that do not fit any of the response categories, and so forth.

5. *Field experiments.* Researchers administer alternative forms of the questionnaire items in field settings and compare results.
6. *Vignettes and debriefing.* Interviewers and respondents are presented with short, invented "lifelike" situations and are asked which questionnaire response category they would use.

THE "MEANING" DIFFICULTY IN SURVEY RESEARCH

How many times in a week do we say to ourselves, "What did she/he mean by that?" Effectively communicating what we "mean" is difficult. The ISS and CSS approaches see this as inevitable, because human meaning is inherently subjective, subject to change, and often fuzzy. Research into survey errors and interview bias has substantiated these views, forcing survey researchers to think seriously about larger issues of how people create social meaning and achieve cultural understanding.[21]

Survey researchers are troubled when the same words have different meanings and implications depending on the social situation, who speaks them, how they are spoken, and the social distance between the survey/interviewer and respondent/listener. Also, respondents who do not understand the social situation of the survey interview or questionnaire may misinterpret the nature of survey research, and may seek clues for how to answer in the wording of questions or subtle actions of the interviewer.

Initially, survey research was based on the **naïve assumption model** (Foddy 1993: 13). This is similar to the naïve assumptions experimental researchers sometimes make as discussed in Chapter 7. Researchers try to improve survey research by reducing the gap between actual experience in conducting surveys and the ideal survey expressed as the model's assumptions. As noted in Table 8.7 researchers should avoid the naïve assumption that asking questions and receiving answers is a fairly straightforward process that yields objective, neutral data.

The critical thinking researcher makes no such assumptions. For example, as an interviewer strives to act in a more neutral and uniform way, he or she reduces the type of bias that causes unreliability because of individual interviewer behavior. Yet, such attempts can result in misinterpretations of meaning on both ends, caused by creating an artificial and counterproductive barrier between researcher and the researched.[22] In complex human interaction, people often add interpretative meaning to simple questions (whether written or oral). For example, my neighbor asks the simple question, "How often do you mow your lawn?" His question could be interpreted in the following ways:

- How often do I personally mow the lawn (versus having someone else mow it for me)?
- How often do I mow it to cut grass (versus run my lawn mower over it to chop up leaves)?

NAÏVE ASSUMPTION MODEL

A model of standardized survey research in which there are no communication problems and respondents' responses perfectly match their thoughts.

TABLE 8.7	Naïve Assumption Model of Survey Interviews

1. Researchers have clearly conceptualized all variables being measured.
2. Questionnaires have no wording, question order, or related effects.
3. Respondents are motivated and willing to answer all the questions asked.
4. Respondents possess complete information and can accurately recall events.
5. Respondents understand each question as the researcher intends it.
6. Respondents give more truthful answers if they do not know the hypotheses.
7. Respondents give more truthful answers if they receive no hints or suggestions.
8. The interview situation and specific interviewers have no effects on answers.
9. The process of the interview has no impact on the respondents' beliefs or attitudes.
10. Respondents' behaviors match their verbal responses in an interview.

- How often do I mow the entire lawn (versus cutting the quick-growing parts only)?
- How often do I mow it during an entire season, a month, a week?
- This isn't really a question but a latent criticism for not mowing my lawn often enough.

Within seconds, I make one of these interpretations and give an answer. The open-ended, ongoing neighborly interaction permits room for clarification and for several follow-up questions that help my neighbor and me to arrive at mutual understanding.

A dilemma arises because a survey interview interaction differs from ordinary conversation. A survey research interview is a standardized, artificial interaction that treats diverse respondents alike to control the communication situation and yield a uniform measure. Ordinary interaction contains built-in features to detect and correct misinterpretation; it relies on nuance and give and take. People achieve social meaning in ordinary conversation by relying on clues in the context, adjusting the interaction flow to specific people involved, and building on a cultural frame (often based on race, class, gender, region, or religion). The fluid interaction of ordinary conversation is self-adjusting because different people do not always assign the same meaning to the same words, phrases, and questions. By standardizing human interaction, the survey research eliminates features in ordinary conversation that provide self-correction, promote the construction of a shared meaning among different people, and increase human mutual understanding.[23]

This critical discussion about quantitative survey interviewing should not be interpreted as a condemnation (not an either-or thinking position). Rather, it simply adds to our critical thinking skills and in-depth understanding about the strengths and limitations of differing research approaches. Indeed, understanding the fallacies of the naïve assumption model encourages survey researchers to collect empirical data in a more rigorous, conscientious, and reflective fashion.

ETHICAL SURVEY RESEARCH

Like all crime and justice research, people can conduct surveys in ethical or unethical ways. A major ethical issue in survey research is the invasion of privacy.[24] Survey researchers can intrude into a respondent's privacy by asking about intimate actions and personal beliefs. People have a right to privacy. Respondents decide when and to whom to reveal personal information. They are likely to provide such information honestly when it is asked for in a comfortable context with mutual trust, when they believe serious answers are needed for legitimate research purposes, and when they believe answers will remain confidential. Researchers should treat all respondents with dignity and reduce discomfort. They are also responsible for protecting the confidentiality of data.

A second issue involves voluntary participation by respondents. Respondents agree to answer questions and can refuse to participate at any time. They give "informed consent" to participate in research. Researchers depend on respondents' voluntary cooperation, so researchers need to ask well-developed questions in a sensitive way, treat respondents with respect, and be very sensitive to confidentiality.

A third issue is the mass media reporting of survey results.[25] Few people reading survey results may appreciate it, but researchers should include details about the survey to reduce the misuse of survey research and increase questions about surveys that lack such information. Survey researchers urge the media to include such information, but it is rarely included. Over 88 percent of reports on surveys in the mass media fail to reveal the researcher who conducted the survey, and only 18 percent provide details on how the survey was conducted.[26] This occurs while the media report more surveys than other types of social research. Highlight 8.6 presents a few of Kraska's experiences in disseminating survey research knowledge to the media.

HIGHLIGHT 8.6
Kraska's Five Minutes of Pain

I assumed the police militarization survey research I completed in the late 1990s would be of interest only to other academics. I published the first article on this research in a well-known sociological journal, *Social Problems*, and assumed few outside academia would notice.

In April 1997, shortly after the *Social Problems* piece came out, William Booth, a journalist from the *Washington Post*, called for an interview. He conducted a two-hour interview. I answered his questions, agreed to send him some details on the survey methodology, and figured nothing would happen. Four days later I found out from a friend that the *Washington Post* had run a front-page article featuring this research: "Exploding Number of SWAT Teams Sets Off Alarms: Critics See Growing Number of Heavily Armed Police Units as 'Militarization' of Law Enforcement." Of course my research was not meant to be so sensational, and despite the inflammatory tone of the title, Booth had done an exceptional job detailing accurately the nature of the research and its findings within the article.

For the next four years I received many more requests for interviews; I ended up working on about seventy different print, radio, and television news stories. With absolutely no previous experience, I found myself giving on-camera interviews attempting to accurately disseminate the findings of my survey research projects to CBS's *60 Minutes*, the *Jim Leher News Hour*, *Peter Jennings World News Tonight*, the *CBS Evening News*, the BBC, the Discovery Channel, *Prime-Time Live*, and *20/20*. I spent numerous hours with print journalists from *The Economist*, the *New York Times*, the *Los Angeles Times*, and regional newspapers. To this day, I still receive about one call a month from print journalists, usually doing a story about a botched quick-knock raid in their community. I am also asked about twice a year to work as an expert witness in SWAT raid cases gone wrong. (I received a call on October 5, 2006, from a journalist in Florida asking questions about a questionable SWAT raid that resulted in the death of the owner of the house. No drugs were found. I received another call from the *Christian Science Monitor* about a story on a botched drug raid in Atlanta, where an eighty-eight-year-old woman was killed after opening fire on police; initial evidence indicates the police were at the wrong address.)

Working this closely with the media has been instructive. I've found television journalists to be in general less professional than print journalists. Print journalists have an interest in research methodology and are quite careful about making sure that research findings have some scientific legitimacy. Many asked questions about the nature of the survey instrument, response rates, and specific statistical techniques. Often fact-checkers will also call and verify the information and its origin. This has generally not been true of television journalists (the only exception was the *Jim Lehrer News Hour*, in an interview conducted by producer Jeffrey Kaye).

The print media stories are referenced in library databases so that future SWAT tragedies can be contextualized within a recorded history of explanations, academic concepts, and events. The print media coverage has, in fact, played a role in reform efforts targeted at developing training standards for SWAT teams, changes in police policies, and changes in no-knock/quick-knock legal procedures in states such as California and Colorado.

Conclusion

In this chapter we discussed survey research. Survey research is versatile and is well suited for exploratory, descriptive, explanatory, and evaluation research. It is widely used by both academics and practitioners, especially in situations in which the researcher wants to study large sample sizes and a large number of variables. We reviewed some principles of writing good survey questions, and the things to avoid when writing questions. We learned about the advantages and disadvantages of four types of survey research: mail, telephone interviews, face-to-face interviews, and Web surveys. We saw that interviewing, especially face-to-face interviewing, can be difficult but productive.

Although this chapter focused on survey research, researchers use questionnaires to measure variables in other types of quantitative research. For example, self-report survey instruments are often used in an experiment that attempts to determine if a treatment (D.A.R.E. program) had an effect on the dependent variable (illegal drug use). The survey, often called the *sample survey* because random sampling is usually used with it, is a distinct technique. It is a process of asking many people the same questions and examining their answers.

We also pointed out how quality survey research requires good interpretive and empathy skills. Although its ultimate goal is to convert social phenomena into quantitative form, it ironically requires the same critical thinking skills espoused by the interpretive social science and qualitative approaches (which questions whether this conversion is even possible). This is a good example, therefore, of how understanding an oppositional perspective can act to strengthen that which it opposes. Still, we need to remain aware of the fact that survey research is limited in its ability to capture the true essence of crime and justice phenomena. For example, asking someone about their values (espoused values) does not necessarily mean that we are accurately measuring the values they actually act upon (values-in-use). Survey research is strong on reliability and less robust when it comes to validity. As we'll discuss further in Chapter 13, we can strengthen the weaknesses of survey research by integrating qualitative methods and analysis (e.g., mixed methods approach).

Key Terms

correlational *176*
prestige bias *180*
double-barreled question *180*
leading (or loaded) question *180*

telescope *181*
self-report surveys *182*
open-ended question *182*
closed-ended question *183*

order effects *186*
cover letter *187*
computer-assisted telephone interviewing (CATI) *189*

survey research interviewing *192*
probe *195*
naïve assumption model *197*

Review Questions

1. Why is the survey research method so important to criminal justice and crime studies? Give one example to substantiate your answer.
2. What is a self-report survey, and why is it important to criminal justice and crime studies?
3. What are the seven types of things surveys often ask about? Give an example of each type, different from the examples given in the book.
4. Why are surveys called correlational, and how do they differ from experiments?
5. What are the two key principles for writing good survey questions? Explain the importance of each.
6. What are four of the eight things to avoid in question writing?
7. What topics are threatening to respondents, and how can a researcher ask about these topics and elicit candid responses?

8. What are advantages and disadvantages of open-ended versus closed-ended questions?
9. What are some of the more important considerations that should go into the design of surveys?
10. What are five of the most important tips to increase mail survey response rates?
11. What are the advantages and disadvantages of: (1) mail and self-administered questionnaires, (2) telephone interviews, (3) face-to-face interviews, and (4) Web surveys?
12. How does ordinary conversation differ from a survey interview?
13. What is interview bias, and how can researchers best avoid this potential problem?
14. What is the "meaning difficulty" in survey research, and what steps can be taken to remedy this potential problem?

Practicing Research

1. Develop a viable survey research study idea that uses college students as the research subjects. Construct a 10–15-item questionnaire, administer the questionnaire to a sample of students (identify the sampling technique used), and record the results. In small groups of four to six students, share your research with your peers and critique each other's work, raising questions about the study's validity and reliability. With such a small-scale study, it won't be necessary to input the data into a statistical computer program (the calculations could be done by hand)—but this would be a good opportunity to try it out. Even many handheld calculators have the ability to input data from a survey into variables and conduct simple statistical calculations. The goal of this exercise is not to conduct a robust study with

detailed statistical analysis but to simply experience how this process works.
2. Locate two survey research articles in a criminal justice/criminology journal. Answer the following questions:
   a. What is the central purpose of each study (e.g., descriptive, explanatory)?
   b. What are the major variables used in the studies and how are they conceptualized?
   c. What sampling techniques were used; what sort of response rate was obtained; what type of delivery method was used (e.g., mail, phone)?
   d. Examine the actual survey questions used in the study (sometimes found in an appendix). Scrutinize the quality of the questions.

e. In light of learning about survey research, what recommendations would you make to the author to improve the study?

3. Develop a viable survey research idea that involves criminal justice agencies divulging information that they might be guarded about (police, courts, probation, juvenile justice, prisons, etc.). Construct a mock cover letter to a survey that would effectively gain the agency's cooperation. Exchange these letters in small groups and discuss with the group members the extent to which they think these letters would persuade an agency to fill out a survey.

4. Develop a short interview instrument (10–15 items) that will be used to ask relatives and friends about their views on terrorism and the war on terrorism. Try to construct the questions in a way that the respondents will understand readily what is being asked. Select four to eight friends or relatives, and using the instrument you constructed, conduct a survey interview. Take note of your comfort level, the extent to which you remained consistent in how you asked the questions across respondents, and make sure that you ask each respondent how he or she felt about the experience and your performance. Report your experiences, making sure to include something about the process of interpreting the meaning of the respondents' answers.

Notes for Further Study

1. See Bannister (1987), Blumer (1991a, 1991b), Blumer and associates (1991), Camic and Xie (1994), Cohen (1991), Deegan (1988), Ross (1991), Sklar (1991), Turner (1991), and Yeo (1991). Also see R. Smith (1996) on how political ideological conflicts and private foundations in the United States in the 1950s and 1960s affected how survey research developed.

2. For a discussion of pilot-testing techniques, see Bishop (1992), Bolton and Bronkhorst (1996), Fowler and Cannell (1996), and Sudman and colleagues (1996).

3. The administration of survey research is discussed in Backstrom and Hursh-Cesar (1981: 38–45), Dillman (1978: 200–281; 1983), Frey (1983: 129–169), Groves and Kahn (1979: 40–78, 186–212), Prewitt (1983), Tanur (1983), and Warwick and Lininger (1975: 20–45, 220–264).

4. See Abelson and associates (1992), Auriat (1993), Bernard and associates (1984), Croyle and Loftus (1992), Gaskell and colleagues (2000), Krosnick and Abelson (1992), Loftus and colleagues (1990), Loftus and colleagues (1992), Pearson and Dawes (1992), and Sudman and colleagues (1996).

5. See Bradburn (1983), Bradburn and Sudman (1980), and Sudman and Bradburn (1983) on threatening or sensitive questions. Backstrom and Hursh-Cesar (1981: 219) and Warwick and Lininger (1975: 150–151) provide useful suggestions as well. Fox and Tracy (1986) discuss the randomized response technique. Also see DeLamater and MacCorquodale (1975) on measuring sexual behavior and Herzberger (1993) for design issues when examining sensitive topics.

6. For studies on survey format and answer honesty, see Holbrook and associates (2003), Johnson et al. (1989), Schaeffer and Presser (2003:75), and Tourangeau and colleagues (2002).

7. For a further discussion of open and closed questions, see Bailey (1987: 117–122), Converse (1984), Converse and Presser (1986: 33–34), deVaus (1986: 74–75), Geer (1988), Moser and Kalton (1972: 341–345), Schuman and Presser (1979; 1981: 79–111), Sudman and Bradburn (1983: 149–155), and Warwick and Lininger (1975: 132–140).

8. The disagree/agree versus specific alternatives debate is discussed in Bradburn and Sudman (1988: 149–151), Converse and Presser (1986: 38–39), Schuman and Presser (1981: 179–223), and Sudman and Bradburn (1983: 119–140). Backstrom and Hursh-Cesar (1981: 136–140) discuss asking Likert, agree/disagree questions.

9. The length of questionnaires is discussed in Dillman (1978: 51–57; 1983), Frey (1983: 48–49), Herzog and Bachman (1981), and Sudman and Bradburn (1983: 226–227).

10. For a discussion of the sequence of questions or question order effects, see Backstrom and Hursh-Cesar (1981: 154–176), Bishop and colleagues (1985), Bradburn (1983: 302–304), Bradburn and Sudman (1988: 153–154), Converse and Presser (1986: 39–40), Dillman (1978: 218–220), McFarland (1981), McKee and O'Brien (1988), Moser and Kalton (1972: 346–347), Schuman and Ludwig (1983), Schuman and Presser (1981: 23–74), Schwartz and Hippler (1995), and Sudman and Bradburn (1983: 207–226). Also see Knäuper (1999), Krosnick (1992), Lacy (2001), and T. Smith (1992) on the issue of question-order effects.

11. For a discussion of format and layout, see Babbie (1990), Backstrom and Hursh-Cesar (1981: 187–236), Dillman (1978, 1983), Mayer and Piper (1982), Sudman and Bradburn (1983: 229–260), Survey Research Center (1976), and Warwick and Lininger (1975: 151–157).

12. For additional discussion of nonresponse and refusal rates, see Backstrom and Hursh-Cesar (1981: 140–141, 274–275), DeMaio (1980), Frey (1983: 38–41), Groves and Couper (1998), Groves and Kahn (1979:218–223), Martin (1985: 701–706), Nederhof (1986), Oksenberg and associates (1986), Schuman and Presser (1981: 331–336), Sigelman (1982), Stech (1981), Sudman and Bradburn (1983), and Yu and Cooper (1983). For a discussion of methods for calculating response rates, see Bailey (1987: 169), Dillman (1978: 49–51), Fowler (1984: 46–52), and Frey (1983: 38).

13. More extensive discussions of how to increase mail questionnaire return rates can be found in Bailey (1987: 153–168), Church (1993), Dillman (1978, 1983), Fox and colleagues (1988), Goyder (1982), Heberlein and

Baumgartner (1978, 1981), Hubbard and Little (1988), Jones (1979), and Willimack and colleagues (1995).

14. CATI is discussed in Bailey (1987: 201–202), Bradburn and Sudman (1988: 100–101), Freeman and Shanks (1983), Frey (1983: 24–25, 143–149), Groves and Kahn (1979:226), Groves and Mathiowetz (1984), and Karweit and Meyers (1983).

15. For Internet usage, see Robyn Greenspan, "Three-Quarters of Americans Have Access from Home," ClickZ News (March 18, 2004), www.clickz.com/news/article.php/ 3328091; Amanda Lenhart, "Who's Not Online," Pew Internet and American Life Project, Washington, D.C. (September 21, 2000), www.pewinternet. org/report_dis-play.asp?r=21. For discussions of Web and e-mail surveys, see Birnhaum (2004), Couper (2000), Couper et al. (2001), Fox and associates (1988), Koch and Emrey (2001), and Tourangeau (2004a: 792–794).

16. For more on interviewing, see Brenner and colleagues (1985), Cannell and Kahn (1968), Converse and Schuman (1974), Dijkstra and van der Zouwen (1982), Foddy (1993), Gorden (1980), Hyman (1975), Moser and Kalton (1972: 270–302), and Survey Research Center (1976). For a discussion of telephone interviewing, see Frey (1983), Groves and Mathiowetz (1984), Jordan and colleagues (1980), and Tucker (1983).

17. See Turner and Martin (1984: 262–269, 282).

18. From Moser and Kalton (1972: 273).

19. The use of probes is discussed in Backstrom and Hursh-Cesar (1981: 266–273), Foddy (1995), Schober and Conrad (1997), and Smith (1989). Gorden (1980: 368–390), Hyman (1975: 236–241), Schober and Conrad (1997), and Smith (1989).

20. See Leal and Hess (1999).

21. See Bateson (1984), Clark and Schober (1992), Foddy (1993), Lessler (1984), and Turner (1984).

22. See Briggs (1986), Cicourel (1982), and Mishler (1986) for critiques of survey research interviewing.

23. For additional discussion of ordinary conversation and survey interviews, see Beatty (1995), Conrad and Schober (2000), Groves and colleagues (1992), Moore (2004), Schaeffer (2004), Schober and Conrad (2004), Smith (1984), and Suchman and Jordan (1992).

24. For a discussion of ethical concerns specific to survey research, see Backstrom and Hursh-Cesar (1981: 46–50), Fowler (1984: 135–144), Frey (1983: 177–185), Kelman (1982: 79–81), and Reynolds (1982: 48–57). Marsh (1982: 125–146) and Miller (1983: 47–96) provided useful discussions for and against the use of survey research. The use of informed consent is discussed in Singer and Frankel (1982) and in Sobal (1984).

25. On reporting survey results in the media, see Channels (1993) and MacKeun (1984).

26. See Singer (1988).

Nonreactive Research: Content Analysis and Existing Documents/Statistics

Digging up Data
   Highlight 9.1 Death on the Roadside
Nonreactive Research in Crime and Justice Studies
   Highlight 9.2 To Map or Not to Map—Derek Paulsen's Crime-Mapping Experiment with the Police
Factors to Consider When Choosing Nonreactive Methods
Nonreactive Research Methods
   The Logic of Nonreactive Research
   Varieties of Nonreactive Observation
      Highlight 9.3 Caught on Camera: Nonreactive Shoplifting Study
   Recording and Documentation
Quantitative Content Analysis
   What Is Content Analysis?
   Topics Appropriate for Content Analysis
   Measurement and Coding
      General Issues
      What Is Measured?
   Coding, Validity, and Reliability
      Manifest Coding
      Latent Coding
      Intercoder Reliability
   Content Analysis with Visual Material
   How to Conduct Content Analysis Research

   Question Formulation
   Units of Analysis
   Sampling
   Variables and Constructing Coding Categories
Inferences
Existing Documents/Statistics
   Topics Appropriate for Existing Documents/Statistics Research
   Locating Data
      Locating Documents
         Highlight 9.4 Counting Death: The Morgue versus Surveys
      Locating Existing Statistics
   Reliability and Validity
      Units of Analysis and Variable Attributes
      Validity
      Reliability
         Highlight 9.5 Racial Assault with a Baseball? Measuring Race-Motivated Aggression
      Missing Data
   Example of Existing Documents/Statistics Research
Conclusion
Key Terms
Review Questions
Practicing Research
Notes for Further Study

DIGGING UP DATA

Imagine a future in which the most dire predictions of climatologists came true: massive global desertification; large land masses of once densely populated coastal areas going under the sea; intense weather patterns that bring a continuous stream of large-scale natural disasters (hurricanes, tornadoes, flooding, heat waves, and tsunamis); and a breakdown in civil order leading to mass migration, social chaos, riots, and rampant crime. Entire populations of people would be displaced, leaving behind mountains of refuse, documents, old computers, and photos. In another few hundred years these same abandoned areas might become valuable sites where archeologists carefully sort through artifacts and crime scenes in an attempt to make sense of the past (similar to today's archeologists studying the cultural artifacts of the ancient Mayan, Roman, or Chinese civilizations).

In a way, the research method used by these archeologists fits the definition of unobtrusive measures provided in Chapter 1: They collect, examine, and analyze what others have left behind (Webb 1981; Webb et al. 2000). Many researchers in crime and justice studies similarly draw upon preexisting documents, figures, and numbers to determine what is really the case in the recent past. Whereas experimental and survey research generate knowledge through actively engaging and manipulating their external environments, **unobtrusive measures** involve collecting what are known as **nonreactive data**. This means that the researcher studies crime and justice phenomena without affecting it—avoiding the problem of research subjects reacting to being researched. They instead gather up what has been left behind (artifacts, existing data, graffiti art, documents, etc.) or they carry out disengaged observation of natural events without intruding (e.g., watching and listening to the activities conducted on a particular street corner using hidden cameras/microphones).

Crime and justice researchers don't, of course, dig through the earth to uncover these data, but they do sometimes have to rummage through dusty governmental storage areas or slog through mountains of paperwork in a police, court, or corrections workplace. In fact, creative researchers have an almost limitless amount of data at their disposal, including diaries, court records, governmental statistics, police records, graffiti, newspapers, television shows, advertisements, music, existing data from previous research, and so on.

Eugene J. Webb and colleagues (1966, 2004) wrote the seminal book about this genre of research, *Nonreactive Research in the Social Sciences*. Webb once described it as the book of "oddball measures." He even considered calling the book *The Bullfighter's Beard*, since some believe bullfighters' beards grow faster on days they fight. Webb cautioned, however, "No one seems to know if the torero's beard really grows faster on that day because of anxiety or if he simply stands farther away from the blade, shaking razor in hand."

Webb outlined three categories of unobtrusive measures:

- **physical traces** (the physical remains of human activities, such as at a crime scene investigation of a murder, or graffiti on a prison cell wall)
- **archival material** (any archived material including government documents, quantitative data sets, photographs, diaries, etc.)
- **unobtrusive observation** (observational data collected by a researcher whose presence is not made known to the observed).

Most nonreactive research involves the second category, archival material, and only a small amount of research is done using physical traces or unobtrusive observation. The bulk of emphasis in this chapter, therefore, will be on the two archival methods discussed in Chapter 1 as content analysis and existing documents/data. Highlight 9.1 provides an example of the interesting research available to the nonreactive researcher.

Although our emphasis in this chapter will be on quantitative methods, it is important to recognize that data collected through unobtrusive means are often approached using historical and qualitative thinking and techniques. As discussed further in Chapter 13, combining both qualitative and quantitative methods within a mixed methods approach is increasingly common.

UNOBTRUSIVE MEASURES

Another name for nonreactive measures that emphasize how the people being studied are not aware of it because the measures do not intrude.

NONREACTIVE DATA

A class of data that are collected in such a way that the people being studied are unaware that they are part of a study.

PHYSICAL TRACES

The physical remains of human activity.

ARCHIVAL MATERIAL

A collection of documents or artifacts that a researcher can use as data.

UNOBTRUSIVE OBSERVATION

Another name for non-reactive measures that emphasizes how the people being studied are not aware of it because the measures do not intrude.

HIGHLIGHT 9.1
Death on the Roadside

©2003 Jeff Ferrell

In the article "Speed Kills," Jeff Ferrell (2002) used nonreactive methods to collect data on roadside shrines (memorials left by surviving family members of a traffic accident victim). His research method was simple—collect photographs of as many different roadside shrines available. His research purpose was clearly aligned with the critical social science approach. Ferrell examined the cultural significance of roadside memorials as a means to expose the inconsistencies in crime and justice ideology when it comes to the high levels of automobile death (43,443 people killed in 2005 alone). His research objective is to get people to think outside dominant ideology. In his own words:

> . . . Overwhelmed by a shrine of especially heartbreaking tragedy—where the children have put up crosses for "Mom" and "Dad" and written "we-love-you-forever" on the blades of a little pinwheel—I think about the notion of hegemony, of domination so thoroughgoing as to become taken-for-granted. I wonder if maybe the culture of the car is so interwoven with contemporary life in the United States—so tightly intertwined with patterns of housing, work, pleasure, and consumption—that critiques have been rendered unimaginable and alternatives unthinkable, even for those accustomed to critique, even in the face of 40,000 fluttering pinwheels a year. (Ferrell 2003: 196)

We'll examine this type of qualitative nonreactive research in Chapter 13.

NONREACTIVE RESEARCH IN CRIME AND JUSTICE STUDIES

Nonreactive research is the second most common research method used in crime and justice studies (recall that survey research is the first). This makes sense, given that the criminal justice apparatus, an immense bureaucratic entity both in the United States and internationally, generates massive volumes of archived information. The possibilities are vast; some of the examples we've drawn so far in this book include crime statistics (UCR, NCVS), the General Social Survey, police and prison records, video-surveillance data, existing self-report data, incarceration trends, drug use statistics, documents concerning prisoners released from death row, and court proceedings documents. Numerous existing information sources are available outside the criminal justice system as well, such as media articles, Web sites, television shows, roadside memorials, hospital records, census reports, and economic data, just to name a few. Crime and justice research is definitely unique in this regard—we generate almost as much knowledge using preexisting information as we do using reactive methods. Highlight 9.2 illustrates the noteworthy work completed by Derek Paulsen combining nonreactive data with experimental research to evaluate whether crime mapping assists police officer decision making.

HIGHLIGHT 9.2

To Map or Not to Map—Derek Paulsen's Crime-Mapping Experiment with the Police

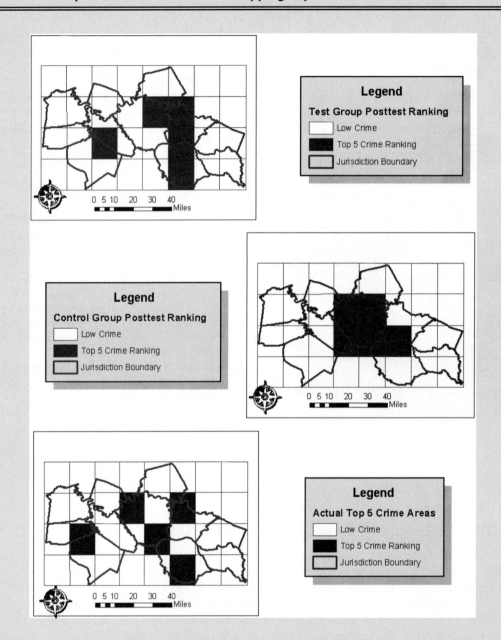

The increased use of crime mapping within policing has been most directly related to the movement away from traditional centralized police operations toward a more intelligence-led proactive style of policing. Variously termed *geographical policing* or *rationalized policing*, this style of policing is heavily influenced by COMSTAT and other such police reform efforts that have received a great deal of publicity over the past ten years. This new style of policing often involves the systematic analysis of crime data to target existing and emerging crime problems more effectively. Specifically, crime data are analyzed to determine "hot spots" of crime to which problem-solving techniques are then applied and police resources committed in order to reduce crime at specific locations.

Central to the success of intelligence-led policing strategies is the ability of individual police officers to accurately identify problem areas within a jurisdiction. In particular, success depends on an expert understanding of crime patterns within a jurisdiction and an officer's ability to quickly and accurately identify those areas most in need of police resources. If police officers have an accurate understanding of crime patterns in their jurisdiction, then it is assumed that resources will be deployed judiciously and that intelligence-led policing strategies will be more likely to have beneficial results. Conversely, if police officers do not have an accurate understanding of crime patterns, then it can be assumed that resources will not be deployed to those areas most in need, lowering the chances of success for intelligence-led policing efforts.

It is this promise of improving officer perceptions through the distribution of crime maps that this research seeks to evaluate. Specifically, can crime information distributed in a crime map form improve officer perception and understanding of crime patterns and problem areas within a jurisdiction? In addition, this research will attempt to ascertain the overall accuracy of officers' spatial perception of crime.

Methods

In order to best ascertain the impact that crime maps have on officers' perceptions of crime locations, a classic experimental method was used, involving test and control groups as well as a pre- and post-test instrument. After randomly splitting forty officers from the test jurisdiction into separate test and control groups, a baseline measure of the officers' spatial perception of crime patterns was gathered using a base map method. In this base map method, officers were given a detailed map of their jurisdiction that had been subdivided into thirty-two equal areas and were asked to list the five areas they felt had the highest crime rates for the jurisdiction. In creating this baseline map, special care was given to making sure that each area contained whole and distinct communities. Subsequently, officers from the test group received daily, weekly, and monthly crime maps that they were asked not to share with other officers. After receiving maps for a two-month period, the posttest instrument was administered to all forty officers in order to assess any changes in the spatial perceptions of crime by either group of officers.

Results

In order to assess the accuracy of officers' perceptions, their baseline maps of the top five high-crime areas were compared with a map indicating the actual top five high-crime areas for the test jurisdiction. The actual high-crime area map was created by taking the locations of all crimes reported to the test jurisdiction for the preceding year and aggregating those crimes to the thirty-two subdivided areas of the baseline map.

In analyzing the results, the test group appears to have been no more accurate in its perception of high-crime areas than the control group, despite having received daily, weekly, and monthly crime maps for two months. As the accompanying figure illustrates, although there are definite differences in the areas that the test and control groups identify as high-crime areas, neither group is very accurate. Both groups correctly identified only two of five actual high-crime areas, giving them an accuracy score of about 40 percent, and, more important, showing no improvement at all over their pretest scores. The findings are consistent with the results of other research and call into question not only police officers' understanding of their jurisdictions, but the ability of maps to assist in intelligence-led policing tactics.

Source: Authored by Derek Paulsen. Used by permission of Derek J. Paulsen. Derek J. Paulsen is the author of the book *Spatial Aspects of Crime: Theory and Practice* by Derek J. Paulsen and Matthew B. Robinson, Allyn & Bacon, 2004.

Availability and convenience are no doubt part of the reason for the popularity of this approach. However, we should not assume that all nonreactive research requires less work. Existing crime and justice information comes in many different forms, sometimes in quantitative data ready to be analyzed, but at other times requiring the researcher to convert it into quantitative variables. Figure 9.1 illustrates the range of forms this information can take. At one end of the continuum,

The Range of Data Forms Found in Nonreactive Research

| Any document(s) or artifact(s); requires collection and conversion into quantitative variables; extensive work | Any organizational data (generally in some type of quantitative form) but which requires reformatting and inputting into a statistical data set | Any existing statistical data set; requires little modification other than variable manipulation and analysis |

| RAW DOCUMENTS | ROUGH DATA | FINISHED DATA SET |

FIGURE 9.1 Forms of Nonreactive Data.

the researcher will need to do extensive work to convert it into quantitative variables; at the other end an existing database allows for immediate analysis.

As we'll discover throughout this chapter, nonreactive research harbors tremendous potential for answering numerous interesting and practical research questions. The possibilities are limited only by our creativity and imagination.

FACTORS TO CONSIDER WHEN CHOOSING NONREACTIVE METHODS

Unobtrusive research has the advantage that the data collection process does not affect the data collected. Collecting existing information or covertly observing an event avoids the problem of data being corrupted by reactive research effects. However, this also means that in the case of using existing data, the researcher is relying on data that have already been processed by state officials. Some criminologists criticize the overreliance on these types of data on the basis that bureaucratic functionaries are more interested in efficiency and/or their own interests than they are in scientific rigor (Haggerty 2001). In addition, when using an existing data set, a researcher has to assume that the original data collection process did not involve strong reactive effects.

A clear strength of using existing documents/data is their ready availability for many crime and justice research topics. Our students have conducted numerous research studies using nonreactive research methods in part because of their accessibility. A student of Kraska collected and analyzed data from over 300 Web sites that deal in the sale and manufacture of illegal performance-enhancing drugs.

This does not necessarily mean that nonreactive research is more convenient and less time consuming. It depends on where the data fall on the continuum found in Figure 9.1. On one hand, collecting and coding data out of thousands of different newspaper articles is an immense amount of work and quite time consuming (recall Chermak's crime and media study). On the other hand, downloading an intact data set from the Internet and conducting a secondary analysis can involve relatively minimal time and effort. Even international comparative analyses of crime and justice phenomenon are possible with minimal time and effort.

Ethical concerns are another limitation of some types of nonreactive methods. Secretly installing a video camera in a classroom to research cheating behavior among students would raise voluntary consent and confidentiality issues. Many types of nonreactive methods, however, only indirectly involve human subjects and in many settings do not even require Internal Review Board (IRB) committee approval (e.g., content analysis of newspaper stories or secondary analysis of existing governmental statistics).

NONREACTIVE RESEARCH METHODS

The Logic of Nonreactive Research

Nonreactive measurement begins when a researcher notices something that indicates a variable of interest. In nonreactive or unobtrusive measures (i.e., measures that are not obtrusive or intrusive), the people being studied are not aware of that fact but leave evidence of their social behavior or actions naturally. The observant researcher infers from the evidence to behavior or attitudes without disrupting those being studied. Unnoticed observation is also a type of nonreactive measure. For example, Highlight 9.3 examines research by Dean Dabneyand colleagues (2004) who studied shoplifting by obtaining camera surveillance footage in various retail stores.

HIGHLIGHT 9.3
Caught on Camera: Nonreactive Shoplifting Study

Photographs are certainly not considered conventional data. Note the woman in the bottom right.

Dabney, Hollinger, and Dugan used a novel approach to study the nature of shoplifting. They were interested in documenting quantitatively who shoplifts and how much occurs. Relying on those already caught (official records) and self-report surveys has obvious limitations. Their approach was direct, unobtrusive observation through the collection and analysis of store surveillance tapes. The researchers gained the cooperation of a drug store that had installed a highly sophisticated color surveillance system. They trained paid observers to operate the cameras and followed an elaborate research protocol throughout (the original article is very impressive in the level of detail used in planning and executing this project). Their final data set analyzed 1,243 drug store shoppers. Of these, 105, or 8.5 percent, were observed shoplifting. They did not find a statistically significant relationship between shoplifting behavior and race/sex; but men were slightly more likely to steal than women, and those who appeared to be poorer rather than middle- and upper-class were more likely to shoplift. They also found that people between the age of thirty-five and fifty-four were more likely to steal than were younger shoppers. The authors generalize their findings and make the following observation:

> . . . one could extrapolate that roughly 2,214,000 incidents of shoplifting occurred in the Atlanta-based stores operated by this single retail chain that year. The Uniform Crime Reports (Federal Bureau of Investigation 2002) indicate that 25,721 cases of larceny-theft were known to police in the city of Atlanta during 2001, and 118,529 cases were reported to police in the 20 counties that make up the Atlanta metropolitan area. While certainly inexact, our extrapolations based on observation data from a single store location produce annual shoplifting numbers that rival the total number of larceny-theft cases known to police in the entire Atlanta metropolitan area!

The authors' point is that the "dark figure of crime" (crime not captured by official UCR statistics) is quite large when it comes to shoplifting.

Source: Dean, Dabney, R. C. Hollinger, and L. Dugan. (2004). "Who Actually Steals? A Study of Covertly Observed Shoplifters," *Justice Quarterly,* 21: 693–729.

Varieties of Nonreactive Observation

Nonreactive measures are varied, and researchers have been creative in inventing indirect ways to measure crime and justice behavior. Researchers have examined graffiti left by inmates on prison walls and graffiti art on trains that travel across the country. Urban anthropologists have examined the contents of garbage dumps to learn about lifestyles from what is thrown away (e.g., drug use paraphernalia). Some have examined high school yearbooks to compare the high school activities of those who had legal problems in later life versus those who did not. Researchers have noted bumper stickers in support of different political candidates to see if one candidate's supporters are more likely than another's to obey traffic laws.[1] As noted in the above example, one variety of unobtrusive research doesn't quite fit the description of studying what has been left behind. This involves the direct and nonreactive observation of events in their natural setting. Of course, the bulk of nonreactive research studies rely on crime and justice agency documents and data.

In criminal justice sciences, in particular, nonreactive measures are very important. They appear chiefly in the form of crime scene forensics. Using biochemical evidence to reconstruct the crime incident and determine guilt, homicide and sexual assault detectives have come to rely on DNA typing. This process, like matching fingerprints, maps and compares unique individual patterns of, in this case, genetic information (or DNA). Its applications are "a powerful criminal justice tool that helps to establish, with a high degree of certitude, the guilt or innocence of suspects. . . . For example, a forensic scientist might compare a semen sample retrieved from a rape victim to a DNA sample taken from a suspect. If fragments appear in both samples, a match is declared" (Hammond and Caskey 1997: 1–2).

Recording and Documentation

Creating nonreactive measures follows the same logic of quantitative measurement in general. A researcher first conceptualizes a construct and then links the construct to nonreactive empirical evidence, which is its measure. The operational definition of the variable includes how the researcher systematically notes and records observations.

Because nonreactive measures indicate a construct indirectly, the researcher needs to rule out reasons for the observation other than the construct of interest. For example, a researcher wants to measure shoplifting in a store. The researcher's measure might be customers placing merchandise into their clothing (instead of the shopping basket). He or she first must clarify the meaning of shoplifting. (E.g., Is placing a piece of merchandise into a pocket stealing or just a way to carry the object?) Next, he or she systematically measures shoplifting behaviors, compares them to other locations, and records results on a regular basis (e.g., every day for three months).

QUANTITATIVE CONTENT ANALYSIS

What Is Content Analysis?

TEXT

A general name for a communication medium from which symbolic meaning is measured in content analysis.

Content analysis is a technique for gathering and analyzing the content of **text**. The content refers to words, meanings, pictures, symbols, ideas, themes, or any message that can be communicated. The text is anything written, visual, or spoken that serves as a medium for communication. It includes books, newspaper or magazine articles, advertisements, speeches, official documents, films or videotapes, musical lyrics, photographs, articles of clothing, or works of art. Content analysis goes back nearly a century and is used in many fields—literature, history, journalism, political science, education, psychology, and so on. At the first meeting of the German Sociological Society, in 1910, Max Weber suggested using it to study newspapers.[2]

CONTENT ANALYSIS

A technique for gathering and analyzing the content of text.

In *quantitative* **content analysis**, a researcher uses objective and systematic counting and recording procedures to produce a numerical description of the symbolic content in a text.[3] There are qualitative versions of content analysis that will be discussed further in Chapter 13. The emphasis here is on quantifying a text's content.

Content analysis is nonreactive because the process of placing words, messages, or symbols in a text to communicate to a reader or receiver occurs without influence from the researcher who analyzes its content. For example, we wrote words or drew diagrams to communicate research methods content to you, the student. The way this book is written and the way you read it are without any knowledge or intention of its ever being content analyzed.

Content analysis reveals the content (i.e., messages, meanings, etc.) in a source of communication (i.e., book, article, movie, etc.). It lets us probe into and discover content in a different way from the ordinary way of reading a book or watching a television program.

With content analysis, a researcher can compare content across many texts and analyze it with quantitative techniques (e.g., charts and tables). In addition, he or she can reveal aspects of the text's content that are difficult to see. For example, someone might have watched the coverage of the Hurricane Katrina disaster and felt that the entire event was constructed by the government and media as a security crisis in need of a strong criminal justice/military response as opposed to a natural disaster requiring humanitarian aid. Content analysis can document—in objective, quantitative terms—whether these vague feelings and impressions based on unsystematic observation are accurate. It yields repeatable, precise results about the text. As a content analysis researcher gathers the data, he or she analyzes them with statistics in the same way that an experimenter or survey researcher would do.

Topics Appropriate for Content Analysis

As noted in Chapter 1, scholars have devoted a significant amount of attention and research to the role the media plays in the construction of views and opinions regarding crime and justice phenomena (referred to as the social construction of the reality of crime and criminal justice). In order to study this process, they often employ quantitative content analysis. Chermak's (1995) research discussed in Chapter 1 is one of the better examples. He coded the content of 2,158 newspaper stories and 506 television stories in order to describe the nature of crime reporting and crime victimization media coverage. He documented quantitatively what many criminologists felt but had little empirical validation for: The media presents a highly distorted and sensationalized presentation of crime, offenders, and victims.

Crime and justice researchers have used content analysis for many purposes: to study themes in songs, crime and justice themes and trends in the topics that newspapers cover, crime control ideology found in newspaper editorials, violence against women stereotypes in textbooks, television shows, and movies, the depiction of race and crime in television commercials and programs, answers to open-ended survey questions, the martial language used in crime and drug control efforts, the content of legal statutes, themes in police and corrections magazine advertising, and so on.

Content analysis is useful for three types of research problems. First, it is helpful for problems involving a large volume of text. A researcher can measure large amounts of text (e.g., years of newspaper articles) with sampling and multiple coders. Second, it is helpful when a topic must be studied at a distance. For example, content analysis can be used to study historical documents, the writings of someone who has died, or broadcasts in a hostile foreign country. Finally, content analysis can reveal messages in a text that are difficult to see with casual observation. The creator of the text or those who read it may not be aware of all its themes, subtext, biases, or hidden ideology. For example, authors of preschool picture books may not consciously intend to portray children in traditional stereotyped sex roles, but a high degree of sex stereotyping has been revealed through content analysis.[4] Agnes Baro and Helen Eigenberg (1993: 3) examined twenty-two crime and justice college textbooks and found that

> women were largely invisible in the educational materials examined: men—
> predominantly white—constituted 81 percent of the individuals in texts, and
> 65 percent of the photos were exclusive portrayals of men. When women were given
> a visual presence, it was as peripheral persons and victims.

Generalizations that researchers make on the basis of content analysis are limited to the cultural communication itself. Content analysis cannot determine the truthfulness of an assertion or evaluate the aesthetic qualities of literature. It reveals the content in text but cannot interpret the content's significance. Researchers must also examine the text directly for its cultural meaning. Holsti (1968: 602) warned, "Content analysis may be considered as a supplement to, not as a substitute for, subjective examination of documents."

Measurement and Coding

GENERAL ISSUES.   Careful measurement is crucial in content analysis because a researcher takes diffuse and murky symbolic communication and turns it into precise, quantitative data. We must carefully design and document procedures for coding to make replication possible. For example, let's say we want to determine whether the media depicts male versus female crime victims in a more personal way. We must first develop a measure of the construct "personal depiction of a crime victim." Our conceptualization may result in a number of indicators of personal depiction, such as whether the victim was referred to by name, a noun (victim), or pronoun (he/she). Anastasio and Costa (2004) conducted a content analysis on this topic and found that women victims are presented in measurably less personal terms. They then presented these types of accounts to 189 undergraduate college students and found that the less personal narratives acted to reduce the level of empathy for the victims (mixing content analysis with survey research methods).

Constructs in content analysis, therefore, must be operationalized with a **coding system,** a set of instructions or rules on how to systematically observe and record content from text. A researcher tailors it to the type of text or communication medium being studied (e.g., television drama, novels, photos in magazine advertisements, etc.). It also depends on the researcher's unit of analysis.

WHAT IS MEASURED?   Measurement in content analysis uses **structured observation**: systematic, careful observation based on written rules. The rules explain how to categorize and classify observations. As with other measurement, categories should be mutually exclusive and exhaustive. Written rules make replication possible and improve reliability. Although researchers begin with preliminary coding rules, they often conduct a pilot study and refine coding on the basis of it. This is an important step. It is not uncommon for a researcher to realize after the data have been collected that they should have coded other important variables. At this point, however, it is usually too late.

Coding systems identify four characteristics of text content: frequency, direction, intensity, and space. A researcher measures from one to all four characteristics in a content analysis research project.

- **Frequency.** Frequency simply means counting whether or not something occurs and, if it occurs, how often. For example, how many non-White crime victims appear on a television program within a given week? What percentage of all characters are they, or in what percentage of programs do they appear?
- **Direction.** Direction is noting the direction of messages in the content along some continuum (e.g., positive or negative, supporting or opposed). For example, a researcher devises a list of ways a crime victim character can act. Some are positive (e.g., friendly, wise, and considerate) and some are negative (e.g., nasty, dull, and selfish).
- **Intensity.** Intensity is the strength or power of a message in a direction. For example, the characteristic of unintelligence can be minor (e.g., not being able to remember simple things) or major (e.g., not being able to understand simple words).
- **Space.** A researcher can record the size of a text message or the amount of space or volume allocated to it. Space in written text is measured by counting words, sentences, paragraphs, or space on a page (e.g., square inches). For video or audio text, space can be measured by the amount of time allocated. For example, a TV character may be present for a few seconds or appear in every scene of a two-hour program.

It is important to note that sometimes researchers code what is *not* present in the text. For example, Elizabeth Rapaport (1991) examined U.S. death penalty statutes and coded the lack of all states' mentioning anything about murder committed within a domestic setting. She concluded

---

CODING SYSTEM

A set of instructions or rules used in content analysis to explain how a researcher systematically converted the symbolic content from text into quantitative data.

STRUCTURED OBSERVATION

A method of watching what is happening in a social setting that is highly organized and follows systematic rules for observation and documentation.

that the law places greater seriousness on economically and stranger-based murder than on domestic murder.

Coding, Validity, and Reliability

MANIFEST CODING.   Coding the visible, surface content in a text is called **manifest coding**. For example, a researcher counts the number of times a phrase or word (e.g., red) appears in written text, or whether a specific action (e.g., a kiss) appears in a photograph or video scene. The coding system lists terms or actions that are then located in text. A researcher can use a computer program to search for words or phrases in text and have a computer do the counting work. To do this, he or she learns about the computer program, develops a comprehensive list of relevant words or phrases, and puts the text into a form that computers can read.[5]

Manifest coding is highly reliable because the phrase or word either is or is not present. Unfortunately, manifest coding does not take the connotations of words or phrases into account. The same word can take on different meanings depending on the context. The possibility that there are multiple meanings of a word limits the measurement validity of manifest coding. For example, we read a book with a red cover that is a real red herring. Unfortunately, its publisher drowned in red ink because the editor could not deal with the red tape that occurs when a book is red hot.

MANIFEST CODING

A type of content analysis coding in which a researcher first develops a list of words, phrases, or symbols and then locates them in a communication medium.

LATENT CODING.   A researcher using **latent coding** (also called semantic analysis) looks for the underlying, implicit meaning in the content of a text. For example, a researcher examines photographs published in major newspapers depicting the "reality" of the Hurricane Katrina disaster. They attempt to determine whether the photos portray African Americans in a negative way. His or her coding system has general rules to guide his or her interpretation of the text and for determining whether particular negative themes are present or not (e.g., assuming that an African American holding a television is looting).

Latent coding tends to be less reliable than manifest coding. It depends on a coder's knowledge of language and social meaning.[6] Training, practice, and written rules improve reliability, but it can still be difficult to consistently identify themes, moods, and the like. Yet, the validity of latent coding can exceed that of manifest coding because people communicate meaning in many implicit ways that depend on context, not just in specific words.

Content analysis research often involves both manifest and latent coding. If the two approaches agree, the final result is strengthened; if they disagree, the researcher may want to reexamine the operational and theoretical definitions.

LATENT CODING

A type of content analysis coding in which a researcher identifies subjective meaning such as themes or motifs and then systematically locates them in a communication medium.

INTERCODER RELIABILITY.   Content analysis usually involves coding information from a very large number of units. A research project might involve observing the content in dozens of books, hundreds of hours of television programming, or thousands of newspaper articles. In addition to coding the information personally, a researcher may hire assistants to help with the coding. He or she teaches coders the coding system and trains them to fill out a recording sheet. Coders should understand the variables, follow the coding system, and ask about ambiguities. A researcher records all decisions he or she makes about how to treat a new specific coding situation after coding begins so that he or she can be consistent.

A researcher who uses several coders must always check for consistency across coders. He or she does this by asking coders to code the same text independently and then checking for consistency across coders. The researcher measures **intercoder reliability**, a type of equivalence reliability, with a statistical coefficient that tells the degree of consistency among coders.[7] The coefficient is always reported with the results of content analysis research.

When the coding process stretches over a considerable time period (e.g., more than three months), the researcher also checks *stability reliability* by having each coder independently code samples of text that were previously coded. He or she then checks to see whether the coding is

INTERCODER RELIABILITY

Equivalence reliability in content analysis with multiple content coders that require a high degree of consistency across coders.

are most interesting to analyze based on the research question. Then, he or she randomly selects articles from those magazines spanning a set period of time. One way to select specific articles is to list all articles published by the weekly magazines between, say, 1976 and 1998. This sampling frame of articles is then used, along with a table of random numbers, to draw the probability sample of news stories. Another way to go about probability sampling is to select random weeks of the year and then analyze relevant articles contained in those corresponding issues of the news magazines. In other words, the researcher decides whether to sample by news story or by week of the year.

Lofquist's (1997) study (mentioned above), on the other hand, used nonprobability purposive sampling. He selected "every relevant story published [in a local newspaper] in the three-month period following the event" (Lofquist: 247). He chose to limit his content analysis to three months of text "because it seemed to provide ample time for developments in each story [i.e., the abduction and the collapse of the mine] and for consideration of their causes" (Lofquist: 247).

VARIABLES AND CONSTRUCTING CODING CATEGORIES.   Lofquist (1997) compared what the local newspaper wrote about two widely reported "crimes" that took place in Rochester, New York, in 1994. As mentioned earlier, one crime was the case of a four-year-old girl who disappeared from in front of her own home; the other was the collapse and flooding of a mine owned by a multinational company. Lofquist coded how the cause of events was described in the newspaper articles. The cause of events was simply categorized as being either "an accident," "negligence," or "a crime." He then simply coded the entire sample of newspaper stories, using manifest and latent coding.

With manifest coding, the researcher could create a list of specific words used to denote whether the event was an accident, due to negligence, or a crime. Words describing the event as an accident would include: *natural disaster, an act of God, beyond the control of,* and so on. The researcher could then literally count the number of times one of the words was used in a news story.

With latent coding, the process is more subtle. The researcher must create rules or guidelines to follow when the meaning of the text becomes implicit, ironic, or in doubt. The rules spell out the criteria for judging the intended meaning of the text. Thus, the word *accident* may appear in the text. But to grasp its intended meaning, the researcher needs to examine the context in which the word or phrase appears. The context will give the researcher clues as to its meaning. This is why latent coding is just as important to researchers as manifest coding. The point is, the meaning of a text must be understood in the context of other words and phrases in the text (see mixed methods research in Chapter 14).

In addition to written rules for coding decisions, a content analysis researcher creates a recording sheet (also called a *coding sheet*) on which to record information. Each unit should have a separate recording sheet. The sheets do not have to be pieces of paper; they can be 3 × 5" or 4 × 6" file cards, or lines in a computer record or file. When a lot of information is recorded for each recording unit, more than one sheet of paper can be used.

As seen in Table 9.1, each recording sheet has a place to record the identification number of the unit and spaces for information about each variable. The researcher should also put identifying information about the research project on the sheet in case he or she wants to go back to it. Finally, in multiple coders, the sheet queues the coder to check intercoder reliability and, if necessary, makes it possible to recode information for inaccurate coders. After completing all recording sheets and checking for accuracy, one can begin data analysis.

Inferences

The inferences a researcher can or cannot make on the basis of results is critical in content analysis. Content analysis describes what is in the text. It cannot reveal the intentions of those who created the text or the effects that messages in the text have on those who receive them. This means that the researcher must be cautious in their interpretation of findings. Demonstrating that a police television show depicts offenders in a racially biased manner does not tell us about

TABLE 9.1	Example of Blank Coding Sheet

A Content Analysis of TV

True Crime Shows

Background Information

1. Coder's name:_____
2. Case number:_____
3. Date of broadcast:_____
4. Length of episode:_____(in minutes:seconds)
5. Location of episode:_____

Portrayal of Suspect

6. Number of suspects (code up to 3 suspects):

Age	Race	Sex	Social Class
___	___	___	___
___	___	___	___
___	___	___	___

7. Does the suspect show remorse (code up to 3 suspects):

Yes	No
___	___
___	___
___	___

8. Suspected crime (code only primary offense for up to 3 suspects):

Violent	Nonviolent
___	___
___	___
___	___

Portrayal of Arresting Officer

9. Number of officers (code up to 3 officers):

Age	Race	Sex	Social Class
___	___	___	___
___	___	___	___
___	___	___	___

10. Does officer use physical force against suspect (code up to 3 officers):

Yes	No
___	___
___	___
___	___

Source: From W. Lawrence Neuman and Bruce Weigand, *Criminal Justice Research Methods, Qualitative and Quantitative Approaches,* 1/e. Published by Allyn and Bacon, 75 Arlington St., Boston, MA 02116. Copyright © 2000 by Pearson Education. Reprinted by permission of the publisher.

the impact this portrayal is having on its viewers. Similarly, the show's producers and creators may be wholly ignorant of their biased portrayal; the researcher cannot infer intent based on a methodology that only measures outcome.

EXISTING DOCUMENTS/STATISTICS

As interesting and productive as content analysis is, the bulk of nonreactive research in crime and justice studies falls into the category *existing documents/statistics* (also referred to as archival research and secondary data analysis). Recall that existing data can come in the form of raw documents in need of conversion into quantitative form, raw data in need of conversion into a useable data set, or an actual statistical database ready for secondary analysis (see Figure 9.1). This section will examine all of these forms under this one heading.

Topics Appropriate for Existing Documents/Statistics Research

The topics available to us in conducting existing documents/statistics research are almost limitless. Any topic on which information has been collected and is available can be studied. In fact, existing documents/statistics projects may not fit neatly into a deductive model of research design. Rather, researchers creatively reorganize the existing information into the variables for a research question after first finding what data are available.

We learned earlier that experiments are best for topics in which the researcher controls a situation and manipulates an independent variable. Survey research is well suited for topics in which the researcher asks questions and learns about reported attitudes or behavior. Content analysis is useful for topics that involve the content of messages in cultural communication. Existing statistics research is best for topics that involve information that has been collected by large bureaucratic organizations. Public or private organizations systematically gather many types of information. Such information is gathered for policy decisions or as a public service. It is rarely collected for purposes directly related to a specific research question. Thus, existing documents/statistics research is appropriate when a researcher wants to test hypotheses involving variables found in official records, reports, or data. Often, such information is collected over long time periods allowing for longitudinal and time-series analyses. The possibilities are vast.

Citing just a few of the many research topics addressed using this approach gives one a sense of how versatile this method is. Highlight 9.4 presents an excellent example of the power and controversial nature of existing document research that deals with counting the dead in the war on terrorism in Iraq. It also demonstrates how existing documents research can be used in conjunction with other methods, such as surveys.

Another example involves examining the relationship of unemployment and crime. Carlson and Michalowski (1997: 224) developed a set of hypotheses about the unemployment/crime relationship and tested the hypotheses using large existing government data sets. The crime data they analyzed were the Uniform Crime Report's annual estimates of crime, beginning in 1933. The unemployment data also came from the U.S. government and was likewise longitudinal. It consisted of the official annual average unemployment rates for the U.S. civilian labor force. These statistics are compiled by the Bureau of the Census in the *Statistical Abstracts of the United States.* Using sophisticated time-series techniques, they concluded that a strong relationship exists between economic trends and crime.

Martin (1997) conducted groundbreaking research into the phenomenon of "dual arrest" for domestic battering (both parties are arrested as opposed to the sole aggressor or primary aggressor in the crime) using existing documents research. The data were collected from court records associated with 4,138 disposed family violence cases. This research documented for the first time the trend toward dual arrest as a result of mandatory arrest laws, with 33 percent of the cases involving dual arrest. The author emphasized the "chilling effect" this trend might have on battered women's willingness to call the police for help.

The opportunities for criminologists to analyze existing documents and statistics are vast. This type of research is especially valuable for international/comparative studies. Every year, more and more data sets become available to researchers around the world, as countries and international agencies improve their research capabilities.

Locating Data

LOCATING DOCUMENTS.   The main sources of existing documents are government agencies involved in crime control. These include any agency that maintains records associated with their activities. Although the obvious entities would include the police, courts, corrections, and juvenile

---

HIGHLIGHT 9.4

Counting Death: The Morgue versus Surveys

The Iraq War has been perhaps the most controversial aspect of the government's war on terrorism efforts. Consistent with the power–knowledge dynamic, generating accurate knowledge about the number of casualties and deaths as a result of this war has been fraught with controversy as well. Just as with John Hagan's research on the crisis in Darfur, researchers are attempting to document the death associated with the Iraq War.

By July of 2007 the media reported that 3,637 U.S. soldiers had died, as well as about 70,000 Iraqi civilians (www.icasualties.org). An article published in a British medical journal by disaster researchers at John Hopkins University in late 2006 ratcheted up the debate significantly. This study estimated, with 95 percent certainty, that the war and its aftermath have resulted in the deaths of between 426,000 and 794,000 Iraqis—with 654,000 being the most likely figure (Bumham 2006).

What explains the discrepancy between 70,000 and 650,000? The lower figure relies on data based on Iraqi government records of the deceased at morgues. The John Hopkins study conducted household surveys at random (much like the NCVS) in forty-seven neighborhood clusters across Iraq. (Imagine the risks involved in this research.) The interviewers asked family members to report deaths and the cause of the deaths, *and obtained death certificates in 92 percent of cases.* Most deaths early in the conflict were due to U.S. military activities; the spike in deaths in 2005–2006 was the result of escalating "sectarian violence."

These data were then generalized to the entire nation of about 26 million people.

The research has met with criticism; there are those who claim that the number is too high to be credible. The study's lead author, Professor Gilbert Bumham, responded as follows:

> The numbers are large, and they surprised us. Yet it is only through population-based sampling that information such as the impact of conflict can be assessed. From isolated numbers taken from morgues and hospitals one cannot arrive at a national figure. Not possible. An active survey is more accurate than a passive [nonreactive] system of counting morgue reports or other lists of the dead, which are often grossly incomplete in a war zone. (Miniter 2006: 1)

Notice that while the John Hopkins study relied on survey methods, its findings would probably have had no impact if it were not for a key piece of nonreactive evidence collected by the researchers—the actual death certificates from family members. The research could have been credibly critiqued on the grounds that many Iraqis overestimated deaths either intentionally (due to animosity against the U.S. government) or unintentionally (reported deaths beyond their immediate families). As stressed in Chapter 5 on research design, measuring variables from multiple angles is desirable if possible (in this case, combining survey research with the collection of unobtrusive documents).

---

justice, recent trends toward the privatization of crime control efforts means that private organizations have to be considered as well. Because these for-profit organizations are not held to the same level of transparency as the government, these data can be more difficult to access. Even some government records are difficult to access. Kraska and Kappeler (1988) conducted survey research on police on-duty illegal drug use (mostly marijuana and amphetamines) and were not allowed access to officer personnel files to cross-validate findings (an understandable refusal). Moreover, the secrecy associated with homeland security, and provisions in the PATRIOT Act that can nullify any Freedom of Information Act request that might have a bearing on national security, are making it more difficult to conduct existing document research in this rapidly expanding area.

We have found that securing existing documents often requires having an "in" within an organization. For example, one of Kraska's graduate students works for the Kentucky State Police (KSP). In trying to come up with an accomplishable thesis project, she noticed a disturbing crime phenomenon that is not discussed in the literature. Victims of identity theft routinely end up with a difficult-to-expunge criminal record, because the identity-theft offender is often arrested for committing a different crime while using the victim's stolen identity. She proposed conducting descriptive research on this unique crime phenomenon and developing a model policy for KSP in handling these situations. Access to this phenomenon and these data would likely not be available to an outsider.

LOCATING EXISTING STATISTICS.   The main sources of existing statistics are government or international agencies and private sources. An enormous volume and variety of information exist. If you plan to conduct existing statistics research, it is wise to discuss your interests with an information professional—in this case, a reference librarian, who can point you in the direction of possible sources.

Many existing statistics are free—that is, publicly available at libraries—but the time and effort it takes to search for specific information can be substantial. Researchers who conduct existing statistics research spend many hours in libraries and on the Internet. After the information is located, it is recorded on cards, graphs, or recording sheets for later analysis. Often, it is already available in a format for computers to read. For example, the U.S. National Institute of Justice (NIJ) has gathered such data sets from its previously funded research. These data sets are available from the National Archive of Criminal Justice Data (NACJD) at the Inter-University Consortium for Political and Social Research (ICPSR) at the University of Michigan.

There are so many sources that only a small sample of what is available is discussed here. The single most valuable source of statistical information about the United States is the *Statistical Abstract of the United States,* which has been published annually (with a few exceptions) since 1878. The *Statistical Abstract* is available in all public libraries and can be purchased from the U.S. Superintendent of Documents. It is a selected compilation of the many official reports and statistical tables produced by U.S. government agencies. It contains the most significant statistical information from hundreds of more detailed government reports. You may want to examine more specific government documents.

Perhaps the single most indispensable source of existing statistics from criminologists in the United States is the annual *Sourcebook of Criminal Justice Statistics* (www.albany.edu/sourcebook). Statistical data are available either in hard copy or on CD-ROM technology. The variety of statistical data sets that are published in the *Sourcebook* is simply amazing (see Table 9.2, www.albany.edu/sourcebook/). Recent additions include data sets on the fear of becoming a victim of terrorism and other crimes, and data related to the federal prosecution of human trafficking.

Another rich source of secondary data is found at the Inter-University Consortium for Political and Social Research (ICPSR) at the University of Michigan (www.icpsr.umich.edu/index.html). It is the world's major archive of social science data. Over 17,000 survey research and related sets of information are stored and made available to researchers either for free or at modest costs. The difficulty in using ICPSR is not locating data, but determining which data set to use. The ICPSR recently made this somewhat easier with the creation of a separate Web page dedicated to crime and justice data sets, National Archive of Criminal Justice Data.

Another widely used source of survey data for the United States is the General Social Survey (GSS), which has been conducted annually by the National Opinion Research Center at the University of Chicago. In recent years, it has covered other nations, as well. The data are made publicly available for secondary analysis at a low cost.[9,10]

Reliability and Validity

Existing documents and data sets are not trouble free just because a government agency or other source gathered the original data. Researchers must be concerned with validity and reliability, as well as with some problems unique to this research technique. Maier (1991) and Webb et al. (1999) detail the many potential problems with their use. This is especially true when using data that have been compiled and processed for bureaucratic reasons and not for social scientific research. The researcher must be diligent in determining how the data were compiled, and what organizational and political factors might have skewed their construction, to avoid the error of naïvely assuming their validity and reliability.

FALLACY OF MISPLACED CONCRETENESS

Using too many digits in a quantitative measure in an attempt to create the (mis)impression that data are accurate.

A common error is the **fallacy of misplaced concreteness**. It occurs when someone gives a false impression of accuracy by quoting statistics in greater detail than warranted by how the statistics are collected and by overloading detail (Horn 1993: 18). For example, to cite agency-constructed data on the negative correlation between juvenile boot camps and reduced recidivism, without really knowing how the data were collected might yield a fundamentally flawed study. Secondary data are useful only provided the researcher understands the underlying research design and its limitations.

| **TABLE 9.2** | Selected Contents of the Thirty-First Annual *Sourcebook of Criminal Justice Statistics* |

A. Statistics on Characteristics of the Criminal Justice System
    1. Expenditures for criminal justice activities
    2. Federal drug control funding
    3. Salaries for police officers and other law enforcement personnel
    4. Criminal cases filed per judgeship in U.S. District Courts
    5. Statutory provisions on firearms

B. Statistics on Public Attitudes toward Crime and Criminal Justice-Related Topics
    1. Most important problems for country and communities
    2. Public confidence in social institutions
    3. Perceptions of crime and safety
    4. Police officials' attitudes toward efforts to reduce the drug problem
    5. Pornography, prostitution, and homosexuality

C. Statistics on Nature and Distribution of Known Offenses
    1. Victim-offender relationship in violent victimization
    2. Reasons for reporting and not reporting crime victimization to the police
    3. Bias-motivated (hate) crimes
    4. Offenses known to the police
    5. Terrorist incidents

D. Statistics on Characteristics and Distribution of Persons Arrested
    1. Number and rate of arrests, national estimates
    2. Arrest rate trends
    3. Drug and property seizure by the U.S. Customs Service
    4. Offenses cleared by arrest
    5. Aliens deported from the United States

E. Statistics on Judicial Processing of Defendants
    1. Requests for immunity by federal prosecutors
    2. Cases filed, terminated, and pending in U.S. District Courts
    3. Time served in prison for offenders sentenced in U.S. District Courts
    4. Criminal tax fraud cases
    5. U.S. Army court-martial cases

F. Statistics on Persons under Correctional Supervision
    1. Adults on probation
    2. Jail inmates with HIV/AIDS
    3. State and federal prisoners executed
    4. Escapes from correctional facilities
    5. Noncitizens in U.S. federal prisons

Source: See http://www.albany.edu/sourcebook.

UNITS OF ANALYSIS AND VARIABLE ATTRIBUTES.   A common problem in existing statistics is finding the appropriate units of analysis. Many statistics are published for aggregates, not the individual. For example, a table in a government document has information (e.g., unemployment rate, crime rate, etc.) for a state, but the unit of analysis for the research question is the individual (e.g., "Are unemployed people more likely to commit property crimes?"). The potential for committing the ecological fallacy is very real in this situation. It is less of a problem for secondary survey analysis because researchers can obtain raw information on each respondent from archives.

    A related problem involves the categories of variable attributes used in existing documents or survey questions. This is not a problem if the initial data were gathered in many highly refined categories. The problem arises when the original data were collected in broad categories or ones that do not match the needs of a researcher.

It would be entirely inappropriate, for example, for a criminologist interested in the relationship of unemployment and crime among Asian Americans to use existing data that categorize ethnicity in terms of "Black," "White," and "Other." The "Other" category includes Asian Americans as well as other ethnic/racial groups. It takes a special effort on the part of researchers to discover existing statistical data that suit the research question being asked.

VALIDITY. Validity problems are a real threat to the legitimacy of existing statistics research. One type of problem occurs when the researcher's theoretical definition does not match that of the government agency or organization that collected the information. Official policies and procedures specify definitions for official statistics, but often criminologists change these definitions to suit their own research purposes.

Carlson and Michalowski's (1997: 224) unemployment and crime study, for example, constructed their own measure of *serious crime* that included "crimes which generate the greatest fear in the general public (homicide, robbery, aggravated assault, and burglary)." Deciding on a definition of *unemployment* was also difficult. They adopted the official definition: "Since most of the research that has led to ambiguous results concerning the unemployment-crime relationship has used the U.S. civilian labor force as a whole, we also use this measure to maintain comparability." The official definition of *unemployment* regards only those who are now actively seeking work (full- or part-time) as unemployed. The official statistics exclude those who have stopped looking, who work part-time out of necessity, or who do not look because they believe no work is available.

A second validity problem arises when official statistics are a surrogate or proxy for a construct in which a researcher is really interested. This is often unavoidable, however, because the researcher cannot collect original data. Crime and justice researchers interested in quantifying the extent of smuggling contraband into the U.S. might decide to make use of official trade data as a proxy for smuggling.

A third validity problem arises because the researcher lacks control over how information is collected. Remember that most existing crime and justice data were originally gathered by people in bureaucracies as part of their jobs. A researcher depends on them for collecting, organizing, reporting, and publishing data accurately. Systematic errors in collecting the initial information (e.g., census takers who avoid poor neighborhoods and make up information, or people who put a false age on a driver's license); errors in organizing and reporting information (e.g., a police department that is sloppy about filing crime reports and loses some); and errors in publishing information (e.g., a typographical error in a table) all reduce measurement validity.

STABILITY RELIABILITY

A technique that checks to see whether the coding is stable or changing.

RELIABILITY. Problems with reliability can also plague existing statistics research. **Stability reliability** problems develop when official definitions or the methods of collecting information change over time. (See Highlight 9.5.) Official definitions of crime, unemployment, and the like change periodically. Even if a researcher learns of such changes, consistent measurement over time is impossible. For example, during the early 1980s, the method for calculating the U.S. unemployment rate changed. Previously, the unemployment rate was calculated as the number of unemployed persons divided by the number in the civilian workforce. The new method divided the number of unemployed by the civilian workforce plus the number of people in the military. Likewise, when police departments computerize their records, there is an apparent increase in crimes reported, not because crime increases but because record keeping improved.

Equivalence reliability can also be a problem. For example, a measure of crime across a nation depends on each police department's providing accurate information. If departments in one region of a country have sloppy bookkeeping, the measure loses equivalence reliability. Likewise, studies of police departments suggest that political pressures to increase arrests are closely related to the number of arrests. For example, political pressure in one city may increase arrests (e.g., a crackdown on crime), whereas pressures in another city may decrease arrests (e.g., to show a drop in crime shortly before an election to make officials look better).

HIGHLIGHT 9.5
Racial Assault with a Baseball? Measuring Race-Motivated Aggression

Validity and reliability problems were not much of a concern for Thomas Timmerman when he was conducting an interesting existing statistics study. Timmerman examined the relationship between race and violence in the context of professional baseball. He coded archival data from 1950 to 1997 on the variable of a batter being hit by a pitch. He uncovered 27,022 individual records and found that race is a significant predictor of being hit by a baseball pitch. Over the entire time period, the rate at which Blacks are hit is about 7.5 percent greater than for Whites and 7.6 percent greater for Hispanics

(he controlled for player ability and league rules). Longitudinal data allowed Timmerman to examine the disparities for differing time periods. He found that Black–White differences were most significant during the 1950s and 1960s, and that from 1990 to 1997, Whites and Hispanics are hit at a significantly higher rate than are Blacks.

Source: From Thomas A. Timmerman. (2002). "Violence and Race in Professional Baseball: Getting Better or Worse?" *Aggressive Behavior*, 28:109–116.

MISSING DATA. Another serious problem that plagues researchers using existing documents/statistics is that of missing data. Sometimes, the data were collected but have been lost. More frequently, the data were never collected. Those who decide what to collect may not collect what another researcher needs to address a research question. Government agencies start or stop collecting information for political, budgetary, or other reasons.

Example of Existing Documents/Statistics Research

Professor Marc Mauer runs an organization called the Sentencing Project (see www.sentencing-project.org). This is a nonprofit organization that attempts to shed academic and empirical light on a host of criminal justice issues—the most important of which is high U.S. incarceration rates. Their mission statement makes clear their perspective (an interesting blend of positivist methods with critical values of change through advocacy):

> As a result of the Sentencing Project's research, publications and advocacy, many people know that this country is the world's leader in incarceration, that one in three young black men is under control of the criminal justice system, that five million Americans can't vote because of felony convictions, and that thousands of women and children have lost welfare, education and housing benefits as the result of convictions for minor drug offenses.

The Sentencing Project relies heavily on existing statistics research. When it advertises the following statement to major media outlets, it is derived from U.S. Department of Justice data and the organization International Centre for Prison Studies (ICPS):

> Bureau of Justice Statistics figures for 2005 indicate that there were nearly 2.2 million inmates in the nation's prisons and jails, representing an increase of 2.6% (56,400) over the previous twelve months. The new figures represent a record 33-year continuous rise in the number of inmates in the U.S. The current incarceration rate of 738 per 100,000 residents places the United States first in the world in this regard.

See Figure 9.2 for a revealing bar graph that compares international incarceration rates.

The ICPS also relies heavily on nonreactive methods. One of its major undertakings is documenting trends in prison practices throughout the world. Roy Walmsley, a research associate, is in charge of collecting prison data from 211 different countries and compiles an important piece of existing document research known as the *World Prison Population List* (2005). Compiling this sort of comprehensive data set from such varied sources is no doubt a highly

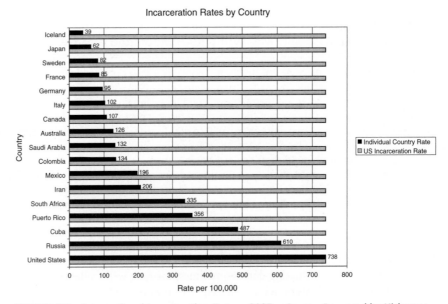

FIGURE 9.2 International Incarceration Rates—2005. *Source:* Prepared by Kishonna Gray, research assistant at Eastern Kentucky University. Data derived from King's College, London, International Centre for Prison Studies (www.prisonstudies.org).

complex undertaking, plagued by missing data and comparability problems. (Some countries, for example, do not differentiate between juvenile and adult offenders.) The advantage, though, is a global view of imprisonment:

- Over 9 million people are held in penal institutions throughout the world; 2.2 million of these are held in the United States alone.
- The United States has the highest imprisonment rate in the world (714 per 100,000 people).
- Nearly 60 percent of the countries examined had quite low imprisonment rates (less than 150 per 100,000 people).
- Prison populations are experiencing marked growth in 73 percent of the countries examined.

Conclusion

Nonreactive research is a valuable set of methods for generating legitimate knowledge in crime and justice studies. These methods potentially reduce the biases that result from the intrusion of a researcher into a research setting. Crime and justice-related documents and data are ubiquitous and can be converted into creative, interesting, and useful research projects. This chapter has provided an overview of several types of nonreactive techniques that result in quantitative data and analysis. We've also demonstrated how these same techniques can be used in conjunction with other types of quantitative methods and can be mixed with qualitative methods as well.

Interestingly, nonreactive methods, particularly content analysis, are somewhat in line with interpretive social science in that they discern the meaning of text.

Of course, this meaning is put into quantitative form but the interpretive skills involved in this process have similarities to the ISS approach. We also saw how CSS researchers have used these quantitative techniques for exposing racial bias, hidden ideology, and the media-distorting effects of crime and justice reality.

We discussed a few potential problems in nonreactive research. First, the availability of existing information restricts the questions that a researcher can address. Second, the nonreactive variables often have weaker validity because they do not measure the construct of interest. Although existing statistics and secondary data analysis are low-cost research techniques, the researcher lacks control over, and substantial knowledge of, the data-collection process. These potential sources of errors mean that researchers need to be especially vigilant and cautious. Finally, the critical thinking researcher must be aware of the potential bias built into existing documents/statistics by those that originally collected these data. Data generated by a police gang unit, for example, could be greatly impacted by biased assumptions and bureaucratic interests (and not necessarily intentionally). Researchers must always be aware that the power–knowledge dynamic can impact all aspects of the research process, including the collection of documents and data by criminal justice practitioners.

In the next chapter, we move from designing research projects and collecting data to analyzing data. The analysis techniques apply to the quantitative data you learned about in the previous chapters. So far, you have seen how to move from a topic, to a research design and measures, to collecting data. Next, you will learn how to look at data and see what they can tell you about a hypothesis or research question.

Key Terms

unobtrusive measures *204*
nonreactive data *204*
physical traces *204*
archival material *204*

unobtrusive observation *204*
text *210*
content analysis *210*
coding system *212*

structured observation *212*
manifest coding *213*
latent coding *213*
intercoder reliability *213*

visual "text" *214*
fallacy of misplaced
　concreteness *220*
stability reliability *222*

Review Questions

1. What is the thinking and logic behind nonreactive methods, and why are they important to criminal justice and crime studies?
2. For what types of research questions is content analysis appropriate?
3. What specifically is measured (four characteristics) when conducting content analysis?
4. Of what reliability problems should the researcher using existing statistical data be aware?
5. How can content analysis be used when studying visual images?
6. What are the major steps taken when conducting content analysis research?

7. How are inferences limited in content analysis?
8. What are the three validity problems in content analysis?
9. What are the advantages and disadvantages of existing documents/statistics analysis?
10. What are three examples of existing documents/statistics analysis discussed?
11. How does a researcher go about finding and collecting existing documents and statistics?
12. What are the major validity and reliability problems associated with existing document/statistics analysis?
13. Of what limitations of using existing statistics should researchers be aware?

Practicing Research

1. Locate an old cemetery either in the city or in the country-side. Using headstones and grave markers as your nonreactive data, decide what information you want to record from the gravesite (e.g., year died, quote, mementos, flowers, style of marker, age of person, any carved images, etc.). Were you able to discern any patterns, associations, or trends? Write a brief report based on what you found. (This exercise was derived from Bruce Berg's 2007 text.)
2. Working in small groups of three to four students, visit a local county or municipal courthouse and inquire into what types of information are available to the public and/or to researchers. Find out what the protocols are in collecting and using this information and how a person might conduct an actual study using these existing documents. If permitted, examine an example of the type of information available, and note what variables could be extracted.

3. Conduct a small content analysis study. It can be on any crime and justice-related topic. The study should only focus on a limited number of newspaper or magazine articles (between 5 and 10), and no more than 5–10 variables need to be coded using a simple code sheet as described in this chapter. Discuss the research process, your findings, and what you learned about this experience in small groups.
4. Find a content analysis study and an existing statistics study in a criminal justice/criminology journal. Take note of the methods used in each study, focusing specifically on:
   • the data source
   • central variables under study
   • data collection techniques (more relevant for the content analysis study)
   • major findings

5. Conduct an Internet search using two sets of keywords: 1. download social research data, and 2. download criminal justice data. Take note of the numerous possibilities for conducting secondary analysis of existing data. Pull up a few Web sites that interest you, including the most comprehensive site mentioned in this chapter, the *Inter-University Consortium* *for Political and Social Research* (www.icpsr.umich.edu/). Write a report, including printed documentation of the Web pages visited, detailing what you learned. An even more |in-depth exercise would be to actually download one of these data sets, open the data set using a statistical package such as SPSS, and examine the variables and cases included.

Notes for Further Study

1. For an inventory of nonreactive measures, see Bouchard (1976) and Webb and associates (1981).
2. See Krippendorff (1980: 13)
3. For definitions of content analysis, see Holsti (1968: 597), Krippendorff (1980: 21–24), Markoff and associates (1974: 5–6), Stone and Weber (1992), and Weber (1985: 81, note 1)
4. Weitzman and colleagues (1995) is a classic in this type of research.
5. Stone and Weber (1992) and Weber (1984, 1985) review computerized content analysis techniques.
6. See Andren (1981: 58–66) on reliability and latent or semantic analysis, and Holsti (1969: 94–126)
7. See Krippendorff (1980, 2003) for various measures of intercoder reliability. Also see Fiske (1982) for the related issue of convergent validity.
8. See, for example, Greek (2006) and Krippendorff (2003).
9. The General Social Survey is described in Alwin (1988) and in Davis and Smith (1986).
10. Other major U.S. archives of survey data include the National Opinion Research Center, University of Chicago; the Survey Research Center, University of California–Berkeley; the Behavioral Sciences Laboratory, University of Cincinnati; Data and Program Library Service, University of Wisconsin–Madison; the Roper Center, University of Connecticut–Storrs; and the Institute for Research in Social Science, University of North Carolina–Chapel Hill. Also see Kiecolt and Nathan (1985) and Parcel (1992).

Analysis of Quantitative Data

Dying for Statistics
Dealing with Data
  Coding Data
  Entering Data
  Cleaning Data
    Highlight 10.1 Neuman's Dealings with Data
Results with One Variable
  Frequency Distributions
  Measures of Central Tendency
  Measures of Variation
    Highlight 10.2 Calculating z-Scores
Results with Two Variables
  A Bivariate Relationship
  Seeing the Relationship: The Scattergram
    What Is a Scattergram?
    How to Construct a Scattergram
    What Can We Learn from the Scattergram?
      ■ *Form*
      ■ *Direction*
      ■ *Precision*
    Highlight 10.3 Graphing Accurately

Bivariate Tables
  What Is a Bivariate Table?
  Constructing Percentaged Tables
  Reading a Percentaged Table
  Bivariate Tables without Percentages
  Measures of Association
Inferential Statistics
  The Purpose of Inferential Statistics
  Statistical Significance
    Highlight 10.4 Chi-Square
  Levels of Significance
  Type I and Type II Errors
Being Critical: Ethics and Statistics
    *Highlight 10.5 Statistical Programs
      on Computers*
Conclusion
Key Terms
Review Questions
Practicing Research
Notes for Further Study

DYING FOR STATISTICS

Chapter 1 noted an interesting paradox in today's society: As research-based knowledge in our society grows exponentially in both size and influence, so has the level of skepticism about its legitimacy. This paradox is also found in our love–hate relationship with statistics: They are essential in today's society for establishing facts, yet their overuse (and sometimes misuse) causes many to be skeptical about their legitimacy. Some have asked whether we're "numb to numbers."

The debate about the war on terrorism is a good example of this paradox. John Mueller (2006) recently wrote an influential article in the journal *Foreign Affairs* in which he raises questions about one of its foundational premises—the dangerousness of the terrorist entity al Qaeda. He reviews arguments by some that we are witnessing the beginnings of World War III, and then relies on statistics to discredit the idea that al Qaeda, post September 11, represents a serious threat to Americans on American soil.

> . . . it is worth remembering that the total number of people killed since 9/11 by al Qaeda or al Qaeda–like operatives outside of Afghanistan and Iraq is not much higher than the number who drown in bathtubs in the United States in a single year, and that the lifetime chance of an American being killed by international terrorism in general is about one in 80,000—about the same chance of being killed by a comet or a meteor. Although it remains heretical to say so, the evidence so far suggests that fears of the omnipotent terrorist may have been overblown, the threat presented within the United States by al Qaeda greatly exaggerated. The massive and expensive homeland security apparatus erected since 9/11 may be persecuting some, spying on many, inconveniencing most, and taxing all to defend the United States against an enemy that scarcely exists.

Mueller's use of statistics in this way angered many and delighted others; the fault line of course divided along ideological preferences. Statistics have the amazing capacity to simultaneously reveal, distort, lie, or inspire. Figure 10.1 provides a government-generated chart by the National Safety Council. As you can see, making sense of Mueller's assertion requires some knowledge about the various causes that bring about our demise overall.

The fact is that all crime and justice researchers work in some way with numbers. There is no getting around it. As social *scientists,* we possess a skeptical appreciation for crime and justice statistics, and how they are collected and analyzed. Quantitative analysis is the mainstay of both basic and applied research in criminology and criminal justice. One would have little more than a pedestrian point of view about the core questions of the field without referencing quantitative research.

The proper way to think about scattergrams, pie charts, correlations, multiple regressions, and tables of numbers is as tools. They are fairly easy tools to learn to use and can wield tremendous influence both positively and negatively; we can't be intimidated by them. By the time you finish reading this chapter, you will have acquired the foundation to comprehend and think through most basic forms of quantitative research.

Causes	Chances of Occurring (Yearly)	Causes	Chances of Occurring (Yearly)
Heart Disease	(1 in 5)	Air/Space Accident	(1 in 5,051)
Cancer	(1 in 7)	Accidental Firearm Discharge	(1 in 5,134)
Motor Vehicle Accident	(1 in 84)	Accidental Electrocution	(1 in 9,968)
Suicide	(1 in 119)	Alcohol Poisoning	(1 in 10,048)
Falling	(1 in 218)	Hot Weather	(1 in 13,729)
Firearm Assault	(1 in 314)	Insect Sting	(1 in 56,789)
Drowning	(1 in 1,008)	Legal Execution	(1 in 62,468)
Motorcycle Accident	(1 in 1,020)	Lightning	(1 in 79,746)
Fire or Smoke	(1 in 1,113)	Flood	(1 in 144,156)

Note: *For the year 2003, as cited by the National Safety Council (www.nsc.org/lrs/statinfo/odds.htm). If you look carefully, it might be confusing how exactly Mueller came up with the "1 in 80,000" statistic for a meteor-caused death when the odds appear the same, at first glance, for a lightning strike. The difference is that Mueller is referring to the chance of death over an entire lifetime, and the NSC statistic cited above is referring to the probability during a one-year time period.

FIGURE 10.1   Greatest to Least Likely Causes of Dying. (in the United States)*

DEALING WITH DATA

Coding Data

Before a crime and justice researcher examines quantitative data to test hypotheses, he or she needs to put them in a different form. We encountered the idea of coding data in the last chapter. Here, data **coding** means systematically reorganizing raw data into a format that is machine readable (i.e., easy to analyze using computers). As with coding in content analysis, researchers create and consistently apply rules for transferring information from one form to another.[1]

Coding can be a simple clerical task when the data are recorded as numbers on well-organized recording sheets, but it is very difficult when, for example, a researcher wants to code answers to open-ended survey questions into numbers in a process similar to latent content analysis.

Researchers use a coding procedure and a codebook for data coding. The **coding procedure** is a set of rules stating that certain numbers are assigned to variable attributes. For example, a researcher codes males as 1 and females as 2. Each category of a variable and missing information needs a code. A **codebook** is a document (i.e., one or more pages) describing the coding procedure and the location of data for variables in a format that computers can use.

When we code data, it is very important to create a well-organized, detailed codebook and make multiple copies of it. If we do not write down the details of the coding procedure, or if we misplace the codebook, we have lost the key to the data and will have to recode the raw data all over again.

Researchers begin thinking about a coding procedure and codebook before they collect data. Survey researchers, for example, often precode their questionnaires before collecting the data. **Precoding** means actually writing the code categories directly on the questionnaire. The codes are contained within the codebook. Figure 10.2 gives an example of a precoded survey question, and Table 10.1 shows an excerpt from the corresponding codebook.

If a researcher does not precode, his or her first step after collecting data is to create a codebook. He or she also gives each case an identification number to keep track of the cases. Next, the researcher transfers the information from each questionnaire into a format that computers can read.

Entering Data

Most computer programs designed for data analysis need the data to be organized in a grid format. In the grid, each row represents a respondent, subject, or case (e.g., "Richmond Police Department"). In computer terminology, these are called data records. Each is the record of data for a single case. A column or set of columns represents specific variables. It is possible to

---

CODING

The systemic reorganization of raw data into a format that is computer readable.

CODING PROCEDURE

A set of rules stating that certain numbers are assigned to variable attributes.

CODEBOOK

A document describing the coding procedure and the location of data for variables in a format that computers can use.

PRECODING

The act of writing the code categories directly on the questionnaire.

"Are there any situations you can imagine in which you would approve of a policeman striking an adult female citizen?"	
Yes	1
No	2
Not sure (volunteered)	3
No response	9

FIGURE 10.2 Precoded Survey Question   *Source:* From W. Lawrence Neuman and Bruce Weigand, *Criminal Justice Research Methods, Qualitative and Quantitative Approaches,* 1/e. Published by Allyn and Bacon, 75 Arlington St., Boston, MA 02116. Copyright © 2000 by Pearson Education. Reprinted by permission of the publisher. Adapted from a General Social Studies Survey question asked of a national sample of Americans as cited in Jean Johnson. "American' Views on Crime and Law Enforcement." *National Institute of Justice Journal* (September 1997): 9–12.

TABLE 10.1	Excerpt from Codebook	
Column	**Variable Name**	**Description**
1–4	ID	Respondent identification number
5–8	Date	Month/Day (e.g., 0525)
9	Interviewer	Interviewer who collected the data:
		1 = Jasmine
		2 = Teddy
		3 = Juan
		4 = Sharon
		5 = Jason
10	Sex	Interviewer report of respondent's sex
		1 = Male, 2 = Female
11	Striking	Approve police striking
		1 = Yes
		2 = No
		3 = Not Sure (volunteered)
		4 = No Response
		Blank = Missing Information

Source: From W. Lawrence Neuman and Bruce Weigand, *Criminal Justice Research Methods, Qualitative and Quantitative Approaches,* 1/e. Published by Allyn and Bacon, 75 Arlington St., Boston, MA 02116. Copyright © 2000 by Pearson Education. Reprinted by permission of the publisher.

DATA FIELD

A column or set of columns assigned to a variable.

CODE SHEETS

A sheet with grids in which the researcher writes code numbers in squares that correspond to a row and column location, and then uses this to type it into a computer.

DIRECT-ENTRY METHOD

A method of data entry where the researcher manually types in the data.

OPTICAL SCAN SHEET

A machine that can read information from questionnaire sheets and insert them directly into a computer file.

go from a column and row location (e.g., row 7, column 5) back to the original source of data (e.g., a questionnaire item on police behavior for respondent 8). A column or set of columns assigned to a variable is called a **data field** or just a *field*.

A researcher transfers information from questionnaires, recording sheets, or similar raw data forms into a format for computers in four ways: code sheets, direct entry, optical scan sheets, and computer-assisted telephone interviewing (CATI). First, he or she can use graph paper or special grid forms for computers (called *transfer* or **code sheets**) by writing code numbers in squares that correspond to a row and column location, then typing it into a computer. Second, the researcher can sit at a computer and directly type in the data. This **direct-entry method** is easiest if information is already in a similar format, as with content analysis recording sheets. Otherwise, it can be very time consuming and error prone. Third, he or she can put data on an **optical scan sheet**. Special machines—optical scanners—read the information from the sheets into a computer. You may have used optical scan sheets, which are used for scoring multiple-choice tests. They are specially printed forms on which a person fills in boxes or circles using a pencil to indicate a response. The researcher can use the last method if his or her project involved telephone interviewing. Computer-assisted telephone interviewing was described in Chapter 9 Interviewers wearing telephone headsets sit at a computer keyboard and enter data directly as respondents answer questions during an interview.

Cleaning Data

Accuracy is extremely important when coding data. Errors made when coding or entering data into a computer threaten the validity of measures and cause misleading results. A researcher who has a perfect sample, perfect measures, and no errors in gathering data but who makes errors in the coding process or in entering data into a computer can ruin a research project. Highlight 10.1 provides an interesting examination of Neuman's dealing with data.

HIGHLIGHT 10.1
Neuman's Dealings with Data

There is no good substitute for getting your hands dirty with the data. Here is an example of data preparation from a study I conducted with my students. My university surveyed about one-third of the students to learn their thinking and experience with sexual harassment on campus. A research team drew a random sample, then developed and distributed a self-administered questionnaire. Respondents put answers on optical scan sheets that were similar to the answer sheets used for multiple-choice exams. The story begins with the delivery of over 3,000 optical scan sheets.

After the sheets arrived, we visually scanned each one for obvious errors. Despite instructions to use pencil and fill in each circle neatly and darkly, we found that about 200 respondents used a pen, and another 200 respondents used a pencil, and another 200 were very sloppy or used very light pencil marks. We cleaned up the sheets and redid them in pencil. We also found about twenty five unusable sheets that were defaced or damaged, or were too incomplete (e.g., only the first two of seventy questions answered).

Next, we read the usable optical scan sheets into a computer. We had the computer produce the number of occurrences, or frequency, of the attributes for each variable. Looking at them, we discovered several kinds of errors. Some respondents had filled in two responses for a question to which only one answer was requested or possible. Some had filled in impossible response codes (e.g., the numeral 4 for sex, when the only legitimate codes were 1 for male and 2 for female), and some had filled in every answer in the same way, suggesting that they did not take the survey seriously. For each case with an error, we returned to the optical scan sheet to see whether we could recover any information. If we could not recover information, we reclassified the case as a nonresponse or recoded a response as missing information.

The questionnaire had two contingency questions. For each, a respondent who answered "no" to one question was to skip the next five questions. We created a table for each question. We looked to see whether all respondents who answered "no" to the first question skipped or left blank the next five. We found about 35 cases in which the respondent answered "no" but then went on to answer the next five questions. We returned to each sheet and tried to figure out which the respondent really intended. In most cases, it appeared that the respondent meant the "no" but failed to read the instructions to skip questions.

Finally, we examined the frequency of attributes for each variable to see whether they made sense. We were very surprised to learn that about 600 respondents had marked "Native American" for the racial heritage question. In addition, over half of those who had done so were freshmen. A check of official records revealed that the university enrolled a total of about twenty Native Americans or American Indians, and that over 90 percent of the students were White, non-Hispanic Caucasians. The percentage of respondents marking Black, African American, or Hispanic-Chicano matched the official records. We concluded that some White Caucasian respondents had been unfamiliar with the term "Native American" for "American Indian." Apparently, they had mistakenly marked it instead of "White, Caucasian." Because we expected about seven Native Americans in the sample, we recoded the "Native American" responses as "White, Caucasian." This meant that we reclassified Native Americans in the sample as Caucasian. At this point, we were ready to analyze the data.

Source: From W. Lawrence Neuman, *Social Research Methods, Qualitative and Quantitative Approaches,* 6/e. Published by Allyn and Bacon, 75 Arlington St., Boston, MA 02116. Copyright © 2006 by Pearson Education. Reprinted by permission of the publisher.

After very careful coding, the researcher checks the accuracy of coding, or "cleans" the data. He or she may code a 10–15 percent random sample of the data a second time. If no coding errors appear, the researcher proceeds; if he or she finds errors, the researcher rechecks all coding.

Researchers verify coding after the data are entered into a computer in two ways. Possible code cleaning (or *wild code checking*) involves checking the categories of all variables for impossible codes. For example, respondent sex is coded 1 = Male, 2 = Female. Finding a 4 for a case in the field for the sex variable indicates a coding error. A second method, contingency cleaning (or *consistency checking*), involves cross-classifying two variables and looking for logically impossible combinations. For example, education is cross-classified by occupation. If a respondent is recorded as never having passed the eighth grade and also is recorded as being a legitimate medical doctor, the researcher checks for a coding error.

A researcher can modify data after they have been entered into a computer. He or she may not use more refined categories than were used when collecting the original data, but may combine or group information. For example, the researcher may group ratio-level income data into five ordinal categories. Also, he or she can combine information from several indicators to create a new variable or add the responses to several questionnaire items into an index score.

RESULTS WITH ONE VARIABLE

Frequency Distributions

STATISTICS

Ways to manipulate and summarize numbers that represent data from a research project.

DESCRIPTIVE STATISTICS

A description of phenomena using numbers.

UNIVARIATE STATISTICS

Statistics describe one variable.

FREQUENCY DISTRIBUTION

A table that shows the distribution of cases into categories of one variable, that is, the number or percent of cases in each category.

HISTOGRAM

A visual technique that summarizes univariate statistical information at the interval level through the use of horizontal bars.

FREQUENCY POLYGON

A visual presentation of statistical information which places frequency of cases along the vertical axis and the values of the variable along the horizontal axis.

The word **statistics** has several meanings. It can mean a set of collected numbers (e.g., numbers of homicides in a city) as well as a branch of applied mathematics used to manipulate and summarize the features of numbers. Criminologists use both types of statistics. Here, we focus on the second type—ways to manipulate and summarize numbers that represent data from a research project.

   Descriptive statistics describe phenomena depicted numerically. They can be categorized by the number of variables involved: univariate, bivariate, or multivariate (for one, two, and three or more variables). **Univariate statistics** describe one variable (*uni-* refers to one; *-variate* refers to variable). The easiest way to describe the numerical data of one variable is with a **frequency distribution**. It can be used with nominal-, ordinal-, interval-, or ratio-level data and takes many forms. For example, O'Toole and colleagues (1994) conducted a survey of 447 business and public-sector organizations in Victoria, Australia, to identify crimes of fraud against them. Table 10.2 summarizes the types of fraud using frequency distribution.

   Besides frequency distributions, criminologists often use graphs and charts to summarize univariate statistics. Some common types of graphic representations are the **histogram**, bar chart, and pie chart. Most people have seen these. The terminology is not exact, but histograms are usually upright bar graphs for interval or ratio data.[2] For interval- or ratio-level data, a researcher often groups the information into categories. The grouped categories should be mutually exclusive. Interval- or ratio-level data are often plotted in a **frequency polygon**. In it, the number of cases or frequency is along the vertical axis, and the values of the variable or scores are along the horizontal axis. A polygon appears when the dots are connected (see Figure 10.3).

TABLE 10.2 Raw Count and Percentage Frequency Distribution		
Type of Fraud	**Frequency**	**Percent**
Misappropriation of stock or equipment	251	25
Misappropriation of cash	162	16
False expense account claims	113	11
Unauthorized use of equipment	79	8
False invoices	50	5
Kickbacks/bribes	45	4
Supplier overcharging	42	4
False claims to obtain credit	41	4
Passing off worthless checks	38	4
Unauthorized use of organization credit cards	30	3
Misuse by employees of organization checks	30	3
Other	129	12
Total	1010	100
		(rounded)

Source: From W. Lawrence Neuman and Bruce Weigand, *Criminal Justice Research Methods, Qualitative and Quantitative Approaches,* 1/e. Published by Allyn and Bacon, 75 Arlington St., Boston, MA 02116. Copyright © 2000 by Pearson Education. Reprinted by permission of the publisher. Adapted from Kevin O'Toole et al. *Fraud against Organizations in Victoria* (Geelong: Deakin University Press, 1994).

Measures of Central Tendency

Researchers often want to summarize the information about one variable into a single number. They use three measures of central tendency, or measures of the center of the frequency distribution: mean, median, and mode, which are often called *averages* (a less precise and less clear way of saying the same thing).

The **mode** is the easiest to use and can be used with nominal, ordinal, interval, or ratio data. It is simply the most common or frequently occurring number. For example, the mode of the following list is 5: 6 5 7 10 9 5 3 5. A distribution can have more than one mode. For example, the mode of this list is both 5 and 7: 5 6 1 2 5 7 4 7. If the list gets long, it is easy to spot the mode

MODE

The most common or frequently occurring number in a distribution of scores.

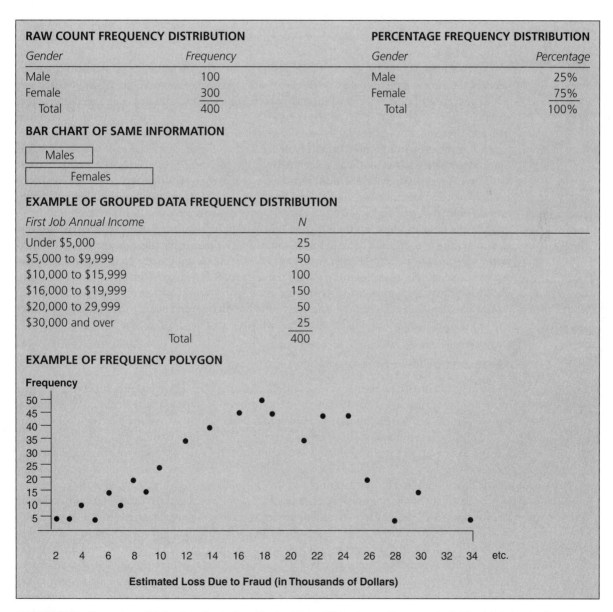

RAW COUNT FREQUENCY DISTRIBUTION		PERCENTAGE FREQUENCY DISTRIBUTION	
Gender	Frequency	Gender	Percentage
Male	100	Male	25%
Female	300	Female	75%
Total	400	Total	100%

BAR CHART OF SAME INFORMATION

Males
Females

EXAMPLE OF GROUPED DATA FREQUENCY DISTRIBUTION

First Job Annual Income	N
Under $5,000	25
$5,000 to $9,999	50
$10,000 to $15,999	100
$16,000 to $19,999	150
$20,000 to 29,999	50
$30,000 and over	25
Total	400

EXAMPLE OF FREQUENCY POLYGON

Frequency

Estimated Loss Due to Fraud (in Thousands of Dollars)

FIGURE 10.3   Examples of Univariate Statistics.   *Source:* From W. Lawrence Neuman, *Social Research Methods, Qualitative and Quantitative Approaches*, 6/e. Published by Allyn and Bacon, 75 Arlington St., Boston, MA 02116. Copyright © 2006 by Pearson Education. Reprinted by permission of the publisher.

in a frequency distribution—just look for the most frequent score. There will always be at least one case with a score that is equal to the mode.

The **median** is the middle point. It is also the 50th percentile, or the point at which half the cases are above it and half below it. It can be used with ordinal-, interval-, or ratio-level data (but not nominal level). We can "eyeball" the mode, but computing a median requires a little more work. The easiest way is first to organize the scores from highest to lowest, then count to the middle. If there is an odd number of scores, it is simple. Seven people are waiting for a bus; their ages are 12 17 20 27 30 55 80. The median age is 27. Note that the median does not change easily. If the 55-year-old and the 80-year-old both got on one bus, and the remaining people were joined by two 31-year-olds, the median remains unchanged. If there is an even number of scores, things are a bit more complicated. For example, six people have the following ages: 17 20 26 30 50 70. The median is somewhere between 26 and 30. Compute the median by adding the two middle scores together and dividing by 2, or $26 + 30 = 56/2 = 28$. The median age is 28, even though no person is 28 years old. Note that there is no mode in the list of six ages because each person has a different age.

The **mean**, also called the arithmetic average, is the most widely used measure of central tendency. It can be used *only* with interval- or ratio-level data. Compute the mean by adding up all scores, then divide by the number of scores. For example, the mean age in the previous example is $17 + 20 + 26 + 30 + 50 + 70 = 213; 213/6 = 35.5$. No one in the list is 35.5 years old, and the mean does not equal the median.

The mean is strongly affected by changes in extreme values (very large or very small values sometimes referred to as "outliers"). For example, the 50- and 70-year-old left and were replaced with two 31-year-olds. The distribution now looks like this: 17 20 26 30 31 31. The median is unchanged: 28. The mean is $17 + 20 + 26 + 30 + 31 + 31 = 155; 155/6 = 25.8$. Thus, the mean dropped a great deal when a few extreme values were removed.[3]

If the frequency distribution forms a "normal" or bell-shaped curve, the three measures of central tendency equal each other. If the distribution is a **skewed distribution** (i.e., more cases are in the upper or lower scores), then the three will not be equal. If most cases have lower scores with a few extreme high scores, the mean will be the highest, the median in the middle, and the mode the lowest. If most cases have higher scores with a few extreme low scores, the mean will be the lowest, the median in the middle, and the mode the highest. In general, the median is best for skewed distributions, although the mean is used in most other statistics (see Figure 10.4).

Measures of Variation

Measures of central tendency are a one-number summary of a distribution; however, they give only its *center*. Another characteristic of a distribution is its spread, dispersion, or variability around the center. Two distributions can have identical measures of central tendency but differ in their spread about the center. For example, seven people are these ages: 25 26 27 30 33 34 35. Both the median and the mean are 30. Another seven people have the identical median and mean, but their ages are 5 10 20 30 40 50 55. The ages of the second group are spread more from the center, or the distribution has more variability.

Variability has important social implications. For example, in city X, the median and mean family income is $25,600 per year, and it has zero variation. *Zero variation* means that every family has an income of exactly $25,600. City Y has the same median and mean family income, but 95 percent of its families have incomes of $8,000 per year and 5 percent have incomes of $300,000 per year. City X has perfect income equality, whereas there is great inequality in city Y. A researcher who does not know the variability of income in the two cities misses very important information.

Researchers measure variation in three ways: *range, percentile, and standard deviation.* **Range** is the simplest. It consists of the largest and smallest scores. For example, the range for the first group is from 25 to 35, or $35 - 25 = 10$ years. If the 35-year-old were replaced by a 60-year-old, the

---

MEDIAN

The middle point of a distribution of scores (1/2 fall below and 1/2 fall above the median).

MEAN

The arithmetic average of a distribution of scores.

SKEWED DISTRIBUTION

A distribution of scores where the three measures of central tendency do not equal each other.

RANGE

The largest and smallest scores within a distribution of scores.

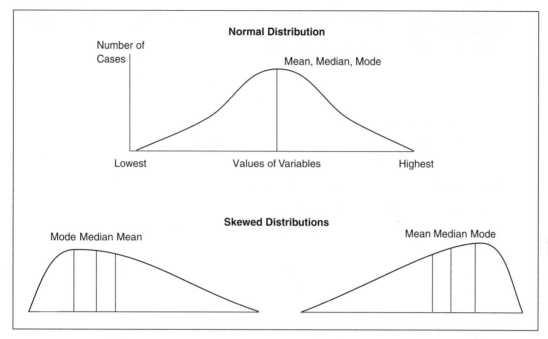

FIGURE 10.4 Measures of Central Tendency. *Source:* From W. Lawrence Neuman and Bruce Weigand, *Criminal Justice Research Methods, Qualitative and Quantitative Approaches*, 1/e. Published by Allyn and Bacon, 75 Arlington St., Boston, MA 02116. Copyright © 2000 by Pearson Education. Reprinted by permission of the publisher.

range would change to $60 - 25 = 45$ years. Range has limitations. For example, here are two groups of six with a range of 35 years: 30 30 30 30 30 65 and 20 45 46 48 50 55.

Percentiles tell the score at a specific place within the distribution. One percentile we already learned is the median, the 50th percentile. Sometimes the 25th and 75th percentiles or the 10th and 90th percentiles are used to describe a distribution. For example, the 25th percentile is the score at which 25 percent of the distribution have either that score or a lower one. The computation of a percentile follows the same logic as the median. If we have 100 people and want to find the 25th percentile, we rank the scores and count up from the bottom until reaching number 25. If the total is not 100, simply adjust the distribution to a percentage basis.

Standard deviation is the most difficult to compute measure of dispersion; it is also the most comprehensive and widely used. The range and percentile are for ordinal-, interval-, and ratio-level data, but the standard deviation requires an interval or ratio level of measurement. It is based on the mean and gives an "average distance" between all scores and the mean. People rarely compute the standard deviation by hand for more than a handful of cases because computers and calculators can do it in seconds.

Look at the calculation of the standard deviation in Table 10.3. If we add up the absolute difference between each score and the mean (i.e., subtract each score from the mean), we get zero. This is because the mean is equally distant from all scores. Also notice that the scores that differ the most from the mean have the largest effect on the sum of squares and on the standard deviation.

The standard deviation is of limited usefulness by itself. It is used for comparison purposes. For example, suppose a researcher was interested in the causal effects of parental education on self-reported delinquency. The researcher has collected data from three classes of students, and parental education was operationalized as parents' years of schooling. The standard deviation for class A is 3.317 years. (The calculations are presented in Table 10.3.) The respective standard deviations for class B and class C are 0.812 and 6.239.

PERCENTILES

Indicate the score at a specific place within a distribution of scores.

STANDARD DEVIATION

A statistic based on the mean and gives an average distance between all scores and the mean.

TABLE 10.3   The Standard Deviation

Steps in Computing the Standard Deviation

1. Compute the mean.
2. Subtract the mean from each score.
3. Square the resulting difference for each score.
4. Total up the squared differences to get the sum of squares.
5. Divide the sum of squares by the number of cases to get the variance.
6. Take the square root of the variance, which is the standard deviation.

Example of Computing the Standard Deviation

[8 respondents, variable = years of schooling]

Score	Score–Mean	Squared (Score–Mean)
15	15 − 12.5 = 2.5	6.25
12	12 − 12.5 = −0.5	25
12	12 − 12.5 = −0.5	25
10	10 − 12.5 = −2.5	6.25
16	16 − 12.5 = 3.5	12.25
18	18 − 12.5 = 5.5	30.25
8	8 − 12.5 = 4.5	20.25
9	9 − 12.5 = −3.5	12.25

Mean = 15 + 12 + 12 + 10 + 16 + 18 + 8 + 9 = 100, 100/8 = 12.5

Some of squares = 6.25 + .25 + .25 + 6.25 + 12.25 + 30.25 + 20.25 + 12.25 = 88

Variance = Sum of squares/Number of cases = 88/8 = 11

Standard deviation = Square root of variance = $\sqrt{11}$ = 3.317 years

Here is the standard deviation in the form of a formula with symbols.

Symbols:

X = SCORE of case Σ = Sigma (Greek letter) for sum, add together

$\bar{X}$ = MEAN N = Number of cases

Formula:[a]

$$\text{Standard deviation} = \sqrt{\frac{\Sigma(X - \bar{X})^2}{N - 1}}$$

[a]There is a slight difference in the formula depending on whether one is using data for the population or a sample to estimate the population parameter.

Source: From W. Lawrence Neuman, *Social Research Methods, Qualitative and Quantitative Approaches,* 6/e. Published by Allyn and Bacon, 75 Arlington St., Boston, MA 02116. Copyright © 2006 by Pearson Education. Reprinted by permission of the publisher.

The standard deviation tells a researcher that the parents of children in class B are very similar, whereas those for class C are very different. In fact, in class B, the schooling of an "average" parent is less than a year above or below than the mean for all parents, so the parents are very homogeneous. In class C, however, the "average" parent is more than six years above or below the mean, so the parents are very heterogeneous.

The standard deviation and the mean are used to create *z*-scores. These *z-scores* let a researcher compare two or more distributions or groups. The *z*-score, also called a standardized score, expresses points or scores on a frequency distribution in terms of a number of standard deviations from the mean. Scores are in terms of their relative position within a distribution, not as absolute values.

HIGHLIGHT 10.2
Calculating Z-Scores

We do not like the formula for z-scores, which is:

Z-score = (Score − Mean)/Standard Deviation   or   in symbols:

$$z = \frac{X - \bar{X}}{\delta}$$

where

X = Score, $\bar{X}$ = mean, δ = standard deviation

We usually rely on a simple conceptual diagram that does the same thing and that shows what z-scores really do. Consider data on the ages of schoolchildren with a mean of seven years and a standard deviation of two years. How do we compute the z-score of five-year-old Miguel, or what if we know that Yashohda's z-score is a + 2 and we need to know her age in years? First, we draw a little chart from −3 to +3 with zero in the middle. We will put the mean value at zero, because a z-score of zero is the mean and z-scores measure distance above or below it. We stop at 3 because virtually all cases fall within 3 standard deviations of the mean in most situations. The chart looks like this:

−3   −2   −1   0   +1   +2   +3

Now, we label the values of the mean and add or subtract standard deviations from it. One standard deviation above the mean (+1) when the mean is 7 and standard deviation is 2 years is just 7 + 2, or 9 years. For a − 2 z-score, I put 3 years. This is because it is 2 standard deviations, of 2 years each (or 4 years), lower than the mean of 7. Our diagram now looks like this:

1	3	5	7	9	11	13	age in years
−3	−2	−1	0	+1	+2	+3	

It is easy to see that Miguel, who is 5 years old, has a z-score of −1, whereas Yashohda's z-score of +2 corresponds to 11 years old. We can read from z-score to age, or age to z-score. For fractions, such as a z-score of −1.5, we just apply the same fraction to age to get 4 years. Likewise, an age of 12 is a z-score of +2.5.

Source: From W. Lawrence Neuman, *Social Research Methods, Qualitative and Quantitative Approaches,* 6/e. Published by Allyn and Bacon, 75 Arlington St., Boston, MA 02116. Copyright © 2006 by Pearson Education. Reprinted by permission of the publisher.

Z-scores are easy to calculate (see Highlight 10.2) from the mean and standard deviation. For example, an employer interviews students from Kings College and Queens College. She learns that the colleges are similar and that both grade on a 4.0 scale. Yet, the mean grade-point average at Kings College is 2.62 with a standard deviation of .05, whereas the mean grade-point average at Queens College is 3.24 with a standard deviation of .40. The employer suspects that grades at Queens College are inflated. Suzette from Kings College has a grade-point average of 3.62, while Jorge from Queens College has a grade-point average of 3.64. Both students took the same courses. The employer wants to adjust the grades for the grading practices of the two colleges (i.e., create standardized scores). She calculates z-scores by subtracting each student's score from the mean, then dividing by the standard deviation. For example, Suzette's z-score is 3.62 − 2.62 = 1.00/.50 = 2, whereas Jorge's z-score is 3.64 − 3.24. = .40/.40 = 1. Thus, the employer learns that Suzette is two standard deviations above the mean in her college, whereas Jorge is only one standard deviation above the mean for his college. Although Suzette's absolute grade-point average is lower than Jorge's, relative to the students in each of their colleges Suzette's grades are much higher than Jorge's.

Z-SCORES

Expresses scores on a frequency distribution in terms of a number of standard deviations from the mean.

RESULTS WITH TWO VARIABLES

A Bivariate Relationship

Univariate statistics describe a single variable in isolation. **Bivariate statistics** are much more valuable. They let a researcher consider two variables together and describe the relationship between variables. Even simple hypotheses require two variables.

Bivariate statistical analysis shows a **statistical relationship** between variables—that is, things that appear together. For example, control theorists have examined the relationship between parental supervision and delinquent behavior. This is a statistical relationship between two variables: the amount of parental supervision and delinquency.

BIVARIATE STATISTICS

Statistics which describe the relationship between two variables.

STATISTICAL RELATIONSHIP

When variables appear together and are associated (they covary).

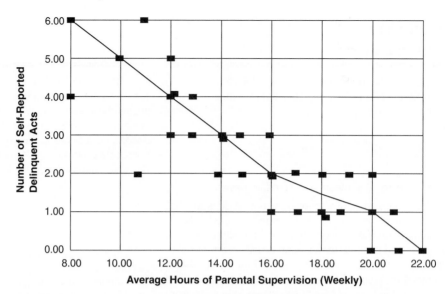

FIGURE 10.5   Example of Scattergram: Self-reported Delinquency and Parental Supervision.   *Source:* From W. Lawrence Neuman and Bruce Weigand, *Criminal Justice Research Methods, Qualitative and Quantitative Approaches*, 1/e. Published by Allyn and Bacon, 75 Arlington St., Boston, MA 02116. Copyright © 2000 by Pearson Education. Reprinted by permission of the publisher.

COVARIATION

Refers to statistical relationships where cases with certain values on one variable are likely to have certain values on the other one.

INDEPENDENCE

The opposite of covariation or no relationship between variables.

Statistical relationships are based on two ideas: covariation and independence. **Covariation** means that things go together or are associated. To *covary* means to vary together: Cases with certain values on one variable are likely to have certain values on the other one. The previous example suggests that as the amount of parental supervision increases, there is a corresponding decrease in the amount of delinquent behavior (see Figure 10.5). To put it differently, knowing one's level of parental supervision reveals the probability of that person engaging in delinquent behavior.

Independence is the opposite of covariation. It means there is no association or no relationship between variables. If two variables are independent, cases with certain values on one variable do not have any particular value on the other variable. Consider, for example, perhaps the most controversial bivariate relationships in criminology: the relationship between social class and crime. Researchers have operationalized the two variables in a variety of ways to explore the causal effect of social class. Some research, indeed, has shown no statistical relationship between the two variables. John Hagan et. al to the Hagan citation. (1996: 15) has addressed this point:

> This is . . . an ideologically charged area of debate that is further complicated by the frequent failure of scientific efforts that use self-report surveys of adolescents to find substantial associations between parental status and delinquency. However, we have argued that when appropriate measures of unemployment are used both among individuals and at higher levels of aggregation [i.e., neighborhoods], consistent relationships are found.

Most researchers state hypotheses in terms of a causal relationship or expected covariation; if they use the null hypothesis, the hypothesis is that there is independence. It is used in formal hypothesis testing and is frequently found in inferential statistics (to be discussed).

Three techniques help researchers decide whether a relationship exists between two variables: (1) a scattergram, or a graph or plot of the relationship; (2) cross-tabulation, or a percentaged table; and (3) measures of association, or statistical measures that express the amount of covariation by a single number (e.g., correlation coefficient). Also see Highlight 10.3 on graphing data.

Seeing the Relationship: The Scattergram

WHAT IS A SCATTERGRAM?   A **scattergram** is a graph on which a researcher plots each case or observation, where each axis represents the value of one variable. It is used for variables measured at the interval or ratio level, rarely for ordinal variables, and never if either variable is nominal. There is no fixed rule for which variable (independent or dependent) to place on the horizontal or vertical axis, but usually the independent variable (symbolized by the letter X) goes on the horizontal axis and the dependent variable (symbolized by Y) on the vertical axis. The lowest value for each should be the lower left corner and the highest value should be at the top or to the right.

HOW TO CONSTRUCT A SCATTERGRAM.   Begin with the range of the two variables. Draw an axis with the values of each variable marked and write numbers on each axis (graph paper is helpful). Next, label each axis with the variable name and put a title at the top. We are now ready for the data. For each case, find the value of each variable and mark the graph at a place corresponding to the two values.

For example, a researcher makes a scattergram of the parental supervision–delinquency relationship for 33 young people. The dependent variable (i.e., self-reported delinquency) forms the vertical (or Y) axis, and the independent variable (i.e., hours of parental supervision) forms the horizontal (or X) axis. The points are plotted accordingly; thus, the first case has four self-reported delinquent acts and eight average hours of parental supervision per week. The second case has six self-reported delinquent acts and eight average hours of supervision, and so on (refer to Figure 10.5). The scattergram in Figure 10.5 is a plot of data for all 33 young people in the survey. As you can see, it shows a *negative relationship* between delinquency and parental supervision. In other words, as the number of hours of parental supervision increases, the self-reported incidences of delinquency decreases.

The scattergram is complete after all the cases have been plotted, which can take some time if there are many cases. Also, some types of computer software can plot a scattergram after the data are in the computer.

WHAT CAN WE LEARN FROM THE SCATTERGRAM?   A researcher can see three aspects of a bivariate relationship in a scattergram: form, direction, and precision.

Form.   Relationships can take three forms: independence, linear, and curvilinear. *Independence* or no relationship is the easiest to see. It looks like a random scatter with no pattern, or a straight line that is exactly parallel to the horizontal or vertical axis. A **linear relationship** means that a straight line can be visualized in the middle of a maze of cases running from one corner to another. A **curvilinear relationship** means that the center of a maze of cases would form a U curve, right side up or upside down, or an S curve.

Direction.   Linear relationships can have a positive or negative direction. The plot of a **positive relationship** looks like a diagonal line from the lower left to the upper right. Higher values on X tend to go with higher values on Y, and vice versa. A **negative relationship** looks like a line from the upper left to the lower right. It means that higher values on one variable go with lower values on the other. For example, people with more education are less likely to have been arrested. If we look at a scattergram of data on a group of males where years of schooling (X axis) are plotted by number of arrests (Y axis), we see that most cases (or men) with many arrests are in the lower right, because most of them completed few years of school. Most cases with few arrests are in the upper left because most have had more schooling. The imaginary line for the relationship can have a shallow or a steep slope. More advanced statistics provide precise numerical measures of the line's slope.

Precision.   Bivariate relationships differ in their degree of precision. **Precision** is the amount of spread in the points on the graph. A high level of precision occurs when the points hug the line that summarizes the relationship. A low level occurs when the points are widely spread around the line. Researchers can "eyeball" a highly precise relationship. They can also use advanced statistics to measure the precision of a relationship in a way that is analogous to the standard deviation for univariate statistics.

SCATTERGRAM

A graph on which a researcher plots each case or observation, and where each axis represents the value of one variable.

LINEAR RELATIONSHIP

A distribution of scores where a straight line can be visualized in the middle of a maze of cases running from one corner to another.

CURVILINEAR RELATIONSHIP

A distribution of cases where the center forms a U curve, right side up or upside down, or an S curve.

POSITIVE RELATIONSHIP

When plotted looks like a diagonal line from the lower left to the upper right. Higher values on X tend to go with higher values on Y, and vice versa.

NEGATIVE RELATIONSHIP

When plotted looks like a line from the upper left to the lower right. It means that higher values on one variable go with lower values on the other.

PRECISION

The amount of spread in the points on the graph. A high level of precision occurs when the points hug the line that summarizes the relationship. A low level occurs when the points are widely spread around the line.

HIGHLIGHT 10.3
Graphing Accurately

The pattern in graph A shows drastic change. A steep drop in 1980 is followed by rapid recovery and instability. The pattern in graph B is much more constant. The decline from 1979 to 1980 is smooth, and the other years are almost level. Both graphs are for identical data, the U.S. business failure rate from 1975 to 1992. The X axis (bottom) for years is the same. The scale of the Y axis is 60–160 in graph A and 0–400 in graph B. The pattern in graph A only looks more dramatic because of the Y axis scale. When reading graphs, be careful to check the scale. Some people purposely choose a scale to minimize or dramatize a pattern in the data.

Source: From W. Lawrence Neuman, _Social Research Methods, Qualitative and Quantitative Approaches_, 6/e. Published by Allyn and Bacon, 75 Arlington St., Boston, MA 02116. Copyright © 2006 by Pearson Education. Reprinted by permission of the publisher.

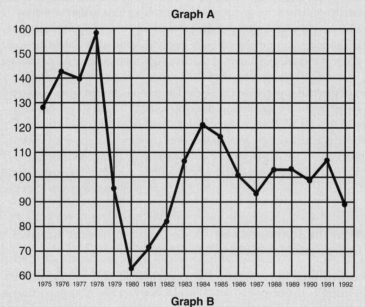

Graph A

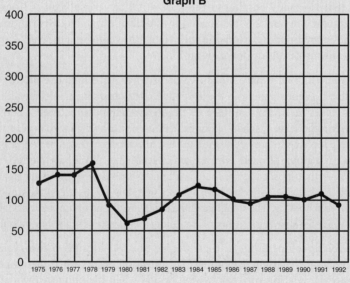

Graph B

Bivariate Tables

WHAT IS A BIVARIATE TABLE?   The **bivariate percentaged table** is widely used. It presents the same information as a scattergram in a more condensed form. The data can be measured at any level of measurement, although interval and ratio data must be grouped if there are many different values. The table is based on **cross-tabulation**: that is, the cases are organized in the table on the basis of two variables at the same time. Bivariate tables usually contain percentages.

CONSTRUCTING PERCENTAGED TABLES.   It is easy to construct a percentaged table, but there are ways to make it look professional. We will first review the steps for constructing a table by hand. The same principles apply if a computer makes the table. We begin with the raw data, which can be organized into a format for computers. They might look like data from an imaginary survey in Table 10.4.

The next step is to create a **compound frequency distribution (CFD)**. This is similar to the frequency distribution, except that it is for each combination of the values of two variables. Suppose, for example, a criminologist wants to see the relationship between age and attitude toward the legalization of marijuana. Since age is measured at the ratio level, it must be grouped into ordinal categories. Ratio- or interval-level data are converted to the ordinal level for percentaged tables. Otherwise, there could be too many categories for a variable, making the table virtually impossible to interpret.

BIVARIATE PERCENTAGED TABLE

A statistical table based on cross-tabulation; that is, the cases are organized in the table on the basis of two variables at the same time. Bivariate tables usually contain percentages.

CROSS-TABULATION

The technique of intersecting two or more variables so that the cases are organized in the same table at the same time.

COMPOUND FREQUENCY DISTRIBUTION (CFD)

Similar to the frequency distribution, except that it is for each combination of the values of two variables.

TABLE 10.4   Raw Data and Frequency Distributions

Example of Raw Data

Case	Age	Gender	Schooling	Attitude toward Legalizing Marijuana
01	21	F	14	1
02	36	M	8	1
03	77	F	12	2
04	41	F	20	2
05	29	M	22	3
06	45	F	12	3
07	19	M	13	2
08	64	M	12	3
09	53	F	10	3
10	44	M	21	1
etc.				

(Attitude scoring, 1 = Agree, 2 = No Opinion, 3 = Disagree)

Two Frequency Distributions: Age and Attitude toward Legalizing Marijuana

Age Group	Number of Cases	Attitude	Number of Cases
Under 30	26		
30–45	30	Agree	38
46–60	35	No Opinion	26
61 and older	15	Disagree	40
Missing	3	Missing	5
Total	109	Total	109

(continued)

Table 10.4 Continued

**Compound Frequency Distribution: Age and Attitude
toward Legalizing Marijuana**

Age	Attitude	Number of Cases
Under 30	Agree	20
Under 30	No Opinion	3
Under 30	Disagree	3
30–45	Agree	10
30–45	No Opinion	10
30–45	Disagree	5
46–60	Agree	4
46–60	No Opinion	10
46–60	Disagree	21
61 and older	Agree	3
61 and older	No Opinion	2
61 and older	Disagree	10
	Subtotal	101
Missing on either variable		8
Total		109

Source: From W. Lawrence Neuman and Bruce Weigand, *Criminal Justice Research Methods, Qualitative and Quantitative Approaches,* 1/e. Published by Allyn and Bacon, 75 Arlington St., Boston, MA 02116. Copyright © 2000 by Pearson Education. Reprinted by permission of the publisher.

The CFD has every combination of categories. Age has four categories and attitude has three, so there are 3 × 4 = 12 rows. The steps to create a CFD are as follows:

1. Figure all possible combinations of variable categories.
2. Make a mark next to the combination category into which each case falls.
3. Add up the marks for the number of cases in a combination category.

If there is no missing information problem, add up the numbers of categories (e.g., all the Agrees, or all the 61 and Olders). In the example, missing data are an issue. The four Agree categories in the CFD add up to 37 (20 + 10 + 4 + 3), not 38, as in the univariate frequency distribution, because one of the 38 cases has missing information for age. The CFD is an intermediate step that makes table construction easier. Computer programs give us the completed table right away.

The next step is to set up the parts of a table (see Figure 10.6) by labeling the rows and columns. The independent variable usually is placed in the columns, but this convention is not always followed. Next, each number from the CFD is placed in a cell in the table that corresponds to the combination of variable categories. For example, the CFD shows that 20 of the under-30-year-olds agree (top number), and so does Figure 10.6 (upper left cell).

Figure 10.6 is a raw count or frequency table. Its cells contain a count of the cases. It is easy to make, but interpreting a raw count table is difficult because the rows or columns can have different totals, and what is of real interest is the relative size of cells compared to others.

Researchers convert raw count tables into percentaged tables to see bivariate relationships. There are three ways to percentage a table: by row, by column, and for the total. The first two are often used and show relationships.

Is it best to percentage by row or column? Either can be appropriate. Let us first review the mechanics of percentaging a table. When calculating column percentages, compute the percentage each cell is of the column total. This includes the total column or marginal for the column variable. For example, the first column total is 26 (there are 26 people under age 30), and the

Raw Count Table

Attitude (b)	AGE GROUP			
	Under 30	*30–45*	*46–60*	*61 and Older*
Agree	20	10	4	3
No opinion	3 (e)	10	10	2
Disagree	3	5	21	10
Total (c)	26	25	35	15
Missing cases (f) = 8			(d)	

The Parts of a Table

a. Give each table a *title*, which names variables and provides background information.

b. Label the row and column variable and give a name to each of the variable categories.

c. Include the totals of the columns and rows. These are called the *marginals*. They equal the univariate frequency distribution for the variable.

d. The numbers with the labeled variable categories and the totals are called the *body of a table*.

e. Each number or place that corresponds to the intersection of a category for each variable is a *cell of a table*.

f. If there is missing information (cases in which a respondent refused to answer, ended interview, said "don't know," etc.), report the number of missing cases near the table to account for all original cases.

FIGURE 10.6 Age Group by Attitude about Legalizing Marijuana Raw Count Table (a).

Source: From W. Lawrence Neuman and Bruce Weigand, *Criminal Justice Research Methods, Qualitative and Quantitative Approaches*, 1/e. Published by Allyn and Bacon, 75 Arlington St., Boston, MA 02116. Copyright © 2000 by Pearson Education. Reprinted by permission of the publisher.

first cell of that column is 20 (there are 20 people under age 30 who agree). The percentage is 20/26 = 0.769 or 76.9 percent. Or, for the first number in the marginal, 37/101 = 0.366 = 36.6 percent (see Table 10.4). Except for rounding, the total should equal 100 percent.

Computing row percentages is similar. Compute the percentage of each cell as a percentage of the row total. For example, using the same cell with 20 in it, we now want to know what percentage it is of the row total of 37, or 20/37 = 0.541 = 54.1 percent. Percentaging by row or column gives different percentages for a cell unless the marginals are the same.

The column and row percentages serve to address different research questions. Column percentages answer questions concerning the distribution of attitudes for a given age group. Thus, of respondents under 30 years of age, 76.9 percent agree with the notion of legalizing marijuana (see Table 10.5. Row percentages, on the other hand, answer questions about the age distribution among those holding a certain attitude. Of respondents agreeing to marijuana legalization, 54.1 percent are under 30 years of age. So, it depends on which question the researcher is asking as to whether he or she should percentage by column or row. One way of percentaging emphasizes people's attitudes at a given age; the other emphasizes people's ages for a given attitude.

A researcher's hypothesis may imply looking at row percentages or the column percentages. When beginning, calculate percentages each way and practice interpreting, or figuring out, what each says. For example, our hypothesis is that age affects attitude, so column percentages are most helpful. However, if our interest was in describing the age makeup of groups of people with different attitudes, then row percentages are appropriate. As Zeisel (1985: 34) noted, whenever one factor in a cross-tabulation can be considered the cause of the other, percentage will be most illuminating if they are computed in the direction of the causal factor.

TABLE 10.5	Age Group by Attitude about Legalizing Marijuana

Column-percentaged Table

Attitude	Age Group Under 30	30–45	46–60	61 and Older	Total
Agree	76.9%	40%	11.4%	20%	36.6%
No opinion	11.5	40	28.6	13.3	24.8
Disagree	11.5	20	60	66.7	38.6
Total	99.9	100	100	100	100
(N)	(26)[a]	(25)[a]	(35)[a]	(15)[a]	(101)[a]

Missing cases = 8

Row-Percentaged Table

Attitude	Age Group Under 30	30–45	46–60	61 and Older	Total	(N)
Agree	54.1%	27%	10.8%	8.1%	100%	(37)[a]
No opinion	12	40	40	8	100	(25)[a]
Disagree	7.7	12.8	53.8	25.6	99.9	(39)[a]
Total	25.7	24.8	34.7	14.9	100.1	(101)[a]

[a]For percentaged tables, provide the number of cases or *N* on which percentages are computed in parentheses near the total or 100 percent. This makes it possible to go back and forth from a percentaged table to a raw count table and vice versa.

Source: From W. Lawrence Neuman and Bruce Weigand, *Criminal Justice Research Methods, Qualitative and Quantitative Approaches,* 1/e. Published by Allyn and Bacon, 75 Arlington St., Boston, MA 02116. Copyright © 2000 by Pearson Education. Reprinted by permission of the publisher.

READING A PERCENTAGED TABLE.   Once we understand how a table is made, reading it and figuring out what it says are much easier. To read a table, first look at the title, the variable labels, and any sources of background information. Next, look at the direction in which percentages have been computed—in rows or columns. Notice that the percentaged tables in Table 10.5 have the same title. This is because the same variables are used. It would have helped to note how the data were percentaged in the title, but this is rarely done. Sometimes, researchers present abbreviated tables and omit the 100 percent total or the marginals, which adds to the confusion. It is best to include all the parts of a table and clear labels.

Researchers read percentaged tables to make comparisons. Comparisons are made in the opposite direction from that in which percentages are computed. A rule of thumb is to compare across rows if the table is percentaged down (i.e., by column) and to compare up and down in columns if the table is percentaged across (i.e., by row).

When reading column-percentaged tables, compare across rows. In Table 10.5, for instance, over three-fourths (76.9 percent) of the youngest group agree, and they are the only group in which a majority agree. Only 11.5 percent disagree, compared to 60 and 66.7 percent, respectively, for the two oldest groups. In row-percentaged tables, compare columns or age groups. In Table 10.5, most of those who agree are in the youngest group, with the proportion declining as age increases. Most no-opinion people are in the middle-age groups. Those who disagree are older, especially in the 46–60 group (53.8 percent). It takes practice to see a relationship in a percentaged table. If there is no relationship in a table, the cell percentages look approximately equal across rows or columns. A linear relationship looks like larger percentages in the diagonal cells. If there is a curvilinear relationship, the largest percentages form a pattern across cells. For example, the largest cells might be the upper right, the bottom middle, and the upper left. It is easiest to see a relationship in a moderate-sized table (9–16 cells) where most cells have some cases (at least five cases are recommended) and the relationship is strong and precise.

Principles of reading a scattergram can help you see a relationship in a percentaged table. Imagine a scattergram that has been divided into twelve equal-sized sections. The cases in each section correspond to the number of cases in the cells of a table that is superimposed onto the scattergram. The table is a condensed form of the scattergram. The bivariate relationship line in a scattergram corresponds to the diagonal cells in a percentaged table. Thus, a simple way to see strong relationships is to circle the largest percentage in each row (for row-percentaged tables) or column (for column-percentaged tables) and see if a line appears.

The circle-the-largest-cell rule works—with one important caveat. The categories in the percentages table *must* be ordinal or interval and in the same order as in a scattergram. In scattergrams, the lowest variable categories begin at the bottom left. If the categories in a table are not ordered the same way, the rule does not work.

BIVARIATE TABLES WITHOUT PERCENTAGES. Very often, researchers present bivariate tables displaying information other than percentages. A measure of central tendency (usually the mean) is reported when one variable is nominal or ordinal (e.g., attitude toward legalizing marijuana) and the other is ordinal- or ratio-level (e.g., age of the respondent). The mean age of those stating the various attitudes is shown in Table 10.6. Such tables are not constructed from the cumulative frequency distribution (CFD). Instead, all cases are divided into the ordinal variable categories (i.e., Agree, No opinion, Disagree); then the mean is calculated from the raw data for the cases in each variable category. Statistical data are commonly reported in tables as rates.

Nationwide, Black men are incarcerated at 9.6 times the rate of White men. In eleven states, Black men are incarcerated at rates that are *twelve to twenty-six* times greater than those of White men (Human Rights Watch 2006). Table 10.7 gives a tabular example. Note that "Black/White ratio" is the ratio of the two incarceration rates.

TABLE 10.6	Attitude toward Legalizing Marijuana by Mean Age of Respondent	
Legalizing Marijuana	**Mean Age**	**(N)**
Agree	26.2	(37)
No opinion	44.5	(25)
Disagree	61.9	(39)
Missing cases = 8		

Source: From W. Lawrence Neuman and Bruce Weigand, *Criminal Justice Research Methods, Qualitative and Quantitative Approaches,* 1/e. Published by Allyn and Bacon, 75 Arlington St., Boston, MA 02116. Copyright © 2000 by Pearson Education. Reprinted by permission of the publisher.

TABLE 10.7	International Comparison of Rates of Imprisonment (per 100,000 persons) by Race, 1990		
	Country		
Race	**United States**	**United Kingdom**	**Australia**
All	474.3	89.3	83.9
Black or Aboriginal	1,860.0	547.0	754.6
White or non-Aboriginal	284.4	80.9	72.7
Black/White ratio	6.5	6.8	18.6

Source: From W. Lawrence Neuman and Bruce Weigand, *Criminal Justice Research Methods, Qualitative and Quantitative Approaches,* 1/e. Published by Allyn and Bacon, 75 Arlington St., Boston, MA 02116. Copyright © 2000 by Pearson Education. Reprinted by permission of the publisher. Adapted from Roderic Broadhurst. "Aborigines and Crime in Australia." *Ethnicity, Crime, and Immigration,* ed. Michael Tonry (Chicago: University of Chicago Press, 1997): 407–468.

Measures of Association

MEASURE OF
ASSOCIATION

A single number that
expresses the strength, and
often the direction, of a
relationship. It condenses
information about a
bivariate relationship into a
single number.

A **measure of association** is a single number that expresses the strength, and often the direction, of a relationship. It condenses information about a bivariate relationship into a single number.

There are many measures of association. The correct one depends on the level of measurement. Many measures are called by letters of the Greek alphabet. Lambda, gamma, tau, chi (squared), and rho are commonly used measures. The emphasis here is on interpreting the measures, not on their calculation. In order to understand each measure, you will need to complete a beginning statistics course.

PROPORTIONATE
REDUCTION IN ERROR
(PRE)

The logic which underlies
most measures of
association. It asks the
question, How much does
knowledge of one variable
reduce the errors that are
made when guessing the
values of the other variable?

Most of the elementary measures discussed here follow a **proportionate reduction in error (PRE)** logic. The logic asks, how much does knowledge of one variable reduce the errors that are made when guessing the values of the other variable? Independence means that knowledge of one variable does not reduce the chance of errors on the other variable. Measures of association equal zero if the variables are independent. If there is a strong association or relationship, then few errors are made predicting a second variable on the basis of knowledge of the first, or the proportion of errors reduced is large. A large number of correct guesses suggests that the measure of association is a nonzero number if an association exists between the variables. Table 10.8 describes five commonly used bivariate measures of association. Notice that most range from -1 to $+1$, with negative numbers indicating a negative relationship and positive numbers a positive relationship. A measure of 1.0 means a 100 percent reduction in errors, or perfect prediction.

TABLE 10.8 Five Measures of Association

Lambda is used for nominal-level data. It is based on a reduction in errors based on the mode and ranges between 0 (independence) and 1.0 (perfect prediction or the strongest possible relationship).

Gamma is used for ordinal-level data. It is based on comparing pairs of variable categories and seeing whether a case has the same rank on each. Gamma ranges from -1.0 to $+1.0$, with 0 meaning no association.

Tau is also used for ordinal-level data. It is based on a different approach than gamma and takes care of a few problems that can occur with gamma. Actually, there are several statistics named tau (it is a popular Greek letter), and the one here is Kendall's tau. Kendall's tau ranges from -1.0 to $+1.0$, with 0 meaning no association.

Rho is also called Pearson's product moment correlation coefficient (named after the famous statistician Karl Pearson and based on a product moment statistical procedure). It is the most commonly used measure of correlation, the correlation statistic people mean if they use the term *Correlation* without identifying it further. It can be used only for data measured at the interval or ratio level. Rho is used for the mean and standard deviation of the variables and tells how far cases are from a relationship (or regression) line in a scatterplot. Rho ranges from -1.0 to $+1.0$, with 0 meaning no association. If the value of rho is squared, sometimes called *R*-squared, it has a unique proportion reduction in error meaning. *R*-squared tells how the percentage in one variable (e.g., the dependent) is accounted for, or explained by, the other variable (e.g., the independent). Rho measures linear relationships only. It cannot measure nonlinear or curvilinear relationships. For example, a rho of zero can indicate either no relationship or a curvilinear relationship.

Chi-squared has two different uses. It can be used as a measure of association in descriptive statistics like the others listed here, or in inferential statistics. Inferential statistics are briefly described next. As a measure of association, chi-squared can be used for nominal and ordinal data. It has an upper limit of infinity and a lower limit of zero, meaning no association (see Summary Table 10.1).

Source: From W. Lawrence Neuman, *Social Research Methods, Qualitative and Quantitative Approaches*, 6/e. Published by Allyn and Bacon, 75 Arlington St., Boston, MA 02116. Copyright © 2006 by Pearson Education. Reprinted by permission of the publisher.

SUMMARY TABLE 10.1	Summary of Measures of Association			
Measure	**Greek Symbol**	**Type of Data**	**High Association**	**Independence**
Lambda	λ	nominal	1.0	0
Gamma	γ	ordinal	$-1.0, -1.0$	0
Tau (Kendall's)	τ	ordinal	$+1.0, -1.0$	0
Rho	ρ	interval, ratio	$+1.0, -1.0$	0
Chi-square	x^2	nominal, ordinal	Infinity	0

TABLE 10.9	Gender and Self-Reported Smoking Behavior		
	No	**Yes**	**N**
Male	77.5(110)	22.5 (32)	100% (142)
Female	76.5 (104)	23.5 (32)	100% (136)

Source: From W. Lawrence Neuman and Bruce Weigand, *Criminal Justice Research Methods, Qualitative and Quantitative Approaches,* 1/e. Published by Allyn and Bacon, 75 Arlington St., Boston, MA 02116. Copyright © 2000 by Pearson Education. Reprinted by permission of the publisher.

TABLE 10.10	Gender and Self-Reported Smoking Behavior, Controlling for Family Type		
	More Patriarchal		
	No	**Yes**	**N**
Male	84.0 (63)	16.0 (12)	100% (75)
Female	75.4 (49)	24.6 (16)	100% (65)
	Less Patriarchal		
	No	**Yes**	**N**
Male	70.1 (147)	29.9 (20)	100% (67)
Female	77.5 (55)	22.5 (16)	100% (71)

Source: From W. Lawrence Neuman and Bruce Weigand, *Criminal Justice Research Methods, Qualitative and Quantitative Approaches,* 1/e. Published by Allyn and Bacon, 75 Arlington St., Boston, MA 02116. Copyright © 2000 by Pearson Education. Reprinted by permission of the publisher. Adapted from Frank Hagan. *Political Crime* (Boston: Allyn & Bacon, 1997).

SUMMARY TABLE 10.2	Summary of Major Types of Descriptive Statistics	
Type of Technique	**Statistical Technique**	**Purpose**
Univariate	Frequency distribution, measures of central tendency, standard deviation, *z*-score	Describe one variable.
Bivariate	Correlation, percentage table, chi-square	Describe a relationship or the association between two variables.

Source: From W. Lawrence Neuman and Bruce Weigand, *Criminal Justice Research Methods, Qualitative and Quantitative Approaches,* 1/e. Published by Allyn and Bacon, 75 Arlington St., Boston, MA 02116. Copyright © 2000 by Pearson Education. Reprinted by permission of the publisher. Adapted from a General Social Studies Survey question asked of a national sample of Americans as cited in Jean Johnson. "Americans' View on Crime and Law Enforcement." *National Institute of Justice Journal* (September 1997): 9–12.

TABLE 10.11	Example of Multiple Regression Results

Dependent Variable is Number of Currency Transaction Report

Independent Variable	Standardized Regression Coefficients
Banks	−.19
Currency	.01
Enforcement	.44
Price	.23
Gross domestic product	−.39
	$R^2 = 38$

Source: From W. Lawrence Neuman and Bruce Weigand, *Criminal Justice Research Methods, Qualitative and Quantitative Approaches,* 1/e. Published by Allyn and Bacon, 75 Arlington St., Boston, MA 02116. Copyright © 2000 by Pearson Education. Reprinted by permission of the publisher.

INFERENTIAL STATISTICS

The Purpose of Inferential Statistics

INFERENTIAL STATISTICS

A genre of statistics that uses probability theory to test hypotheses formally, permit inferences from a sample to a population, and test whether descriptive results are likely to be due to random factors or to a real relationship.

The statistics discussed so far in this chapter are descriptive statistics. But researchers often want to do more than describe; they want to test hypotheses, know whether sample results hold true in a population, and decide whether differences in results (e.g., between the mean scores of two groups) are big enough to indicate that a relationship really exists. **Inferential statistics** use probability theory to test hypotheses formally, permit inferences from a sample to a population, and test whether descriptive results are likely to be due to random factors or to a real relationship.

This section explains the basic ideas of inferential statistics but does not deal with inferential statistics in any detail. This area is more complex than descriptive statistics and requires a background in statistics.

Inferential statistics rely on principles from probability sampling, in which a researcher uses a random process (e.g., a random number table) to select cases from the entire population. Inferential statistics are a precise way to talk about how confident a researcher can be when inferring from the results in a sample to the population.

We have already encountered the basic thinking behind inferential statistics in Chapter 6 on sampling (recall the notions of "statistical significance" or results "significant at the .05 level"). Researchers use them to conduct various statistical tests (e.g., a *t*-test or an *F*-test). Statistical significance is also used in formal hypothesis testing, which is a precise way to decide whether to accept or to reject a null hypothesis.[4]

Statistical Significance

STATISTICAL SIGNIFICANCE

The foundational idea behind inferential statistics. It means that results are not likely to be due to chance factors. It indicates the probability of finding a relationship in the sample when there is none in the population.

Statistical significance means that results are not likely to be due to chance factors. It indicates the probability of finding a relationship in the sample when there is none in the population. Because probability samples involve a random process, it is always possible that sample results will differ from a population parameter. A researcher wants to estimate the odds that sample results are due to a true population parameter or to chance factors of random sampling. Statistical significance uses probability theory and specific statistical tests to tell a researcher whether the results (e.g., an association, a difference between two means, a regression coefficient) are produced by random error in random sampling.

Statistical significance only tells what is likely. It cannot prove anything with absolute certainty. It states that particular outcomes are more or less probable. Statistical significance is *not* the same as practical, substantive, or theoretical significance. Results can be statistically significant but theoretically meaningless or trivial. For example, two variables can have a statistically significant association due to coincidence, with no logical connection between them (e.g., length of fingernails and ability to speak French).

HIGHLIGHT 10.4
Chi-Square

The chi-square (χ^2) is used in two ways. This creates confusion. As a *descriptive statistic*, it tells us the strength of the association between two variables; as an *inferential statistic*, it tells us the probability that any association we find is likely to be due to chance factors. The chi-square is a widely used and powerful way to look at variables measured at the ordinal level. It is a more precise way to tell whether there is an association in a bivariate percentaged table than by just "eyeballing" it.

Logically, we first figure out "expected values" in a table. We do this based on information from the marginals alone. Recall that marginals are frequency distributions of each variable alone. An expected value can be thought of as our "best guess" without looking at the body of the table.

Next, we look at the data to see how much differs from the "expected value." If it differs by a lot, then there may be an association between the variables. If the data in a table are identical or very close to the expected values, then the variables are not associated; they are independent. In other words, *independence* means "what is not going on" in a table is what we would expect based on the marginals alone. Chi-square is zero if there is independence and gets bigger as the association gets stronger. If the data in the table greatly differ from the expected values, then we know something is "going on" beyond what we would expect from the marginals alone (i.e., an association between the variables). See the example of an association race and court disposition.

RAW OR OBSERVED DATA TABLE

Court Disposition

RACE	Acquitted	Prison	Noncustodial	TOTAL
White	30	10	10	50
Black	10	30	10	50
Other	30	20	50	100
Total	70	60	70	200

EXPECTED VALUES TABLE

Expected value = (Column $\times$ total Row total) / Grand total. EXAMPLE (70 $\times$ 50) / 200 = 17.5

Court Disposition

RACE	Acquitted	Prison	Noncustodial	TOTAL
White	17.5	15	17.5	50
Black	17.5	15	17.5	50
Other	35	30	35	100
Total	70	60	70	200

DIFFERENCE TABLE

Difference = (Observed − Expected) EXAMPLE (30 − 17.5) = 12.5

Court Disposition

RACE	Acquitted	Prison	Noncustodial	TOTAL
White	12.5	−5	−7.5	0
Black	−7.5	15	−7.5	0
Other	−5	−10	15	0
Total	0	0	0	0

TABLE 10.12 Example of Chi-Square

Higher Court Dispositions by Aboriginality, 1990 (In Percent)

	N	Noncustodial	Prison
Aborigine	298	40.3	59.7
Non-Aborigine	1,177	54.8	45.2
Unknown	125	58.4	41.6

Note: Chi−square, $dt = 2$; $p < 0.001$.

Source: From W. Lawrence Neuman and Bruce Weigand, *Criminal Justice Research Methods, Qualitative and Quantitative Approaches,* 1/e. Published by Allyn and Bacon, 75 Arlington St., Boston, MA 02116. Copyright © 2000 by Pearson Education. Reprinted by permission of the publisher. Adapted from Roderic Broadhurst. "Aborigines and Crime in Australia." *Ethnicity, Crime, and Immigration,* ed. Michael Tonry (Chicago: University of Chicago Press, 1997): 407–468.

Levels of Significance

Researchers usually express statistical significance in terms of levels (e.g., a test is statistically significant at a specific level) rather than giving the specific probability. The **level of statistical significance** (usually .05, .01, or .001) is a way of talking about the likelihood that results are due to chance factors—that is, that a relationship appears in the sample when there is none in the population. If a researcher says that results are significant at the .05 level, this means the following:

- Results like these are due to chance factors only 5 in 100 times.
- There is a 95 percent chance that the sample results are not due to chance factors alone, but reflect the population accurately.
- The odds of such results based on chance alone are .05, or 5 percent.
- One can be 95 percent confident that the results are due to a real relationship in the population, not chance factors.

These all say the same thing in different ways. This may sound like the discussion of sampling distributions and the central limit theorem in the chapter on sampling. It is not an accident. Both are based on probability theory, which researchers use to link sample data to a population. Probability theory lets us predict what happens in the long run over many events when a random process is used. In other words, it allows precise prediction over many situations in the long run, but not for a specific situation. Since we have one sample and we want to infer to the population, probability theory helps us estimate the odds that our particular sample represents the population. We cannot know for certain unless we have the whole population, but probability theory lets us state our confidence—how likely it is that the sample shows one thing while something else is true in the population.

Take, for example, a study of some 1,600 court dispositions in Australia that showed Aborigines are relatively more likely to be sentenced to prison (Broadhurst 1997). The question is, does the sample of 1,600 represent all court dispositions? Is it discrimination? Or is it just chance finding? Using a chi-square statistic (see Highlight 10.4), the researcher can state his or her findings with much more confidence (see Table 10.12). And, given the probability of 1 out of 1,000, one can confidently say that there is a relationship between aboriginality and court dispositions.

Type I and Type II Errors

If the logic of statistical significance is based on stating whether chance factors produce results, why use the .05 level? It means a 5 percent chance that randomness could cause the results. Why not use a more certain standard—for example, a 1 in 1,000 probability of random chance? This gives a smaller chance that randomness versus a true relationship caused the results.

TABLE 10.13	Type I and Type II Errors	

True Situation in The World

What the Researcher Says	No Relationship	Causal Relationship
No relationship	No error	Type II error
Causal relationship	Type I error	No error

Source: From W. Lawrence Neuman and Bruce Weigand, *Criminal Justice Research Methods, Qualitative and Quantitative Approaches,* 1/e. Published by Allyn and Bacon, 75 Arlington St., Boston, MA 02116. Copyright © 2000 by Pearson Education. Reprinted by permission of the publisher.

There are two answers to this way of thinking. The simple answer is that the scientific community has informally agreed to use .05 as a rule of thumb for most purposes. Being 95 percent confident of results is the accepted standard for explaining the social world.

A second, more complex answer involves a trade-off between making Type I and Type II errors (see Table 10.13). A researcher can make two kinds of logical errors. A **Type I error** occurs when the researcher says that a relationship exists when in fact none exists. It means falsely rejecting a null hypothesis. A **Type II error** occurs when a researcher says that a relationship does not exist, when in fact it does. It means falsely accepting a null hypothesis. Of course, researchers want to avoid both errors. They want to say that there is a relationship in the data only when it does exist and that there is no relationship only when there really is none, but they face a dilemma: As the odds of making one type of error decline, the odds of making the opposite error increase.

The idea of Type I and Type II errors may seem difficult at first, but the same logical dilemma appears outside research settings. For example, a jury can err by deciding that an accused person is guilty when in fact he or she is innocent. Or the jury can err by deciding that a person is innocent when in fact he or she is guilty. The jury does not want to make either error. It does not want to jail the innocent or to free the guilty, but the jury must make a judgment using limited information. Likewise, a pharmaceutical company has to decide whether to sell a new drug. The company can err by stating that the drug has no side-effects when, in fact, it has the side-effect of causing blindness. Or it can err by holding back a drug because of fear of serious side-effects when in fact there are none. The company does not want to make either error. If it makes the first error, the company will face lawsuits and injure people. The second error will prevent the company from selling a drug that may cure illness and produce profits.

Let us put the ideas of statistical significance and the two types of error together. An overly cautious researcher sets a high level of significance and is likely to make one kind of error. For example, the researcher might use the .0001 level. He or she attributes the results to chance unless they are so rare that they would occur by chance only 1 in 10,000 times. Such a high standard means that the researcher is most likely to err by saying results are due to chance when in fact they are not. He or she may falsely accept the null hypothesis when there is a causal relationship (a Type II error). By contrast, a risk-taking researcher sets a low level of significance, such as .10. His or her results indicate a relationship would occur by chance 1 in 10 times. He or she is likely to err by saying that a causal relationship exists, when in fact random factors (e.g., random sampling error) actually cause the results. The researcher is likely to falsely reject the null hypothesis (Type I error). In sum, the .05 level is a compromise between Type I and Type II errors.

This section outlines the basics of inferential statistics. The statistical techniques are precise and rely on the relationship between sampling error, sample size, and central limit theorem. The power of inferential statistics is their ability to let a researcher state, with specific degrees of certainty, that specific sample results are likely to be true in a population. Highlight 10.5 examines statistical programs for the computer.

Tests for inferential statistics are useful but limited. The data must come from a random sample, and tests only take into account sampling errors. Nonsampling errors (e.g., a poor sampling frame or a poorly designed measure) are not considered. Do not be fooled into thinking that such tests offer easy, final answers.

TYPE I ERROR

Type I error occurs when the researcher says that a relationship exists when in fact none exists. It means falsely rejecting a null hypothesis.

TYPE II ERROR

Type II error occurs when a researcher says that a relationship does not exist, when in fact it does.

BEING CRITICAL: ETHICS AND STATISTICS

Statistics don't lie any more than guns kill. However, guns make it a lot easier to kill as do statistics make it easier to effectively lie. Ultimately it is the behavior of the people using these powerful tools that matters.

Statistics are a tool that must be wielded with responsibility and a strong sense of research ethics. It is quite easy to deceive others through the distortion or fraudulent use of statistics. There is even a well-known book, *How to Lie with Statistics*, which is basically a manual for how to spot unethical uses of statistics (Huff and Geis 1993). You may have noticed that each side of any major political issue—whether it be global warming, the why of the crime rate drop, or deaths in the war on terrorism—usually presents a cornucopia of colorful charts and impressive numbers to "prove" the accuracy of their position. Simple co-varying associations are presented as causes, trend lines are made to look more or less dramatic, and sometimes the statistics used are outright fabricated.

The tendency is in some ways understandable—after all, we're just dealing with a simple number—why not exaggerate it slightly if our overall position is correct and noble? Similarly, if a simple statistic can mean the difference between a criminal justice agency grant's success and continuation, or a professor's chances at receiving tenure and the respect and recognition of her or his peers, the benefits might seem to outweigh the costs. Remaining ethical can be even more problematic when academics use high-end statistical techniques. These usually involve a moderate level of researcher discretion in how variables will be analyzed, and are quite easily manipulated. Ethical researchers must continually ask themselves whether they are conducting their analyses and presenting their data in the most objective manner possible.

We cannot throw up our hands and assume all statistics are suspect and therefore unusable. We need statistics to rigorously evaluate crime control programs, make theoretical sense of crime and justice phenomena, and to debate important crime and justice issues facing society. The key is to remain ever diligent about scrutinizing the origin and presentation of these statistics; in other words, *be critical*. Joel Best (2001: 13), in his book *Damned Lies and Statistics: Untangling Numbers from the Media, Politicians, and Activists*, encourages us with the following passage.

HIGHLIGHT 10.5
Statistical programs on Computers

Almost every crime and justice researcher who needs to calculate many statistics does so with a computer program. One can do some statistics using a basic spreadsheet program, such as Excel. Unfortunately, spreadsheets are designed for accounting and bookkeeping functions. They include statistics, but are clumsy and limited for that purpose. There are many computer programs designed for calculating general statistics. The marketplace can be confusing to a beginner, for products rapidly evolve with changing computer technology. One or two decades ago, one had to know a computer language or do simple programming to have a computer calculate statistics.

In recent years, the software has become less demanding for a user. The most popular programs in the social sciences are Minitab, Microcase, and SPSS (Statistical package for the Social Sciences). Others include SAS (Statistical Analysis System), BMPD (bought out by SPSS, Inc), STATISTICA by StratSoft, and Strata. Many began as simple, low-cost programs for research purposes. Today, private corporations own many of these and are interested in selling a sophisticated set of software products to many diverse corporate and government users.

The most widely used program for statistics in the social sciences in SPSS. Its advantages are that crime and justice researchers have used it extensively for over three decades, it includes many ways to manipulate quantitative data, and it contains most statistical measures. Its disadvantage is that it can take a long time to learn because of its many options and complex statistics. Also, it is expensive to purchase unless one gets an inexpensive, "stripped down" student version included with a textbook or workbook.

As computer technology makes using a statistics program easier, the danger increases that some people will use the programs but not understand statistics or what the programs are doing. They can easily violate basic assumptions required by a statistical produce, use the statistics improperly, and produce results that are pure nonsense yet look very technically sophisticated.

Statistics are not magical. Nor are they always true—or always false. Nor need they be incomprehensible. Adopting a critical approach offers an effective way of responding to the numbers we are sure to encounter. Being critical requires more thought, but failing to adapt a critical mind-set makes us powerless to evaluate what others tell us. When we fail to think critically, the statistics we hear might just as well be magical.

Conclusion

In this chapter, we learned how to organize and analyze quantitative data. We now have the foundation for understanding quantitative analysis in crime and justice research. We know how data must first be coded before being analyzed by univariate, bivariate, and, finally, multivariate statistics. We also know that bivariate relationships might be spurious, thus requiring the use of control variables.

Beginning researchers sometimes feel as though they have done something wrong if the data do not support their hypothesis. *There is nothing wrong with rejecting a hypothesis.* Hypotheses are educated guesses based on limited knowledge; they need to be tested. Good research depends on high-quality methodology, not on supporting a pet theory. If you recall Popper's thinking, falsifying a theory should be actually held in higher regard then substantiation (although this is not usually the case in the real world of the journal review process).

Good researchers must guard against possible errors in research. Errors can occur throughout the research process: research designing, measuring, collecting data, coding, calculating statistics, assembling tables, or interpreting results. All of this must be accounted for as he or she asks what the research means. The only way to assign meaning to tables, charts, and statistics is with the use of crime and criminal justice theory.

Facts do not speak for themselves. It is the social scientist's understanding of concepts and their relationships that unlocks the meaning of quantitative data. This is not to say, however, that we should not be open to new ideas that will inevitably result from doing the research. Consider these new ideas and reflect on how they might fit into the research at hand. This is what top scientists do in every field of study.

Statistics are susceptible to the knowledge–power dynamic. Statistics are a powerful tool of persuasion and at the same time can be adversely influenced by power. Journalists, politicians, activists, and professionals increasingly use statistical results to promote a particular point of view or agenda. The cliché that you can prove anything with statistics is false; however, people can and do misuse statistics. Critical thinking, and becoming intelligent consumers of research knowledge, is the only corrective.

In the next section of this book, we turn to the fascinating topic of qualitative research. Crime and justice studies has a rich tradition when it comes to qualitative research, striving to study the world of deviants, criminals, and the criminal justice system from the inside, so to speak. This requires a different approach to research, as reviewed in our earlier discussion of positivist, interpretive, and critical approaches to crime and justice inquiry.

Key Terms

coding *229*
coding procedure *229*
codebook *220*
precoding *229*
data field *230*
code sheets *230*
direct-entry method *230*
optical scan sheet *230*
statistics *232*
descriptive statistics *232*
univariate statistics *232*
frequency distribution *232*

histogram *232*
frequency polygon *232*
mode *233*
median *235*
mean *234*
skewed distribution *234*
range *235*
percentiles *235*
standard deviation *235*
z-scores *237*
bivariate statistics *237*
statistical relationship *237*

covariation *238*
independence *238*
scattergram *240*
linear relationship *240*
curvilinear
   relationship *240*
positive relationship *240*
negative relationship *240*
precision *240*
bivariate percentaged
   table *241*
cross-tabulation *241*

compound frequency
   distribution (CFD) *241*
measure of
   association *246*
proportionate reduction in
   error (PRE) *246*
inferential statistics *248*
statistical significance *248*
level of statistical
   significance *250*
Type I error *251*
Type II error *251*

Review Questions

1. What is a codebook and how is it used in research?
2. How do researchers clean data and check their coding?
3. Describe how researchers use the optical scan sheets.
4. In what ways can a researcher display frequency distribution information?
5. Describe the differences between mean, median, and mode.
6. What three features of a relationship can be seen from a scattergram?

7. What is a covariation and how is it used?
8. When can a researcher generalize from a scattergram to a percentaged table to find a relationship among variables?
9. What does it mean to say "statistically significant at the .001 level," and what type of error is more likely: Type I or Type II?

Practicing Research

1. There are numerous Web sites on the Internet that provide free access SPSS tutorials (e.g., www.utexas.edu/its/rc/tutorials/stat/spss/spss1/ or www.ats.ucla.edu/STAT/spss/sk/default.htm). Access one of these Web sites and go through the beginning steps of learning how to use this software program (data input, defining variables, and simple frequency distributions). Print out the work you did, and write a short essay describing what you learned.

2. Using the data collected from one of the previous exercises found in Chapter 6, 7, or 8, input this data into a statistical program (ideally SPSS, but there are other free statistical packages available on the Internet; many calculators have statistical abilities, and even spread sheets (e.g., Microsoft Excel) can conduct simple statistics). Conduct some simple statistics including frequency distributions, mode/median/mean, and bivariate statistics.

3. Determine the mean, median, and mode for the following numbers: 1, 1, 1, 2, 3, 4, 4, 4, 5, 7, 7, 7, 13, 16, 29. Are these data skewed? Which measure of central tendency do you think best represents the central tendency of these data?

4. Over a one-week period, take note of the media's use of statistics (e.g., crime statistics, health statistics, and political polling statistics). Attempt to uncover instances where the statistics cited are likely to confuse or distort rather than responsibly educate. One example to look for is the irresponsible reporting of health studies. In July 2007, the media reported a study that linked drinking one soda a day (even diet sodas) with a 48 percent increased risk of metabolic syndrome which leads to heart disease. A more careful reading of the research, however, would reveal a lack of statistical control for research subject lifestyle.

5. Using Douglas A. Smith and Christy A. Visher's article "Street-Level Justice: Situational Determinants of Police Arrest Decisions" (*Social Problems*, Vol. 29, No. 2, Dec., 1981, pp. 167–177), answer the following questions.

    1. What central variables were studied?
    2. How did the authors use and present their descriptive statistics?
    3. How did the authors employ statistical analysis in presenting their findings?
    4. How did the authors make use of the idea of "statistical significance"?

Notes for Further Study

1. Some of the best practical advice on coding and handling quantitative data come from survey research. See discussions in Babbie (1998: 366–372), Backstrom and Hursh-Cesar (1981: 309–400), Fowler (1984: 127–133), Sonquist and Dunkelberg (1977: 210–215), and Warwick and Lininger (1975: 234–291).

2. For discussions of many different ways to display quantitative data, see Fox (1992), Henry (1995), Tufte (1983, 1991), and Zeisel (1985: 14–33).

3. There are other statistics to measure a special kind of mean for ordinal data and for other special situations, which are beyond the level of discussion in this book.

4. In formal hypothesis testing, researchers test the *null hypothesis*. They usually want to reject the null because rejection of the null indirectly supports the alternative hypothesis to the null, the one they deduced from theory as a tentative explanation. The null hypotheis was discussed in Chapter 6.

PART FOUR

Qualitative Research, Mixed Methods, and Presenting Research

This next section requires us to shift our methodological gears—or perhaps the more accurate analogy would be to jump into a new car. The last several chapters have focused on positivist thinking and methods. Emphasis was placed on deductive theory testing, transforming social phenomena into quantitative form, collecting data using standardized quantitative methods, and testing hypotheses and examining relationships using statistics. As you discovered in learning about the ISS approach (interpretive social science), qualitative research methods and analysis are simply a different make and model. It relies on nonnumerical data such as words (spoken and written) and pictures (still and video). It tends to produce knowledge inductively (recall the notion of grounded theory); studies the social world as it naturally occurs; depicts social reality with rich ("thick") descriptions, theoretical narratives, and even visual media; and strives for *verstehen* (empathetic understanding). (We are not inferring that they are incompatible, as seen in Chapter 13, on mixed methods research.)

You have also been exposed to a number of qualitative research studies at this point in the book. We'll list a few just to jog your memory.

- Wright and Decker's armed robbery ethnography
- Ferrell's graffiti artist ethnography and roadside memorial study
- Rafter's historical study of the origins of criminology (horse-slasher)
- Athens's in-depth interviews of violent, dangerous criminals
- Marquart's prison guard ethnography
- Humphrey's Tearoom Trade ethnography
- Brent's research on cage-fighting
- Bussard's ethnography of the illegal steroid marketplace

Criminology and criminal justice textbooks have traditionally devoted only superficial attention to qualitative research. Even though we have a rich history of invaluable qualitative studies, its influence faded considerably under the shining light of scientific positivism during the 1970s and most of the 1980s. In fact, the dominant view saw qualitative research as insignificant at best and as illegitimate at worst (some hard-core traditionalists of course still do). It's not an overstatement to say that we've witnessed a sea change only in the last ten years. A few of the more important reasons for such a change include the following:

1. a growing European influence that values qualitative scholarship,
2. the influential contribution of feminist scholars,
3. the emergence of a new subfield known as "cultural criminology,"

4. a number of prominent mainstream criminologists conducting qualitative studies, and

5. the fact that most other social science disciplines surrounding us are embracing qualitative methods and the mixed methods approach.

Qualitative knowledge production has rapidly become a mainstream and essential tool in our field's methodological handbag.

This last section of the book also includes something missing from most other research textbooks in our field—mixed methods research. We will examine the thinking that underlies a mixed methods approach, and what various mixed methods projects might look like. The philosophy behind mixed methods—namely, one of inclusion, compatibility, and pragmatism—is representative of the approach we've taken throughout this book, and is therefore a fitting anchor to the rest of the methods reviewed. We conclude this section, and the book, with a final chapter on writing and presenting our research to a wider audience.

The Nature of Qualitative Research

Home-Grown Terrorism Data

Qualitative Research Basics

Qualitative "Versus" Quantitative Research
  Linear and Nonlinear Paths
  Objectivity and Integrity
  Reliability and Validity
    Reliability
    Validity

Features of Qualitative Research
  Grounded Theory
  The Context Is Critical
  Bricolage
  The Case and Process
  Interpretation

Qualitative Document Analysis (QDA)

The General Idea of QDA
  Possible Applications of QDA
  Highlight 11.1 Deciphering Meaning from a Photograph
  How to Conduct QDA (Steps)
  Highlight 11.2 Semiotics and the Study of Crime and Justice
  Highlight 11.3 Visual Crime and Justice Studies
  QDA Wrap-Up

Conclusion

Key Terms

Review Questions

Practicing Research

Notes for Further Study

HOME-GROWN TERRORISM DATA

The hand that shook U.S. army general Norman Schwarzkopf's after Iraq's defeat in the first Gulf War is the same hand that lit the fuse of the deadliest domestic terrorist bomb detonated in U.S. history. On April 19, 1995, Timothy McVeigh parked a Ryder rental truck in front of the Alfred P. Murrah Federal Building in Oklahoma City and walked away from an explosion that killed 169 children, women, and men. Six years after the crime, the federal government executed McVeigh by lethal injection.

McVeigh's behavior brought anguished cries for an explanation—a way to make sense of a seemingly senseless act. Most were comfortable with the simplest of theories: McVeigh was evil. The difficulty, though, was that McVeigh, up until this event, seemed normal in every way: a patriotic young man who earned numerous medals for valor while serving in the first Iraq war and had no prior record of any wrongdoing. Producing credible knowledge that would give us theoretical insight into the why of this crime seemed to be an essential endeavor. Not only would it answer some fascinating crime theory questions, it could also provide useful knowledge that might help to prevent future acts of domestic terrorism.

Think for a second about trying to answer this research question using the quantitative methods so far reviewed in this book. Conducting an experiment or survey, or analyzing existing quantitative data would

The remains of automobiles with the bombed Federal Building in the background. What do you think about McVeigh's stated motivations?

obviously not work. The only feasible approach for uncovering McVeigh's reasons/motivations would be to talk to him, observe him, study his correspondence, or read his psychological files. We would refer to such a study as qualitative inquiry—meaning that the researcher would inquire into McVeigh's biographical history, his mind-set, his actions, and the larger cultural or historical context in which his motivations were formed (e.g., right-wing extremism).

A talented and ambitious student in Kraska's theory course, Carl Root, decided to embark on such a project. He spent two years collecting, scouring through, and making sense of a massive amount of qualitative data for the purpose of better understanding McVeigh's crime—and the larger cultural context from which it was spawned. Of course, Carl had to rely on preexisting documents and interviews because McVeigh had been executed by then. Fortunately, he and Kraska managed to secure access to a treasure trove of original qualitative data. In a soon-to-be-published paper, Kraska and Root write,

> McVeigh granted the most access to Lou Michel and Dan Herbeck who eventually wrote the book *American Terrorist: Timothy McVeigh & the Oklahoma City Bombing*. Michel and Herbeck not only interviewed McVeigh for over 75 hours, they also gathered an immense collection of source materials from McVeigh, his attorney's, his family members, his psychiatrists, and other key players. These materials were archived and sealed from public view since they finished their book in 2001. In securing a grant to conduct this research, Root and Kraska convinced Michel and Herbeck to allow us access to this treasure trove of original data. These data proved invaluable for examining in-depth McVeigh's thinking and biographical history.

Carl discovered in sorting through these materials that explaining this crime was quite complicated (and as he described, "a dark undertaking"), requiring an examination of McVeigh's military experience, his return to the United States after the war, his anger at the U.S. government for foreclosing on family farms in his home-town community, and his involvement in extremist right-wing subculture.

However, none of these contributing factors was as central to McVeigh's reasons as the age-old motive of revenge—examined through the CIA's concept of "blowback." McVeigh wanted to strategically, and with military precision, retaliate against the federal government for its military-style assault on the Branch Davidian's residence in Waco, Texas, that resulted in the deaths of twenty-five children and fifty-one adults. McVeigh, quite simply, was engaging in a familiar pattern of behavior found in many cultures—to use lethal violence as a means to get even for a similar harmful act perceived to be unjust. When asked by *60 Minutes* whether it is acceptable to use violence against the government, McVeigh said, "If government is the teacher, violence would be an acceptable option. What did we do to Sudan? What did we do to Afghanistan? Belgrade? Iraq? What are we doing with the death penalty? It appears they [the government] use violence as an option all the time" (Bradley 2001).

A few months before his death, McVeigh sent a letter to a news agency articulating his motivations. As seen in Figure 11.1, it makes for a very revealing piece of qualitative data, and it certainly corroborates much of what Carl Root discovered through his research. Note how McVeigh begins his explanation.

<table>
<tr><td>

McVeigh's Apr. 26 Letter to Fox News

Thursday, April 26, 2001

The following letter has been authenticated and was sent to Fox News Correspondent Rita Cosby on April 26, 2001.

I explain herein why I bombed the Murrah Federal Building in Oklahoma City. I explain this not for publicity, nor seeking to win an argument of right or wrong. I explain so that the record is clear as to my thinking and motivations in bombing a government installation.

I chose to bomb a federal building because such an action served more purposes than other options. Foremost, the bombing was a retaliatory strike; a counter attack, for the cumulative raids (and subsequent violence and damage) that federal agents had participated in over the preceding years (including, but not limited to, Waco.) From the formation of such units as the FBI's "Hostage Rescue" and other assault teams amongst federal agencies during the '80's; culminating in the Waco incident, federal actions grew increasingly militaristic and violent, to the point where at Waco, our government—like the Chinese—was deploying tanks against its own citizens.

Knowledge of these multiple and ever-more aggressive raids across the country constituted an identifiable pattern of conduct within and by the federal government and amongst its various agencies. (see enclosed) For all intents and purposes, federal agents had become "soldiers" (using military training, tactics, techniques, equipment, language, dress, organization, and mindset) and they were escalating their behavior.

</td><td>

Therefore, this bombing was also meant as a pre-emptive (or pro-active) strike against these forces and their command and control centers within the federal building. When an aggressor force continually launches attacks from a particular base of operation, it is sound military strategy to take the fight to the enemy.

Additionally, borrowing a page from U.S. foreign policy, I decided to send a message to a government that was becoming increasingly hostile, by bombing a government building and the government employees within that building who represent that government. Bombing the Murrah Federal Building was morally and strategically equivalent to the U.S. hitting a government building in Serbia, Iraq, or other nations. (see enclosed) Based on observations of the policies of my own government, I viewed this action as an acceptable option. From this perspective, what occurred in Oklahoma City was no different than what Americans rain on the heads of others all the time, and subsequently, my mindset was and is one of clinical detachment. (The bombing of the Murrah building was not personal, no more than when Air Force, Army, Navy, or Marine personnel bomb or launch cruise missiles against government installations and their personnel.)

I hope that this clarification amply addresses your question.

Sincerely,

Timothy J. McVeigh

USP Terre Haute (IN)

Source: Find additional documents at: www.foxnews.com/story/ 0,2933,17500,00.html.

</td></tr>
</table>

FIGURE 11.1   Inside the Mind of Domestic Terrorist.

> . . . this is not for publicity. . . . I explain so that the record is clear as to my thinking and motivations in bombing a government installation. . . . The bombing was a retaliatory strike; a counter attack, for the cumulative raids (and subsequent violence and damage) that federal agents had participated in over the preceding years (including, but not limited to, Waco).

While the "McVeigh is pure evil" explanation may be more comforting for much of the public, crime and justice analysts need methods that can help us to truly understand (not sympathize with) these types of crimes. We need methods that can uncover and interpret systematically the culture, meanings, and motivations embedded in both crime and criminal justice phenomena. This requires us to immerse ourselves into the real-life natural settings of our objects of study and to collect qualitative data through observation, experience, talking, listening, and feeling.

This chapter is designed to give you a solid sense of the nature of qualitative inquiry and research. The major example of a qualitative technique employed in this chapter—discussed in Chapter 1 as "qualitative document analysis"—will hopefully provide a good starting place. The next chapter (Chapter 12) on ethnographic field research details the ins and outs of conducting qualitative research in natural human settings. Note that there are many different approaches to doing qualitative research; this book is going to cover just a few. (Appendix C on qualitative data analysis provides a good discussion of some of these, including biography and case studies).

QUALITATIVE RESEARCH BASICS

Recall that research is simply the systematic production of knowledge. And the core purpose of producing knowledge is answering the question, "what is really the case?" Qualitative research is merely another avenue for answering this question using qualitative sources of data—as opposed to quantitative. As demonstrated above, explaining "what's really the case" with regard to McVeigh's crime necessitates qualitative inquiry. Carl studied thousands of pages of documents not knowing what he would find. In this way Carl's research—as is generally the case with qualitative inquiry—was exploratory and his understanding of this crime progressed inductively (i.e., from specific pieces of empirical data to more general ideas about the why of terrorism). Carl referred to this process as "falling down the rabbit hole," inferring that it was the data that dictated the trajectory of his "fall," as opposed to testing a preexisting theory as one might do in quantitative research. Even though Carl never met or talked with McVeigh, the process of developing *verstehen* (empathetic understanding) was quite unsettling, yet at the same time intellectually exhilarating.

Your authors recognize that the qualitative–quantitative data distinction can be confusing: Aren't most of our observations, conversations, documents, and so on originally in qualitative form? The answer is yes; however, the quantitative approach converts these into numbers while the qualitative approach keeps them in their raw form. Hence, qualitative data usually are found in three forms: (1) in-depth interviews; (2) electronic or hard copy documents (e.g., McVeigh's psychological evaluation or court transcripts of his trial); and (3) direct observation. Visual materials (e.g., photographs or video recordings) will also be discussed later in this chapter as a form of qualitative data.

Although qualitative research can be revealing, fascinating, and even fun, wrapping our minds around its winding contours is not easy. As with the label *quantitative research*, *qualitative research* is just a generic term for a multitude of differing types. Some methods texts are only concerned with qualitative field research (Chapter 12). This is where a researcher studies the culture of people within their natural environment. However, there are other important styles used by crime and justice scholars, such as historical, qualitative document analysis, academic legal research, and mixed methods (as found in Chapter 1). Appendix C details with how researchers analyze their qualitative data regardless of the style.

It is easy to perceive of qualitative research as almost mystical. The language of "empathetic understanding," "taken-for-granted reality," "the social construction of meaning," and "interpretive analysis" can seem abstract and fuzzy. Keep in mind, though, these words, and qualitative research in general, operate from the same tradition and mind-set with which we approach our everyday life. We go through life observing, listening, interacting with others, and reading texts (like this book). A thousand times a day we interpret the meaning of these experiences and stimuli, and synthesize them into a comprehendible and useable form. Our interpretation and synthesis form narratives in our mind, and sometimes on paper (e.g., a personal journal) that are similar to stories (or interpretive constructs) that help us make sense of our surroundings. We usually keep these stories to ourselves, but we sometimes share them with others by communicating them orally, visually, or in writing. Qualitative research is similar, except that it is a more formalized, cognizant, and systematic method of generating the same types of real-life knowledge to make sense of people and society. Collecting and analyzing qualitative data, and converting these data into communicable knowledge, therefore, should be far from foreign or mystical; its approach is similar to what we've been doing our whole lives.

QUALITATIVE "VERSUS" QUANTITATIVE RESEARCH

While this book does not want to promote the "qualitative versus quantitative" mind-set, contrasting the two does help us to better understand the nature of qualitative inquiry. Your understanding from Chapter 3 of the philosophical differences between interpretive social science (qualitative) and positivist social science (quantitative) will help (and it may be worth you while to review those few pages of text). This section will discuss some more concrete differences. It is worth another look at the summary table presented in Chapter 1.

Quantitative Approach	Qualitative Approach
Measure objective facts	Construct social reality, culture
Focus on variables	Focus on interactive process, meaning
Reliability is key	Authenticity is key
Data are quantitative; precise measurement	Data are qualitative: words, images, categories
Analysis looks for statistical relationships	Analysis looks for patterns, themes, holistic features
Researcher is detached	Researcher is involved
Deductive process (top down)	Inductive process (bottom up)

It might help to first present some quantitative data on the use of each of these approaches in our discipline. Using the same data set discussed in Chapter 1 (based on four of our leading crime and justice journals), about 75 percent of researchers choose to rely exclusively on quantitative methods, whereas 25 percent use qualitative methods alone or in conjunction with quantitative. It is important to note, however, that qualitative research is more often presented in book form than in journal articles—meaning that these data likely underestimate the presence of qualitative methods. Moreover, our data indicate a slow but certain increase in the use of qualitative methods—particularly mixed methods.

A recent article in the journal *Criminology* is illustrative. In a highly quantitative piece ("Does Crime Just Move around the Corner? A Controlled Study of Spatial Displacement and Diffusion of Crime Control Benefits")—produced by researchers who lean heavily toward quantitative methods—the team of authors uses numerous insights and quotes from ethnographic research within their research site to make better theoretical sense of their quantitative findings. For example, in discovering that intensified crime control efforts did not simply displace crime within the particular location they studied, they offered the following quote from a street prostitute to provide some deeper insight:

> I was tired of being tired. Sick of running. Then it started to scare me. It seemed like there would be stings (police roundups) constantly. I got scared of going to jail. . . . I had been told that I had a warrant (arrest warrant). I didn't want to do it (prostitution) anymore. Or my drug habit anymore. (Brisgone 2004: 205)

All crime and justice researchers, whether quantitative or qualitative, systematically collect and analyze empirical data and carefully examine the patterns in them to understand and explain their objects of study. One of the differences between the two styles comes from the nature of the data. **Soft data**, in the form of impressions, words, sentences, photos, symbols, and so forth, dictate different research strategies and data collection techniques than do **hard data**, in the form of numbers. Another difference is in their respective research objectives. Recall that qualitative research's (ISS) objective is understanding (*verstehen*), whereas quantitative (PSS) is prediction and control. People who judge qualitative research by standards of quantitative research are often disappointed, and vice versa. It is best to appreciate the strengths each style offers on its own terms.

SOFT DATA

Data that come in the form of impressions, words, photographs, etc.

HARD DATA

Data that come in the form of numbers.

Linear and Nonlinear Paths

Qualitative research also differs from quantitative in that it follows a nonlinear research path. It requires a high level of flexibility in which the researcher must adapt to both changing conditions within the environment they're working, and changes in understanding the research topic in new ways. In this way, it follows an incremental, inductive approach. Qualitative researchers speak a language of "cases and contexts." They emphasize conducting detailed examinations of cases that arise in the natural flow of social life.

Most quantitative researchers, on the other hand, follow a linear research path as guided by formal, universal, and systematic rules. They speak a language of "variables and hypotheses."

Quantitative researchers emphasize precisely measuring variables and testing hypotheses that are linked to general causal explanations.

Researchers who use one style alone do not always communicate well with those using the other. People who are used to the direct, linear approach may be impatient with a less direct cyclical path. From a strict linear perspective, a cyclical path can appear inefficient and sloppy. But the diffuse cyclical approach found in qualitative research is not merely disorganized, undefined chaos. It can be highly effective for creating a feeling for the whole, for grasping subtle shades of meaning, for pulling together divergent information, and for switching perspectives. The languages and orientations of quantitative and qualitative research are mutually intelligible. It takes time and effort, however, to understand both styles and to see how they can be complementary.

Objectivity and Integrity

All crime and justice researchers strive to be fair, honest, truthful, and unbiased in their research activity. Qualitative and quantitative styles emphasize different ways to ensure honest, truthful research.

Qualitative researchers emphasize intimate firsthand knowledge of the research setting; they avoid distancing themselves from the people or events they study. This does not mean arbitrarily interjecting personal opinion, being sloppy about data collection, or using evidence selectively to support personal prejudices. It means taking advantage of personal insight, feelings, and human perspectives to understand the subject matter more fully. The researcher makes his or her presence explicit and is sensitive to prior assumptions. In place of objective techniques, the qualitative researcher is forthright and open about his or her personal involvement.

Researcher integrity is central to both qualitative and quantitative research. Quantitative researchers stress objectivity and specific mechanical techniques in an attempt to ensure objectivity. They use the principle of replication, adhere to standardized methodological procedures, measure with numbers, and then analyze the data with statistics.[1] Quantitative research tries to control or eliminate the human factor. Consequently, quantitative research addresses the issue of integrity by relying on an objective technology—such as precise statements, standard techniques, numerical measures, statistics, and replication. This is the same as in the natural sciences.

Qualitative researchers emphasize trustworthiness as a parallel idea to objective standards in quantitative research design. This ensures that their research is dependable and credible.[2] Qualitative researchers also have checks on their evidence.[3] For example, the field researcher listens to and records a student who says, "Professor Smith threw an eraser at Professor Jones." The field researcher treats this evidence carefully. To strengthen the claim, the researcher considers what other people say, looks for confirming evidence, and checks for internal consistency. The researcher asks whether the student has firsthand knowledge of the event and whether the student's feelings or self-interest would lead him to lie (e.g., the student might dislike Professor Smith for some reason). Similarly, the researcher examining historical or legal evidence uses techniques for verifying and cross-checking the authenticity of sources and the data found in those sources.

Another check is the great volume of detailed notes and/or photographs that qualitative researchers generate. Besides a detailed verbatim description of the evidence, notes include references to the sources, commentaries by the researcher, and key terms to help organize the notes, as well as quotes, photographs, maps, diagrams, paraphrasing, and counts. The cage-fighting study conducted by John Brent discussed earlier in the book resulted in over 800 typed pages of notes.

The most important way that a qualitative researcher creates trust is how she or he presents evidence. A qualitative researcher constructs a matrix of interlocking details, providing sufficient texture and detail so that the readers feel immersed in the "story." A qualitative researcher's firsthand knowledge of events, people, and situations cuts two ways. It raises questions of bias, but it also provides a sense of immediacy, direct contact, and intimate knowledge. Lonnie Athens's research of dangerous violent criminals, featured in Chapter 2, is a solid example. His writing is so rich with detailed notes and profound insights that the reader grasps immediately the depth of his understanding and experience with the research subjects. Summary Table 11.1 overviews the key differences between quantitative and qualitative research.

| **SUMMARY TABLE 11.1** | Key Differences between Quantitative and Qualitative Research |

Quantitative Research

- *Test hypothesis that the researcher begins with.*
- *Concepts are in the form of distinct variables.*
- *Measures are systematically created before data collection and are standardized.*
- *Data are in the form of numbers from precise measurement.*
- *Theory is largely causal and is deductive.*
- *Procedures are standard, and replication is frequent.*
- *Analysis proceeds by using statistics, tables, or charts and by discussing how what they show relates to hypotheses.*

Qualitative Research

- *Capture and discover meaning once the researcher becomes immersed in the data.*
- *Concepts are in the form of themes, motifs, generalizations, and taxonomies.*
- *Measures are created in an ad hoc manner and are often specific to the individual setting or researcher.*
- *Data are in the form of words and images from documents, observations, and transcripts.*
- *Theory can be causal or noncausal and is often inductive.*
- *Research procedures are particular, and replication is very rare.*
- *Analysis proceeds by extracting themes or generalizations from evidence and organizing data to present a coherent, consistent picture.*

Reliability and Validity

Most qualitative researchers accept the basic principles of reliability and validity, but rarely use the terms because of their association with quantitative measurement. In addition, qualitative researchers apply the principles in a different manner.

RELIABILITY. Reliability for a qualitative researcher simply means dependability or consistency. Qualitative researchers use a variety of techniques (e.g., interviews, participation, photographs, document studies, etc.) to record their observations consistently. Qualitative researchers want to be consistent (i.e., not vacillating and erratic) in how, over time, they make observations, similar to the idea of stability reliability. One difficulty is that they often study processes that are not stable over time. Moreover, they emphasize the value of a changing or developing interaction between the researcher and what he or she studies. Qualitative researchers believe that the subject matter and a researcher's relationship to it should be an evolving process. The metaphor for the relationship between a researcher and the data is one of an evolving relationship or living organism (e.g., a plant) that naturally matures.

Most qualitative researchers see the quantitative approach to reliability as a fixed mechanical instrument that one repeatedly applies to some static object of study. Qualitative researchers focus instead on a range of data sources and employ multiple measurement methods. They question the quantitative-positivist ideas of replication, equivalence, and subpopulation reliability. They accept that sometimes different researchers or researchers using alternative measures will get distinctive results. Data collection from this perspective is an interactive process in which particular researchers operate in an evolving setting, and the setting's context dictates using a unique mix of measures that are difficult to replicate. However, they do hope that if a major finding of their research were reexamined, similar conclusions would be drawn. For example, Jeff Ferrell would expect that if another researcher spent considerable time with the same group of graffiti artists he studied, that person would also conclude that their motivation was not vandalism but the production of art.

VALIDITY.   Validity means accuracy or truthfulness. Qualitative researchers are more interested in real-world authenticity than in the idea of a single version of truth. Authenticity means giving a fair, honest, and balanced account and interpretation of some crime and justice phenomenon from the viewpoint of those who live it every day. Qualitative researchers are less concerned with matching an abstract construct to empirical data and more concerned with giving a candid and accurate portrayal and interpretation of social life that is true to the experiences of people being studied. Most qualitative researchers concentrate on capturing an inside view and providing a detailed account of how those being studied understand events.

The essence of validity in qualitative research, therefore, is the accurate interpretation of meaning. To use the same question asked throughout this book, did the researcher accurately capture what is really the case? This is verified in historical research based on internal and external criticisms to determine whether the evidence the researcher has is real or he or she believes it to be. Ethnography often involves cross-validating a study by asking the research subjects about their opinions as to its accuracy. At its heart, then, qualitative researchers adhere to the core principle of being truthful and avoiding false or distorted accounts. They try to create a tight fit between their understanding, ideas, and statements and what is actually occurring in it.

FEATURES OF QUALITATIVE RESEARCH

Qualitative researchers only infrequently use variables and test relationships quantitatively. They instead view the social world as intrinsically qualitative. To them, qualitative data are not imprecise or deficient; they are highly meaningful. Instead of trying to convert social life into numbers, qualitative researchers borrow ideas from the people they study and place them within the context of a natural setting. They examine motifs, themes, distinctions, and ideas instead of variables, and they adopt the inductive approach of grounded theory (discussed below and in Chapter 3).

Qualitative data are sometimes misunderstood as being intangible, fuzzy, and elusive. As any quality historical book demonstrates, however, describing and explaining social events through concepts, ideas, stories, quotations from real people, and clear narratives is quite effective in relaying "what really is the case." Qualitative data involve documenting real events, recording what people say (with words, gestures, and tone), observing what they do, studying written documents, and examining visual images. These are all concrete aspects of the social world.

Qualitative research, therefore, has its own unique features essential for understanding its nature. These include the following:

1. grounded theory
2. the context is critical
3. bricolage
4. the case and process, and
5. interpretation.

Grounded Theory

As described in Carl Root's research on McVeigh, the inductive method means that theory is built from data, or grounded in the data. It makes qualitative research flexible and lets data and theory interact. Qualitative researchers remain open to the unexpected, are willing to change the direction or theoretical focus of a research project, and may abandon their original research question in the middle of a project.[4] Recall Ryan Bussard who researched illicit steroid manufacturing and trafficking. He didn't settle on his actual research focus until he was well into his data collection, at which point his primary informant revealed how he could convert $500.00 worth of legally purchased precursor chemicals from the Internet into a nearly $15,000.00 profit.

A qualitative researcher builds her or his explanations of what he or she is studying by making comparisons. For example, when a researcher observes an event (e.g., a police officer confronting a speeding motorist), he or she immediately ponders questions and looks for similarities and differences. When watching a police officer stop a speeder, a qualitative researcher asks, does the police officer always radio in the car's license number before proceeding? After radioing the car's location, does the officer ask the motorist to get out of the car sometimes, but in others casually walk up to the car and talk to the seated driver? When data collection and theorizing are interspersed, theoretical questions arise that suggest future observations, so new data are tailored to answer theoretical questions that came from thinking about previous data.

This approach to developing theory, although not normally associated with positivism, is not unscientific. Indeed, **Charles Darwin**, the father of the theory of evolution, used this approach in developing one of our most important scientific theories. After receiving his bachelor's degree from Cambridge University, he embarked on a five-year scientific expedition aboard a British ship to study plants and animals throughout the world. Darwin's approach was inductive—he meticulously collected data over a several-year period, letting the data drive his thinking. This interactive process between his observations and developing his theoretical ideas and concepts came to a high point on the Galápagos Islands in the Pacific Ocean. He found fossils of extinct animals that were clearly related to modern species and plants and animals similar to those found in remote areas of South America. He formally constructed and refined his theory after returning home, using the voluminous data he had collected (Quammen 2006).

CHARLES DARWIN

The father of the theory of evolution, used here as an example of how researchers can develop theory inductively.

The Context Is Critical

Another feature of qualitative research is that it relies on context for understanding crime and criminal justice phenomena. It holds that the meaning of our actions or statements depends on the context in which they appear. When a researcher removes an event, social action, answer to a question, or conversation from the context in which it appears, social meaning and significance are distorted. Attention to social context means that a qualitative researcher notes what came before or what surrounds the focus of study (e.g., historical and cultural context). Even on the microlevel, we define the meaning of a behavior depending on the context in which it occurs. Slight changes in context can dramatically alter meaning. Consider the essential bodily act of urinating. In the context of a bathroom, it is acceptable. In public restrooms, men often engage in this act communally, standing side by side. However, change the physical context a mere few feet, outside a bathroom, and the same behavior would result in the criminal charge of public urination, public indecency (particularly if done communally, side by side), or, in some jurisdictions, would be defined as a sex crime requiring the offenders' placement on a sex offender registry. Both are public acts—but it is the context that provides its meaning.

Lonnie Athens (Chapter 2) and Jeff Ferrell (Chapters 1 and 2) relied on context for understanding their objects of study. By interviewing convicted violent criminals, Athens placed their horrific acts of violence within the context of a shared brutalization process they went through as children. Ferrell helped us better understand graffiti, beyond the simplistic notion of vandalism, by situating the behavior within the context of political and economic oppression, and resistance to that oppression. Jody Miller (2001) had to situate female gangs within the larger context of the poor urban environment in which they formed their subculture.

The careful reader could easily be confused. Does not the error of reductionism say that we cannot make statements about individuals using macrotheories? Almost; however, the error of reductionism refers to using microlevel data to explain macrolevel events. Qualitative researchers are attempting to explain microlevel events by placing them within a macrocontext. We make theoretical sense of things in this way every day without committing a logical error. If we had scored a ninety-eight on an exam, we might attribute it to our hard work, unless we placed it within a larger university environment that has allowed grade inflation to push average scores into the ninety-five-plus range. We assign meaning and significance to the event of scoring a ninety-eight depending on the context in which it occurred. Qualitative researchers, therefore, believe it is imperative to understand ground-level phenomena by situating them within a larger context.

The steroid trafficking article mentioned above includes a passage that exemplifies the importance of placing microlevel findings within a larger context.

> At the root of our analysis is the way in which late-modern society has become preoccupied with the health and aesthetics of the *body*. Recall earlier how the various research subjects characterized their goals: "being ripped/shredded," "being massive," "looking scary," "being scary strong," and "wanting the ultimate body." Clearly these subjects' personal and group identities are constructed in large part around the pursuit of today's hyper-masculine norm of bodily perfection—the muscular, low-body fat, well-proportioned physique. . . .
>
> Moreover, the body has been converted into an object to be modified, altered, re-engineered, and perfected—not just for reasons of health or increased athleticism, but maybe just as important, for visual imagery. This cultural obsession with the body-aesthetic is fueled by a pervasive commodification of the ideal body-image as found in the health, beauty, fashion, and sports industries. (Baudrillard 1970; Featherstone, Hepworth, and Turner 1991; Kraska, Bussard, and Brent 2010: 22; Petersen 2007)

Bricolage

BRICOLAGE

Improvising by drawing on diverse materials that are lying about and using them in creative ways to accomplish a pragmatic task.

Bricolage (pronounced breko′lazh) means working with one's hands and being pragmatic at using an assortment of odds and ends in an inventive manner to accomplish a specific task. It requires having a deep knowledge of one's materials, a collection of esoteric skills, and the capacity to combine them flexibly. The mixture of using diverse materials, applying disparate approaches, and assembling bits and pieces gives qualitative researchers the aura of being similar to a skilled craftsperson who seems able to make or repair almost anything. Qualitative researchers are bricoleurs; they learn to be adept at doing many things, drawing on a variety of sources and methods, and making do with whatever is at hand.[5]

The qualitative style emphasizes developing an ability to draw on a variety of skills, materials, and approaches as they may be needed, usually without being able to plan for them in advance. They then weave together a representation of what they are studying—a patchwork quilt, if you will—that helps the reader develop a deeper understanding of the object of study. Similar to storytelling, the qualitative researcher "stitches, edits, and puts slices of reality together" to create a new, more comprehendible representation of that reality (Denzin and Lincoln 2003: 7).

The Case and Process

Qualitative researchers tend to use a "case-oriented approach [that] places cases, not variables, center stage" (Ragin 1992: 5). They examine in depth a wide variety of aspects of only a few cases. Their analyses emphasize contingencies in "messy" natural settings (i.e., the co-occurrence of many specific factors and events in one place and time). Explanations or interpretations are complex and may be in the form of an unfolding plot or a narrative story about particular people or specific events. Rich detail and astute insight into the cases replace the sophisticated statistical analysis of precise measures across a huge number of units or cases found in quantitative research.

The passage of time is integral to qualitative research. Qualitative researchers look at the sequence of events and pay attention to what happens first, second, third, and so on. Because qualitative researchers examine the same case or set of cases over time, they can see an issue evolve, a conflict emerge, or a social relationship develop. The researcher can detect process and causal relations. In historical research, the passage of time may involve years or decades. In field research, the passage of time is shorter. Nevertheless, in both, a researcher notes what is occurring at different points in time and recognizes that when something that occurs is often important.

Patricia and Peter Alder (1994) befriended and studied a group of cocaine users and dealers for a seven-year period. This lengthy ethnography allowed them a long range of experience in these research subjects' lifestyles—both good and bad. One of their main informants, in fact, was convicted and sent to prison, which allowed the researchers insights into the effects on "Dave's" wife and kids, as well as his continued drug dealing.

Interpretation

Interpretation means to explain the meaning of something. Quantitative research expresses meaning by using numbers (e.g., percentages or statistical coefficients), and a researcher tells how they relate to hypotheses.

Qualitative research reports only occasionally include tables with numbers, and these are supplementary to the textual evidence. It more often involves visual presentations of data including maps, photographs, or causal/conceptual diagrams showing how ideas are related. A researcher weaves the data into discussions of their deeper significance and meaning. The bulk of the data are presented in the form of quotes and rich descriptions of particular events and settings.

A qualitative researcher gives data meaning, translates them, or makes them understandable. He or she begins with the point of view of the people being studied, and then finds out how the people being studied see the world, how they define the situation, or what it means for them.

The first step in qualitative interpretation is to learn about its meaning for the people being studied.[6] The people who created the social behavior have personal reasons or motives for their actions. This is first-order interpretation. A researcher's discovery and reconstruction of this **first-order interpretation** is a second-order interpretation, because the researcher comes in from the outside to discover what has occurred. In a **second-order interpretation**, the researcher elicits an underlying coherence or sense of meaning in the data. Because meaning develops within a set of other meanings, not in a vacuum, a second-order interpretation places the human action being studied in the *stream of behavior*, or events to which it is related—its context.

A researcher who adopts a strict interpretive approach may stop at a second-order interpretation—that is, once he or she understands the significance of the action for the people being studied. Many qualitative researchers go further, however, and link the second-order interpretation to general theory and larger social/cultural/historical contexts. They move to a broader level of interpretation and context, or **third-order interpretation**. This is the point at which a researcher assigns a broader-based theoretical significance to the findings. Kraska's research on the criminalization of accidents, for example, would make sense of the situation in which the nephew was imprisoned for accidentally killing his uncle by placing it into the context of the current societal era known as late modernity. A major feature of late-modern society is a preoccupation with safety, leading to extremely punitive reactions to risky and unsafe actions. Of course, this linkage between a microevent and macroprocesses would be credible only if the empirical research evidence indicated the trend of criminalizing negligence as legitimate. Figure 11.2 provides a visual review of these three orders of qualitative interpretation.

QUALITATIVE DOCUMENT ANALYSIS (QDA)

The McVeigh study at its essence was an interpretive analysis of the thousands of pages of documents that Carl Root and Kraska were able to secure. An appropriate label for this kind of research would be "qualitative document analysis." We will next examine in detail this particular method to provide a more tangible rendering—aside from the next chapter on ethnographic field research—of qualitative inquiry.

The General Idea of QDA

As we outlined in Chapter 9, quantitative content analysis is a valuable research method for documenting quantitatively patterns, themes, biases, or distortions among a set of documents. We examined in Chapters 2 and 9 how crime and justice studies has used content analysis to examine the bias and distortion in the media's coverage of crime and justice phenomena and issues. Converting existing text or images to numbers, however, limits our ability to decipher their deeper

---

INTERPRETATION

To explain the meaning of something.

FIRST-ORDER INTERPRETATION

Interpretations from the point of view of the people being studied.

SECOND-ORDER INTERPRETATION

Interpretation that involves the researcher's point of view, eliciting an underlying coherence or sense of meaning in the data.

THIRD-ORDER INTERPRETATION

Interpretation where the researcher links the second-order interpretation to general theories and larger social/cultural/ historical contexts.

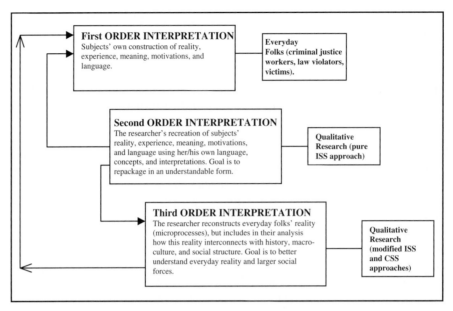

FIGURE 11.2   Qualitative Interpretation—First through Third Order.

QUALITATIVE DOCUMENT ANALYSIS

A research method that involves collecting and analyzing interpretively a systematically selected set of documents, including text and/or visual images, in an effort to uncover their meaning, themes, and cultural and social significance revolving.

meaning and cultural/social significance. This is where **qualitative document analysis (QDA)** is helpful. It is also sometimes called qualitative content analysis. It is defined as the collection and interpretive analysis of a systematically selected set of documents, including text and/or visual images, in an effort to uncover their meaning, themes, and cultural and social significance. It generally uses nonreactive data (what others have left behind), but could be applied to text or images collected firsthand by the researcher.

QDA uses the same logic as ethnographic field research in deciphering meaning, developing understanding, and constructing grounded theory. Instead of immersing ourselves into a natural environment of human activity, however, QDA involves our immersion into documents. In a sense, then, the QDA researcher enters the life of the documents and inquires into their meaning. This again should not be viewed as mystical or foreign; we spend our entire lives engaging in a similar, albeit unsystematic, type of interpretive pursuit whenever we read text or view still or video images. (Highlight 11.1 illustrates this point further.) The difference is that QDA systematizes our approach and is targeted at answering well-defined research questions.

POSSIBLE APPLICATIONS OF QDA.   QDA can be used for a wide range of applications. Revisiting the lynching example used throughout this text, one example can be found within a data-collection project known as Without Sanctuary. James Allen has traveled the United States for years and collected hundreds of lynching photographs and postcards taken as souvenirs by professional and amateur photographers. Analyzed interpretively, these photographs along with their associated text (the personal note written to a friend or loved one) would provide a fascinating opportunity to delve into an in-depth understanding of their cultural meaning and significance. Although no one has conducted a formal qualitative document analysis of these documents, Allen's interpretive notes analyzing the meaning of these gruesome postcards reveal their potential for QDA.[7]

> It wasn't the corpses that bewildered me as much as the canine-thin faces of the pack, lingering in the woods, circling after the kill. Hundreds of flea markets later a trader pulled me aside and in conspiratorial tones offered me a second card, this one of Laura Nelson, caught so pitiful and tattered and beyond retrieving—like a child's paper kite snagged on a utility wire. The sight of Laura layered a pall of grief over all my fears.

HIGHLIGHT 11.1
Deciphering Meaning from a Photograph

To demonstrate how we all routinely decipher meaning from documents, examine the photograph. What does it tell you? What is its meaning? When and where did this take place? If this is a representative snapshot of someone's life, what does it tell you about him or her?

Oftentimes a photograph will have an associated caption. Imagine how the following caption might alter your interpretation: "As the floodwaters gained ground, many decided to evacuate their homes." Qualitative analysis of documents sometimes requires us to consider the interplay between text and image to accurately decipher the meaning (see the section below on semiotics).

(By the way, this is actually a photograph of preparations to go to grandmother's house for the holidays. Is there any evidence that the dog got to go on the trip? Any clues to where they might be headed?)

I believe the photographer was more than a perceptive spectator at lynchings. The photographic art played as significant a role in the ritual as torture or souvenir grabbing—a sort of two-dimensional biblical swine, a receptacle for a collective sinful self. Lust propelled their commercial reproduction and distribution, facilitating the endless replay of anguish. Even dead, the victims were without sanctuary.

Studying crime and justice phenomena provides us many opportunities for conducting qualitative document analysis. Aside from lynching postcards, we might study:

- a collection of advertisements in police or corrections magazines,
- a series of newspaper articles that act to construct and perpetuate a crime or criminal justice myth,
- a sample of Web pages on such topics as conspiratorial thinking about September 11 or Web sites that feature video coverage of amateur fighting contests,
- a collection of computer communication correspondence between police patrol cars,
- a series of video-taped "cell extractions" taken by correctional rapid response teams,
- a set of open-ended responses found in a questionnaire or survey,
- an interpretive analysis of twenty-five years of disciplinary reports found in a juvenile detention center for girls,
- a series of photographs of their everyday lives taken by juveniles serving on probation, or perhaps
- a collection of newspaper stories over a ten-year period that tracks changes in how society is redefining accidents and acts of negligence as crime.

Each of these data sets would be collected and analyzed with particular research questions in mind. For example, criminal justice practitioner trade magazine advertisements could be used to examine changes over time in occupational culture—as reflected in what advertisers believe is appealing to their audience. Another research question might center on the genesis and nature of a crime myth—such as the crack baby phenomenon discussed in Chapter 2. QDA would examine the process and techniques involved in the construction of the crack baby myth, focusing on the role of government sources, the rhetorical tactics used, the way in which moral discourse was used, the use of anecdotes as reliable evidence, and the reliance on politicians' or experts' opinions. In other words, the QDA researcher would not be so much concerned about the quantitative frequency or duration of certain themes or words; rather, she or he would decipher how this mythical knowledge claim came to pass and what it means for us as a society.

How to Conduct QDA (steps)

The steps in a QDA research project are similar to that of any qualitative project.

1. *Select Topic and Focus the Question.* Selecting a topic and focusing that topic into a clear, workable research question is the first step in conducting qualitative document analysis. As seen above, the QDA researcher has many research topics from which to choose. Data availability is a key determinant as to whether a topic is viable. QDA works best with a well-defined body of preexisting documents (text and/or visual), but data created by the researcher (a set of photographs or interviews, for example) can also work. Focusing the question requires the researcher to think carefully about the purpose of the project. Most QDA projects attempt to deconstruct the meaning found in text and visual data, and then reconstruct it in an intelligible form for their audience. As with all qualitative forms of research, the focus of the study can shift throughout the entire duration of the project.

2. *Design Study.* Designing a QDA study is similar to designing any qualitative project. Design considerations begin with the realization that analyzing qualitatively a set of documents will require flexibility and adaptation. The first design issue involves the selection of the data itself. QDA mimics traditional content analysis in that the data collection should be systematic (see step 3). The researcher also has to consider the advantages and disadvantages of using one or more data analyzers. Another deals with whether the research would benefit from some quantitative techniques. If studying the impact the media had on the government's reaction to the Hurricane Katrina disaster, it might be helpful to document quantitatively the intensity and timing of the media's theme of "crime and disorder." One more design issue might be whether the researcher uses a qualitative software analysis program to assist in selecting themes, patterns, and ideas found in the data set (discussed in Appendix C).

3. *Collect Data.* Robust data collection is key to this method. QDA will select data primarily based on the extent to which it best answers the research question. This might mean that reliability is quite important—as illustrated in the fear study noted above—because the researcher has to establish with a high degree of reliability changes over time. Other studies will be concerned more with validity—such as a QDA study of photographs taken by juvenile probationers of their lived worlds.

QDA most often involves collecting nonreactive data. In one police QDA, researchers collected preexisting government documents from the U.S. Department of Justice; these documents were attempting to educate police practitioners about the thinking behind and benefits of community policing. The rhetoric used within these documents was approached as the data. In the authors' words: "Here we deconstruct a key representation of community policing discourse (official CP literature from the U.S. Department of Justice). Our purpose is to dissect a well-known and seemingly straightforward community policing narrative to expose the subtext of its meaning" (Kappeler and Kraska 1998: 297).

4. *Analysis and Interpretation of the Data.* QDA analyzes and interprets text and images using various analytical techniques. Many of these are discussed in the next chapter on qualitative data analysis (e.g., narrative analysis); suffice it to say that they all involve deciphering the meaning and cultural significance from a data set of text and/or visual images. The analytical approach is similar to ethnographical field research. The actual qualitative analysis technique employed will depend in great part on the purpose of the research question and the theoretical framework through which the researcher is working.

For example, a project geared at deciphering inductively the causal connections and pathways of the government/media's construction of Hurricane Katrina as a security crisis, as opposed to a humanitarian one, would rely on "grounded theory" techniques. A researcher operating from a social constructionist paradigm might use a narrative analysis technique to tease out the rhetorical methods used by the government and media to construct a moral panic using newspapers or television news coverage as their communication medium.

The community policing example noted above relied on a document analysis technique known as **semiotics**. Highlight 11.2 provides a brief glimpse at what this interesting and useful

---

HIGHLIGHT 11.2
Semiotics and the Study of Crime and Justice

Semiotics is one of the most powerful, and paradoxically underutilized, forms of analysis in crime and justice studies. The power of semiotic analysis comes from its ability to be used from a number of theoretical perspectives and its applicability to a variety of objects of study. We can use semiotics to study words, images, objects, or speeches; and we can invoke it to question the variables used in empirical studies of crime and criminal justice. A brief definition of semiotics and a few examples might help to illustrate the power of this form of analysis.

Semiotics is the study of the production and interpretation of signs. It involves studying the relationships within and between signs, system, and codes. *Sign* is a general term that includes any act, object, or symbol that conveys information and meaning (practically anything discernible with the human senses). Signs may include language, gesture, image, sound, depiction, and action. In studying the associations among signs, one looks at sign systems or collections or groupings of signs to better understand how complex sign relationships create meaning. From this approach, crime and justice are not seen as objective and naturally occurring phenomena, but rather complex constructs imbued with both experience and meaning.

Semiotic analysis often focuses on words and language because these are the vehicles that turn our experiences into conceptual reality. Words allow us to vicariously share experiences and descriptions of reality that may or may not be fully grounded in experience. Words, even if they are carefully chosen to describe experience, do not replicate experience. Words are representations and abstractions of reality. Much like an artist's painting of a landscape, the image should not be confused with the actual landscape. The painting is merely the artist's representation of what he or she sees or wants us to see—a single interpretation of reality. Similarly, words create associations with our experiences; the language we use to depict these experiences, then, frame and alter our understanding of those experiences; semiotics focuses on these transformations.

Because crime and justice are multifaceted phenomena, we represent through images and words only selective aspects of them. More often than not, when we react to crime, when we appeal to justice, or when we demand action, we are reacting to crime's semiotic representation—not an objective material reality.

For example, when people are victimized by crime, what influences their reaction? Is it strictly a product of the actual crime experience or is it a product of symbols that contextualize the experience and give it meaning? Are we obligated to experience victimization in a certain way? Consider two different scenarios in which two identical pieces of property are stolen. In one situation, the item is stolen from a car; in the other, it is taken from a home. Both incidents are property crimes. The significance and meaning we give these acts come not just from the experience of loss, but also from the meaning (or "sign-ificance") we attach to the place in which the property is stolen. A home carries with it the connotation of individual ownership, belonging, privacy, and refuge. It may be our place of origin or where our domestic affections are centered. In other words, crime gains its meaning from its relationship to different systems of meaning that are composed of signs—how we think about and represent property and place. These relational systems inform us on how to experience crime. So it is little wonder that we react to the theft of property from a vehicle quite differently than we do to a theft from our home. The signification of a behavior as *criminal* invokes a very selective, complex, and powerful web of symbolic meaning. Semiotics seeks to illuminate these webs.

Semiotics assumes, similar to the ISS approach, that our entire understanding of the world is captured and stored in symbolic form. When we communicate about crime and

(continued)

theoretical synthesis research, Ericson incorporates some good examples of QDA techniques. The book's purpose is succinctly presented in its first two sentences:

> This book investigates the alarming trend across Western countries of treating every imaginable source of harm as a crime. I argue that this urge to criminalize is rooted in neo-liberal political cultures that are obsessed with uncertainty. (Ericson 2007: 1)

Later in the book, Ericson examines the tactics the Department of Homeland Security (DHS) uses to socially construct the reality of safeguarding against the uncertainty and risk of domestic terrorism. The DHS uses its partner organization the America Prepared Campaign (APC) to overcome what they see as the American public's general skepticism about terrorism and terrorism preparedness. He highlights one media campaign in which the APC takes out advertisements in magazines. "Each ad features a particular consumer item in a household closet or cabinet that have been consumed in excess: shoes, lipstick. . . . The picture of excessive consumption is overlain with 'But Do You Have a _____' " (Ericson 2007: 66). The blank is filled in with a security item such as a whistle or duct tape. The bottom of the ad continues: "You have the things that make you happy. Get the things that make you prepared."

Ericson's interpretation of these advertisements is comprehensive, but his overall point is to expose the subtle yet effective tactics the architects of the war on terrorism employ to inculcate into Americans' minds and everyday routines a "terrorism threat consciousness." Highlight 13.3 looks at the trend toward approaching images, both still and video, as credible data used in conducting crime and justice research.

QDA Wrap-Up

Qualitative document analysis is a broad category of research that analyzes interpretively the meaning and significance of textual and visual data. Generally, this involves a carefully selected set of documents, but in some instances a single document could be used (e.g., the U.S. PATRIOT Act). It is a particularly powerful research method when coupled with quantitative content analysis. Analyzing language and images qualitatively represents a cutting-edge development that several important academics have been encouraging for some time.[8] The emphasis is to deconstruct and make sense of the way in which language and images form a particular version of reality.

As discussed in Highlight 11.2, the way we conceive of crime and justice reality is based partially in how those with a vested interest want us to conceive it. This does not imply any type of conscious conspiracy; rather, language and images simply act to frame our perception of things in a way that benefits some people's worldviews and agendas. Employing the language of homeland and homeland security, for example, is a new development in U.S. politics that frames our thinking about domestic and national security in a particular manner. QDA provides a valuable tool for deciphering the origin, use, and social/political meaning of this emerging use of language. Can you conceive of a QDA research project that would inquire into this research topic?

Conclusion

In this chapter, we explored the nature of qualitative research. We saw how differences in the qualitative and quantitative styles direct a researcher to approach a study differently. All crime and justice researchers narrow their topic into a more specific, focused research question. The styles of research suggest a different form and sequence of decisions, and different answers to when and how to focus the research. The style that a researcher uses will depend on the topic he or she selects, the researcher's purpose and intended use of study results, the orientation toward social science that he or she adopts, and the individual researcher's own assumptions and beliefs.

Key Terms

soft data *261*

hard data *261*

Charles
  Darwin *265*

bricolage *266*

interpretation *267*

first-order
  interpretation *267*

second-order
  interpretation *267*

third-order
  interpretation *267*

qualitative document
  analysis (QDA) *268*

semiotics *271*

Review Questions

1. What are the basics of qualitative research, including its major differences when compared to quantitative research?
2. What is grounded theory and how does it help us to understand the nature of qualitative research?
3. What is qualitative document analysis, and what are some of its possible applications in crime and criminal justice studies?
4. What are the major steps involved in conducting qualitative document analysis?
5. What is semiotics and how can it help us understand crime and criminal justice phenomena?
6. Explain how qualitative researchers approach the issue of interpreting data. Refer to first-, second-, and third-order interpretations.

Practicing Research

1. Conduct a microqualitative document analysis study. Select a set of documents (visual or text) and analyze them qualitatively. The key here is to look for patterns of meaning and clues to these documents' social significance. It may be fruitful to use Kappeler's essay on semiotics to help make interpretive sense of your data.
2. Find a qualitative document analysis article. Write a review of this article, including its purpose, various methods used, and major findings.
3. Three key qualitative research concepts discussed in this chapter include case study, context, and interpretation. Qualitative researchers often study and interpret the meaning of a particular case by placing that case within a larger context. Think about some event that has been especially meaningful in your life, and imagine how a qualitative research project might make sense of that event by placing it within a larger context. For example, Kraska had a several-ton oak log fall on his leg a few years ago that, needless to say, was a life-threatening situation. If someone were to examine this event in depth, he or she might help tease out its significance and meaning by examining the changing nature of the rural community in which he lives. Write an essay detailing your thinking and analysis as applied to an important even in your life.
4. Find three qualitative research articles (one good place to look for these is in the *Journal of Contemporary Ethnography*), and applying the key concepts and ideas outlined in this chapter, write a short review of each.

Notes for Further Study

1. On the issue of using quantitative, statistical techniques as a substitute for trust, see Collins (1984), Porter (1995), and Smith and Heshusius (2004).
2. For discussion, see Schwandt (1997), Swanborn (1996), and Tashakkori and Teddlie (1998: 90–93).
3. For examples of checking, see Agar (1980) and Becker (1970c).
4. For place of theory in qualitative research, see Hammersley (1995).
5. See Harper (1987: 9, 74–75) and Schwandt (1997: 10–11).
6. See Blee and Billings (1986), Ricoeur (1970), and Schneider (1987) on the interpretation of text in qualitative research.
7. See www.withoutsanctuary.org/main.html
8. See Altheide (1996, 2001), Arrigo (2005), Kappeler (forthcoming), and Manning and Cullum-Swan (1994).

12

Crime and Justice Ethnographic Field Research

Home-Brewing Steroids: Generating Grounded Theory

The Roots of Ethnographic Field Research
Early Beginnings
Chicago School of Sociology
Conceptual/Theoretical Underpinnings
Highlight 12.1 An Excerpt from Clifford Geertz's Famous Description of a Balinese Cockfight

Ethnographic Field Research in Crime and Justice Studies

Appropriate Questions for Ethnographic Field Research

The Logic of Field Research
What Is Ethnographic Field Research?
Steps in a Field Research Project
Flexibility
Organized Flexibility

Choosing a Site and Gaining Access
Selecting a Site
Where to Observe
Level of Involvement
Gatekeepers
Informants
Strategy for Entering
Planning
Negotiation
Disclosure
Entering the Field
Presentation of Self
Highlight 12.2 Entering the Field with Active Burglars

Researcher as Instrument
An Attitude of Strangeness
Highlight 12.3 Enjoying Militarism
Building Rapport
Charm and Trust
Understanding

Relations in the Field
Roles in the Field
Preexisting versus Created Roles
Negotiations and Danger
Learning the Ropes
Stress
Normalizing Crime and Justice Research
Acceptable Incompetent
Maintaining Relations
Small Favors
Conflicts in the Field
Appearing Interested

Observing and Collecting Data
Watching and Listening with Care
Keenly Observant
Argot or Specialized Language
Taking Notes
Types of Field Notes
- *Jotted Notes*
- *Direct Observation Notes*
- *Researcher Inference Notes*
- *Analytic Memos*
- *Personal Notes*
- *Maps and Diagrams*
- *Machine Recordings to Supplement Memory*
- *Interview Notes*
Data Quality in Ethnographic Field Research

The Meaning of Quality
Reliability in Field Research
Validity in Field Research
Sampling
The Field Research Interview
Focus Group Research
The Field Interview
Life History
*Highlight 12.4 The Life History or Life Story
Interview*
Types of Questions in Field Interviews

Leaving the Field
Ethical Dilemmas of Field Research
Deception
Confidentiality
Involvement with Criminals/Deviants
Publishing Ethnographic Field Reports
Conclusion
Key Terms
Review Questions
Practicing Research
Notes for Further Study

HOME-BREWING STEROIDS: GENERATING GROUNDED THEORY

Numerous performance-enhancing drug scandals have rocked both professional and Olympic sports. A few examples include the sentencing of Marion Jones (Olympic track star) to a six-month imprisonment for lying to a steroid investigative body, the constant turmoil surrounding Tour-de-France cycling race over positive drug tests, and numerous high-profile baseball players being accused of and admitting to using anabolic steroids and human growth hormone. The attention on illegal steroids and professional sports has also generated a more general concern about the extent to which everyday athletes (both young and old), weightlifters, bodybuilders, and people interested in losing weight or living longer are buying and using these illicit substances (McCallum 2008). The media (particularly the sports media) have adopted it as a part of their daily news cycle. The U.S. Congress has launched hearings, conducted in-depth investigations, and passed new steroid control legislation (Shipley 2007; Tucker 2007). The moralizing about steroids reached the presidential level during a State of the Union Address in 2004:

> the use of performance-enhancing drugs like steroids in base-ball, football, and other sports is dangerous, and it sends the wrong message—that there are shortcuts to accomplishment, and that performance is more important than character.

Despite the obvious importance of this phenomenon, criminal justice/criminology has yet to provide any research or scholarly discussion about the steroid-trafficking industry. As mentioned earlier in this text, Ryan Bussard, John Brent, and Kraska sought to remedy this gap by providing the first in-depth study into steroid trafficking (Kraska, Bussard, and Brent 2010). Our interest was in developing grounded data that would provide our field with an accurate picture of the real world of steroid trafficking. What we discovered was noteworthy: The central informant in our ethnography had established a large and very lucrative steroid-trafficking operation that involved ordering from the Internet a variety of precursor chemicals off foreign Web sites and then "homebrewing" these into injectable, powerful, and highly desired solutions. His customers included bodybuilders, collegiate athletes, police officers, firefighters, and a large number of middle-aged men attempting to attain a lean and youthful physique. The genre of research we relied on is referred to as ethnographic field research. (The study also employed a large content analysis component making it actually a "mixed methods" study as discussed in Chapter 13) As Emerson defines it,

> Field research is the study of people acting in the natural courses of their daily lives. The fieldworker ventures into the worlds of others in order to learn firsthand about how they live, how they talk and behave, and what captivates and distresses them. . . . It is also seen as a method of study whose practitioners try to understand the meanings that activities observed have for those engaging in them. (Emerson 1983: 1)

The type of qualitative research we'll examine in this chapter—ethnographic field research—exemplifies this line of inquiry. This method encourages researchers to engage the real world, to directly observe and participate to varying degrees in crime and criminal justice natural settings to describe and make sense of their culture. Ethnographic reports can be fascinating accounts of unfamiliar social worlds: street prostitution, K-9 police units, upper-class drug use, crack trafficking, undercover police work, street gangs, juvenile detention facilities, terrorist networks, or domestic violence settings. As a method, it appeals to those who are keenly observant and have an ability to get along easily with others. Through interaction over months or years, the researcher learns about them; their life histories; their hobbies and interests; and their habits, hopes, fears, and dreams. Meeting new people, developing friendships, and discovering new social worlds can be enjoyable. It is also time consuming, emotionally taxing, and sometimes, especially in crime and justice studies, physically dangerous.

THE ROOTS OF ETHNOGRAPHIC FIELD RESEARCH

Early Beginnings

Academic field research began in the late nineteenth century with anthropology. The first anthropologists only read the reports of explorers, government officials, or missionaries, and therefore lacked direct contact with the people they studied. The reports focused on the exotic and were highly racist and ethnocentric. Travelers rarely spoke the local language and had to rely on interpreters. Not until the 1890s did European anthropologists begin to travel to faraway lands to learn about other cultures.

British social anthropologist Bronislaw Malinowski (1844–1942) was the first researcher to live with a group of people for a long period of time and write about collecting data. In the 1920s, he presented intensive fieldwork as a new method and argued for separating direct observation and native statements from the observer's inferences. He said that social researchers should directly interact with and live among the native peoples, and learn their customs, beliefs, and social processes.

Researchers also used field research to study their own society. The observations of the London poor by Charles Booth and Beatrice Webb in the 1890s began the movement toward conducting field research outside of anthropology. Booth and Webb directly observed people in natural settings and used an inductive data-gathering approach. Participant observation may have originated in Germany in 1890. Paul Gohre worked and lived as a factory apprentice for three months and took detailed notes each night at home to study factory life. His published work influenced scholars in the universities, including the sociologist Max Weber.

Chicago School of Sociology

Sociological field research in the United States began at the University of Chicago's Department of Sociology. The Chicago school's influence on field research had two phases. In the first phase, from the 1910s to 1930s, the school used a variety of methods based on the case study or life history approach, including direct observation, informal interviews, and review of documents or official records. Important influences came from Booker T. Washington, William James, and John Dewey. In 1916, Robert E. Park (1864–1944) drew up a research program for the social investigation of the city of Chicago. Influenced by his background as a newspaper reporter, and by the work of anthropologists, he said that social researchers should leave the libraries and "get their hands dirty" by direct observations and conversations on street corners, in barrooms, and in luxury hotel lobbies. Early studies such as *The Hobo* (Anderson 1923), *The Jack Roller* (Shaw 1930), and *The Gang* (Thrasher 1927) established early Chicago school sociology as the descriptive study of street life.

Journalistic and anthropological models of research were combined in the first phase. The journalistic model has a researcher get behind the scenes, use informants, look for conflict, and expose what is "really happening." In the anthropological model, a researcher attaches himself or herself to a small group for an extended period of time and reports on the members' activities and views of the world.

In the second phase, from the 1940s to the 1960s, the Chicago school developed participant observation as a distinct technique. It expanded the anthropological model to groups and settings in the researcher's society. Three principles emerged:

1. Study people in their natural settings.
2. Study people by directly interacting with them.
3. Gain an understanding of the social world and make theoretical statements based on the members' perspective.

After World War II, field research fell out of favor because of the popularity of survey and quantitative research, but was rejuvenated in the 1970s and 1980s. Ethnographic field researchers started to draw heavily from the more developed ideas and techniques found in cognitive psychology and cultural anthropology. They wrote more rigorously about its epistemological underpinnings and became more systematic about it as a research technique.

Conceptual/Theoretical Underpinnings

Today most see ethnographic field research's foundation as symbolic interactionism, and to a lesser extent social constructionism (Chapter 3's discussion of the ISS approach reviewed this thinking in depth). These theoretical orientations do not see people as a neutral medium through which social forces operate, nor do they see social meanings as something "out there" to observe and measure. Instead, they hold that people create and define meaning, or their reality, through their interactions with other people. As Berg (2007: 10) states, "Meanings allow people to produce various realities that constitute the sensory world (the so-called real world), but because these realities are related to how people create meanings, reality becomes an interpretation of various definitional options."

Our reality and our shared realities (culture), therefore, are socially constructed through an intricate process of learning and constructing meanings and definitions of situations through language, symbols, and interactions with other people. Human experiences are filtered through this subjective reality, which affects how people see, define, and act in the social world. Thus, ethnographers focus on the everyday, face-to-face social processes of negotiation, discussion, and bargaining to construct social meaning. They simultaneously describe and interpret this socially constructed reality.

The term **ethnography** comes from cultural anthropology.[1] *Ethno-* means people or folk, and *-graphy* means to describe something. Thus, ethnography means describing a culture and understanding another way of life from the native point of view. As Franke (1983: 61) stated, "Culture, the object of our description, resides within the thinking of natives." Ethnography assumes that people make inferences—that is, go beyond what is explicitly seen or said to what is meant or implied. People display their culture (what people think, ponder, or believe) through actions, language, or rituals. These do not give meaning; rather, meaning is inferred, or someone figures out meaning. Moving from what is heard or observed to what is meant is at the center of ethnography.

ETHNOGRAPHY

A form of research that describes a culture and understanding another way of life from the native point of view.

For example, when a police officer is invited to a "get together," he or she infers that it is an informal party exclusive to other police officers and their significant others, and things will be discussed and humor will be used that "the public" wouldn't understand. These assumptions are based on his or her cultural knowledge of police lifestyle. Cultural knowledge includes symbols, songs, sayings, facts, informal rules, ways of behaving, and objects (e.g., telephones, newspapers). We learn culture through working on the job, being in the school, attending a church, watching television, listening to parents, interacting with peers, and the like. This is not to infer that culture resides in a vacuum. As we learned in Chapter 1, most see culture and social structure mutually transforming and reinforcing one another in dialectical fashion.

Cultural knowledge includes both **explicit knowledge**, what we know and talk about, and **tacit knowledge**, what we rarely acknowledge. For example, explicit knowledge includes the social event (e.g., a "get together"). Most attendees could describe what happens at one. Tacit knowledge includes the unspoken cultural norm for the proper distance to stand from others, or what is acceptable to say and what's not. People are often unaware of these more tacit norms. They feel unease or discomfort when the norms are violated, but it is difficult to pinpoint the source of discomfort. Ethnographers describe the explicit and tacit cultural knowledge that members use. Their detailed descriptions and careful analysis take what is described apart and put it back together.

Anthropologist Clifford Geertz stated that a critical part of ethnography is **thick description**, a rich, detailed description of specifics (as opposed to summary, standardization, generalization, or variables).[2] A thick description of a three-minute event may go on for pages. It captures what occurred and the drama of events, thereby permitting multiple interpretations, much like you might read in a good novel. It places events in a context so that the reader of an ethnographic report can infer cultural meaning. Highlight 12.1 quotes a famous passage from Geertz's best-known work. It is a classic example of "thick description."

EXPLICIT KNOWLEDGE

Knowledge that people are aware of and readily discuss.

TACIT KNOWLEDGE

Knowledge that people rarely acknowledge and may not be explicitly aware of.

THICK DESCRIPTION

Qualitative data in which a researcher attempts to capture all the details of a social setting in an extremely detailed description and convey an intimate feel for the setting and the inner lives of people in it.

HIGHLIGHT 12.1

An Excerpt from Clifford Geertz's Famous Description of a Balinese Cockfight

Cockfights (tetadjen; sabungan) are held in a ring about fifty-feet square. Usually they begin toward late afternoon and run three or four hours until sunset.

. . .A match made, the other hopefuls retire with the same deliberate indifference, and the selected cocks have their spurs (tadji) affixed—razor sharp, pointed steel swords, four or five inches long. This is a delicate job which only a small proportion of men, a half-dozen or so in most villages, know how to do properly. The man who attaches the spurs also provides them, and if the rooster he assists wins its owner awards him the spur-leg of the victim. The spurs are affixed by winding a long length of string around the foot of the spur and the leg of the cock.

. . . The spurs affixed, the two cocks are placed by their handlers (who may or may not be their owners) facing one another in the center of the ring. A coconut pierced with a small hole is placed in a pail of water, in which it takes about twenty-one seconds to sink, a period known as a tjeng and marked at beginning and end by the beating of a slit gong. During these twenty-one seconds the handlers (pengangkeb) are not permitted to touch their roosters. If, as sometimes happens, the animals have not fought during this time, they are picked up, fluffed, pulled, prodded, and otherwise insulted, and put back in the center of the ring and the process begins again. Sometimes they refuse to fight at all, or one keeps running away, in which case they are imprisoned together under a wicker cage, which usually gets them engaged.

Most of the time, in any case, the cocks fly almost immediately at one another in a wing-beating, head-thrusting, leg-kicking explosion of animal fury so pure, so absolute, and in its own way so beautiful, as to be almost abstract, a Platonic concept of hate. Within moments one or the other drives home a solid blow with his spur. The handler whose cock has delivered the blow immediately picks it up so that it will not get a return blow, for if he does not the match is likely to end in a mutually mortal tie as the two birds wildly hack each other to pieces. This is particularly true if, as often happens, the spur sticks in its victim's body, for then the aggressor is at the mercy of his wounded foe.

During this interval, slightly over two minutes, the handler of the wounded cock has been working frantically over it, like a trainer patching a mauled boxer between rounds, to get it in shape for a last, desperate try for victory. He blows in its mouth, putting the whole chicken head in his own mouth and sucking and blowing, fluffs it, stuffs its wounds with various sorts of medicines, and generally tries anything he can think of to arouse the last ounce of spirit which may be hidden somewhere within it. By the time he is forced to put it back down he is usually drenched in chicken blood, but, as in prize fighting, a good handler is worth his weight in gold. Some of them can virtually make the dead walk, at least long enough for the second and final round.

You can read the rest of Geertz's famous description, and the entire article itself, on the Internet, where the essay in its entirety is posted on several different Web sites (use keywords "Geertz Balinese Cockfight").

Source: From Clifford Geertz, "Deep Play: Notes on the Balinese Cockfight," *Daedalus*, 101:1 (Winter, 1972), pp. 1–38. © 1972 by the American Academy of Arts and Sciences. Reprinted by permission of MIT Press Journals.

ETHNOGRAPHIC FIELD RESEARCH IN CRIME AND JUSTICE STUDIES

We already mentioned the difficulty qualitative research has had in finding a comfortable home in crime and justice studies. This seems incompatible with the fact that many of the foundational studies in crime, deviance, prisons, police, and courts were conducted using ethnographic field research. As part of our field's growing pains, some positivists attempted to ignore, and sometimes outright rejected, ethnography as a legitimate research technique. Ethnographers, for their part, oftentimes framed their arguments for their approach as a rejection of positivism. After years of debate and struggle, the past five years have seen a new level of respect and tolerance. A large number of well-done, intensely researched ethnographies on a range of crime and criminal justice subjects seem to have solidified its standing as a credible and worthwhile method for producing knowledge.

Two brief empirical indicators of this change are worth mentioning. First, the American Society of Criminology awarded Darrell Steffensmeier and Jeffery Ulmer's (2005) *Confessions of a Dying Thief: Understanding Criminal Careers and Illegal Enterprises* the 2006 book of the year. It is a remarkable piece of ethnographic research that spans decades. It epitomizes Weber's verstehen in providing a backstage and deeply personal view of crime. It is ethnography at its best.

The other indicator is a new qualitative journal, *Crime, Media, Culture*, that received the Best New Journal award from the prestigious Association of Learned and Professional Society of Publishers (see http://cmc.sagepub.com/). This crime and justice journal competed with new journals found in all social science disciplines worldwide. The journal is committed to expanding the discipline's boundaries to include ethnographic field research, as well as a range of other qualitative methods.

A quick review of the recent literature would reveal numerous examples of ethnographic field studies in the areas of crime and crime control, including domestic violence, racial dynamics in prisons, street gangs, motorcycle gangs, the work of probation officers, crack dealing, dumpster diving, robbery, white-collar crime, juvenile detention workers, and police arrest practices.

One brief example that demonstrates the accessibility and value of this approach is found in the *Journal of Contemporary Ethnography* published in 2006. Clinton Sanders published a study on the subculture of police K-9 units, looking specifically at the relationship between K-9 police dog handlers and their canine companions. He spent several months with police officers and their dogs, and became interested in the ambivalence the officers experience in treating their dog as a functional tool (and the

U.S. Customs and Border Protection officers make extensive use of bomb and contraband sniffing dogs.

training they receive is designed to make them feel this way) versus a sentient being (their good friend and pet). A quote from a trainer captures the difficulty.

> In some states the dog is classified as a police officer. . . . I always have to tell handler trainees that the dog is a tool. You cannot use lethal force if someone is threatening the dog. But, in the excitement of the moment when the adrenaline is up, it is hard to think about that. To a handler, harming his dog is like harming a person. But the dog is just a tool. (Sanders 2006: 165)

APPROPRIATE QUESTIONS FOR ETHNOGRAPHIC FIELD RESEARCH

When should we use ethnographic field research? This method is appropriate when the research question involves learning about, understanding, or describing a group of interacting people. It is usually best when the question is, how do people do Y in the social world? or what is the cultural world of X like? It can be used when other methods (e.g., survey, experiments) are not practical, as in studying street gangs or corporate criminals. This method can be used to accomplish any of the major goals of research—exploration, description, explanation, and evaluation (but only occasionally for evaluation purposes). It is increasingly used in conjunction with quantitative methods.

Field researchers study people in their own setting. It has been generally used to study relatively small groups, or even a particular individual within a group, who interact with each other on a regular basis in a relatively fixed setting. Field research is also used to study amorphous social experiences that are not fixed in place, but where intensive interviewing and observation are the only way to gain access to the experience—for example, the feelings of a person who has been mugged, or the widow of someone who committed suicide.[3]

THE LOGIC OF FIELD RESEARCH

What is Ethnographic Field Research?

Ethnographic field research is more of an orientation toward research than a fixed set of techniques to apply.[4] A field researcher uses various methods to obtain information. As Schatzman and Strauss (1973: 14) said, "Field method is more like an umbrella of activity beneath which any technique may be used for gaining the desired knowledge, and for processes of thinking about this information." A field researcher is a "methodological pragmatist" (Schatzman and Strauss 1973: 7), a resourceful, talented individual who has ingenuity, and an ability to think on his or her feet while in the field.

NATURALISM

The principle that researchers should examine events as they occur in natural, everyday ongoing social settings.

Field research is based on **naturalism,** which is a notion derived from the biological sciences used to study oceans, animals, plants, forests, and so forth. Naturalism involves observing ordinary events in natural settings, not in contrived, invented, or researcher-created settings. Research occurs in the field and outside the safe settings of an office, laboratory, or classroom. Ferrell (1997: 3) sees that approach as benefiting our understanding of both crime and criminal justice.

> Although I focus on field research inside criminal worlds and in illegal settings, I suggest that such immersion can provide equally important insights into the experiences of crime victims, crime control agents, and others. I propose that experiential immersion by field researchers can begin to unravel the lived meanings of both crime and criminal justice.

A field researcher examines social meanings and grasps multiple perspectives in natural social settings. He or she gets inside the meaning system of members and then goes back to an outside or research viewpoint. As Van Maanen (1982: 139), a renowned police ethnographer, noted, "Fieldwork means involvement and detachment, both loyalty and betrayal, both openness and secrecy, and most likely, love and hate." The researcher switches perspectives and sees the setting from multiple points of view simultaneously.

Research is usually conducted by a single individual, although small teams have been effective. A researcher is directly engaged in the cultural world studied, so his or her personal characteristics are relevant. Wax (1979: 509) noted:

> In informal and quantitative methods, the peculiarities of the individual tend to go unnoticed. Electronic data processing pays no heed to the age, gender, or ethnicity of the research director or programmer. But, in fieldwork, these basic aspects of personal identity become salient; they drastically affect the process of field research.

Ethnographic field research, then, is a systematic process of gathering data through observation, participation, and interviews to describe, understand, and even explain a specific natural setting. As Berg (2007: 179) notes, a unique characteristic of this approach is that the researcher must be aware of his or her **reflexive** role in the research process.

> Reflexivity implies a shift in the way we understand data and their collection. To accomplish this, the researcher must make use of an internal dialogue that repeatedly examines *what the researcher knows and how the researcher came to know this.* . . . The ideal result from this process is reflexive knowledge: information that provides insights into the workings of the world and insights on how that knowledge came to be.

Table 12.1 provides a simple summary of what ethnographic field researchers do.

ETHNOGRAPHIC FIELD RESEARCH

A systematic process of gathering data through observation, participation, and interviews to describe, understand, and even explain a specific natural setting.

REFLEXIVITY

The field research technique that allows the researcher to use his or her own personal reaction to one's experience as part of the data and analysis.

TABLE 12.1 What Do Field Researchers Do?

A field researcher does the following:

1. Observes ordinary events and everyday activities as they happen in natural settings, in addition to any unusual occurrences
2. Becomes directly involved with the people being studied and personally experiences the process of daily social life in the field setting
3. Acquires an insider's point of view while maintaining the analytic perspective or distance of an outsider
4. Uses a variety of techniques and social skills in a flexible manner as the situation demands
5. Produces data in the form of extensive written notes, as well as diagrams, maps, or pictures to provide very detailed descriptions
6. Sees events holistically (e.g., as a whole unit, not in pieces) and individually in their social context
7. Understands and develops empathy for members in a field setting, and does not only record "cold" objective facts
8. Notices both explicit (recognized, conscious, spoken) and tacit (less recognized, implicit, unspoken) aspects of culture
9. Observes ongoing social processes without imposing an outside point of view
10. Copes with high levels of personal stress, uncertainty, ethical dilemmas, and ambiguity

Source: From W. Lawrence Neuman, *Social Research Methods, Qualitative and Quantitative Approaches,* 6/e. Published by Allyn and Bacon, 75 Arlington St., Boston, MA 02116. Copyright © 2006 by Pearson Education. Reprinted by permission of the publisher.

TABLE 12.2 Steps in Field Research

1. Prepare oneself, read the literature, and defocus.
2. Select a field site and gain access to it.
3. Enter the field and establish social relations with members.
4. Adopt a social role, learn the ropes, and get along with members.
5. Watch, listen, and collect quality data.
6. Begin to analyze data and to generate and evaluate working hypotheses.
7. Focus on specific aspects of the setting and use theoretical sampling.
8. Conduct field interviews with member informants.
9. Disengage and physically leave the setting.
10. Complete the analyses and write the research report.

Note: There is no fixed percentage of time needed for each step. For a rough approximation, Junker (1960:12) suggested that, once in the field, the researcher should expect to spend approximately one-sixth of his or her time observing; one-third, recording data; one-third of the time analyzing data; and one-sixth, reporting results. Also see Denzin (1989:176) for eight steps of field research.

Source: From W. Lawrence Neuman, *Social Research Methods, Qualitative and Quantitative Approaches,* 6/e. Published by Allyn and Bacon, 75 Arlington St., Boston, MA 02116. Copyright © 2006 by Pearson Education. Reprinted by permission of the publisher.

Steps in a Field Research Project

Field research is less structured than quantitative research. This makes it essential to be well organized and prepared before entering the field. As seen in Table 12.2, the steps of a project only serve as an approximate guide or road map.

FLEXIBILITY. Field researchers rarely follow fixed steps. Flexibility is a key advantage of field research, which lets a researcher shift direction and follow leads. Good field researchers recognize and seize opportunities, "play it by ear," and rapidly adjust to fluid social situations.

A field researcher does not begin with a set of methods to apply or explicit hypotheses to test. Rather, he or she chooses techniques on the basis of their value for providing information. In the beginning, the researcher expects little control over data and little focus. Once socialized to the setting, however, he or she focuses the inquiry.

ORGANIZED FLEXIBILITY. Human and personal factors can play a role in any research project, but they are crucial in field research. Field projects often begin with chance occurrences or a personal interest. Field researchers can begin with their own experiences or the experiences of friends or families.[5] One of Kraska's research methods students interviewed her aunt who ran an illegal prescription drug operation out of her home (small-term projects such as these are sometimes called *microethnographies*).

Field researchers use the skills of careful looking and listening, short-term memory, and regular writing. Before entering the field, we should practice observing the ordinary details of situations and later writing them down. Attention to details and short-term memory can improve with practice. Likewise, keeping a daily diary or personal journal is good practice for writing field notes.

As with all crime and justice research, reading the scholarly literature helps us learn concepts, potential pitfalls, data collection methods, and techniques for resolving conflicts. In addition, we may find diaries, novels, journalistic accounts, and autobiographies useful for gaining familiarity and preparing emotionally for the field. Of course, we have to be careful not to form ideas and theories prior to our data collection. We must remain open to discovering new ideas. Finding the right questions to ask about the field takes time.

Another preparation for field research is self-knowledge (reflexivity). A field researcher needs to know him or herself and reflect on personal experiences. We should expect anxiety, self-doubt, frustration, and uncertainty in the field. Especially in the beginning, a researcher may feel disoriented and suffer from emotional turmoil, isolation, and confusion. He or she may feel doubly marginal: an outsider in the field setting and also more distant from friends, family, and other researchers.[6] The relevance of our emotional makeup, personal biography, and cultural experiences makes it important to be aware of our personal commitments and inner conflicts (see the later section on stress in this chapter).

Fieldwork can have a strong impact on a researcher's identity and outlook. Researchers have been personally transformed by the field experience. Some adopt new values, interests, and moral commitments, or change their religion or political ideology.[7] Jeff Ferrell (1997: 2) admits to "going native" in his research on graffiti artists, even to the point of being arrested.

> By this time I have engaged in almost two years of intensive participant observation inside the underground—that is, inside the world of nongang graffiti writers. . . . Suddenly two cars round the corner into the alley a block and a half away. . . . The other writers and I run for it. . . . In the next instant I am pinned against the fence by a policeman. . . . A month later I appear in court.

Ferrell notes the numerous other ethnographic researchers who also blurred the line between criminality and criminology—including Becker's famous study of marijuana-smoking jazz musicians and Adler's study of cocaine dealers. As you remember from the ethics chapter, ethnographic field research can get quite sticky ethically.

CHOOSING A SITE AND GAINING ACCESS

Although a field research project does not proceed by fixed steps, some common concerns arise in the early stages. These include selecting a site, gaining access to the site, entering the field, and developing rapport with members in the field.

Selecting a Site

WHERE TO OBSERVE.   Field researchers talk about doing research on a setting, or **field site,** but this term is misleading. A site is the context in which events or activities occur, a socially defined territory with shifting boundaries. A social group may interact across several physical sites. For example, Polsky's (1997) fieldwork with heroin users and dealers illustrates the shifting boundaries of his field site: "During the summer of 1960 . . . I spent much time with people involved in heroin use and distribution, in their natural settings: on rooftops, in apartments, in tenement hallways, on stoops, in streets, in automobiles, in parks and taverns" (p. 224).

The field site and research question are bound up together, but choosing a site is not the same as focusing on a case for study. A case is a social relationship or activity; it can extend beyond the boundaries of the site and have links to other social settings. A researcher selects a site, and then identifies cases to examine within it—for example, how football team members relate to authority figures.

Selecting a field site is an important decision, and we should take notes on the site selection processes. Three factors are relevant when choosing a field research site: richness of data, unfamiliarity, and suitability.[8] Some sites are more likely than others to provide rich data. Sites that present a web of social relations, a variety of activities, and diverse events over time provide richer, more interesting data. Beginning field researchers should choose an unfamiliar setting because it is easier to see cultural events and social relations in a new site. Bogdan and Taylor (1975: 28) noted, "We would recommend that researchers choose settings in which the subjects are strangers and in which they have no particular professional knowledge or expertise." When "casing" possible field sites, we must consider such practical issues as your time and skills, serious conflicts among people in the site, personal characteristics and feelings, and access to parts of a site.

FIELD SITE

The one or more natural locations where a researcher conducts field research.

Our ascriptive characteristics can limit access. For example, an African-American researcher cannot hope to study the Ku Klux Klan or neo-Nazis, although some researchers have successfully crossed ascriptive lines.[9] Sometimes "insider" and "outsider" teams can work together. Skolnick's (1994: 35) participant observation of the Westville police serves as a good example of this:

> I could walk into a bar looking for a dangerous armed robber who was reportedly there without undergoing much danger myself because I would not be recognized as a police officer. Similarly, I could drive a disguised truck, with a couple of officers hidden in the rear, up to a building without the lookout recognizing me.

LEVEL OF INVOLVEMENT. Field roles can be arranged on a continuum by the degree of detachment or involvement a researcher has with members. At one extreme is a detached outsider; at the other extreme is an intimately involved insider. The range of field roles is described in three systems developed by Junker, Gans, and the Adlers.

Adler and Adler (1987) suggest three roles.

- *Peripheral membership* means maintaining distance between self and those studied, or setting limits by the researcher's beliefs or discomfort with the members' activities.
- *Active membership* means that the researcher assumes a membership role and goes through a similar induction into membership and participates like a member. The researcher maintains high levels of trust and can withdraw from the field periodically.
- *Complete membership* means converting and **going native.** As a fully committed member, the researcher experiences the same emotions as others and finds it very difficult or impossible to leave the field and return to being a researcher.

The researcher's level of involvement depends on negotiations with members, specifics of the field setting, personal comfort level, and the particular role adopted in the field. Sometimes the level of involvement changes over the course of the research. Each level has its advantages and disadvantages. Different field researchers advocate different levels of involvement. For example, the Adlers's or Ferrell's complete member role is criticized by some for overinvolvement and loss of a researcher's perspective. Others argue that it is the only way to really understand a member's social world. Full involvement facilitates empathy and sharing of a member's experience and culture. Nevertheless, a lack of distance from or too much sympathy for members could compromise objectivity. This is because reports may be questioned, there can be a dramatic impact on the self, and the distance needed for analysis may be hard to attain.[10]

GOING NATIVE

When a researcher in field research gets overly involved and loses all distance or objectivity and becomes joined with the people being studied.

GATEKEEPER

Anyone the field research encounters who has formal or informal authority to control access to a site.

GATEKEEPERS. A **gatekeeper** is someone with the formal or informal authority to control access to a site. It can be the thug on the corner, an administrator of a hospital, or the owner of a business. Most formal organizations have authorities from whom permission to enter must be obtained.

We should expect to negotiate with gatekeepers and bargain for access. The gatekeepers may not appreciate the need for conceptual distance or ethical balance. We need to set nonnegotiable limits to protect research integrity. If there are many restrictions initially, we can often reopen negotiations later, and gatekeepers may forget their initial demands as trust develops. It is ethically and politically astute to call on gatekeepers. Many gatekeepers do not care about the findings, except insofar as these findings might provide evidence for someone to criticize them.

Richard Wright has been remarkably successful gaining access and valuable qualitative data from active criminals. In the following quote, he describes the importance of effectively using gatekeepers. Jacobs and Wright (2000: 11) relied on their trusted relationship with two street-based "field recruiters" to identify research subjects.

Each recruiter was himself an active member of the criminal underworld. Each also had extensive connections to networks of street offenders and, within those networks, enjoyed a solid reputation for integrity and trustworthiness. As Walker and Lidz (1977) remind us, when access to secret worlds is needed, "the individual who will establish the researcher's credentials must be well thought of by the other participants in the system." Without the properly located "gatekeeper," research of the type undertaken has virtually no chance of success.

INFORMANTS.　An **informant** or key actor in field research is a member with whom a field researcher develops a relationship and who tells about, or informs on, the field. Who makes a good informant? As seen in Table 12.3, the ideal informant has four characteristics.

　　The field researcher may use several types of informants. Contrasting types of informants who provide useful perspectives include rookies and old-timers, people in the center of events and those on the fringes of activity, people who recently changed status (e.g., through promotion) and those who are static, frustrated or needy people and happy or secure people, the leader in charge and the subordinate who follows.

INFORMANT

A key actor in field research with whom an ethnographer develops a relationship and who tells about, or informs on, the field.

Strategy for Entering

PLANNING.　Entering and gaining access to a field site depend on commonsense judgment and social skills. Field sites usually have different levels or areas, and entry is an issue for each. Entry is more analogous to peeling the layers of an onion than to opening a door. Moreover, bargains and promises of entry may not remain stable over time. We need fallback plans or may have to return later for renegotiation. Because the specific focus of research may not emerge until later in the research process or may change, it is best to avoid being locked into specifics by gatekeepers.

　　As seen in Figure 12.1, entry and access can be visualized as an **access ladder**. We begin at the bottom rung, where access is easy and where you are an outsider looking for public information. The next rung requires increased access. Once close on-site observation begins, we become a passive observer, not questioning what members say. With time in the field, we observe specific activities that are potentially sensitive or seek clarification of what we see or hear. Reaching this access rung is more difficult. Finally, we may try to shape interaction so that it reveals specific information, or we may want to see highly sensitive material. This highest rung of the access ladder is difficult to access and requires deep trust.[11]

ACCESS LADDER

Field researchers may be able to see and learn about only public, noncontroversial events in the beginning, but with time and effort they can gain entry to more hidden, intimate, and controversial information.

TABLE 12.3	The Ideal Field Research Informant

1. The informant who is totally familiar with the culture and is in position to witness significant events makes a good informant. He or she lives and breathes the culture, and engages in routines in the setting without thinking about them. The individual has years of intimate experience in the culture; he or she is not a novice.
2. The individual is currently involved in the field. Ex-members who have reflected on the field may provide useful insights, but the longer they have been away from direct involvement, the more likely it is that they have reconstructed their recollections.
3. The person can spend time with the researcher. Interviewing may take many hours, and some members are simply not available for extensive interviewing.
4. Nonanalytic individuals make better informants. A nonanalytic informant is familiar with and uses native folk theory or pragmatic common sense. This is in contrast to the analytic member, who preanalyzes the setting, using categories from the media or education. Even members educated in the social sciences can learn to respond in a nonanalytic manner, but only if they set aside their education and use the member perspective.

Source: From W. Lawrence Neuman, *Social Research Methods, Qualitative and Quantitative Approaches,* 6/e. Published by Allyn and Bacon, 75 Arlington St., Boston, MA 02116. Copyright © 2006 by Pearson Education. Reprinted by permission of the publisher.

FIGURE 12.1 The Access Ladder *Source:* From W. Lawrence Neuman, *Social Research Methods, Qualitative and Quantitative Approaches,* 6/e. Published by Allyn and Bacon, 75 Arlington St., Boston, MA 02116. Copyright © 2006 by Pearson Education. Reprinted by permission of the publisher.

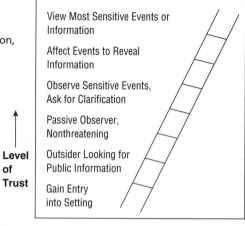

NEGOTIATION.   Social relations are negotiated and formed throughout the process of field-work.[12] Negotiation occurs with each new member until a stable relationship develops to gain access, develop trust, obtain information, and reduce hostile reactions. We should expect to negotiate and explain what we are doing over and over in the field (see the discussion of normalizing social research, to follow).

Deviant groups and elites often require special negotiations for gaining access. To gain access to deviant subcultures, field researchers have used contacts from the researcher's private life, gone to social welfare or law enforcement agencies where the deviants are processed, advertised for volunteers, offered a service (e.g., counseling) in exchange for access, or gone to a location where deviants hang out and joined a group. For example, Harper (1982) gained access by living in a skid-row mission without any money and befriending homeless men who knew street life. Bart (1987) argued that her background as a feminist activist and her nonprofessional demeanor were essential for gaining access to an illegal feminist abortion clinic.[13]

Polsky (1997: 22) suggested a rather novel technique:

Getting an initial introduction or two is not nearly so difficult as it might seem. Among students whom I have had perform the experiment of asking their relatives and friends to see if any could provide an introduction to a career criminal, fully a third reported that they could get such introductions.

Kraska, in his qualitative research classes over the years, has had students write about their families' or friends' involvement in drug dealing, making moonshine, snake handling (as part of a religious ceremony), dog and rooster fighting, burglary, domestic violence, police crime and deviance, courtroom corruption, and juvenile detention officer abuse of juveniles, to name just a few. The real world is filled with ethnographic field research opportunities—we just have to look.

DISCLOSURE.   We must decide how much to reveal about ourselves and the research project. Disclosing details about our personal life, hobbies, interests, and background can build trust and close relationships, but we also lose privacy and we need to ensure that the focus remains on events in the field.

Disclosure ranges on a continuum from fully covert research, in which no one in the field is aware that research is taking place, to the opposite end, where everyone knows the specifics of the research project (see Chapter 1 on covert research). The degree and timing of disclosure depend on a researcher's judgment and particulars in the setting. Disclosure may unfold over time as the researcher feels more secure.

Entering the Field

After a field site is selected and access obtained, we must learn the ropes, develop rapport with members, adopt a role in the setting, and maintain social relations. Before confronting such issues, we should ask, How will I present myself? What does it mean for me to be a "measurement instrument"? How can I assume an "attitude of strangeness"? Highlight 12.2 provides a look at Richard Wright's means of entry into the field.

PRESENTATION OF SELF.   People explicitly and implicitly manage the impression of themselves to others. We display who we are—the type of person we are or would like to be—through our physical appearance, what we say, and how we act. The presentation of self sends a symbolic message. It may be, "I'm a serious, hard-working student," "I'm a warm and caring person," "I'm a cool jock," or "I'm a rebel and wanna-be anarchist." Many selves are possible, and presentations of selves can differ depending on the occasion.

A good field researcher is very conscious of the presentation of self in the field. For example, how should we dress in the field? The best guide is to respect both yourself and those being studied. We don't want to overdress so as to offend or stand out, but copying the dress of those being studied is not always necessary. A professor who studies street people does not have to dress or act like one; dressing and acting informally are sufficient. Likewise, more formal dress and professional demeanor are usually required when studying corporate executives or top criminal justice officials.[14]

A researcher must be aware that self-presentation will influence field relations to some degree. It is difficult to present a highly deceptive front or to present oneself in a way that deviates sharply from the person one is ordinarily.

Patricia Gangé (1996) used ethnographic field research to better understand Appalachian culture and its relationship to domestic violence and patriarchal control. She describes how she had to act out a different identity to gain access to her research members. She needed to convince the "head of the household" that she was sympathetic to the "man's point of view."

HIGHLIGHT 12.2
Entering the Field with Active Burglars

Richard Wright et al. (1992: 150), in the article "A Snowball's Chance in Hell: Doing Fieldwork with Active Residential Burglars," describe the unique and efficient tactic they used to gain access to active burglars.

> A commonly suggested means of making initial contact with active offenders . . . involves frequenting locales favored by criminals. This strategy, however, requires an extraordinary investment of time as the researcher establishes a street reputation as an "all right square" (Irwin 1972: 123) who can be trusted. Fortunately we were able to shortcut that process by hiring an ex-offender (who, despite committing hundreds of serious crimes, had few arrests and no felony convictions) with high status among several groups of Black street criminals in St. Louis. This person retired from crime after being shot and paralyzed in a gangland-style execution attempt.

He then attended a university and earned a bachelor's degree, but continued to live in his old neighborhood, remaining friendly, albeit superficially, with local criminals. We initially met him when he attended a colloquium in our department. . . .

> This approach offers the advantage that such a person already has contacts and trust in the criminal subculture and can vouch for the legitimacy of the research. In order to exploit this advantage fully, however, the ex-offender selected must be someone with a solid street reputation for integrity and must have a strong commitment to accomplishing the goals of the study.

Despite the importance of making solid contacts, a researcher would still have to be quite skilled in presenting oneself in a manner that wouldn't generate suspicion or disrespect.

To gain his trust, she presented herself in a manner very foreign to her actual identity, by behaving according to feminine gender norms within the community . . . washing the dishes, cleaning the house, asking permission to leave the house, and deferring to men's decisions about daily activities. In short, she emulated women in the community through presentation of self. Over time she gained his trust, and he began to serve as both a guide, explaining the cultural significance of local events and relationships, and as a patron, securing the trust of men in the community. (Tewksbury and Gangé 1996: 57)

RESEARCHER AS INSTRUMENT. The researcher is the instrument for measuring field data. This has two implications. First, it puts pressure on the researcher to be alert and sensitive to what happens in the field and to be disciplined about recording data. Second, it has personal consequences. Fieldwork involves social relationships and personal feelings. Field researchers are flexible about what to include as data and admit their own subjective insights and feelings, or "experiential data."[15] Consistent with the notion of reflexivity, personal, subjective experiences are part of field data. They are valuable both in themselves and for interpreting events in the field. Instead of trying to be objective and eliminate personal reactions, field researchers treat their feelings toward field events as data. For example, as seen in Highlight 12.3, Kraska (2001a) used his simultaneous feelings of enjoyment and discomfort while training with SWAT officers as an opportunity for theorizing.

Field research can heighten a researcher's awareness of personal feelings, and these personal feelings can be highly instructive. The researchers' own feelings of repulsion, surprise, indignation, or questioning are key opportunities for reflection and theoretical insight.[16]

AN ATTITUDE OF STRANGENESS. It is hard to recognize what we take for granted. The everyday world we inhabit is filled with thousands of details. If we paid attention to everything all the time, we would suffer from severe information overload. We manage by ignoring much of what is around us and by engaging in habitual thinking. Unfortunately, we fail to see the familiar as distinctive, and assume that others experience reality just as we do. We tend to treat our own way of living as natural or normal.

HIGHLIGHT 12.3
Enjoying Militarism

The following quote is found in the conclusion of an article based on a two-year ethnography with rural SWAT teams and military personnel involved in their formation. Reflexivity allows the researcher to use personal reactions to his or her experience as part of the data, and to make *third-order interpretations* (Chapter 4). "Mike" and "Steve" were the two main informants.

> . . . This ethnography illustrates the powerful and enduring nature of militarism. My enjoyment of and effortless blending into these paramilitary rituals tapped into my own deeply embedded militarized scripts. As importantly, it provides a window through which to view broader processes of militarism and militarization as they relate to the criminal justice apparatus.
>
> The identities of Mike and Steve are products of a long-standing cultural environment which actively promotes the notion that a man's

worth increases in proportion to his ability to be a warrior. This influential spirit of militarism is unmistakable in video and computer games, toys, television shows, and movies marketed to boys. The appeal of these pedagogical devices derives from their recreational nature. As with my own ethnographic experience, militarism is enjoyed and embraced, as well as imposed. Through learning, enjoying, and internalizing the tenets of militarism, the personal ideological framework for many of our youths is pre-constructed to be receptive to violence and war, whether with other nations, other gangs, drug law violators, or the police. Growing older, for many, only changes and amplifies the organization, hardware, and the consequences. Militarism has been historically and continues to be today a seductive, pleasurable, and embedded component of social life. (Kraska 2001a: 154)

Familiarity can blind us to important observations. In fact, "intimate acquaintance with one's own culture can create as much blindness as insight" (McCracken 1988: 12). By studying other cultures, researchers often encounter dramatically different assumptions about what is important and how things are done. This confrontation of cultures, or *culture shock*, has two benefits: It makes it easier to see cultural elements and it facilitates self-discovery. Researchers adopt the **attitude of strangeness** to gain these benefits. The attitude of strangeness means we question and notice ordinary details or look at the ordinary through the eyes of a stranger. Strangeness helps us to overcome the boredom of observing ordinary details. It helps us see in a way that reveals aspects of the setting of which members are not consciously aware.

Building Rapport

A field researcher **builds rapport** by getting along with members in the field. He or she forges a friendly relationship, shares the same language, and laughs and cries with members. This is a step toward obtaining an understanding of members and moving beyond understanding to empathy—that is, seeing and feeling events from another's perspective.

It is not always easy to build rapport. The social world is not all in harmony, with warm, friendly people. A setting may contain fear, tension, and conflict. Members may be unpleasant, untrustworthy, or untruthful; they may do things that disturb or disgust a researcher. An experienced researcher is prepared for a range of events and relationships. He or she may find, however, that it is impossible to get really close to members. Settings in which cooperation, sympathy, and collaboration are impossible require different techniques.[17] Also, the researcher accepts what he or she hears or sees at face value, but without being gullible. As Schatzman and Strauss (1973: 69) remarked, "The researcher believes 'everything' and 'nothing' simultaneously."

CHARM AND TRUST.   We need social skills and personal charm to build rapport. Trust, friendly feelings, and being well liked facilitate communication and help us understand the inner feelings of others. There is no magical way to do this. Showing a genuine concern for and interest in others, being honest, and sharing feelings are good strategies, but they are not foolproof. It depends on the specific setting and members.

Many factors affect trust and rapport—how we present ourselves; the role we choose for the field; and the events that encourage, limit, or make it impossible to achieve trust. Trust is not gained once and for all. It is a developmental process built up over time through many social nuances (e.g., sharing of personal experiences, storytelling, gestures, hints, and facial expressions). It is constantly re-created and seems easier to lose once it has been built up than to gain in the first place.

Establishing trust is important, but it does not ensure that all information will be revealed. It may be limited to specific areas of inquiry. Trust is also often tested in the field and must be constantly reaffirmed, as the following quote suggests:

> A number of [robbery] offenders tested us by asking what a criminal associate said about a particular matter. We declined to discuss such issues, explaining that the promise of confidentiality extended to all those participating in our research. (Wright et al. 1996: 5)

A high level of trust can also come from friendship. Steffensmeier (2005: 20) gained such a rapport and trust with his informant-friend Sam Goodman that Sam even confessed to a murder during a deathbed interview. In Sam's words,

> I had to put a motherfucker to sleep. I did it because I had to. I would've ended up with a lotta time otherwise. . . . Wasn't really a decision on my part. Knew what I had to do. He was hurt bad. Needed to go to the hospital, get sewed up. But then questions would be asked. It would come out what happened and I'm back doing time. . . . You have to do what you have to do. I wish there had been another way.

UNDERSTANDING.   Rapport helps us understand members, but understanding is a precondition for greater depth, not an end in itself. It slowly develops in the field as we overcome an initial bewilderment with a new or unusual language and system of social meaning. Once we attain an understanding of the member's point of view, the next step is to learn how to think and act within a member's perspective. This is empathy, or adopting another's perspective. Empathy does not necessarily mean sympathy, agreement, or approval; it means feeling things as another does.[18] Criminological **verstehen**

> denotes a researcher's subjective understanding of crime's [and criminal justice's] situational meanings and emotions—its moments of pleasure and pain, its emergent logic, and excitement. . . . It further implies that a researcher, through attentiveness and participation, at least can begin to apprehend and appreciate the specific roles and experiences of criminals, crime victims, and crime control agents. . . . Ferrell (1997: 10)

Rapport helps create understanding and ultimately empathy, and the development of empathy facilitates greater rapport.

VERSTEHEN

A central objective of the ethnographic field research that requires a deep empathy with those being studied and their culture.

RELATIONS IN THE FIELD

We play many social roles in daily life—daughter/son, student, customer, and sports fan—and maintain social relations with others. We choose some roles and others are structured for us. Few have a choice but to play the role of son or daughter. Some roles are formal (e.g., bank teller, police chief), others are informal (e.g., flirt, elder statesperson, buddy). We can switch roles, play multiple roles, and play a role in a particular way. Field researchers play roles in the field. In addition, they learn the ropes and maintain relations with members.

Roles in the Field

PREEXISTING VERSUS CREATED ROLES.   At times, a researcher adopts an existing role. Some existing roles provide access to all areas of the site, the ability to observe and interact with all members, the freedom to move around, and a way to balance the requirements of researcher and member. At other times, a researcher modifies an existing role or even creates a new role. Wright and associates (1996), for example, played the role of a helper, which fostered rapport with their subjects (i.e., currently active residential burglars):

> We took subjects to job interviews or work, helped some enroll in school, and gave others advice on legal matters. We even assisted a juvenile offender who was injured while running away from the police, to arrange for emergency surgery when his parents, fearing that they would be charged for the operation, refused to give their consent. (p. 5)

The adoption of a field role takes time and will probably evolve during the course of the fieldwork. Let it happen.

NEGOTIATIONS AND DANGER.   Most field sites contain informal groups, hierarchies, and rivalries. The researcher must therefore take heed in the relations he or she is forming that one does not unnecessarily close off other parts of the field site. Again, the field study of burglars by Wright, Decker, and colleagues (1996) is instructive. The following passage points to the delicate negotiations that field researchers must do to keep rapport and channels of communication open and free flowing:

> Over the course of the research, numerous disputes arose between offenders and informants over the payment of referral fees. We resisted becoming involved in these disputes, reckoning that such involvement could only result in the alienation of one or both parties. Instead, we made it clear that our funds were intended as interview payments and thus would be given only to interviewees. (p. 4)

In short, the researcher needs to be aware that by adopting a role, he or she may be forming allies and enemies who can assist or limit the fieldwork.

Danger and high risk are aspects of some settings (e.g., police work and violent criminal gangs). A field researcher should be aware of risks to his or her safety, assess the risks, and then decide what he or she is willing to do. Some observers argue that a field researcher needs to share in the risks and danger of a setting to truly understand it and the experiences of participants. For example, Westmarland (2000) argued that only by putting on a safety vest while rushing to the scene of violent crime and then dodging bullets along with police officers can a researcher acquire an insider's view. Taking risks means that some researchers have had "near misses" or been injured.

Learning the Ropes

As a researcher learns the ropes on the field site, he or she learns how to cope with personal stress, how to normalize the social research, and how to act like an "acceptable incompetent."

STRESS.   Fieldwork can be highly rewarding, exciting, and fulfilling, but it also can be difficult:

> Fieldwork must certainly rank with the more disagreeable activities that humanity has fashioned for itself. It is usually inconvenient, to say the least, sometimes physically uncomfortable, frequently embarrassing, and, to a degree, always tense. (Shaffir et al. 1980: 3)

New researchers face embarrassment, experience discomfort, and are overwhelmed by the details in the field.

Instead of suppressing emotional responses, the field researcher is sensitive to emotional reactions. He or she copes in the field by keeping a personal diary, emotional journal, or written record of inner feelings, or by having sympathetic people outside the field site to confide.[19]

NORMALIZING CRIME AND JUSTICE RESEARCH.   A field researcher not only observes and investigates members in the field but is observed and investigated by members as well:

> In studying a criminal it is important to realize that he will be studying you, and to let him study you. Don't evade or shut off any questions he might have about your personal life, even if those questions are designed to "take you down," for example, designed to force you to admit that you too have knowingly violated the law. He has got to define you satisfactorily to himself and his colleagues if you are to get anywhere, and answering his questions frankly helps this process along. (Polsky 1997: 223)

In overt field research, members are usually initially uncomfortable with the presence of a researcher. Most are unfamiliar with field research and fail to distinguish between criminologists, crime control workers, or social workers. They may see the researcher as an outside critic or spy, or as a savior or all-knowing expert.

An overt field researcher must **normalize field research**—that is, help members redefine research from something unknown and threatening to something normal and predictable. He or she can help members manage research by presenting his or her own biography, explaining field research a little at a time, appearing nonthreatening, or accepting minor deviance in the setting (e.g., minor violations of official rules).[20]

Another way to normalize research is to explain it in terms members understand. Sometimes, members' excitement about being written up in a book is useful. And sometimes it is

NORMALIZE FIELD RESEARCH

Techniques in field research to make the people being studied feel more comfortable with the research process and to help them accept the researcher's presence.

not, as Klockars (1974: 201–202), in his classic work *The Fence*, found out when trying to convince "Knuckles," a professional fence, to cooperate in the field research:

> My strategy in trying to convince Knuckles to talk to me was to offer him a kind of anonymous immortality in exchange for information. To have someone want to write a book about you is for most people, I suspect, flattering. I hoped to convince Knuckles that he could have a book written about him even if the details had to be changed to protect his true identity. The day after I talked to Knuckles on the phone I visited him at the hospital. I brought a copy of Sutherland's *The Professional Thief* with me. . . . I hoped it would serve as a precedent—as evidence that another criminal had seen fit to work with a college professor in recounting the details of his occupation. . . . Although I think the strategy was sound, it did not work.

ACCEPTABLE INCOMPETENT. A researcher is in the field to learn, not to be an expert. Depending on the setting, he or she appears to be a friendly but naive outsider, an acceptable incompetent who is interested in learning about the social life of the field. An **acceptable incompetent** is someone who is partially competent (skilled or knowledgeable) in the setting but who is accepted as a nonthreatening person who needs to be taught.[21] As Schatzman and Strauss (1973: 25) noted, "The researcher should play down any expertise or profound knowledge he may have on the subject on which the hosts may claim to be expert; the researcher is and should act the learner, indicating no inclination to evaluate the host's activities."

A field researcher may know little about the setting or subculture at first. He or she may be seen as a fool who is hoodwinked or short-changed, and may be the butt of jokes for his or her lack of adeptness in the setting. Even when the researcher is knowledgeable, he or she displays less than full information to draw out a member's knowledge. Of course, the researcher can overdo this and appear so ignorant or incompetent that he or she de-legitimizes oneself.

Maintaining Relations

SMALL FAVORS. **Exchange relationships** develop in the field, in which small tokens or favors, including deference and respect, are exchanged.[22] A researcher may gain acceptance by helping out in small ways. Exchange helps when access to sensitive issues is limited. A researcher may offer small favors but not burden members by asking for return favors. As the researcher and members share experiences and see each other again, members recall the favors and reciprocate by allowing access. This was certainly Steffensmeier's (2005) experience where he became very close friends with his main informant, Sam Goodman, even up to the time of Sam's death. Similarly, Klockars (1974: 219) described a close relationship with his informant "Vincent," a professional fence:

> I ate with him, drank with him, learned from him, invited him to my home, brought him cakes my wife had baked, brought my family to his store, drove him in my car, visited him in the hospital, sent him birthday cards, and showed him my son's baby pictures.

Some feminist ethnographers, in fact, encourage this type of human connection, and believe that helping women in need is as important as the collection of data.

CONFLICTS IN THE FIELD. Fights, conflict, and disagreements can erupt in the field, or a researcher may study groups with opposing positions. In such situations, the researcher will feel pressure to take sides and will be tested to see if he or she can be trusted. In such occasions, a researcher usually stays on the neutral sidelines and walks a tightrope between opposing sides. This is because once he or she becomes aligned with one side, the researcher will cut off access to the other side, and in some cases, his or her personal safety may be at stake.[23]

ACCEPTABLE INCOMPETENT

When a field researcher pretends to be less skilled or knowledgeable in order to learn more about a field site.

EXCHANGE RELATIONSHIPS

A relationship between ethnographer and informant in which small tokens or favors, including deference and respect, are exchanged.

In addition, he or she will see the situation from only one point of view. Nevertheless, some (e.g., Van Maanen 1982: 115) argue that true neutrality is illusory. As a researcher becomes involved with members and embroiled in webs of relationships and commitments, neutrality becomes almost impossible.

APPEARING INTERESTED.   Field researchers maintain an **appearance of interest** in the field. An experienced researcher appears to be interested in and involved with field events by statements and behaviors (e.g., facial expression, going for coffee, organizing a party) even if he or she is not truly interested. This is because field relations may be disrupted if the researcher appears to be bored or distracted. Putting up such a temporary front of involvement is a common small deception in daily life and is part of being polite.[24]

Of course, selective inattention (i.e., not staring or appearing not to notice) is also part of acting polite. If a person makes a social mistake (e.g., accidentally uses an incorrect word, passes gas), the polite thing to do is to ignore it. Selective inattention is used in fieldwork, as well. It gives an alert researcher an opportunity to learn by casually eavesdropping on conversations or observing events not meant to be public.

APPEARANCE OF INTEREST

An experienced researcher appears to be interested in and involved with field events by statements and behaviors (e.g., facial expression, going for coffee, or organizing a party) even if he or she is not truly interested.

OBSERVING AND COLLECTING DATA

This section looks at how to get good qualitative field data. Field data are what we experience, remember, and record in field notes.

Watching and Listening with Care

KEENLY OBSERVANT.   A great deal of what researchers do in the field is to pay close attention, watch, and listen carefully. They use all the senses, noticing what is seen, heard, smelled, tasted, or touched. The researcher becomes an instrument that absorbs all sources of information.

A field researcher carefully scrutinizes the physical setting to capture its atmosphere. He or she asks the following questions: What is the color of the floor, walls, ceiling? How large is a room? Where are the windows and doors? How is the furniture arranged, and what is its condition (e.g., new or old and worn, dirty or clean)? What type of lighting is there? Are there signs, paintings, or plants? What are the sounds or smells?

Why bother with such details? You may have noticed that stores and restaurants often plan lighting, colors, and piped-in music to create a certain atmosphere. Maybe you know that used-car salespeople spray a new-car scent into cars, or that shops in shopping malls intentionally send out the odor of freshly made cookies. These subtle, unconscious signals influence human behavior.

Observing in field research is often detailed, tedious work. Silverman (1993: 30) noted, "If you go to the cinema to see action [car chases, hold-ups, etc.], then it is unlikely that you will find it easy to be a good observer." Instead of the quick flash, motivation arises out of a deep curiosity about the details. Good ethnographic field researchers are intrigued about details that reveal "what's going on here" through careful listening and watching. They believe that the core of social life and its meaning is communicated through the mundane, trivial, everyday minutia. This is what people often overlook, but field researchers need to learn how to notice.

We must record such details because something of significance might be revealed. It is better to err by including everything than to ignore potentially significant details. For example, "the tall, White muscular nineteen-year-old male in a torn tee shirt and dirty jeans sprinted into the brightly lit room just as the short, overweight light-skinned Black woman in her sixties who was professionally dressed eased into a battered chair" says much more than "one person entered, another sat down."

We should also note aspects of physical appearance such as neatness, dress, and hairstyle because they express meaning. Criminals, victims, and criminal justice practitioners can spend a great deal of time and money selecting clothes, styling and combing hair, grooming with makeup, shaving, ironing clothes, and using deodorant or perfumes. These are part of their presentation of self.

Even people who do not groom, shave, or wear deodorant present themselves and send a symbolic message by their appearance. For example, if a police department's road patrol officers' hairstyle of choice is the traditional marine-style haircut, it potentially tells us something about their subculture.

What people do is also significant. A field researcher notices where people sit or stand, the pace at which they walk, and their nonverbal communication. People express social information, feelings, and attitudes through nonverbal communication, including gestures, facial expressions, and how one stands or sits (standing stiffly, sitting in a slouched position, etc.). People express relationships by how they position themselves in a group and through eye contact. A researcher may read social communication by noting that people are standing close together, looking relaxed, and making eye contact. We can also notice the context in which events occur: Who was present? Who just arrived or left the scene? Was the room hot and stuffy? Such details may help us assign meaning and understand why an event occurred. If they are not noticed, the details are lost, as is a full understanding of the event. Remember when we mentioned earlier how qualitative research draws on the skills we learn in everyday life? We assess all of these signs, although sometimes subconsciously, thousands of times a day. Noticing and inferring meaning to these cultural signs is critical to quality ethnographic field research.

A good field researcher listens carefully to phrases, accents, and incorrect grammar, listening both to what is said and how it is said or what was implied. Single phrases can harbor literally pages worth of meaning, and sometimes end up framing an entire project. A child being abused by a parent, for example, might say, "I never get to sleep," likely meant both literally and figuratively. Upon further examination, this phrase might reveal stress-induced insomnia (literal meaning), as well as a home environment so unsafe physically and sexually that true rest is not possible (figurative meaning).

ARGOT OR SPECIALIZED LANGUAGE. People who interact with each other over a period of time develop shared symbols and terminology. They create new words or assign new meanings to ordinary words. New words develop out of specific events, assumptions, or relations. Knowing and using the language can signal membership in a distinct subculture. A field researcher learns the specialized language, or **argot.**[25]

ARGOT

The special language or terminology used by the members of a subculture or group that interacts regularly.

A field researcher discovers how the argot fits into social relations or meanings. The argot gives a researcher clues to what is important to members and how they see the world. In Sutherland's classic field study, *The Professional Thief* (1937), slang terms are used to refer to amateur thieves. A few of them are "snatch-and-grab thief," "boot-and-shoe thief," and "raw-jaw" method. These terms clearly convey the low opinion professionals have of amateurs.

Wright and colleagues (1996:5) familiarized themselves with the field argot of burglars before conducting the fieldwork, as indicated here:

> We made an effort to "fit in" by learning the distinctive terminology and phrases used by the offenders. Here again, the assistance of the ex-offender proved invaluable. Prior to entering the field, he suggested ways in which questions might be asked so that the subjects would better understand them, and provided us with a working knowledge of popular street terms (e.g., "boy" for heroin, "girl" for cocaine) and pronunciations (e.g., "hair ron" for heroin).

Taking Notes

Most field research data are in the form of field notes. Full field notes can contain maps, diagrams, photographs, interviews, tape recordings, videotapes, memos, objects from the field, notes jotted in the field, and detailed notes written away from the field. We can expect to fill many notebooks or the equivalent in computer memory. We may spend more time writing notes than being in the field. Some researchers produce forty single-spaced pages of notes for three hours of observation. With practice, we should produce several pages of notes for each hour in the field.

Writing notes is often boring, tedious work that requires self-discipline. The notes contain extensive descriptive detail drawn from memory. Emerson and colleagues (1995: 40) argued that good field notes are as much a mind-set as an activity, and remarked, "Perhaps more crucial than how long the ethnographer spends in the field is the timing of writing up field notes. . . . Writing field notes immediately after leaving the setting provides fresher, more detailed recollections . . ." If possible, write notes before the day's thoughts and excitement begin to fade, without retelling events to others. Pouring fresh memories into the notes with an intense immediacy often triggers an emotional release and stimulates insightful reflection. Sometimes a researcher's most important theoretical insights can reveal themselves at this time. A good rule of thumb is to allocate about a half an hour to writing field notes for each hour spent in the field site.

The notes must be neat and organized because the researcher returns to them over and over again. Most researchers today store them on computer files so that they can use qualitative software packages to help in the analysis. Once written, the notes are private and valuable. They must be treated with care. Members have the right to remain anonymous, and researchers often use pseudonyms (false names) in notes. Field notes may be of interest to hostile parties, blackmailers, or legal officials, so some researchers write field notes in code.

TYPES OF FIELD NOTES.   Field researchers take notes in many ways (see Figure 12.2). Full field notes have several types or levels. Five levels will be described. It is usually best to keep all the notes together for an observation period and to distinguish types of notes by separate pages or computer files. Some researchers include inferences and insights along with direct observations and then clearly delineate the two with a visible device such as brackets, colored ink, or underlining. The quantity of notes varies across types. For example, six hours in the field might result in one page of jotted notes; forty pages of direct observation; five pages of researcher inference; and two pages total for methodological, theoretical, and personal notes. See Table 12.4.

Jotted Notes.   It is nearly impossible to take good notes in the field. Even a known observer in a public setting looks strange when furiously writing. More important, when looking down and writing, the researcher cannot see and hear what is happening. The attention given to note writing is taken from field observation where it belongs. The specific setting determines whether any notes in the field can be taken. The researcher may be able to write, and members may expect it, or he or she may have to be secretive (e.g., go to the restroom or use a digital recording device).

Jotted notes are written in the field. They are short, temporary memory triggers such as words, phrases, or drawings taken inconspicuously, often scribbled on any convenient item (e.g.,

JOTTED NOTES

Field notes inconspicuously written while in the field site on whatever is convenient to "jog the memory" later.

Direct Observation	Inference	Analytic	Personal Journal
Sunday, October 4. Kay's Kafe 3:00 pm. Large White male in mid-40s, overweight, enters. He wears worn brown suit. He is alone; sits at booth #2. Kay comes by, asks, "What'll it be?" Man says, "Coffee, black for now." She leaves and he lights cigarette and reads menu. 3:15 pm. Kay turns on radio.	Kay seems friendly today, humming. She becomes solemn and watchful. I think she puts on the radio when nervous.	Women are afraid of men who come in alone since the robbery.	It is raining. I am feeling comfortable with Kay but am bored today.

FIGURE 12.2 Types of Field Notes *Source:* From W. Lawrence Neuman, *Social Research Methods, Qualitative and Quantitative Approaches,* 6/e. Published by Allyn and Bacon, 75 Arlington St., Boston, MA 02116. Copyright © 2006 by Pearson Education. Reprinted by permission of the publisher.

TABLE 12.4	Recommendations for Taking Field Notes

1. Record notes as soon as possible after each period in the field, and do not talk with others until observations are recorded.
2. Begin the record of each field visit with a new page, with the date and time noted.
3. Use jotted notes only as a temporary memory aid, with keywords or terms, or the first and last things said.
4. Use wide margins to make it easy to add to notes at any time. Go back and add to the notes if you remember something later.
5. Plan to type notes and keep each level of notes separate so it will be easy to go back to them later.
6. Record events in the order in which they occurred, and note how long they lasted (e.g., a fifteen-minute wait, a one-hour ride).
7. Make notes as concrete, complete, and comprehensible as possible.
8. Use frequent paragraphs and quotation marks. Exact recall of phrases is best, with double quotes; use single quotes for paraphrasing.
9. Record small talk or routines that do not appear to be significant at the time; they may become important later.
10. "Let your feelings flow" and write quickly without worrying about spelling or "wild ideas." Assume that no one else will see the notes, but use pseudonyms.
11. Never substitute tape recordings completely for field notes.
12. Include diagrams or maps of the setting, and outline your own movements and those of others during the period of observation.
13. Include the researcher's own words and behavior in the notes. Also record emotions and feelings and private thoughts in a separate section.
14. Avoid evaluative summarizing words. Instead of "The sink looked disgusting," say, "The sink was rust-stained and looked as though it had not been cleaned in a long time. Pieces of food and dirty dishes looked as though they had been piled in it for several days."
15. Reread notes periodically and record ideas generated by the rereading.
16. Always make one or more backup copies, keep them in a locked location, and store the copies in different places in case of fire, flood, or theft.

Source: From W. Lawrence Neuman, *Social Research Methods, Qualitative and Quantitative Approaches,* 6/e. Published by Allyn and Bacon, 75 Arlington St., Boston, MA 02116. Copyright © 2006 by Pearson Education. Reprinted by permission of the publisher.

DIRECT OBSERVATION NOTES

Field research notes that attempt to include all details and specifics of what the researcher heard or saw in a field site, and are written to permit multiple interpretations later.

napkin, matchbook). They are incorporated into **direct observation notes** but are never substituted for them. These notes can sometimes be recorded into a digital recorder. Kraska has found these very helpful because of their small, inconspicuous size (some resemble a small cell phone) and their ability to record digitally—meaning that they can be easily converted into digital text.

Direct Observation Notes. The basic sources of field data are notes a researcher writes immediately after leaving the field, which he or she can add to later. The notes should be ordered chronologically with the date, time, and place noted on each entry. They serve as a detailed description of what the researcher heard and saw in concrete, specific terms. To the extent possible, they are an exact recording of the particular words, phrases, or actions.

An ethnographic field researcher's memory improves with practice. Verbatim statements should be written with double quote marks to distinguish them from paraphrases. Dialogue accessories (nonverbal communication, props, tone, speed, volume, gestures) should be recorded as well. Slang and slogans can be especially important to record accurately because they can contain rich meaning.

One SWAT officer Kraska researched, for example, wore a T-shirt during a training session that pictured an inner city under military siege—the caption read "Operation Ghetto Storm." Another SWAT commander had a framed pencil drawing on his office wall that showed two squad members suiting up to go on a deployment—the caption read "Time to Take out the

Garbage." Extracting the meaning from these visual images and the associated captions yielded rich insights about police paramilitary subculture.

Researcher Inference Notes.   Carefully listening to members and the visual worlds they reside in is critical to developing empathetic understanding.[26] This involves a three-step process: Listen without applying analytical categories; compare what is heard to what was heard at other times and to what others say; then apply our own interpretation to infer or figure out what it means. In ordinary interaction, we do all three steps simultaneously and jump quickly to our own inferences. A field researcher learns to look and listen without inferring or imposing an interpretation. His or her observations without inferences go into direct observation notes.

We can record inferences in a separate section that is keyed to direct observations. We never see social relationships, emotions, or meaning. We see specific physical actions and hear words, then use background cultural knowledge, clues from the context, and what is done or said to assign social meaning. For example, we do not see love or anger; we see and hear specific actions (red face, loud voice, wild gestures, and obscenities) and draw inferences from them (the person is angry).

Analytic Memos.   Researchers make many decisions about how to proceed while in the field. Some acts are planned (e.g., to conduct an interview, to observe a particular activity) and others seem to occur almost out of thin air. Field researchers keep methodological ideas in analytic notes to record their plans, tactics, ethical and procedural decisions, and self-critiques of tactics.

Theory emerges in field research during data collection and when reviewing field notes. Analytic notes have a running account of a researcher's attempts to give meaning to field events. He or she thinks out loud in the notes by suggesting links between ideas, creating hypotheses, proposing conjectures, and developing new concepts.

Analytic memos are part of the theoretical notes. They are systematic digressions into theory, where a researcher elaborates on ideas in depth, expands on ideas while still in the field, and modifies or develops more complex theory by re-reading and thinking about the memos.

Personal Notes.   As discussed earlier in our discussion of reflexivity, personal feelings and emotional reactions become part of the data and color what a researcher sees or hears in the field. A researcher keeps a section of notes that is like a personal diary. He or she records personal life events and feelings in it ("I'm tense today; I wonder if it's because of the fight I had yesterday with . . . "; "I've got a headache on this gloomy, overcast day and not sure if I want to deal with X's whining"). Personal notes provide a way to cope with stress; they are also a source of data about personal reactions; they help to evaluate direct observation or inference notes when the notes are later reread. More ethnographers are including their emotional and intellectual reactions to their field experiences within their scholarly writing.

Maps and Diagrams.   Ethnographic field researchers often make maps and draw diagrams or pictures of the features of a field site. This serves two purposes: It helps organize complex events and arrangements in the field and it helps convey a field site to others. For example, a researcher studying dog fighting in a rural barn in eastern Kentucky might keep the map written up by the informant and diagram the seating arrangement in relation to the "gaming pen." Field researchers develop maps that revolve around people, physical space, or even power dynamics.

Machine Recordings to Supplement Memory.   Tape recorders, cameras, and video cameras can be helpful supplements in field research. This is especially true today because many of these devices are small and inconspicuous. More and more people are comfortable with someone in their peer group recording their activities. They cannot be introduced into all field sites and can be used only after a researcher develops rapport. Recordings, photographs, and videotapes provide a close approximation to what occurred and a permanent record that others can review. They help a researcher recall events and observe what does not happen, or nonresponses, which are easy to miss.

Web-based academic journals exist that allow video links and photographs to be attached to an article, potentially providing the reader a more accurate and interesting visual sense of the

ANALYTIC MEMOS

Notes a qualitative researcher takes while developing more abstract ideas, themes, or hypotheses from an examination of details in the data.

Jeff Ferrell participates in the underground world of "scrounging."

FACE SHEET

A page at the beginning of interview or field notes with information on the date, place of observations, interviews, the context, and so on.

research setting. Jeff Ferrell's (2006) latest book, *Empire of Scrounge: Inside the Urban Underground of Dumpster Diving, Trash Picking, and Street Scavenging*, is replete with his own personal photographs of urban landscapes and the activity he studied and participated in. His work likely represents the future of ethnographic crime and justice field research where visual data are used both as a data collection tool and as powerful new form of presentation.

Interview Notes.   If a researcher conducts field interviews (to be discussed), he or she keeps the interview notes separate.[27] In addition to recording questions and answers, he or she creates a **face sheet.** This is a page placed at the beginning of the notes with information such as the date, place of interview, characteristics of interviewee, content of the interview, and so on. It helps the interviewer when re-reading and making sense of the notes.

Data Quality in Ethnographic Field Research

THE MEANING OF QUALITY.   What does the term *high-quality data* mean in field research, and what does a researcher do to get such data?[28] For a quantitative researcher, high-quality data are reliable and valid; they give precise, consistent measures of the same objective truth for all researchers. An interpretive approach suggests a different kind of data quality. Instead of assuming one single, objective truth, field researchers hold that members subjectively interpret experiences within a social context. What a member takes to be true results from social interaction and interpretation. Thus, high-quality field data capture such subcultural processes and provide an understanding of the member's viewpoint.

A field researcher does not eliminate subjective views to get quality data; rather, quality data include his or her subjective responses and experiences. Quality field data are detailed descriptions from the researcher's immersion and authentic experiences in the social world of members.[29]

INTERNAL CONSISTENCY

A way to achieve data reliability in field research in which a researcher examines the plausibility of data to see whether they form a coherent whole, fit all else that is known about a person or event, and avoid common forms of deception.

EXTERNAL CONSISTENCY

A way to achieve reliability of data in field research in which the researcher cross-checks and verifies qualitative data using multiple sources of information.

RELIABILITY IN FIELD RESEARCH.   The reliability of field data addresses the question, are researcher observations about a member or field event internally and externally consistent? **Internal consistency** refers to whether the data are plausible given all that is known about a person or event, eliminating common forms of human deception. In other words, do the pieces fit together into a coherent picture? For example, are a member's actions consistent over time and in different social contexts?

External consistency is achieved by verifying or cross-checking observations with other, divergent sources of data. In other words, does it all fit into the overall context? For example, can others verify what a researcher observed about a person? Does other evidence confirm the researcher's observations? Sometimes a microlevel study is being done on a well-documented macrolevel phenomenon. For example, a field researcher studying police sexual harassment within a single police department can cross-validate his or her experiences and findings with that of larger quantitative studies that have documented its existence and nature. In this way, a field researcher can use his or her microlevel data to make macrolevel connections.

Obstacles to reliability include behaviors that can mislead a researcher: misinformation, evasions, and lies.[30] Misinformation is an unintended falsehood caused by the uncertainty and complexity of life. Evasions are intentional acts of not revealing information. Common evasions include not answering questions, answering a different question than was asked, switching topics, or answering in a purposefully vague and ambiguous manner. For example, a corporate manager feels uncomfortable when the topic of using prostitutes to get customers comes up at a dinner party. He says, "Yes, a lot of people use them." But later, alone, after careful questioning, the manager is drawn out and reveals that he himself uses the practice.

Lies are untruths intended to mislead or to give a false view. For example, a gang member gives the researcher a false name and address, or a church minister gives an inflated membership figure to look more successful. Douglas (1976: 73) noted, "In all other research settings I've known about in any detail, lying was common, both among members and to researchers, especially about the things that were really important to the members."

VALIDITY IN FIELD RESEARCH.　Validity in field research comes from a researcher's analysis and data as accurate representations of the social world in the field. Essential aspects of the field change: the social events and context change, the members are different, the individual researcher differs, and so on. There are four kinds of validity or tests of research accuracy: ecological validity, natural history, member validation, and competent insider performance.

- **Ecological validity** is the degree to which the social world described by a researcher matches the world of members. It asks, is the natural setting described relatively undisturbed by the researcher's presence or procedures? A study has ecological validity if events would have occurred without a researcher's presence.
- **Natural history** is a detailed description of how the project was conducted. It is a full and candid disclosure of a researcher's actions, assumptions, and procedures for others to evaluate. A study is valid in terms of natural history if outsiders see and accept the field site and the researcher's actions.
- **Member validation** occurs when a researcher takes field results back to members, who judge their adequacy. A study is member valid if members recognize and understand the researcher's description as reflecting their intimate social world. Member validation has limitations because conflicting perspectives in a setting produce disagreement with the researcher's observations, and members may object when results do not portray their group in a favorable light. In addition, members may not recognize the description because it is not from their perspective or does not fit with their purposes.[31]
- **Competent insider performance** is the ability of a nonmember to interact effectively as a member or pass as one. This includes the ability to tell and understand insider jokes. A valid study gives enough of a flavor of the social life in the field and sufficient detail so that an outsider can act as a member. Its limitation is that it is not possible to know the social rules for every situation. Also, an outsider might be able to pass simply because members are being polite and do not want to point out social mistakes.[32]

Sampling

As noted in Chapter 6 in the section on nonprobability sampling, field research sampling differs from quantitative-based sampling.[33] A field researcher often uses snowball sampling by developing his or her theoretical research objectives. Field researchers sample times, situations, types of events, locations, types of people, or contexts of interest. For example, a researcher samples time by observing a setting at different times. He or she observes at all times of the day, on every day of the week, and in all seasons to get a full sense of how the field site stays the same or changes. It is often best to overlap when sampling (e.g., to have sampling times from 7:00 a.m. to 9:00 a.m., from 8:00 a.m. to 10:00 a.m., from 9:00 a.m. to 11:00 a.m.).

A researcher samples locations because one location may give depth, but a narrow perspective. Sitting or standing in different locations helps the researcher get a sense of the whole site. For example, the peer-to-peer behavior of gang members can occur at night in a car or out on the streets, but it also occurs at their homes, during the day, after they get off work. The two locations would likely yield different attitudes, demeanors, and customs.

Field researchers sample people by focusing their attention or interaction on different kinds of people (old-timers and newcomers, old and young, males and females, leaders and followers). As a researcher identifies types of people, or people with opposing outlooks, he or she tries to interact with and learn about all types.

ECOLOGICAL VALIDITY

Demonstrating the authenticity and trustworthiness of a study by showing that the researcher's descriptions of the field site match those of the members and that the field researcher's presence was not a disturbance.

NATURAL HISTORY

A method field researchers use to demonstrate the authenticity and trustworthiness of a study by fully disclosing actions and procedures in depth as they occurred over time.

MEMBER VALIDATION

A method field researchers use to demonstrate the authenticity and trustworthiness of a study by having the people who were studied read and confirm as being true that which the researchers have reported.

COMPETENT INSIDER PERFORMANCE

A method field researchers use to demonstrate the authenticity and trustworthiness of a study by the researcher "passing" as a member of the group under study.

THE FIELD RESEARCH INTERVIEW

FOCUS GROUPS

A special qualitative
research technique in which
people are informally
interviewed in a group
discussion setting.

So far, we have learned how field researchers observe and take notes. They also interview members, but field interviews differ from survey research interviews. This section introduces the field interview. One important technique available to the field researcher is known as **focus groups.** Focus group interviewing is often used in evaluative field research.

Focus Group Research

The focus group is a special qualitative research technique in which people are informally "interviewed" in a group-discussion setting. Focus group research has grown rapidly in the past twenty years. The procedure is that a researcher gathers together six to twelve people in a room with a moderator to discuss a few issues. Most focus groups last about ninety minutes. The moderator is trained to be nondirective and to facilitate free, open discussion by all group members (i.e., not let one person dominate the discussion). Group members should be homogeneous, but not include close friends or relatives. In a typical study, a researcher uses four to six separate groups. Focus group topics might include public attitudes (e.g., race relations and workplace equality), personal behaviors (e.g., dealing with AIDS), a new product (e.g., breakfast cereal), or a political candidate. Researchers often combine focus groups with quantitative research, and the procedure has its own specific strengths and weaknesses (see below in the following paragraphs).

Several years ago, Neuman conducted an applied study on why parents and students chose a private high school over public ones. In addition to collecting quantitative survey data, he formed six focus groups, each with eight to ten students from the high school. A trained college-student moderator asked questions, elicited comments from group members, and prevented one person from dominating discussions. The six groups were co-ed and contained members of either one grade level or two adjacent grades (e.g., freshmen and sophomores). Students discussed their reasons for attending the high school and whether specific factors were important. He tape-recorded the discussions, which lasted about forty-five minutes, then analyzed the tapes to understand what the students saw as important to their decisions. In addition, the data helped when interpreting the survey data (see mixed methods research in Chapter 1).

The advantages of focus group research are as follows:

- The natural setting allows people to express opinions/ideas freely.
- Open expression among members of marginalized social groups is encouraged.
- People tend to feel empowered, especially in action-oriented research projects.
- Survey researchers are provided a window into how people talk about survey topics.
- The interpretation of quantitative survey results is facilitated.
- Participants may query one another and explain their answers to each others.

The limitations of focus group research are as follows:

- A "polarization effect" exists (attitudes become more extreme after group discussion).
- Only one or a few topics can be discussed in a focus group session.
- A moderator may unknowingly limit open, free expression of group members.
- Focus group participants produce fewer ideas than in individual interviews.
- Focus group studies rarely report all the details of study design/procedure.
- Researchers cannot reconcile the differences that arise between individual-only and focus group–context responses.

The Field Interview

Field researchers use unstructured, nondirective, in-depth interviews, which differ from formal survey research interviews in many ways, Table 12.5 contrasts survey interviews with field interviews to help in seeing the difference.[34] The field interview involves asking questions, listening, expressing interest, and recording what was said. It is more similar to what we think of as a conversation than an interview.

TABLE 12.5 Survey Interviews versus Field Research Interviews

Typical Survey Interview	Typical Field Interview
1. It has a clear beginning and end.	1. The beginning and end are not clear. The interview can be picked up later.
2. The same standard questions are asked of all respondents in the same sequence.	2. The questions and the order in which they are asked are tailored to specific people and situations.
3. The interviewer appears neutral at all times.	3. The interviewer shows interest in responses, and encourages elaboration.
4. The interviewer asks questions, and the respondent answers.	4. It is like a friendly conversational exchange, but with more interviewer questions.
5. It is almost always with one respondent alone.	5. It can occur in group setting or with others in area, but varies.
6. It has a professional tone and businesslike focus; diversions are ignored.	6. It is interspersed with jokes, asides, stories, diversions, and anecdotes, which are recorded.
7. Closed-ended questions are common, with infrequent probes.	7. Open-ended questions are common, and probes are frequent.
8. The interviewer alone controls the pace and direction of the interview.	8. The interviewer and member jointly control the pace and direction of the interview.
9. The social context in which the interview occurs is ignored and assumed to make little difference.	9. The social context of the interview is noted and seen as important for interpreting the meaning of responses.
10. The interviewer attempts to mold the communication pattern into a standard framework.	10. The interviewer adjusts to the member's norms and language usage.

Source: From W. Lawrence Neuman, *Social Research Methods, Qualitative and Quantitative Approaches,* 6/e. Published by Allyn and Bacon, 75 Arlington St., Boston, MA 02116. Copyright © 2006 by Pearson Education. Reprinted by permission of the publisher. Adapted from the following sources: Charles L. Briggs. *Learning How to Ask: A Sociolinguistic Appraisal of the Role of the Interview in Social Science Research.* New York: Cambridge University Press, 1986; Norman K. Denzin. *The Research Act: A Theoretical Introduction to Sociological Methods,* 3/e. Englewood Cliffs, NJ: Prentice-Hall, 1989; Jack D. Douglas. *Creative Interviewing.* Beverly Hills, CA: Sage, 1985; Elliot G. Mishler. *Research Interviewing: Context and Narrative.* Cambridge, MA: Harvard University Press, 1986; and James P. Spadley. *The Ethnographic Observation.* New York: Holt, Rinehart and Winston, 1979.

The field interview is a joint production between a researcher and a member. Members are active participants whose insights, feelings, and cooperation are essential parts of a discussion process that reveals subjective meanings. "The interviewer's presence and form of involvement—how he or she listens, attends, encourages, interrupts, digresses, initiates topics, and terminates responses—is integral to the respondent's account" (Mishler 1986: 82).

Field research interviews go by many names: unstructured, depth, ethnographic, open ended, informal, and long. Generally, they involve one or more people being present, occur in the field, and are informal and nondirective (i.e., the respondent may take the interview in various directions).[35]

A field interview involves a mutual sharing of experiences. It is often a process of mutual discovery. In field interviews, members express themselves in the forms in which they normally speak, think, and organize reality. We want to retain members' jokes and narrative stories in their natural form and not to repackage them into a standardized format. We focus on the member's perspective and experiences. In order to stay close to the member's experience, we ask questions in terms of concrete examples or situations—for example, "Could you tell me things that led up to your quitting in June?" instead of asking, "Why did you quit your job?"

Field interviews occur in a series over time. We begin by building rapport and steering the conversation away from evaluative or highly sensitive topics. We usually avoid probing inner feelings until intimacy is established. After many meetings, we may be able to probe more deeply into sensitive issues and seek clarification of less sensitive issues. In later interviews, we may return to topics and check past answers by restating them in a nonjudgmental tone and asking for verification—for example, "The last time we talked, you said that you started taking things from the store after they reduced your pay. Is that right?"

The field interview is a "speech event," closer to a friendly conversation than the stimulus–response model found in a survey research interview (see Chapter 8). We approach field interviews as we would a friendly conversation, but unless we are conducting covert research, both parties understand that the researcher is gathering information. It has an explicit purpose—to learn about the informant and setting.

Sam Good's deathbed confession of murder likely surprised Steffensmeier, so he asked for more clarification the next morning when visiting him.

> I did it with my hand. Choked him. Dumped his body in a quarry that had filled with water. Tied rocks, weighed him down. The car I burnt. They never found him. Five six years ago, I heard they drained the quarry. I wondered if they had found the body, the bones. But never heard anything. . . . There was no hesitation on my part. I knew what had to be done. I snuffed him out with hand. Gag, gaaggh. It was over for him. (Steffensmeier and Ulman 2005: 20)

Life History

LIFE HISTORY INTERVIEW

Open-ended interview with one person who describes his or her entire life. It can be considered a subtype of oral history.

Life history, life story, or a biographical interview is a special type of field interviewing. It overlaps with oral history (as seen in Chapter 13).[36] There are multiple purposes for stories of the past and these may shape the forms of interview. In a life history interview, researchers interview and gather documentary material about a particular individual's life, usually someone who is old. "The concept of life story is used to designate the retrospective information itself without the corroborative evidence often implied by the term life history" (Tagg 1985: 163). Researchers ask open-ended questions to capture how the person understands his or her own past. Exact accuracy in the story is less critical than the story itself. Researchers recognize that the person may reconstruct or add present interpretations to the past; the person may "rewrite" his or her story. As seen in Highlight 12.4 the main purpose is to get at how the respondent sees/remembers the past, not just some kind of objective truth.

HIGHLIGHT 12.4
The life History or Life Story Interview

Life history or life story interviews usually involve two to ten open-ended interviews, usually recorded, of sixty to ninety minutes. These interviews serve several purposes. First, they can assist the informant being interviewed in reconstructing his or her life memories. Retelling and remembering one's life events as a narrative story can have therapeutic benefits and pass on personal wisdom to a new generation. Second, these interviews can create new qualitative data on the life cycle, the development of self, and how people experience events that can be archived and added to similar data (e.g., The Center for Life Stories at University of Southern Maine is such an archive). Third, life story interviews can provide the interviewer with an in-depth look at another's life. This is often an enriching experience that creates a close personal relationship and encourages self-reflection in ways that enhance personal integrity. Steps in the process are as follows:

1. The researcher prepares with background reading, refines his or her interview skills, contacts the informant, gets permission for the interview, and promises anonymity.
2. The researcher conducts a series of interviews, audio- or video-recording them. The interviewer suspends any prior history with an informant and gives his or her total respect, always showing sincere interest in

what another says. He or she asks open-ended questions, but is flexible and never forces a question. The interviewer acts as a guide, knowing when to ask a question that will open up stories; gives intense attentiveness; and is completely nonjudgmental and supportive. Often, the interviewer offers photographs or objects to help spark memories and past feelings.

3. The researcher transcribes the recorded interviews in four stages: (a) prepares a summary of each tape; (b) makes a verbatim transcription, with minor editing (e.g., adds sentences, paragraphs) and stage direction (e.g., laughter, coughing); (c) reviews the whole transcript for clarity of meaning and does further editing and minor rearranging; and (d) has the informant review the transcript for any corrections and modifications.

4. The researchers sends a note of appreciation to the informant and prepares a commentary on major themes and/or sends it to an archive.

Source: From W. Lawrence Neumann, *Social Research Methods, Qualitative and Quantitative Approaches,* 6/e. Published by Allyn and Bacon, 75 Arlington St., Boston, MA 02116. Copyright © 2006 by Pearson Education. Reprinted by permission of the publisher. Adapted from Robert Atkinson, *The Life Story Interview.* Thousand Oaks, CA: Sage Publications, 1998.

Researchers sometimes use a life story grid in which they ask the person what happened at various dates and in several areas of life. A grid may consist of categories such as migration, occupation, education, or family events for each of ten different ages in the person's life. Researchers often supplement the interview information with artifacts (e.g., old photos) and may present them during the interview to stimulate discussion or recollection. "Life writing as an empirical exercise feeds on data: letters, documents, interviews" (Smith 1994: 290). McCracken (1988: 20) gave an example of how objects aided the interview by helping him understand how the person being interviewed saw things. When interviewing a seventy-five-year-old woman in her living room, McCracken initially thought the room just contained a lot of cluttered physical objects. After having the woman explain the meaning of each item, it was clear that she saw each as a memorial or a memento. The room was a museum to key events in her life. Only after the author looked at the objects in this new way did he begin to see the furniture and objects not as inanimate things but as objects that radiated meaning.

Sometimes, researchers find an existing archive with a person; other times, they search out the documents and create an archive. Locating such documentary data can be a tremendous task, followed by reviewing, cataloging, and organizing the information. The interview and documentary data together form the basis of the life story.

Types of Questions in Field Interviews

Field researchers ask three types of questions in a field interview: descriptive, structural, and contrast questions. All are asked concurrently, but each type is more frequent at a different stage in the research process (see Figure 12.3).

A researcher asks a descriptive question to explore the setting and learn about members. Descriptive questions can be about time and space—for example, "Where is the bathroom?" "What are the scales for?" "What Web sites do you use to order the precursor chemicals?"

A researcher uses a structural question after spending time in the field and is starting to analyze data. It begins after a researcher organizes specific field events, situations, and conversations into categories. For example, a researcher's observations of illegal steroid buyers reveal that they fall into several conceptual categories of kinds of customers. The researcher might discuss these informally with the dealer to verify their accuracy.

One way to pose a structural question is to ask the members whether a category includes elements in addition to those already identified by a researcher—for example, "Are there any types of customers other than bone-heads, meat-heads, wanna-be jocks, and athletes?" In addition, a researcher asks for confirmation, "Is a meat-head always a competitive bodybuilder?"

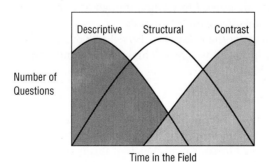

FIGURE 12.3 Types of Questions in Field Research Interviews *Source:* From W. Lawrence Neuman, *Social Research Methods, Qualitative and Quantitative Approaches,* 6/e. Published by Allyn and Bacon, 75 Arlington St., Boston, MA 02116. Copyright © 2006 by Pearson Education. Reprinted by permission of the publisher.

The contrast question builds on the analysis that has been verified by structural questions. Questions focus on similarities or differences between elements in categories or between categories as the researcher asks members to verify similarities and differences: "You seem to have a number of different kinds of buyers. I've heard you call some customers bone-heads and some wanna-be jocks—what's the difference between the two?"

LEAVING THE FIELD

Work in the field can last for a few weeks to a dozen years.[37] In either case, at some point work in the field ends. Some researchers suggest that the end comes naturally when theory building ceases or reaches a closure; others feel that fieldwork could go on without end and that a firm decision to cut off relations is needed.

Experienced field researchers anticipate a process of disengaging and exiting the field. Depending on the intensity of involvement and the length of time in the field, the process can be disruptive or emotionally painful for both the researcher and the members. A researcher may experience the emotional pain of breaking intimate friendships when leaving the field. He or she may feel guilty and depressed immediately before and after leaving. He or she may find it difficult to let go because of personal and emotional entanglements. If the involvement in the field was intense and long, and the field site differed from his or her native culture, the researcher may need months of adjustment before feeling at home with his or her original cultural surroundings. Imagine how James Marquart must have felt after leaving his correctional officer ethnography discussed in Chapter 4. These types of intense field research experiences can deeply impact someone for the rest of his or her life.

Once they decide to leave—because the project reaches a natural end and little new is being learned, or because external factors force it to end (e.g., end of a job, gatekeepers order the researcher out)—we choose a method of exiting. We can leave by a quick exit (simply not return one day) or slowly withdraw, reducing involvement over weeks. We also need to decide how to tell members and how much advance warning to give. Unless impossible, it is vital to leave the project's participants on good terms.

The exit process depends on the specific field setting and the relationships developed. In general, we let members know a short period ahead of time. We should fulfill any bargains or commitments that were built up and leave with a clean slate. Sometimes, a ritual or ceremony, such as a going-away party or shaking hands with everyone, helps signal the break for members. Maintaining friendships with members after exiting is also advocated and is preferred by feminist researchers.

Exiting affects members. Some may feel hurt or rejected because a close social relationship is ending. They may react by trying to pull the researcher back into the field, or they may become angry and resentful. They may grow cool and distant because of an awareness that the researcher was merely an outsider all along. Most often, though, if done properly, the researcher leaves under favorable terms and often with new friends.

Leaving can also affect the researcher. Ferrell (2006: 200) describes how his scrounging ethnography, where he spent almost a year of his life jobless and living off only what he could find in the streets, changed his outlook.

> In writing an illicit map of the city, scrounging made a new map out of me. In the same way that it confirmed for me the existential pleasures of slowing down, it affirmed the possibilities available in an everyday life on the margins, a life reconstructed by back alleys and abandoned urban spaces. Much of this personal transformation merged with, and emerged from, what I might call *existential ethnography*. With no research grant, no book contract—hell, with no job, academic or otherwise—I was able at least to approach the point of "becoming the phenomenon," scrounging the city not as a research project or field experiment, but as existence.

ETHICAL DILEMMAS OF FIELD RESEARCH

The direct personal involvement of a field researcher in the social lives and activities of criminals, criminal justice practitioners, and other people raises many ethical dilemmas. The dilemmas arise when a researcher is alone in the field and has little time to make a moral decision. Although he or she may be aware of general ethical issues before entering the field, they arise unexpectedly in the course of observing and interacting in the field. We will look at four ethical issues in field research: deception, confidentiality, involvement with deviants and the powerful, and publishing reports.[38]

Deception

As discussed in Chapter 4, the most hotly debated of the ethical issues arising from deception is that of covert versus overt field research.[39] Deception arises in several ways in field research: The research may be covert; or may assume a false role, name, or identity; or may mislead members in some way. Some support it and see it as necessary for entering into and gaining a full knowledge of many areas of social life. Others oppose it and argue that it undermines a trust between researchers and society.[40]

Confidentiality

A researcher learns intimate knowledge that is given in confidence. He or she has a moral obligation to uphold the confidentiality of data. This includes keeping information confidential from others in the field and disguising members' names in field notes. Take, for instance, Sullivan's (1989) fieldwork on youth crime and employment in three neighborhoods in Brooklyn, New York. Sullivan stated:

> The neighborhoods we studied are referred to here by pseudonyms. . . . [My] descriptions of the neighborhoods are written so as to convey what needs to be known about them without making them precisely identifiable. . . . La Barriada is a mixed Latino and white neighborhood, though all the youths we studied here were Latino, either first- or second-generation migrants to New York from Puerto Rico. . . . Projectville is a predominantly black neighborhood in which there is a large concentration of public housing. . . . Hamilton Park is a predominantly white neighborhood in which most families are supported by relatively high-paying blue-collar jobs. (pp. 18–20)

Involvement with Criminals/Deviants

Researchers who conduct field research on people who engage in illegal, immoral, or unethical behavior face additional dilemmas. They know of and are sometimes involved in illegal activity. Fetterman (1989) called this **guilty knowledge**. Such knowledge is of interest not only to law enforcement officials but also to other field site members. The researcher faces a dilemma of building trust and rapport with the members, yet not becoming so involved as to violate his or her basic personal moral standards.

GUILTY KNOWLEDGE
When a researcher learns of illegal, unethical, or immoral actions by the people in the field site that are not widely known.

Publishing Ethnographic Field Reports

The intimate knowledge obtained and reported creates a dilemma between the right of privacy and the right to know. We cannot publicize member secrets, violate privacy, or harm reputations. Yet, if we cannot publish anything that might offend or harm someone, what we have learned will remain hidden, and it may be difficult for others to believe the report if critical details are omitted.

Some researchers suggest asking members to look at a report to verify its accuracy and to approve of their portrayal in print. For marginal groups (e.g., addicts, prostitutes, and crack users), this may not be feasible, but researchers must always respect member privacy. On the other hand, censorship or self-censorship can be a danger. A compromise position is that truthful but unflattering material may be published only if it is essential to the researchers' larger arguments.[41]

Conclusion

In this chapter, we learned about ethnographic field research and the field research process (choosing a site and gaining access, relations in the field, observing and collecting data, and the field interview). Field researchers begin data analysis and theorizing during the data collection phase.

Armed with this knowledge, you can now appreciate the implication of saying that in ethnographic field research, the researcher engages the real world of his or her object of study, immersing oneself into a natural setting and dealing directly with the culture and activities of those being studied. Doing ethnographic field research usually has a greater impact on the researcher's emotions, personal life, and sense of self than any other type. Field research is difficult to conduct, but it is a valuable way to study parts of the crime and justice world that otherwise could not be studied.

Good field research requires a combination of skills. In addition to a strong sense of self, the best field researchers possess a keen ability to listen and absorb details, tremendous patience, sensitivity and empathy for others, superb social skills, a talent to think very quickly "on one's feet," the ability to see subtle interconnections among people/events, and a superior ability to express oneself in writing. We realize this chapter reviewed many difficult-to-execute ethnographic projects, and we do not want you to get the wrong impression. Yes, ethnography is difficult, but it is also a readily accomplishable research method. We've also reviewed some smaller, less time consuming, and safe ethnographic projects, including those that can be conducted online (virtual ethnographies).

Key Terms

ethnography *279*
explicit knowledge *280*
tacit knowledge *280*
thick description *280*
naturalism *282*
Ethnographic field
   research *283*
reflexivity *283*
field site *285*

going native *286*
gatekeeper *286*
informant *287*
access ladder *287*
attitude of strangeness *291*
building rapport *291*
verstehen *292*
normalize field research *293*
acceptable incompetent *294*

exchange relationships *294*
appearance of interest *295*
argot *296*
jotted notes *297*
direct observation notes
   298
analytic memos *299*
face sheet *300*
internal consistency *300*

external consistency *300*
ecological validity *301*
natural history *301*
member validation *301*
competent insider
   performance *301*
focus groups *302*
life history interview *304*
guilty knowledge *307*

Review Questions

1. What were the two major phases in the development of the Chicago school? Describe the connection ethnographic field research has to the discipline of anthropology.
2. What is the logic and thinking that underpins ethnographic field research?
3. List five of the ten things the "methodological pragmatist" field researcher does.
4. Why is it important for a field researcher to read the literature before beginning fieldwork? How does this relate to defocusing?
5. Identify the characteristics of a field site that make it a good one for a beginning field researcher.
6. What are the roles of a gatekeeper and an informant?
7. How does the "presentation of self" affect a field researcher's work?

8. What is the attitude of strangeness and why is it important?
9. What are relevant considerations when choosing roles in the field, and how can the degree of researcher involvement vary?
10. Identify three ways to ensure quality field research data.
11. Compare differences between a field research and a survey research interview, and between a field interview and a friendly conversation.
12. What does it mean for a field researcher to remain keenly observant?
13. What are the different types or levels of field notes, and what purpose does each serve?
14. What are some of the potential ethical issues associated with ethnographic field research?

Practicing Research

1. Reviewing published ethnographic studies is essential for grasping what exactly this genre of research is all about. Locate a scholarly book that relies primarily on this method, and read through the introduction, methodology, conclusion, and other key parts of the book (it may not be realistic to read the entire book, but if possible, it might be worth your while). Numerous well-known works are cited in this chapter, but many others exist. Write a detailed review of the work you selected .

   One variation of this same exercise would be to find one journal article that uses ethnographic field research. The *Journal of Contemporary Ethnography* is a quality resource that publishes both small- and large-scale ethnographies.

2. Using the concepts and ideas in this chapter, discuss in small groups the types of contacts that each group member might have that would make for an interesting crime and justice ethnography. Speculate about how entry might be gained, the difficulties that might be encountered in gaining the trust and cooperation of the research subjects, and the likely reaction of an IRB committee.

3. Using the concepts, ideas, and processes discussed in this chapter, conduct a microethnography. This could be a semester-long project or something that only lasts one to three days. Our students, for example, have conducted microethnographies of their family's Thanksgiving dinner, an interesting workplace, a police ride-along, the local courthouse, and a friend or relative involved in an interesting recreational or ceremonial activity. Make sure and discuss with your professor the ethical issues that might be involved.

4. In groups of five to seven students, conduct a mock focus group interview. You will have to select a topic that will facilitate a good deal of discussion, design open-ended questions that revolve around the topic, and record with quality notes and/or audio-visual means what transpired. If a single topic and set of questions are selected for the entire class, have all the focus groups meet collectively and compare the findings.

Notes for Further Study

1. Ethnography is described in Agar (1986), Franke (1983), Hammersley and Atkinson (1983), Sanday (1983), and Spradley (1979a: 3–12; 1979b: 3–16).

2. See Geertz (1973, 1979) on "thick description." Also see Denzin (1989: 159–160) for additional discussion.

3. See Lofland and Lofland (1995: 6, 18–19).

4. For a general discussion of field research and naturalism, see Adler and Adler (1994), Georges and Jones (1980), Holy (1984), and Pearsall (1970). For discussions of contrasting types of field research, see Clammer (1984), Gonor (1977), Holstein and Gubrium (1994), Morse (1994), Schwandt (1994), and Strauss and Corbin (1994).

5. See Georges and Jones (1980: 21–42) and Lofland and Lofland (1995: 11–15).

6. See Lofland (1976: 13–23) and Shaffir and colleagues (1980: 18–20) on feeling marginal.

7. See Adler and Adler (1987: 67–78).

8. See Hammersley and Atkinson (1983: 42–45) and Lofland and Lofland (1995: 16–30).

9. Jewish researchers have studied Christians (Kleinman 1980), Whites have studied African Americans (Liebow 1967), and adult researchers have become intimate with youngsters (Fine 1987; Fine and Glassner 1979; Thorne and Luria 1986). Also see Eichler (1988), Hunt (1989), and Wax (1979) on the role of race, sex, and age in field research.

10. Roy (1970) argued for the "Ernie Pyle" role based on his study of union organizing in the southern United States. In this role, named after a World War II battle journalist, the researcher "goes with the troops" as a type of participant as observer. Trice (1970) discussed the advantages of an outsider role. Schwartz and Schwartz (1969) discussed various roles.

11. Adapted from Gray (1980: 311). See also Hicks (1984) and Schatzman and Strauss (1973: 58–63).

12. Negotiation in the field is discussed in Gans (1982), Johnson (1975: 58–59, 76–77), and Schatzman and Strauss (1973: 22–23).

13. On entering and gaining access to field sites with deviant groups, see Becker (1970a: 31–38), Hammersley and Atkinson (1983: 54–76), Lofland and Lofland (1995: 31–41), and West (1980). Elite access is discussed by Hoffmann (1980).

14. For more on roles in field settings, see Barnes (1970: 241–244), Emerson (1981: 364), Hammersley and Atkinson (1983: 88–104), Warren and Rasmussen (1977), and Wax (1979). On dress, see Bogdan and Taylor (1975: 45) and Douglas (1976).

15. See Strauss (1987: 10–11).

16. See Georges and Jones (1980: 105–133) and Johnson (1975: 159). Clarke (1975) noted that it is not necessarily "subjectivism" to recognize this in field research.

17. See Douglas (1976), Emerson (1981: 367–368), and Johnson (1975: 124–129) on being patient, polite, and considerate.

18. See Wax (1971: 13).

19. See Douglas (1976: 216) and Corsino (1987).

20. For discussion of "normalizing," see Gans (1982: 57–59), Georges and Jones (1980: 43–164), Hammersley and Atkinson (1983: 70–76), Harkens and Warren (1993), Johnson (1975), and Wax (1971). Mann (1970) discussed how to teach members about a researcher's role.

21. The acceptable incompetent or learner role is discussed in Bogdan and Taylor (1975: 46), Douglas (1976), Hammersley and Atkinson (1983: 92–94), Lofland and Lofland (1995: 56), and Schatman and Strauss (1973: 25).

22. Also see Adler and Adler (1987: 40–42), Bogdan and Taylor (1975: 35–37), Douglas (1976), and Gray (1980: 321).

23. See Bogdan and Taylor (1975: 50–51), Lofland and Lofland (1995: 57–58), Shupe and Bromley (1980), and Wax (1971).

24. See Johnson (1975: 105–108).

25. See Becker and Geer (1970), Spradley (1979a, 1979b), and Schatzman and Strauss (1973) on argot.

26. See Schatzman and Strauss (1973: 69) on inference.

27. See Burgess (1982b), Lofland and Lofland (1995: 89–98), and Spradley (1979a, 1979b) on notes for field interviews.

28. For additional discussion of data quality, see Becker (1970b), Dean and Whyte (1969), Douglas (1976: 7), Kirk and Miller (1986), and McCall (1969).

29. Douglas (1976: 115) argued that it is easier to "lie" with "hard numbers" than with detailed observations of natural settings.

30. Adapted from Douglas (1976: 56–104).

31. See Bloor (1983) and Douglas (1976: 126).

32. For more on validity in field research, see Briggs (1986: 24), Bogdan and Taylor (1975), Douglas (1976), Emerson (1981: 361–363), and Sanjek (1990).

33. See Denzin (1989: 71–73, 86–92), Glaser and Strauss (1967), Hammersley and Atkinson (1983: 45–53), Honigmann (1982), and Weiss (1994: 25–29) on sampling in field research.

34. Discussion of field interviewing can be found in Banaka (1971), Bogdan and Taylor (1975: 95–124), Briggs (1986), Burgess (1982c), Denzin (1989: 103–120), Douglas (1985), Lofland and Lofland (1995: 78–88), Spradley (1979a), and Whyte (1982).

35. See Fontana and Frey (1994).

36. See Atkinson (1998), Denzin (1989: 182–209), Nash and McCurdy (1989), Smith (1994), and Tagg (1985) on life history interviews.

37. Altheide (1980), Bogdan and Taylor (1975: 75–76), Lofland and Lofland (1995: 61), Maines and colleagues (1980), and Roadburg (1980) discuss leaving the field.

38. See Lofland and Lofland (1995: 26, 63, 75, 168–177), Miles and Huberman (1994: 288–297), and Punch (1986).

39. Covert, sensitive study is discussed in Ayella (1993), Edwards (1993), and Mitchell (1993).

40. See Douglas (1976), Erikson (1970), and Johnson (1975).

41. See Barnes (1970), Becker (1969), Fichter and Kolb (1970), Goward (1984), Lofland and Lofland (1995: 204–230), Miles and Huberman (1994: 298–307), and Wolcott (1994) on publishing field research results.

Historical, Academic Legal, and Mixed Methods Research

Historical Research
  The General Idea of Historical Research
    The Specific Case of Historical-Comparative Research
    Highlight 13.1 Seeing Past Events in a New Light, Racial Boundaries in the United States
  Major Features of Historical Research
  How to Conduct Historical and Historical-Comparative Research
    Primary Sources
    Highlight 13.2 Using Archival Data
    Secondary Sources
    Highlight 13.3 World War II, Military Justice, and Racism
    Running Records
    Recollections
    Highlight 13.4 Women of the Klan
  Limits of Secondary Sources
  Limits of Primary Sources
  Steps Taken in a Historical Research Project
  Conclusion to Historical Research

Academic Legal Research (ALR)
  Justifying ALR
  The General Idea of ALR
    Highlight 13.5 A Quick Guide to Using Westlaw and Westlaw Campus
    The Specific Case of Socio-Legal Research
  How to Conduct Legal Research
  Conclusion to Legal Research

Mixed Methods Research
  Beyond Conflict and Exclusion
  The General Idea of Mixed Methods Research
    Highlight 13.6 Discovering the Benefits of Mixed Methods Research
  Major Features of Mixed Methods Research
  How to Conduct Mixed Methods Research
  Conclusion to Mixed Methods Research

Conclusion

Key Terms

Review Questions

Practicing Research

Notes for Further Study

Chapter 12 examined what most consider the foundational qualitative research method, ethnographic field research. We will now examine other possibilities, including major sections on historical research and academic legal research. The third section examines the thinking behind, and the techniques used, in mixed methods research (combining qualitative and quantitative approaches). Despite their lack of coverage in most research methods texts, these research methods, as we'll demonstrate, are quite important to crime and justice studies in generating systematic knowledge about crime and justice phenomena.

HISTORICAL RESEARCH

Throughout this text, we referenced the public spectacle of lynching in late nineteenth- and early twentieth-century America. Perhaps the most well-known discussion of public torture and execution is found in Michel Foucault's (1977: 3) description of the French government's execution of Damiens on March 2, 1757:

> On 2 March 1757 Damiens the regicide was condemned "to make the *amende honorable* before the main door of the Church of Paris," where he was to be "taken and conveyed in a cart, wearing nothing but a shirt, holding a torch of burning wax weighing two pounds"; then, "in the said cart, to the Place de Grève, where, on a scaffold that will be erected there, the flesh will be torn from his breasts, arms, thighs and calves with red-hot pincers, his right hand, holding the knife with which he committed the said parricide, burnt with sulphur, and, on those places where the flesh will be torn away, poured molten lead, boiling oil, burning resin, wax and sulphur melted together and then his body drawn and quartered by four horses and his limbs and body consumed by fire, reduced to ashes and his ashes thrown to the winds." (*Pièces originales. . .*, pp. 372–374)

Foucault's sweeping historical analysis of the modernization of punishment still serves as the theoretical foundation for a wealth of academic scholarship and research about corrections and punishment.

Historical research, in fact, has played a quiet yet central role in understanding the police, corrections, courts, law, and crime. Textbooks all rely on the work of historical scholars who have produced a wealth of knowledge about nearly every facet of crime and criminal justice. This work in its original form is more often found in books than it is in journal articles, and some of it emanates from other disciplines (such as Foucault's work). Due to the dominance of positivist social science, though, it has not been recognized in research methods texts as a legitimate knowledge production method.[1] Indeed, it is barely mentioned in most leading methods texts.[2] This is unfortunate, because collecting historical materials and synthesizing them into a coherent story about the past can be highly rewarding and useful. The purpose of this section is to introduce you to the ideas, features, and a few techniques used in historical research, and its close cousin, historical-comparative research.

The General Idea of Historical Research

HISTORICAL RESEARCH

Systematically collecting historical materials and analyzing those materials for constructing a descriptive and/or theoretical account of what has happened in the past.

History is usually thought of as the study of past human events. As a method, **historical research** involves systematically collecting historical materials and analyzing those materials for constructing a descriptive and/or theoretical account of what has happened in the past. The purpose of these studies is sometimes descriptive (e.g., relaying an accurate account of events), sometimes explanatory (theorizing about the evolution of events), and oftentimes both descriptive and explanatory.

Developing credible knowledge about the crime and justice past is an essential undertaking. Samuel Walker (1980: 5), a scholar who has produced an impressive body of historical work, makes the following case:

> One might well ask, why bother to study the history of criminal justice? How does an understanding of colonial forms of punishment or the early forms of police administration possibly contribute to the solutions of our present problems? . . . The study of history can have enormous contemporary relevance. Recent scholarship on slavery and the black experience, for example, has contributed greatly to our understanding of the contemporary racial problems. . . . Properly organized and interpreted, the facts of history can illuminate the dynamics of change. The study of history can tell us something about how people in different times viewed their own problems and how new ideas became translated into social policy.

David C. McCullough, a famous historian, sums up these sentiments: "History is a guide to navigation in perilous times. History is who we are and why we are the way we are."[3] Criminal justice/criminology is witnessing an increasing interest in historical research. The emergence of new research evidence has begun to dramatically alter our preconceptions about the past. We looked at Nicole Rafter's historical research, for example, in Chapter 2 ("The Horse-Slasher"), which raised serious questions about the dominant view that Lombroso's work represents the first attempts to study crime scientifically. Police study is also having to rethink its standard historical narrative. There is growing evidence that the first police agencies in the United States were not formed in the mid-1800s in urban centers of the Northeast, but instead in the South.

> As early as the 1780s, Charleston introduced a paramilitary municipal police force primarily to control the city's large concentration of slaves. . . . These police forces, usually called city guards, wore uniforms and carried formidable weapons. City guardsmen were municipal employees. . . . (Rousey 1994: 3)

Historians are documenting how these first U.S. police departments in Charleston, Savannah, Mobile, Richmond, and New Orleans were created out of a fear of slave crime and rebellion.[4] Their appearance and tactics—both modeled after the military—were designed to promote fear among rebellious Blacks and respond to lawbreaking with a high degree of force. Thinking about the origins of police in terms of slave patrols, versus the English model of unarmed watchmen, renders a very different image of our past.

THE SPECIFIC CASE OF HISTORICAL-COMPARATIVE RESEARCH.   An important branch of historical research is called **historical-comparative research**. Its emergence intersects with crime and justice studies' increasing interest in international/comparative research. **Comparative research** generates knowledge about crime and justice phenomena by making comparisons (qualitative and quantitative) across different countries or cultures. As Richard Bennett (2004) noted in his presidential address to the Academy of Criminal Justice Sciences (ACJS), the confluence of globalization and the events of September 11, 2001, has solidified the place of comparative research in our field. Historical-comparative research examines aspects of social and political life across different *cultures* and *eras*. Sometimes researchers focus on one historical period or several, compare one or more cultures, or mix historical periods and cultures. It combines theory with data collection. Researchers use a mix of evidence, including existing statistics, documents (e.g., books, newspapers, diaries, photographs, and maps), observations, and interviews.

Historical-comparative research is a powerful method for addressing big questions: How did major societal shifts in views on crime take place across different countries? What fundamental features of crime control are common to most societies? Why did current police arrangements take a certain form in some societies but not in others? Why did one country experience a high level of criminal justice system growth as compared to other countries?

A historical-comparative perspective allows us the opportunity to see things not only in relation to the past but also in relation to other cultures and governments. Chapter 9, for example, examined the widely varying rates of incarceration associated with differing countries. Examining the historical reasons for these variations (experiences with governmental repression, for example) and the cultural differences between countries that might cultivate a punitive versus nonpunitive ethos would make for interesting historical-comparative research. Historical-comparative research, then, can strengthen conceptualization and theory building. By looking at historical events and diverse cultural contexts, a researcher can generate new concepts and broaden his or her perspectives. Concepts are less likely to be restricted to a single historical time or to a single culture. General concepts can be grounded in the experiences of people living in specific cultural and historical contexts.[5]

Highlight 13.1 provides an interesting example of historical-comparative research.

HISTORICAL-COMPARATIVE RESEARCH

A type of research that examines aspects of social and political life across different *cultures* and *eras*. Sometimes researchers focus on one historical period or several, compare one or more cultures, or mix historical periods and cultures.

COMPARATIVE RESEARCH

A type of research that generates knowledge about crime and justice phenomena by making comparisons (qualitative and quantitative) across different countries or cultures.

HIGHLIGHT 13.1

Seeing Past Events in a New Light, Racial Boundaries in the United States

Historical-comparative researchers reorganize data and use theory to see events in new ways. Olzak and Shanahan (2003) did this in a study of past racial conflicts in the United States. They noted that before 1870, the U.S. racial divide was between Whites, understood as people from a few northwestern European countries, and all others, and Whites alone had full citizenship. After an 1870 law granted citizenship rights to African Americans and large-scale immigration from Southern or Eastern Europe and Asia, the line between being White and others began to blur. In the 1890s, Southern and Eastern Europeans (e.g., Italians) were called colored and lynched as Blacks, and Asians who tried to become naturalized citizens were turned down by the courts using a 1790 law that limited U.S. citizenship to "white persons."

Competition theory states that when racial barriers weaken between two groups in the same social economic position, competition and conflict between the groups will grow. The authors argued that legal action affecting the dominant racial group's exclusive position can increase intergroup conflict. They examined historical records of racial-ethnic relations and immigration, information on new laws and court rulings, and newspaper reports of racial conflict in seventy-six local settings between 1869 and 1924. They documented patterns of White attacks on Asian and African Americans and found that laws clarifying racial divisions and reinforcing a new "White" identity to include all people of European ancestry were associated with greater attacks on African Americans and Asians. U.S. courts rulings sharpened a new racial division, placing all European-origin immigrants on one side, and African Americans and Asians on the other. Mob attacks and the court rulings or new laws were dual strategies to exclude non-Whites, with the legal action legitimating attacks on non-Whites. The authors concluded, as a result of the legal policy, "race became a master identity for newcomers and racial boundaries become salient to many types of interaction" (p. 506).

Source: From W. Lawrence Neuman, *Social Research Methods, Qualitative and Quantitative Approaches,* 6/e. Published by Allyn and Bacon, 75 Arlington St., Boston, MA 02116. Copyright © 2006 by Pearson Education. Reprinted by permission of the publisher.

Major Features of Historical Research

One major feature of historical research is that the available data are generally limited and indirect. This means that the historical researcher relies heavily on existing government documents, firsthand written accounts, artifacts, maps, drawings, and photographs (referred to below as primary sources). The data are generally, therefore, nonreactive. However, this depends on the time frame being studied. Oftentimes, a more recent historical study will involve interviewing key historical figures who are still alive (e.g., the fourteen surviving World War I veterans as of November 2006).

In fact, historical research shares some key features with ethnographic field research. Historical researchers are similar to ethnographers in that they immerse themselves into a particular historical setting (using records and accounts of that time period), and then through a process of interpretation, attempt to convert these historical materials into a coherent narrative. There are other similarities:

1. The historical researcher, as does the ethnographer, recognizes that in the process of interpreting and reconstructing past events, the researcher's point of view is an unavoidable part of the knowledge produced. Both require the researcher to immerse herself in the data to gain an empathetic understanding of events and people; quality historical research can even transport the reader into the past.

2. Both also rely on inductive theory generation (i.e., grounded theory). Both examine the data without fixed hypotheses. Instead, they develop and modify their organizing concepts and theory through a dialogue with the data, then apply theory to reorganize the evidence. Thus, historical data collection and theory building interact (e.g., grounded theory).

3. Another similarity is that they approach the idea of "change over time" with a similar level of complexity. Both are sensitive to how human agency/choice influences societal structure, and how societal structure influences and changes human agency/choice (discussed in Chapter 3 as a mutually transformative process or dialectic). A competent historical narrative, for example, will examine simultaneously not only the role a highly influential person might have played in some societal shift (e.g., Robert Martinson's academic report criticizing prison

rehabilitation studies) but also the larger societal context in which that person's influence took hold (e.g., the ideological shift toward more conservative crime control politics that did not support prison rehabilitation efforts).

How to Conduct Historical and Historical-Comparative Research

Historical and ethnographic research are also similar in that they both collect primarily qualitative data. Historical researchers, though, have their own terminology and techniques with regard to their data. When studying the past, researchers draw on four types of historical evidence:

- primary sources
- secondary sources
- running records
- recollections

Traditional historians rely on primary sources. Most historical research in our field usually involves a mixture of primary and secondary sources.

PRIMARY SOURCES. The letters, diaries, newspapers, movies, novels, articles of clothing, photographs, ledgers, and so forth of those who lived in the past and have survived to the present are **primary sources**. They are found in archives (a place where documents are stored), in private collections, in family closets, or in museums (see Highlight 13.2). Today's documents and objects

PRIMARY SOURCES

Qualitative or quantitative data about past events that were created and used in the past time period.

HIGHLIGHT 13.2
Using Archival Data

The archive is the main source for primary historical materials. Archives are accumulations of documentary materials (papers, photos, letters, etc.) in private collections, museums, libraries, or formal archives.

Location and Access

Finding whether a collection exists on a topic, organization, or individual can be a long, frustrating task of many letters, phone calls, and referrals. If the material on a person or topic does exist, it may be scattered in multiple locations. Gaining access may depend on an appeal to a family member's kindness for private collections or traveling to distant libraries and verifying one's reason for examining many dusty boxes of old letters. Also, the researcher may discover limited hours (e.g., an archive is open only four days a week from 10 a.m. to 5 p.m., but the researcher needs to inspect the material for forty hours).

Sorting and Organization

Archival material may be unsorted or organized in a variety of ways. The organization may reflect criteria that are unrelated to the researcher's interests. For example, letters and papers may be in chronological order, but the researcher is interested only in letters to four professional colleagues over three decades, not daily bills, family correspondence, and so on.

Technology and Control

Archival materials may be in their original form, on microforms, or, more rarely, in an electronic form. Researchers may be allowed only to take notes, not make copies, or they may be allowed only to see select parts of the whole collection. Researchers become frustrated with the limitations of having to read dusty papers in one specific room and being allowed only to take notes by pencil for the few hours a day the archive is open to the public.

Tracking and Tracing

One of the most difficult tasks in archival research is tracing common events or persons through the materials. Even if all materials are in one location, the same event or relationship may appear in several places in many forms. Researchers sort through mounds of paper to find bits of evidence here and there.

Drudgery, Luck, and Serendipity

Archival research is often painstakingly slow. Spending many hours pouring over partially legible documents can be very tedious. Also, researchers will often discover holes in collections, gaps in a series of papers, or destroyed documents. Yet, careful reading and inspection of previously untouched material can yield startling new connections or ideas. The researcher may discover unexpected evidence that opens new lines of inquiry (see Elder et al. 1993, and Hill 1993).

Source: From W. Lawrence Neuman, *Social Research Methods, Qualitative and Quantitative Approaches,* 6/e. Published by Allyn and Bacon, 75 Arlington St., Boston, MA 02116. Copyright © 2006 by Pearson Education. Reprinted by permission of the publisher.

(our letters, television programs, commercials, clothing, and automobiles) will be primary sources for future historians. An example of a classic primary source is a bundle of yellowed letters written by a husband away at war to his wife and found in an attic by a researcher.

For example, in a historical study on poverty in one Kentucky community, Billings and Blee's (2000) data included manuscripts from a federal census (1850–1910) for both individuals and agriculture as well as tax rolls, deeds, wills, and court records; newspapers; state accounting board records; letters and reports by visiting preachers; and official data at the county and state level. They were able to link individuals, relationships, and households to create longitudinal files on individuals and families for a sixty-year period.

Published and unpublished written documents are the most important types of primary sources. Researchers find them in their original form or preserved in microfiche or on film. They are often the only surviving record of the words, thoughts, and feelings of people in the past. Written documents are helpful for studying societies and historical periods with writing and literate people. Robert Lilly, in his article "Dirty Details: Executing U.S. Soldiers During World War II," relied on official written documents and records in his fascinating historical study of the U.S. military's execution of eighteen soldiers in England from 1943 to 1945.[6] Highlight 13.3 examines Lilly and Thomson's (1997) noteworthy findings and conclusions in a

HIGHLIGHT 13.3
World War II, Military Justice, and Racism

More than half a million African-American soldiers served in Europe during World War II. This photograph was taken in Italy.

J. Robert Lilly and J. Michael Thomson (1997: 282–283) published an important article in the *British Journal of Criminology* on the U.S. military's use of capital punishment in England during World War II. It captures a fascinating and previously untold piece of criminal justice history. Notice how the authors, in summarizing their research and findings, contextualize this historical event within its own time frame so that the reader can better understand what happened and why.

The capital punishment literature suggests particular variables favour its use: people of colour, the socially disadvantaged, and offenders committing acts of violence. All three are powerful predictors of who is selected for execution. In "occupied" England, US execution files were disproportionately represented by soldiers of colour (African American and Mexican American), low ranks and by soldiers committing acts of violence. This paper uses an analysis of primary and secondary sources to examine another powerful explanatory tool: context. This is demonstrated by the paucity of the defence in these 18 capital cases, and the predominance of sex-related crimes, especially in a country where rape is not a capital offence. Each represents an example of how the military as a context influence the selection and outcome of capital cases.

We argue that the U.S. military is an institution fraught with concern with its legitimacy, which employs "military justice" as a disciplinary tool. It uses and abuses command influence, even at the highest levels of military discipline—executions. World War II ETO [European Theatre Operations] defense strategies in capital trials were especially weak because of overt and subtle command pressure to dispose of cases without questioning due process. The U.S. ETO military embraced a policy of Jim Crow segregation to defuse the powder keg of race relations, especially problems arising from the fraternization of African-American troops with British women. Violators were subject to the severest of penalties. When combined, the two contexts examined here dominated and illuminated the selection of racially mixed sex cases as a prime target for the hangman's noose.

related study dealing with military capital punishment and sexual racism. Another study by Brian Donovan (2005) analyzed the courtroom narratives found in fifteen sexual coercion cases tried in New York City from 1903 to 1918. The purpose of this historical research was to examine how early constructions of masculinity and femininity framed the court's discourse and outcomes.

A frequent criticism of these types of written sources is that most were written by elites or those in official organizations (notice above how Foucault relied on an official description of Damiens's execution). Thus, the views of the oppressed, or those outside official social institutions, are often overlooked. For example, it was illegal for slaves in the United States to read or write, and thus written sources on the experience of slavery have been indirect or difficult to find.

The written word on paper was the main medium of communication to record events and ideas prior to the widespread use of telecommunications, computers, and video technology. In fact, the spread of forms of communication that do not leave a permanent physical record (e.g., telephone conversations, computer records, and live television or radio broadcasts), and that have largely replaced letters, written ledgers, and newspapers, may make the work of future historians more difficult.

SECONDARY SOURCES.   Primary sources have realism and authenticity, but the practical limitation of time and access can restrict research on many primary sources to a narrow time frame or location. To get a broader picture, most historical researchers also use **secondary sources**, the writings of specialist historians who have spent years studying primary sources. Sam Walker's (1980) historical research discussed earlier relied mostly on secondary sources. Leonard and Leonard (2003: 5) recently completed a noteworthy historical study that "surveys the historiography of violence in America through the 1990s" concentrating on interpersonal violence (criminal homicide). Through the use of secondary sources, this piece provides an effective theoretical narrative, arguing, among other things, that the widespread availability of firearms is likely one reason that the United States has been uniquely violent as compared to other countries.

SECONDARY SOURCES

Qualitative data and quantitative data used in historical research. Information about events or settings are documented, or written later by historians or others who did not directly participate in the events or settings.

RUNNING RECORDS.   **Running records** consist of files or existing statistical documents maintained by organizations. An example of a running record is a file in a local sheriff's office that contains a record of every homicide in a county from 1875 to the present.

RECOLLECTIONS.   The statements or writings of individuals about their past lives or experiences based on memory are **recollections**. These can be in the form of memoirs, autobiographies, or interviews. Because memory is imperfect, recollections are often distorted in ways that primary sources are not. For example, Blee (1991) interviewed a woman in her late eighties about being in the Ku Klux Klan (see Highlight 13.4).

In gathering oral history, a type of recollection, a researcher conducts unstructured interviews with people about their lives or events in the past. This approach is especially valuable for nonelite groups or the illiterate. The oral history technique began in the 1930s and now has a professional association and scholarly journal devoted to it.[7] As demonstrated in Table 13.1, studies on memory suggest caution when a researcher uses oral history or recollections. As Schacter (2001: 9) remarked,

RUNNING RECORDS

Existing statistics research based on files, records, or documents that are maintained in a relatively consistent matter over a long period of time.

RECOLLECTIONS

Statements or writings about past experiences collected over time and based on a memory or stimulated by a review of old objects, photos, or notes.

> We tend to think of memories as snapshots from family albums that, if stored properly, could be retrieved in precisely the same condition in which they were put away. But we now know that we do not record our experience in the way a camera records them. . . . We extract key elements of our experience and store them. We then recreate or reconstruct our experiences rather than retrieve copies of them. Sometimes, in the process of reconstructing we add on feelings, beliefs, or even knowledge we have obtained after the experience.

HIGHLIGHT 13.4
Women of the Klan

In *Women of the Klan,* Kathleen Blee (1991) noted that, prior to her research, no one had studied the estimated 500,000 women in the largest racist, right-wing movement in the United States. She suggested that this might have been due to an assumption that women were apolitical and passive. Her six years of research into the unknown members of a secret society over sixty years previous shows the ingenuity needed in historical research.

Blee focused on the state of Indiana, where as many as 32 percent of White Protestant women were members of the Ku Klux Klan at its peak in the 1920s. In addition to reviewing published studies on the Klan, her documentary investigation included newspapers, pamphlets, and unpublished reports. She conducted library research on primary and secondary materials at over half a dozen college, government, and historical libraries. The historical photographs, sketches, and maps in the book give readers a feel for the topic.

Finding information was difficult. Blee did not have access to membership lists. She identified Klan women by piecing together a few surviving rosters, locating newspaper obituaries that identified women as Klan members, scrutinizing public notices or anti-Klan documents for the names of Klan women, and interviewing surviving women of the Klan.

To locate survivors sixty years after the Klan was active, Blee had to be persistent and ingenious. She mailed a notice about her research to every local newspaper, church bulletin, advertising supplement, historical society, and public library in Indiana. She obtained three written recollections, three unrecorded interviews, and fifteen recorded interviews. Most of her informants were over age eighty. They recalled the Klan as an important part of their lives. Blee verified parts of their memories through newspaper and other documentary evidence.

Membership in the Klan remains controversial. In the interviews, Blee did not reveal her opinions about the Klan. Although she was tested, Blee remained neutral and did not denounce the Klan. She stated, "My own background in Indiana (where I lived from primary school through college) and white skin led informants to assume—lacking spoken evidence to the contrary—that I shared their world-view" (p. 5). She did not find Klan women brutal, ignorant, and full of hatred. Blee got an unexpected response to a question on why the women had joined the Klan. Most were puzzled by the question. To them it needed no explanation—it was just "a way of growing up" and "to get together and enjoy."

Source: From W. Lawrence Neuman, *Social Research Methods, Qualitative and Quantitative Approaches,* 6/e. Published by Allyn and Bacon, 75 Arlington St., Boston, MA 02116. Copyright © 2006 by Pearson Education. Reprinted by permission of the publisher.

TABLE 13.1 Seven Deadly Sins of Memory

Schacter (2001) observed that memory loss or mistaken memory takes several forms:

1. *Transience.* Experiencing the slow, continuous decay of memory over time, such that the more distance in the past an event occurred, the less detail is recalled about it
2. *Absent-mindedness.* Focusing on one idea or thing so much that it misdirects one's attention so that other, simple things, are forgotten (e.g., focusing on a major project but forgetting to pick up the car keys)
3. *Blocking.* Searching unsuccessfully for information that the person possesses but cannot recall despite trying to do so at the moment (often phrased as "it is on the tip of my tongue")
4. *Misattribution.* Mistaking fantasy for reality, or what one heard from a friend or what one saw in a movie for one's own experience
5. *Suggestibility.* Being asked questions in such a way that a person begins to distort his or her memory and believe things happened that did not happen
6. *Bias.* Recalling things in a distorted way, often interjecting ideas, feelings, o beliefs that occurred later in time, or after the remembered event, into it
7. *Persistence.* Being unable to forget something despite trying

Source: From W. Lawrence Neuman, *Social Research Methods, Qualitative and Quantitative Approaches,* 6/e. Published by Allyn and Bacon, 75 Arlington St., Boston, MA 02116. Copyright © 2006 by Pearson Education. Reprinted by permission of the publisher.

Some people "rewrite" the past to make it more consistent with current beliefs or remember the past in a self-enhancing way (i.e., inaccurately recall themselves in a more positive way). Older adults (usually beginning sometime in their fifties) tend to lose the memory of specific details about past events more than do younger people. More highly educated, mentally active older adults show less memory loss, but some degree of individual or collective memory distortion is relatively frequent.[8]

Limits of Secondary Sources

The two major limitations of secondary historical evidence include (1) problems of inaccurate historical accounts written by other researchers, and (2) a lack of historical research in crime and justice research. Often, though, the problem is one of too much information. The many volumes of secondary sources present a maze of details and interpretations for the historical researcher. She or he must transform the mass of descriptive studies into an intelligible picture. This picture needs to be consistent with and reflective of the richness of the evidence. It also must bridge the many specific time periods or locales.

Another limitation is in reading the works of historians.[9] Historians do not present theory-free, objective facts. They implicitly frame raw data, categorize information, and shape evidence using the organizing concepts of their preference. These concepts are often a mixture drawn from journalism, the language of historical actors, ideologies, philosophy, everyday language in the present, and social science. They may be vague, applied inconsistently, and not mutually exclusive nor exhaustive. For example, a historian describes a group of people in a nineteenth-century town as *upper class*. But he or she never defines the term and fails to link it to a theory of social classes.

A second problem is that the historian's selection procedure is not transparent. Historians select some information from all possible evidence. As Carr (1961: 138) noted, "History therefore is a process of selection in terms of historical significance . . . from the infinite oceans of facts the historian selects those which are significant for his purpose." Yet, the historical researcher does not know how this was done. Without knowing the selection process, a historical researcher must rely on the historian's judgments, which can contain biases.[10] For example, a historian reads 10,000 pages of newspapers, letters, and diaries, and then boils down this information into summaries and selected quotes in a 100-page book. We do not know whether information that the historian left out is relevant for our purposes.

Another issue is in the organization of the evidence. Historians organize evidence as they write narrative history. This compounds problems of undefined concepts, the selection of evidence, and theoretical preferences. In the historical narrative, the writer organizes material chronologically around a single coherent "story." Each part of the story is connected to each other part by its place in the time order of events. Together, all the parts form a unity or whole. Telling the story necessarily involves causal thinking—that is, if X (or X plus Z) occurred, then Y would occur, and if X (or X plus Z) had not occurred, something else would have followed. The researcher must recreate a logical interdependency between earlier and later events. The historical theoretical narrative differs from quantitative explanation in which the researcher identifies and tests statistical patterns to infer causes.

A difficulty of the narrative is that the organizing tool—time order or position in a sequence of events—does not alone denote theoretical or historical causality. In other words, the narrative may fail to address all three criteria (temporal order, association, and the elimination of plausible alternatives) for establishing causality. The narrative method can, therefore, obscure underlying causal models or processes when a sloppy historian includes events in the narrative that have no causal significance (e.g., adding them to enrich the background or context to add color).

Limits of Primary Sources

The major difficulty the historical researcher has to deal with when using secondary sources is the historian. When using primary sources, the major issue is that only a fraction of everything written or used in the past has survived into the present. Moreover, what survived is a nonrandom sample of what once existed. Lowenthal (1985: 191–192) observed, "The surviving residues of past thoughts and things represent a tiny fraction of previous generations' contemporary fabric."

Historical researchers attempt to read primary sources with the eyes and assumptions of a contemporary who lived in the past. They "bracket" or hold back knowledge of subsequent events and modern values. Cantor and Schneider (1967: 46) wrote, "If you do not read the primary sources with an open mind and an intention to get inside the minds of the writings and look at things the way they saw them, you are wasting your time."

For example, when reading a source produced by a slaveholder, moralizing against slavery or faulting the author for not seeing its evil is not worthwhile. The researcher holds back moral judgments and becomes a moral relativist while reading primary sources. He or she must "think and believe like his subjects, discover how they performed in their own eyes" (Shafer 1980: 165) (remember Weber's *verstehen*).

Another problem is that locating primary documents is a time-consuming task. A researcher must search through specialized indexes and travel to archives or specialized libraries. Primary sources are often located in a dusty, out-of-the-way room full of stacked cardboard boxes containing masses of fading documents. These may be incomplete, unorganized, and in various stages of disarray. Once the documents or other primary sources are located, the researcher evaluates them by subjecting them to external and internal criticism (depicted in Figure 13.1).

External criticism means we evaluate the authenticity of a document itself to be certain that it is not a fake or a forgery. Criticism involves asking, was the document created when it is claimed to have been, in the place where it was supposed to be, and by the person who claims to be its author? Why was the document produced to begin with, and how did it survive?

Once the document passes as being authentic, we use **internal criticism**, an examination of the document's contents to establish credibility. We evaluate whether what is recorded was based on what the author directly witnessed or is secondhand information. This requires examining both the literal meaning of what is recorded and the subtle connotations or intentions. We note other events, sources, or people mentioned in the document and ask whether they can be verified.

Many types of distortions can appear in primary documents. One is **bowdlerization**—a deliberate distortion designed to protect moral standards or furnish a particular image. For example, a photograph is taken of the front of a building. Trash and beer cans are scattered all around this building, and the paint is faded. The photograph, however, is taken of the one part of the building that has little trash and is framed so that the trash does not show; darkroom techniques make the faded paint look new.

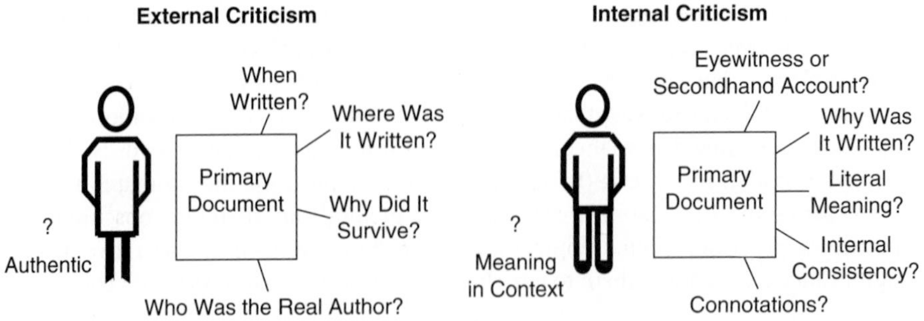

EXTERNAL CRITICISM

Checking the authenticity of primary historical sources by accurately locating the place and time of its creation (e.g., it is not a forgery).

INTERNAL CRITICISM

A way to establish the authenticity and credibility of primary historical sources and determine its accuracy as an account of what occurred in the past.

BOWDLERIZATION

A deliberate distortion of the past designed to protect the appearance of a particular image.

FIGURE 13.1 Internal and External Criticism *Source:* From W. Lawrence Neuman, *Social Research Methods, Qualitative and Quantitative Approaches,* 6/e. Published by Allyn and Bacon, 75 Arlington St., Boston, MA 02116. Copyright © 2006 by Pearson Education. Reprinted by permission of the publisher.

Steps Taken in a Historical Research Project

1. Conceptualizing the Object of Inquiry. As with all research, historical researchers begin with a vague idea of what to study. They next become familiar with the historical setting of their study and conceptualize what exactly will be studied through reading several general historical works. This process assists in assembling organizing concepts and developing a list of research questions. Researchers may start with a loose model or set of preliminary concepts and apply them to a specific setting. The initial working concepts contain implicit assumptions or organizing categories that they use to see the world, "package" observations, and search through evidence. Historical researchers recognize that their initial orientation is guided to some extent by their own ideological and theoretical assumptions. They take care to avoid what is called the Baconian fallacy. Named for Francis Bacon (1561–1626), it assumes that a researcher operates without preconceived questions, hypotheses, ideas, assumptions, theories, paradigms, postulates, prejudices, or presumptions of any kind.

2. Locating Evidence. Next, a researcher locates and gathers evidence through extensive bibliographic work. A researcher uses many indexes, catalogs, and reference works that list what libraries contain. The researcher frequently spends many weeks searching for sources in libraries, travels to several different specialized research libraries, and spends months or years reading books and articles. In historical-comparative research, the researcher sometimes has to become familiar with a foreign language.

As the researcher masters the literature and takes detailed notes, he or she completes many specific tasks: creating a bibliography list (on cards or computer) with complete citations, taking notes that are neither too skimpy nor too extensive (i.e., more than one sentence but less than dozens of pages of quotes), and developing a file on themes or working hypotheses.

A researcher adjusts initial concepts, questions, or focus on the basis of what he or she discovers in the evidence. New issues and questions arise as she or he reads and considers a range of research reports at different levels of analysis (e.g., general context and detailed narratives on specific topics) and multiple studies on a topic, crossing topic boundaries.

3. Evaluating Quality of Evidence. As a historical researcher gathers evidence, he or she asks two questions: How relevant is the evidence to emerging research questions and evolving concepts? How accurate and strong is the evidence?

The question of relevance is a difficult one. As the focus of research shifts, evidence that was not relevant can become relevant. Likewise, some evidence may stimulate new avenues of inquiry and a search for additional confirming evidence.

The researcher reads evidence for three things: the implicit conceptual framework, particular details, and empirical generalizations (factual statements on which there is agreement). He or she evaluates alternative interpretations of evidence and looks for "silences," or cases in which the evidence fails to address an event, topic, or issue. For example, when examining a group of leading male merchants, a researcher may find documents that ignore their wives and many servants.

Researchers try to avoid fallacies in the evidence. Fischer (1970) provided an extensive list of such fallacies. For example, the fallacy of **pseudoproof** is a failure to place something into its full context. The evidence might state that there was a 50 percent increase in income taxes, but its impact is not meaningful outside of a context. The researcher must ask, Did other taxes decline? Did income increase? Did the tax increase apply to all income? Was everyone affected equally? Another fallacy to avoid with historical evidence is **anachronism**, when an event appears to have occurred before or after the time it actually did. A researcher should be precise about the sequence of events and note discrepancies in dating events in evidence.

4. Organizing the Evidence. As a researcher gathers evidence and locates new sources, he or she begins to organize the data. Obviously, it is unwise to take notes madly and let them pile up haphazardly. A researcher begins a preliminary analysis by noting low-level generalizations or themes. For example, in a study of political revolution, a researcher develops a theme: The rich

PSEUDOPROOF

A failure to place a historical event within its full context.

ANACHRONISM

An error whereby a historical researcher locates an event before or after when it actually occurred.

peasants supported the old regime. He or she can record this theme in his or her notes and later assign it significance.

Next, a researcher organizes evidence, using theoretical insights to stimulate new ways to organize data and for new questions to ask of evidence. The interaction of data and theory means that a researcher goes beyond a surface examination of the evidence to develop new concepts by critically evaluating the evidence based on theory.

5. Synthesizing. The next step is the analytical process of synthesizing evidence. The researcher refines concepts and moves toward a solid historical description, and a general explanatory model after most of the evidence is in. Old themes or concepts are revised, and new ones are created. Concrete events give meaning to concepts. The researcher looks for patterns across time or cultures, and draws out similarities and differences with analogies. He or she organizes divergent events into sequences and groups them together to create a larger coherent picture. Plausible explanations are then developed that subsume both concepts and evidence into an articulate whole. The researcher then reads and rereads notes and sorts and resorts them on the basis of organizing schemes. She or he looks for links or connections while looking at the evidence in different ways.

Synthesis links evidence with ideas. Historical researchers often use metaphors. For example, large increases in incarceration are like a "runaway train without brakes." Each element of the metaphor has to be elaborated for it to work (e.g., what types of limits, or brakes, are missing). Metaphors can be powerful sensitizing devices.

6. Writing a Report. The last step is to combine evidence, concepts, and synthesis into a research report. The careful crafting of evidence, description, and explanation makes or breaks historical or historical-comparative research. A researcher distills mountains of evidence into exposition and prepares extensive footnotes. She or he weaves together evidence and arguments to communicate a coherent, convincing picture and story to readers (see Chapter 14). In quantitative research it is primarily the quantitative data and analysis that convinces the readers of its credibility. In historical research, it is the extent to which the historical narrative comes across as rigorous, intellectually honest, logically consistent, empirically grounded, and theoretically plausible.

Conclusion to Historical Research

This section provides a brief look at historical research ideas and methods. Historical and historical-comparative research are important methods for generating knowledge in our field. As crime and justice studies matures and diversifies, interest has steadily grown about the historical and global context of crime and justice phenomena. Placing what we study into historical context can be a highly revealing and powerfully sensitizing experience. Particular interest lately is being paid to those voices of the past not normally heard from. The views and experiences of the historically marginalized—children, women, minorities, poor—are critical for gaining a true understanding of their realities, and for a more thoughtful consideration of the linkages between the discrimination of the past and the continuing problems of today.

ACADEMIC LEGAL RESEARCH (ALR)

Justifying ALR

Legal research is generally not seen as a social science research method. Its placement within a research methods text, a book steeped in the social sciences, is unique and needs a brief explanation and justification.

Crime and justice studies has struggled with its study of the law. In an effort to establish itself as a legitimate social science discipline, criminology and criminal justice has strived to differentiate itself from the legal profession (what lawyers and legal scholars do). Consequently, studying the legal dimension of our field using legal research and analysis methods, while not uncommon, is not formally recognized as a legitimate means to generate knowledge.

This mind-set has changed significantly, however, in the last ten years. A growing number of researchers publish academic studies within crime and justice journals relying exclusively on legal research for their data collection and analysis (see Chapter 1), and a much larger number incorporate legal research methods within studies that use more traditional social science approaches. There is an increasing realization that comprehensive studies of most crime or criminal justice topics require an examination of its legal dimension—rendering a working knowledge of legal research methods essential, even if the study itself is primarily social science oriented. Moreover, generating knowledge through legal research methods can be a highly valuable skill for the practitioner or future practitioner.

We must emphasize, though, that this section is not concerned so much with the type of legal research that practicing attorneys and paralegals conduct. Their research revolves around establishing what is known as *legal authority* to convince the court of an argument about the law. We labeled this in Chapter 1 as **technical legal research**. What we're concerned with is **academic legal research** (ALR). Academic legal research can be defined as the systematic collection and legal analysis of law-related sources in order to generate knowledge about a given crime and justice subject. ALR is used in scholarly law journals, a host of crime and justice journals, numerous social science journals, and scholarly books.

We'll explore in this section how the ALR process has parallels to the social scientific research process. The basic research steps, for example, are quite similar, in addition to its various purposes (exploratory, descriptive, explanatory, and evaluative). The analysis process is similar in that it examines a body of work and deciphers it for patterns, themes, and meaning. However, legal research and thinking are also unique in that they follow their own system of legal logic (as opposed to scientific logic), their own rules for data collection, and some unique methods to analyze these data. Our coverage of this complex methodology, steeped in a long and rich tradition, will be admittedly cursory.

The General Idea of ALR

Let's revisit the basic question that encapsulates what most research tries to determine: What is really the case? The academic legal researcher tries to ascertain what the case is with regard to a legal controversy, ambiguity, trend, or problem. The data collected to figure this out are found in the written documents associated with the legal system; for example: constitutions (e.g., the U.S. Constitution); federal and state law enacted by legislatures; and the body of case law set forth by judicial rulings within individual legal cases. Similar to historical or QDA research, the ALR researcher then analyzes these data by figuring out what they mean in relation to some research question.

Let's say, for instance, that we have questions about the growing use of police "dynamic entries" into private residences for the purposes of searching for contraband—usually drugs, guns, and illegally obtained cash. (As noted in previous chapters, the United States has experienced a significant growth in "no-knock" drug raids conducted by SWAT teams.) Our research question originates from reading a local newspaper story in October 2002 that detailed a situation where a fifty-two-officer SWAT team in Eugene, Oregon, conducted a surprise predawn drug raid on a couple's home (and their two rental houses) because the couple was suspected of growing marijuana. We read that the SWAT team set off flash-bang grenades, forcibly entered the home from multiple directions using a "no-knock" warrant, and threw the couple onto the floor from their bed while the house was ransacked. Further, they refused to let the woman arrestee get dressed, and then tied a black hood over her head and led her, mostly naked, out of the house into a patrol car. The raid yielded no drugs and no drug conviction.[11]

Perhaps we had previously assumed that the U.S. Constitution ensured the inner sanctity of the home against unreasonable government intrusion, and this case piqued our curiosity. We decide to research the constitutional and case law associated with no-knock police raids and the rules associated with police knocking and announcing before entering a private residence. Our research

TECHNICAL LEGAL RESEARCH

The search for legal authority conducted by legal professionals designed to convince the courts of a particular legal position.

ACADEMIC LEGAL RESEARCH

The systematic collection and legal analysis of law-related sources to generate knowledge about a given crime and justice subject.

evaluative. Kopel's research on the Darfur genocide is quite broad in its coverage (exploratory), but it ultimately is geared toward answering an evaluative question: Does international law provide the targets of genocide the legal right to arm and defend themselves against such governmental behavior? The hate-crime research reviewed above is explanatory: What explains the wide disparity between hate-crime legislation and its implementation in practice? The topic of criminalizing accidents is exploratory: documenting and exploring the nature of the criminal law system reacting to accidents and negligence as serious crime.

3. *Design Study.* ALR basically involves the collection and analysis of documents—similar to content analysis. A body of law—both statutes and case law—is collected and then examined to determine general trends, clarify issues, evaluate effectiveness, or shed light on a historical event. Its design, just as with content analysis, involves thinking through the research questions to be answered, what documents will be collected, and how they will be analyzed. Another important consideration is whether legal research techniques will be married with more traditional research methods (socio-legal research).

Craig Hemmens and Daniel Levin (2000) published an interesting piece of legal research on the topic of the right to resist unlawful arrest. The researchers designed the study to include an examination of common-law cases and thinking regarding a citizen's right to resist an unlawful police arrest, as well as a review of recent cases to shed light on where the law is headed. They conclude that the recent and significant legal erosion of the right to resist arrest is "based on a misunderstanding of the original justifications for the right and that there remains a great need for the right, particularly as new police tactics increase the probability of arbitrary assertions of authority" (Hemmens and Levin 2000: 472).

4. *Collect Data.* Entire books are dedicated to locating and collecting legal research data. The law is basically a highly complex set of rules found in common-law cases; a voluminous array of federal, state, and municipal statutes; and a massive body of case law found at the appellate law level (both federal and state) and in local court rulings. The original source of these rules is what legal researchers refer to as primary sources of authority (see above). The hate-crime study discussed above collected primary sources of authority in the form of the original hate-crime statutes and its subsequent case law. Similarly, Kopel's Darfur legal research collected international law passed by the United Nations dealing with the crime, genocide. Secondary sources of authority are also collected—these include law journal articles, comments from members of the judiciary (e.g., Supreme Court justice giving a speech), and scholarly legal treatises.

Most legal researchers recommend starting with secondary sources. This allows us to first find out what research has been done in our area of interest, and second draw from the work of other legal scholars, potentially eliminating the need to conduct exhaustive research in some area related to our study using original sources. For example, two crime and justice scholars—Craig Hemmens and David Jones—have published articles on recent Supreme Court rulings associated with no-knock drug raids.[14] Using these secondary sources of authority could potentially eliminate a lot of work if we were inquiring into this area of the law.

Collecting accurate and comprehensive legal data poses a significant challenge. However, as reviewed in detail in Highlight 13.5, computerized legal search engines such as *Westlaw* and *LexisNexis* simplify the task and provide great opportunities for documenting and making sense of national legal trends. The services not only provide valuable search engines they also contain most of the original documents (both primary and secondary) needed to conduct legal research. Vaughn and Collins (2004), for example, used Westlaw to collect litigation cases from across the United States that dealt with the issue of medical malpractice in jails and prisons. Through collecting an exhaustive database of medical malpractice legal cases in correctional facilities, they were able to develop four areas of concern: (1) inadequate and inappropriate medication; (2) inappropriate medical procedures; (3) inappropriate diagnosis of serious medical conditions, and (4) undertreatment of serious medical problems.

5. *Analyze the Data.* The next step involves the analysis of the primary and secondary sources of authority collected. ALR analysis is similar to qualitative document analysis, or historical research, in that the researcher uses an inductive process of making sense of the data through developing chronologies, making categorizations, organizing concepts, and providing explanations. Collecting legal data and conducting the analysis are often done simultaneously.

There is one analytical technique unique to legal research that needs reviewing. Perhaps the most important skill the academic legal researcher must possess is the ability to read and decipher the meaning found in judicial rulings. The legal world is in some ways a self-contained system of language and logic. Competent ALR requires a close familiarity with this language and its logic.

Recall that case law is established through rulings made by judges. These are published in federal and state reports, and can be found in their original form in law libraries, and in electronic form within legal data services such as Westlaw. Remember that these rulings, especially those made by the appellate courts, establish precedent based on certain legal principles. A central task of ALR, then, is to be able to identify and accurately interpret the court's rulings and reasoning for these rulings.

Analyzing the legal meaning of these rulings involves sifting carefully through a judicial ruling and succinctly capturing the following:

- understanding the facts of the case,
- identifying the central legal issue or controversy,
- uncovering the principle of the case (or its *ratio decidendi*), and
- detailing the legal reasoning used in the case.

Conducting these **case reviews** can be quite time consuming for the uninitiated; however, with practice, the essence of even lengthy rulings can be discerned fairly quickly.

6. *Interpret Data.* Interpreting legal data generally involves a process of synthesis, where a large body of information is merged into a coherent narrative that answers our research questions. Michael Vaughn (1999), for example, analyzed hundreds of judicial rulings related to police officers committing acts of sexual violence against female citizens while on duty. He completed a case review for each relevant case. These cases ranged from full body-cavity searches on females detained for traffic violations to the actual on-duty rape of female citizens. He was interested in the extent to which the court has addressed this problem and its application of criminal and civil law in these cases. His interpretation of these judicial rulings was that police departments are often found legally liable for these acts of police sexual violence against citizens, especially when the acts of the officer are "incidental to authorized agency activities." Vaughn concludes that both police administrators and police academics should recognize police sexual violence as a serious problem.

7. *Inform Others.* Most academic legal research informs others by publishing their research and findings in academic journals. As mentioned in Chapter 1, though, some academicians use their legal research when providing expert witness testimony in civil litigation cases—whether testifying either for or against criminal justice agencies.

CASE REVIEWS

A method of reviewing the narrative contained in a court ruling that captures the facts of the case, the central legal issue, the legal principle at the heart of the case, and the legal reasoning employed.

Conclusion to Legal Research

Even though our research methods are founded in the social sciences, crime and justice studies cannot avoid the necessity of generating credible knowledge about the law. This section examined the methods used to collect and analyze legal data for purposes of answering academic research questions. Oftentimes, this endeavor mixes traditional social science approaches to research with legal research, which we referred to as socio-legal research. Academic legal research methods are also emerging as an essential tool in the comparative researcher's handbag. Studying international trends in crime and crime control requires an ability to collect, analyze, and make sense of the rapidly evolving arena of international law.

MIXED METHODS RESEARCH

Beyond Conflict and Exclusion

We have referred throughout this book, with a certain level of caution, to the opportunities for mixing qualitative and quantitative research methods. Our position has been that these two types of research can be seen and applied in a complementary fashion. The uninitiated might wonder, why this is even an issue, why the caution, and why wouldn't we mix them? The answer lies in how knowledge progresses, the nature of academic politics, and how organizations establish their identities.

What we've experienced in the development of crime and justice studies is a common pattern in organizational dynamics: As a young organization attempts to establish its identity (who it is, what it does, and why it does what it does), differing factions within that organization vie for power, carve out territory, and establish their own identities. Conflicts and power struggles erupt between factions, each attempting to make over the organization's institutional identity in their own image. The factions tend to dismiss, if not outright malign, the views and activities of rival factions in an effort to discredit them. The objective is to dominate, marginalize, and, if possible, eliminate the competition—blinding them to the potential worth and benefits of the other factions' views and activities. Sharp lines are drawn around the differing factions' supposedly distinct positions and ideas. This process is similar to Thomas Kuhn's theory diagrammed in Chapter 2, which illustrates how the progression of knowledge in scientific disciplines evolves from normal science to conflict, to new paradigms.

Such has been the case in crime and justice studies. Using the scenario above, we can simply replace "organization" with "crime and justice studies," and "factions" with "qualitative versus quantitative approaches." Each faction (*quants vs. quals*) have traditionally viewed the other in adversarial terms (us vs. them), and therefore adopted a type of binary or exclusionary logic, in which our methodological choices are limited to either one or the other approach, with both camps viewing each other's as inferior.

It is in this context that discussing a mixed approach—a third choice that emphasizes inclusion and compatibility—is quite different from historical precedent. Our discipline, by recently demonstrating a willingness to embrace this middle way, has matured considerably in just the last ten years. The old dismissive and exclusionary mind-set of the past is giving way to a new, more nuanced outlook that allows for a diversity of approaches. Valuing diversity can be seen as a form of triangulation, in which crime and justice phenomena can be studied and viewed from differing angles, allowing for a more holistic and rigorous answer to the question, what is really the case? Although the process is nowhere near complete, our disciplinary identity is being reconstructed to embrace a paradigm of inclusion rather than exclusion. Highlight 13.6 examines your authors' first experiences with mixed methods research.

The mixed methods research approach will likely in the near future constitute the third major methodological movement in crime and justice research (qualitative and quantitative being the other two).[15] Our field, in fact, is on the cutting edge of mixing qualitative and quantitative data in its study of crime and criminal justice phenomena.

The General Idea of Mixed Methods Research

In everyday life, when we need to solve a problem, we use whatever knowledge we have at our disposal to make good decisions. Suppose we're faced, for example, with a health issue. If we need additional knowledge, we might talk to a doctor, talk to other people who have experienced the same ailment, look up the scientific research on the Internet, explore what people in other countries do (e.g., German society has fully embraced the use of medicinal herbs and plants), or even conduct an informal survey of opinions found in medical chat rooms on the Internet. Generating comprehensive information, and then using it to answer the question competently, is the objective, not whether the "correct" approach to knowledge generation is employed. Results trumps allegiance to a particular approach to generating knowledge.

HIGHLIGHT 13.6
Discovering the Benefits of Mixed Methods Research

We are advocates of the mixed methods approach. We originally came to this position for pragmatic reasons, rather than philosophical. While Kraska was conducting his ethnographic field study on SWAT teams, he sensed that his microexperience with local SWAT teams likely reflected a much larger shift in the police institution as a whole. Being trained in the PSS tradition, he knew that he needed national-level, representative data, to test his grounded observations. So while he was still conducting the ethnography, he began planning a survey research project to determine if his ethnographic experiences represented national trends. Within a year after finishing the ethnography, he and his research team sent out two surveys: one to a representative sample of all police departments serving jurisdictions of 50,000 people or more, and then a second to agencies serving jurisdictions between 25,000 and 50,000 people.

The surveys provided difficult-to-refute quantitative data that documented a steep growth trend in the number of police paramilitary units nationwide and a massive increase in annual deployments. It also revealed some surprising developments that needed further clarification. For example, almost half of the respondents said that they trained with active-duty military personnel; in addition, nearly 20 percent said that they used their SWAT team to routinely conduct aggressive patrol functions in high-crime areas. As a way to follow up on these quantitative findings, the research team then conducted eighty-one in-depth telephone interviews with SWAT commanders from all over the country, asking them to provide qualitative data and insights regarding these unexpected findings.

Mixing qualitative and quantitative approaches yielded immediate and tangible benefits.

- The ethnography was invaluable for developing a knowledge survey instrument, based on insider information, ensuring a high response rate and the ability to document a host of important trends that only an insider would have known to ask about.
- The survey data were invaluable for establishing hard data about the growth and normalization of SWAT teams in the United States.
- The follow-up interviews provided context and qualitative depth to some of the more surprising and controversial quantitative findings.

One finding, for example, surprised the researchers. Even though on the surface it seemed community policing and militarized policing contradicted each other, the police themselves cited them as complementary when responding to the survey. The in-depth interviews of SWAT team commanders revealed their rationale.

We conduct a lot of saturation patrol. We do Terry stops and aggressive field interviews. These tactics are successful as long as the pressure stays on relentlessly. The key to our success is that we're an elite crime-fighting team that's not bogged down in the regular bureaucracy. We focus on *quality of life* issues like illegal parking, loud music, bums, neighborhood troubles. We have the freedom to stay in a hot area and clean it up—particularly gangs. Our tactical enforcement team works nicely with our department's emphasis on community policing. (Kraska and Cubellis 1997: 624)

In addition to the principles of inclusion and compatibility, the philosophy behind using mixed methods is pragmatic. The mixed methods approach assumes that mixing qualitative methods with quantitative methods will yield more complete knowledge about a research question than any one type might alone—what's known as **monomethod**. It matters little that the goals of interpretive social science (ISS) approach (empathetic understanding) differ from positivist social science (the development of causal laws). The principle of inclusiveness found in the mixed methods approach takes the position that both goals are worth pursuing. Whether we mix ethnography with survey research, content analysis with qualitative document analysis, historical with secondary data analysis, experimental with in-depth interviews, or a slew of other possible combinations, the idea is that all are potentially compatible and mutually beneficial.

Johnson and Christensen's (2006: 411) fundamental principle of mixed methods research is instructive: "Researchers should collect and analyze multiple sets of data using different approaches and methods in such a way that the resulting mixture or combination has complementary strengths and non-overlapping weaknesses." In other words, mixing quantitative and qualitative methods draws on the strengths of each while minimizing their weaknesses. For example, whereas survey research is able to generate general knowledge about large numbers of people, qualitative research

MONOMETHOD
A label used to describe a research study that relies on only one method of data collection and analysis.

Researchers studying domestic violence are increasingly relying on mixed methods to collect a comprehensive picture.

generates in-depth, context-based knowledge about a small group of individuals. If a national-level survey study of juvenile probation officers, for example, documents low worker morale as measured through a reliable index, in-depth qualitative interviews could provide important interpretive-based information. Combining quantitative findings with qualitative insights is invaluable for effectively exposing the nature of the phenomena under study.

A quick search of the research literature will demonstrate that crime and justice studies is clearly a leader in the mixed methods movement. In an important article published in the journal *Violence against Women*, T. K. Logan, Lisa Shannon, and Robert Walker (2005) studied the nature of the protective order process for domestic violence situations in rural and urban areas. Through a comprehensive approach, they found that rural women experience unique and in some ways significantly worse domestic violence problems than do women living in urban areas. Criminal justice measures such as protective orders are poorly implemented in rural versus urban areas, and the culture in rural communities, including within the legal system itself, is a serious impediment to effective implementation. The authors used government documents, interviews, focus groups, and other methods to construct a comprehensive and multiperspective view of the phenomenon under study.

This approach coincides with the general premise posited throughout this text that viewing a phenomenon through more than one theoretical and/or methodological lens yields a more complete picture of our object of study. As Norman K. Denzin said in 1978, "The bias inherent in any particular data source, investigators, and particularly method will be cancelled out when used in conjunction with other data sources, investigators and methods. . . . The result will be a convergence upon the truth about some social phenomena" (p. 14).

Major Features of Mixed Methods Research

We can define **mixed methods research**, therefore, as that class of research in which quantitative and qualitative data collection and analysis techniques are used in a single study, or series of studies, examining a particular object of study. "Its central premise is that the use of quantitative and qualitative approaches in combination provides a better understanding of research problems than either approach alone" (Creswell and Clark 2006: 5).

Let's look now at how these two approaches might be mixed. As seen in Figure 13.3, we can conceptualize mixed methods research on a three-part continuum. In general, we have pure qualitative research at one end, pure quantitative at the other end, and fully integrated in the middle. Mixing quantitative and qualitative usually involves one of three approaches:

MIXED METHODS RESEARCH

That class of research in which quantitative and qualitative data collection and analysis techniques are used in a single study, or series of studies, examining a particular object of study.

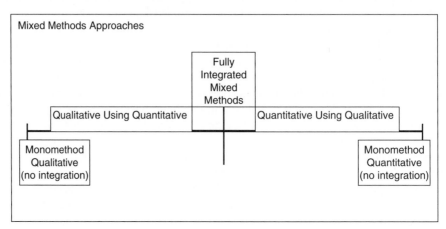

FIGURE 13.3 Mixed Methods Approach on a Continuum

1. A predominantly quantitative study employs qualitative data and analysis to shed additional light on their quantitative findings
2. A predominantly qualitative study employs quantitative data and analysis to bolster their qualitative findings.
3. Both quantitative and qualitative data and analysis are used in a fully integrated fashion.

The survey research on police paramilitary units seen in Highlight 13.6 uses qualitative data and analysis to shed light on the quantitative findings (#1). Logan's study on domestic violence protective orders is an example of a full integration and mixture of methods (although the actual article emphasizes quantitative over qualitative findings) (#3).

The decision for the mixed methods researcher boils down to whether she or he is going to emphasize a positivist approach over the interpretive, vice versa, or treat them as equal. Another important decision—and a key distinction in the mixed methods approach—is timing: Will the qualitative and quantitative components of the study be conducted concurrently (at the same time) or sequentially (one after the other)? The concurrent route most often includes both qualitative and quantitative findings in a single study. The sequential approach usually involves two studies or more, each reporting on either qualitative or quantitative data. The SWAT research in Highlight 13.6 was conducted sequentially (first the ethnography and then the survey research), and concurrently (survey research and the in-depth interviews conducted simultaneously) (see Table 13.2).

TABLE 13.2 Mixed Data Sources/Analysis

1. **Archival analysis.** Review the records of the college program since inception (1997), tracking rates of persistence, women drafted, dropout rates, racial and ethnic distribution, percent in precollege and college courses.
2. **Inmate-initiated research.** The impact of college, which consisted of one-on-one interviews of four to five women each by 15 inmates (N = 65 interviews by 15 inmates). The interviews were typically conducted with women who lived on the floor of the researchers.
3. **Focus group interviews with inmates.** Selected on the basis of the women's status in the program: dropout; GED students; precollege students; first-time college students; adolescent children of women in college; college leaders/mentors; women in the ESL class (N = 43). Each focus group lasted between 45 minutes and 1 hour, was tape-recorded, and transcribed.
4. **Individual interviews.** Women who were in college at Bedford Hills, postrelease from prison (N = 15). These women were randomly selected from a list of recently released women in the New York City area for whom sufficient contact information was available. Each interview was conducted at the Graduate Center of the City University of New York, and lasted anywhere from 1–3 hours. Women were compensated $50 for participating in the interview.
5. **Participant observations.** The research team met every 2–3 weeks for 4 years. During this time, we were able to gather much data from our participation and observations within the Learning Center, as well as ongoing conversations with the superintendent, students in the Learning Center, and the prison-based members of the research team.
6. **Interviews with correctional administrators and officers.** In order to understand the impact of the college program on the prison environment, interviews with administrators and correctional officers would be essential. The superintendent, deputy superintendent for programs, and four correctional officers were interviewed (N = 6). Each interview lasted between 20 and 40 minutes.
7. **Focus group and surveys of educators.** In order to document the impact of the college program on educators and the college communities, a focus group with college faculty (N = 20) was conducted by the research team in 1999. A survey was distributed in 2000 to faculty of the Spring 2000 semester.
8. **Quantitative recidivism analysis.** 274 women who had attended college while in prison and 2,031 who did not attend college, tracked over 36 months.

Source: Adapted from Torre, Maria, and Michelle Fine (2005). "Bar none: Extending affirmative action to higher education in prison." *Journal of Social Issues.* 61:569–594. Adapted with permission of Blackwell Publishing and the authors.

How to Conduct Mixed Methods Research

Mixed methods research is appropriate for exploratory, descriptive, explanatory, and evaluative research questions. Multiple methods are very helpful for exploring a new research area, as well as attempts to describe phenomena. In both instances, mixing statistics with qualitative observations and insights yields a more complete empirical picture. Examining the why of something is greatly enhanced by studying it both inductively and deductively.

Finally, even though we usually associate quantitative methods with evaluation research, qualitative methods can reveal key explanations for the success or failure of a policy or program that could only be extracted using qualitative techniques. A growing number of evaluative studies are collecting and analyzing qualitative data as a way to make more detailed and nuanced sense of their quantitative findings. As two mixed methods researchers stated in their study on African-American boys' involvement in drug trafficking, "By using a combination of qualitative and quantitative data gathering techniques, investigators can better clarify subtleties, cross-validate findings, and inform efforts to plan, implement, and evaluate intervention strategies" (Black and Ricardo 1994: 1066).

You might recall from Chapter 2 that progression of quantitative and qualitative studies differ—with quantitative being linear and fairly sequential, and qualitative being more contingent and flexible. When mixing the two, the best we can do is present a very generic approach.

1. *Determining Whether Mixed Methods Is Appropriate.* Our research topic will determine to some extent whether we use a mixed methods approach. If it is a fairly narrow topic that only attempts to answer a quantitative- or qualitative-oriented research question, then a monomethod approach is more appropriate. For example, if we want to test whether Headstart programs reduce a child's chances for engaging in criminality, then quantitative methods alone will suffice. However, if we want to understand the impact Headstart has had on its participants, from their point of view, a combination of survey research and in-depth qualitative interviews would be more appropriate.

When deciding on whether a mixed approach is desirable, we also need to consider the advantages and disadvantages (Table 13.3 provides a summary). We've already discussed the advantages; the disadvantages can be formidable. The first deals with the limitations of the researcher. Some researchers are quite uncomfortable with numbers and others are uncomfortable with empathetic understanding. Becoming well versed in both approaches can be time consuming and taxing. Another disadvantage is cost and time. Conducting a fully integrated mixed methods study can be much more work than concentrating on a single method. Sixty in-depth telephone interviews used to supplement a survey research study could mean additional

---

TABLE 13.3	Advantages and Disadvantages of Mixed Methods

Advantages
- Qualitative information (words, pictures) can add meaning and depth to numbers.
- Quantitative information can add clarity and precision to words and pictures.
- Enhances the researcher's ability to answer a greater range of research questions.
- Potentially enhances both validity and reliability.
- Examining an object of study using multiple approaches allows for more complete knowledge.

Disadvantages
- Carrying out multiple methods simultaneously can be taxing.
- The researcher has to be competent in multiple research approaches.
- Potential to be criticized by methodological purists.
- It is potentially more expensive and time consuming.

Source: Adapted from Johnson and Christensen's (2004: 414).

160-plus hours of work. The decision could hinge on whether the study involves one versus a team of researchers, and how many research assistants are available. Clearly Logan's research examined earlier could have only been conducted using a team approach.

2. *Selecting the Mixed Methods Design.* The possibilities in constructing a mixed design are vast. We have all the quantitative and qualitative approaches available to us, and they can be combined in any number of ways. Because the underlying philosophy is one of pragmatism, we are not constrained by epistemological concerns. The sole decision-making criterion is whether the design will yield credible and worthwhile data about our object of study. Several designs have already been noted throughout this section. Let's look at one more example.

Randy Gainey, Sara Steen, and Rodney Engen (2005) published an article in *Justice Quarterly*, "Exercising Options: An Assessment of the Use of Alternative Sanctions for Drug Offenders." Their research goal was to describe which drug offenders receive alternative sentences for drug offenses, which do not, and why. Put differently, their study inquires into the judicial decision-making process. Their quantitative data were derived from the state of Washington's sentencing commission. It included 25,028 felony drug arrestees that were processed over a three-year period. It also included a host of legal and extralegal variables that allowed for correlational analysis. Their qualitative data consisted of field interviews with twenty-three different prosecutors, defense attorneys, and judges.

The authors found that their dominant approach using quantitative analysis provided valuable findings, but they provided no context for understanding them. For example, the quantitative data demonstrated that Hispanic offenders were much less likely than Whites or Blacks to receive alternative sanctions. In-depth field interviews revealed several interesting explanations, including that most assume Hispanics will be deported and receiving treatment to be reintegrated into the community makes no sense. The researchers also found out that the high rate of all offenders receiving some sort of alternative sentence was likely motivated by legislative penalties that those in the courtroom work group feel are too harsh. As one judge put it:

> . . . I think that they're [mandatory sentencing guidelines] much, much too harsh. And what happens is the legislature makes political hay by making the penalties really harsh. And then they pass these little alternatives. . . . And that is the way the prosecutors and defense attorneys get rid of these cases without having to deal with the harsh penalties (Gainey et al. 2005: 498).

Gainey and colleagues used a highly feasible, and generally fruitful, mixed methods design—secondary data analysis combined with qualitative field interviews.

3. *Collect the Data.* Mixed methods researchers can employ any of the data collection methods reviewed in this book. This methodological freedom can of course lead to a confusing number of choices. The key is to keep in mind what combination will be most appropriate for the research purpose, for the research questions examined, and the practical constraints of the researcher (time and money). The alternative sentencing study should demonstrate that collecting the data does not have to be as comprehensive as the domestic violence protective order study, or the higher education for women prisoner study.

4. *Analyze and Interpret the Data.* The data analysis and interpretation process is the same in mixed methods research as it is for all the methods discussed in this book. The process, however, can be more dynamic and complex because the research at some point in the analysis and interpretation process compares their qualitative findings with the quantitative findings. This requires both the skills of the interpretive paradigm as well as those of the positivist. Consider the undertaking that Torre and Fine must have been confronted with in sorting through and making sense of these multiple sources and levels of data. In this way, mixed methods research will push crime and justice researchers to be better synthesizers of data and research findings.

5. *Inform Others.* The final step is writing up the report and disseminating the findings. This can come in the form of journal publication, agency report, consulting report, in-person presentation, or Internet presentation. Mixed methods can be presented in traditional form by presenting quantitative findings in one publication, qualitative findings in another, and then possibly synthesizing both into a larger book project. It is also ideally suited for the creative presentation of research. As noted earlier, many researchers are beginning to incorporate visual data and methods into their research projects, which happens to be a natural fit for the mixed methods approach.

Conclusion to Mixed Methods Research

Mixed methods research requires our field to change its traditional exclusionary way of thinking about qualitative and quantitative approaches. The methods we use to study our object of study should match our research objectives. In addition, trying to determine what is really the case from using differing approaches yields more complete knowledge about our object of study. We reviewed several different ways to approach mixed methods research, and looked at the various steps involved. Perhaps someday we will view monomethod research projects as the exception and mixed methods as the norm.

Conclusion

This chapter has reviewed three different approaches to the production of knowledge. Most are not discussed in crime and research textbooks, even though they are all quite important to our field. We hope this chapter has made clear that qualitative research methods go beyond ethnographic field research, and the qualitative researcher has many options available. We also hope that our discussion of mixed methods research has demonstrated that the traditional thinking of *quants versus quals* is unnecessary and inhibiting. Perhaps one day mixing methods will be the norm as opposed to the exception.

Key Terms

historical research *312*
historical-comparative
   research *313*
comparative
   research *313*
primary sources *315*
secondary sources *317*

running records *317*
recollections *317*
external criticism *320*
internal criticism *320*
bowdlerization *320*
pseudoproof *321*
anachronism *321*

technical legal
   research *323*
academic legal
   research *323*
legal authority *324*
stare decisis *324*
primary authority *324*

secondary authority *324*
Westlaw *324*
socio-legal research *326*
case reviews *329*
monomethod *331*
mixed methods
   research *332*

Review Questions

1. What is historical research, and what is historical-comparative research?
2. What are the similarities between field research and historical-comparative research?
3. What are the major features of historical research?
4. What questions are asked by a researcher using external criticism?
5. What are the limitations of using secondary sources?
6. What is academic legal research, and why does it belong in a social science-based research methods text?

7. What is stare decisis and what role does it play in conducting academic legal research?
8. What is socio-legal research? Give one example.
9. What are the major steps involved in conducting academic legal research?
10. What are the two major philosophical underpinnings to mixed methods research?
11. What is Johnson and Christensen's fundamental principle of mixed methods research?
12. Describe the mixed methods continuum.

Practicing Research

1. Find out what primary sources of historical data are available from your university or local library. Are any of these related to crime and justice phenomena or issues? If so, look through the documents and try to conceive a viable historical study using these materials. Write up your findings, and discuss your report in small groups.
2. Conduct a microqualitative document analysis study. Select a set of documents (visual or text) and analyze them qualitatively. The key here is to look for patterns of meaning and clues to these documents' social significance. It may be fruitful to use Kappeler's essay on semiotics to help make interpretive sense of your data.
3. Find one of the legal articles discussed in the academic legal research section of this chapter. Write a review of this article, including its purpose, methods, and major findings.
4. Find one of the mixed methods articles discussed in this chapter. Write a review of this article, including its purpose, various methods used, and major findings.

Notes for Further Study

1. Bruce Berg (2007) makes an excellent case for acknowledging the importance of historical research methods to our field.
2. The most often used textbook in our field, Maxfield and Babbie (2005), doesn't mention historical research.
3. See www.neh.gov/whoweare/mccullough/biography.html).
4. See Sally Hadden's (2001) authoritative book on slave patrols.
5. See Calhoun (1996), McDaniel (1978), Przeworski and Teune (1970), and Stinchcombe (1978) for additional discussion.
6. See Lilly (1996) and Lilly and Thomson (1997).
7. For additional information on oral history, see Dunaway and Baum (1984), Sitton and colleagues (1983), and P. Thompson (1978). Also see Prucha (1987: 78–80) for a guide to major collections of oral histories in the United States.
8. See Schacter (1995) and Schacter (2001: 20–21).
9. The word *read*, as used here, means to bring a theoretical framework and analytic purpose to the text. Specific details and the historian's interpretations are read "through" (i.e., passed, but not without notice) in order to discover patterns of relations in underlying structures. See Sumner (1979) for discussion. This relates to the objectivity question in historiography in Novick (1988) and Winkler (1989).
10. Bonnell (1980: 161), Finley (1977: 132), and Goldthorpe (1977: 189–190) discussed how historians use concepts. Selection in this context is discussed by Abrams (1982: 194) and Ben-Yehuda (1983).
11. For a complete description of this event along with the relevant legal cites, see Balko (2006).
12. Although beyond the scope of this book, there are also striking parallels between the major schools of thought in the law—(1) legal formalism, (2) legal realism, and (3) critical legal studies—and in social science research—(1) positivist, (2) interpretive, and (3) critical.
13. *Wilson v. Arkansas*, 514 U.S. 927 (1995); *Hudson v. Michigan*, 547 U.S. (2006).
14. See Hemmens and Mathias (2004) and Jones (2002). See also, Craig Hemmens and Chris Mathias, "*United States v. Banks*: The Knock and Announce Rule Returns to the Supreme Court," *Idaho Law Review* forthcoming.
15. The mixed methods approach has rapidly ascended in the social sciences due in large part to some excellent books that provide useful guides for understanding and execution. Our discussion in this section draws heavily from several of these books, especially those authored by John Creswell (1994, 1998, 2003, 2007) and Tashakkori and Teddlie (1998, 2003).

14

Presenting Crime
and Justice Research

Communing with Our Audience

Why Write a Report?

Writing Considerations
  Your Audience
  Style and Tone
  Organizing Thoughts
  Back to the Library

The Writing Process
    Highlight 14.1 Suggestions for Ending Writer's
      Block
  Rewriting

The Quantitative Research Report
  Abstract or Executive Summary
    Highlight 14.2 Suggestions for Rewriting
  Introduction and Presenting the Problem
  Describing the Methods
  Results and Tables Section
  Discussion Section

Drawing Conclusions

The Qualitative Research Report
    Highlight 14.3 Why Qualitative Research
      Reports Are Longer
  Ethnographic Field Research Reports
  Historical Research
    Highlight 14.4 Features to Consider in the
      Historical-Comparative Research Report

The Research Proposal
  Proposals to Fund Research

What Happens to the Research?

Conclusion

Conclusion to the Book

Key Terms

Review Questions

Practicing Research

Notes for Further Study

COMMUNING WITH OUR AUDIENCE

> But that's our business: to arrange ideas in so rational an order that another person can make sense of them. We have to deal with that problem on two levels. We have to arrange the ideas in a theory or narrative, to describe causes and conditions that lead to the effects that we want to explain, and do it in an order that is logically and empirically correct . . . . Finally, we want our prose to make the order we have constructed clear. We don't want imperfection in our prose to interfere with our readers' understanding. These two jobs converge and cannot be separated. (Becker 1986: 133).

This quote is taken from a valuable book, Howard Becker's *Writing for Social Scientists*. It's designed to help the social scientist write clearly, efficiently, and effectively. In the previous chapters, we have looked at how to design studies, gather data, and analyze the data. Yet, a research project is not complete until the researcher shares the results with others. Communicating the method used and results is a critical last step in the research process, and usually comes in the form of a written report. In Chapter 2, we saw how the norm of communalism emphasizes that researchers make public how they conducted their research and their findings. In Chapter 4, we saw how to locate previous studies in the scholarly literature. In this chapter, you will learn about presenting the knowledge we have generated.

In this last chapter, we examine how to write both quantitative and qualitative reports. We must describe to an audience how we conducted our study and the findings in a research report. The writing process is a serious endeavor. Conducting a study and reporting its results can create controversy. As we learned from the knowledge–power dynamic, the politics of research can affect not only how one conducts a study but also how its findings are disseminated and ultimately used. It is critical to present our research in such a clear, unambiguous manner that they are hard to be misused, misconstrued, or distorted—whether unintentionally or not. Crime and research may be imperfect, but its ultimate goals are to discover knowledge, expand understanding, and seek truth. We want to effectively and openly share the method and findings of our research with the social scientific community, perhaps the policy-making and practitioner community, and even beyond. It is not an overstatement to say that the clarity of our presentation is as important as the research itself.

WHY WRITE A REPORT?

After a researcher completes a project or a significant phase of a large project, she or he must communicate the findings to others through a research report. One can learn a lot about writing a research report by reading other reports and taking a course in scientific and/or creative writing.

A research report is a written document (or oral presentation based on a written document) that communicates the methods and findings of a research project to others. It is more than a summary of findings; it is a record of the research process. A researcher cannot wait until the research is done to think about the report; he or she must think ahead about the report and keep careful records while conducting research. In addition to findings, the report includes the reasons for initiating the project, a description of the project's steps, a presentation of data, and a discussion of how the data relate to the research question or topic. All these components are ideally woven together seamlessly.

The report tells others what you, the researcher, did, and what you discovered. It is a way of disseminating knowledge. As we've seen throughout this book, the research report plays a significant role in binding together the scientific community, and in communicating clearly with practitioners and the public. Other reasons for writing a report are to fulfill an educational or job assignment, to meet an obligation to an organization that paid for the research, to persuade a professional group about specific aspects of a problem, or to report about the effectiveness of a policy or program to a criminal justice organization. Communicating with the general public is rarely the primary method for communication of scientific results; it is usually a second stage of dissemination.

WRITING CONSIDERATIONS

Your Audience

Professional writers say, always know for whom you are writing. This is because communication is more effective when it is tailored to a specific audience. We write a research report differently depending on whether the primary audience is an instructor, students, professional social scientists, practitioners, or the general public. Whatever the audience, the writing should be clear, accurate, and well organized.

Instructors assign a report for different reasons and may place requirements on how it is written. In general, instructors want to see writing that reflects clear, logical thinking. Student reports should demonstrate a solid grasp of substantive and methodological concepts. A good way to do this is to use technical terms explicitly when appropriate; however, they should not be used excessively or incorrectly.

When writing for the uninitiated, it is best to define technical terms and label each part of the report. The discussion should proceed in a logical, step-by-step manner, using many specific examples. Use straightforward language to explain how and why you conducted the various steps of the research project. One strategy is to begin with the research question, then structure the report as an answer.

Scholars generally do not need definitions of technical terms or explanations of why standard procedures (e.g., random sampling) were used. They are most interested in how the research is linked to abstract theory or previous findings in the literature. They want a condensed, detailed description of research design. They pay close attention to how variables are measured, what type of research was done in the field, or the methods of data collection. Scholars like a compact, tightly written, but extensive section on data analysis, with a meticulous discussion of results.

Practitioners, because of their need for bottom-line knowledge, prefer a short summary of how the study was conducted. They also prefer the results of the study to be presented in a few simple charts and graphs. They like to see an outline of alternative paths of action implied by results with the practical outcomes of pursuing each path. It is best to place the details of research design and results in an appendix.

When writing for the general public, we use simple language, provide concrete examples, and focus on the practical implications of the findings. We only sometimes include details of research design or of results, and we're careful not to make unsupported claims. Informing the public is an important service, which can help nonspecialists make better judgments about public issues.

Style and Tone

Technical research reports are written in a narrow range of styles and have a distinct tone. Their purpose is to communicate clearly the research method and findings. Books based on an extensive research project or projects, on the other hand, often take more liberty in being creative, informal, and thought provoking.

Style refers to the types of words chosen by the writer, the cadence in the placement of words, and the length and form of sentences or paragraphs used. *Tone* is the writer's attitude or relation toward the subject matter. For example, an informal, conversational style (e.g., colloquial words, idioms, clichés, and incomplete sentences) with a personal tone (e.g., these are my feelings) is appropriate for writing a letter to a close friend, but generally not for research reports. Research reports have a formal and succinct (saying a lot in few words) style. The tone expresses distance from the subject matter; it is professional and serious. Qualitative researchers are more apt to use an informal style and a personal tone, but even here there are limits. Academic writing generally avoids moralizing, polemics, and flowery language. The goal is usually to inform using the data (letting the data speak for itself), not to passionately advocate a position or to entertain. Some academics have the ability, however, to do both.

A research report should be written with utmost accuracy and clarity. We should check and recheck details (e.g., page references in citations) and fully disclose how we conducted the research project. If readers detect carelessness in writing, they may question the knowledge itself. The details of a research project can be complex, and such complexity means that confusion is always a danger. It makes clear writing essential. Clear writing is best achieved by:

- thinking and rethinking the research problem, purpose, and design,
- explicitly and clearly defining all terms and concepts,
- mixing longer, more complex sentences and ideas with short, declarative sentences,
- using the simplest possible words available (e.g., "use" instead of "utilize"), and
- limiting conclusions to what is supported by the evidence.

Organizing Thoughts

Writing does not happen magically or simply flow out of a person when he or she puts pen to paper (or fingers to keyboard). Rather, it is hard work, which emanates only from careful preparation. It involves a sequence of steps and activities that result in a final product. Writing a research report is not radically different from other types of writing, although some steps differ and the level of complexity may be greater. *Students can get bogged down in the notion of sounding* "academic" *or* "profound." *They should instead think of writing as merely articulating thoughts on paper*—much like we do when we write a letter, a poem, a set of instructions, or a short story.

To prepare properly, the writer needs something about which to write. The "something" in the research report includes the topic, research question, design and measures, data collection techniques, results, and implications. With so many parts to write about, organization is essential. The most basic tool for organizing writing is the outline. Outlines help a writer ensure that all ideas are included and that the relationship between them is clear. Outlines are made up of topics (words or phrases) or sentences. Most of us are familiar with the basic form of an outline (see Table 14.1).

Outlines can help the writer, but they can also become a barrier if they are used improperly. An outline is simply a tool to help the writer organize ideas. It helps to: (1) put ideas in a sequence (e.g., what will be said first, second, and third), (2) group related ideas together (e.g., these are similar to each other, but differ from those), and (3) separate the more general, or higher-level, ideas from more specific ideas, and the specific ideas from very specific details.

Some students feel that they need a complete outline before writing, and that once an outline is prepared, they should avoid deviating from it. Few seasoned writers begin with a complete outline. The initial outline is sketchy because it is impossible to put all ideas in a sequence, group them together, or separate the general from the specific from the outset. For most writers, new ideas develop or become clearer in the process of writing itself, and the original outline is modified significantly.

The process of writing may not only reveal or clarify ideas for the writer, but it may also stimulate new ideas, new connections between ideas, a different sequence, or new relations between the general and the specific. In addition, the process of writing may stimulate reanalysis or a reexamination of the literature or findings. This does not mean beginning all over again. Rather, it means keeping an open mind to new insights and being candid about the research project.

TABLE 14.1 Form of Outline	
First major topic	One of the most important
A. Subtopic of topic 1	Second level of importance
1. Subtopic of A	Third level of importance
a. Subtopic of 1	Fourth level of importance
b. Subtopic of 1	"
(1) Subtopic of b	Fifth level of importance
(2) Subtopic of b	"
(a) Subtopic of (2)	Sixth level of importance
(b) Subtopic of (2)	"
i. Subtopic of (b)	Seventh level of importance
ii. Subtopic of (b)	"
2. Subtopic of A	Third level of importance
B. Subtopic of topic 1	Second level of importance
1. Second major topic	One of the most important

Source: From W. Lawrence Neuman, *Social Research Methods, Qualitative and Quantitative Approaches,* 6/e. Published by Allyn and Bacon, 75 Arlington St., Boston, MA 02116. Copyright © 2006 by Pearson Education. Reprinted by permission of the publisher.

Introduction and Presenting the Problem

The introduction to a research report establishes the tone and direction for the rest of the piece. It should capture the reader's attention and make clear the purpose and importance of the study. Remember that the reader is asking the so what? question as he or she begins to read; the introduction must establish in the reader's mind immediately why exactly the paper or book is worthwhile.

Overall, the first section of the report defines the research problem. It can be placed in one or more sections with titles such as "Introduction," "Problem Definition," "Literature Review," "Hypotheses," or "Background Assumptions." Although the subheadings vary, the contents include a statement of the research problem and a rationale for what is being examined. We explain the significance of and provide a background to the research question. We explain the significance of the research by showing how different solutions to the problem lead to different applications or theoretical conclusions. This is where researchers will sometimes explain their modification to a crime or criminal justice theory, or possibly review the conceptual background to their project.

Describing the Methods

The next section of the report describes how we designed the study and collected the data. It goes by several names (e.g., "Methods," "Research Design," or "Data") and may be subdivided into other parts (e.g., "Measures," "Sampling," or "Manipulations"). It is the most important section for evaluating the methodology of the project. The section answers several questions for the reader:

1. What type of study (e.g., experiment and survey) was conducted?
2. Exactly how were the data collected (e.g., study design, type of survey, time and location of data collection, and experimental design used)?
3. How were variables measured? Are the measures reliable and valid?
4. What is the sample? How many subjects or respondents are involved in the study? How were they selected?
5. How were ethical issues and specific concerns of the design dealt with?

Results and Tables Section

After describing how data were collected, methods of sampling, and measurement, we then present the data. This section should merely present the findings; it keeps discussion, analysis, and interpretation of the data to a minimum. Some researchers combine the "Results" section with the next section, called "Discussion" or "Findings."

We must make choices in how to present the data.[7] When analyzing the data, we look at dozens of univariate, bivariate, and multivariate tables and statistics to get a feel for the data. This does not mean that we include every statistic or table in a final report. Rather, we select the minimum number of charts or tables that fully inform the reader. We use data analysis techniques to summarize the data and test hypotheses (e.g., frequency distributions, tables with means and standard deviations, correlations, and other statistics).

We want to give a complete picture of the data without overwhelming the reader. Detailed summary statistics belong in appendixes.

Discussion Section

In the discussion section, we give the reader a concise, unambiguous interpretation of the data's meaning. The discussion is not a selective emphasis or partisan interpretation; rather, it is an intellectually honest discussion of what was found in the results section. The discussion section is separated from the results so that a reader can examine the data and arrive at different interpretations. Grosof and Sardy (1985: 386) warned, "The arrangement of your presentation should reflect a strict separation between data (the record of your observations) and their summary and analysis on one hand, and your interpretations, conclusion, and comment on the other."

Beginning researchers often find it difficult to organize a discussion section. One approach is to organize the discussion according to hypotheses, and to discuss how the data relate to each hypothesis. In addition, researchers should discuss unanticipated findings, possible alternative explanations of results, and weaknesses or limitations.

Drawing Conclusions

We should restate the research question and summarize findings in the conclusion. One of its purposes is to summarize the report. The other is to afford the author some liberty in stepping back and engaging in some more speculative commentary about the theoretical, legal, or practical implications of her or his research, and to make some recommendations for future studies. In an applied study, this is where we would articulate the policy implications of our study for crime and justice practice.

The only sections after the conclusion are the references and appendixes. The references section contains only sources that were referred to in the text or notes of the report. Appendixes, if used, usually contain additional information on methods of data collection (e.g., questionnaire wording) or results (e.g., descriptive statistics). The footnotes or endnotes in quantitative research reports expand or elaborate on information in the text. We use them sparingly to provide secondary information that clarifies the text. They should not distract from the flow of the reading.

THE QUALITATIVE RESEARCH REPORT

Compared to quantitative research, it is often more difficult to write a report on qualitative crime and justice research. It has fewer rules and less structure. Nevertheless, the purpose is the same: to clearly communicate the research process, the data collected, and the discoveries and findings. Quantitative reports present hypotheses and evidence in a logically tight and condensed style. By contrast, qualitative reports tend to be longer, and book-length reports are common (see Highlight 14.3). This section will examine how to present just two of the qualitative research approaches discussed in Chapters 12 and 13 (ethnographic field research and historical/historical-comparative research).

HIGHLIGHT 14.3
Why Qualitative Research Reports Are Longer

1. The data in a qualitative report are more difficult to condense. Data are in the form of words, pictures, or sentences and include many quotes and examples.

2. Qualitative researchers try to create a subjective sense of empathy and understanding among readers in addition to presenting factual evidence and analytic interpretations. Detailed descriptions of specific settings and situations help readers better understand or get a feel for settings. Researchers attempt to transport the reader into the subjective worldview and meaning system of a social setting.

3. Qualitative researchers use less standardized techniques of gathering data, creating analytic categories, and organizing evidence. The techniques applied may be particular to individual researchers or unique settings. Thus, researchers explain what they did and why, because it has not been done before.

4. Exploring new settings or constructing new theory is a common goal in qualitative research. The development of new concepts and examination of relationships among them adds to the length of reports. Theory flows out of evidence, and detailed descriptions demonstrate how the researcher created interpretations.

5. Qualitative researchers may use more varied writing styles, which increases length. They have greater freedom to employ literary devices to tell a story or recount a tale.

Source: From W. Lawrence Neuman, *Social Research Methods, Qualitative and Quantitative Approaches,* 6/e. Published by Allyn and Bacon, 75 Arlington St., Boston, MA 02116. Copyright © 2006 by Pearson Education. Reprinted by permission of the publisher.

Ethnographic Field Research Reports

Ethnographic field research reports rarely follow a fixed format with standard sections. Theoretical generalizations and data are usually not separated into distinct sections.[8] Generalizations are intertwined with the evidence, which takes the form of a detailed description with frequent quotes.

Researchers balance the presentation of data and analysis to avoid an excessive separation of data from analysis, called the **error of segregation**. This occurs when researchers separate data from analysis so much so that readers cannot see the connection.[9]

The tone of field research reports is less objective and formal, and more personal. Field research reports may be written in the first person (i.e., using the pronoun *I*) because the researcher was directly involved in the setting, interacted with the people studied, and was the measurement "instrument." The decisions or indecisions, feelings, reactions, and personal experiences of the researcher are parts of the field research process (i.e., reflexivity).

Field research reports often face more skepticism than quantitative reports do. This makes it essential to assess an audience's demands for evidence and to establish credibility. The key is to provide readers with enough evidence so that they believe the recounted events and accept the interpretations as plausible. A degree of selective observation is accepted in field research, so the critical issue is whether other observers could reach the same conclusion if they examined the same data.[10]

Field researchers face a data reduction dilemma when presenting evidence. Data usually consist of an enormous volume of documents and field notes, but a researcher cannot directly share all the observations or recorded conversations with the readers. For example, in their study of medical students, *Boys in White*, Becker and Geer had about 5,000 pages of single-spaced field notes. Field researchers include only about 5 percent of their field notes in a report as quotes. The remaining 95 percent is not wasted; there is just no room for it. Thus, writers select representative quotes and indirectly convey the rest of the data to readers.

There is no fixed organization for a field research report, although a literature review often appears near the beginning. There are many acceptable organizational forms. Lofland (1976) suggests the following:

1. Introduction
   a. Most general aspects of situation
   b. Main contours of the general situation
   c. How materials were collected
   d. Details about the setting
   e. How the report is organized
2. The situation
   a. Analytic categories
   b. Contrast between situation and other situations
   c. Development of situation over time
3. Strategies
4. Summary and implications

Devices for organizing evidence and analysis also vary a great deal.[11] For example, writers can organize the report in terms of a natural history, an unfolding of events as discovered, or as a chronology, following the developmental cycle or career of an aspect of the setting or people in it. Another possibility is to organize the report as a **zoom lens**, beginning broadly and then focusing increasingly narrowly on a specific topic. Statements can move from universal statements about all cultures to general statements about a specific cultures, to statements about a specific cultural scene, to specific statements about an aspect of culture, to specific statements about specific incidents.[12]

Field researchers also organize reports by themes. A writer chooses between using abstract analytic themes and using themes from the categories used by the people who were studied. The latter gives readers a vivid description of the setting and displays knowledge of the language, concepts, categories, and beliefs of those being written about.[13]

ERROR OF
SEGREGATION

A mistake when writing qualitative research in which a writer creates too large a separation between empirical details and abstract theorizing.

ZOOM LENS

A method of organizing a field research report in which the author begins broadly with a topic, then increasingly focuses it more narrowly and specifically.

Field researchers discuss the methods used in the report, but its location and form vary. One technique is to interweave a description of the setting, the means of gaining access, the role of the researcher, and the subject–researcher relationship into the discussion of evidence and analysis. This is intensified if the writer adopts what Van Maanen (1988: 73) called a "confessional" style of writing. A chronological, zoom lens, or theme-based organization allows placing the data collection method near the beginning or the end. In book-length reports, methodological issues are usually discussed in a separate appendix.

Field research reports can contain transcriptions of tape recordings, maps, photographs, or charts, illustrating analytic categories. They supplement the discussion and are placed near the discussion they complement. Qualitative field research can use creative formats that differ from the usual written text with examples from field notes. Photographs give a visual inventory of the settings described in the text and present the meanings of settings in the terms of those being studied. For example, field research articles have appeared in the form of being all photographs, a script for a play, or a documentary film.[14]

Direct personal involvement in the intimate details of a social setting heightens ethical concerns. Researchers write in a manner that protects the privacy of those being studied and helps prevent the publication of a report from harming those who were studied.[15] They usually change the names of members and exact locations in field reports. Personal involvement in field research leads researchers to include a short autobiography. For example, in the appendix to *Street Corner Society* the author, William Foote Whyte, gave a detailed account of the occupations of his father and grandfather, his hobbies and interests, the jobs he held, how he ended up going to graduate school, and how his research was affected by his getting married.

Historical Research

There is no single way to write a report on historical or historical-comparative research. Most frequently, researchers "tell a story" or describe details in general analytic categories. The writing usually goes beyond description and includes limited generalizations and abstract concepts. These reports are published in both journal articles and scholarly books.

Historical researchers do not describe their methods in great detail. Explicit sections of the report or an appendix that describes the methods used are unusual. Occasionally, a book-length report contains a bibliographic essay that discusses major sources used. More often, numerous detailed footnotes or endnotes describe the sources and evidence. For example, a twenty-page report on quantitative or field research typically has five to ten notes, whereas a historical or historical-comparative research report of equal length may have forty to one hundred notes.

Historical reports can contain photographs, maps, diagrams, charts, or tables of statistics throughout the report and in the section that discusses evidence that relates to them. The charts, tables, and so forth supplement a discussion or give the reader a better feel for the places and people being described. They are used in conjunction with frequent quotes as one among several types of evidence. Historical reports rarely summarize data to test specific hypotheses as quantitative research does. Instead, the writer builds a web of meaning or descriptive detail and organizes the evidence itself to convey interpretations and generalizations.

There are two basic modes of organizing historical/historical-comparative research reports: by topic and chronologically. Most writers mix the two types. For example, information is organized chronologically within topics or organized by topic within chronological periods. Occasionally other forms of organization are used—by place, by individual person, or by major events. If the report is truly comparative, the writer has additional options, such as making comparisons within topics. Highlight 14.4 provides a sample of some techniques used by historical-comparative researchers to organize evidence and analysis.[16]

We discuss narrative analysis in Appendix C. Researchers who use this strategy often adopt a narrative style of report writing. Researchers who use the narrative style organize data chronologically and "tell a story" around specific individuals and events.

6. See Mullins (1977: 11–30) for a discussion of outlines and the organization of quantitative research reports. Also see Williams and Wolfe (1979: 85–116) for good hints on how to organize ideas in a paper.

7. Grosof and Sardy (1985: 386–389) have provided suggestions on how to explain quantitative findings.

8. Lofland (1974) inductively discovered what he identifies as five major writing styles for reporting field research (generic, novel, elaborated, eventful, and interpenetrated) and discusses how they are evaluated.

9. The error of segregation is discussed in Lofland and Lofland (1984: 146).

10. See Becker and Geer (1982: 244) and Schatzman and Strauss (1973: 130) for a discussion of this and related issues.

11. See Hammersley and Atkinson (1983) and Van Maanen (1988).

12. Discussed in Spradley (1970: 162–167).

13. See Van Maanen (1988:13).

14. See Dabbs (1982) and Jackson (1978).

15. For a discussion of ethical concerns in writing field research reports, see Becker (1969), Punch (1986), and Wax (1971).

16. See Barzun and Graff (1970) and Shafer (1980) for excellent suggestions on writing about historical research.

17. For more on writing proposals to fund research projects, see Bauer (1988), Locke and associates (1987), and Quarles (1986). A somewhat dated but useful short introduction to proposal writing is Krathwohl (1965).

APPENDIX A

Epistemology Elaborated

POSITIVIST SOCIAL SCIENCE FEATURES

Positivist social science (PSS) is used widely, and positivism, broadly defined, is the approach of the natural sciences. In fact, most people assume that the positivist approach is science. Positivism arose from a nineteenth-century school of thought founded by the Frenchman who is the father of sociology—Auguste Comte (1798–1857). Classical French sociologist Émile Durkheim (1858–1917) also outlined a version of positivism in his classic text, *Rules of the Sociological Method* (1895). Criminologists usually trace the rise of positivism in our field to Italian criminologist Cesare Lombroso but recall the "horse-slasher" clarification found in Chapter 2 (see Highlight 2.2).[1]

PSS researchers prefer precise quantitative data and often use experiments, surveys, and statistics. They emulate the hard sciences by emphasizing on rigorous, exact measures and the statistical testing of hypotheses. Positivist social science, *thus, is a method for combining deductive logic with precise empirical observations in order to discover and confirm a set of probabilistic causal laws that can be used to predict general patterns of human activity*.

1. *Purpose of PSS.* Perhaps the most important distinction between PSS, ISS, and CSS is what they assume is their purpose—in other words, the ultimate objective of research. The ultimate purpose of research for PSS is scientific explanation—to discover and document universal causal laws of human behavior. Developing causal laws provides us a tool, in turn, that allows us to predict, based on probability statements of what will likely occur in the future. In this way we can exercise control over our external environment. Put simply, if we know the cause of something, we can better control its effect. This is the premise behind using PSS as a tool to control crime and administer justice rationally.

This instrumental form of knowledge sees research results as a tool or instrument people use to master or control events in the world around them. Consequently, PSS has a more technical perspective toward applying knowledge. It is perceived as a valuable tool for solving problems and enhancing the quality of decisions in organizations.

2. *Nature of Reality.* Modern positivists adopt an essentialist orientation to reality: Reality is real; it exists "out there" and is waiting to be discovered. Human perception and intellect may be flawed, and reality may be difficult to pin down, but it does exist. Moreover, social reality is not random; it is patterned and has order. Without this assumption (i.e., the world is not chaotic and without regularity), logic and prediction would be impossible. Science lets humans discover this order and the laws of nature. "The basic, observational laws of science are considered to be true, primary and certain, because they are built into the fabric of the natural world. Discovering a law is like discovering America, in the sense that both are already waiting to be revealed" (Mulkay 1979: 21).

An essentialist position states that what people see and touch (i.e., empirical reality) is not overly complex. Thus, quantitative measurements of crime, race, and gender may be difficult but still accomplishable. An essentialist assumption about time is that it is linear or flows in a straight line. This means that what happened in the past will not be directly repeated, because time moves in only one direction—forward to the future.

3. *Human Nature.* PSS assumes humans are self-interested, pleasure seeking, rational mammals. A cause will, within a probability range, have the same effect on everyone. We can learn about people by observing their behavior, what we see in external reality. This is more important than what happens in internal, subjective reality. Sometimes, this is called a behaviorist approach. It means people respond to external forces that are as real as physical forces on objects. Durkheim (1938: 27) stated, "Social phenomena are things and ought to be studied as things."

4. *Free Will versus Determinism.* PSS looks at how external forces and pressures (e.g., child abuse) that operate on individuals, groups, organizations, or societies produce outcomes (resulting in adult criminality). Although few positivists believe in absolute determinism, PSS downplays an individual's subjective or internal reasons and any sense of free choice or volition. Mental processes are less central than the structural forces or conditions beyond individual control that exert influence over choices and behavior. Although individual people may feel that they can act freely and can make any decision, positivists emphasize the powerful pressures and situations that operate on people to shape most, if not all, of their actions. Even positivists who use rational choice explanations focus less on how individuals reason and make choices than they do on identifying sets of conditions that allow them to predict what people will choose. They assume that once they know external factors, individual reasoning will largely follow a machinelike rational logic of decision making.

Consequently, researchers can estimate the odds of a predicted behavior. In other words, scientific causal laws enable us to make accurate predictions of how often a social behavior will occur within a large group. The causal laws cannot predict the specific behavior of a specific person in each situation. However, they can say that under conditions X, Y, and Z, there is a 95 percent probability that half of the people will engage in a specified behavior.

5. *Views on Common Sense.* PSS sees a clear separation between science and nonscience. Of the many ways to seek truth, science is special—the best way. Scientific knowledge is better than and will eventually replace the inferior ways of gaining knowledge (e.g., magic, religion, astrology, personal experience, and tradition). Science borrows some ideas from common sense, but it replaces the parts of common sense that are sloppy, logically inconsistent, unsystematic, and full of bias. The scientific community—with its special norms, scientific attitudes, and techniques—can regularly produce truth, whereas common sense does so infrequently and inconsistently.

6. *Determining the Truth.* PSS explanations must meet two conditions: They must (1) have no logical contradictions and (2) be consistent with observed facts. Yet, this is not sufficient. Replication is also needed.[2] Any researcher can replicate or reproduce the results of others. This puts a check on the whole system for creating knowledge. It ensures honesty because it repeatedly tests explanations against hard, objective facts. An open competition exists among opposing explanations, impartial rules are used, neutral facts are accurately observed, and logic is rigorously followed. Over time, scientific knowledge accumulates as different researchers conduct independent tests of a theory and add up the findings. Recall the NIJ-sponsored mandatory arrest for domestic violence experiments. Numerous replications raised serious doubts about the original finding that mandatory arrest practices reduce domestic violence.

7. *Good Evidence.* PSS is dualist; it assumes that the cold, observable facts are fundamentally distinct from ideas, values, or theories. Empirical facts exist apart from personal ideas or thoughts. We can observe them by using our senses (sight, smell, hearing, and touch) or special instruments that extend the senses (e.g., telescopes, microscopes, and Geiger counters). Knowledge of observable reality obtained using our senses allows us to separate true from false ideas about social life.

Many positivists also endorse the falsification doctrine outlined by the Anglo-Austrian philosopher Sir Karl Popper (1902–1991) in *The Logic of Scientific Discovery* (1934). Popper argued that claims to knowledge "can never be proven or fully justified, they can only be refuted" (Phillips 1987: 3). Evidence for a causal law requires more than piling up supporting facts; it involves looking for evidence that contradicts the causal law. Popper's view of science is one in which even a researcher's most cherished theories and beliefs are approached skeptically, and revised or jettisoned if needed. In a classic example, if we want to test the claim that all swans are white, and I find 5,000 white swans, we have not totally confirmed a causal law or pattern. All it takes is locating one black swan to refute our claim—one piece of negative evidence. This means that researchers search for disconfirming evidence, and even then, the best they can say is, "Thus far, I have not been able to locate any, so the claim is probably right." Of course, when working with social phenomena there are almost always exceptions. We have to rely, therefore, on less rigorous standards, such as the body of evidence.

8. *Role of Values.* PSS argues for value-free, objective science. There are two meanings of the term objective: (1) Observers agree on what they see, and (2) scientific knowledge is not based on values, opinions, attitudes, or beliefs.[3] Positivists see science as a special, distinctive part of society that is free of personal, political, or religious values. It assumes it can operate independently of the social and cultural forces affecting other human activity because it involves applying strict rational thinking and systematic observation in a manner that transcends personal prejudices, biases, and values. PSS has had an immense impact on how researchers see ethical issues and legitimate knowledge:

> To the degree that a positivist theory of scientific knowledge has become the criterion for all knowledge, moral insights and political commitments have been delegitimized as irrational or reduced to mere subjective inclination. Ethical judgments are now thought of as personal opinion (Brown 1989: 37).

PSS CONCLUSION.   Many PSS assumptions will reappear when you read about quantitative research techniques and measurement in later chapters. A positivist approach implies that a researcher begins with a cause–effect relationship that he or she logically derives from a possible causal law in general theory. He or she logically links the abstract ideas to precise measurements of the social world. The researcher remains detached, neutral, and objective as he or she measures aspects of social life, examines evidence, and replicates the research of others. These processes lead to an empirical test of and confirmation for the laws of social life as outlined in a theory.

INTERPRETIVE SOCIAL SCIENCE FEATURES.   Interpretive social science (ISS) can be traced to German sociologist Max Weber (1864–1920) and German philosopher Wilhelm Dilthey (1833–1911). Dilthey argued that there were two fundamentally different types of science: *Naturwissenschaft* and *Geisteswissenschaft*. The first is based on positivist explanation. The latter is rooted in an empathetic understanding, or verstehen, of the everyday lived experience of people in specific cultural settings. Weber embraced *verstehen* and felt that we must learn the personal reasons, motives, and cultural context that shape a person's internal feelings and guide decisions to act in particular ways. Here's how one criminologist describes this concept:

> I can't seem to find an ethnographic moment away from Max Weber. His notion of *Verstehen* all but overwhelms me. . . . He showed up regularly in one of my research projects: the documentation of the roadside shrines that families and friends build for loved ones lost to automotive violence. Sometimes the rush of sympathetic understanding overtakes me at the edge of a roadway as a big automobile blasts by, offering me the visceral proximity of violent death. . . . Such moments sparkle with human possibility, with intellectual excitement, because they ground analysis in experience—and because they situate our analysis and experience inside the everyday lives of others. (Ferrell 2004a: 299)

There are several varieties of ISS: hermeneutics, social constructionism, symbolic interactionism, and phenomenology.[4] *Hermeneutics*, for example, comes from the name of a god in Greek mythology, Hermes, who had the job of communicating the desires of the gods to mortals. It "literally means making the obscure plain" (Blaikie 1993: 28). Hermeneutics emphasizes a detailed reading or examination of text, which could refer to a conversation, written words, or pictures. A researcher conducts a reading to discover the meaning embedded within text (similar to the research in Chapter 1 on rap lyrics). When studying the text, the researcher/reader tries to absorb or get inside the text to develop a deep understanding of its meaning. True meaning is rarely obvious on the surface; one reaches it only through a detailed study of the text, contemplating its many messages, both implicit and explicit, and seeking the connections among its parts.

In sum, the interpretive approach is the systematic analysis and detailed study of people and text to arrive at understandings and interpretations of how people construct and maintain meaning within their social worlds.

1. *Ultimate Purpose of ISS.* The goal of interpretive research is to develop an understanding of social life and discover how people construct meaning in natural settings—in a word, *verstehen*. An interpretive researcher wants to learn what is meaningful or relevant to the people being studied, or how individuals experience daily life. The researcher does this by getting to know a particular social setting and seeing it from the point of view of those in it. Recall Wright and Decker's research of armed robbers in Chapter 1 and Athens's research on violent criminals in Chapter 2.

The researcher must take into account the social actor's reasons and the social context of action. For example, a physical reflex such as eye blinking is human behavior that is rarely an intentional social action (i.e., done for a reason or with human motivation), but in some situations, it can be such a social action (i.e., a wink). Human action, therefore, has little inherent meaning. People construct meaning by interacting with others. Interpretative social scientists' ultimate purpose thus is to learn about how the world works so they can acquire an in-depth understanding of other people, appreciate the wide diversity of lived human experience, and better acknowledge shared humanity. Instead of viewing knowledge as a kind of tool or instrument, ISS researchers try to capture the inner lives and subjective experience of ordinary people.

2. *Nature of Reality.* The interpretive approach sees human social life intentionally created out of the purposeful actions of interacting social beings. In contrast to the positivist view that social life is out there waiting to be discovered, ISS states that the social world is largely what people perceive it and construct it to be. Social life exists as people experience it and give it meaning. It is fluid and fragile. People construct it by interacting with others in ongoing processes of communication, conflict, and negotiation. What we call crime, for example, is a human construction that varies across time and place. Consider that when your authors were growing up, a fistfight among children at school was seen at worst as a situation requiring parental involvement. Today, many states require by law that any incidence of so-called violence on school grounds to be reported to the police—even at the elementary school level. What was previously handled as a minor childhood transgression is increasingly being redefined as serious criminality (Kappeler and Potter 2006).

ISS assumes that this ongoing construction of meaning creates our reality (referred to as the social construction of reality). There is no inner essence that causes the reality people see; it is a product of social and political processes. For example, when you see a chair, there is no "chairness" in it; rather, what you see as a chair arises from what a people of a particular society define, accept, and understand to be a chair. Imagine coming from a culture that had no chairs. A chair would have no meaning—it would be merely a peculiar inanimate object (until someone sat in it).

What we see, then, as solid empirical reality is actually a fluid process of appearances that we have come to be defined as real. Just because our reality is socially constructed does not render it immaterial or unimportant. Once people accept their creations as facts, or as real, very real consequences follow. For example, if socially constructed reality instructs us that women are generally less capable of competent police work than are men, only a marginal percentage of a police force will be made up of women. Not only will this socially constructed reality guide the behavior of police departments, it might also affect women who might otherwise pursue a career in law enforcement.

3. *Human Nature.* Ordinary people are engaged in an ongoing process of creating systems of meaning through social interaction. They then use such meanings to interpret their social world and make sense of their lives. Human behavior may be patterned and regular, as PSS asserts, but this is not due to preexisting laws waiting to be discovered. The patterns result from evolving meaning systems or social conventions that people generate as they socially interact.

Important questions for the interpretive researcher are as follows: What do people believe to be true? What do they hold to be relevant? How do they define what they are doing? As opposed to concentrating on people as things, therefore, interpretive researchers want to discover what actions mean to the people who engage in them. People have their own reasons for their actions, and researchers need to learn the reasons people use. Individual intents and motives are crucial to consider.

4. *Free Will versus Determinism.* Whereas PSS assumes determinism, ISS emphasizes voluntary individual free choice, sometimes called human agency. ISS sees people as having volition and being able to make conscious choices. Social settings and subjective points of view help to shape the choices a person makes, but people create and change those settings and have the ability to develop or form an alternative point of view. ISS researchers emphasize the importance of taking into account individual decision-making processes, subjective feelings, and ways to understanding events.

5. *Views on Common Sense.* Positivists see little value in common sense—a form of knowledge fraught with potential error and bias. Interpretive researchers argue that common sense guides people in their daily lives; it is a stockpile of everyday theories people use to organize and explain events in the world.

An interpretive approach says that common sense and the positivist's laws are alternative ways to interpret the world; that is, they are distinct meaning systems. Neither common sense nor scientific law has all the answers. Instead, interpretive researchers see each as important in its own domain; each is created in a different way for a different purpose.

Ordinary people could not function in daily life if they based their actions on science alone. For example, in order to boil an egg, people use unsystematic experiences, habits, and guesswork. A strict application of natural science would require one to know the laws of physics that determine heating the water and the chemical laws that govern the changes in the egg's internal composition. Even natural scientists use common sense when they are not "doing science."

6. *Determining the Truth.* PSS logically deduces from theory, collects data, and analyzes facts in ways that allow replication. For ISS, a theory is true if it makes sense to those being studied and if it allows others to enter the reality of those being studied. The theory or description is accurate if the researcher conveys a deep understanding of the way others reason, feel, and see things. Prediction may be possible, but it is a type of prediction that occurs when two people are very close, as when they have been married for a long time. An interpretive explanation documents the actor's point of view and translates it into a form that is intelligible to readers.

7. *Good Evidence.* Good evidence in positivism is observable, quantitatively measurable, precise, and independent of theory and values. By contrast, ISS sees PSS, by reducing human experience to numbers, as distorting the true nature of human social life. Evidence about social action cannot be isolated from the context in which it occurs or the meanings assigned to it by the social actors involved. As Weber (1978: 5) said, "Empathic or appreciative accuracy is attained when, through sympathetic participation, we can adequately grasp the emotional context in which the action took place."

For ISS, facts are fluid and embedded within a culture or subculture; they are not impartial, objective, and neutral. Facts are contingent and context specific; they depend on combinations of specific events with particular people in a social setting. What the positivist assumes—that neutral outsiders observe behavior and see unambiguous, objective facts—an ISS researcher takes as a question to be addressed: How do people observe ambiguities in social life and assign meaning? Interpretive researchers say that social situations are filled with ambiguity. Most behaviors or statements can have several meanings and can be interpreted in multiple ways.

For example, we might all agree when standing in a forest looking at a tree that it is a tree (assuming we all use the same symbolic sound "tree" to represent this massive brown, gray, and green object in front of us). PSS views this scene as clear evidence of an objective fact. ISS, however, would argue that there is a tremendous amount of ambiguity in what this object means (what is its reality), depending on whether a corporate logging executive or passionate conservationist is interpreting its meaning. To one it's a commodity to be cut down and used for human consumption and profit; to the other it's a living organism essential for the health and well-being of our natural environment (example modified from Blumer): one object—two very different realities based on differing interpretive values.

8. *Role of Values.* The PSS researcher calls for eliminating values and operating within an apolitical environment. The ISS researcher, by contrast, argues that researchers should reflect on, reexamine, and analyze value positions as a part of the process of studying others and their cultures. The ISS researcher needs, at least temporarily, to empathize with and share in the social and political commitments or values of those he or she studies. This is why ISS adopts the position of relativism with regard to values.

ISS questions PSS's assumption of being value free because interpretive research sees values and meaning infused everywhere in everything. What PSS calls value freedom is just another meaning of system and value—the value of positivist science. The interpretive researcher adopts a position, therefore, of value relativism and does not assume that any one set of values is better or worse. Values should be recognized and be made explicit.

ISS CONCLUSION.   The interpretive approach existed for many years as the loyal opposition to positivism. Although some positivist social researchers resist viewing the interpretive approach as scientific research (see Chapter 2), most now concede its credibility as a means to produce knowledge. You will read again about the interpretive outlook in various parts of this book concentrating on qualitative research—especially historical, ethnographic field research, and qualitative document analysis. The interpretive approach is the foundation of social research techniques that are sensitive to context, that get inside the ways others see the world, and that are more concerned with achieving an empathic understanding than with testing lawlike theories of human behavior.

CRITICAL SOCIAL SCIENCE FEATURES.   Critical social science (CSS) agrees with many of the criticisms the interpretive approach directs at PSS, but it adds some of its own and disagrees with ISS on some points. This approach's roots are traced to Karl Marx (1818–1883) and Sigmund Freud (1856–1939), and were elaborated on by Theodor Adorno (1903–1969), Erich Fromm (1900–1980), and Herbert Marcuse (1898–1979). CSS is usually associated with conflict theory, feminist analysis, and critical psychotherapy. It is also tied to critical theory, first developed by the Frankfurt School in Germany in the 1930s.[5] In crime and justice studies, the areas of scholarship most associated with CSS include a broad-based area of interest usually referred to as critical criminology, as well as feminist criminology and race-based criminology. The common thread running through each is a concern for researching oppression and injustice, the role of the criminal justice system in that oppression and injustice, and the measures needed to eliminate or improve these conditions.

As outlined below, CSS researchers critique ISS for being too subjective and relativist. CSS states that the interpretive approach treats people's ideas and subjective experiences as more important than actual economic and political conditions. By focusing on localized, microlevel, short-term settings, ISS tends to ignore the broader and long-term context. CSS believes researchers should link both microprocesses and concerns to macrostructures and concerns (the larger economic system, for example). To CSS researchers, ISS and PSS are also amoral and passive. They fail to take a value position or actively help people to see false illusions around them so that they can improve their lives. *In general, then, CSS defines social science as a critical process of inquiry that generates liberating knowledge so as to reveal structural and cultural inhibiting forces in an attempt to help people change their living conditions and build a better world for themselves.* It is important to caution that even if one is not predisposed to accept some of the alternative ideas associated with CSS, its views on research and knowledge are formidable and highlight important shortcomings and potential solutions to PSS and ISS approaches.

1. *Ultimate Purpose of CSS.* The purpose of critical research is not simply to study the social world but to change it. CSS researchers conduct research to critique and transform inhibiting social conditions by revealing the underlying sources of these conditions and empowering people, especially less powerful people. More specifically, they uncover deep-seated ideologies, reveal hidden truths, and help people to change the world for themselves. In CSS, the purpose is "to explain a social order in such a way that it becomes itself the catalyst which leads to the transformation of this social order" (Fay 1987: 27).

The CSS researcher asks normally unmentionable questions, exposes hypocrisy, and investigates oppressive conditions. "The point of all science, indeed all learning, is to change and develop out of our understandings and reduce illusion. . . . Learning is the reducing of illusion and ignorance; it can help free us from domination by hitherto unacknowledged constraints, dogmas and falsehoods" (Sayer 1992: 252).

For example, a CSS researcher conducts a study documenting that there is illegal racial discrimination in rental housing. White landlords refuse to rent to minority tenants. The CSS ethic dictates that not only will the researcher publish his or her research in an academic journal, he or she will also take action: contact appropriate enforcement officials, give the published work to newspapers, and possibly meet with grassroots organizations to discuss the results of the study. The goal is to promote social justice through knowledge and empowerment.

For CSS, then, knowledge is not an instrument for people to manipulate, nor is it a capturing and rendering of people's inner, subjective experiences; instead, knowledge means active change in the world. Knowledge can free people from the shackles of past thinking and help them take control of events around them. It is not a thing to be possessed, but a process that combines greater awareness with taking action. The relevance of knowledge is its ability to connect consciousness with people engaging in concrete actions, reflecting on the consequences of those actions, and then advancing consciousness to a new level in an ongoing cycle.

2. *Nature of Reality.* CSS bridges a divide between PSS and ISS. It shares PSS's premise that there is an empirical reality independent of our perceptions, and agrees with ISS's position that we simultaneously construct what we take to be reality from our subjective experiences, cultural beliefs, and social interactions. Although seemingly irreconcilable, CSS views this, and many other societal contradictions, as operating in a dialectical fashion. Put simply, *PSS reality and ISS reality mutually transform one another; it's not one or the other in operation but both transforming and influencing each other simultaneously.*

Similarly, causal mechanisms in society often have internal contradictions and operate in a paradoxical manner, creating structural conflicts. They may contain forces or processes that appear to be opposites, or to be in conflict, but are actually parts of a single larger process. A biological analogy helps illustrate this idea. We see birth and life as the opposites of death. Yet, death begins the day we are born and each day of living moves us toward death as our body ages and decays. There is a contradiction between life and death; to live we move toward its opposite, death. Living and dying appear to be opposites, but actually they are two parts of a single process. Discovering and understanding such paradoxical processes, what CSS researchers call the dialectic, is a central task in CSS.

Laying bare and making sense of society's paradoxes and contradictions reveal what critical social scientists refer to as "deep structure." An example would be how the deep structure of patriarchy—a cultural and structural system of male privilege—shapes and structures the everyday actions of men and women. With theoretical insight and careful investigation, researchers can uncover these deep structures, expose the unfair assumptions and the power they wield, and then help to reconstruct them in a way that no longer disadvantages or harms women. (Patriarchy is also seen by feminists as quite harmful to boys and men as well.) Feminist CSS researchers would certainly argue that the educative power of knowledge has made advances in the United States—but would quickly point out how far we still have to go. They would note the virulent backlash in contemporary U.S. society against the deconstruction of patriarchy, and the complete lack of progress made with regard to women's oppression in much of the rest of the world.

For CSS, therefore, social change and conflict are not always apparent or easily observable. As illustrated in Highlight 3.1 using the *Matrix* movies, the social world is full of illusion, myth, and distortion. These illusions, what some CSS theorists call dominant ideology, benefit and work to the advantage of those with cultural, political, and economic power. Responsible research, from this perspective, should expose the flaws in dominant ideology and work to empower those who are oppressed by it.

3. *Human Nature.* PSS sees humans as rationally acting individuals. ISS sees humans as fundamentally social beings defined by their capacity to create and sustain social meanings. CSS recognizes that people are both rational decision makers who are shaped by social structures, and creative beings that construct meaning and social structures. Society exists prior to and apart from people, yet it can exist only with their active involvement. People create society and society creates people, who in turn create society, in a continuous process.6 Thus, human beings exist again, within a mutually transformative process.

CSS notes that humans can be misled and have unrealized potential. One important way this happens is through reification. Reification occurs when we become detached from and lose sight of our connection to something that we created ourselves (e.g., Frankenstein syndrome). We take our human constructions for granted to the point that they become invisible, rendering an unquestioning level of control over us. CSS researchers would cite capitalism, patriarchy, or a punitive criminal justice apparatus as examples of human constructions that, despite the pain and injustice they create, are seen as inevitable and invisible by most people. Although humans are filled with tremendous potential, it often goes unrealized because we find it difficult to break free from reified beliefs, conditions, and situations.

4. *Free Will versus Determinism.* CSS blends determinism and voluntarism into a single idea labeled bounded autonomy. Bounded autonomy suggests that free will, choices, and decision making are not unlimited or open ended; rather, they stay within restricted boundaries of options—both culturally and materially derived. In other words, a CSS researcher identifies a range of options, or at least what people see as being realistic alternatives, and allows for some volition among those options. People make choices, but the choices are confined to what they feel is possible. Material factors (e.g., natural resources and physical abilities) and cultural-subjective schemes (e.g., beliefs, core values, and deeply felt norms) set what people feel to be possible or impossible, and people act based on what they believe is possible.

5. *Views on Common Sense.* The CSS position on common sense is based on the idea of false consciousness—that ways of thinking are constructed by powerful forces in society that are false and act against our best interests as defined in objective reality. Objective reality lies behind ideological myth and illusion. For example, one false belief based in feminist thinking, that operates against the best interests of women (and men), is that men are inherently more capable and worthy of major leadership positions in politics, corporations, and government. Clearly, the objective reality differs, yet a large segment of the U.S. population (both male and female), and an even larger segment worldwide, assumes with little reflection that this is true.

The notion of false consciousness plays little role in pure ISS because it implies that a social actor uses a meaning system that is false or out of touch with objective reality. ISS states that people create and use such systems and that researchers can only describe such systems, not judge their value. CSS states that social researchers should study subjective ideas and common sense because these shape human behavior. Yet, they contain myth and illusion that can mask an objective world in which there is oppression and injustice.

A researcher must use research and theory to dig beneath the veneer of ideology, myth, distortion, and false appearances. Explanatory critique often will enlighten and help to emancipate people. As the explanation reveals aspects of reality beyond the surface level, people are awakened to see the underlying structures of society (e.g., much like Neo taking the red pill and unplugging from the Matrix; see Highlight 3.1). As it reveals deep causal mechanisms, people learn how to change those structures. In this way, the explanations are critiques that show a pathway for taking action and achieving change.

6. *Determining the Truth.* PSS deduces hypotheses, tests hypotheses with replicated observations, and then combines results to confirm causal laws. ISS asks whether the meaning system and rules of behavior make sense to those being studied. CSS develops and tests theory through both positivist and interpretive means with the aim of exposing the forces of underlying structures, both past and present, and then applying that knowledge to bring about change.

CSS, therefore, informs practical action and is modified on the basis of its utility. Because CSS tries to explain and change the world by revealing hidden structures that are in flux, the test of an explanation is not static. Testing theory is a dynamic, ongoing process of applying theory and modifying it. Knowledge grows by an ongoing process of eroding ignorance and enlarging insights through action—an approach captured by the notion of praxis. Praxis is where simultaneously theory informs practice and practice informs theory. As seen in the Möbius strip in Figure 3.1, theory and practice are simultaneously separate entities, yet are inextricably interwoven. The ethic of praxis minimizes the division between the researcher and those being researched, and the distinction between scientific inquiry and everyday life. Highlight 3.2 features a type of research referred to as participatory action research. It is a good example of CSS's commitment to the mutually transformative relationship between theory and practice.

7. *Good Evidence.* CSS researchers believe that our observations and experiences with empirical reality are not pure, neutral, and unmediated; rather, preexisting ideas, beliefs, and interpretations color what we see and how we interpret it. Our knowledge of empirical reality can capture the way things really are, yet in an incomplete manner, because our experiences of it depend on ideas and beliefs. What the PSS researcher calls facts are actually only interpretation of the "real" within a framework of preconstructed values, theory, and meaning.

In CSS, theory is a type of map telling researchers where to look for facts and how to interpret them once they are uncovered. It claims this is true in the natural sciences as well. For example, a biologist looks into a microscope and sees red blood cells—a fact based on a theory about blood and cells and a biologist's education about microscopic phenomena. Without this theory and education, a biologist sees only meaningless spots. Clearly, then, facts and theories are interrelated. And if all theory has values embedded within them, then values play a critical role in all research.

8. *Role of Values.* CSS sees all research, therefore, whether acknowledged or not, as a moral-political activity that involves a value position. CSS rejects PSS value freedom and pure objectivity as a myth. It also differs with ISS for its value relativism. For CSS, being objective is not being value free. Denying that a researcher has a point of view is itself a point of view. It is a technician's point of view: Conduct research and ignore or gloss over the moral questions and value implications. In its extreme form, such a view says that science is a mere tool or instrument anyone can use. This notion of pure science was strongly criticized when Nazi scientists conducted inhumane experiments and then claimed that they were blameless because they just followed orders and were doing science (see Chapter 4). The same criticisms were made about the U.S. scientific project, dubbed the Manhattan Project, to build the atom bomb. Chapter 4 on ethics will review several other examples of human atrocities committed under the justification of value-free science.

In the view of the CSS approach, PSS produces technocratic knowledge—a form of knowledge best suited for use by the people in power to dominate or control other people.[7] Their emphasis would be on acknowledging the importance of values and morals in generating knowledge—especially when researching notions of harm, punishment, and justice, as in crime and justice and research.

CSS CONCLUSION.   The CSS approach captures many of the more important criticisms of both the positivist and interpretive approaches. It constitutes an important presence and influence in crime and justice studies. Despite CSS's critique of positivism, it is important to realize that there is actually a large range of activism associated with CSS (from passive rhetoric to serious activist work), as there is with positivist social science. Remember that these categories are ideal types, and most researchers incorporate elements of all three orientations at some time in their work. We have already discussed several researchers—such as Francis Cullen, Todd Clear, Robin Haarr, and John Hagan—who rely primarily on the PSS approach, and yet are committed to bringing about social changes consistent with the value position of social justice (see Chapters 1, 2, and 3).

Notes for Further Study

1. Halfpenny (1982) and Turner (1984) have provided overviews of positivism in sociology. Also see Giddens (1978). Lenzer (1975) for an excellent introduction to Auguste Comte.
2. See Hegtvedt (1992).
3. For a discussion, see Derksen and Gartell (1992: 1715).
4. In addition to the works in note 3, interpretive science approaches are discussed in Berger and Luckman (1967), Bleicher (1980), Cicourel (1973), Garfinkel (1967, 1974), Geertz (1979), Glaser and Strauss (1967), Holstein and Gubrium (1994), Leiter (1980), Mehan and Wood (1975), Silverman (1972), and Weber (1974, 1981).
5. For a discussion of the Frankfurt School, see Bottomore (1984), Held (1980), Martin (1973), and Slater (1977). Also, for more on the works of Habermas, see Holub (1991), McCarthy (1978), Pusey (1987), and Roderick (1986).

   In addition to the works cited above, additional critical science approaches are discussed in Burawoy (1990), Dickson (1984), Fay (1987), Glucksmann (1974), Harding (1986), Harvey (1990), Keat (1981), Lane (1970), Lemert (1981), Mayhew (1980, 1981), Sohn-Rethel (1978), Veltmeyer (1978), Wardell (1979), Warner (1971), and Wilson (1982).
6. See Swartz (1997) on Bourdieu.
7. See Habermas (1971, 1973, 1979) for a critical science critique of positivism as being technocratic and used for domination. He has suggested an emancipatory alternative.

APPENDIX B

All About Researching and Reviewing Literature

REVIEWING THE LITERATURE

In Chapter 5 we discussed the story of Michelle Grant, who wanted to conduct research on surveillance by the police in U.S. society. A crucial first step was to familiarize herself with the literature so that she could determine whether her idea was viable, necessary, focused, and interesting. The first book she came across was Gary Marx's *Undercover Policing: The Rise of the Surveillance Society*. She found it fascinating and it further piqued her interest. Kraska then recommended a scholarly book by David Lyon (1994) and some solid scholarship written by Kevin Haggerty (2000). These sources were not so much based on research, as on ideas and theory; consequently, she learned new organizing concepts, theoretical perspectives, and research issues.

Her search then continued into the actual research articles published in the area of surveillance, as well as police trade magazines that discussed the latest uses of surveillance within the police community. As noted above, she was pleased to find out that despite the voluminous literature on surveillance, no one had attempted to document the extent of government-controlled surveillance systems in the United States. Michelle was ready to proceed with her project.

Studying the accumulated knowledge about a potential research question is an essential early step in the research process. As in other areas of life, it is best to find out what is already known about a question before trying to answer it yourself. As Michelle's experience demonstrated, the existing literature can help us to (1) better understand the object of study, (2) refine our research question, and (3) suggest the most successful research method. It is also used when we write our final paper, which generally includes a review of the preexisting literature.

We begin this section by looking at the various purposes our review of the literature can serve. We will also discuss what the literature is, where to find it, and what it contains. Next, we will explore techniques for systematically conducting a review. Finally, we will look at how to write a review and its place in a research report.

Reasons for and Types of Literature Reviews

A literature review is based on the assumption that knowledge accumulates and that people learn from and build on what others have done. Scientific research is a collective effort of many researchers who share their results with one another as a community. Although some studies may be especially important, a specific research project is just a tiny part of the overall process of creating knowledge. Today's studies build on those of yesterday. Researchers read studies to compare, replicate, or criticize them for weaknesses.

A thorough review of the literature is pursued for four main reasons. These objectives include (see Summary Table B.1):

1. *To demonstrate a familiarity with a body of knowledge and establish credibility.* A review tells a reader that the researcher knows the research in an area and knows the major issues. A good review increases a reader's confidence in the researcher's professional competence, ability, and background.

SUMMARY TABLE B.1 Four Objectives of Reviewing the Literature
1. To demonstrate a familiarity with a body of knowledge and establish credibility.
2. To show the path of prior research and how a current project is linked to it.
3. To integrate and summarize what is known in an area.
4. To learn from others and stimulate new ideas.

SUMMARY TABLE B.2 Five Types of Literature Reviews
1. Context review (*most common in quantitative research*)
2. Historical review (*most common in qualitative research*)
3. Integrative review (*both qualitative and quantitative research*)
4. Methodological review (*most common in quantitative research*)
5. Theoretical review (*both quantitative and qualitative research*)

2. *To show the path of prior research and how a current project is linked to it.* A review outlines the direction of research on a question and shows the development of knowledge and the gaps in that knowledge in need of new thinking and research. A good review places a research project in a context and demonstrates its relevance by making connections to a body of knowledge.

3. *To integrate and summarize what is known in an area.* A review pulls together and synthesizes different results. A good review points out areas where prior studies agree, where they disagree, and where major questions remain. It collects what is known up to a point in time and indicates the direction for future research.

4. *To learn from others and stimulate new ideas.* A review tells what others have found so that a researcher can benefit from the efforts of others. A good review identifies interesting theoretical concepts and ideas, and suggests hypotheses for thought or replication. It divulges procedures, techniques, and research designs worth copying so that a researcher can better focus hypotheses and gain new insights.

Reviews vary in scope and depth. There are several different types of reviews (see Summary Table B.2). Each fulfills one or another of the four objectives reviewed above. However, the type of review to be used often depends on whether the study is quantitative or qualitative. The five types of literature reviews include the following:

1. *A context review.* A common type of review in which the author links a specific study to a larger body of knowledge. It often appears at the beginning of a research report and introduces the study by situating it within a broader framework and showing how it continues or builds on a developing line of thought or study. This approach is most common in quantitative research.

2. *A historical review.* A specialized review in which the author traces an issue over time. It can be merged with a theoretical or methodological review to show how concept, theory, or research method developed over time. This approach is most common in qualitative research.

3. *An integrative review.* A common type of review in which the author presents and summarizes the current state of knowledge on a topic, highlighting agreements and disagreements within it. It is often combined with a context review or may be published as an independent article as a service to other researchers. It is used in both quantitative and qualitative studies.

4. *A methodological review.* A specialized type of integrative review in which the author compares and evaluates the relative methodological strength of various studies and shows how different methodologies (e.g., research designs, measures, and samples) account for different results. This is generally used in quantitative research.

5. *A theoretical review.* A specialized review in which the author reviews various theories or concepts focused on explaining some crime and justice phenomena and compares/synthesizes them on the basis of assumptions, logical consistency, and scope of explanation. This type of review is found in both quantitative and qualitative research. It is also found in stand-alone theoretical articles that develop theoretical ideas without presenting actual research.

It may take a researcher over a year to complete an extensive professional summary review of all the literature on a broad question. The same researcher might complete a highly focused review in a very specialized area in a week. When beginning a review, a researcher decides on a topic, how much depth to go into, and the kind of review to conduct.

The five kinds of literature review are ideal types. A specific review often combines features of several kinds.

Where to Find Research Literature

Researchers, whether academic or practitioner, report their research projects in books, scholarly journal articles, dissertations, government documents, policy reports, and agency reports. They sometimes present them as papers at the meetings of professional societies. This section briefly discusses each type and gives you a simple road map on how to access them.

PERIODICALS. You can find crime and justice research in newspapers, in popular magazines, on television or radio broadcasts, and in Internet news summaries. These, of course, are not the full, complete reports of research required to prepare a proper literature review. They are selected, condensed summaries prepared by journalists for a general audience, but they are still useful in completing a comprehensive search. Textbooks and encyclopedias also present condensed summaries of research, but these must only be used as a way to find relevant research. Locating and reviewing the original research articles are still necessary.

Navigating published articles often confuses beginning research students. This is not surprising. When asked to do a literature review, many students first go to familiar nonscholarly magazines or newspaper articles they may have used for a high school term paper or freshman-level report. It is important, however, to learn to distinguish between scholarly publications that report on research studies and popular or layperson entertainment or news articles for the general public. Researchers rely primarily on scholarly publications written for a professional audience. The important exception is in exploratory research where there often is no body of preexisting work. Sometimes the only sources are journalistic periodicals. Remember, too, that print journalists sometimes conduct cutting-edge and well-done exploratory research, usually documenting some controversial phenomenon.

Academic researchers present the results of empirical studies in one of several forms: academic research books (often called monographs), articles in scholarly journals, chapters in edited academic books, and papers presented at professional meetings. One can also read about these studies, in a summarized, simplified, abbreviated, and "predigested" form, in textbooks written for students who are first learning about a topic. However, simplified summaries can give an incomplete or distorted picture of the full original study. Whenever possible, go to the original scholarly journal article to see what the author has said and the data show.

Upper-level students writing a term paper or a serious research paper should rely primarily on the academic literature. Sometimes these scholarly sources are highly technical and difficult to follow. The upside is that the articles are original reports—and not another person's (mis)reading of the original. They also have been carefully reviewed for professional use and most are of high quality. (As you develop your skills as a critical consumer of research, you'll soon discover that there is a wide range of quality even among refereed academic publications.)

SCHOLARLY JOURNALS. The primary type of periodical to use for a literature review is the scholarly journal filled with peer-reviewed reports of research (see the list of sample crime and justice journals in Chapter 2). One rarely finds them outside of college and university libraries. Recall from Chapter 2 that scholarly journals are where most researchers disseminate findings of new studies, and they are the heart of the scientific community's communication system.

Some scholarly journals are specialized. Instead of reports of research studies, they have only book reviews that provide commentary and evaluations on a book (e.g., *Criminal Justice Review*), or they contain only literature review essays (e.g., *Annual Review of Sociology, Annual Review of Criminology*) in which researchers give a "state of the field" essay for others. Publications that specialize in literature reviews can be quite helpful if an article was recently published on an object of study. Many scholarly journals have a mix of literature reviews, book reviews, reports on research studies, and theoretical essays.

You may wonder if anyone ever reads all the articles published in journals. One study found that in a sample of 379 sociology articles, 43 percent were cited in another study in the first year after publication and 83 percent within six years.[1] As mentioned in Chapter 1, scholarly journals vary by prestige and acceptance rates, with some prestigious journals rejecting as much as 90 percent of the reports submitted to them. Overall rejection rates are higher in the social sciences than in other academic fields and these rates have been rising.[2] This does not mean that researchers are doing lower-quality studies. Rather, the review process is becoming more rigorous, standards are rising, and more researchers are conducting studies, thus increasing the competition to publish in a well-respected journal.

Most, but not all, scholarly journals may be viewed via the Internet. Usually, this depends on the years selected and the availability each library provides. A few Internet services provide full, exact copies of scholarly journal articles over the Internet. For example, JSTOR provides exact copies, but only for a small number of scholarly journals and only for a few years. Other Internet services, such as ProQuest or EBSCOhost, offer a full-text version of recent articles for a limited number of scholarly journals.

Despite the growing electronic availability of articles, it is still a good idea to actually step foot into the library and see what a full-print version of the scholarly article looks like in the actual journal. This makes it easy for you to browse the table of contents of the journals, and browsing can be very useful for generating new ideas for research topics, seeing an established topic in creative ways, or expanding an idea into new areas. Only a handful of new Internet-only scholarly journals, called e-journals, present their work only over the Internet.

Your college library has a section for scholarly journals and magazines, or, in some cases, they may be mixed with books. Look at a map of library facilities or ask a librarian to find this section. The most recent issues, which look like magazines, are often physically separate in a "current periodicals" section. This is done to store them temporarily and make them available until the library receives all the issues of a volume. Most often, libraries bind all issues of a volume together in book form before adding it to their permanent collection.

To assist in locating articles, scholars have a system for tracking scholarly journals and the articles in them. Each issue is assigned a date, volume number, and issue number. This information makes it easier to locate an article. Such information—along with details such as author, title, and page number—is called an article's citation and is used in bibliographies. When a journal is first published, it begins with volume 1, number 1, and continues increasing the numbers thereafter. For most journals, each volume is one year. If you see a journal issue with volume 52, for example, it probably means that the journal has been in existence for 52 years.

Most crime and justice journals number pages by volume, not by issue. The first issue of a volume usually begins with page 1, and page numbering continues throughout the entire volume. For example, the first page of volume 52, issue 4, might be page 547. Most journals have an index for each volume and a table of contents for each issue that lists the title, the author's or authors' names, and the page on which the article begins. The articles often have abstracts, which are short summaries that appear on the first page of the article or are grouped together at the beginning of the issue.

Many libraries do not retain physical paper copies of older journals. To save space and costs, they retain only digital versions. Sometimes you may have to borrow a journal or photocopy of an article from a distant library through an interlibrary loan service, a system by which libraries lend books or materials to other libraries. Library Internet services are slowly making interlibrary loan services less relevant (but not yet for books, though).

Citation Formats.   An article's citation is the key to locating it. Suppose Michelle Grant wanted to read more work from Gary Marx in the area of surveillance and found the following article cited in one of his books:

> *Marx, Gary T. (2003). "A Tack in the Shoe: Neutralizing and Resisting the New Surveillance." Journal of Social Issues 59(2):369–385.*

It tells you to go to an issue of the scholarly journal *Journal of Social Issues* published in 2003. The citation does not provide the issue or months, but it gives the volume number (59), the issue number (2), and the page numbers (369–385).

There are many ways to cite the literature. Formats for citing literature in the text itself vary. Citation formats can get complex. Two major reference tools on the topic in the social sciences are *The Chicago Manual of Style*, which has nearly eighty pages on bibliographies and reference formats, and the *Publication Manual of the American Psychological Association*, which devotes about sixty pages to the topic. To make things more confusing, many journals adopt their own unique format citations.

SCHOLARLY BOOKS. Researchers are usually interested in those books containing reports of original research or collections of research articles. Libraries shelve these books and assign call numbers to them, as they do with other types of books. You can find citation information on them (e.g., title, author, or publisher) in the library's catalog system.

It is not easy to distinguish a book that reports on research from other books. You are more likely to find such books in a college or university library. Some publishers, such as university presses, specialize in publishing them. Nevertheless, there is no guaranteed method for identifying one without reading it.

Some types of crime and justice research are more likely to appear in book form than others. Large-scale ethnographic studies and complex theoretical or philosophical discussions usually appear as books. Sometimes an academic author communicates to both scholarly peers and the general public within a book that bridges the scholarly, academic style and a popular nonfiction style. Good examples are James Q. Wilson's (1981) *Thinking about Crime* or Elliot Currie's (1995) *Confronting Crime*.

Locating original research articles in books can be difficult because there is no single source listing them. Three types of books contain collections of articles or research reports. The first is designed for teaching purposes. Such books, called readers, may include original research reports. Usually, articles on a topic from scholarly journals are gathered and edited to be easier for students to read and understand.

The second type of collection is designed for scholars and may gather journal articles or may contain original research or theoretical essays on a specific topic. These are usually referred to as edited scholarly books. These may include original research reports organized around a specialized topic. Libraries shelve these collections with other books, and most libraries' computerized catalog systems include article or chapter titles.

Citations or references to books are shorter than article citations. They include the author's name, book title, year and place of publication, and publisher's name.

DISSERTATIONS. All graduate students who receive a PhD degree are required to complete a work of original research, which they write up as a dissertation or thesis. The dissertation is bound and shelved in the library of the university that granted the PhD. Because dissertations report on original research, they can be valuable sources of information.

Specialized indexes list dissertations completed by students at accredited universities. For example, Dissertation Abstracts International lists dissertations with their authors, titles, and universities. This index is organized by topic and contains an abstract of each dissertation.

GOVERNMENT DOCUMENTS. The federal government of the United States, the governments of other nations, state- or provincial-level governments, the United Nations, and other international agencies, such as the World Bank, all sponsor studies and publish reports of the research. Many college and university libraries have these documents in their holdings, usually in a special "government documents" section. These reports are rarely found in the catalog system. You must use specialized computerized search systems and indexes, usually with the help of a librarian, to locate these reports. Most college and university libraries hold only the most frequently requested documents and reports.

Many of these valuable sources can also be obtained over the Internet. For example, most government reports of research conducted by the U.S. Department of Justice are available on their various Web sites (e.g., NIJ, BJS, and FBI). The United Nations also makes available hundreds of reports related to crime and justice issues. These Web sites generally require a high-speed Internet connection, and the files are usually in PDF format, requiring Adobe Acrobat to successfully download them. Figure B.1 illustrates a typical government document cover produced by the Government Accounting Office (an agency noted in Chapter 1).

October 2005

Highlights of GAO-06-104, a report to the Chairman, Committee on the Judiciary, House of Representatives

COMMUNITY POLICING GRANTS

COPS Grants Were a Modest Contributor to Declines in Crime in the 1990s

Why GAO Did This Study

Between 1994 and 2001, the Office of Community Oriented Policing Services (COPS) provided more than $7.6 billion in grants to state and local communities to hire police officers and promote community policing as an effective strategy to prevent crime. Studies of the impact of the grants on crime have been inconclusive.

GAO was asked to evaluate the effect of the COPS program on the decline in crime during the 1990s. GAO developed and analyzed a database containing annual observations on crime, police officers, COPS funds, and other factors related to crime, covering years prior to and during the COPS program, or from 1990 through 2001. GAO analyzed survey data on policing practices that agencies reportedly implemented and reviewed studies of policing practices. GAO assessed: (1) how COPS obligations were distributed and how much was spent; (2) the extent to which COPS expenditures contributed to increases in the number of police officers and declines in crime nationwide; and (3) the extent to which COPS grants during the 1990s were associated with policing practices that crime literature indicates could be effective.

In commenting on a draft of this report, the COPS Office said that our findings are important and support conclusions reached by others.

www.gao.gov/cgi-bin/getrpt?GAO-06-104.

To view the full product, including the scope and methodology, click on the link above. For more information, contact Laurie Ekstrand at (202) 512-8777 or ekstrandl@gao.gov.

What GAO Found

About half of the COPS funds distributed from 1994 through 2001 went to law enforcement agencies in localities of fewer than 150,000 persons and the remainder to agencies in larger communities. This distribution roughly corresponded to the distribution of major property crimes but less so to the distribution of violent crimes. For example, agencies in larger communities received about 47 percent of COPS funds but accounted for 58 percent of the violent crimes nationwide. From 1994 through 2001, COPS expenditures constituted about 1 percent of total local expenditures for police services.

For the years 1994 through 2001, expenditures of COPS grants by grant recipients resulted in varying amounts of additional officers above the levels that would have been expected without the expenditures. For example, during 2000, the peak year of COPS expenditures by grant recipients, they led to an increase of about 3 percent in the level of sworn officers—or about 17,000 officers. Adding up the number of additional officers in each year from 1994 through 2001, GAO estimated that COPS expenditures yielded about 88,000 additional officer-years. GAO obtained its results from fixed-effects regression models that controlled for pre-1994 trends in the growth rate of officers, other federal expenditures, and local- and state-level factors that could affect officer levels.

From its analysis of the effects of increases in officers on declines in crime, GAO estimated that COPS funds contributed to declines in the crime rate that, while modest in size, varied over time and among categories of crime. For example, between 1993 and 2000, COPS funds contributed to a 1.3 percent decline in the overall crime rate and a 2.5 percent decline in the violent crime rate from the 1993 levels. The effects of COPS funds on crime held when GAO controlled for other crime-related factors—such as local economic conditions and state-level policy changes—in its regression models, and the effects were commensurate with COPS funds' contribution to local spending on police protection. Factors other than COPS funds accounted for the majority of the decline in crime during this period. For example, between 1993 and 2000, the overall crime rate declined by 26 percent, and the 1.3 percent decline due to COPS, amounted to about 5 percent of the overall decline. Similarly, COPS contributed about 7 percent of the 32 percent decline in violent crime from 1993 to 2000.

From 1993 though 1997, agencies that received and spent COPS grants reported larger changes in policing practices and in the subsets of practices that focus on solving crime problems or focus on places where crime is concentrated than did agencies that did not receive the grants. The differences held after GAO controlled for underlying trends in the reported use of these policing practices. From 1996 to 2000, there was no overall increase in policing practices associated with COPS grants. In its review of studies on policing practices, GAO found that problem-solving and place-oriented practices can be effective in reducing crime.

_____ United States Government Accountability Office

FIGURE B.1 Government Document from the Government Accounting Office *Source:* From United States General Accounting Office, Oct. 2005. www.gao.gov/cgi-bin/getrpt? GAO-06-104.

SUMMARY TABLE B.3	Where to Look for Relevant Literature

1. **Periodicals**—*Newspapers and magazines found using periodical search engines*
2. **Scholarly journals**—*Academic articles found using academic search engines (e.g., CJ Abstracts, Google Scholar) and perusing library shelves*
3. **Scholarly books**—*University press, edited books found using academic search engines and perusing library shelves*
4. **Dissertations**—*Original research found in dissertation abstracts*
5. **Government documents**—*Reports, hearings, and evaluation research found using various search engines and Web sites*
6. **Policy reports, agency reports, and presented papers**—*Research institute reports (e.g., The Brookings Institution, Cato Institute) and academic papers presented at conferences*

POLICY REPORTS, AGENCY REPORTS, AND PRESENTED PAPERS. A researcher conducting a thorough review of the literature will examine these three additional sources. Research institutes and policy centers (e.g., The Brookings Institution, Institute for Research on Poverty, Rand Corporation, Cato Institute, and Justice Institute) publish papers and reports. Oftentimes their Internet sites make them available to the general public. Paid-for consultants usually conduct agency reports; these are tough to track down unless perhaps your professor can point you to the right person.

Each year, professional associations in crime and justice studies from around the world hold annual meetings. Thousands of researchers assemble to give, listen to, or discuss oral reports of recent research. People who do not attend the meetings but who are members of the association receive a program of the meeting, listing each paper to be presented with its title, author, and author's place of employment (recall the list of paper presentation topics provided in Chapter 1). These associations' Web sites also usually provide these programs. You can write directly to the author and request a copy of the paper. Summary Table B.3 reviews the various locations for finding relevant literature.

How to Conduct a Systematic Literature Review

DEFINE AND REFINE A TOPIC. Michelle Grant's research topic could be constructed around the broad notion of surveillance, or it could focus more narrowly on governmental surveillance, or it could concentrate specifically on fixed surveillance systems used by governmental police agencies. A good literature review begins with a clearly defined, well-focused research question. For example, the notion of surveillance is much too broad. A context review for a research project should be slightly broader than the specific research question being examined. Often, a researcher will not finalize a specific research question for a study until he or she has reviewed the literature. As in Michelle's case, researching the literature usually helps bring greater focus to an initial research interest.

DESIGN A SEARCH. After choosing a focused research question for the review, the next step is to plan a search strategy. You must decide on the type of review, its extent, and the types of materials to include. The key is to be careful, systematic, and organized. Set parameters on your search: how much time you will devote to it, how far back in time you will look, the minimum number of research reports you will examine, how many libraries you will visit, and so forth.

Also, decide how to record the bibliographic citation for each reference you find and how to take notes (e.g., in a notebook, on 3 × 5 cards, or in a computer file). Develop a schedule, because several visits are usually necessary. You should begin a file folder or computer file in which you can place possible sources and ideas for new sources. As the review proceeds, it should become more focused.

LOCATE RESEARCH REPORTS. Locating research reports depends on the type of report or outlet of research being searched. As a general rule, you should use multiple search strategies to counteract the limitations of a single search method.

Articles in Scholarly Journals. The task of searching for articles can be formidable. Luckily, specialized publications and high-power search engines found in most libraries make the task easier. In perhaps one of the most important developments for researchers since the card catalog, Google has put in place the search engine **Google Scholar**. Highlight B.1 describes how this site works, its strengths and limitations, and what it might portend for the future.

One particularly important computerized search source is CJ Abstracts. There is also the Social Sciences Index and the Educational Resources Information Center (ERIC) system. There are over hundred such source tools. You can usually find them in the reference section of a library or on the Internet.

Researchers organize computerized searches in several ways—by author, by article title, by subject, or by keyword. A keyword is an important term for a topic that is likely to be found in a title. You will want to use six to eight keywords in most computer-based searches and consider several synonyms. Often, figuring out the correct keywords means the difference between success and failure. The computer's searching method can vary, and most look for a keyword only in a title or abstract. If you choose too few words or very narrow terms, you will miss a lot of relevant articles. If you choose too many words or very broad terms, you will get a huge number of irrelevant articles. The best way to learn the appropriate breadth and number of keywords is by trial and error.

Kraska (2001a) has discovered, for example, that in his research on the blurring distinction between the military and police that only a single phrase will generally yield worthwhile

HIGHLIGHT B.1
"Schoogle": The Emergence of Google Scholar

Searching for academic articles and books used to be a highly time-consuming and cumbersome process. With today's advanced computerized search engines, most academic articles and books on a particular topic, or by a particular author, are easily uncovered and accessed. While many students and libraries have relied on the subscription service EBSCOhost (a fee-based system), Google Corporation in 2004 launched an ambitious project known as Google Scholar. Google Scholar is the first free Internet-based search engine that targets scholarly literature, including peer-reviewed papers, theses, books, preprints, abstracts, and technical reports from all broad areas of research. Many libraries link their system to Google Scholar so that all free articles available to a student or faculty affiliated with a particular library can be accessed. For example, let's say Neuman wanted to search for literature examining crime rates across different countries (known as cross-national crime research). Google Scholar would instantly pull up those various academic books and articles on this topic (along with an occasional irrelevant citation), and rank them according to how often they are cited in the literature. Neuman would notice that one of his own articles is listed ("Competing Perspectives on Cross-National Crime: An Evaluation of Theory and Evidence" in *Sociological Quarterly*, 1988), and by clicking on the link "Cited by 20"

he could pull up the full citations of those twenty articles that have cited his work. There is also a feature that would allow him to select all "Related Articles"—a function that could significantly reduce the amount of time spent researching for relevant literature. If his library subscribes to a particular journal, he would be able to pull a full-length PDF copy of the journal up for free.

Google has ambitious plans for making scholarly information available on the Internet for free. Their latest undertaking involves scanning the entire text of millions of books and posting them on the Internet. The possibilities for research junkies are amazing. While some professors lament the use of Google as students' first and last research resource, the increasing sophistication of Google Scholar and the Google Books Library Project, when combined with access rights afforded by a university library, will likely provide a formidable research resource.

Google has long said it plans to make the world's information accessible and searchable, and a cornerstone to its mission would be to bring libraries to life online. For now, in our experience, Google Scholar is an excellent tool when used as a supplement to other, more traditional library search methods. The day may be coming, though, when the bulk of literature research will be conducted almost exclusively through search engines such as Google Scholar.

references. (It is a Latin phrase, *posse comitatus*, which refers to the Posse Comitatus Act of 1878, which prohibits the military from engaging in civilian police functions and activities.) In a study Neuman conducted on how college students define sexual harassment (Neuman 1992), he used the following keywords: sexual harassment, sexual assault, harassment, gender equity, gender fairness, and sex discrimination. He later discovered a few important studies that lacked any of these keywords in their titles. He also tried the keywords "college student and rape," but got huge numbers of unrelated articles that were not worth reviewing.

There are numerous computer-assisted search databases or systems. A person with a computer and an Internet hookup can search some article index collections, the catalogs of libraries, and other information sources around the globe if they are available on the Internet.

Scholarly Books and Dissertations.   Finding scholarly books on a subject can be difficult. The subject topics of library catalog systems are usually incomplete and too broad to be useful. Moreover, they list only books that are in a particular library system, although you may be able to search other libraries for interlibrary loan books. Libraries organize books by call numbers based on subject matter. Librarians can help you locate books from other libraries. Google Scholar is sometimes a good place to start. As mentioned earlier, Dissertation Abstracts International lists most dissertations. Like the indexes and abstracts for journal articles, it organizes dissertations by broad subject category, author, and date.

Government Documents.   Government-based Web sites are one good option. The "government documents" sections of libraries also contain specialized lists of government documents. A useful index for documents issued by the U.S. federal government is the *Monthly Catalog of United States Government Publications*, which is available online as the GPO Monthly Catalog. Indexes to congressional hearings, another useful source, lists committees and subjects going back to the late 1930s. The *Congressional Record* contains debate of the U.S. Congress with synopses of bills, voting records, and changes in bills. These are both excellent sources for historical research. The *United States Statutes at Large* lists each individual U.S. federal law by year and subject. The *Federal Register*, a daily publication of the U.S. government, contains all rules, regulations, and announcements of federal agencies. It has both monthly and annual indexes.

Policy Reports, Agency Reports, and Presented Papers.   The most difficult sources to locate are policy reports and presented papers. They are listed in some bibliographies of published studies; some are listed in the abstracts or indexes. Relevant Web sites are the best place to begin. Writing to research centers and authors of work found in journal sources can also be fruitful.

Evaluating Research Articles

After you locate published studies, you need to read and evaluate them. This section will review some general guidelines to help you read and evaluate the research and literature you uncover. First, look at the title carefully. A good title is specific yet not too technical, and it indicates the nature of the research without describing the results.

Next, read the abstract. A good abstract summarizes critical information about a study. It gives the study's purpose, tells methods used, and highlights major findings. It will avoid vague references to future implications.

We recommend a two-stage screening process. Use the title and abstract to determine initial relevance. If it appears relevant, quickly scan the introduction and conclusion sections to decide whether it is a real "keeper" and worth investing in a slow, careful reading of the entire article or picking out a few details. Most likely, you will discover a few articles are very central to your purpose and many others have tangential relevance and are only worth skimming to locate one or two specific relevant details. Exercise caution not to pull specific details out of context.

Three factors will influence the amount of time, effort, and overall payoff from reading a scholarly article. The time and effort are lower and results greater when

1. the article is of high quality with a well-defined purpose, clear writing, and smooth, logical organization;
2. the reader is sharply focused on a particular research issue or question; and
3. the reader has a solid theoretical background, knows a great deal about the substantive topic, and is familiar with multiple research methodologies.

A great deal depends on reader preparation. A reader who can quickly size up an article by recognizing the dimensions of a study (see Chapter 2), its use of theory (Chapter 3), and the author's approach to conducting research (Chapter 3) will find it less burdensome to read, evaluate, and extract information from a scholarly article. These skills can only be obtained through reading numerous journal articles (a requirement in Kraska's and Neuman's research methods classes) and learning crime and criminal justice theories.

When you read what seems to be a highly relevant article, begin with the introduction section. The introduction section has three purposes: (1) introduce a broad topic and show a transition to a specific research question that is the primary focus of the study, (2) establish the significance of the problem (in terms of expanding knowledge, linking to past studies, or addressing an applied concern), and (3) outline the theoretical framework and define major concepts being used. Sometimes an article blends the introduction with a context literature review; at other times, the literature review is a separate section.

A good literature review is selective, comprehensive, critical, and current. By being selective, it does not list everything ever written on a topic, but picks the most relevant past studies. By being comprehensive, it includes past studies that are highly relevant and does not omit any important ones. More than merely recounting past studies, the review should be critically evaluative. This means it comments on the details of some specific studies and evaluates them as they relate to current study. Because the writer does not know everything about a study until it is done, a literature review prepared before conducting a study must be fine-tuned and rewritten after the study is completed.

Depending on the type of research study, a hypothesis or methods section may follow the literature review. They outline what will be examined in detail, inform readers of specific data sources or methods of data collection, describe how variables were measured and whether sampling was used, and, if so, details about it. These sections are usually tightly written and packed with technical details. They are often longer in quantitative studies than in qualitative studies.

After a methods section comes the results or findings. The results section is a descriptive essay. If it is quantitative research, it needs to do more than present a collection of statistical tables or coefficients and percentages. If it is qualitative research, it should be more than a list of quotations or straight description.

Each paragraph flows sequentially, describing results in a logical order. The organization of data presentation usually begins simply, painting a broad scope, and then goes into complexities and specific findings. Data presentation includes a straightforward discussion of the central findings and notes their significance. In quantitative research, it is not necessary to discuss every detail in a table or chart, but to note major findings and any unexpected or unusual findings. The author guides the reader through the data, pointing out what is in the study, but lets the reader see details for himself or herself. In qualitative research, the organization of data often tells a story or presents a line of reasoning. Readers follow the author's story but are free to make inquiries of it.

Some researchers combine a discussion section with a results section; others keep them separate. A discussion section goes beyond straight description to elaborating on the implications of results for past findings, theory, or applied issues. Implications and interpretation include several forms: (1) implications for the building of knowledge as outlined in the literature review,

(2) implications for the specific research question of this study, as well as what was unexpected, and (3) implications for policy and practice.

Researchers usually include methodological limitations in the discussion or conclusion. An author may state how the specific measures, sampling, cases, location, or other factors restrict the generalizability of findings or open up alternative explanations. Full candor and openness are expected. An author should show readers that he or she was self-critical and has thought through the results.

Last, read through the conclusion or summary at the end. A good conclusion/summary reviews the research problem, major findings, and significant unexpected results. It also outlines future implications, directions, and theoretical insights. It is sometimes useful to read the introduction and skim the conclusion before reading through the entire report step by step. This allows you to comprehend the big picture before becoming mired in the details. You also want to review the reference or bibliography section. An article's bibliography often gives important leads to finding the mainstay references within an area of study.

Reading and critically evaluating scholarly articles improve with practice. Despite the peer-review process and manuscript rejection rates, articles vary in quality and may contain errors, sloppy logic, or gaps. A careful reader will evaluate how the study was done, how logically the parts of an article fit together, and whether the major conclusions really flow from all the findings.

Taking Notes

As you gather the relevant research literature, it is easy to feel overwhelmed by the quantity of information, so you need a system for taking notes. Before computers, the usual approach was to write notes on index cards, and then shift and sort the note cards, looking for connections among them to develop an outline for a report or paper. This method still works. Today, however, most people use word-processing software and gather photocopies or printed versions of many articles.

As you discover sources, it is a good idea to create two kinds of files for your note cards or computer documents: a Source File and a Content File. Record all the bibliographic information for each source in the Source File, even though you may not use some and later erase them.

Your note cards or computer documents go into the Content File. This file contains substantive information of interest from a source, usually its major findings, details of methodology, definitions of concepts, or interesting quotes. If you directly quote from a source or want to take some specific information from a source, you need to record the specific page number(s) on which the quote appears. Link the files by putting key source information, such as author and date, on each content file.

WHAT TO RECORD. Researchers have to decide what to record about an article, book, or other source. It is better to err in the direction of recording too much rather than too little. In general, record the hypotheses tested, valuable insights, how major concepts were measured, the main findings, the basic design of the research, the group or sample used, and ideas for future study.

Photocopying all relevant articles or reports will save you time recording notes and is highly recommended. Also, you can make notes on the photocopy. Each photocopy can be numbered, and then these numbers can be applied to different sections of the article when writing your report. Figure B.2 provides a tangible example of how to go about taking notes from Miller's (2001) path-breaking article on the "dual arrest" phenomenon in domestic violence.

ORGANIZE NOTES. After gathering a large number of references and notes, you need an organizing scheme. One approach is to group studies or specific findings by skimming notes and creating a mental map of how they fit together. Try several organizing schemes before settling on a final one. In the process of organizing notes, you will find that some references and notes do not fit and should be discarded as irrelevant. Also, you may discover gaps or areas and topics that are relevant but that you did not examine. This necessitates return visits to the library.

RESEARCH TOPIC: DUAL ARREST IN DOMESTIC VIOLENCE FULL CITATION (SOURCE FILE)

Miller, L. Miller (2001) "The Paradox of Women Arrested for Domestic Violence: Criminal Justice Professionals and Service Providers Respond." Violence Against Women, 7,12: 1139-1376.

NOTE CARD (CONTENT FILE)

Susan Miller 2001   Topics: Dual Arrest; CJ Response; Mandatory
                                     Arrest Laws; Police Training; Primary Aggressor

Abstract (cut and pasted directly form PDF file)
"Increasingly, women are being arrested for domestic violence charges as part of dual arrests (when their partner is also arrested) or as a result of their own actions. Could this phenomenon be explained by women's greater willingness to use violence against their abusive partners, or by a strict adherence by police and prosecutors to follow mandatory or pro-arrest laws without examining the context of the incidents, or something else? This article explores this issue by examining one state's experience, using interview data from criminal justice professionals and service providers who deal directly with women arrested for domestic violence charges."

Relevance to Research:
A highly relevant piece to this research topic that overviews—using a combination of interviews, quantitative data, and previous research information—the larger phenomenon of battered women being arrested for domestic violence. Miller explains the "paradox" as such:

"This paradox gets to the crux of the matter: What is the appropriate criminal justice response to battered women who assault (as legally defined) their abuser or do other illegal acts and end up getting arrested, particularly when these acts of violence committed by victims are qualitatively different from acts of violence committed by batterers? The situation in which many battered women now find themselves is assuredly not the response that was envisioned when the cry for the criminalization of domestic violence was first heard."

This article provides numerous other sources of research conducted on the dual arrest phenomenon, and also includes evidence that proper police training can ameliorate this problem (while still noting that this type of training is the exception rather than the rule). The following quote captures Miller's thoughts.

"Research demonstrates that following the implementation of mandatory arrest policies, dual arrests directly attributable to the policy change have dramatically increased (for example, in Connecticut, 18% of approximately 25,000 annual arrests are dual arrests, which represents a significant increase in the number of dual arrests) (Martin, 1997). Some jurisdictions have recognized this unintended consequence and have either enacted "primary aggressor" laws (Zorza, 1992) or instituted new police training policies. For instance, a 6% dual arrest rate reported in Dallas was reduced to 1% after instituting new training that taught police to arrest the person determined to be most culpable or most dangerous (Martin, 1997). Primary aggressor laws are very promising; for instance, following this kind of policy change, Los Angeles reduced the number of women arrested by one third using this new contextual training."

The article concludes discussing the unintended consequences of new policy, the role the police can play in fixing the problem, and the various hindrances to a solution.

FIGURE B.2 Example of Student Notes on an Article Used in a Master's Thesis Research Project

There are many organizing schemes. The best one depends on the purpose of the review. A context review implies organizing recent reports around a specific research question. A historical review implies organizing studies by major theme and by the date of publication. An integrative review implies organizing studies around core common findings of a field and the main hypotheses tested. A methodological review implies organizing studies by the topic and, within the topic, by the design or method used. A theoretical review implies organizing studies by the theories and major thinkers being examined.

What Does a Good Literature Review Look Like?

A quality literature review requires planning and clear writing. All the rules of good writing (e.g., clear organizational structure, an introduction and conclusion, and transitions between sections) apply to writing a literature review. Keep your purposes in mind when you write, and communicate clearly and effectively.

An author should communicate a review's purpose to the reader by its organization. The wrong way to write a review is to list a series of research reports with a summary of the findings of each. The right way to write a review is to organize common findings or arguments together (see Highlight B.2). A well-accepted approach is to address the most important ideas first, to logically link statements or findings, and to note discrepancies or weaknesses in the research. Qualitative researchers often integrate the review of the literature within the analysis and findings section, as opposed to a separate section.

A Brief Word on the Internet

The Internet has revolutionized how crime and justice researchers work. Only a decade ago, it was rarely used; today, most researchers use the Internet regularly to help them review the literature, to communicate with other researchers, and to search for other information sources. Kraska has

---

HIGHLIGHT B.2
Example of a Bad and Good Review

Example of a Bad Review

Sexual harassment has many consequences. Adams et al. (1983) found that some women students said they avoided taking a class or working with certain professors because of the risk of harassment. They also found that men and women students reacted differently. Their research was a survey of 1,000 men and women graduate and undergraduate students. Benson and Thomson's study in *Social Problems* (1982) lists many problems created by sexual harassment. In their excellent book, *The Lecherous Professor*, Dziech and Weiner (1990) give a long list of difficulties that victims have suffered.

Researchers study the topic in different ways. Hunter and McClelland (1991) conducted a study of undergraduates at a small liberal arts college. They had a sample of 300 students, and students were given multiple vignettes that varied by the reaction of the victim and the situation. Jaschik and Fretz (1991) showed ninety women students at a mideastern university a videotape with a classic example of sexual harassment by a teaching assistant. Before it was labeled as sexual harassment, few women called it that. When asked whether it was sexual harassment, 98 percent agreed. Weber-Burdin and Rossi (1982) replicated a previous study on sexual harassment—only difference is they used students at the University of Massachusetts. They had fifty-nine students rate forty hypothetical situations. Reilley et al. (1982) conducted a study of 250 female and 150 male undergraduates at the University of California, Santa Barbara. They also had a sample of fifty-two faculty. Both samples completed a questionnaire in which respondents were presented vignettes of sexual-harassing situations that they were to rate. Popovich et al. (1986) created a nine-item scale of sexual harassment. They studied 209 undergraduates at a medium-sized university in groups of fifteen to twenty-five. They found disagreement and confusion among students.

Example of a Better Review

The victims of sexual harassment suffer a range of consequences, from lowered self-esteem and loss of self-confidence to withdrawal from social interaction, changed career goals, and depression (Adams et al. 1983; Benson and Thomson 1982; Dziech and Weiner 1990). For example, Adams et al. (1983) noted that 13 percent of women students said they avoided taking a class or working with certain professors because of the risk of harassment.

Research into campus sexual harassment has taken several approaches. In addition to survey research, many have experimented with vignettes or presented hypothetical scenarios (Hunter and McClelland 1991; Jaschik and Fretz 1991; Popovich et al. 1986; Reilley et al. 1982; Rossi and Anderson 1982; Valentine-French and Radtke 1989; Weber-Burdin and Rossi 1982). Victim verbal responses and situational factors appear to affect whether observers label a behavior as harassment. There is confusion over the application of a sexual harassment label for inappropriate behavior. For example, Jaschik and Fretz (1991) found that only 3 percent of the women students shown a videotape with a classic example of sexual harassment by a teaching assistant initially labeled it as sexual harassment. Instead, they called it "sexist," "rude," "unprofessional," or "demeaning." When asked whether it was sexual harassment, 98 percent agreed. Roscoe et al. (1987) reported similar labeling difficulties.

found that it can also be a valuable tool for the collection of research data. One of Kraska's recent research assistants visited over 115 Web sites dedicated to the online sale of anabolic steroids and human growth hormone. He conducted a content analysis of these sites, recording numerous variables, including whether the supplier contacted him after making an initial inquiry. With the Internet continually transforming and expanding, the opportunities for using it to conduct research and collect literature will likely only increase.

Of course, it has still been a mixed blessing, and has not proved to be the panacea that some people first thought it might be. Although the Internet provides new and important ways to find information, it can mislead and supply erroneous information. Anyone can put together an impressive-appearing Web site and fill it with fabricated data, bogus findings, and misinformation. It is best thought of as another valuable tool as opposed to a replacement for traditional library research.

Conclusion

We have examined in depth the process by which we obtain knowledge from the preexisting literature. Aside from including a section in our research report called "literature review," the activity of reviewing the existing literature is invaluable in other ways: It helps us to refine our ideas, develop our organizing concepts, and focus our research question, and assists us in determining our research method. Perhaps, most important, it allows us to answer that ever-important question: So what? Why is my research study important?

Notes for Further Study

1. From Hargens (1988).

2. Based on Hargens (1991).

APPENDIX C

Qualitative Data Analysis Techniques

ANALYSIS OF QUALITATIVE DATA

Just as with quantitative research, qualitative studies involve large amounts of data that have to be analyzed, reduced, and synthesized into a coherent form easily communicated to others. Even the most seasoned researcher can become overwhelmed by this task. It can be intimidating to analyze lengthy interview transcripts; hundreds of pages of thickly described field experiences; photographs; documents; collected items; and a large number of rough ideas, concepts, and potential theories contained in researcher notes. This process requires patience, creativity, solid interpretive skills, and some specific tactics and techniques reviewed in this chapter.

A common criticism of qualitative research has been that even though its methods of data collection are discussed at length, its methods of analysis were unclear and not open to inspection. Qualitative researchers have, in the past ten years, though, moved toward articulating an analytical approach that now seems as scientific as it does artistic (a change some qualitative researchers would bemoan). Admittedly, qualitative analysis cannot be entirely learned, like a recipe in a cookbook fashion. Still, much has been done to make the process of analyzing qualitative data more explicit and systematic.[1] Keep in mind that no single analytic plan will work in all cases. But there are techniques for analyzing qualitative data that work better with ethnographic field research, and others that work better with historical or qualitative document analysis research.

As you read through these different analytical techniques, try not to lose sight of the big picture. Keep in mind that the analysis of qualitative data is similar to how we make sense of our surroundings every day. The qualitative researcher reviews all the data he or she has collected and attempts to find in those data important themes, accurate typologies, rich descriptions of meaningful settings or events, important theoretical insights, new organizing concepts, and narratives that accurately reflect the researcher's understanding of his or her object of study. True to the inductive process, qualitative researchers claim that a deep familiarity with their subject allows the data to speak to them—revealing their themes, significance, and insights.

CONCEPT FORMATION AND CODING

Conceptualization in Qualitative Research

Quantitative researchers conceptualize variables and refine concepts as part of the process of measuring variables. By contrast, qualitative researchers form new concepts or refine concepts that are grounded in the data. Concept formation is an integral part of data analysis and begins during data collection. Thus, conceptualization is one way that a qualitative researcher organizes and makes sense of data.

A qualitative researcher analyzes data by organizing them into categories on the basis of themes, concepts, or similar features. He or she develops new concepts, formulates conceptual definitions, and examines the relationships among concepts. Eventually, he or she links concepts to each other in terms of a sequence, as oppositional sets (X is the opposite of Y), or as sets of similar categories that he or she interweaves into theoretical statements. Researchers form concepts as they read through and ask critical questions of data (e.g., field notes, historical documents, photographs, and secondary sources). The questions can come from the abstract vocabulary of a discipline such as criminology, for example, Is this a case of class conflict? Was role conflict present in that situation? Is this a social movement? Questions can also be logical, for example, What was the sequence of events? How does the way it happened here compare to over there? Are these the same or different, general or specific cases?[2]

In qualitative research, ideas and evidence are mutually interdependent. This applies particularly to case-study analysis. Cases are not given preestablished empirical units or theoretical categories apart from data; they are defined by data and theory. By analyzing a situation, the researcher organizes data and applies ideas to create or specify a case. Making or creating a case brings the data and theory together.

Coding Qualitative Data

Quantitative research codes data by measuring variables into a machine-readable form for statistical analysis. Coding data has a different meaning and role in qualitative research. A researcher organizes the raw data into conceptual categories and creates themes or concepts. Instead of a clerical data management task, qualitative coding is an integral part of data analysis. It is guided by the research question and leads to new questions. It frees a researcher from entanglement in the details of the raw data and encourages higher-level thinking about them. It also moves him or her toward theory and generalizations:

> Codes are tags or labels for assigning units of meaning to the descriptive or inferential information compiled during a study. Codes usually are attached to "chunks" of varying size—words, phrases, sentences or whole paragraphs, connected or unconnected to a specific setting. (Miles and Huberman 1994: 56)

Coding involves two simultaneous activities: mechanical data reduction and analytic categorization of data. The researcher imposes order on the data. "Contrasted with the weeks and weeks in which she will be engaged in mechanical processing, the truly analytic moments will occur during bursts of insight or pattern recognition" (Wolcott 1994: 24). Coding data is the hard work of reducing large mountains of raw data into small, manageable piles. Ferrell (2006), for example, in his study on urban scrounging, collected a storage shed full of discarded items. He had to separate and organize them into a comprehendible system. In doing so, he was able to analyze the large collection of personal photographs and memorabilia that the deceased had left behind, and ponder the social significance of people's lives discarded in the trash. In addition to making the data manageable, coding allows a researcher to quickly retrieve relevant parts of it. Between the moments of thrill and inspiration, a great deal of coding qualitative data, or file-work, can be wearisome and tedious.

Strauss (1987) defined three kinds of qualitative data coding: open coding, axial coding, and selective coding.

OPEN CODING. Open coding is performed during a first pass through recently collected data. The researcher locates themes and assigns initial codes in a first attempt to condense the mass of data into categories. He or she slowly reads field notes, historical sources, or other data, looking for critical terms, central people, key events, or themes, which are then noted. Next, he or she writes a preliminary concept or label at the edge of a note card or computer record and highlights it with a different color or in some similar way. The researcher is open to creating new themes and to changing these initial codes in subsequent analysis. A theoretical framework helps if it is used in a flexible manner.

Open coding brings themes to the surface from deep inside the data. The themes are at a low level of abstraction and come from the researcher's initial research question, concepts in the literature, terms used by members in the social setting, or new thoughts stimulated by immersion in the data. It is important for researchers to see abstract concepts in concrete data and to move back and forth between abstract concepts and specific details.

For example, Lucia's description of the murders was specific in detail. She described "camouflaged uniforms . . . [of] various colors that she has seen soldiers in the street wearing." Good qualitative researchers are able to identify abstract concepts based on concrete details.

Concepts such as *political crime, paramilitary crime, civil war,* and so on come to mind from reading Lucia's declaration.

Historical-comparative researchers also use open coding. For example, the concepts that emerge from coding Lucia's eyewitness account of the murders can be easily combined together into interesting substantive relationships: What is the relationship between death squad activity and religion? What role do the military and police play in the death squad activity? Is there a relationship between U.S. foreign aid to El Salvador and the death squads? What political and economic interests in El Salvador perceive the Jesuits as a threat? As this example illustrates, coding helps make related themes and concepts buried in the qualitative data more explicit.

We urge the novice in qualitative analysis to convert relatively inert abstractions into stories— even with plots. Although some researchers suggest that you begin coding with a list of concepts, researchers generate most coding themes while reading data notes. Regardless of whether you begin with a list of themes, you make a list of themes after open coding. Such a list serves three purposes:

1. It helps you see the emerging themes at a glance.
2. It stimulates you to find themes in future open coding.
3. You can use the list to build a universe of all themes in the study, which you reorganize, sort, combine, discard, or extend in further analysis.

Qualitative researchers vary in how completely and in how much detail they code. Some code every line or every few words; others code paragraphs or pages. Some of the data are not coded and are dross or left over. The degree of detail in coding depends on the research question, the richness of the data, and the researcher's purposes

AXIAL CODING. Axial coding is done on the second pass through the data. During open coding, we focus on the actual data and assign code labels for themes. There is no concern about making connections among themes or elaborating the concepts that the themes represent. By contrast, in axial coding, we begin with an organized set of initial codes or preliminary concepts. In this second pass, we focus on the initial coded themes more than on the data. Additional codes or new ideas may emerge during this pass, and we should note them; but our primary task is to review and examine initial codes. We move toward organizing ideas or themes and identifying the axis of key concepts in analysis. Miles and Huberman (1994: 62) have warned:

> Whether codes are created and revised early or late is basically less important than whether they have some conceptual and structural order. Codes should relate to one another in coherent, study-important ways; they should be part of a governing structure.

During axial coding, we ask about causes and consequences, conditions and interactions, and strategies and processes, and look for categories or concepts that cluster together. We should ask questions such as, Can I divide existing concepts into subdimensions or subcategories? Can I combine several closely related concepts into one more general one? Can I organize categories into a sequence (i.e., A, then B, then C), or by their physical location (i.e., where they occur), or their relationship to a major topic of interest?

A criminologist doing research on paramilitary death squads, for example, may decide to make the concept of *social class* a major theme. In selective coding he or she would go back through the qualitative data and look for information regarding the social class of the victims, the social class of the death squad murders, the social class interests that challenge the death squad worldview, and so on. The array of themes and concepts identified in axial coding helps the researcher discover interesting new research questions and conceptual relationships to explore.

Axial coding not only stimulates thinking about linkages between concepts or themes but it also raises new questions. It can suggest dropping some themes or examining others in more depth. In addition, it reinforces the connections between evidence and concepts. As we consolidate codes, we may find evidence in many places for core themes and build a dense web of support in the qualitative data for them. This is analogous to the idea of multiple indicators described with regard to reliability and measuring variables. The connection between a theme and data is strengthened by multiple instances of empirical evidence.[3]

SELECTIVE CODING. By the time we are ready for this last pass through the data, we have identified the major themes of the research project. Selective coding involves scanning all the data and previous codes. We look selectively for cases that illustrate themes and make comparisons and contrasts after most or all data collection is complete. We begin after we have well-developed concepts and have started to organize the overall analysis around several core generalizations or ideas. During selective coding, major themes or concepts ultimately guide the search. We reorganize specific themes identified in earlier coding and elaborate more than one major theme.

ANALYTIC STRATEGY FOR QUALITATIVE DATA

In general, data analysis means a search for patterns in data—recurrent behaviors, objects, phases, or ideas. Once a pattern is identified, it is interpreted in terms of a social theory or the setting in which it occurred. This allows the qualitative researcher to move from the description of a historical event or social setting to a more general interpretation. In this section you will learn about strategies researchers use to analyze qualitative data: the ideal type, successive approximation, the illustrative method, domain analysis, analytic comparison, narrative analysis, and negative case method.

A source of confusion is that data take multiple forms in various stages of qualitative research. For example, field research data include raw sense data that a researcher experiences, recorded data in field notes, and selected or processed data that appear in a final report (see Figure C.1). Data analysis involves examining, sorting, categorizing, evaluating, comparing,

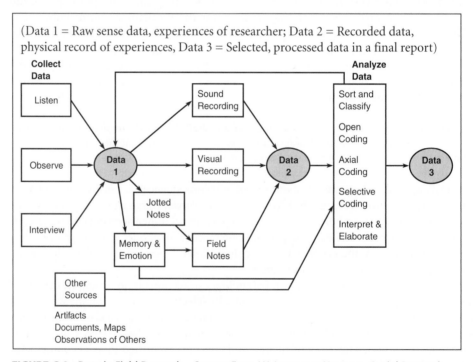

FIGURE C.1 Data in Field Research *Source:* From W. Lawrence Neuman, *Social Research Methods, Qualitative and Quantitative Approaches,* 6/e. Published by Allyn and Bacon, 75 Arlington St., Boston, MA 02116. Copyright © 2006 by Pearson Education. Reprinted by permission of the publisher. Adapted from R. F. Ellen, ed. *Ethnographic Research: A Guide to General Conduct.* Orlando: Academic Press, 1984.

synthesizing, and contemplating the coded data as well as reviewing the raw and recorded data. Probably the best example of an analytic strategy is narrative analysis.

Narrative Analysis

The concept *narrative* has multiple meanings and is used in anthropology, archaeology, history, linguistics, literary criticism, political science, psychology, and criminology/criminal justice.[4] A **narrative** refers to a type of qualitative data, a form of inquiry and data gathering, a way to discuss and present data, a set of qualitative data analysis techniques, and a kind of theoretical explanation. As Griffin (1992: 419) observed, "Narrative is both a rhetorical form and a generic, logical form of explanation that merges theorized description of an event with its explanation."

Despite the diversity of its uses, a narrative shares six core elements: (1) telling a story or tale (i.e., presenting unfolding events from a point of view), (2) a sense of movement or process (i.e., a before and after condition), (3) interrelations or connections within a complex, detailed context, (4) an involved individual or collectivity that engages in action and makes choices, (5) coherence or the whole holds together, and (6) the temporal sequencing of a chain of events. Next we briefly consider several kinds of narrative, and then turn to examine narrative analysis, a type of qualitative data analysis.

As raw data, a narrative refers to the condition of social life. Narratives are how people organize their everyday practices and subjective understandings, and they appear in oral or written texts to express the understandings. It is a quality of lived experience and a form by which people construct their identities and locate themselves in what is happening around them, at the micro- and macrolevels.[5] Narrative text is a storylike format people apply to organize and express meaning and understandings in social life. Narratives appear in stories in novels, poems, myths, epic tales, dramatic performances, film, newspaper or other media reports, sermons, oral histories, interviews, and in the telling of events of a person's life.

More than a form of expression, narrative is also a practice. Narrative practice is the storylike form through which people subjectively experience and give meaning to their daily lives and their actions in the world. A narrative organizes information, events, and experiences that flow across time, providing a story line or plot from a particular point of view. The point of view is that of a motivated actor who expresses intentions. The narrative plot is embedded in a complex constellation of particular details, making universal generalizations difficult. McVeigh's chilling letter represents a type of narrative, as does the hundreds of interviews that Woods conducted with rural peasants in El Salvador, as well as the rich narratives that Steffensmeier collected from Sam Goodman (*Confessions of a Dying Thief*).

Narrative inquiry is a method of investigation and data collection that tries to retain a narrativelike quality that exists in social life. The researcher using narrative inquiry tries to capture people's ordinary lived experience without disrupting, destroying, or reducing its narrative character. The researcher's inquiry is self-reflective; that is, the researcher places himself or herself in a flow of events and self-consciously becomes a part of the "plot." The research sees inquiry itself—engaging participant-observers in a field setting or examining historical-comparative documents—in narrative terms; that is, as a tale with a sense of movement and a coherent sequence of events about an engaged social actor in a specific context.[6]

A narrative style of presenting and describing data grows out of the interpretative social science approach, and is highly valued by feminist researchers. It is sometimes called *storytelling* (Berger and Quinney 2004). This mode of presentation blends description, empathetic understanding, and interpretation. It seeks to dissolve any gap between the researcher and those being researched, making the researcher an integral aspect of the description, discussion, and interpretation in a study. Researcher and the researched coparticipate in creating or gathering data and in reflecting on them, so the researcher's life and those of the people being studied are interwoven. The researcher, as an individual social actor, is inseparable from the research process and from data presentation. His or her personal biography and life situation are a part of the story format in which data are presented, discussed, and interpreted. Besides giving voice to the people who are studied, the researcher's voice, presence, and subjectivity are also included. The researcher is a storyteller, not a disembodied voice or detached observer; rather, he or she is a storyteller whose emotions, personal experiences, and life events are a part of the story that is being told.

Last, narrative is a method for analyzing data and providing an explanation. This take several forms and goes by several names—such as analytic narrative, narrative explanation, narrative structural analysis, or sequence analysis. Besides recognizing the core elements of a narrative (listed earlier), researchers who use narrative analysis techniques try to systematically "map out" the narrative and give it a formalized grammar or structure. They not only recognize the narrative character of social life but also analyze data in ways that retain and unveil that character. They portray the narrative as an outline or model that also serves as an explanation.

Some authors apply a few analytic concepts to qualitative data, whereas others employ complex logical systems to detect or outline the structure of a narrative, often with the aid of computer software. As a researcher examines and analyzes qualitative data for its narrative form and elements—whether it is an individual's life history, a particular historical event, the evolution of an organization over the years, or a macrolevel historical process—he or she focuses on events (rather than variables, individuals, or cases); connections among events; and temporal features, such as the order, pace, duration, and frequency. The researcher treats the sequence of events itself as an object of inquiry.

TOOLS OF NARRATIVE ANALYSIS. We next examine three analytic tools qualitative researchers use in narrative analysis:

- path dependency
- periodization
- historical contingency[7]

Path dependency refers to how a unique beginning can trigger a sequence of events and create a deterministic path that is followed in the chain of subsequent events. The path constrains or limits the direction of the ongoing events that follow. In explanations that use path dependency, the outcome is highly sensitive to events that occurred very early in the process. Path dependency explanations emphasize how the choices of one period limit future options, shape later choices, and even accelerate events toward future crises in which options may be restricted.

When building a path-dependent explanation, a researcher starts with an outcome. He or she then shows how the outcome follows from a sequence of prior events. As he or she traces back and demonstrates each event's effect on another, the researcher goes backward in the process to initial events or conditions. The initial conditions a researcher identifies are a "historical fork in the road" (Haydu 1998: 352). Timothy McVeigh wrote numerous letters to a local newspaper that illustrate his growing disenfranchisement with the U.S. government. These letters show that the potential "fork in the road" came when the government foreclosed on numerous family farms in his hometown community, a set of events that infuriated him and likely was a factor in leading him down the path of becoming a right-wing extremist.

There are two types of path dependency: self-reinforcing and reactive sequence.[8] A researcher using a self-reinforcing path dependency explanation looks at how, once set into motion, events continue to operate on their own, or propel later events in a direction that resists external factors. Thus, the initial trigger event constrains, or places limits on, the direction of a process. Once a process begins, inertia comes into play to continue the process along the same path or track. The events surrounding September 11, 2001, for example, could be seen as the trigger event with the subsequent war on terrorism taking on its own inertia.

The reactive sequence path dependency emphasizes a different process. Researchers focus on how each event responds to an immediately preceding one. Thus, instead of tracing a process back to its origins, the researcher examines each step in the process to see how one step influences the next one. The interest is in whether the moving sequence of events transforms or reverses the flow of direction from the initial event. The path does not have to be unidirectional or linear; it can "bend" or even reverse course to negate its previous direction.

One way to see reactive sequence path dependency is that a sequence of events can be like a pendulum that swings back and forth. A single event may set into motion a reaction that changes or reverses the direction of the events that preceded it. For example, as part of the long process of the U.S. civil rights movement, the assassination of Martin Luther King Jr. triggered more vigorous civil rights law enforcement and an expansion of welfare programs. Events had been moving in the direction of greater social equality, reduced discrimination, and expanded legal rights. Yet, vigorous civil rights enforcement and welfare expansion disrupted existing status and power relations. This created tensions that triggered a backlash by resentful Whites. The White backlash tried to restrict or reverse civil rights law enforcement and cut back social welfare programs. A reaction to events in the sequence reversed the direction of its path.

A historical-comparative researcher believes that historical reality has discontinuous stages or steps. He or she may divide 100 years of history into periods by breaking continuous time into discrete units or periods and define the periods theoretically. This is known as periodization. Theory helps him or her identify what is significant and what is common within periods or between different periods. As Carr (1961: 76) remarked, "The division of history into periods is not a fact, but a necessary hypothesis." The breaks between periods are artificial; they are not natural in history, but they are not arbitrary.

The researcher cannot determine the number and size of periods and the breaks between them until after the evidence has been examined. He or she may begin with a general idea of how many periods to create and what distinguishes them, but will adjust the number and size of the periods and the location of the breaks after reviewing the evidence. He or she then reexamines the evidence with added data, readjusts the periodization, and so forth. After several cycles, he or she approximates a set of periods in 100 years on the basis of successively theorizing and looking at evidence.

Historical contingency refers to a unique combination of particular factors or specific circumstances that may not be repeated. The combination is idiosyncratic and unexpected from the flow of prior conditions. As Mahoney (2000: 513) explained, "Contingency refers to the inability of theory to predict or explain, either deterministically or probabilistically, the occurrence of a specific outcome. A contingent event is therefore an occurrence that was not expected to take place." A contingent situation may be unexpected, but once it occurs, it can profoundly influence subsequent events. Because many possible idiosyncratic combinations of events occur, a researcher uses theory to identify important contingent events for an explanation.

A critical juncture is often a part of historical contingency. Researchers explain how several viable options may exist at a specific point in time. Once one option is selected by the coming together of many idiosyncratic events, it has a powerful continuing influence. Researchers combine historical contingency and path dependency The path dependency may be self-reinforcing to continue with inertia along one direction, or particular events might set off a reaction that alters its direction (e.g., the war on terrorism direction might be altered due to the war in Iraq not proceeding as planned). Along the flowing sequence of events across time, periodic critical junctures may occur. The process or conditions that were initially set into motion may resist change, or the contingent conditions may be powerful enough to trigger a major change in direction and initiate a new path of events.

ONE OTHER QUALITATIVE ANALYTIC TECHNIQUE

Event-Structure Analysis

Many qualitative researchers organize data chronologically in a narrative analysis. Event-structure analysis (ESA) is a method to help researchers organize the sequence of events in ways that facilitate seeing causal relations. The method usually involves the use of the qualitative software program ETHNO. In ESA, the researcher first organizes the data into events, and then places the events in a temporal sequence.[9] It can be very helpful in organizing the events in a complex historical research project.

ESA is a type of narrative analysis in which the researcher outlines a set of links between important events. The researcher separates what had to happen before other events from what could have happened. The computer program forces the researcher to answer questions about the logical relationships among events. For example, a situation has events A, B, C, X, and Y. The researcher is asked, must event A occur prior to X's causing Y (i.e., is A a necessary precondition for the X:Y causal relationship?) or would X affect Y without A? If it is required, A must recur before X will affect Y again. This process forces a researcher to explain whether the causal relation between two events is a unique and one-time relation or a recurring relationship that can be repeated either indefinitely or a limited number of cycles.

Griffin's (1993) analysis of a lynching illustrates the benefits of ESA. Based on many oral histories, a book, and newspaper reports, he reconstructed the sequence of events surrounding the lynching of David Harris in Bolivar County, Mississippi, in April 1930. After answering many yes/no questions about possible linkages among a long series of events and analyzing the linkages, Griffin was able to conclude that the critical factor was the inaction of the local deputy who could have stopped the process. An abbreviated summary of the ESA diagram is presented in Figure C.2.

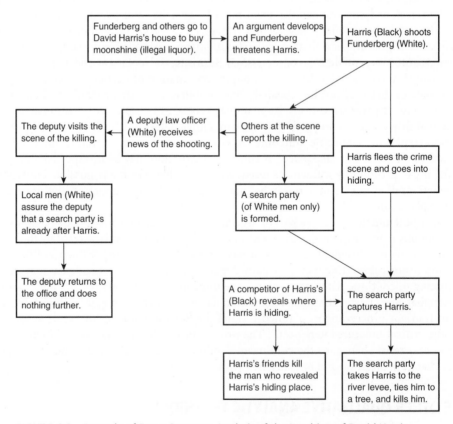

FIGURE C.2 Example of Event-Structure Analysis of the Lynching of David Harris
Source: From W. Lawrence Neuman, *Social Research Methods, Qualitative and Quantitative Approaches*, 6/e. Published by Allyn and Bacon, 75 Arlington St., Boston, MA 02116. Copyright © 2006 by Pearson Education. Reprinted by permission of the publisher. Adapted from Larry J. Griffin. "Narrative, Event Structure Analysis and Causal Interpretation in Historical Sociology." *American Journal of Sociology*, v. 98 (1993): 1094–1133.

ANALYSIS SOFTWARE FOR QUALITATIVE DATA

Quantitative researchers have used computers for four decades to generate tables, graphs, and charts to analyze and present numerical data. By contrast, qualitative researchers moved to computers and diagrams only in the past fifteen years.[10] A researcher who enters notes in a word-processing program may quickly search for words and phrases that can be adapted to coding data and linking codes to analytic memos. Word processing can also help a researcher revise and move codes and parts of field notes.

Here, we will consider software specifically created for qualitative data analysis. Many are new and are quickly changing. New computer programs are continuously being developed or modified, and most come with highly detailed and program-specific user manuals, so we will not go into detail about specific software. There are numerous quality Web sites that both review and advertise the latest in qualitative research software developments (one good example can be found at www.datasense.org).

TEXT RETRIEVAL. Some programs perform searches of text documents, similar to the search function in word-processing software. The specialized text retrieval programs are faster and have the capability of finding close matches, slight misspellings, similar sounding words, or synonyms. For example, when a researcher looks for the keyword "boat," the program might also tell whether any of the following appeared: ship, battleship, frigate, rowboat, schooner, vessel, yacht, steamer, ocean liner, tug, canoe, skiff, cutter, aircraft carrier, dinghy, scow, galley, ark, cruiser, destroyer, flagship, and submarine.

In addition, some programs permit the combination of words or phrases using logical terms (AND, OR, NOT) in what are called Boolean searches. For example, a researcher may search long documents for instances where the keywords "college student" and "marijuana smoking" occur within four sentences of each other, but only when the word "fraternity" is not present in the block of text. This Boolean search seeks the intersection of "college student" with either of two behaviors that are connected by the logical term.

TEXTBASE MANAGERS. Textbase managers are similar to text retrieval programs. The key difference is their ability to organize or sort information about search results. Many programs create subsets of text data that help a researcher compare and sort notes by a key idea or to add factual information. For example, in cases where the data are detailed notes on interviews, a researcher can add information on the date and length of the interview, gender of interviewee, location of interview, and so on. The researcher can then sort and organize each interview or part of the interview notes using a combination of keywords and added information.

CODE-AND-RETRIEVE PROGRAMS. Researchers often assign codes or abstract terms to qualitative data (text field notes, interview records, and video- or audio-tape transcripts). Code-and-retrieve programs allow a researcher to attach codes to lines, sentences, paragraphs, or blocks of text. The programs may permit multiple codes for the same data. In addition to attaching codes, most programs also allow the researcher to organize the codes. For example, a program can help a researcher make outlines or "trees" of connections (e.g., trunks, branches, and twigs) among the codes, and among the data to which the codes refer. The qualitative data are rearranged in the program based on the researcher's codes and the relations among codes that a researcher specifies

CODE-BASED THEORY BUILDERS. Qualitative researchers are often interested in the evaluation and generation of theory. Code-based theory builders require that a researcher first assign codes to the data. The programs provide ways for manipulating or drawing contrasts and comparisons among the codes. The relationships among the codes then become the basis for a researcher to test or generate theory.

As noted above, the computer software ETHNO asks for logical connections among the events (e.g., time order, necessary precondition, and co-occurrence), and then shows the pattern among events. In contrast to other qualitative programs, code-based theory builders have a powerful ability to manipulate codes to reveal patterns or show relations in data that are not immediately evident. It becomes easier for researchers to compare and classify categories of data.

CONCEPTUAL NETWORK BUILDERS. This category of programs helps a researcher build and test theory by presenting graphic displays or networks. The displays do more than diagram data; they help organize a researcher's concepts or thinking about the data. The programs use nodes, or key concepts, that the researcher identifies in data. They then show links or relationships among the nodes. Most programs give graphic presentations with boxes or circles connected by lines with arrows. The output looks similar to a flowchart diagram, with a web or network of connections among concepts. For example, the data might be a family tree in which the relationships among several generations of family members are presented. Relations among family members (X is a sibling of Y; Z is married to Y; G is an offspring of X) can be used to discuss and analyze features of the network.

Conclusion to Qualitative Analysis

Angus Vail (2001: 720) sums up nicely the crux of qualitative analysis.

> In essence, the ethnographer's task is to filter through the myriad of relationships that make up our social worlds and show how they work together in ways that make sense to those who enact them. We accomplish this goal by using our specialized ethnographic skills to help our readers experience the unfamiliar in terms that make it familiar and vice versa. In essence, we try to impose a little order on what could quite easily seem like chaos.

Re-creating a comprehendible and valid narrative out of what could be easily seen as chaos is an apt description of what qualitative analysis is all about. Just as statistical analysis assists the quantitative researcher, the techniques reviewed in this chapter help the qualitative researcher make sense of the data through figuring out the progression of events, making causal connections, deciphering the meaning of everyday language, constructing typologies, and developing new organizing concepts.

Most forms of qualitative data analysis involve coding and writing analytic memos. Both are labor-intensive efforts by the researcher to read over data carefully and think about them seriously. In addition, we learned about methods that researchers have used for the analysis of qualitative data. They are only a sample of the many methods of qualitative data analysis.

Notes for Further Study

1. See Miles and Huberman (1994) and Ragin (1987). These should not be confused with statistical techniques for "qualitative" data (see Haberman 1978). These are sophisticated statistical techniques (e.g., logit and log linear) for quantitative variables where the data are at the nominal or ordinal level. They are better labeled as techniques for categorical data.

2. See Hammersley and Atkinson (1983: 174–206) for a discussion of questions.

3. See Boyatzis (1998), Lofland and Lofland (1995: 192–193), Miles and Huberman (1994: 57–71), Sanjek (1990: 388–392), and Wolcott (1994) for additional discussions of coding.

4. On various uses see Abbott (1995) and Franzosi (1998).

5. On narrative as a condition of social life, see Abbott (2001) and Somers (1994).

6. The six core elements are derived from discussion of narrative in the following: Abell (2001, 2004), Abbott (1995, 2001), Büthe (2002), Franzosi (1998), Griffin (1992b, 1993), Gubrium and Holstein (1998), Haydu (1998), Mahoney (2000a), Pedriana (2005), Sewell (1992, 1996), and Stryker (1996).

7. On debates about causality in narrative analysis and narrative as explanation, see Abbott (2001: 290), Abell (2004), Büthe (2002), Griffin (1993), and Mahoney (2000b). For debate about the narrative, see Haydu (1998), Mahoney (1999), Sewell (1996), and Stryker (1996). Researchers such as

Goldthorpe (1991, 1997) and Lieberson (1991) question the approach, whereas Goldstone (1997) and Rueschemeyer and Stephens (1997) defend its utility. See Haydu (1998: 353) with regard to path dependency.

8. Mahoney (2000a) gives a detailed description of the path dependency method and provides many examples of its use. Altman (2000) provides a discussion from the economics literature. Also see Blute (1997) and Pedriana (2005).

9. For a more in-depth discussion of event-structure analysis, see Abbott (1992), Griffin (1993), Griffin and Ragin (1994), Heise (1991), and Isaac and colleagues (1994).

10. See Dohan and Sanchez-Jankowski (1998) and Weitzman and Miles (1995) for a comprehensive review of software programs for qualitative data analysis. Also see Fielding and Lee (1991) and Richards and Richards (1994).

BIBLIOGRAPHY

Abbott, Andrew. (1992). From causes to events: Notes on narrative positivism. *Sociological Methods and Research,* 20:428–455.

Abbott, Andrew. (1995). Sequence analysis. *Annual Review of Sociology,* 21:93–113.

Abbott, Andrew. (2001). *Time matters: On theory and method.* Chicago, IL: University of Chicago Press.

Abell, Peter. (2001). Causality and low-frequency complex events. *Sociological Methods and Research,* 30:57–80.

Abell, Peter. (2004). Narrative explanation. *Annual Review of Sociology,* 30:287–310.

Abelson, Robert P., Elizabeth F. Loftus, and Anthony G. Greenwald. (1992). Attempts to improve the accuracy of self-reports of voting. In *Questions about questions: Inquiries into the cognitive bases of surveys,* edited by J. Turner, pp. 138–153. New York: Russell Sage Foundation.

Abrams, Philip. (1982). *Historical sociology.* Ithaca, NY: Cornell University Press.

Adams, J. W., Kottke, J. L., and J. S. Padgitt. (1983). Sexual harassment of university students. *Journal of College Student Personnel,* 24(6):484–490.

Adler, Patricia A. (1985). *Wheeling and dealing.* New York: Columbia University Press.

Adler, Patricia A., and Peter Adler. (1987). *Membership roles in field research.* Beverly Hills, CA: Sage.

Adler, Patricia A., and Peter Adler. (1993). Ethical issues in self-censorship: Ethnographic research on sensitive topics. In *Research on sensitive topics,* edited by C. Renzetti and R. Lee, pp. 249–266. Thousand Oaks, CA: Sage.

Adler, Patricia A., and Peter Adler. (1994). Observational techniques. In *Handbook of qualitative research,* edited by N. Denzin and Y. Lincoln, pp. 377–392. Thousand Oaks, CA: Sage.

Agar, Michael. (1980). Getting better quality stuff: Methodological competition in an interdisciplinary niche. *Urban Life,* 9:34–50.

Agar, Michael. (1986). *Speaking of ethnography.* Beverly Hills, CA: Sage.

Agger, Ben. (1991). Critical theory, post-structuralism, postmodernism: Their sociological relevance. *Annual Review of Sociology,* 17:105–131.

Allison, Paul D. (2001). *Missing data.* Thousand Oaks, CA: Sage.

Altheide, David L. (1980). Leaving the newsroom. In *Fieldwork experience,* edited by W. B. Shaffir, R. Stebbins, and A. Turowetz, pp. 301–310. New York: St. Martin's Press.

Altheide, David L. (1987). Ethnographic content analysis. *Qualitative Sociology,* 10(1):65–77.

Altheide, David L. (1996). *Qualitative media analysis.* Thousand Oaks, CA: Sage.

Altheide, David L., and Sam Michalowski, R. (1999). Fear in the news: A discourse of control. *The Sociological Quarterly,* 40(3):475–503.

Altman, Lawrence K. (1997, April 16). Drug firm, relenting, allows unflattering study to appear. *New York Times.*

Altman, Morris. (2000). A behavioral model of path dependency: The economics of profitable inefficiency and market failure. *Journal of Socio-Economics,* 29:127–145.

Alwin, Duane F. (1988). The general social survey: A national data resource for the social sciences. *PS: Political Science and Politics,* 21:90–94.

Anderson, N. (1923). *The hobo: The sociology of the homeless man.* Chicago, IL: University of Chicago Press.

Anderson, Andy B., Alexander Basilevsky, and Derek P. J. Hum. (1983). Measurement: Theory and techniques. In *Handbook of survey research,* edited by P. Rossi, J. D. Wright, and A. Anderson, pp. 231–287. New York: Academic Press.

Anderson, Barbara A., Brian D. Silver, and Paul R. Abramson. (1988). The effects of the race of interviewer on race-related attitudes of black respondents in SRC/CPS national election studies. *Public Opinion Quarterly,* 52:289–324.

Andren, Gunnar. (1981). Reliability and content analysis. In *Advances in content analysis,* edited by K. Rosengren, pp. 43–67. Beverly Hills, CA: Sage.

Applebaum, Richard. (1978). Marxist method: Structural constraints and social praxis. *American Sociologist,* 13:73–81.

Aquilino, William S., and Leonard Losciuto. (1990). Effects of interview mode on self-reported drug use. *Public Opinion Quarterly,* 54:362–395.

Aronson, Elliot, and J. Merrill Carlsmith. (1968). Experimentation in social psychology. In *The handbook of social psychology,* vol. 2: *Research methods,* edited by G. Lindzey and E. Aronson, pp. 1–78. Reading, MA: Addison-Wesley.

Arrigo, Bruce A., Dragan Milovanovic, and Robert Schehr. (2005). *The French connection in criminology: Rediscovering crime, law and social change.* Albany, NY: State University of New York Press.

Athens, Lonnie H. (1992). *The creation of dangerous violent criminals.* Champaign: University of Illinois Press.

Athens, Lonnie H. (1997). *Violent criminal acts and actors revisited.* Champaign, IL: University of Illinois Press.

Atkinson, Robert. (1998). *The life story interview.* Thousand Oaks, CA: Sage.

Auriat, Nadia. (1993). My wife knows best: A comparison of event dating accuracy between the wife, the husband, the couple, and the Belgium population register. *Public Opinion Quarterly,* 57:165–190.

Ayella, Marybeth. (1993). "They must be crazy:" Some of the difficulties in researching cults. In *Research on sensitive topics,* edited by C. Renzetti and R. Lee, pp. 108–124. Thousand Oaks, CA: Sage.

Babbie, Earl. (1990). *Survey research methods,* 2nd ed. Belmont, CA: Wadsworth.

Babbie, Earl. (1998). *The practice of social research,* 8th ed. Belmont, CA: Wadsworth.

Bachman, Ronet, and Bruce H. Taylor. (1994). The measurement of family violence and rape by the redesigned national crime victimization survey. *Justice Quarterly,* 11(3):499–512.

Backstrom, Charles H., and Gerald Hursh-Cesar. (1981). *Survey research,* 2nd ed. New York: Wiley.

Bailey, Kenneth D. (1987). *Methods of social research,* 3rd ed. New York: Free Press.

Balko, Radley. (2006). *Overkill: The rise of paramilitary police raids in America.* Washington, DC: Cato Institute.

Ball, Richard A., and G. David Curry. (1995). The logic of definition in criminology: Purposes and methods for defining "gangs." *Criminology,* 33:225–245.

Baller, Robert D., and Kelly K. Richardson. (2002). Social integration, imitation and the geographic patterning of suicide. *American Sociological Review,* 67:873–888.

Banaka, William H. (1971). *Training in depth interviewing.* New York: Harper & Row.

Banks, Marcus, and Howard Murphy. (2001). *Rethinking visual anthropology.* London: Routledge.

Bannister, Robert C. (1987). *Sociology and scientism: The American quest for objectivity 1880–1940.* Chapel Hill, NC: University of North Carolina Press.

Barlow, Melissa Hickman, David E. Barlow, and Theodore G. Chiricos. (1995). Economic conditions and ideologies of crime in the media: A content analysis of crime news. *Crime and Delinquency,* 41:3–19.

Barnes, John A. (1970). Some ethical problems in modern fieldwork. In *Qualitative methodology,* edited by W. J. Filstead, pp. 235–251. Chicago, IL: Markham.

Barnes, John A. (1979). *Who should know what? Social science, privacy and ethics.* New York: Cambridge University Press.

Baro, Agnes, and Helen Eigenberg. (1993). Images of gender: A content analysis of photographs in introductory criminology and criminal justice textbooks. *Women and Criminal Justice,* 5:3–36.

Baron, Stephen W. (2006). Street youth, strain theory, and crime. *Journal of Criminal Justice,* 34:209–223.

Barry, Brian. (1975). On analogy. *Political Studies,* 23:208–224.

Bart, Pauline. (1987). Seizing the means of reproduction: An illegal feminist abortion collective—How and why it worked. *Qualitative Sociology,* 10:339–357.

Barzun, Jacques, and Henry F. Graff. (1970). *The modern researcher,* rev. ed. New York: Harcourt, Brace and World.

Bateson, Nicholas. (1984). *Data construction in social surveys.* Boston, MA: George Allen and Unwin.

Baudrillard, Jean. (1970). *The consumer society.* London: Sage.

Bauer, David G. (1988). *The "how to" grants manual,* 2nd ed. New York: Macmillan.

Beatty, Paul. (1995). Understanding the standardization. *Journal of Official Statistics,* 11:147–160.

Beck, Bernard. (1970). Cooking welfare stew. In *Pathways to data,* edited by R. W. Habenstein, pp. 7–29. Chicago, IL: Aldine.

Beck, Ulrich. (1992). *Risk society, towards a new modernity.* Trans. Mark Ritter, and with an Introduction by Scott Lash and Brian Wynne. London: Sage Publications.

Becker, Howard S. (1967). Whose side are we on? *Social Problems,* 14:239–247.

Becker, Howard S. (1969). Problems in the publication of field studies. In *Issues in participant observation,* edited by G. McCall and J. L. Simmons, pp. 260–275. Reading, MA: Addison-Wesley.

Becker, Howard S. (1970a). Practitioners of vice and crime. In *Pathways to data,* edited by R. W. Habenstein, pp. 30–49. Chicago, IL: Aldine.

Becker, Howard S. (1970b). Problems of inference and proof in participant observation. In *Qualitative methodology: Firsthand involvement with the social world,* edited by W. J. Filstead, pp. 189–201. Chicago, IL: Markham.

Becker, Howard S. (1970c). Whose side are we on? In *Qualitative methodology,* edited by W. J. Filstead, pp. 15–26. Chicago, IL: Markham.

Becker, Howard S. (1986). *Writing for social scientists: How to start and finish your thesis, book or article.* Chicago, IL: University of Chicago Press.

Becker, Howard S., and Blanche Geer. (1970). Participant observation and interviewing: A comparison. In *Qualitative methodology,* edited by W. J. Filstead, pp. 133–142. Chicago, IL: Markham.

Becker, Howard S., and Blanche Geer. (1982). Participant observation: The analysis of qualitative field data.

In *Field research: A sourcebook and field manual,* edited by R. G. Burgess, pp. 239–250. Boston, MA: George Allen and Unwin.

Beecher, Henry K. (1970). *Research and the individual: Human studies.* Boston, MA: Little, Brown.

Belenky, Mary Field, Blythe McVicker Clinchy, Nancy Rule Goldberger, and Jill MattuckTarule. (1986). *Women's ways of knowing: The development of self, voice and mind.* New York: Basic Books.

Ben-David, Joseph. (1971). *The scientist's role in society.* Englewood Cliffs, NJ: Prentice-Hall.

Bennett, Richard R. (1994). Comparative criminology and criminal justice research: The state of our knowledge. *Justice Quarterly,* 21:1–21.

Benson, Donna J., and Gregg E. Thomson. (1982). Sexual harassment on a university campus: The confluence of authority relations, sexual interest, and gender stratification. *Social Problems,* 29(3):236–251.

Benton, Ted. (1977). *Philosophical foundations of the three sociologies.* Boston, MA: Routledge and Kegan Paul.

Ben-Yehuda, Nachman. (1983). History, selection and random-ness—towards an analysis of social historical explanations. *Quality and Quantity,* 17:347–367.

Berg, Bruce. (2007). *Qualitative research for the social sciences.* Boston, MA: Pearson/Allyn and Bacon.

Berger, Peter, and Thomas Luckman. (1967). *The social construction of reality: A treatise in the sociology of knowledge.* Garden City, NY: Anchor.

Berger, Ronald, and Richard Quinney. (2004). *Storytelling sociology: Narrative as social inquiry.* Boulder, CO: Lynne Reinner.

Bernard, H. Russell, Peter Killworth, David Kronenfeld, and Lee Sailer. (1984). The problem of information accuracy: The validity of retrospective data. *Annual Review of Anthropology,* 13:495–517.

Best, Joel. (2001). *Damned lies and statistics.* Berkeley, CA: University of California Press.

Bhaskar, Roy. (1975). *A realist theory of science.* Atlantic Highlands, NJ: Humanities.

Bhaskar, Roy. (2003). *From science to emancipation: Alienation and enlightenment.* Thousand Oaks, CA: Sage.

Bhayani, Paras D. (2006). EPA official decries climate change. *Harvard Crimson* <http://www.thecrimson.harvard.edu/article.aspx?ref=512937>.

Billings, Dwight B., and Kathleen Blee. (2000). *The road to poverty.* New York and London: Cambridge University Press.

Birnbaum, Michael H. (2004) Human research and data collection via the internet. *Annual Review of Psychology,* 55(1):803.

Bishop, George F. (1987). Experiments with the middle response alternative in survey questions. *Public Opinion Quarterly,* 51:220–232.

Bishop, George F. (1992). Qualitative analysis of question-order and context effects. In *Context effects in social and psychological research,* edited by N. Schwarz and S. Sudman, pp. 149–162. New York: Springer-Verlag.

Bishop, George F., Robert W. Oldendick, and Alfred J. Tuchfarber. (1983). Effects of filter questions in public opinion surveys. *Public Opinion Quarterly,* 47:528–546.

Bishop, George F., Robert W. Oldendick, and Alfred J. Tuchfarber. (1984). What must my interest in politics be if I just told you "I don't know"? *Public Opinion Quarterly,* 48:510–519.

Bishop, George F., Robert W. Oldendick, and Alfred J. Tuchfarber. (1985). The importance of replicating a failure to replicate: Order effects on abortion items. *Public Opinion Quarterly,* 49:105–114.

Bishop, George F., Alfred J. Tuchfarber, and Robert W. Oldendick. (1986). Opinions on fictitious issues: The pressure to answer survey questions. *Public Opinion Quarterly,* 50:240–251.

Black, Maureen M., and Izabel B. Ricardo. (1994). Drug use, drug trafficking, and weapon carrying among low-income, African-American, early adolescent boys. *Pediatrics,* 93:1065–1072.

Blaikie, Norman. (1993). *Approaches to social enquiry.* Cambridge, MA: Polity.

Blalock, Hubert M., Jr. (1969). *Theory construction: From verbal to mathematical formulations.* Englewood Cliffs, NJ: Prentice-Hall.

Blalock, Hubert M., Jr. (1979). Measurement and conceptualization problems: The major obstacle to integrating theory and research. *American Sociological Review,* 44:881–894.

Blalock, Hubert M., Jr. (1982). *Conceptualization and measurement in the social sciences.* Beverly Hills, CA: Sage.

Blee, Kathleen M. (1991). *Women of the Klan: Racism and gender in the 1920s.* Berkeley, CA: University of California Press.

Blee, Kathleen M., and Dwight B. Billings. (1986). Reconstructing daily life in the past: An hermeneutical approach to ethnographic data. *Sociological Quarterly,* 27:443–462.

Bleicher, Josef. (1980). *Contemporary hermeneutics.* Boston, MA: Routledge and Kegan Paul.

Bloor, Michael J. (1983). Notes on member validation. In *Contemporary field research,* edited by R. M. Emerson, pp. 156–171. Boston, MA: Little, Brown.

Blume, Stuart S. (1974). *Toward a political sociology of science.* New York: Free Press.

Blumer, Martin. (1991a). W. E. B. DuBois as a social investigator: The Philadelphia Negro 1889. In *The social survey in historical perspective, 1880–1940,* edited by M. Blumer, K. Bales, and K. Sklar, pp. 170–188. New York: Cambridge University Press.

Blumer, Martin. (1991b). The decline of the social survey movement and the rise of American empirical sociology. In *The social survey in historical perspective, 1880–1940,* edited by M. Blumer, K. Bales, and K. Sklar, pp. 271–315. New York: Cambridge University Press.

Blumer, Martin, Kevin Bales, and Katryn Sklar. (1991). The social survey in historical perspective. In *The social survey in historical perspective, 1880—1940,* edited by M. Blumer, K. Bales, and K. Sklar, pp. 1–48. New York: Cambridge University Press.

Blumstein, Alfred. (1974). Seriousness weights in an index of crime. *American Sociological Review,* 39:854–864.

Blumstein, Alfred, and Joel Wallman. (2000, 2006). *The crime drop in America.* New York: Cambridge University Press.

Blute, Marion. (1997). History versus science: The evolutionary solution. *Canadian Journal of Sociology,* 22:345–364.

Bogdan, Robert, and Steven J. Taylor. (1975). *Introduction to qualitative research methods: A phenomenological approach to the social sciences.* New York: Wiley.

Bohm, Robert, and Jeffrey Walker. (2006). *Demystifying crime and criminal justice.* Los Angeles,: Roxbury Press.

Bohrnstedt, George. (1992). Reliability. In *Encyclopedia of Sociology,* vol. 3, edited by E. and M. Borgatta, pp. 1626–1632. New York: Macmillan.

Bolton, Ruth N., and Tina Bronkhorst. (1996). Questionnaire pretesting: Computer-assisting coding of concurrent protocols. In *Answering questions,* edited by N. Schwarz and S. Sudman, pp. 37–64. San Francisco: Jossey-Bass.

Bond, Charles F., Jr., and Evan L. Anderson. (1987). The reluctance to transmit bad news: Private discomfort or public display? *Journal of Experimental Social Psychology,* 23:176–187.

Bonnell, Victoria E. (1980). The uses of theory, concepts and comparison in historical sociology. *Comparative Studies in Society and History,* 22:156–173.

Borgatta, Edgar F., and George W. Bohrnstedt. (1980). Level of measurement: Once over again. *Sociological Methods and Research,* 9:147–160.

Boruch, Robert F. (1982). Methods for revolving privacy problems in social research. In *Ethical issues in social science research,* edited by T. Beauchamp, R. Faden, R. J. Wallace, and L. Walters, pp. 292–313. Baltimore, MD: Johns Hopkins University Press. Bottomore, Thomas. (1984). *The Frankfurt School.* New York: Tavistock.

Bouchard, Thomas J., Jr. (1976). Unobtrusive measures: An inventory of uses. *Sociological Methods and Research,* 4:267–300.

Boyatzis, Richard E. (1998). *Transforming qualitative information: Thematic analysis and code development.* Thousand Oaks, CA: Sage.

Boyer, Ernest L. (1997). *Scholarship reconsidered.* San Francisco, CA: Jossey-Bass.

Bradburn, Norman M. (1983). Response effects. In *Handbook of survey research,* edited by P. Rossi, J. Wright, and A. Anderson, pp. 289–328. Orlando, FL: Academic.

Bradburn, Norman M., and Seymour Sudman. (1980). *Improving interview method and questionnaire design.* San Francisco, CA: Jossey-Bass.

Bradburn, Norman M., and Seymour Sudman. (1988). *Polls and surveys: Understanding what they tell us.* San Francisco, PA: Jossey-Bass.

Bradsher, Keith. (2002). *High and mighty.* New York: Public Affairs.

Bredo, Eric, and Walter Feinberg, eds. (1982). *Knowledge and values in social and educational research.* Philadelphia, PA: Temple University Press.

Brehm, John. (1994). Stubbing our toes for a foot in the door? Prior contact, incentives and survey response. *International Journal of Public Opinion Research,* 6:45–63.

Brenner, Michael, Jennifer Brown, and David Canter, eds. (1985). *The research interview: Uses and approaches.* Orlando, FL: Academic Press.

Briggs, Charles L. (1986). *Learning how to ask: A sociolinguistic appraisal of the role of the interview in social science research.* New York: Cambridge University Press.

Brinberg, David, and Joseph E. McGrath. (1982). A network of validity concepts. In *Forms of validity in research,* edited by D. Brinberg and L. Kidder, pp. 5–21. San Francisco, CA: Jossey-Bass.

Brisgone, Regina. (2004). Report on qualitative analysis of displacement in a prostitution site. In *Does crime just move around the corner? A study of displacement and diffusion in Jersey City, NJ,* edited by David Weisburd, Laura A. Wyckoff, Justin Ready, John E. Eck, Joshua C. Hinkle, and Frank Gajewski. Report submitted to National Institute of Justice. Grant No. 97-IJ-CX-0055. Washington, DC: U.S. Department of Justice.

Broad, William J., and Nicholas Wade. (1982). *Betrayers of the truth.* New York: Simon and Schuster.

Broadhurst, Roderic. (1997). Aborigines and crime in Australia. In *Ethnicity, crime, and immigration,* edited by Michael Tonry, pp. 407–468. Chicago, IL: University of Chicago Press.

Brodsky, Stanley L., and O'Neal Smitherman, H. (1983). *Handbook of scales for research in crime and delinquency.* New York: Plenum.

Brody, Charles J. (1986). Things are rarely black or white: Admitting gray into the converse model of attitude stability. *American Journal of Sociology,* 92:657–677.

Brown, Elizabeth K. (2006). The dog that did not bark: Punitive social views and the "professional middle classes." *Punishment and Society*, 8(3):287–312.

Brown, Richard Harvey. (1989). *Social science as civic discourse: Essays on the invention, legitimation and uses of social theory.* Chicago, IL: University of Chicago Press.

Burawoy, Michael. (1990). Marxism as science: Historical challenges and theoretical growth. *American Sociological Review*, 55:775–793.

Burgess, Robert G. (1982a). Keeping field notes. In *Field research*, edited by R. G. Burgess, pp. 191–194. Boston, MA: George Allen and Unwin.

Burgess, Robert G. (1982b). The unstructured interview as a conversation. In *Field research*, edited by R. G. Burgess, pp. 107–110. Boston, MA: George Allen and Unwin.

Burnham, Gilbert, Riyadh Lafta, Shannon Doocy, and Les Roberts. (2006). Mortality after the 2003 invasion of Iraq: A cross-sectional cluster sample survey. *The Lancet*, 368(9545):1421–1428.

Büthe, Tim. (2002). Taking temporality seriously: Modeling history and the use of narratives as evidence. *American Political Science Review*, 96:481–493.

Calhoun, Craig. (1996). The rise and domestication of historical sociology. In *The historical turn in the human sciences*, edited by T. J. McDonald, pp. 305–337. Ann Arbor, MI: University of Michigan Press.

Callanan, Valerie J. (2005). *Feeding the fear of crime: Crime-related media and support for three strikes.* New York: LFB Scholarly Publications.

Camic, Charles, and Yu Xie. (1994). The statistical turn in American social science: Columbia University, 1890–1915. *American Sociological Review*, 59:773–805.

Campbell, Donald T., and Julian C. Stanley. (1963). *Experimental and quasi-experimental designs for research.* Chicago: Rand McNally.

Campbell, John P., Richard L. Daft, and Charles L. Hulin. (1982). *What to study: Generating and developing research questions.* Beverly Hills, CA: Sage.

Cannell, Charles F., and Robert L. Kahn. (1968). Interviewing. In *Handbook of social psychology*, 2nd ed., vol. 2, edited by G. Lindzey and E. Aronson, pp. 526–595. Reading, MA: Addison-Wesley.

Canon, Kevin D. (2005). Ain't no faggot gonna rob me!: Anti-gay attitudes of criminal justice undergraduate majors. *Journal of Criminal Justice Education*, 16(2):226–243.

Cantor, Norman F., and Richard I. Schneider. (1967). *How to study history.* New York: Thomas Y. Crowell.

Capron, Alexander Morgan. (1982). Is consent always necessary in social science research? In *Ethical issues in social science research*, edited by T. Beauchamp, R. Faden, R. J. Wallace, and L. Walters, pp. 215–231. Baltimore, MD: Johns Hopkins University Press.

Carlson, Susan M., and Raymond J. Michalowski. (1997). Crime, unemployment, and social structures of accumulation: An inquiry into historical contingency. *Justice Quarterly*, 14:209–242.

Carmines, Edward G., and Richard A. Zeller. (1979). *Reliability and validity assessment.* Beverly Hills, CA: Sage.

Carr, Edward Hallett. (1961). *What is history?* New York: Vintage.

Carr, Wilfred, and Stephen Kemmis. (1986). *Becoming critical: Education, knowledge, and action research.* Philadelphia, PA: Falmer Press.

Catania, Joseph, Diane Binson, Jesse Canchola, Lance M. Pollack, Walter Hauck, and Thomas Coates. (1996). Effects of interviewer gender, interviewer choice and item wording on responses to questions concerning sexual behavior. *Public Opinion Quarterly*, 60:345–375.

Chafetz, Janet Saltzman. (1978). *A primer on the construction and testing of theories in sociology.* Itasca, IL: Peacock.

Channels, Noreen L. (1993). Anticipating media coverage: Methodological decisions regarding criminal justice research. In *Research on sensitive topics*, edited by C. Renzetti and R. Lee, pp. 267–280. Thousand Oaks, CA: Sage.

Charmaz, Kathy. (2003). Grounded theory: Objectivist and constructionist methods. In *Strategies of qualitative inquiry*, 2nd ed., edited by N. Denzin and Y. Lincoln, pp. 249–291. Thousand Oaks, CA: Sage.

Charmaz, Kathy. (2006). *Constructing grounded theory: A practical guide through qualitative analysis.* Thousand Oaks, CA: Sage.

Chavez, Leo R. (2001). *Covering immigration: Popular images and politics of the nation.* Berkeley, CA: University of California Press.

Chermak, Steven. (1995). *Victims in the news: Crime and the American news media.* Boulder, CO: Westview Press.

Christians, Clifford G. (2003). Ethics and politics in qualitative research. In *The landscape of qualitative research*, 2nd ed., edited by N. Denzin and Y. Lincoln, pp. 208–244. Thousand Oaks CA: Sage.

Christie, Nils. (2000). *Crime control as industry.* New York: Routledge.

Church, Allan H. (1993). Estimating the effect of incentives on mail survey response rates: A meta analysis. *Public Opinion Quarterly*, 57:62–80.

Churchill, Gilbert A., Jr. (1983). *Marketing research: Methodological foundations*, 3rd ed. New York: Dryden.

Cicourel, Aaron. (1973). *Cognitive sociology.* London: Macmillan.

Cicourel, Aaron. (1982). Interviews, surveys, and the problem of ecological validity. *American Sociologist*, 17:11–20.

Clammer, John. (1984). Approaches to ethnographic research. In *Ethnographic research: A guide to general conduct*, edited by R. F. Ellen, pp. 63–85. Orlando, FL: Academic Press.

Clark, Herbert H., and Michael F. Schober. (1992). Asking questions and influencing answers. In *Questions about questions: Inquiries into the cognitive bases of surveys*, edited by J. Turner, pp. 15–18. New York: Russell Sage Foundation.

Clarke, Michael. (1975). Survival in the field: Implications of personal experience in field work. *Theory and Society*, 2:95–123.

Clear, Todd R. (1994). *Harm in American penology: Offenders, victims, and their communities*. Albany, NY: State University of New York Press.

Clemens, Elizabeth, and Walter Powell. (1995). Careers in print: Books, journals, and scholarly reputations. *American Journal of Sociology*, 101:433–497.

Cohen, Stephen R. (1991). The Pittsburg survey and the social survey movement: A sociological road not taken. In *The social survey in historical perspective, 1880–1940*, edited by M. Blumer, K. Bales, and K. Sklar, pp. 245–268. New York: Cambridge University Press.

Cole, Jonathan R., and Stephen Cole. (1973). *Social stratification in science*. Chicago, IL: University of Chicago Press.

Cole, Stephen. (1978). Scientific reward systems: A comparative analysis. *Research in the Sociology of Knowledge, Science and Art*, 1:167–190.

Cole, Stephen. (1983). The hierarchy of the sciences? *American Journal of Sociology*, 89:111–139.

Cole, Stephen. (1994). Why sociology doesn't make progress like the natural sciences. *Sociological Forum*, 9:133–154.

Cole, Stephen, Jonathan Cole, and Gary A. Simon. (1981). Chance and consensus in peer review. *Science*, 214:881–885.

Collins, Harry M. (1983). The sociology of scientific knowledge: Studies of contemporary science. *American Review of Sociology*, 9:265–285.

Collins, Randall. (1984). Statistics versus words. *Sociological Theory*, 2:329–362.

Collins, Randall. (1989). Sociology: Pro-science or anti-science? *American Sociological Review*, 54:124–139.

Collins, Randall, and Sal Restivo. (1983). Development, diversity and conflict in the sociology of science. *Sociological Quarterly*, 24:185–200.

Collins, Sue Carter, and Michael S. Vaughn. (2004). Liability for sexual harassment in criminal justice agencies. *Journal of Criminal Justice*, 32(6):531–545.

Conrad, Frederick, and Michael Schober. (2000). Clarifying question meaning in a household telephone survey. *Public Opinion Quarterly*, 64:1–28.

Converse, Jean M. (1984). Strong arguments and weak evidence: The open/closed questioning controversy of the 1940s. *Public Opinion Quarterly*, 48:267–282.

Converse, Jean M. (1987). *Survey research in the United States: Roots and emergence, 1890—1960.* Berkeley: University of California Press.

Converse, Jean M., and Howard Schuman. (1974). *Conversations at random: Survey research as interviewers see it.* Ann Harbor, MI: Wiley & Sons.

Converse, Jean M., and Stanley Presser. (1986). *Survey questions: Handcrafting the standardized questionnaire.* Beverly Hills, CA: Sage.

Cook, Thomas D., and Donald T. Campbell. (1979). *Quasi-experimentation: Design and analysis issues for field settings.* Chicago, IL: Rand McNally.

Corsino, Louis. (1987). Fieldworkers blues: Emotional stress and research underinvolvement in fieldwork settings. *Social Science Journal*, 24:275–285.

Costner, Herbert L. (1985). Theory, deduction and rules of correspondence. In *Causal models in the social sciences*, 2nd ed., edited by H. M. Blalock Jr., pp. 229–250. New York: Aldine.

Cotter, Patrick R., Jeffrey Cohen, and Philip B. Coulter. (1982). Race of interview effects in telephone interviews. *Public Opinion Quarterly*, 46:278–286.

Couper, Mick P. (2000). Review: Web surveys. *Public Opinion Quarterly*, 64:464–495.

Couper, Mick P., and Benjamin Rowe. (1996). Evaluation of a computer assisted self-interview component in a computer-assisted personal interview survey. *Public Opinion Quarterly*, 60:89–105.

Couper, Mick P., Eleanor Singer, and Richard A. Kulka. (1998). Participation in the 1990 decennial census. *American Politics Quarterly*, 26:59–81.

Couper, Mick P., Eleanor Singer, and Roger Tourangeau. (2003). Understanding the effects of audio-CASI on self-reports of sensitive behavior. *Public Opinion Quarterly*, 67:385–395.

Couper, Mick P., Michael Traugott, and Mark Lamias. (2001). Web survey design and administration. *Public Opinion Quarterly*, 65:230–253.

Craib, Ian. (1984). *Modern social theory: From Parsons to Habermas.* New York: St. Martin's Press.

Creswell, John W. (1994). *Research design: Qualitative and quantitative approaches.* Thousand Oaks, CA: Sage.

Creswell, John W., and Vicki L. Clark. (2006). *Designing and conducting mixed methods research.* Thousand Oaks CA: Sage.

Croyle, Robert T., and Elizabeth Loftus. (1992). Improving episodic memory performance of survey respondents. In *Questions* *about questions: Inquiries into the cognitive bases of surveys,* edited by J. Turner, pp. 95–101. New York: Russell Sage Foundation.

Cullen, Francis T. (2005). The twelve people who saved rehabilitation: How the science of criminology made a difference. *Criminology,* 43(1):1–42.

Cullen, Francis T., Bruce Link, and Craig Polanzi. (1982). The seriousness of crime revisited: Have attitudes toward white collar crime changed? *Criminology,* 20:83–102.

Currie, Elliot. (1985). *Confronting crime: An American challenge.* New York: Pantheon Books.

Dabbs, James M., Jr. (1982). Making things visible. In *Varieties of qualitative research,* edited by J. Van Maanen, J. Dabbs, Jr., and R. R. Faulkner, pp. 31–64. Beverly Hills, CA: Sage.

Dabney, Dean A., Richard C. Hollinger, and Laura Dugan. (2004). Who actually steals? A study of covertly observed shoplifters. *Justice Quarterly,* 21:693–732.

Davis, Darren W. (1997). The direction of race of interviewer effects among African-Americans: Donning the black mask. *American Journal of Political Science,* 41:309–322.

Davis, Fred. (1973). The Martian and the convert: Ontological polarities in social research. *Urban Life,* 2:333–343.

Davis, James A. (1985). *The logic of causal order.* Beverly Hills, CA: Sage.

Davis, James A., and Tom W. Smith. (1986). *General social surveys 1972—1986 cumulative codebook.* Chicago, IL: National Opinion Research Center, University of Chicago.

Davis, James A., and Tom W. Smith. (1992). *The NORC General Social Survey: A user's guide.* Newbury Park, CA: Sage.

Davis, W. Rees, Bruce Johnson, Hilary Liberty, and Randolph Doris. (2004). Characteristics of hidden status among users of crack, powder cocaine, and heroin in central Harlem. *Journal of Drug Issues,* 34(1):15–28.

Dean, John P., and William Foote Whyte. (1969). How do you know if the informant is telling the truth? In *Issues in participant observation,* edited by G. McCall and J. L. Simmons, pp. 105–115. Reading, MA: Addison-Wesley.

Decker, Scott H., and Barrik Van Winkle. (1996). *Life in the gang: Family, friends and violence.* Cambridge: Cambridge University Press.

Deegan, Mary Jo. (1988). *Jane Addams and the men of the Chicago School, 1892–1918.* New Brunswick, NJ: Transaction.

De Heer, Wim. (1999). International response trends: Results from an international survey. *Journal of Official Statistics,* 15:129–142.

DeKeseredy, Walter S., and Martin D. Schwartz. (1998). *Woman abuse on campus: Results from the Canadian national survey.* Thousand Oaks, CA: Sage.

DeLamater, John, and Pat MacCorquodale. (1975). The effects of interview schedule variations on reported sexual behavior. *Sociological Methods and Research,* 4:215–236.

DeMaio, Theresa J. (1980). Refusals: Who, where and why? *Public Opinion Quarterly,* 44:223–233.

DeMaio, Theresa J. (1984). Social desirability and survey measurement: A review. In *Surveying subjective phenomena,* vol. 2, edited by C. Turner and E. Martin, pp. 257–282. New York: Russell Sage Foundation.

Denzin, Norman K. (1989). *The research act: A theoretical introduction to sociological methods,* 3rd ed. Englewood Cliffs, NJ: Prentice-Hall.

Denzin, Norman K., and Kai Erikson. (1982). On the ethics of disguised observation: An exchange. In *Social research ethics,* edited by M. Blume. New York: Macmillan.

Denzin, Norman K., and Yvonna S. Lincoln. (2003). Introduction. In *Strategies of qualitative inquiry,* 2nd ed., edited by N. Denzin and Y. Lincoln, pp. 1–45. Thousand Oaks, CA: Sage.

Derksen, Linda, and John Gartell. (1992). Scientific explanation. In *Encyclopedia of sociology,* vol. 4, edited by E. and M. Borgatta, pp. 1711–1720. New York: Macmillan.

Devault, Marjorie L. (1990). Talking and listening from women's standpoint: Feminist strategies for interviewing and analysis. *Social Problems,* 37:96–116.

de Vaus, David A. (1986). *Surveys in social research.* Boston, MA: George Allen and Unwin.

de Vise, Daniel . (2005, March 19). Defense dept. surveys academy sex assaults: 1 woman in 7 reports being attacked. *Washington Post,* p. A01.

Dickson, David. (1984). *The new politics of science.* Chicago, IL: University of Chicago Press.

DiCristina, Bruce. (1995). *Method in criminology: A philosophical primer.* New York: Harrow and Heston.

Diener, Edward, and Rick Crandall. (1978). *Ethics in social and behavioral research.* Chicago, IL: University of Chicago Press.

Dijkstra, Wil, and Johannes van der Zouwen, eds. (1982). *Response behavior in the survey interview.* New York: Academic Press.

Dillman, Don A. (1978). *Mail and telephone surveys: The total design method.* New York: Wiley.

Dillman, Don A. (1983). Mail and other self-administered questionnaires. In *Handbook of survey research,* edited by P. Rossi, J. Wright, and A. Anderson, pp. 359–377. Orlando, FL: Academic Press.

Dillman, Don A. (2000). *Mail and Internet surveys: The tailored design method,* 2nd ed. New York: Wiley.

Dillman, Don A., and Cleo Redline. (2004). Testing paper self-administered questionnaires. In *Methods for testing and evaluating survey questionnaires,* edited by Stanley Presser et al., pp. 299–318. New York: Wiley.

Dohan, Daniel, and Martin Sanchez-Jankowski. (1998). Using computers to analysis ethnographic field data. *Annual Review of Sociology,* 24:477–498.

Dokoupil, Tony. (2006). A grim calculation: The first scientifically rigorous estimate of the death toll in Darfur shows that the pessimists were right. *Newsweek* <www.msnbc.msn.com/id/14840118/site/newsweek>.

Donald, Robert B., et al. (1983). *Writing clear paragraphs,* 2nd ed. Englewood Cliffs, NJ: Prentice-Hall.

Dooley, David. (1984). *Social research methods.* Englewood Cliffs, NJ: Prentice-Hall.

Douglas, Jack D. (1976). *Investigative social research.* Beverly Hills, CA: Sage.

Douglas, Jack D. (1985). *Creative interviewing.* Beverly Hills, CA: Sage.

Dunaway, David K., and Willa K. Baum, eds. (1984). *Oral history.* Nashville, TN: Association for State and Local History.

Duncan, Otis Dudley. (1984). *Notes on social measurement: Historical and critical.* New York: Russell Sage Foundation.

Duncan, Otis Dudley, and Magnus Stenbeck. (1988). No opinion or not sure? *Public Opinion Quarterly,* 52:513–525.

Durkheim, Émile. (1938). *Rules of the sociological method.* Trans. Sarah Solovay and John Mueller, edited by G. Catlin. Chicago, IL: University of Chicago Press.

Dziech, Billie W., and Linda Weiner. (1990). *The lecherous professor: Sexual harassment on campus,* 2nd ed. Urbana, IL: University of Illinois Press.

Eastrope, Gary. (1974). *History of social research methods.* London: Longman.

Edwards, Allen L. (1957). *Techniques of attitude scale construction.* New York: Appleton-Century-Crofts.

Edwards, Rosalind. (1993). An education in interviewing: Placing the researcher and research. In *Research on sensitive topics,* edited by C. Renzetti and R. Lee, pp. 181–196. Thousand Oaks, CA: Sage.

Eggen, Dan. (2006, December 19). Violent crime is up for 2nd straight year. *Washington Post,* p. A01.

Eichler, Margrit. (1988). *Nonsexist research methods: A practical guide.* Boston, MA: George Allen and Unwin.

Eilperin, Juliet. (2006). Censorship is alleged at NOAA. *Washington Post* <http://www .washingtonpost.com/wpdyn/content/article/2006/02/10/AR2006021001766.html>.

Elder, Glen H. Jr., Eliza Pavalko, and Elizabeth Clipp. (1993). *Working with archival data: Studying lives.* Thousand Oakes, CA: Sage.

Emerson, Robert M. (1981). Observational field work. *Annual Review of Sociology,* 7:351–378.

Emerson, Robert M. (1983). Introduction. In *Contemporary field research,* edited by R. M. Emerson, pp. 1–16. Boston, MA: Little, Brown.

Emerson, Robert M., Rachel Fretz, and Linda Shaw. (1995). *Writing ethnographic field notes.* Chicago, MA: University of Chicago Press.

Ericson, Richard. (2007). *Crime in an insecure world.* Cambridge: Polity Press.

Erikson, Kai T. (1970). A comment on disguised observation in sociology. In *Qualitative methodology,* edited by W. J. Filstead, pp. 252–260. Chicago, IL: Markham.

Eysenck, Hans J. (2006). *The structure and measurement of intelligence.* Edison, NJ: Transaction Books.

Fagan, Jeff. (2005). Deterrence and the death penalty: A critical review of new evidence. *Testimony to the New York State Assembly Standing Committee on Judiciary* <http://www.death-penaltyinfo .org/FaganTestimony.pdf>.

Farrington, David P. (2003). A short history of randomized experiments in criminology. *Evaluation Review,* 27(3):218–227.

Fay, Brian. (1975). *Social theory and political practice.* London: George Allen and Unwin.

Fay, Brian. (1987). *Critical social science: Liberation and its limits.* Ithaca, NY: Cornell University Press.

Ferrell, Jeff. (1993). *Crimes of style: Urban graffiti and the politics of criminality.* New York: Garland Publishing.

Ferrell, Jeff. (2003). 'Speed Kills.' *Critical Criminology* 11(3):185–198.

Ferrell, Jeff. (2004a). Boredom, crime and criminology. *Theoretical Criminology,* 8:287–302.

Ferrell, Jeff. (2006). *Empire of scrounge: Inside the urban underground of dumpster diving, trash picking, and street scavenging.* New York: New York University Press.

Ferrell, Jeff, and Mark Hamm. (1998). *Ethnography at the edge: Crime, deviance, and field research.* Boston, MA: Northeastern University Press.

Fetterman, David M. (1989). *Ethnography: Step by step.* Newbury Park, CA: Sage.

Fichter, Joseph H., and William L. Kolb. (1970). Ethical limitations on sociological reporting. In *Qualitative methodology,* edited by W. J. Filstead, pp. 261–270. Chicago, IL: Markham.

Fielding, Nigel G., and Raymond M. Lee, eds. (1991). *Using computers in qualitative research.* Newbury Park, CA: Sage.

Fine, Gary Alan. (1980). Cracking diamonds: Observer role in Little League baseball settings and the acquisition of social competence. In *Fieldwork experience,* edited by W. B. Shaffir, R. A. Stebbins, and A. Turowetz, pp. 117–132. New York: St. Martin's Press.

Fine, Gary Alan. (1987). *With the boys: Little League baseball and preadolescent culture.* Chicago, IL: University of Chicago Press.

Fine, Gary Alan. (1988). The ten commandments of writing. *The American Sociologist,* 19:152–157.

Fine, Gary Alan. (1999). Field labor and ethnographic reality. *Journal of Contemporary Ethnography,* 28:532–540.

Fine, Gary Alan, and Barry Glassner. (1979). Participant observation with children: Promise and problems. *Urban Life,* 8:153–174.

Finkel, Steven E., Thomas M. Guterbock, and Marian J. Borg. (1991). Race-of-interviewer effects in a preelection poll: Virginia 1989. *Public Opinion Quarterly,* 55:313–330.

Finley, M. I. (1977, Summer). Progress in historiography. *Daedalus,* pp. 125–142.

Fisher, Bonnie S., Francis T. Cullen, and Michael G. Turner. (2000). *The sexual victimization of college women.* BJS Research Report. Washington, DC: U.S. Department of Justice.

Fischer, David H. (1970). *Historians' fallacies: Towards a logic of historical thought.* New York: Harper & Row.

Fischer, Frank. (1985). Critical evaluation of public policy: A methodological case study. In *Critical theory and public life,* edited by J. Forester, pp. 231–257. Cambridge, MA: MIT Press.

Fiske, Donald W. (1982). Convergent-discriminant validation in measurements and research strategies. In *Forms of validation in research,* edited by D. Brinberg and L. H. Kidder, pp. 72–92. San Francisco, CA: Jossey-Bass.

Fletcher, Colin. (1974). *Beneath the surface: An account of three styles of sociological research.* Boston, MA: Routledge and Kegan Paul.

Flick, Uwe. (1998). *An introduction to qualitative research.* Thousand Oaks, CA: Sage.

Foddy, William. (1993). *Constructing questions for interviews and questionnaires: Theory and practice in social research.* New York: Cambridge University Press.

Foddy, William. (1995). Probing: A dangerous practice in social surveys? *Quality and Quantity,* 29:73–86.

Fontana, Andrea, and James H. Frey. (1994). Interviewing: The art of science. In *Handbook of qualitative research,* edited by N. Denzin and Y. Lincoln, pp. 361–376. Thousand Oaks, CA: Sage.

Foucault, Michel. (1977). *Discipline and punish: The birth of the prison.* New York: Penguin.

Fowler, Floyd Jackson., Jr. (1984). *Survey research methods.* Beverly Hills, CA: Sage.

Fowler, Floyd Jackson, Jr. (1992). How unclear terms affect survey research. *Public Opinion Quarterly,* 56(2):218–232.

Fowler, Floyd Jackson, Jr. (2004). The case for more split-sample experiments in developing survey instruments. In *Methods for testing and evaluating survey questionnaires,* edited by S. Presser, M. Couper, J. Lessler, E. Martin, J. Martin, J. Tothgeb, E. Singer, pp. 173–188. New York: Wiley.

Fowler, Floyd Jackson, Jr., and Charles Cannell. (1996). Using behavioral coding to identify cognitive problems with survey questions. In *Answering questions,* edited by N. Schwarz and S. Sudman, pp. 15–36. San Francisco, CA: Jossey-Bass.

Fox, James Alan, and Paul E. Tracy. (1986). *Randomized response: A method for sensitive surveys.* Beverly Hills, CA: Sage.

Fox, John. (1992). Statistical graphics. In *Encyclopedia of sociology,* vol. 4, edited by E. and M. Borgatta, pp. 2054–2073. New York: Macmillan.

Fox, Richard, Melvin R. Crask, and Jonghoon Kim. (1988). Mail survey response rate: A meta-analysis of selected techniques for inducing response. *Public Opinion Quarterly,* 52:467–491.

Franke, Charles O. (1983). Ethnography. In *Contemporary field research,* edited by R. M. Emerson, pp. 60–67. Boston, MA: Little, Brown.

Franke, Richard H., and James D. Kaul. (1978). The Hawthorne experiments: First statistical interpretation. *American Sociological Review,* 43:623–643.

Frankel, Martin. (1983). Sampling theory. In *Handbook of survey research,* edited by P. Rossi, J. Wright, and A. Anderson, pp. 21–67. Orlando, FL: Academic Press.

Franzosi, Roberto. (1998). Narrative analysis—or why (and how) sociologists should be interested in narrative. *Annual Review of Sociology,* 24:517–554.

Freeman, Howard, and Merrill J. Shanks, eds. (1983). The emergence of computer assisted survey research. *Sociological Methods and Research,* 23:115–230.

Freire, Paulo. (1970). *Pedagogy of the oppressed.* Trans. Myra Bergman Ramos. New York: Seabury.

Frey, James H. (1983). *Survey research by telephone.* Beverly Hills, CA: Sage.

Friday, Paul, Elmar Weitekamp, Hans Kerner, and Terrence Taylor. (2005). A Chinese birth cohort: Theoretical implications. *Journal of Research in Crime and Delinquency,* 42(2):176–192.

Fuchs, Stephan, and Jonathan H. Turner. (1986). What makes a science "mature"? Patterns of organizational control in scientific production. *Sociological Theory,* 4:143–150.

Gaines, Larry K., and Peter Kraska. (2005). *Drugs, crime, and justice.* Long Grove, IL: Waveland.

Gainey, Randy R., Sara Steen, and Rodney L. Engen. (2005). Exercising options: An assessment of the use of alternative sanctions for drug offenders. *Justice Quarterly,* 22:488–520.

Gagne, Patricia. (1996). Identity, strategy, and feminist politics: Clemency for battered women who kill. *Social Problems,* 43:77–93.

Galaskiewicz, Joseph. (1985). Professional networks and the institutionalization of a single mind set. *American Sociological Review,* 50:639–658.

Gans, Herbert J. (1982). The participant observer as a human being: Observations on the personal aspects of fieldwork. In *Field research,* edited by R. G. Burgess, pp. 53–61. Boston, MA: George Allen and Unwin.

Garfinkel, Harold. (1967). *Studies in ethnomethodology.* Englewood Cliffs, NJ: Prentice-Hall.

Garfinkel, Harold. (1974). The rational properties of scientific and common sense activities. In *Positivism and sociology,* edited by A. Giddens, pp. 53–74. London: Heinemann.

Garland, David. (2001). *Culture of control: Crime and social order in contemporary society.* Chicago, IL: University of Chicago Press.

Garland, David. (2005). Penal excess and surplus meaning: Public torture lynchings in twentieth-century America. *Law and Society Review,* 39(4):793–833.

Garner, Joel H., and Christy A. Visher. (2003). The production of criminological experiments. *Evaluation Review,* 27(3):316–335.

Gaskell, George, Daniel Wright, and Colm O'Muircheartaigh. (2000). Telescoping landmark events. *Public Opinion Quarterly,* 64:77–89.

Gaston, Jerry. (1978). *The reward system in British and American science.* New York: Wiley.

Geer, John G. (1988). What do open-ended questions measure? *Public Opinion Quarterly,* 52:365–371.

Geertz, Clifford. (1973). *The interpretation of cultures.* New York: Basic Books.

Geertz, Clifford. (1979). From the native's point of view: On the nature of anthropological understanding. In *Interpretative social science: A reader,* edited by P. Rabinow and W. Sullivan, pp. 225–242. Berkeley, CA: University of California Press.

Gelsthorpe, Loraine, and Allison Morris. (1990). *Feminist perspectives in criminology.* Philadelphia, PA: Open University.

Georges, Robert A., and Michael O. Jones. (1980). *People studying people.* Berkeley, CA: University of California Press.

Gibbs, Jack. (1989). Conceptualization of terrorism. *American Sociological Review,* 54:329–340.

Giddens, Anthony. (1976). *New rules of sociological method: Positivist critique of interpretative sociologies.* New York: Basic Books.

Giddens, Anthony. (1978). Positivism and its critics. In *A history of sociological analysis,* edited by T. Bottomore and R. Nisbet. New York: Basic Books.

Gillespie, Richard. (1988). The Hawthorne experiments and the politics of experimentation. In *The rise of experimentation in American psychology,* edited by J. Morawski, pp. 114–137. New Haven, CT: Yale University Press.

Gillespie, Richard. (1991). *Manufacturing knowledge: A history of the Hawthorne experiments.* New York: Cambridge University Press.

Gilljam, Mikael, and David Granberg. (1993). Should we take Don't Know for an answer? *Public Opinion Quarterly,* 57:348–357.

Glaser, Barney, and Anselm Strauss. (1967). *The discovery of grounded theory.* Chicago, IL: Aldine.

Glasser, Gerald J., and Gale O. Metzger. (1972). Random digit dialing as a method of telephone sampling. *Journal of Marketing Research,* 9:59–64.

Glucksmann, Miriam. (1974). *Structuralist analysis in contemporary social thought: A comparison of the theories of Claude Levi-Strauss and Louis Althusser.* Boston, MA: Routledge and Kegan Paul.

Gold, Raymond L. (1969). Roles in sociological field observation. In *Issues in participant observation,* edited by G. J. McCall and J. L. Simmons, pp. 30–38. Reading, MA: Addison-Wesley.

Goldstone, Jack A. (1997). Methodological issues in comparative macrosociology. *Comparative Social Research,* 16:107–120.

Goldthorpe, John. (1977). The relevance of history to sociology. In *Sociological research methods,* edited by M. Bulmer, pp. 178–191. London: Macmillan.

Goldthorpe, John. (1991). The uses of history in sociology: Reflections on some recent tendencies. *British Journal of Sociology,* 42:211–230.

Goldthorpe, John H. (1997). Current issues in comparative macrosociology: A debate on methodological issues. *Comparative Social Research,* 16:1–26.

Gonor, George. (1977). "Situation" versus "frame": The "interactionist" and the "structuralist" analysis of everyday life. *American Sociological Review,* 42:854–867.

Gorden, Raymond. (1980). *Interviewing: Strategy, techniques and tactics,* 3rd ed. Homewood, IL: Dorsey Press.

Gottfredson, Michael R., and Travis Hirschi. (1990). *A general theory of crime.* Stanford, CA: Stanford University Press.

Gover, Angela R., John MacDonald, and Geoffrey Alpert. (2003). Combating domestic violence: Findings from an evaluation of a local domestic violence court. *Criminology and Public Policy,* 3(1):109–132.

Goward, Nicola. (1984). Publications on fieldwork experiences. In *Ethnographic research: A guide to general conduct,* edited by R. F. Ellen, pp. 88–100. Orlando, FL: Academic Press.

Gowda, Rajeev, and Jeffrey C. Fox, eds. (2002). *Judgments, decisions, and public policy.* New York: Cambridge University Press.

Goyder, John C. (1982). Factors affecting response rates to mailed questionnaires. *American Sociological Review,* 47:550–554.

Graham, Sandra. (1992). Most of the subjects were white and middle class: Trends in published research on African Americans in selected APA journals, 1970–1989. *American Psychologist,* 47:629–639.

Granovetter, Mark. (1976). Network sampling: Some first steps. *American Journal of Sociology,* 81:1287–1303.

Grattet, Ryken, and Valerie Jenness. (2005). The reconstitution of law in local settings: Agency discretion, ambiguity, and a surplus of law in the policing of hate crime. *Law and Society Review,* 39(4):893–942.

Gray, Bradford H. (1982). The regulatory context of social and behavioral research. In *Ethical issues in social science research,* edited by T. Beauchamp, R. Faden, R. J. Wallace, and L. Walters, pp. 329–354. Baltimore, MD: Johns Hopkins University Press.

Gray, Paul S. (1980). Exchange and access in field work. *Urban Life,* 9:309–331.

Greek, Cecil E. (2006). Visual criminology. Posted on Cecil Greek's Web site at <www.criminology.fsu.edu/faculty/greek/VisualCriminology.pdf>.

Griffin, Larry J. (1992). Temporality, events and explanation in historical sociology. *Sociological Methods and Research,* 20:403–427.

Griffin, Larry J. (1993). Narrative, event structure analysis and causal interpretation in historical sociology. *American Journal of Sociology,* 98:1094–1133.

Griffin, Larry J., and Charles Ragin. (1994). Some observations on formal methods of qualitative analysis. *Sociological Methods and Research,* 23:4–22.

Grinnell, Frederick. (1987). *The scientific attitude.* Boulder, CO: Westview.

Grosof, Miriam, and Hyman Sardy. (1985). *A research primer for the social and behavioral sciences.* Orlando: FL: Academic Press.

Groves, Robert M., and Mick Couper. (1998). *Nonresponse in household interview surveys.* New York: Wiley.

Groves, Robert M., Nancy H. Fultz, and Elizabeth Martin. (1992). Direct questioning about comprehension in a survey setting. In *Questions about questions: Inquiries into the cognitive bases of surveys,* edited by J. Turner, pp. 49–61. New York: Russell Sage Foundation.

Groves, Robert M., and Nancy Mathiowetz. (1984). Computer assisted telephone interviewing: Effects on interviewers and respondents. *Public Opinion Quarterly,* 48:356–369.

Groves, Robert M., and Robert L. Kahn. (1979). *Surveys by telephone: A national comparison with personal interviews.* New York: Academic Press.

Guba, Egon G., and Yvonna S. Lincoln. (1994). Competing paradigms in qualitative research. In *Handbook of qualitative research,* edited by N. Denzin and Y. Lincoln, pp. 105–117. Thousand Oaks, CA: Sage.

Gubrium, Jaber F., and James A. Holstein. (1998). Narrative practice and the coherence of personal stories. *Sociological Quarterly,* 39:163–187.

Gunsalus, C. Kristina. (2005). *Improving the system for protecting human subjects: Counteracting IRB mission creep.* Center for Advanced Study <http://www.law .uiuc.edu/-conferences/whitepaper/>.

Gurevitch, Zali D. (1988). The other side of the dialogue: On making the other strange and the experience of otherness. *American Journal of Sociology,* 93:1179–1199.

Gustin, Bernard H. (1973). Charisma, recognition and the motivation of scientists. *American Journal of Sociology,* 86:1119–1134.

Haarr, Robin N. (2007). Violence against women in marriage: A general population study in Khatlon Oblast, Tajikistan. *Feminist criminology,* 2(3):245–270.

Haberman, Shelby J. (1978). *Analysis of qualitative data.* New York: Academic Press.

Habermas, Jurgen. (1971). *Knowledge and human interests.* Boston, MA: Beacon.

Habermas, Jurgen. (1973). *Theory and practice.* Boston, MA: Beacon.

Habermas, Jurgen. (1976). *Legitimation crisis.* Boston, MA: Beacon.

Habermas, Jurgen. (1979). *Communication and the evolution of society.* Boston, MA: Beacon.

Hadden, Sally E. (2001). *Slave patrols: Law and violence in Virginia and the Carolinas.* Cambridge, MA: Harvard University Press.

Hagan, John, A. R. Gillis, and David Brownfield. (1996). *Criminological controversies.* Boulder, CO: Westview.

Hagan, John, Wenona Rymond-Richmond, and Patricia Parker. (2005) The criminology of genocide: The death and rape of Darfur. *Criminology,* 43:525–561.

Hage, Jerald. (1972). *Techniques and problems of theory construction in sociology.* New York: Wiley.

Haggerty, Kevin D. (2001). *Making crime count.* Buffalo, NY: University of Toronto Press.

Haggerty, Kevin D., and Richard V. Ericson. (2000). The surveillant assemblage. *Journal of Sociology,* 51(4):605–622.

Hagstrom, Warren. (1965). *The scientific community.* New York: Basic Books.

Halfpenny, Peter. (1982). *Positivism and sociology: Explaining social life.* London: George Allen and Unwin.

Hamm, Mark S. (1997). *Apocalypse in Oklahoma: Waco and Ruby Ridge revenged.* Boston, MA: Northeastern University Press.

Hammersley, Martyn. (1995). Theory and evidence in qualitative research. *Quality and Quantity,* 29:55–66.

Hammersley, Martyn, and Paul Atkinson. (1983). *Ethnography: Principles in practice.* London: Tavistock.

Hannan, Michael T. (1985). Problems of aggregation. In *Causal models in the social sciences,* 2nd ed., edited by H. Blalock, Jr., pp. 403–439. Chicago, IL: Aldine.

Harcourt, Bernard E. (2006, March 11). Order and law: Broken windows diverts cops from policing violent crime. *Rocky Mountain News.*

Harding, Sandra. (1986). *The science question in feminism.* Ithaca, NY: Cornell University Press.

Hargens, Lowell L. (1988). Scholarly consensus and journal rejection rates. *American Sociological Review,* 53:139–151.

Hargens, Lowell L. (1991). Impressions and misimpressions about sociology journals. *Contemporary Sociology,* 20:343–349.

Harkens, Shirley, and Carol Warren. (1993). The social relations of intensive interviewing: Constellations of strangeness and science. *Sociological Methods and Research,* 21:317–339.

Harkness, Janet, Fons van de Vijver, and Timothy Johnson. (2003). Questionnaire design in comparative research. In *Cross-cultural survey methods,* edited by J. Harkness, F. Van de Vijver, and P. Mohler, pp. 19–34. Hoboken, NJ: Wiley.

Harper, Douglas. (1982). *Good company.* Chicago, IL: University of Chicago Press.

Harper, Douglas. (1987). *Working knowledge.* Chicago, IL: University of Chicago Press.

Harper, Douglas. (1994). On the authority of the image: Visual methods at the crossroads. In *Handbook of qualitative research,* edited by N. Denzin and Y. Lincoln, pp. 403–412. Thousand Oaks, CA: Sage.

Harré, Rom. (1972). *The philosophies of science.* London: Oxford University Press.

Harvey, Lee. (1990). *Critical social research.* London: Urwin Hyman.

Haydu, Jeffrey. (1998). Making use of the past: Time periods as cases to compare and as sequences of problem solving. *American Journal of Sociology,* 104:339–371.

Hayward, Keith. (2006). Personal conversation.

Hearnshaw, Leslie S. (1979). *Cyril Burt: Psychologist.* London: Holder and Stoughten.

Heberlein, Thomas A., and Robert Baumgartner. (1978). Factors affecting response rates to mailed questionnaires: A quantitative analysis of the published literature. *American Sociological Review,* 43:447–462.

Heberlein, Thomas A., and Robert Baumgartner. (1981). Is a questionnaire necessary in a second mailing? *Public Opinion Quarterly,* 45:102–107.

Heckathorn, Douglas D. (1997). Respondent-driven sampling: A new approach to the study of hidden populations. *Social Problems,* 44:174–199.

Heckathorn, Douglas D. (2002). Respondent-driven sampling II: Deriving valid population estimates from chain-referral samples of hidden populations. *Social Problems,* 49:11–35.

Hegtvedt, Karen A. (1992). Replication. In *Encyclopedia of sociology,* vol. 3, edited by E. and M. Borgatta, pp. 1661–1663. New York: Macmillan.

Heise, David. (1991). Event structure analysis. In *Using computers in qualitative research,* edited by N. Fielding and R. Lee, pp. 136–163. Newbury Park, CA: Sage.

Held, David. (1980). *Introduction to critical theory: Horkheimer to Habermas.* Berkeley, CA: University of California Press.

Hemmens, Craig, and Chris Mathias. (2004). United States v. Banks: The Knock and Announce Rule Returns to the Supreme Court. *Idaho Law Review,* 41(1):1–36.

Hemmens, Craig, and Daniel Levin. (2000). Resistance is futile: The right to resist unlawful arrest in an era of aggressive policing. *Crime and Delinquency,* 46:472–496.

Henry, Gray T. (1995). *Graphing data: Techniques for display and analysis.* Thousand Oaks, CA: Sage.

Herting, Jerald R. (1985). Multiple indicator models using LISREL. In *Causal models in the social sciences,* 2nd ed., edited by H. Blalock, Jr., pp. 263–320. New York: Aldine.

Herting, Jerald R., and Herbert L. Costner. (1985). Re-specification in multiple indicator models. In *Causal models in the social sciences,* 2nd ed., edited by H. Blalock, Jr., pp. 321–394. Chicago, IL: Aldine.

Hertsgaard, Mark. (2006, April 20). While Washington slept. *Vanity Fair,* pp. 66–115.

Herzberger, Sharon D. (1993). The cyclical pattern of child abuse: A study of research methodology. In *Research on sensitive topics,* edited by C. Renzetti and R. Lee, pp. 33–51. Thousand Oaks, CA: Sage.

Herzog, A. Regula, and Jerald G. Bachman. (1981). Effects of questionnaire length on response quality. *Public Opinion Quarterly,* 45:549–559.

Hesse, Mary B. (1970). *Models and analogies in science.* Notre Dame, IN: Notre Dame Press.

Hicks, David. (1984). Getting into the field and establishing routines. In *Ethnographic research: A guide to general conduct,* edited by R. F. Ellen, pp. 192–199. Orlando: Academic Press.

Higher Education Research Institute. (2004). *Recent findings* <www.gseis.ucla.edu/ heri/findings.html>

Hill, Michael R. (1993). *Archival strategies and techniques.* Thousand Oaks, CA: Sage.

Hoffmann, Joan Eakin. (1980). Problems of access in the study of social elites and boards of directors. In *Fieldwork experience,* edited by W. B. Shaffir, R. A. Stebbins, and A. Turowetz, pp. 45–56. New York: St. Martin's Press.

Holbrook, Allyson, Melanie Green, and Jon Krosnick. (2003). Telephone versus face-to-face interviewing of national probability samples with long questionnaires. *Public Opinion Quarterly,* 67:79–125.

Holstein, James A., and Jaber F. Gubrium. (1994). Phenomenology, ethnomethodology and interpretative practice. In *Handbook of qualitative research,* edited by N. Denzin and Y. Lincoln, pp. 262–272. Thousand Oaks, CA: Sage.

Holsti, Ole R. (1968). Content analysis. In *Handbook of social psychology,* 2nd ed., vol. 2, edited by G. Lindzey and E. Aronson, pp. 596–692. Reading, MA: Addison-Wesley.Holub, Robert C. (1991). *Jürgen Habermas: Critic in the public sphere.* New York: Routledge.

Holy, Ladislav. (1984). Theory, methodology and the research process. In *Ethnographic research: A guide to general conduct,* edited by R. F. Ellen, pp. 13–34. Orlando, FL: Academic Press.

Homan, Roger. (1980). The ethics of covert methods. *British Journal of Sociology,* 31:46–57.

Honigmann, John J. (1982). Sampling in ethnographic fieldwork. In *Field research,* edited by R. G. Burgess, pp. 79–90. Boston, MA: Allen and Unwin.

Horn, Robert V. (1993). *Statistical indicators for the economic and social sciences.* Cambridge: Cambridge University Press.

Hornstein, Gail A. (1988). Quantifying psychological phenomena: Debates, dilemmas and implications. In *The rise of experimentation in American psychology,* edited by J. Morawski, pp. 1–34. New Haven, CT: Yale University Press.

Hubbard, Raymond, and Eldon Little. (1988). Promised contributions to charity and mail survey responses: Replication with extension. *Public Opinion Quarterly,* 52:223–230.

Huff, Darrell, and Irving Geis. (1993). *How to lie with statistics.* New York: W.W. Norton.

Humphreys, Laud. (1975). *Tearoom trade: Impersonal sex in public places,* enlarged ed. Chicago, IL: Aldine.

Hunt, Lynn. (1989). Introduction. In *The new cultural history,* edited by L. Hunt, pp. 1–22. Berkeley, CA: University of California Press.

Hunter, Christopher., and Kent McClelland. (1991). Honoring accounts for sexual harassment: A factorial survey analysis. *Sex Roles,* 24(11–12):725–751.

Hyman, Herbert H. (1975). *Interviewing in social research.* Chicago, IL: University of Chicago Press.

Inciardi, James A., Anne E. Pottieger, and Hilary L. Surratt. (1996). African Americans and the crack-crime connection. In *The American pipe dream: Crack cocaine in the inner city,* edited by Dale Chitwood, James E. Rivers, and James A. Inciardi, pp. 56–70. Fort Worth, TX: Harcourt Brace.

Isaac, Larry W., Debra A. Street, and Stan J. Knapp. (1994). Analyzing historical contingency with formal methods: The case of the "relief explosion" and 1968. *Sociological Methods and Research,* 23:114–141.

Jackson, Bruce. (1978). Killing time: Life in the Arkansas penitentiary. *Qualitative Sociology,* 1:21–32.

Jackson, Shelly, Lynette Feder, David Forde, Robert Davis, Christopher Maxwell, and Bruce Taylor. (2003). *Batterer intervention programs: Where do we go from here?* National Institute of Justice Research Report. Washington, DC: NIJ.

Jacobs, Bruce. (2000). *Robbing drug dealers.* New York: Aldine de Gruyter.

Jacobs, Jerry. (1974). *Fun city: An ethnographic study of a retirement community.* New York: Holt, Rinehart, and Winston.

Jaschick, Mollie L., and Bruce R. Fretz. (1991). Women's perception and labeling of sexual harassment. *Sex Roles.* 25(1–2):19–23.

Johnson, Burke, and Larry Christensen. (2004). *Educational research: Quantitative, qualitative, and mixed approaches.* Boston, IL: Allyn and Bacon.

Johnson, John M. (1975). *Doing field research.* New York: Free Press.

Johnson, P. Timothy, James G. Hougland, Jr., and Richard R. Clayton. (1989). Obtaining reports of sensitive behavior: A comparison of substance-use reports from telephone and face-to-face interviews. *Social Science Quarterly,* 70:173–183.

Jones, James H. (1981). *Bad blood: The Tuskegee syphilis experiment.* New York: Free Press.

Jones, Wesley H. (1979). Generalizing mail survey inducement methods: Populations' interactions with anonymity and sponsorship. *Public Opinion Quarterly,* 43:102–111.

Jordan, Lawrence A., Alfred C. Marcus, and Leo G. Reeder. (1980). Response styles in telephone and household interviewing: A field experiment. *Public Opinion Quarterly,* 44:210–222.

Junker, Buford H. (1960). *Field work.* Chicago, IL: University of Chicago Press.

Kalton, Graham. (1983). *Introduction to survey sampling.* Beverly Hills, CA: Sage.

Kane, Emily W., and Laura J. MacAulay. (1993). Interview gender and gender attitudes. *Public Opinion Quarterly,* 57:1–28.

Kaplan, Abraham. (1964). *The conduct of inquiry: Methodology for behavioral science.* New York: Harper & Row.

Kappeler, Victor E. (2004). Inventing criminal justice: Myth and social construction. In *Theorizing criminal justice: Eight essential orientations,* edited by Peter Kraska, pp. 167–176. Prospect Heights, IL: Waveland Press.

Kappeler, Victor E. (2006). *Critical issues in civil liability.* Prospect Heights, IL: Waveland.

Kappeler, Victor E. (Forthcoming). *Speaking of crime: An invitation to semiotic criminology.* Prospect Heights, IL: Waveland.

Kappeler, Victor E., and Gary Potter. (2006). *The mythology of crime and criminal justice.* Prospect Heights, IL: Waveland.

Kappeler, Victor E., and Peter B. Kraska. (1998). A textual critique of community policing: Police adaptation to high modernity. *Policing,* 21:293–313.

Karjane, Heather, Bonnie Fisher, and Francis Cullen. (2005). Sexual assault on campus: What colleges and universities are doing about it. *National Institute of Justice Research for Practice.* Washington, DC: U.S. Department of Justice.

Karp, David, and Todd Clear. (2000). Community justice: A conceptual framework. *Boundary Changes in Criminal Justice Organizations.* Washington, DC: U.S. Department of Justice.

Karweit, Nancy, and Edmund D. Meyers, Jr. (1983). Computers in survey research. In *Handbook of survey research,* edited by P. Rossi, J. Wright, and A. Anderson, pp. 379–414. Orlando, FL: Academic Press.

Katz, Charles M. (2003). Issues in the production and dissemination of gang statistics. *Crime and Delinquency,* 49:485–516.

Katz, Charles M., and Vincent Webb. (2005). *Policing gangs in America.* Cambridge: Cambridge University Press.

Keat, Russell. (1981). *The politics of social theory: Habermas, Freud and the critique of positivism.* Chicago, IL: University of Chicago Press.

Keat, Russell, and John Urry. (1975). *Social theory as science.* London: Routledge and Kegan Paul.

Keeter, Scott. (1995). Estimating telephone noncoverage bias with a telephone survey. *Public Opinion Quarterly,* 59:196–217.

Keeter, Scott, Carolyn Miller, Andrew Kohut, Robert M. Groves, and Stanley Presser. (2000). Consequences of reducing non-response in a national telephone survey. *Public Opinion Quarterly,* 64:125–148.

Kelling, George, Robert Wasserman, and Mike Wagers. (2006, March 26). Order and law: Attack minor offenses, theory goes, and major ones diminish. *Rocky Mountain News* (March 11).

Kelman, Herbert. (1982). Ethical issues in different social science methods. In *Ethical issues in social science research,* edited by T. Beauchamp, R. Faden, R. J. Wallace, and L. Walters, pp. 40–99. Baltimore, MD: Johns Hopkins University Press.

Kemmis, Stephen, and Robin McTaggart. (2003). Participatory action research. In *Strategies of qualitative inquiry,* 2nd ed., edited by N. Denzin and Y. Lincoln, pp. 336–396. Thousand Oaks CA: Sage.

Kercher, Kyle. (1992). Quasi-experimental research designs. In *Encyclopedia of sociology,* vol. 3, edited by E. and M. Borgatta, pp. 1595–1613. New York: Macmillan.

Kidder, Louise H., and Charles M. Judd. (1986). *Research methods in social relations,* 5th ed. New York: Holt, Rinehart and Winston.

Kiecolt, K. Jill, and Laura E. Nathan. (1985). *Secondary analysis of survey data.* Beverly Hills, CA: Sage.

Kilzer, Lou. (2006). Fighting graffiti to cut down on crime. *Rocky Mountain News.*

Kindermann, Charles, James Lynch, and David Cantor. (1997). *Effects of the redesign on victimization estimates.* Washington, DC: U.S. Bureau of Justice Statistics.

King, Desmond. (1998). The politics of social research: Institutionalizing public funding regimes in the United States and Britain. *British Journal of Political Science,* 28:415–144.

Kirk, Jerome, and Marc L. Miller. (1986). *Reliability and validity in qualitative research.* Beverly Hills, CA: Sage.

Kiser, Edgar, and April Linton. (2002). The hinges of history: State making and revolt in early modern France. *American Sociological Review,* 62:889–910.

Kish, Leslie. (1965). *Survey sampling.* New York: Wiley.

Kleinman, Sherry. (1980). Learning the ropes as fieldwork analysis. In *Fieldwork experience,* edited by W. B. Shaffir, R. A. Stebbins, and A. Turowetz, pp. 171–183. New York: St. Martin's Press.

Klockars, Carl B. (1974). *The professional fence.* New York: Free Press.

Knäuper, Bärbel. (1999). The impact of age and education on response order effects in attitude measurement. *Public Opinion Quarterly,* 63:347–370.

Koch, Nadine S., and Jolly A. Emrey. (2001). The Internet and opinion measurement: Surveying marginalized populations. *Social Science Quarterly,* 82:131–138.

Koetting, Mark, and Vincent Schiraldi. (1997). Singapore west: The incarceration of 200,000 Californians. *Social Justice,* 24:145–176.

Kopel, David B., Paul Gallant, and Joanne D. Eisen. (2006). Is resisting genocide a human right? *Notre Dame Law Review,* 81(4):1275–1346.

Kraemer, Helena Chmura, and Sue Thiemann. (1987). *How many subjects? Statistical power analysis in research.* Newbury Park, CA: Sage.

Kraska, Peter B. (2001). Policing Kentucky's school children: Issues and trends. *Kentucky Justice and Safety Research Bulletin,* 3(2):1–14.

Kraska, Peter B. (2004). *Theorizing criminal justice: Eight essential orientations.* Prospect Heights, IL: Waveland.

Kraska, Peter B. (2006). Criminal justice theory: Towards an infrastructure. *Justice Quarterly,* 23:167–185.

Kraska, Peter B., Charles R. Bussard, and John J. Brent. (2010). Trafficking in bodily perfection: Examining the late-modern steroid marketplace and its criminalization. *Justice Quarterly,* 27(2):159–185.

Kraska, Peter B., and Kishonna Gray. (2006). Examining the relevance of real-world theory. Paper presented at the Academy of Criminal Justice Sciences meeting, Baltimore, Maryland.

Kraska, Peter B., and Louis J. Cubellis. (1997). Militarizing Mayberry and beyond: Making sense of American paramilitary policing. *Justice Quarterly,* 14(4):607–629.

Kraska, Peter B. and Matthew T. DeMichele. (2001, November). Policing Kentucky's School Children: Issues and Trends. Kentucky Justice & Safety Research Bulletin, 3(2), 8.

Kraska, Peter B., and Victor E. Kappeler. (1988). Police on-duty drug use: A theoretical and descriptive examination. *American Journal of Police,* 7(1):1–28.

Kraska, Peter B., and Victor E. Kappeler. (1997). Militarizing American police: The rise and normalization of paramilitary units. *Social Problems,* 44(1):1–18.

Krathwohl, David R. (1965). *How to prepare a research proposal.* Syracuse, NY: Syracuse University Bookstore.

Krienert, Jessie L. (2005). Bridging the gap between prison and community employment: An initial assessment of current information. *Criminal Justice Studies,* 18:293–303.

Krippendorff, Klaus. (1980). *Content analysis: An introduction to its methodology.* Beverly Hills, CA: Sage.

Krippendorff, Klaus. (2003). *Content analysis: An introduction to its methodology.* Thousand Oaks, CA: Sage.

Krosnick, Jon A. (1992). The impact of cognitive sophistication and attitude importance on response-order and question-order effects. In *Context effects,* edited by N. Schwarz and Sudman, pp. 203–218. New York: Springer-Verlag.

Krosnick, Jon A., Holbrook, A., and Berent, M. (2002). The impact of "no opinion" response options on data quality. *Public Opinion Quarterly,* 66:371–403.

Krosnick, Jon A., and Robert P. Abelson. (1992). The case for measuring attitude strength in surveys. In *Questions about questions: Inquiries into the cognitive bases of surveys,* edited by J. Turner, pp. 177–203. New York: Russell Sage Foundation.

Krueger, Richard A. (1988). *Focus groups: A practical guide for applied research.* Beverly Hills, CA: Sage.

Kubrin, Charles E. (2005). Gangstas, thugs, and hustlas: Identity and the code of the street in rap music. *Social Problems,* 52:360–378.

Kuhn, Thomas S. (1963). *The structure of scientific revolutions.* Chicago, IL: University of Chicago Press.

Kuhn, Thomas S. (1970). *The structure of scientific revolutions,* 2nd ed. Chicago, IL: University of Chicago Press.

Kuhn, Thomas S. (1979). The relations between history and the history of science. In *Interpretive social science: A reader,* edited by P. Rabinow and W. Sullivan. Berkeley, CA: University of California Press.

Kusserow, Richard P. (1989, March). *Misconduct in scientific research.* Report of the Inspector General of the U.S. Department of Health and Human Services. Washington, DC: Department of Health and Human Services.

Kviz, Frederick J. (1984). Bias in a directory sample for mail survey of rural households. *Public Opinion Quarterly,* 48:801–806.

Labaw, Patricia J. (1980). *Advanced questionnaire design.* Cambridge, MA: Abt Books.

Lacy, Dean. (2001). A theory of nonseparable preferences in survey responses. *American Journal of Political Science,* 45:239–258.

LaFree, Gary. (1998). Social institutions and the crime "bust" of the 1990s. *Journal of Criminal Law and Criminology,* 88(1):325–1368.

LaFree, Gary. (1999). Declining violent crime rates in the 1990s: Predicting crime booms and busts. *Annual Review of Sociology,* 25:145–168.

Lane, Jodi, Susan Turner, Terry Fain, and Amber Sehgal. (2005). Evaluating an experimental intensive juvenile probation program: Supervision and official outcomes. *Crime and Delinquency,* 51(1):26–52.

Lane, Michael. (1970). *Structuralism.* London: Jonathan Cape.

Lang, Eric. (1992). Hawthorne effect. In *Encyclopedia of sociology,* vol. 2, edited by E. and M. Borgatta, pp. 793–794. New York: Macmillan.

Lanier, Mark, and Stuart Henry. (2004). *Essential criminology,* 2nd ed. Boulder, CO: Westview.

Laslett, Barbara. (1992). Gender in/and social history. *Social Science History,* 16:177–196.

Laurence, Matt. (2004). *Like a splinter in your mind: The philosophy behind the Matrix trilogy.* Malden, MA: Blackwell.

Leal, David L., and Frederick Hess. (1999). Survey bias on the front porch: Are all subjects interviewed equally? *American Politics Quarterly*, 27:468–487.

Leggett, Glenn, C. David Mean, and William Charvat. (1965). *Prentice-Hall handbook for writers*, 4th ed. Englewood Cliffs, NJ: Prentice-Hall.

Leiter, Kenneth. (1980). *A primer on ethnomethodology.* New York: Oxford University Press.

Lemert, Charles. (1979). Science, religion and secularization. *Sociological Quarterly*, 20:445–461.

Lemert, Charles, ed. (1981). *French sociology: Rupture and renewal since 1968.* New York: Columbia University Press.

Lenzer, Gertrud, ed. (1975). *Auguste Comte and positivism: Essential writings.* New York: Harper & Row.

Leonard, Ira M., and Christopher C. Leonard. (2003). The historiography of American violence. *Homicide Studies*, 7:99–153.

Lessler, Judith T. (1984). Measurement error in surveys. In *Surveying subject phenomena*, vol. 2, edited by Charles F. Turner and Elizabeth Martin, pp. 405–440. New York: Russell Sage Foundation.

Lester, Marilyn, and Stuart C. Hadden. (1980). Ethnomethodology and grounded theory methodology: An integration of perspective and method. *Urban Life*, 9:3–33.

Levine, Joel H. (1993). *Exceptions are the rule: An inquiry into methods in the social sciences.* Boulder, CO: Westview.

Lewis, George H., and Jonathan F. Lewis. (1980). The dog in the night-time: Negative evidence in social research. *British Journal of Sociology*, 31:544–558.

Lieberson, Stanley. (1985). *Making it count: The improvement of social research and theory.* Berkeley, CA: University of California Press.

Lieberson, Stanley. (1991). Small N's and big conclusions: An examination of the reasoning of comparative studies based on a small number of cases. *Social Forces*, 70:307–320.

Liebow, Elliot. (1967). *Talley's corner.* Boston, MA: Little, Brown.

Lifton, Robert J. (1986). *Nazi doctors.* New York: Basic Books.

Lilly, J. Robert. (1996). Dirty details: Executing U.S. soldiers during World War II. *Crime and Delinquency*, 42:491–516.

Lilly, J. Robert, and Michael Thomson. (1997). Executing U.S. soldiers in England, World War II: Command influence and sexual racism. *British Journal of Criminology*, 37:262–288.

Lindzey, Gardner, and Donn Byrne. (1968). Measurement of social choice and interpersonal attractiveness. In *The handbook of social psychology*, vol. 2: *Research methods*, edited by G. Lindzey and E. Aronson, pp. 452–525. Reading, MA: Addison-Wesley.

Little, Daniel. (1991). *Varieties of social explanation: An introduction to the philosophy of science.* Boulder, CO: Westview.

Lloyd, Christopher. (1986). *Explanation in social history.* New York: Basil Blackwell.

Locke, Lawrence F., Warren Wyrick Spirduso, and Stephen J. Silverman. (1987). *Proposals that work: A guide for planning dissertations and grant proposals*, 2nd ed. Beverly Hills, CA: Sage.

Locy, Toni. (2005). Murder, violence rates fall, FBI says. *USA Today* <http://www.usatoday.com/news/nation/2005-06-06-crime-drop_x.htm?POE=NEWISVA>.

Lofland, John. (1974). Styles of reporting qualitative field research. *American Sociologist*, 9:101–111.

Lofland, John. (1976). *Doing social life: The qualitative study of human interaction in natural settings.* New York: Wiley.

Lofland, John, and Lyn H. Lofland. (1984). *Analyzing social settings*, 2nd ed. Belmont, CA: Wadsworth.

Lofland, John, and Lyn H. Lofland. (1995). *Analyzing social settings*, 3rd ed. Belmont, CA: Wadsworth.

Lofquist, William S. (1997). Constructing crime: Media coverage of individual and organizational wrongdoing. *Justice Quarterly*, 14:243–263.

Loftus, Elizabeth, Kyle D. Smith, Mark R. Klinger, and Judith Fiedler. (1992). Memory and mismemory of health events.In *Questions about questions: Inquiries into the cognitive bases of surveys*, edited by J. Turner, pp. 102–137. New York: Russell Sage Foundation.

Loftus, Elizabeth, Mark Klinger, Kyle Smith, and Judith Fiedler. (1990). A tale of two questions: Benefit of asking more than one question. *Public Opinion Quarterly*, 54:330–345.

Logan, T. K., Lisa Shannon, and Robert Walker. (2005). Protective order in rural and urban areas: A multiple perspective study. *Violence Against Women*, 11:876–911.

Long, J. Scott. (1978). Productivity and academic positions in a scientific career. *American Sociological Review*, 43:889–908.

Lowenthal, David. (1985). *The past is a foreign country.* New York: Cambridge University Press.

Lutze, Faith A. (2006). Boot camp prisons and corrections policy: Moving from militarism to an ethic of care. *Criminology and Public Policy*, 5(2):389–400.

Lyon, David. (1994). *The electronic eye: The rise of the surveillance society.* Minneapolis, MN: University of Minnesota Press.

MacKenzie, Doris L., David B. Wilson, and Suzanne Kider. (2001). Effects of correctional boot camps on offending. *The ANNALS*, 578(1):126–143.

MacKeun, Michael B. (1984). Reality, the press and citizens' political agendas. In *Surveying subjective phenomena*, vol. 2, edited by C. Turner and E. Martin, pp. 443–473. New York: Russell Sage Foundation.

Maguire, Kathleen, and Ann L. Pastore, eds. (1997). *Sourcebook of criminal justice statistics 1996.* U.S. Department of Justice, Bureau of Justice Statistics. Washington, DC: U.S. Government Printing Office.

Mahoney, James. (1999). Nominal, ordinal, and narrative appraisal in macrocausal analysis. *American Journal of Sociology,* 104:1154–1196.

Mahoney, James. (2000). Path dependence in historical sociology. *Theory and Society,* 9:507–548.

Maier, Mark H. (1991). *The data game: Controversies in social science statistics.* Armonk, NY: M. E. Sharpe.

Maines, David R., William Shaffir, and Allan Turowetz. (1980). Leaving the field in ethnographic research. In *The fieldwork experience: Qualitative approaches to social research,* edited by W. B. Shaffir, R. Stebbins, and A. Turowetz, pp. 261–280. New York: St. Martin's Press.

Maloney, Dennis M. (1984). *Protection of human research subjects: A practical guide to federal laws and regulations.* New York: Plenum.

Mann, Floyd C. (1970). Human relations skills in social research. In *Qualitative methodology,* edited by W. J. Filstead. Chicago, IL: Markham.

Manning, Peter K., and Betsy Cullum-Swan. (1994). Narrative content, and semiotic analysis. In *Handbook of qualitative research,* edited by N. K. Denzin and Y. S. Lincoln, pp. 463–83. New York: Sage.

Marenin, Otwin. (1996). *Policing change, changing police: International perspectives.* New York: Garland.

Markoff, John. (1997, March 12). Dispute over unauthorized reviews leaves intel embarassed. *New York Times.*

Marquart, James W. (1986). Doing research in prison: The strengths and weaknesses of full participation as a guard. *Justice Quarterly,* 3(1):15–32.

Marquart, James W. (2001). Doing research in prison: The strengths and weaknesses of full participation as a guard. In *Extreme methods: Innovative approaches to social science research,* edited by Mitchell Miller and Richard Tewksbury. Boston, MA: Allyn and Bacon.

Marquart, James W., Sheldon Ekland-Olson, and Jonathan Sorensen. (1989). Gazing into the crystal ball: Can jurors accurately predict dangerousness in capital cases? *Law and Society Review,* 23:449–468.

Marsh, Catherine. (1982). *The survey method: The contribution of surveys to sociological explanation.* Boston, MA: George Allen and Unwin.

Martin, Elizabeth. (1985). Surveys as social indicators: Problems of monitoring trends. In *Handbook of survey research,* edited by P. Rossi, J. Wright, and A. Anderson, pp. 677–743. Orlando, FL: Academic.

Martin, Elizabeth. (2004). Vignettes and respondent debriefing for questionnaire design. In *Methods for testing and evaluating survey questionnaires,* edited by S. Presser, M. Couper, J. Lessler, E. Martin, J. Martin, J. Tothgeb, E. Singer, pp. 149–172. New York: Wiley.

Martin, Jay. (1973). *The dialectical imagination.* Boston, MA: Little, Brown.

Martin, John L., and Laura Dean. (1993). Developing a community sample of gay men for an epidemiological study of AIDS. In *Research on sensitive topics,* edited by C. Renzetti and R. Lee, pp. 82–100. Thousand Oaks, CA: Sage.

Martin, Margaret E. (1997). Double your trouble: Dual arrest in family violence. *Journal of Family Violence,* 12:139–157.

Marvasti, Amir B. (2004). *Qualitative research in sociology.* Thousand Oaks CA: Sage.

Marx, Anthony W. (1998). *Making race and nation: A comparison of the United States, South Africa and Brazil.* New York: Cambridge University Press.

Maxfield, Michael G., and Earl Babbie. (2005). *Research methods for criminal justice and criminology.* Belmont, CA: Wadsworth.

Mayer, Charles S., and Cindy Piper. (1982). A note on the importance of layout in self-administered questionnaires. *Journal of Marketing Research,* 19:390–391.

Mayhew, Bruce H. (1980). Structuralism versus individualism, Part I: Shadowboxing in the dark. *Social Forces,* 59:335–375.

Mayhew, Bruce H. (1981). Structuralism versus individualism, Part II: Ideological and other obfuscations. *Social Forces,* 59:627–648.

McCall, George. (1969). Quality control in participant observation. In *Issues in participant observation,* edited by G. McCall and J. L. Simmons, pp. 128–141. Reading, MA: Addison-Wesley.

McCarthy, Thomas. (1978). *The critical theory of Jurgen Habermas.* Cambridge, MA: MIT Press.

McCord, Joan. (2001). Crime prevention: A cautionary tale. Paper presented at the Proceedings of the Third International Inter-Disciplinary Studies conference. New York, NY.

McCracken, Grant. (1988). *The long interview.* Thousand Oaks, CA: Sage.

McDaniel, Timothy. (1978). Meaning and comparative concepts. *Theory and Society,* 6:93–118.

McFarland, Sam G. (1981). Effects of question order on survey responses. *Public Opinion Quarterly,* 45:208–215.

McIver, John P., and Edward G. Carmines. (1981). *Unidimensional scaling.* Beverly Hills, CA: Sage.

McKee, J. McClendon, and David J. O'Brien. (1988). Question order effects on the determinants of subjective well being. *Public Opinion Quarterly,* 52:351–364.

McVeigh, Rory, Michael Welch, and Thoroddur Bjarnason. (2003). Hate crime reporting as a successful social movement outcome. *American Sociological Review,* 68:843–867.

Meadows, Arthur Jack. (1974). *Communication in science.* Toronto: Butterworths.

Mehan, Hugh, and Houston Wood. (1975). *The reality of ethnomethodology.* New York: Wiley.

Meier, Barry. (1998, May 7). Philip Morris censored data about addiction. *New York Times.*

Mendelberg, Tali. (1997). Executing Hortons: Racial crime and the 1988 presidential campaign. *Public Opinion Quarterly,* 61:134–157.

Mendenhall, William, Lyman Ott, and Richard L. Scheaffer. (1971). *Elementary survey sampling.* Belmont, CA: Duxbury Press.

Merton, Robert K. (1957). *Social theory and social structure.* New York: Free Press.

Merton, Robert K. (1970). *Science, technology and society in seventeenth century England.* New York: Harper & Row.

Merton, Robert K. (1973). *The sociology of science.* Chicago, IL: University of Chicago Press.

Miles, Matthew B., and Michael Huberman, A. (1994). *Qualitative data analysis,* 2nd ed. Thousand Oaks, CA: Sage.

Milgram, Stanley. (1963). Behavioral study of obedience. *Journal of Abnormal and Social Psychology,* 6:371–378.

Milgram, Stanley. (1965). Some conditions of obedience and disobedience to authority. *Human Relations,* 18:57–76.

Milgram, Stanley. (1974). *Obedience to authority.* New York: Harper & Row.

Miller, Delbert C. (1991). *Handbook of research design and social measurement,* 5th ed. Newbury Park, CA: Sage.

Miller, J. Mitchell, and Richard Tewksbury, eds. (2000). *Extreme methods: Innovative approaches to social science research.* New York: Addison Wesley, Longman.

Miller, Jody. (2000). Feminism and the study of girls' delinquency. *DivisionNews* Winter 2000–2001. American Society of Criminology <www.ou.edu/soc/dwc/ newsletter4.htm>.

Miller, Jody. (2001). *One of the guys: Girls, gangs and gender.* New York: Oxford University Press.

Miller, Jody. (2006). The status of qualitative research in criminology. In *Workshop on interdisciplinary standards for systematic qualitative research.* Washington, DC: National Science Foundation.

Miller, Richard. (1987). *Fact and method: Explanation, confirmation and reality in the natural and social sciences.* Princeton, NJ: Princeton University Press.

Miller, Susan. (2001). The paradox of women arrested for domestic violence. *Violence Against Women,* 7(12):1339–1376.

Miller, William L. (1983). *The survey method in the social and political sciences: Achievements, failures and prospects.* London: Frances Pinter.

Mills, C. Wright. (1959). *The sociological imagination.* New York: Oxford University Press.

Miniter, Richard. (2006). Jousting with the lancet. *Pajamasmedia* <http://pajamasmedia.com/2006/10/joisting_with_the_lancet_the_p.php>.

Mishler, Elliot G. (1986). *Research interviewing: Context and narrative.* Cambridge, MA: Harvard University Press.

Mitchell, Alison. (1997, May 17). Survivors of Tuskegee study get apology from Clinton. *New York Times.*

Mitchell, Mark, and Janina Jolley. (1988). *Research design explained.* New York: Holt, Rinehart and Winston.

Mitchell, Richard G., Jr. (1993). *Secrecy and fieldwork.* Thousand Oaks, CA: Sage.

Mitroff, Ian. (1974). Norms and counter-norms in a select group of the Apollo moon scientists: A case study of ambivalence of scientists. *American Sociology Review,* 39:579–595.

Molotch, Harvey, William Freudenburg, and Krista Paulsen. (2000). History repeats itself, but how? City character, urban tradition, and the accomplishment of place. *American Sociological Review,* 65:791–823.

Moore, Joan. (1973). Social constraints on sociological knowledge: Academic and research concerning minorities. *Social Problems,* 21:65–77.

Moore, Robert J. (2004). Managing troubles in answering survey questions: Respondents' uses of projective reporting. *Social Psychology Quarterly,* 67:50–69.

Morrison, Brenda, and Eliza Ahmed. (2006). Restorative justice and civil society: Emerging practice, theory, and evidence. *Journal of Social Issues,* 62(2):209–215.

Morse, Janice M. (1994). Designing funded qualitative research. In *Handbook of qualitative research,* edited by N. Denzin and Y. Lincoln, pp. 220–235. Thousand Oaks, CA: Sage.

Moser, Claus Adolf, and Graham G. W. Kalton. (1972). *Survey methods in social investigation.* New York: Basic Books.

Mostyn, Barbara. (1985). The content analysis of qualitative research data: A dynamic approach. In *The research interview: Uses and approaches,* edited by M. Brenner, J. Brown, and D. Canter, pp. 115–145. New York: Academic Press.

Mueller, John. (2006). Is there still a terrorist threat? The myth of the omnipresent enemy. *Foreign Affairs* <http://www.foreignaffairs.org/20060901facomment85501/john-mueller/is-there-still-a-terrorist-threat.html>.

Mulkay, Michael. (1979). *Science and the sociology of knowledge.* London: George Allen and Unwin.

Mullins, Carolyn J. (1977). *A guide to writing and publishing in the social and behavioral sciences.* New York: Wiley.

Mullins, Nicholas C. (1971). *The art of theory: Construction and use.* New York: Harper & Row.

Nash, Jeffrey E., and David W. McCurdy. (1989). Cultural knowledge and systems of knowing. *Sociological Inquiry,* 59:117–126.

Nederhof, Anton J. (1986). Effects of research experiences of respondents. *Quality and Quantity,* 20:277–284.

Neuman, W. Lawrence. (1992). Gender, race and age differences in student definitions of sexual harassment. *Wisconsin Sociologist,* 29:63–75.

Novick, Peter. (1988). *That noble dream: The "objectivity question" and the American historical profession.* New York: Cambridge University Press.

Nunnally, Jum C. (1978). *Psychometric theory.* New York: McGraw-Hill.

Oksenberg, Lois, Lerita Coleman, and Charles F. Cannell. (1986). Interviewers' voices and refusal rates in telephone surveys. *Public Opinion Quarterly,* 50:97–111.

Olsen, Virginia. (1994). Feminism and models of qualitative research. In *Handbook of qualitative research,* edited by N. Denzin and Y. Lincoln, pp. 158–174. Thousand Oaks, CA: Sage.

Olzak, Susan, and Suzanne Shanahan. (2003). Racial Policy and Racial conflict in the United States, 1869–1924. *Social Forces,* 82:481–518.

Ong, Andy S. J., and Colleen A. Ward. (1999). The effects of sex and power schemas, attitudes toward women, and victim resistance on rape attributions. *Journal of Applied Social Psychology,* 29:362–376.

Oreskes, Naomi. (2004). Beyond the ivory tower: The scientific consensus on climate change. *Science,* 306(5702):1686–1698.

O'Toole, Kevin, Neville Millen, and Ranjut Murugason. (1994). *Fraud against organizations in Victoria.* Geelong, Australia: Deakin University Press.

Ouimet, Marc. (2004). Explaining the American and Canadian crime drop in the 1990s. *Champ Penal/Penal Field,* 44:33–50.

Paige, Jeffrey M. (1975). *Agrarian revolution.* New York: Free Press.

Parcel, Toby L. (1992). Secondary data analysis and data archives. In *Encyclopedia of sociology,* vol. 4, edited by E. and M. Borgatta, pp. 1720–1728. New York: Macmillan.

Patrick, Steven, Robert Marsh, Wade Bundy, Susan Mimura, and Tina Perkins. (2004). Control group study of juvenile diversion programs. *Social Science Journal,* 41:129–35.

Paulos, John Allen. (2001). *Innumeracy: Mathematical illiteracy and its consequences.* New York: Hill and Wang.

Pauwels, Lieven, and Stefaan Pleysier. (2005). Assessing cross-cultural validity of fear of crime measures through comparisons between linguistic communities in Belgium. *European Journal of Criminology,* 2(2):139–159.

Pearsall, Marion. (1970). Participant observation as role and method in behavioral research. In *Qualitative methodology,* edited by W. J. Filstead, pp. 340–352. Chicago, IL: Markham.

Pearson, Michael Ross, and Robyn M. Dawes. (1992). Personal recall and the limits of retrospective questions in surveys. In *Questions about questions: Inquiries into the cognitive bases of surveys,* edited by J. Turner, pp. 65–94. New York: Russell Sage Foundation.

Pedriana, Nicholas. (2005). Rational choice, structural context, and increased return. *Sociological Methods and Research,* 33:349–382.

Pettit, Becky, and Bruce Western. (2004). Mass imprisonment and the life course. *American Sociological Review,* 69:151–169.

Phillips, Denis Charles. (1987). *Philosophy, science and social inquiry: Contemporary methodological controversies in social science and related applied fields of research.* New York: Pergamon.

Piquero, Alex R., Robert Brame, Jeffrey Fagan, and Terrie Moffitt. (2005). Assessing the offending activity of criminal domestic violence suspects. Final Report, Washington, DC: U.S. Department of Justice.

Poe, Gail S., Isadore Seeman, Joseph McLaughlin, Eric Mehl, and Michael Dietz. (1988). "Don't know" boxes in factual questions in a mail questionnaire: Effects on level and quality of response. *Public Opinion Quarterly,* 52:212–222.

Politics and Science. (2006). The science on global warming. *Government Reform Minority Office* <http://oversight.house.gov/features/politics_and_science/index.htm>.

Polsky, Ned. (1969) *Hustlers, beats, and others.* Garden City, NY: Anchor Books.

Polsky, Ned. (1997). Research method, morality, and criminology. In *The subcultures reader,* edited by Ken Gelder and Sarah Thornton, pp. 217–230. London: Routledge.

Popkin, Margaret L. (2000). *Peace without justice: Obstacles to building the rule of law in El Salvador.* University Park, PA: Penn State University Press.

Popovich, Paula M., Betty Jo Licata, Deeann Nokovich, Theresa Martelli, and Sheryl Zoloty. (1986). Assessing the incidence and perceptions of sexual harassment behaviors among American undergraduates. *The Journal of Psychology: Interdisciplinary and Applied.* 120(4):387–396.

Popper, Karl. (1959/1934). *The logic of scientific discovery.* New York: Basic Books.

Porter, Theodore M. (1995). *Trust in numbers: The pursuit of objectivity in science and the public life.* Princeton, NJ: Princeton University Press.

Powers, Edwin, and Helen Witmer. (1951). *An experiment in the prevention of delinquency: The Cambridge-Somerville Youth Study.* New York: Columbia University Press.

Pratt, Travis C., Michael J. Gaffney, and Nicholas P. Lovrich. (2006). This isn't CSI: Estimating the national backlog of forensic DNA cases and the barriers associated with case processing. *Criminal Justice Police Review,* 17(1):32–47.

Prewitt, Kenneth. (1983). Management of survey organizations. In *Handbook of social research,* edited by P. Rossi, J. Wright, and A. Anderson, pp. 123–143. Orlando, FL: Academic Press.

Prucha, Francis Paul. (1987). *Handbook for research in American history: A guide to bibliographies and other reference works.* Lincoln, NE: University of Nebraska Press.

Przeworski, Adam, and Henry Teune. (1970). *The logic of comparative inquiry.* New York: Wiley.

Punch, Maurice. (1986). *The politics and ethics of fieldwork.* Beverly Hills, CA: Sage.

Pusey, Michael. (1987). *Jügen Habermas.* New York: Tavistock.

Quammen, David. (2006). *The reluctant Mr. Darwin: An intimate portrait of Charles Darwin and the making of his theory of evolution.* New York: W.W. Norton.

Quarles, Susan D., ed. (1986). *Guide to federal funding for social scientists.* New York: Russell Sage Foundation.

Rafter, Nicole. (2004). The unrepentant horse-slasher: Moral insanity and the origins of criminological thought. *Criminology,* 42(4):979–1008.

Ragin, Charles C. (1987). *The comparative method.* Berkeley, CA: University of California Press.

Ragin, Charles C. (1989). New directions in comparative research. In *Cross-national research in sociology,* edited by M. Kohn, pp. 57–76. Newbury Park, CA: Sage.

Ragin, Charles C. (1992). Introduction: Cases of "what is a case?" In *What is a case: Exploring the foundations of social inquiry,* edited by C. Ragin and H. Becker, pp. 1–18. New York: Cambridge University Press.

Ragin, Charles C. (1994). *Constructing social research.* Thousand Oaks, CA: Pine Forge Press.

Rawls, John. (2005). *A theory of justice.* Cambridge, MA: Harvard University Press.

Rebellon, Cesar, and Karen Gundy. (2005). Can control theory explain the link between parental physical abuse and delinquency? A longitudinal analysis. *Journal of Research in Crime and Delinquency,* 42(3):247–274.

Reese, Stephen, Wayne A. Danielson, Pamela J. Shoemaker, Tsan-Kuo Chang, and Huei-Ling Hsu. (1986). Ethnicity of interview effects among Mexican Americans and Anglos. *Public Opinion Quarterly,* 50:563–572.

Reilly, T., Carpenter, S., Dull, V., and Bartlett, K. (1982). The factorial survey technique: An approach to defining sexual harassment on campus. *Journal of Social Issues,* 38, 99–110.

Reinharz, Shulamit. (1992). *Feminist methods in social research.* New York: Oxford University Press.

Reskin, Barbara. (1977). Scientific productivity and the reward structure of science. *American Sociological Review,* 42:491–504.

Reynolds, Paul Davidson. (1971). *A primer in theory construction.* Indianapolis, IN: Bobbs-Merrill.

Reynolds, Paul Davidson. (1979). *Ethical dilemmas and social science research.* San Francisco, CA: Jossey-Bass.

Reynolds, Paul Davidson. (1982). *Ethics and social science research.* Englewood Cliffs, NJ: Prentice-Hall.

Rhodes, Richard. (1999). *Why they kill: The discoveries of a maverick criminologist.* New York: Random House.

Richards, Thomas J., and Lyn Richards. (1994). Using computers in qualitative research. In *Handbook of qualitative research,* edited by N. Denzin and Y. Lincoln, pp. 445–462. Thousand Oaks, CA: Sage.

Ricoeur, Paul. (1970). The model of the text: Meaningful action considered as a text. In *Interpretative social science: A reader,* edited by P. Rabinow and W. Sullivan, pp. 73–102. Berkeley, CA: University of California Press.

Rifkin, Jeremy. (1995). *The end of work.* New York: Putnam.

Risman, Barbara J. (2001). Calling the bluff of value-free science. *American Sociological Review,* 66:605–618.

Ritzer, George. (1975). *Sociology: A multi-paradigm science.* Boston, MA: Allyn and Bacon.

Roadburg, Alan. (1980). Breaking relationships with field subjects: Some problems and suggestions. In *Fieldwork experience,* edited by W. B. Shaffir, R. Stebbins, and A. Turowetz, pp. 281–291. New York: St. Martin's Press.

Robertson, John A. (1982). The social scientist's right to research and the IRB system. In *Ethical issues in social science research,* edited by T. L. Beauchamp, R. Faden, R. J. Wallace, and L. Walters, pp. 356–372. Baltimore, MD: Johns Hopkins University Press.

Robinson, John P., Jerrold G. Rusk, and Kendra B. Head. (1972). *Measures of political attitudes.* Ann Arbor, MI: Center for Political Studies, Institute for Social Research, University of Michigan.

Robinson, John P., and Philip R. Shaver. (1969). *Measures of social psychological attitudes.* Ann Arbor, IN: Survey Research Center, Institute for Social Research, University of Michigan.

Roderick, Rick. (1986). *Habermas and the foundations of critical theory.* New York: St. Martin's Press.

Roethlisberger, Fritz J., and William J. Dickenson. (1939). *Management and the worker.* Cambridge, MA: Harvard University Press.

Rosenbaum, Dennis P., and Gordon S. Hanson. (1998). Assessing the effects of school-based drug education: A six-year multilevel analysis of project D.A.R.E. *Journal of Research in Crime and Delinquency,* 35(4):381–412.

Rosenberg, Morris. (1968). *The logic of survey analysis.* New York: Basic Books.

Ross, Dorothy. (1991). *The origins of American social science.* New York: Cambridge University Press.

Rossi, Peter Henry., and Andy B. Anderson. (1982). The factorial survey approach: An introduction. In *Measuring social judgments,* edited by P. H. Rossi and S. L. Nock.

Rotton, James, and Ellen G. Cohn. (2000). Weather, disorderly conduct, and assaults. *Environment and Behavior,* 32(5):651–673.

Rousey, Dennis. (1996). *Policing the Southern City: New Orleans, 1805–1889.* Baton Rouge, LA: Louisiana State University Press.

Roy, Donald. (1970). The study of southern labor union organizing campaigns. In *Pathways to data,* edited by R. W. Habenstein, pp. 216–244. Chicago, IL: Aldine.

Rueschemeyer, Dietrich, and John Stephens. (1997). Comparing historical sequences: A powerful tool for causal analysis. *Comparative Social Research,* 16:55–72.

Sabia, Daniel R., Jr., and Jerald T. Wallulis. (1983). *Changing social science: Changing theory and other critical perspectives.* Albany, NY: State University of New York at Albany.

Sagarin, Edward. (1973). The research setting and the right not to be researched. *Social Problems,* 21:52–64.

Sanday, Peggy Reeves. (1983). The ethnographic paradigm(s). In *Qualitative methodology,* edited by J. Van Maanen, pp. 19–36. Beverly Hills, CA: Sage.

Sanders, Clinton R. (2006). The dog you deserve. *Journal of Contemporary Ethnography,* 35:148–172.

Sanjek, Roger. (1990). On ethnographic validity. In *Field notes: The makings of anthropology,* edited by R. Sanjek, pp. 385–418. Ithaca, NY: Cornell University Press.

Savelsberg, Joachim J., Ryan King, and Lara Cleveland. (2002). Politicized scholarship? Science on crime and the state. *Social Problems,* 49:327–48.

Savelsberg, Joachim J., and Sarah M. Flood. (2004). Criminological knowledge: Period and cohort effects in scholarship. *Criminology,* 42(4):1009–1041.

Sayer, Andrew. (1992). *Method in social science: A realist approach,* 2nd ed. New York: Routledge.

Scarce, Rik. (1995). Scholarly ethics and courtroom antics: Where researchers stand in the eyes of the law. *American Sociologist,* 26(1):87–112.

Schacter, Daniel L., ed. (1995). *Memory distortion: How minds, brains, and societies reconstruct the past.* Cambridge, MA: Harvard University Press.

Schacter, Daniel L. (2001). *The seven deadly sins of memory: How the mind forgets and remembers.* Boston, MA: Houghton Mifflin.

Schaefer, David R., and Don A. Dillman. (1998). Development of a standard e-mail methodology. *Public Opinion Quarterly,* 62:378–397.

Schaeffer, Nora Cate. (1980). Evaluating race-of-interviewer effects in a national survey. *Sociological Methods and Research,* 8:400–419.

Schaeffer, Nora Cate. (2004). Conversation with a purpose—or conversation? In *Standardization and tacit knowledge,* edited by Douglas W. Maynard, pp. 95–123. New York: Wiley.

Schaeffer, Nora Cate, and Stanley Presser. (2003). The science of asking questions. *Annual Review of Sociology,* 29:65–88.

Schatzman, Leonard, and Anselm L. Strauss. (1973). *Field research: Strategies for a natural sociology.* Englewood Cliffs, NJ: Prentice-Hall.

Scheuch, Erwin K. (1990). The development of comparative research: Towards causal explanations. In *Comparative methodology,* edited by E. Ø[Q1]yen, pp. 19–37. Newbury Park, CA: Sage.

Schneider, Mark A. (1987). Culture-as-text in the work of Clifford Geertz. *Theory and Society,* 16:809–883.

Schober, Michael, and Frederick G. Conrad. (1997). Does conversational interviewing reduce survey measurement error? *Public Opinion Quarterly,* 61:576–602.

Schober, Michael, and Frederick G. Conrad. (2004). A collaborative view of standardized survey interview. In S*tandardization and tacit knowledge,* edited by Douglas W. Maynard et al., pp. 67–94. New York: Wiley.

Schuessler, Karl. (1982). *Measuring social life feelings.* San Francisco, CA: Jossey-Bass.

Schuman, Howard. (1992). Context effects: State of the past/state of the art. In *Context effects in social and psychological research,* edited by N. Schwarz and S. Sudman, pp. 5–20. New York: Springer-Verlag.

Schuman, Howard, and Jacob Ludwig. (1983). The norm of even-handedness in surveys as in life. *American Sociological Review,* 48:112–120.

Schuman, Howard, and Jean M. Converse. (1971). Effects of black and white interviewers on black response in 1968. *Public Opinion Quarterly,* 65:44–68.

Schuman, Howard, and Stanley Presser. (1979). The open and closed question. *American Sociological Review,* 44:692–712.

Schuman, Howard, and Stanley Presser. (1981). *Questions and answers in attitude surveys: Experiments on question form, wording and content.* New York: Academic Press.

Schwandt, Thomas A. (1994). Constructivist, interpretivist approaches to human inquiry. In *Handbook of qualitative research,* edited by N. Denzin and Y. Lincoln, pp. 118–137. Thousand Oaks, CA: Sage.

Schwandt, Thomas A. (1997). *Qualitative inquiry: A dictionary of terms.* Thousand Oaks, CA: Sage.

Schwartz, Morris, and Charlotte Green Schwartz. (1969). Problems in field observation. In *Issues in participant observation,* edited by G. J. McCall and J. L. Simmons, pp. 89–105. Reading, MA: Addison-Wesley.

Schwartz, Norbert, and Hans-J. Hippler. (1995). Subsequent questions may influence answers to preceding questions in mail surveys. *Public Opinion Quarterly,* 59:93–97.

Scott, William A. (1968). Attitude measurement. In *The handbook of social psychology,* vol. 2: *Research methods,* edited by G. Lindzey and E. Aronson, pp. 204–273. Reading, MA: Addison-Wesley.

Selvin, Hanan C., and Everett K. Wilson. (1984). On sharpening sociologists' prose. *Sociological Quarterly,* 25:205–223.

Sewell, William H., Jr. (1992). Introduction: Narratives and social identities. *Social Science History,* 16:479–488.

Sewell, William H., Jr. (1996). Three temporalities: toward an eventful sociology. In *The historical turn in the human sciences,* edited by T. McDonald, pp. 245–280. Ann Arbor, MI: University of Michigan Press.

Shadish, William R., Thomas D. Cook, and Donald T. Campbell. (2002). *Experimental and quasi-experimental designs for generalized causal inference.* Boston, MA: Houghton Mifflin.

Shafer, Robert Jones. (1980). *A guide to historical method,* 3rd ed. Homewood, IL: Dorsey.

Shaffir, William B., Robert A. Stebbins, and Allan Turowetz. (1980). Introduction. In *Fieldwork experience,* edited by W. B. Shaffir, R. Stebbins, and A. Turowetz, pp. 3–22. New York: St. Martin's Press.

Shaw, Clifford R. (1930). *The jack-roller: A delinquent boy's own story.* Chicago, IL: University of Chicago Press.

Sheatsley, Paul B. (1983). Questionnaire construction and item writing. In *Handbook of social research,* edited by P. Rossi, J. Wright, and A. Anderson, pp. 195–230. Orlando, FL: Academic Press.

Sherman, Lawrence W. (2003). Misleading evidence and evidence-led policy: Making social science more experimental. *The ANNALS,* 589(1):6–19.

Shupe, Anston D., Jr., and David G. Bromley. (1980). Walking a tightrope: Dilemmas of participation observation of groups in conflict. *Qualitative Sociology,* 2:3–21.

Sieber, Joan, ed. (1982). *The ethics of social research: Fieldwork, regulation, and publication.* New York: Springer-Verlag.

Sigelman, Lee. (1982). The uncooperative interviewee. *Quality and Quantity,* 16:345–353.

Silverman, David. (1972). Some neglected questions about social reality. In *New directions in sociological theory,* edited by P. Filmer, M. Phillipson, D. Silverman. Cambridge, MA: MIT Press.

Silverman, David. (1993). *Interpreting qualitative data.* Thousand Oaks, CA: Sage.

Singer, Eleanor. (1978). Informed consent: Consequences for response rate and response quality in social survey. *American Sociological Review,* 43:144–162.

Singer, Eleanor. (1988). Surveys in the mass media. In *Surveying social life: Papers in honor of Herbert H. Hyman,* edited by H. O'Gorman, pp. 413–436. Middletown, CT: Wesleyan University Press.

Singer, Eleanor, Dawn R. Von Thurn, and Ester R. Miller. (1995). Confidentiality assurances and response: A quantitative review of the experimental literature. *Public Opinion Quarterly,* 59:66–77.

Singer, Eleanor, and Luane Kohnke-Aguirre. (1979). Interviewer expectation effects: A replication and extension. *Public Opinion Quarterly,* 43:245–260.

Singer, Eleanor, and Martin R. Frankel. (1982). Informed consent procedures in telephone interviews. *American Sociological Review,* 47:416–126.

Singleton, Royce, Jr., Bruce C. Straits, Margaret Straits, and Ronald McAllister. (1988). *Approaches to social research.* New York: Oxford University Press.

Sitton, Thad, George L. Mehaffy, and Davis, O. L., Jr. (1983). *Oral history.* Austin, TX: University of Texas Press.

Skidmore, William. (1979). *Theoretical thinking in sociology,* 2nd ed. New York: Cambridge University Press.

Sklar, Kathryn Kish. (1991). Hull House maps and papers: Social science as women's work in the 1890s. In *The social survey in historical perspective, 1880–1940,* edited by M. Blumer, K. Bales, and K. Sklar, pp. 111–147. New York: Cambridge University Press.

Skocpol, Theda. (1984). Emerging agendas and recurrent strategies in historical sociology. In *Vision and method in historical sociology,* edited by T. Skocpol, pp. 356–392. Cambridge: Cambridge University Press.

Skocpol, Theda, and Margaret Somers. (1980). The uses of comparative history in macrosocial inquiry. *Comparative Studies in Society and History,* 22:174–197.

Skolnick, Jerome H. (1994). *Justice without trial.* New York: Macmillan.

Slater, Phil. (1977). *Origin and significance of the Frankfurt School.* Boston, MA: Routledge and Kegan Paul.

Smart, Barry. (1976). *Sociology, phenomenology, and Marxian analysis: A critical discussion of the theory and practice of a science of society.* Boston: Routledge and Kegan Paul.

Smelser, Neil J. (1959). *Social change in the industrial revolution.* Chicago, IL: University of Chicago Press.

Smelser, Neil J. (1976). *Comparative methods in the social sciences.* Englewood Cliffs, NJ: Prentice-Hall.

Smith, Daniel. (2005). Political science. *New York Times* <http://www.nytimes.com/2005/09/04/magazine/04SCIENCE.html?ex=1283486400&en=db44d8e77dacc23d&ei=5088&partner=rssnyt&emc=rss>.

Smith, John K., and Lous Heshusius. (1996). Closing down the conversation: the end of the quantitative-qualitative debate among educational inquirers. *Educational Researcher,* 15(1):4–12.

Smith, Louis M. (1994). Biographical method. In *Handbook of qualitative research,* edited by N. Denzin and Y. Lincoln, pp. 286–305. Thousand Oaks, CA: Sage.

Smith, Mary Lee, and Gene V. Glass. (1987). *Research and evaluation in education and the social sciences.* Englewood Cliffs, NJ: Prentice-Hall.

Smith, Rogers M. (1996). Science, non-science and politics. In *The historic turn in the human sciences,* edited by T. McDonald, pp. 119–159. Ann Arbor, MI: University of Michigan Press.

Smith, Tom W. (1984). The subjectivity of ethnicity. In *Surveying subjective phenomena,* vol. 2, edited by C. Turner and E. Martin, pp. 117–128. New York: Russell Sage Foundation.

Smith, Tom W. (1989). Random probes of GSS questions. *International Journal of Public Opinion Research,* 1:305–325.

Smith, Tom W. (1992). Thoughts on the nature of context effects. In *Context effects in social and psychological research,* edited by N. Schwarz and S. Sudman, pp. 163–184. New York: Springer-Verlag.

Smith, Tom W. (1995). Trends in non-response rates. *International Journal of Public Opinion Research,* 7:156–171.

Sobal, Jeffery. (1984). The content of survey introductions and the provision of informed consent. *Public Opinion Quarterly,* 48:788–793.

Sociology Writing Group, UCLA. (1991). *A guide to writing sociology papers,* 2nd ed. New York: St. Martin's Press.

Sohn-Rethel, Alfred. (1978). *Intellectual and manual labor: A critique of epistemology.* New York: Macmillan.

Somers, Margaret R. (1994). Reclaiming the epistemological "other": Narrative and the social construction of identity. In *Social theory and the politics of identity,* edited by Craig Calhoun, pp. 37–99. Cambridge MA: Blackwell.

Sonquist, John A., and William C. Dunkelberg. (1977). *Survey and opinion research: Procedures for processing and analysis.* Englewood Cliffs, NJ: Prentice-Hall.

Spector, Paul E. (1981). *Research designs.* Beverly Hills, CA: Sage.

Spector, Paul E. (1992). *Summated rating scale construction.* Newbury Park, CA: Sage.

Spradley, James P. (1970). *You owe yourself a drunk.* Boston: Little, Brown.

Spradley, James P. (1979a). *The ethnographic interview.* New York: Holt, Rinehart and Winston.

Spradley, James P. (1979b). *Participant observation.* New York: Holt, Rinehart and Winston.

Sprague, Joey, and Mary K. Zimmerman. (1989). Quality and quantity: Reconstructing feminist methodology. *American Sociologist,* 20:71–86.

Stack, Carol. (1989). Doing research in the flats. In *In the field,* edited by C. Smith and W. Kornblum, pp. 21–26. New York: Praeger.

Steensland, Brian, Jerry Z. Park, Mark D. Regnerus, Lynn D. Robinson, Bradford Wilcox, W., and Robert D. Woodberry. (2000). The measure of American religion: Toward improving the state of the art. *Social Forces,* 79(1):291–318.

Stech, Charlotte G. (1981). Trends in nonresponse rates, 1952–1979. *Public Opinion Quarterly,* 45:40–57.

Steffensmeier, Darrell J., and Jeffery T. Ulmer. (2005). *Confessions of a dying thief: Understanding criminal careers and illegal enterprise.* New Brunswick, NJ: Aldine/Transaction.

Stinchcombe, Arthur L. (1968). *Constructing social theories.* New York: Harcourt, Brace and World.

Stinchcombe, Arthur L. (1973). Theoretical domains and measurement, Part 1. *Acta Sociologica,* 16:3–12.

Stinchcombe, Arthur L. (1978). *Theoretical methods in social history.* New York: Academic Press.

Stone, Philip J., and Robert P. Weber. (1992). Content analysis. In *Encyclopedia of sociology,* vol. 1, edited by E. and M. Borgatta, pp. 290–295. New York: Macmillan.

Stoner, Norman W. (1966). *The social system of science.* New York: Holt, Rinehart and Winston.

Strauss, Anselm L. (1987). *Qualitative analysis for social scientists.* New York: Cambridge University Press.

Strauss, Anselm L., and Juliet Corbin. (1990). *Basics of qualitative research: Grounded theory procedures and techniques.* Newbury Park, CA: Sage.

Strauss, Anselm L., and Juliet Corbin. (1994). Grounding theory methodology: An overview. In *Handbook of qualitative research,* edited by N. Denzin and Y. Lincoln, pp. 273–285. Thousand Oaks, CA: Sage.

Stryker, Robin. (1996). Beyond history versus theory: Strategic narrative and sociological explanation. *Sociological Methods and Research,* 24:304–352.

Suchman, Luch, and Brigitte Jordan. (1992). Validity and the collaborative construction of meaning in face-to-face surveys. In *Questions about questions: Inquiries into the cognitive bases of surveys,* edited by J. Turner, pp. 241–267. New York: Russell Sage Foundation.

Sudman, Seymour. (1976a). *Applied sampling.* New York: Academic Press.

Sudman, Seymour. (1976b). Sample surveys. *Annual Review of Sociology,* 2:107–120.

Sudman, Seymour, and Norman M. Bradburn. (1983). *Asking questions: A practical guide to questionnaire design.* San Francisco, CA: Jossey-Bass.

Sudman, Seymour, Norman M. Bradburn, and Norbert Schwarz. (1996). *Thinking about answers: The application of cognitive processes to survey research.* San Francisco, CA: Jossey-Bass.

Sullivan, John L., and Stanley Feldman. (1979). *Multiple indicators: An introduction.* Beverly Hills, CA: Sage.

Sullivan, Mercer. (1989). *Getting paid: Youth crime and work in the inner city.* Ithaca, NY: Cornell University Press.

Suls, Jerry M., and Ralph L. Rosnow. (1988). Concerns about artifacts in psychological experiments. In *The rise of experimentation in American psychology,* edited by J. Morawski, pp. 153–187. New Haven, CT: Yale University Press.

Sumner, Colin. (1979). *Reading ideologies.* New York: Academic Press.

Survey Research Center, Institute for Social Research. (1976). *Interviewer's manual,* rev. ed. Ann Arbor, MI: University of Michigan.

Sutherland, Edwin. (1937). The professional thief. Chicago, IL: University of Chicago Press.

Sutton, John R. (2000). Imprisonment and social classification in five common-law democracies, 1955–1985. *American Journal of Sociology,* 106:350–386.

Sutton, Robbie M., and Stephen Farrall. (2005). Gender, socially desirable responding and the *fear of crime*: Are women really more anxious about *crime? British Journal of Criminology,* 45(2):212–224.

Swanborn, Peter G. (1996). A common base for quality control criteria in quantitative and qualitative research. *Quality and Quantity,* 30:19–35.

Swartz, David. (1997). *Culture and power: The sociology of Pierre Bourdieu.* Chicago, IL: University of Chicago Press.

Tagg, Stephen K. (1985). Life story interviews and their interpretation. In *The research interview: Uses and approaches,* edited by M. Brenner, J. Brown, and D. Canter, pp. 163–199. New York: Academic Press.

Tanur, Judith M. (1983). Methods for large scale surveys and experiments. In *Sociological methodology, 1983–1984,* edited by S. Leinhardt, pp. 1–71. San Francisco, CA: Jossey-Bass.

Tark, Jongyeon, and Gary Kleck. (2004). Resisting crime: The effects of victim action on the outcomes of crime. *Criminology,* 42:861–910.

Tarnai, John, and Dillman, D. (1992). Questionnaire context as a source of response differences in mail and telephone surveys. In *Context effects,* edited by N. Schwarz and S. Sudman, pp 115–129. New York: Springer-Verlag.

Tashakkori, Abbas, and Charles Teddlie. (1998). *Mixed methodology: Combining qualitative and quantitative approaches.* Thousand Oaks, CA: Sage.

Thompson, Edward P. (1978). *The poverty of theory and other essays.* New York: Monthly Review Press.

Thompson, Paul. (1978). *The voice of the past: Oral history.* New York: Oxford University Press.

Thornberry, Terence P. and Marvin D. Krohn. (2000). The self-report method for measuring delinquency and crime. *Criminal Justice,* 4:33–83.

Thorne, Barrie, and Zella Luria. (1986). Sexuality and gender in children's daily world. *Social Problems,* 33:176–190.

Thrasher, Frederic. (1927). *The Gang.* Chicago, IL: University of Chicago Press.

Timmerman, Thomas A. (2002). Violence and race in professional baseball: Getting better or worse? *Aggressive Behavior,* 28:109–116.

Tjaden, Patricia, and Nancy Thoennes. (1998). Full report of the prevalence, incidence, and consequences of violence against women. *National Institute of Justice and the Centers for Disease Control and Prevention* <http://www.ncjrs .gov/txtfiles1/nij/183781.txt>.

Todorov, Alexander. (2000a). Context effects in national health surveys. *Public Opinion Quarterly,* 64:65–76.

Todorov, Alexander. (2000b). The accessibility and applicability of knowledge: Predicting context effects in national surveys. *Public Opinion Quarterly,* 64:429–451.

Torre, Maria, and Michelle Fine. (2005). Bar none: Extending Affirmative Action to higher education in prison. *Journal of Social Issues,* 61:569–594.

Tourangeau, Roger. (1992). Context effects on responses to attitude questions. In *Context effects in social and psychological research,* edited by N. Schwarz and S. Sudman, pp. 35–47. New York: Springer-Verlag.

Tourangeau, Roger. (2004a). Survey research and societal change. *Annual Review of Psychology,* 55:775–801.

Tourangeau, Roger. (2004b). Experimental design considerations for testing and evaluating questionnaires. In *Methods for testing and evaluating survey questionnaires,* edited by Stanley Presser et al., pp. 209–224. New York: Wiley.

Tourangeau, Roger, and Tom Smith. (1996). Asking sensitive questions: The impact of data collection mode, question format and question context. *Public Opinion Quarterly,* 60:275–304.

Tourangeau, Roger, Darby Steiger, and David Wilson. (2002). Self-Administered Questions by Telephone. *Public Opinion Quarterly,* 66:265–278.

Trice, Harrison M. (1970). The "outsider's" role in field study. In *Qualitative methodology,* edited by W. J. Filstead, pp. 77–82. Chicago, IL: Markham.

Tropp, Richard A. (1982). A regulatory perspective on social science research. In *Ethical issues in social science research,* edited by T. Beauchamp, R. Faden, R. J. Wallace, and L. Walters, pp. 391–415. Baltimore, MD: Johns Hopkins University Press.

Tucker, Clyde. (1983). Interviewer effects in telephone interviewing. *Public Opinion Quarterly,* 47:84–95.

Tufte, Edward. (1983). *The visual display of quantitative information.* Cheshire, CT: Graphics Press.

Tufte, Edward. (1991). *Envisioning information,* rev. ed. Cheshire, CT: Graphics Press.

Tuma, Nancy B., and Andrew Grimes. (1981). A comparison of models of role orientations of professionals in a research oriented university. *Administrative Science Quarterly,* 21:187–206.

Turner, Charles. (1984). Why do surveys disagree? Some preliminary hypotheses and some disagreeable examples. In *Surveying subjective phenomena,* vol. 2, edited by C. Turner and E. Martin, pp. 157–214. New York: Russell Sage Foundation.

Turner, Charles, and Elizabeth Martin, eds. (1984). *Surveying subjective phenomena,* vol. 1. New York: Russell Sage Foundation.

Turner, Stephen P. (1980). *Sociological explanation as translation.* New York: Cambridge University Press.

Turner, Stephen P. (1991). The world of academic quantifiers: The Columbia University family and its connections. In *The social survey in historical perspective, 1880–1940,* edited by M. Blumer, K. Bales, and K. Sklar, pp. 269–290. New York: Cambridge University Press.

Turner, Stephen P., and Jonathan H. Turner. (1991). *The impossible science: An institutional analysis of American sociology.* Newbury Park, CA: Sage.

Ursula, Hoffman-Lange. (1987). Surveying national elites in the federal republic of Germany. In *Research methods for elite studies,* edited by George Moyser and Margaret Wagstaffe, pp. 27–47. Boston, MA: Allen and Unwin.

Vail, Angus. (2001). Researching from afar: Distance, ethnography, and testing the edge. *Journal of Contemporary Ethnography,* 30:704–725.

Valentine-French, Suzanne, and H. Lorraine Radtke. (1989). Attributions of responsibility for an incident of sexual harassment in a university setting. *Sex Roles,* 21:545–555.

Van der Zouwen, Johannes, and Johannes Smit. (2004). Evaluating survey questions by analyzing patterns of behavior codes and question-answer sequences. In *Methods for testing and evaluating survey questionnaires,* edited by S. Presser, M. Couper, J. Lessler, E. Martin, J. Martin, J. Tothgeb, E. Singer, pp. 109–130. New York: Wiley.

Van Maanen, John. (1973). Observations on the making of policemen. *Human Organization,* 32:407–418.

Van Maanen, John. (1982). Fieldwork on the beat. In *Varieties of qualitative research,* edited by J. Van Maanen, J. Dabbs, Jr., and R. Faulkner, pp. 103–151. Beverly Hills, CA: Sage.

Van Maanen, John. (1988). *Tales of the field: On writing ethnography.* Chicago, IL: University of Chicago Press.

Van Poppel, Frans, and Day, L. (1996). A test of Durkheim's theory of suicide—without committing the "ecological fallacy." *American Sociological Review,* 61:500–507.

Vaughn, Michael S. (1999). Police sexual violence: Civil liability under state tort law. *Crime and Delinquency,* 45:334–357.

Vaughn, Michael S., and Sue Carter Collins. (2004). Medical malpractice in correctional facilities: State tort remedies for inappropriate and inadequate health care administered to prisoners. *The Prison Journal,* 84(4):503–534.

Vaughan, Ted R. (1967). Government intervention in social research: Political and ethical dimensions of the Wichita jury recordings. In *Ethics, politics and social research,* edited by G. Sjøberg. New York: Schenck-man.

Veltmeyer, Henry. (1978). Marx's two methods of sociological analysis. *Sociological Inquiry,* 48:101–112.

Verrengia, Joseph. (2005). Katrina reignites global warming debate. *USA Today* <www.usatoday.com/tech/science/2005-09-01-katrina-global-warming_x.htm>.

Villarreal, Andrés. (2002). Political competition and violence in Mexico. *American Sociological Review,* 67:477–498.

Villarreal, Andrés. (2004). The social ecology of rural violence. *American Journal of Sociology,* 110:349–399.

Wade, Nicholas. (1976). IQ and heredity: Suspicion of fraud beclouds classic experiment. *Science,* 194:916–919.

Waksberg, Joseph. (1978). Sampling methods for random digit dialing. *Journal of the American Statistical Association,* 73:40–46.

Walker, Samuel. (1998). *Popular justice: A history of American criminal justice.* New York: Oxford University Press.

Wallace, Walter. (1971). *The logic of science in sociology.* Chicago, IL: Aldine.

Walmsley, Roy. (2005). World prison population list. *International Centre for Prison Studies* <http://www.kcl.ac.uk/depsta/rel/icps/world-prison-population-list-2005.pdf>.

Wardell, Mark L. (1979). Marx and his method: A commentary. *Sociological Quarterly,* 20:425–436.

Warner, R. Stephen. (1971). The methodology of Marx's comparative analysis of modes of production. In *Comparative methods in sociology,* edited by I. Vallier, pp. 49–74. Berkeley, CA: University of California Press.

Warren, Carol A. B., and Paul K. Rasmussen. (1977). Sex and gender in field research. *Urban Life,* 6:349–369.

Warren, Carol A. B., and Tracy X. Karner. (2005). *Discovering qualitative methods.* Los Angeles, CA: Roxbury Press.

Warwick, Donald P. (1982). Types of harm in social science research. In *Ethical issues in social science research,* edited by T. Beauchamp, R. Faden, R. J. Wallace, and L. Walters, pp. 101–123. Baltimore, MD: Johns Hopkins University Press.

Warwick, Donald P., and Charles A. Lininger. (1975). *The sample survey: Theory and practice.* New York: McGraw-Hill.

Wax, Rosalie H. (1971). *Doing fieldwork: Warnings and advice.* Chicago, IL: University of Chicago Press.

Wax, Rosalie H. (1979). Gender and age in fieldwork and field-work education: No good thing is done by any man alone. *Social Problems,* 26:509–522.

Webb, Eugene J. (1981). *Nonreactive measures in the social sciences.* Boston, MA: Houghton Mifflin.

Webb, Eugene J., Donald Campbell, Lee Sechrest, and Richard Schwartz. (2000). *Unobtrusive measures.* Thousand Oaks, CA: Sage.

Webb, Eugene J., Donald T. Campbell, Richard D. Schwartz, Lee Sechrest, and Janet Belew Grove. (1981). *Non-reactive measures in the social sciences,* 2nd ed. Boston, MA: Houghton Mifflin.

Weber, Max. (1974). Subjectivity and determinism. In *Positivism and sociology,* edited by A. Giddens, pp. 23–32. London: Heinemann.

Weber, Max. (1978). *Economy and society,* vol. 1, edited by G. Roth and C. Wittich. Berkeley, CA: University of California Press.

Weber, Max. (1981). Some categories of interpretative sociology. *Sociological Quarterly,* 22:151–180.

Weber, Robert P. (1984). Computer assisted content analysis: A short primer. *Qualitative Sociology,* 7:126–149.

Weber, Robert P. (1985). *Basic content analysis.* Beverly Hills, CA: Sage.

Weber-Burden, Eleanor, and Peter H. Rossi. (1982). Defining sexual harassment on campus: A replication and extension. *Journal of Social Issues,* 38, 111–120.

Weeks, Michael F., and R. Paul Moore. (1981). Ethnicity of interviewer effects on ethnic respondents. *Public Opinion Quarterly,* 45:245–249.

Weinstein, Deena. (1979). Fraud in science. *Social Science Quarterly,* 59:639–652.

Weisburd, David. (2000). Randomized experiments in criminal justice policy: Prospects and problems. *Crime and Delinquency,* 46(2):181–193.

Weisburd, David, Laura Wyckoff, Justin Ready, John Eck, Joshua Hinkle, and Frank Gajewski. (2006). Does crime just move around the corner? A controlled study of spatial displacement and diffusion of crime control benefits. *Criminology,* 44(3):549–592.

Weiss, Robert S. (1994). *Learning from strangers: The arts and method of qualitative interview studies.* New York: Free Press.

Weitzman, Eben, and Matthew Miles. (1995). *Computer programs for qualitative data analysis.* Thousand Oaks, CA: Sage.

Wells, Gary L., and Elizabeth A. Olson. (2003). Eyewitness testimony. *Annual Review of Psychology,* 54:277–295.

Wells, Gary L., Elizabeth A. Olson, and Steve Charman. (2003). Distorted retrospective eyewitness reports as functions of feedback and delay. *Journal of Experimental Psychology, Applied,* 9:42–52.

West, W. Gordon. (1980). Access to adolescent deviants and deviance. In *Fieldwork experience,* edited by W. B. Shaffir, R. A. Stebbins, and A. Turowetz, pp. 31–44. New York: St. Martin's Press.

Westmarland, Louise. (2000). Taking the flak: Operational policing, fear, and violence. In *Danger in the field,* edited by G. Lee-Treweek and S. Linkogle, pp. 26–42. New York: Routledge.

Whyte, William Foote. (1982). Interviewing in field research. In *Field research,* edited by R. G. Burgess, pp. 111–122. Boston, MA: George Allen and Unwin.

Williams, Bill. (1978). *A sampler on sampling.* New York: Wiley.

Williams, Carol I., and Gary K. Wolfe. (1979). *Elements of research: A guide for writers.* Palo Alto, CA: Mayfield.

Willimack, Diane K., Howard Schuman, Beth-Ellen Pennell, and James M. Lepkowski. (1995). Effects of prepaid non-monetary incentives on response rates and response quality in face-to-face survey. *Public Opinion Quarterly,* 59:78–92.

Willis, Gordon B. (2004). Cognitive interviewing revisited. In *Methods for testing and evaluating survey questionnaires,* edited by S. Presser, M. Couper, J. Lessler, E. Martin, J. Martin, J. Tothgeb, E. Singer, pp. 23–44. New York: Wiley.

Wilson, James Q. (1975). *Thinking about crime.* New York: Basic Books.

Wilson, John. (1982). Realist philosophy as a foundation for Marx's social theory. *Current Perspectives in Social Theory,* 3:243–263.

Wilson, Thomas P. (1970). Normative and interpretative paradigms in sociology. In *Understanding everyday life: Toward the reconstruction of sociological knowledge,* edited by J. Douglas, pp. 57–79. New York: Aldine.

Wilson, Timothy D., and Elizabeth W. Dunn. (2004). Self-knowledge: Its limits, value, and potential for improvement. *Annual Review of Psychology,* 55:493–518.

Winkler, Karen J. (1989, January 11). Dispute over validity of historical approaches pits traditionalists against advocates of new methods. *Chronicle of Higher Education,* pp. A4ff.

Winston, Chester. (1974). *Theory and measurement in sociology.* New York: Wiley.

Wolcott, Harry F. (1994). *Transforming qualitative data: Description, analysis and interpretation.* Thousand Oaks, CA: Sage.

Wood, Elisabeth Jean. (2003). *Insurgent collection action and civil war in El Salvador.* Cambridge: Cambridge University Press.

Wright, Debra L., William S. Aquilino, and Andrew J. Supple. (1998). A comparison of computer-assisted and paper-and-pencil administered questionnaires in a survey on smoking, alcohol and drug use. *Public Opinion Quarterly,* 62:311–353.

Wright, Richard T., and Scott H. Decker. (1997). *Armed robbers in action: Stickups and street culture.* Boston, MA: Northeastern University Press.

Wright, Richard T., Scott H. Decker, Allison K. Redfern, and Dietrich L. Smith. (1996). A snowball's chance in hell: Fieldwork with active residential burglars. In *In their own words*, edited by Paul Cromwell, pp. 1–7. Los Angeles, CA: Roxbury.

Wuthnow, Robert. (1979). The emergence of modern science and world system theory. *Theory and Society,* 8:215–243.

Wysong, Earl, Richard Aniskiewicz, and David Wright. (1994). Truth and DARE: Tracking drug education from graduation and symbolic politics. *Social Problems,* 41:448–468.

Yammarino, Francis, Steven Skiner, and Terry Childers. (1991). Understanding mail survey response behavior: A meta-analysis. *Public Opinion Quarterly,* 55:613–640.

Yeo, Eileen James. (1991). The social survey in social perspective, 1830–1930. In *The social survey in historical perspective, 1880–1940,* edited by M. Blumer, K. Bales, and K. Sklar, pp. 49–65. New York: Cambridge University Press.

Yu, Julie, and Harris Cooper. (1983). A quantitative review of research design effects on response rates to questionnaires. *Journal of Marketing Research,* 20:36–44.

Zeisel, Hans. (1985). *Say it with figures,* 6th ed. New York: Harper & Row.

Zhang, Sheldon X., and Lening Zhang. (2005). An experimental study of the Los Angeles County repeat offender prevention program: Its implementation and evaluation. *Criminology and Public Policy,* 4(2):205–236.

Ziman, John. (1968). *Public knowledge: An essay concerning the social dimension of science.* New York: Cambridge University Press.

Ziman, John. (1976). *The force of knowledge: The scientific dimension of society.* New York: Cambridge University Press.

Zimbardo, Philip G. (1972). Pathology of imprisonment. *Society,* 9:4–6.

Zimbardo, Philip G. (1973). On the ethics of intervention in human psychological research. *Cognition,* 2:243–256.

Zimbardo, P. G., Haney, C., and Banks, W. C. (1973, April 8). The mind is a formidable jailer: A pirandellian prison. *New York Times Magazine,* 122:38–60.

Zimbardo, P. G., Haney, C., and Banks, W. C. (1974). The psychology of imprisonment: Privation, power and pathology. In *Doing unto others,* edited by Z. Rubin. Englewood Cliffs, NJ: Prentice-Hall.

Zuckerman, Harriet. (1978). Theory choice and problem choice in science. In *Sociology of science,* edited by J. Gaston, pp. 65–95. San Francisco, CA: Jossey-Bass.

INDEX

A

Abbreviations, in survey questions, 179
Abstract, of quantitative research report, 344–345
Academic freedom, 96–97
Academic legal research (ALR), 17
  conducting, 327–329
  general idea of, 323–326
  justifying, 322–323
  socio-legal research, 326–327
Academy of Criminal Justice Sciences (ACJS), 94
Acceptable incompetent, 294
Access ladder, 287
Active membership, 286
Adler, P. A., 89, 286
African Americans
  lynchings, 16
  media myths regarding, 31
Agency reports, 373, 375
Agree/disagree responses, 185
AIDS research, 143
Ambiguity in survey questions, 179
Anachronism, 321
Analytic memos, 299
Anastasio, 212
Anderson, N., 279
Anonymity, special populations and, 92–93
Appearance of interest, 295
Applied research, 19–20
Archival material, 204
Argot, 296
Association
  for causality, 67
  measures of, 246
Assumptions, theoretical, 63
Athens, L. H., 43–45
Atkins v. Virginia (2002), 107
Attitude of strangeness, 290–291
Attitudes, research question regarding, 175
Attributes, 67
Attrition, 163
Audience
  communing with, 338–339
  knowing who it is, 339–340
  authority knowledge, 29
  axial coding, 383–384
Authority knowledge, 29

B

Bad Blood (Tuskegee Syphilis Study), 86
Ball, R. A., 64, 110
Baro, A., 211
Bart, P., 288
Basic research, 18–19
Becker, H. S., 338, 348
Behavior
  coding, 196
  compensatory, 164
  research question regarding, 175
Belenky, M. F., 113
Beliefs, research question regarding, 175
Bennett, R., 455
Berg, B., 48, 412, 416

Berger, R., 511
Best, J., 402
Bias
  interviewer, 196
  prestige, in survey questions, 180
  selection, 162–163
  social desirability, 182
Billings, D. B., 316
Binet, Alfred, 151
Biologically based theories of crime, 65
Bivariate statistics, 237
Bivariate tables
  percentaged, 244–245
  without percentages, 245
BJS (Bureau of Justice Statistics), 8, 223
Black, M. M., 334
Blaikie, N., 359
Blee, K. M., 316
Blind review, 39
Blumstein, A., 161, 353
Bogdan, R., 285
Bond, C. F., 163
Bounded autonomy, 58
Bowdlerization, 320
Bradley, 258
Bricolage, 266
Brisgone, R., 261
Broadhurst, R., 250
Brown, R. H., 359
Building rapport, 291
Bureau of Justice Statistics (BJS), 8, 223

C

Campbell, D. T., 166
Cannon, K. D., 12, 45
Cantor, N. F., 320
Carlson, S. M., 218, 222
Carr, E. H., 319, 387
Case and process, in qualitative research, 266–267
Case reviews, 329
CATI (computer-assisted telephone interviewing), 189
Causal explanation, 66–67
  potential errors in, 72
Causal hypothesis, 70–75
Causal inference, 150
Causality, inferring, 67
Causal variables, 152
Central limit theorem, 131–132
Central tendency, measures of, 233–234, 235
Chain referral sampling, 141
Characteristics
  research question regarding, 175
  of text content, 212
Chavez, L. R., 214
Chermak, S., 14, 211
Chicago school of sociology, 278–279
Child abuse, 41–45
Citation formats, for journal articles, 370–371
Classical experimental design, 157
Cleaning data, 230–232
Clear, Todd R., 98
Closed-ended question, 182–184
Cluster sampling, 135–136

Code-and-retrieve programs, 389
Code-based theory builders, 390–391
Codebook, 229, 230
Code of ethics, 94
Code sheets, 230
Coding
  categories, 216
  data, 229
  procedure, 229
  qualitative data, 382–384
Coding system, in content analysis, 349–350
Coercion, special populations and, 149
Cohort study, 86–87
Collaborative encounter model, 331
Collins, R., 98
Collins, S. C., 49
Common sense knowledge, 68
Common sense views
  CSS, 364
  ISS, 361
  PSS, 358
Communalism, 36
Community, social science, 35–36
Comparative research, 313
Compensatory behavior, 164
Competent insider performance, 301
Complete membership, 286
Compound frequency distribution (CFD), 241–242
Computer-assisted telephone interviewing (CATI), 189
Concepts, as part of theory, 63–64
Conceptualization, 109–113
  of the object of inquiry, 321
  in qualitative research, 347–348
Conceptual network builders, 390
Conceptual underpinnings of ethnographic field research, 279–280
Conclusion section, of research report, 347
Concurrent validity, 115
Conducting experiments, steps in, 156
Conducting research, 18–24
  applied research, 19–20
  basic research, 18–19
  beyond basic/applied distinction, 20
  four purposes of research, 20–24
  legal research, 327–329
  mixed methods research, 334–336
  QDA, 270–274
Confidence intervals, 132
Confidentiality
  in field research, 307
  special populations and, 93
Conflict
  in the field, 294–295
  in mixed methods research, 330
Confusion, in survey questions, 179
Consciousness, false, 60, 364
Consistency checking, 231
Constructs, clear conceptualization of, 111
Construct validity, 116
Contamination, 164
Content analysis, 13–14
  ethnographic, 18
  quantitative, 210–217

Content validity, 115
Context
   in qualitative research, 264–265
Context review of literature, 368
Contingency cleaning, 231
Continuous variables, 119
Continuum of field roles, 286
Control, in experimental research, 157
Control group, 150
Control variable, 176
Convenience sampling, 140
Convergent validity, 116
Corporate secrecy, 98–99
Correlational, survey research as, 176
Covariation, 238
Cover letter, 187
Covert observation, 90–91
Creswell, J. W., 332
Crime, fear of, 106–107
Crime and justice phenomena, 6
Crime and justice research, 4
   codes of ethics in, 94
   communing with audience, 338–339
   ethics in, 81–99
   experimental design
      logic of, 155–157
      types of, 157–161
   experiments
      choosing, 152–153
      as gold standard, 150
      meta-analysis of, 168
   importance of random assignment, 154–155
   internal and external validity, 162–167
   naïve realism and, 169
   normalizing, 293–294
   philosophical foundations, 50–76
   practical considerations, 167–168
   report writing, 339
   theory in, 62–75
   writing process
      back to the library, 342
      freewriting, 343
      know your audience, 339–340
      organizing thoughts, 341
      prewriting, 342
      rewriting, 342–344
      style and tone, 340
Crime and justice studies, 5
   ethnographic field research in, 281–282
   experimental research in, 151–152
   nonreactive research in, 205–208
   survey research in, 174
Crime and justice phenomena, 6
Criterion validity, 115–116
Critical social science (CSS), 57–60
Critical thinking, 5, 82
Cross-sectional research, 45
Cross-tabulation, 241
CSI television show, 28, 31
Cullen, F. T., 19, 23, 60, 168
Currie, E., 371
Curvilinear relationship, 239

D

Dabney, D. A., 208, 209
Danger, in the field, 292–293
D.A.R.E. (Drug Abuse Resistance Education),
   23–24, 152
Darwin, Charles, 265

Data
   cleaning, 230–232
   coding, 229
   digging it up, 204
   entering, 229–230
   hard and soft, 261
   for legal research, 328–329
   locating, 218–219
   missing, 223
   for mixed methods research, 330–336
   for QDA, 267–274
   qualitative, 14–18
   for qualitative research, 40–41
   quality, in ethnographic field research,
      300–301
   quantitative, 11–14, 147–254
   for quantitative research, 39–40
   social science, 35–36
   on terrorism, 257–259
Databases, Westlaw, 329
Data field, 230
Davis, F., 175
Death penalty, 24
Debriefing, 197
Deception
   in experimental research, 157
   in field research, 307
   of research participants, 88–89
Decker, S. H., 15, 82, 292, 353
Deductive theorizing, 65
Deep cover, 90
Demand characteristics, 166–167
Denzin, N. K., 43, 303, 332
Dependent variable, 64, 155–156
Description, thick, 280
Descriptive research, 22
Descriptive statistics, 232
Design
   experimental
      classical, 157
      factorial, 158–159
      Latin square, 158
      parts of experiment, 155–156
      preexperimental or weak, 159
      quasi-experimental, 160
      Solomon four-group, 158
      staying in control, 157
      steps in conducting an experiment, 156
      two-group posttest-only, 157–158
   legal research study, 328
   QDA study, 270
   of questionnaires, 185–188
   of research questions, 103–105
Determinism, free will *vs.,* 56, 58, 358, 361, 364
Deviant case sampling, 141–142
Developing theory, 65–66
Diagrams, in qualitative analysis, 299
Dialectic relationship, 58
Diffusion of treatment, 164
Dillman, D. A., 191, 192, 196
Direct entry method, 230
Direct observation notes, 298–299
Disclosure, 288
Discrete variables, 119
Discriminant validity, 116
Discussion section, of research report,
   346–347
Disinterested knowledge, 18
Disinterestedness, 36

Dissertations, as source of research literature,
   371, 375
Documentation, nonreactive measures, 210
Dominant ideology, 58
Donovan, B., 317
Double-barreled question, 180
Double-blind experiment, 164–165
Douglas, J. D., 301
Drug Abuse Resistance Education (D.A.R.E.),
   23–24, 152
Dual arrest, 377
Durkheim, E., 69

E

Ecological fallacy, 73
Ecological validity, 301
Editing, 344
Emerson, R. M., 278, 295
Emotional language, in survey questions, 180
Empirical evidence, 35
Epistemology, 51
Equivalence reliability, 114
Equivalent time-series design, 161
Ericson, R., 273–274
Error of segregation, 348
Essentialism, 53
Ethical dilemmas, of field research, 307
Ethics
   in crime and justice research, 80–99
   in experimental research, 151–152
   statistics and, 252–253
   in survey research, 198
Ethnographic content analysis, 13–14
Ethnographic field research, 14–15
   appropriate questions for, 282
   Chicago school of sociology, 278–279
   choosing a site and gaining access, 285–292
   conceptual/theoretical underpinnings,
      279–280
   in crime and justice studies, 281–282
   early beginnings, 278
   ethical dilemmas of, 307
   field interview, 302–304
   leaving the field, 306
   life history, 304–305
   observing and collecting data, 295–301
   relations in the field, 292–295
   reports, 348–349
   steps in a research project, 283–285
   types of questions in interviews, 305–306
   what it is, 282–283
Ethnography, 279
Evaluation
   of quality of evidence, 321
   of research articles, 375–377
Evaluation research, 23–24
Event-structure analysis, 387–388
Evidence
   empirical, 35
   evaluating quality of, 321
   good
      CSS, 58, 60, 365
      ISS, 56, 361
      PSS, 54, 358
   locating, 321
   negative, 71, 358
   organizing, 321–322
Evidence-based practice, 19
Exchange relationship, 294

Executions, IQ-based, 106–107
Executive summary, 344, 345
Existing documents/statistics
 research, 13
 example (Sentencing Project), 223–224
 locating data, 218–220
 reliability and validity, 220
 topics appropriate for, 218
Expectations, research question regarding, 175
Experimental group, 150
Experimental hypothesis, 71
Experimental mortality, 163
Experimental research, 11–12
 choosing an experiment, 152–153
 in crime and justice studies, 151–152
 design, logic of, 155–157
Experimenter expectancy, 164–165
Expert evaluation, 196
Expert witness, research and testimony, 8
Explanatory research, 22–23, 174
Explicit cover, 90
Explicit knowledge, 280
Exploratory research, 20–22
External consistency, 300–301
External criticism, 320
External validity, 165–166
Extreme case sampling, *See* Deviant case
 sampling
Eysenck, H. J., 104

F

Face sheet, 300
Face-to-face interviews, 190
Face validity, 115
Factorial design, 158–159
Fagan, J., 166
Fallacy of misplaced concreteness, 220
False consciousness, 60, 364
False premises, in survey questions, 180–181
Falsification evidence, 43
Farrington, D. P., 150, 152
Fay, B., 57, 362
Fear of crime, 106–107
Ferrell, J., 15, 29, 55, 96, 141, 263, 265, 282,
 285–286, 300, 306, 359, 382
Fetterman, D. M., 307
Field experiments, 197
Field interview, 302–304
Field notes
 analytic memos, 299
 direct observation, 298–299
 interview, 300
 jotted, 297–298
 levels, 297
 machine recordings, 299–300
 maps and diagrams, 299
 personal, 299
 researcher inference, 299
Field site, selection of, 285
Fine, G. A., 90
First-order interpretation, 267
Fischer, D. H., 321
Flexibility, organized, 284–285
Flick, U., 140
Focus group research, 302
Foddy, W., 197
Foucault, M., 45, 51, 312
Fowler, F. J., 196
Fraud, research, 82

Freedom of Information Act, 9
Free will *vs.* determinism
 CSS, 58, 364
 ISS, 56, 361
 PSS, 53–54, 358
Freewriting, 343
Frequency distributions, 232
 compound (CFD), 241–242
Frequency polygon, 232
Friday, P., 48
Full-filter question, 180
Funding
 of research, 351–353
 sponsored, 97

G

Gangé, P., 289
Gaines, L. K., 74
Gainey, R. R., 335
Garland, D., 16, 23, 255
Garner, J. H., 168
Gatekeeper, 286–287
General Social Survey (GSS), 225, 220
Gibbs, J., 110
Global warming, 51, 115, 161, 252
Good evidence
 CSS, 58, 365
 ISS, 56, 361
 PSS, 54, 358
Going native, 286
Google Scholar, 353
Gottfredson, M. R., 42
Gover, A. R., 161
Governmental research, 8
 literature review of government documents,
 371–372, 375
Governmental secrecy, 98–99
Graffiti artists, 15, 20, 29, 141, 263, 285
Grantsmanship, 351
Grattet, R., 327
Griffin, L. J., 385, 388
Grosof, M., 346
Grounded theory, 66, 264–265, 271, 277–278
Guilty knowledge, 307

H

Haarr, R. N., 22, 45, 60, 178, 365
Hagan, J., 12, 60, 238, 365
Haggerty, K. D., 208, 367
Halo effect, 32
Hamm, M., 96
Hammond, 210
Haphazard sampling, 140
Hard data, 261
Harper, D., 288
Hawthorne effect, 166
Haydu, J., 386
Heckathorn, D. D., 144
Hemmens, C., 327–328
Hidden populations, 143–144
Histogram, 232
Historical-comparative research, 16, 313
Historical contingency, 387
Historical research, 15–16
 evidence drawn upon, 314–319
 general idea of, 312–314
 limits of primary sources, 319–320
 limits of secondary sources, 319
 major features of, 314–315

project steps, 321–322
 report writing, 349
Historical review of literature, 368
History
 of ethnographic field research, 278–280
 life, 304–305
 of survey research, 173–174
History effects, 163
Holsti, O. R., 211
Honest answers, to survey questions, 182–185
Horn, R. V., 220
Huff, D., 252
Human agency, 56
Human nature
 CSS, 364
 ISS, 360
 PSS, 357
Human Rights Watch, 245
Humphreys, L., 87–88, 92
Humphreys's tearoom trade, 87–88
Hurricane Katrina, 50–51
Hypothesis, 95
 from research question to, 70
 testing and refining, 66–67, 70–71
 types of, 158, 71

I

ICPSR (Inter-University Consortium for
 Political and Social Research), 220
Independence, 238
Independent variable, 64, 67–69
Indexes, 119–120
 purpose of, 121
 weighting, 122
Inductive theorizing, 124–125, 314
Inferences, 216–217
 researcher inference notes, 299
Inferential statistics
 levels of significance, 250
 purpose of, 248
 statistical significance, 248
 type I and type II errors, 250–251
Informant, 287
Informed consent, 89–90
Institutional review boards (IRBs), 94, 95–96
Instrumentation, 163
Integrative review of literature, 368
Integrity
 in research, 262
 treatment, 156–157, 164, 167
Interactive voice response (IVR), 189
Intercoder reliability, 213–214
Internal consistency, 300
Internal criticism, 320
Internal validity, 117
 logic of, 162
 threats to, 162–167
Internet
 doing research via, 379–380
 surveys via, 191–192
Interpretation
 of legal research data, 329
 of QDA data, 270–271
 qualitative, 267
Interpretive social science (ISS), 102–106
Interrupted time-series design, 279–281
Inter-University Consortium for Political and
 Social Research (ICPSR), 359
Interval-level measurement, 224

Intervening variable, 185
Interview
    field research, 302–304
    notes, by field researcher, 300
    postexperimental, 167–168
    quantitative and qualitative, 331
    stages of, 195–196
    as type of survey, 192
Interviewer
    bias, 196
    role of, 192–195
IVR (interactive voice response), 189

J

Jackson, S., 156
Jacobs, 286
James, William, 151, 279
Jargon, in survey questions, 179
Johnson, B., 331
Jotted notes, 297–298
Journalists, as researchers, 8–9
Journals
    Crime, Media, Culture, 273, 281
    scholarly, 369–371
Judgmental sampling, 141
Junker, B. H., 286

K

Kappeler, V. E., 18, 28, 55, 110, 219, 270, 273, 324, 327, 360
Katz, C. M., 8
Klockars, C. B., 294
Knowledge
    disinterested, 18
    explicit, 280
    guilty, 307
    research-based, alternatives to, 28–33
    research question regarding, 175
    sharing, 37–39
    tacit, 280
Knowledge/power dynamic, 3–4
Koetting, M., 13
Kopel, D. B., 327–328
Kraska, P. B., 18, 97, 63, 174, 186, 215, 219, 277, 290
Kubrin, C. E., 14, 45
Kuhn's progression of knowledge, 34
Kuhn, T., 34

L

Lane, J., 157
Language
    emotional, in survey questions, 180
    of experiments, 155
    specialized, 296
Latent coding, 213, 216
Latin square design, 158
Layout of questionnaire, 187
Leading (or loaded) question, 180
Learning the ropes, in the field, 293–294
Leaving the field, 306
Legal authority, 324
Legal harm, to research participants, 87–88
Legal research, academic, 17
Leggett, G., 344
Leonard, I. M., 317
Level of involvement, in ethnographic research, 286

Level of statistical significance, 250
Levels of measurement, 117–119
Levine, 10
Life history interview, 304–305
Likert scales, 122–123
Lilly, J. R., 316
Linear relationship, 239
Linear research path, 261–262
Listening, by field researcher, 295–300
Literature review
    dissertations, 371
    evaluating research articles, 375–377
    government documents, 371
    periodicals, 369
    policy reports, 373
    reasons and types of, 367–368
    role of Internet, 379–380
    scholarly books, 371
    scholarly journals, 369–371
    systematic, conducting, 373–375
    taking notes, 377–378
Lofland, J., 348
Lofquist, W. S., 215–216
Logan, T. K., 332–333
Longitude/latitude (LL) system, 158
Longitudinal research, 46–48
Lowenthal, D., 320
Lyon, D., 367

M

Mahoney, J., 387
Maier, M. H., 220
Mail questionnaires, 188–189
Main effect/interaction effect, 158
Manifest coding, 213, 216
Maps
    in field research, 299
Marenin, O., 110
Marquart, J., 88
Martin, E., 196
Martin, J. L., 143
Martin, M. E., 218
Marx, A. W., 16
Marx, G. T., 370
Matching, *vs.* random assignment, 154–155
Maturation effect, 163
McCallum, 277
McCord, J., 11–12
McCracken, G., 291, 305
Mean, 234
Meaning, in survey research, 197–198
Measurement
    in content analysis, 212–213
    levels of, 117
    quantitative, 117–120, 119–120
Measures
    of association, 246
    of central tendency, 233–234
    unobtrusive, 204
    of variation, 234–237
Media
    mass, reporting of survey results, 198
    role in constructing views and opinions, 14, 211
Media knowledge, 31
Median, 234
Media/political myths, 31
Medical research, in prisons, 86–87

Membership, peripheral, active, and complete, 286
Member validation, 301
Meta-analysis, 168
Method section, of research report, 346
Methodological review literature, 368
Miles, M. B., 382, 383
Milgram, S., 87
Milgram's obedience study, 87
Miller, J., 265
Miller, J. M., 90
Misconduct, scientific, 82
Mishler, E. G., 303
Missing children phenomenon, 9
Missing data, 223
Mixed methods research, 17–18
    beyond conflict and exclusion, 330
    conducting, 333–336
    general idea of, 330–332
    major features of, 332–333
Mixed sampling approaches, 143–144
Mode, 233
Monomethod, 331
Morale, 110–112
Morrison, B., 30
Mortality, experimental, 163
Mueller, J., 227–229
Mulkay, M., 357

N

Naïve assumption model, 197
Naïveté, in experimental research, 169
Narrative, historical, 319
Narrative analysis, 385–387
National Crime Victimization Survey (NCVS), 8, 45, 136, 174
National Institute of Justice (NIJ), 8, 220
Natural history, 301
Naturalism, 282
Nature of reality
    CSS, 58, 363
    ISS, 55–56, 360
    PSS, 53, 357
NCVS (National Crime Victimization Survey), 8, 45, 136, 174
Negative relationship, 239
Negotiation, 288
    in the field, 292–293
Network sampling, 141
Neuman, W. L., 375
New inequalities, special populations and, 92
NIJ (National Institute of Justice), 8, 220
No-knock entries, 324
Nominal-level measurement, 118
Nonlinear research path, 261–262
Nonprobability sampling
    deviant case sampling, 141–142
    haphazard or convenience sampling, 140
    purposive or judgmental sampling, 141
    quota sampling, 140–141
    sequential sampling, 142
    snowball sampling, 141
    theoretical sampling, 142
Nonrandom sample, 140
Nonreactive data, 204, 270
Nonreactive research
    content analysis, 13–14
    in crime and justice studies, 205–208
    existing documents/statistics research, 13

nonreactive methods, 208–210
  as unobtrusive collection of data, 12
Nonresponses to questionnaire, 187, 188
Normalize field research, 293
Note taking, 296–297
  by field researcher, 297–300
  from review of literature, 377–380
Null hypothesis, 71
Nuremberg Code, 94

O

Obedience, Milgram's study of, 87
Objective(s)
  as defined by PSS, 53, 357, 358
  of literature reviews, 367–368
Objectivity, in research, 262
Object of inquiry, conceptualizing, 321
Objects of study, 5
Observation
  and collection of data in the field, 295–301
  covert, 90–91
  nonreactive, 209–210
  structured, 212
  unobtrusive, 204
One-group pretest-posttest design, 159–160
One-shot case-study design, 159
Ong, A. S. J., 158
Open coding, 382–383
Open-ended question, 182–184
Operational definition, 112
Operationalization, 109
Opinions, research question regarding, 175
Optical scan sheet, 230
Order effects, 186
Ordinal-level measurement, 118
Organization
  of evidence, 321–322
  of notes, 377–378
  of questionnaire, 186
  of thoughts, 341
O'Toole, K., 232
Overgeneralization, 32

P

Panel study, 46
Paraphrasing, 342
Park, Robert E., 279
Participatory action research, 60
Path dependency, 386
Percentaged tables, 241–243
Percentile, 235
Periodicals, as source of research literature, 369
Periodization, 387
Peripheral membership, 286
Personal experience knowledge, 31–32
Personal notes, 299
Personal theoretical framework, 62
Phenomenology, 31
Phillips, D. C., 358
Photocopying of articles, 377
Physical harm, of research participants, 86–87
Physical traces, 204
Pilot tests, 167, 196–197
Piquero, A. R., 12
Placebo effect, 167
Plagiarism, 82, 342
Planning
  for entering field site, 287
  experimental, 167

Policies, research question regarding, 175
Policing research, 94, 96
Policy reports, 373, 375
Politicians
  as sources of knowledge, 29
  and tautology, 73
Politics
  of crime and justice research, 80–99
  science and, 96–99
Polsky, 285, 288, 293
Population parameter, 129
Populations, 129
  hidden, 143
  special, 91–92
Population validity, 166
Positive relationship, 239
Positivist social science (PSS), 53–54, 357–359
Possible code cleaning, 231
Postexperimental interview, 167–168
Posttest, as part of an experiment, 155
Power, in knowledge/power dynamic, 3–4
Powers, E., 11PQI (index score of program quality), 121
Practitioner-based research, 8
Pratt, T. C., 31
Praxis, 365
Precision, 239
Precoding, 229
Predictive validity, 115
Preexperimental designs, 159
Premature closure, 32
Presentation of self, in the field, 289–290
Presented papers, 373, 375
Prestige bias, in survey questions, 180
Pretests, as part of an experiment, 155
Prewriting, 342
Primary authority, 324
Primary sources
  in historical research, 315–317
  limits of, 319–320
Principal investigator (PI), 352
Prisons, medical research, 86–87
Privacy, special populations and, 92
Probability proportionate to size (PPS), 136
Probability sampling
  necessity for randomness, 129–130
  populations, cases, and sampling frames, 129
  sample size, 137, 139
  types of probability samples, 130–137
  vocabulary of, 129
Probe, 195
Problem presentation, in quantitative research report, 346
Professors, as researchers, 7–8
Proportionate reduction in error (PRE), 246
Proposition, 64
Pseudoproof, 321
Psychological abuse, of research participants, 87
Publishing, ethnographic field reports, 307
Purpose of CSS, 57, 362–363
Purpose of ISS, 55, 360
Purpose of PSS, 53, 357
Purposes of research
  description, 22
  evaluation, 23–24
  explanation, 22–23
  exploration, 20–22
Purposive sampling, 141

Q

Qualitative data, 18–22
  analysis techniques, 381
  analytic strategies for, 384–387
  coding, 382–384
  software, 389–390
Qualitative document analysis (QDA), 15
  applications, 268–270
  conducting, 270–271, 273–274
  general idea of, 267–268
  Wrap-Up, 274
Qualitative research, 10–18
  basics, 260
  conceptualization in, 381–382
  example: violent criminals, 43–45
  features of, 264–267
  vs. quantitative research, 260–264
  report, 347–349
  steps, 40–41
Quality field data, 300
Quammen, D., 265
Quantitative content analysis
  coding, validity, and reliability, 213–214
  inferences, 216–217
  measurement and coding, 212–213
  research, 214–215
  topics appropriate for, 211
  with visual material, 214
  what it is, 210–211
Quantitative data analysis
  dealing with data, 229–232
  ethics and statistics, 252–253
  inferential statistics, 248–251
  results with one variable, 232–237
  results with two variables, 237–246
  statistics on causes of dying, 227–228
Quantitative measurement, 178–179
  levels of measurement, 117–119
  scales and indexes, 119–120
Quantitative research, 10–18
  conceptualization and operationalization, 112–113
  example: child abuse, 41–43
  qualitative vs., 260–264
  reliability and validity, 114–117
  report, 504, 344–347
  steps, 39–40
Quasi-experimental designs, 160–161
Questionnaire construction
  agree/disagree or ratings, 185
  aiding respondent recall, 181–182
  avoiding nonresponses, 187–188
  design issues, 185–186
  format and layout, 187
  getting honest answers, 182–184
  open-ended and closed-ended questions, 182–184
  principles of good question writing, 178–179
Questions
  for ethnographic field research, 282
  in field interviews, 305–306
  focusing
    for legal research, 327–328
    for QDA, 270
  formulation for content analysis research, 214–215
  for research, See Research questions
Quota sampling, 140–141

R

Ragin, C. C., 266
Random assignment, 153–155
Random-digit dialing (RDD), 136–137
Random sample, 129–130
Range, 234
Rapaport, E., 212
Rapport building, 291
Ratio-level measurement, 118–119
Raw count tables, 242
Rawls, J., 355
Reactivity, 166–167
Reading a percentaged table, 244–245
Reality, nature of
   CSS, 58, 363
   ISS, 55–56, 360
   PSS, 53, 357
Rebellon, C., 42, 45–46, 48
Recall, respondent, 181–182
Recollections, 317–319
Recording
   by machine, in field research, 299–300
   of nonreactive measures, 210
Recording sheet, 216
Reductionism, 73–74
Rees, 144
Refining a hypothesis, 70–71
Reflexivity, 283
Regression, statistical, 163–164
Reification, 364
Reliability
   content analysis, 213–214
   existing documents/statistics, 220
   in field research, 300–301
   in qualitative *vs.* quantitative research, 263
   relationship to validity, 116
Replication, 358
Report writing, 322, 273
   qualitative research, 347–349
   quantitative research, 344–347
   reasons for, 339
Representative reliability, 114
Reputational sampling, 141
Request for proposals (RFP), 352
Research, *See also specific types of research*
   conducting, 10–18
      applied research, 19–20
      basic research, 18–19
      four purposes of research, 20–24
      legal research, 327–329
      mixed methods research, 330–336
      QDA, 270–274
   experimental, 11–12
      in crime and justice studies, 151–152
   focus group, 302
   ideals, *vs.* political realities, 96–97
   policing of, 94–96
   qualitative *vs.* quantitative, 260–264
   relevance of, 4–5
   report
      impact of, 353
      qualitative, 347–349
      quantitative, 344–347
Research atrocities, 84
Research fraud, 82
Research honesty, 36
Researcher inference notes, 299
Researchers
   exploratory, 20–22

governmental research, 8
   as instrument, 290
   journalists, 8–9
   practitioner-based research, 8
   professors in practice, 7–8
   students, 9–10
Research fraud, 82
Research proposal, 351–353
Research questions
   appropriate for survey research, 175
   designing, 103–105
   hypotheses following from, 70
Resistance, as self-protection measure, 13
Resources, access to, 104
Response categories, overlapping or
      unbalanced, 181
Results section, of research report, 346
Results with one variable
   frequency distributions, 232
   measures of central tendency, 233–234
   measures of variation, 234–237
Results with two variables
   bivariate relationship, 237–238
   bivariate tables, 241–245
   measures of association, 246
   scattergram, 239
Retrospective interviews, 196
Revising, 344
Rewriting, 342–344
Rifkin, J., 73
Risks in the field, 292–293
Roles in the field
   negotiations and danger, 292–293
   preexisting *vs.* created roles, 292
Rosenbaum, D. P., 24
Rousey, D., 313
Running records, 317
Ryder, N. B., 48

S

Sample size, 137–139, 137–139
Sampling
   for content analysis, 215–216
   ethnographic, 301
   mixed, for hidden populations, 143–144
   nonprobability, 139–142
   probability, 129–139
   sexual coercion and, 126–129
Sampling case, 129
Sampling distribution, 131
Sampling error, 130
Sampling frame, 129
Sampling interval, 133
Sampling ratio, 139
Sanders, C. R., 282
Savelsberg, J. J., 98
Sayer, A., 57, 363
Scales, 119–120
   Likert, 122–123
   logic and purpose of, 122
   Thurstone scaling, 123–124
Scarce, R., 93
Scattergram, 239
Schacter, D. L., 317
Schatzman, L., 282, 291, 294
Scholarly publications, 37–39
Science
   and politics, 96–99
   wars, 3
Scientific misconduct, 82

Scientific research
   process
      qualitative research steps, 40–41, 43–45
      quantitative research steps, 39–40
   and time, 45–48
Secondary authority, 324
Secondary sources
   in historical research, 317
   limits of, 319
Second-order interpretation, 267
Secrecy, governmental and corporate, 98–99
Selection bias, 162–163
Selective coding, 384
Selective observation, 32
Self-administered questionnaires, 189
Self-classification, research question
      regarding, 175
Self-report surveys, 182
Semiotics, 273
Sentencing Project, 223
Sequential sampling, 142
Sexual coercion and sampling, 126–129
Shadish, W. R., 165, 169
Shafer, R. J., 320
Shafiir, W., 293
Shallow cover, 90
Shaw, C., 279
Sherman, L. W., 152
Shipley, 277
Silverman, D., 33, 295
Simple random sample, 130–133
Singer, E., 89–90
Skewed distribution, 234
Skinner, B. F., 151
Skolnick, 286
Slang, in survey questions, 179
Snowball sampling, 141
Social construction of reality, 55
Social relations, of field researcher, 288
Social science
   community of, 35–37
   critical, 57–60, 362–365
   interpretive, 54–56, 359–362
   positivist, 53–54, 357–359
   research, history of experiment in, 150–151
   and science, 33–35
   sharing knowledge via scholarly
      publications, 37–39
Social skills, in building rapport, 291
Socio-legal research, 326–327
Soft data, 261
Software, for qualitative data analysis, 389–390
Solomon four-group design, 158
Special populations
   and coercion, 91–92
   new inequalities, 91–92
   privacy and anonymity issues, 92–93
Sponsored funding, 97
Spuriousness, 74
Spurious relationship, 74
Stability reliability, 114, 213, 222
Standard deviation, 235
Stare decisis, 324
Statistical regression, 163–164
Statistical relationship, 237
Statistical significance, 248
Statistical validity, 117
Statistics
   bivariate, 237
   on causes of dying, 227–228

defined, 232
ethics and, 252–253
existing, locating, 219–220
inferential, 248–251
Steffensmeier, D. J., 281, 291, 294, 304
Steps in conduction of
legal research, 327–329
mixed methods research, 334–336
QDA, 270–274
a survey, 176–178
Steps in field research project, 284–285
Steroids, home-brewing, 277–278
Strangeness, attitude of, 290
Stratified sampling, 133–135
Strauss, A., 382
Stress of fieldwork, 293
Structured observation, 212
Students as researchers, 9–10
Study design
qualitative research, 43
quantitative research, 42
Style of writing, 340
Subjects, instructions to, 167
Sullivan, M., 307
Survey and interview research, 12
Survey research
appropriateness of, 174–175
in crime and justice studies, 174
ethical, 198
history or, 173–174
logic of, 176–178
"meaning" difficulty in, 197–198
questionnaire construction, 178–188
types of surveys, 189–197
Survey research interviewing, 192
SWAT teams, 16–17
Synthesis of evidence, 322
Systematic literature review, 373–375
Systematic sampling, 133

T

Tables section, of research report, 346
Tacit knowledge, 280
Tagg, S. K., 304
Targeted probes, 196
Target population, 129
Tark, J., 13, 45
Tautology, 73
Taylor, Frederick W., 151
Tearoom trade, Humphreys's, 87
Technical legal research, 323
Techniques of qualitative analysis, 381–390
Teleology, 73
Telephone interviews, 189–190
Telescope, 181–182
Temporal order, 67
Terrorism
home-grown data, 257–259
and statistics on causes of dying, 227–228
Testing a hypothesis, 70–71
Testing effect, 163
Tewksbury, 90, 290
Text
content analysis and, 210–211
retrieval, 389
visual, 214
Textbase managers, 389
Theoretical assumptions, 63

Theoretical review of literature, 368
Theoretical sampling, 142
Theoretical underpinnings of ethnographic field research, 279–280
Theorizing, direction of, 65–66
Theory
causal, 70–71
in crime and justice research, 62–75
grounded, 66, 264–265
parts of, 63–64
Thick description, 280
Think aloud interviews, 196
Third-order interpretation, 267
Thrasher, F. M., 279
Thurstone scaling, 123–124
Time, and scientific research, 45–48
Time-series experimental design
equivalent, 161
interrupted, 161
Time-series research, 46
Tone of writing, 340
Tools of narrative analysis, 386–387
Torre, M., 333, 335
Tourangeau, R., 192, 196
Traditional knowledge, 29–30
Treatment
diffusion of, 164
as part of an experiment, 155
Treatment integrity, 156, 167
Trust, in building rapport, 291
Truth, determining
by CSS, 364–365
by ISS, 361
by PSS, 358
Tucker, 277
Turk, 110
Turner, C., 192, 266
Tuskegee Syphilis Study, 84, 86
Two-group posttest-only design, 157–158
Type I error, 250–251
Type II error, 250–251

U

Ultimate purpose
of CSS, 57, 362–363
of ISS, 55, 360
of PSS, 53, 357
Understanding, in building rapport, 292
Unidimensionality, 120
Uniform Crime Reports, 12, 46
Units of analysis, 215, 221–222
existing statistics, 221
mismatched, 73
Univariate statistics, 232
Universalism, 36
Unobtrusive measures, 204
Unobtrusive observation, 204
Utilitarian balance, 82–83
Utilitarianism, 83

V

Vagueness, in survey questions, 175
Validity
content analysis, 213–214
existing documents/statistics, 220
external, 165–167
in field research, 301
internal, 162–165

population, 166
in qualitative research, 264
in quantitative research, 113–116
relationship to reliability, 116
types of, 115–116
Values, role in science, 359, 362, 365
van der Zouwen, J., 196
Van Maanen, J., 88, 283, 295, 349
Variables, 154–156
causal, 67–69
for content analysis, 221–222
control, 176
independent and dependent, 64
one, results with, 232–237
two, results with, 237–246
types of, 69–70
Variation, measures of, 234–237
Vaughn, M. S., 329
Verstehen, 54, 292
Victims, self-protection measures, 13
Vignettes, 197
Violent criminals, 43–45
Visual text, 214
Voluntary consent, 88

W

Walker, S., 312, 317
Watson, John B., 151
Wax, R. H., 283
Weak experimental designs, 159
Webb, 220
Webb, E., 12
Webb, E. J., 204
Weber, M., 56
Web surveys, 191–192
Weighted index, 122
Weisburd, D., 152, 168
Westlaw, 324
Westmarland, L., 293
Wild code checking, 231
Willis, G. B., 196
Wilson, J. Q., 371
Wolcott, H. F., 382
Wright, R., 15, 353
Wright, R. T., 292, 296
Writing
report, *See* Report writing
survey research questions, 178–181
Writing process
back to the library, 342
freewriting, 343
knowing your audience, 339–340
organizing thoughts, 341
prewriting, 342
rewriting, 343–344
style and tone, 340
Wundt, Wilhelm M., 150–151

Y

Yammarino, F., 188

Z

Zeisel, H., 243
Zero variation, 234
Zhang, S. X., 157, 163
Zimbardo, P. G., 86
Zimbardo prison experiment, 86
Zoom lens, 348
Z-score, 236–237

CREDITS

Chapter 1: p. 12, Michael Newman/ PhotoEdit Inc.; p.13, Getty Images, Inc - Stock Image; p.24, ©Syracuse Newspapers / The Image Works.

Chapter 2: p.28, Courtesy Everett Collection; p.41, Fotolia, LLC - Royalty Free.

Chapter 3: p.51, JAMES NIELSEN/AFP/Getty Images; p.55, Fotolia, LLC - Royalty Free; p.56, Fotolia, LLC - Royalty Free; p.56, Shutterstock; p.59, Courtesy Everett Collection.

Chapter 4: p.81, Shutterstock; p.83, CORBIS- NY; p.88, Getty Images, Inc - Stock Image.

Chapter 5: p.102, Matt Cardy/Stringer/Getty Images News; p.108, CORBIS- NY; p.113, Allen Eyestone/ AP Wide World Photos; p.120, Redux Pictures.

Chapter 6: p.127, Deborah Davis/ PhotoEdit Inc.; p.130, (c)Thaves. Reprinted by permission.; p.133, © Mikael Karlsson / Alamy.

Chapter 7: p.150, Shutterstock; p. 168, Copyright © Robin Nelson / Photo Edit.

Chapter 8: p.176, U. S. Army Photograph; p.194, © John Sturrock / Alamy.

Chapter 9: p.205, Dr. Jeff Ferrell; p.209, AP Image/Bedford, N.H. Police Department; p.215, AP Image/Denis Porgy.

Chapter 11: p. 258, US Department of Defense; p.269, Peter Kraska; p.271, Thomas Michael Corcoran/ PhotoEdit Inc.

Chapter 12: p.277, Arresting Images; p.281, US Department of Defense; p.300, Dr. Jeff Ferrell.

Chapter 13: p.316, © Bettmann/CORBIS All Rights Reserved; p.332, Arresting Images.